Zoë Elliston.

MW01196993

# THE ROADMAP TO LITERACY

## A Guide to Teaching Language Arts in Waldorf Schools
## Grades 1 through 3

# THE ROADMAP TO LITERACY

A Guide to Teaching Language Arts in Waldorf Schools
Grades 1 through 3

## JANET LANGLEY & JENNIFER MILITZER-KOPPERL

### WITH CONTRIBUTIONS FROM PATTI CONNOLLY

MILL CITY PRESS

Mill City Press, Inc.
2301 Lucien Way #415
Maitland, FL 32751
407·339·4217
www.millcitypress.net

© 2018 by JANET LANGLEY & JENNIFER MILITZER-KOPPERL

All rights reserved solely by the authors. The authors guarantee all contents are original and do not infringe upon the legal rights of any other person or work. No part of this book may be reproduced in any form without the permission of the authors. The views expressed in this book are not necessarily those of the publisher.

No part of this publication may be reproduced, stored in a retrieval system, or transmitted in any form or by any means—electronic, mechanical, photocopy, recording, or any other—without the prior permission of the authors.

**ACKNOWLEDGMENTS**

For each of the selections listed below, grateful acknowledgment is made for permission to reprint copyrighted material.

Figure 3.2.4: D'Nealian: Print and Figure 3.2.5: D'Nealian: Cursive. Used with permission of Donald N. Thurber. www.dnealian.com.

Figure 5.5.1 Schema of Nature Spirits. Used with permission of Dr. Patrick Wakeford-Evans.

Printed in the United States of America.

ISBN-13: 978-1-54566-023-2

# BOOK DEDICATIONS

To Christof Wiechert, Past Director of the Pedagogical Section of the Anthroposophical Society, for inspiring me to write this book for English-speaking Waldorf teachers.

*Janet Langley*

To all of my teachers and to my parents, my first teachers.

*Jennifer Militzer-Kopperl*

# FOREWORD

It is a great joy to teach using the rich vocabulary that is found in the storytelling tradition of Waldorf education. Teachers in the early grades are delighted when they experience the wonder dawn in the eyes of their students as the spoken word and oral tradition of these stories touch their souls. However, every teacher faces the challenge of teaching her students the skills needed to look at the written words on a page and resurrect them into pictures, colors, and feelings. The teacher longs to see that moment of recognition when the child moves from word to meaning and becomes the captain of his own reading journey. To some children, this comes naturally, like breathing or the acquisition of the mother tongue. However, many students will need their teacher to be their guide on the road to reading, and the teacher needs her roadmap

Whether the reader is an experienced Waldorf teacher or new to Waldorf teaching, *The Roadmap to Literacy* offers support and guidance. It is comprehensive and well organized, and its direct manner will serve the reader well as she embarks upon the journey of language arts in the early grades. It truly lives up to its title… and more!

Just a quick glance at the table of contents offers the new Waldorf teacher a certain reassurance that the authors know what is needed. They seem to have anticipated which questions to ask, which traditions to challenge, and what to explore before the reader has thought of these things for herself. For the experienced Waldorf teacher, there is the challenge to reexamine what is held as unbreakable traditions (i.e., *Sacred Nothings*). The experienced teacher may feel the need to speak back and thus arrive at a conscious articulation about her own approach to teaching. Then, she can ask if she is a 'responsible innovator' as defined herein and if she has something more to offer to this great journey of education.

This book opens with a pragmatic, straightforward thesis. First, it is necessary to define where the problems of teaching reading in Waldorf schools may originate. How does American English compare to the native tongue of the founder of Waldorf education (i.e., Rudolf Steiner's German)? When Steiner was guiding the first Waldorf faculty in Stuttgart, he focused on imparting the quality and character of the German language. What of this rich work translates to application in an American Waldorf School classroom? Second, it is important to consider not only the imaginative, pictorial presentation of new material such as the letters but also the young child's need to practice and acquire stability of skill.

As I read this book, I recognized the wisdom of its organization. Section 1 unfolds the essential questions of English language learning. It first explores the question 'Why': Why is learning English skills different from other, more simple or predictable languages? Then it addresses the 'What' question: What is the origin and development of the English language? Next, 'How': How does the young child recapitulate the acquisition of literacy and the development of the English language? And finally, 'If': If the child is guided by a knowledgeable teacher, who seeks to integrate the best of the various ways of teaching reading, will this child experience a sense of mastery and re-birthed wonder at the mystery of the written word?

Section 2 examines the essentials of good planning and the underlying understandings of the Waldorf approach to education. The reader is introduced to or reminded of 14 core essential practices of the Waldorf teacher who seeks to foster and support the healthy development of the child's body, soul, and spirit. Herein, the notion of teacher and students as authoring either independently or collaboratively is spoken of. The basic approaches within Waldorf education, which are grounded in the child's cognitive and emotional readiness, are highlighted. Much of what is explored here falls within the category of essential, good teaching practices. However, some of the content approaches, in a very direct and lucid manner, the essential core principles of Waldorf education.

Juxtaposed to these essentials are the 'Sacred Nothings' or unhelpful traditions that have grown up over the years. Many of these practices are not necessarily grounded in a theory based on the developmental needs of the child or the class. For example, the authors question the use of the 'birthday' or 'report' verse, often written by the teacher for a specific child. In practice, the children recite their verses on a weekly basis before the class. In examining this practice, one must ask, what is the value if it takes an inordinate amount of time in large classes, or if it becomes 'dead air' not listened to by classmates and said with a rote or unengaged tone without a sense of import? If a teacher senses the value of this practice, how is it kept alive and how does the teacher craft language to serve the inmost needs of the child? And, most importantly, does this 'Waldorf myth' take away from valuable time needed for practicing more essential skills in the early grades? This is only one of the Sacred Nothings that are examined. As I read these Sacred Nothings, I began to ponder how they got started in this country and what the origin and original intent were behind these practices. It is a timely and needed query and deserves even more exploration than this book is able to offer given its primary focus.

Section 2 culminates in valuable definitions of the practical aspects of planning the teaching day, week, and year. The authors touch on what Steiner defined as economy in teaching. They then address the different needs of classroom learners and how the teacher addresses them. A focus toward the importance of pacing and addressing the specific and general needs of the students contributes to a deeper understanding of how these foster classroom harmony and a more intrinsic classroom management style. A well-planned and well-managed lesson imparts a sense of security and peace in the students. This in turn evokes trust in the authority of the teacher and culminates as a love for the teacher and for learning.

For the teacher wishing to explore more of the concepts of section 2, a natural jump is to section 5, wherein more depth of planning and sequencing of instruction are elucidated. Herein one finds very practical and helpful advice for planning the day, the monthly blocks of learning, and the year. Primary or 'key aspects' of each of the first three grades are explored. An exploration of a primary grades block entitled *Home Surroundings* is worked through and made more accessible to a teacher who may not be familiar with this particular block. This block is a reinterpretation of Steiner's intent for certain explorations in the early grades. The teacher is asked to look around her area of the world and identify the natural resources and human responses to these resources that the children can experience directly. I was touched by and excited to encounter these ideas as they made me rethink my own current teaching and block preparation in the first three grades. It is always exciting and challenging to keep growing after so many years in Waldorf education.

When one arrives at section 3, the purpose, intent, and value of the book becomes apparent. This section focuses on 15 essential aspects of language arts and how these aspects are approached from a developmental phase of readiness in the young student. The questions of 'how to' from phonemic awareness through spelling, writing, speech, grammar, reading, etc. are covered in an openly accessible and useful way. Each of the 15 chapters has a similar method of presentation: why the concept matters, preparation for teaching it, scheduling, introducing the concept, and so forth. The organization and clarity are so helpful that a sense of order and peace in approaching and teaching new concepts is imparted. To culminate this section, the reader is given the Curriculum Chart for the 15 Aspects of Language Arts in a Waldorf school.

Section 4 offers the teacher an organized and clear reference for teaching the 33 major phonics skills necessary for every skilled reader and writer. The new teacher and experienced teacher alike will be so grateful for the examples the authors give as teaching methods to approach these rules. Again, it is very clearly and methodically presented and organized. The reader is given the essentials for planning to teach a rule: First the time it will take to teach it, practice it, and be certain it is a learned skill/capacity from which to scaffold new material. Next the reader is given a deeper understanding of the rule, an introductory image, and activities to help students learn the rule and to practice it. Finally, advice on how to anchor the concept within the child's own phonics rules book is touched upon. As I read the examples and ideas given under an individual rule, I saw the wisdom in a deeply integrated approach to the learning.

Many children can read but do not have good spelling habits. Phonics rules can help them too. Just a glance at this very full section should make the early grades teacher feel assured that guidance is right at her fingertips. Keep this book nearby!

Section 6 is near and dear to my heart in that it asserts that it is one thing to teach something, it is quite another to be held accountable for the learning. This section reads like a mentor to a mentee teacher. It is a 'how to' use the information to create mutual understandings between teacher and student, teacher and parent, and more. It offers very valuable information for the teacher to discern the appropriate and most useful way to assess, record progress, and plan future teaching. An introduction to the basic usefulness of teacher-made assessments as formative in nature is given. The teacher can use these simple, intimate assessment techniques to inform her about which skills students have learned, which ones need further practice, and which concepts or skills may not be fully understood by the class as a whole.

Waldorf places emphasis on the teacher's relationship with the individual and the class as a whole. Ideally the teacher stays with a group of children for a long period of time. This length of experience gives her the imagination, inspiration, and intuition needed to meet the needs of her class. Given this relationship, teacher assessments can not only be informative but also provide for laughs and self-reflection.

Beyond these intimate but subjective assessments are the more standardized assessments which are objective and reveal how an individual or class stands in relationship to a norm established by the test. In some settings, this summative testing is required and used at or near the end of a grade. In most states, this does not occur until the 3rd Grade. It is important for the Waldorf teacher, no matter her setting, to be familiar with the standards and assessment tools so as to address them in the most developmentally appropriate way for her class and school.

The final chapter of section 6 addresses children who display learning difficulties and provides specific remedial approaches for these children. The teacher considers the individual needs and how to approach the child's needs. The usefulness of working with Therapeutic Eurythmy and Extra Lesson is also touched upon and encouraged whenever available. The authors mention other more mainstream approaches to specific learning needs. In my experience, the very ones that they mention are the most effective that I have experienced.

The Waldorf teacher is entreated to know that she is not alone when facing a child with specific challenges. Steiner spoke of children in ever growing numbers who will incarnate with cognitive, emotional, and learning needs. He said their purpose is to evoke love-filled curiosity so that the teacher will ask for others to also observe the child. This joining together of teacher and others generates even more love for the child and by that action, for the world. That is a strong imagination of the purpose of the encounter with a child who presents difficulties in learning! The overall mood of this final chapter is to affirm the teacher's journey toward such a love for a child. The teacher, through intense, focused observation and an effort to meet the child, evokes such a love. The ultimate gift of such an effort is to recognize one's own higher humanity.

The authors' years of Waldorf teaching experience guided them in this great labor of love. They also were fortunate to work with Christof Wiechert, past head of the Pedagogical Section of the Anthroposophical Society. His advice and depth of knowledge served them as they articulated a truly American approach to teaching language arts to the young children in English-speaking Waldorf Schools.

I feel an immense gratitude for having been asked to write this foreword. These women have taken on a Task of Great Importance. *The Roadmap to Literacy* will echo into many classrooms, affirm many teachers, and create many happy and imaginative Waldorf readers.

Bonnie River, M.Ed.

Co-Founder, Gradalis Teacher Training Program

# ACKNOWLEDGMENTS

No book is ever solely the work of the authors.

We would like to acknowledge the many contributions made by our colleague, **Patti Connolly.** Patti, a Waldorf teacher, mentor, and adult educator, was an integral part of the initial planning stages of *The Roadmap to Literacy*. Her research, reflections, and initial drafts serve as the inspirations for several of the book's chapters. In particular, we are indebted for her initial drafts of the chapters on teaching composition skills, reading, and speech and to her contributions to the chapter on reading and the brain. We are also appreciative of the invaluable insights that she gave us after reading the first draft of the book as it came back from the publishers. The book would not have been the same without her contributions.

Next we would like to acknowledge **Christof Wiechert**, a former Waldorf teacher of 30 years and the Head of the Pedagogical Section of the Anthroposophical Society from 2001–2010. In his capacity as Section head, Christof's task was to encourage, educate, and inspire Waldorf teachers around the world. He visited North America many times, lecturing at conferences, giving workshops, and visiting schools and teacher education institutes. In 2006 Janet attended one of these workshops where she heard him speak about *Sacred Nothings* or 'Waldorf Myths' and the need for teachers to teach not out of tradition but out of knowledge of what their students need (see chapter 2.2). This lecture changed Janet's entire approach to teaching. Over the following years, Janet has had many conversations with Christof about the art of teaching. This book is in part a result of those conversations. Today Christof continues to travel the world supporting teachers with great energy, wisdom, insight, and humor.

We would also like to recognize another colleague, **Patrick Wakeford-Evans,** for his contributions to chapter 5.5 (Working with Stories). Patrick shared his process for creating original nature stories and two of his original creations. His insights were the inspiration for this chapter.

Offering to be a **Beta Reader** for a book of this magnitude is truly a selfless task. We want to thank the following three educators for their willingness to read our book and give us feedback as to its efficacy. *The Roadmap to Literacy* is all the better as a result of their suggestions and reflections.

**Bethany Chaffin** is the founder and Administrator of the Willow Tree Charter School, a school in Fallbrook, California that embraces Waldorf Methodology. She has a Masters in Educational Administration, was San Diego County's 2014 Teacher of the Year, and has been a classroom teacher since 2001. Bethany has also studied schooling systems in the following countries: Japan, China, Vietnam, Malaysia, India, Israel, Turkey, Italy, and Morocco. She is the founder and Board President of a private Waldorf preschool serving ages two through six years (Rock Rose).

**Heather Handy** is a teacher and mentor at the Waldorf School on the Roaring Fork in Carbondale, Colorado. She has a BS in Special Education from the University of Maine and a M.Ed. in Elementary Education with a Waldorf Teaching Certificate from Antioch University-New England. Heather has been working in Waldorf education since 2001 including taking a class from 1st through 8th Grade.

**Bonnie River** (*also author of our foreword*) has a M.Ed. and has been involved in Waldorf education for over 40 years. She has served on the faculty and in founding positions of five independent Waldorf schools and two public Waldorf schools. She taught kindergarten for 15 years, took a class from 1st through 8th Grade, taught sciences in a Waldorf high school, and picked up other grades along the way.

Bonnie has also completed the Remedial Education Training and Chirophonetics Training both of which combine the work of the doctor, therapist, and teacher on behalf of students. Currently Bonnie is on the faculty of the Gradalis Teacher Training program, which she co-founded, and teaches in a new initiative in Truckee, California.

We also would like to acknowledge **Suzanne Coutchie**, MA and reading coach, for providing us with research on how long it takes German and English-speaking students to master reading and for recommendations regarding good spelling programs.

In addition, Eurythmist **Ruth Bucklin** came through in a pinch with information about archetypal vowels and their soul gestures.

The following added their artistic skills to our book and we thank them:

Francesca Lohmann (Janet's past student): Figure 1.6.1–painting of a beach scene (You can see more of Francesca's work on: www.francescalohmann.com) Ute Luebeck (colleague and friend): Figure 3.1.3- drawing of a goose Elliot Drake-Maurer (Janet's past student): excerpt from his poem "My Garden" found on page 349 (Elliot's poetry and prose have appeared in the journals Aqueous and Mosaic, Northland College's Literary and Visual Arts magazine.)

**Cover Art:** The cover art for *The Roadmap to Literacy* was created by **Nani Pacal**, one of Janet's Waldorf graduates (Class of 2001). We sat down with Nani, now a professional artist, and shared with her our goal of writing a book that would serve as a roadmap for teachers to help them avoid the brambles and pitfalls of teaching English. She took our verbal description and created this beautiful metaphorical painting, which so clearly illustrates how easy it is to get lost when teaching English if you do not have a clear roadmap to guide you. (You can see more of Nani's amazing art at *https://ecosilkart.com.*)

And last, but not at all least, we would like to thank our husbands, **Jerry and Ben**. They supported us emotionally (and at times financially) for the five years it took us to write this book. Jerry also provided countless hours of much-needed technical support. They believed in our mission, and we are grateful.

# A FEW NOTES TO HELP YOU NAVIGATE THIS BOOK

This book is a reference book. It is organized to help you create a language arts curriculum.

Read the book in its entirety first. The first two sections provide background information. The last four sections are a reference for planning your curriculum.

The following conventions apply:

- Letters of the alphabet are written in uppercase italics (e.g., *S*).
- Phonemes (sounds) are written in lowercase inside two forward slashes (e.g., /s/). To read a phoneme, make the letter's sound. For example, sssssss.
- The pronouns *she* and *her* are used for both teachers and students.
- The names of students have been changed to protect their privacy.

# TABLE OF CONTENTS

## SECTION 1
### *Essential Background Information*

## SECTION 2
### *Waldorf Methodologies*

# SECTION 3
*The 15 Aspects of Language Arts*

# SECTION 4
*Phonics Rules*

# SECTION 5
*Curriculum and Lesson Planning*

# SECTION 6
*Assessment and Remediation*

# APPENDICES AND BIBLIOGRAPHY

# THE ROADMAP TO LITERACY

A Guide to Teaching Language Arts in Waldorf Schools
Grades 1 through 3

# SECTION 1

Essential Background Information

# 1.1 WHY IS TEACHING READING SUCH A STRUGGLE?

*When mentoring 1st and 2nd Grade Waldorf teachers, I hear them ask the same question that I did when I first began teaching: "Now that I've taught the alphabet, what do I do?"*

Janet Langley shares:

As a new 1st Grade teacher, I jumped into my first language arts block with gusto. The story "Snow White and Rose Red" helped me introduce the letter *B* and the students had lots of fun combing the room for all of the items they could find that began with the sound /b/. My students continued this foray into the world of *B* by drawing the letter *B* in sand, on the sidewalk, in the air, etc. For several days the classroom was immersed in this wonderful letter and sound. I spent most of the year teaching each of the letters of the alphabet in this way. In the spring, the class was able to decode (sound out) **CVC words** (Consonant-Vowel-Consonant words, like *hut*) and they learned about the Wizard *E* who could magically change a *can* into a *cane* and a *dam* into a *dame*. I counted the year a success.

In 2nd Grade, the situation changed. I did not know what to teach next and consulting books by Rudolf Steiner, the creator of Waldorf education, was no help at all because he offered no pertinent directions. I was lost. "What should I do now?" and "What concepts should I be teaching and when should I teach them?" were the questions I constantly lived with. For most of 2nd and 3rd Grade, I did what many dedicated, English-speaking Waldorf teachers do: I spent hours furtively pouring over English skills resources that I found in mainstream teacher supply stores. From these books, I slowly cobbled together a Waldorf language arts curriculum.

First, I taught myself the fundamentals of teaching children how to read in English. Then I chose the concepts I wanted to teach. Finally, I figured out how to bring these concepts in a Waldorf way. This approach was often exhausting, and I was never confident that what I was doing was covering all of the bases. When I spoke with my peers at various Waldorf conferences, I discovered that I was not alone: They, too, were trying their best to create an effective teaching plan using the same seat-of-your-pants approach I was following. My colleagues and I were all exhausted and agreed that we could use more guidance. Our students became literate, but at what a cost to us!

As a mentor, I routinely see teachers running into the same frustrations I had. Many teachers are desperately trying to piece together an effective language arts curriculum for English. It seems that everyone is trying to reinvent the wheel, with varying degrees of success. Many schools lose enrollment because parents do not feel that their children are getting an adequate language arts education. Furthermore, in some schools I find that 30–50% of the students are being recommended for (or are currently receiving) remedial support in reading, spelling, and writing.

I began to ask myself this question: What could explain the high number of students requiring tutoring when so many come from well-educated families that put a high value on education? Something was clearly not working, but what?

# 1. English is Not German

In the fall of 2012, I was mentoring teachers at a local Waldorf school. This position brought me in contact with Jennifer Militzer-Kopperl, a Waldorf-trained, Lindamood-Bell tutor who worked with some of the students at the school. I decided to ask her if she had any thoughts about why so many Waldorf students needed tutoring in reading and writing.

She looked me in the eye, smiled, and said, "Janet, I have been waiting for years for someone to ask that question. The answer is really simple. English is not German."

Jennifer went on to explain that if English-speaking teachers limit themselves to Steiner's indications for literacy, they will inevitably find themselves going straight into the wilderness without a roadmap She explained that in phonetic German, it is a straight shot from learning the alphabet to learning to read and write, but that in partially-phonetic English, learning the alphabet is only the first leg of the journey. Steiner's indications for literacy are brilliant for German, but they are just the beginning for English. Waldorf teachers need to know what to do after that first stage.

As fate would have it, Christof Wiechert, Head of the Pedagogical Section of the Anthroposophical Society (2001–2010), the organization that guides and supports Waldorf schools around the world, was visiting the school where Jennifer and I were working. When I shared Jennifer's comment with Christof, he insisted on meeting to discuss the topic further. In our meeting, I first described what many Waldorf teachers were going through in order to create an English literacy program. Then Jennifer shared her insights about the difference between what is needed to teach English and what is needed to teach German. Upon hearing this, Christof enthusiastically charged us to do further research and get this information out to other English-speaking Waldorf teachers. And so we have.

Jennifer and I began this book as a means to address the missing stages of English literacy instruction. However, we soon found two additional roadblocks that made teaching literacy in Waldorf classrooms even more difficult. The first one centers on the confusion over the type of instruction that is needed to teach a fundamental skill vs. that necessary to teach a subject. This realization also encompassed an exploration into the role of practice in relationship to learning foundational skills. The second one had to do with what Christof refers to as *Sacred Nothings* or *Waldorf Myths* that have come into vogue over time and are of questionable value. We realized that we were going to have to address all three roadblocks if we wished to provide English-speaking Waldorf teachers a clear roadmap to teaching literacy.

# 2. Subject vs. Skill: The Importance of Practice

Most non-Waldorf schools in Grades 1–3 have ongoing classes in reading, writing, and spelling instruction. These classes usually meet daily throughout the school year. However, Waldorf schools use a different schedule: blocks of study. While blocks work well for subjects, they are much less effective for developing skills.

The block system is scheduled as follows: For three or four weeks, students focus on one subject for two hours a day. Waldorf teachers bring poems, music, artistic activities, stories, and assignments related to the subject of study. At the end of the block, the subject matter changes. The block system allows the teacher and students to delve deeply into a subject and then set it aside (or 'put it to sleep') for at least a month before taking it up in a new way.

Block study is an effective approach to teaching subjects such as history, science, geography, etc. In the 5th Grade, teaching a block on ancient India at the beginning of the year, ancient Egypt in January, and ancient

Greece at the end of the year works very well. Students do not need to practice subjects like history to study them successfully. However, blocks do not work well when it comes to learning foundational <u>skills</u> such as reading or math. Learning a skill requires a different approach.

There are two important points to keep in mind. First, students must practice skills until they become abilities. This concept is covered in chapter 1.2. Second, skills are not static but keep progressing over the years. For example, once students learn to read, they have to build their fluency with higher and higher levels of text in each passing grade. Students need ongoing practice to meet these fluency goals. For example, starting in 3rd Grade on, they should read <u>at least</u> a total of 30 minutes a day from books/texts at an appropriate level. Daily practice is the key to developing reading fluency skills, just as it is the key for developing all skills. Ongoing practice is as critical as the initial introduction.

More and more Waldorf schools are turning to practice classes as the solution to the limitations found in a main lesson block-based schedule. These language skills practice classes occur during the off block (i.e., when math is the focus of the current main lesson block) and afford additional time for mastering the skills introduced the previous month. However, as they are currently used, many of these practice classes have three problems: 1) They only meet two or three times a week, which is an inadequate amount of time; 2) They are often used for activities other than language arts practice (e.g., nature walks, making birthday cards, etc.) and; 3) They are only used to review skills taught in the past block, not teach new ones.

Teaching language arts for only half the year (i.e., every other block) in Grades 1–3 does not provide enough continuity to cover an adequate language arts curriculum for English. A different schedule is needed.

The germ of this idea is already present among some Waldorf educators. The authors of *The Educational Tasks and Content of the Steiner Waldorf Curriculum* state:

> Steiner Waldorf [School] differentiates between skills needing regular practice (foreign languages, music, math, spelling, etc.) and the introduction of new content. New experiences or teaching content are often best introduced after a period during which the assimilation of previously taught material can occur. Acquiring new skills and practicing them until they become ability are two different processes requiring different rhythms. (Avison 2014, 31)

We concur that there needs to be a different rhythm for skills. Furthermore, we add reading and writing to the top of Avison's list of skills that require regular practice.

Here is the guiding principle: Academic <u>subjects</u> (history, science, geography, etc.) benefit from being 'put to sleep' at the end of a block to be reawakened at a later time. Academic <u>skills</u> (readin', 'riting, and 'rithmetic) require daily instruction and/or practice. They should never be 'put to sleep.'

## 3.   Sacred Nothings

There is one final area that makes teaching an effective Waldorf literacy program a challenge. This roadblock centers on a number of Waldorf educational practices that have sprung up over the years that are of questionable value. These practices have been called *Waldorf Myths* or *Sacred Nothings* by Christof Wiechert. As we began to articulate a language arts curriculum, we kept running into these Sacred Nothings. One example is having students use art supplies for writing (e.g., crayons or colored pencils) rather than graphite pencils with an eraser. Sacred Nothings are covered in more depth in chapter 2.2 and are addressed as they come up in the language skills involved in *The Roadmap to Literacy's* curriculum.

In summary, there are three reasons why teaching literacy is such a struggle for Waldorf teachers: 1) English literacy requires additional instruction which is not always part of Waldorf teacher trainings because these trainings tend to focus on Steiner's indications, which are for teaching the German language; 2) Reading, writing, and spelling are skills, not subjects, and require daily practice. These skills should never be 'put to sleep'; 3) Some Waldorf practices which have sprung up over the years undermine the delivery of an effective literacy curriculum (i.e., Sacred Nothings).

## 4. The Solution: The Roadmap to Literacy

In this book, Jennifer Militzer-Kopperl and I have developed an approach to teaching English language arts that we refer to as *The Roadmap to Literacy*. This approach is based upon three things: brain development, the recapitulation of the history of English, and the recapitulation of the development of written language. As the reader will see in the upcoming chapters, combining brain development with the history of both English and written language results in five phases of reading and spelling development. These five phases are the basis for what to teach and how to assess.

This book is laid out as follows:

Section 1: Essential Background Information

Section 2: Waldorf Methodologies

Section 3: The 15 Aspects of Language Arts

Section 4: Phonics Rules

Section 5: Curriculum and Lesson Planning

Section 6: Assessment and Remediation

Our goal is for all Waldorf students to graduate from the 3rd Grade with the language arts skills necessary to do well in any 4th Grade curriculum, a goal shared by Rudolf Steiner. He writes, "In my letter to the authorities, I stated that, on completion of the third school year, our students would have reached the same standards of basic education as those achieved in other schools and thus would be able to change schools without difficulty" (Steiner 2003, 126).

By the end of 3rd Grade, Waldorf students should no longer need to *learn to read* but should be ready to *read to learn*. This ability will allow them to transition successfully into 4th Grade. Regardless of the school they attend, they will begin to read about the subjects they will be studying. *The Roadmap to Literacy* will help teachers and students meet this goal.

Teachers who worked with this book prior to its publication all recommend that it be read through in its entirety before it is used as a resource book. Once you have done so, you will know how best to utilize the book to plan and teach your curriculum, and you will be able to speak knowledgably to current and prospective parents about your language arts curriculum across these three grades.

Following the approach outlined in this book will save you hours of pouring over teaching materials because it answers that ubiquitous question: "What do I teach now that I have taught the alphabet?"

# 1.2 CRACKING THE CODE: READING AND THE BRAIN

*It simply is not true that there are hundreds of ways to learn to read. Every child is unique...but when it comes to reading, all have roughly the same brain that imposes the same constraints and the same learning sequence.*

—Stanislas Dehaene, *Reading in the Brain: The New Science of How We Read* (218)

*It was December in 2nd Grade when Beth came running into the classroom, calling out, " Mrs. Connolly, Mrs. Connolly, I can read!" Her classmates looked on as she jumped into my lap and opened the book she had brought from home. "Oh, Beth," I exclaimed, "Read to me!" And so she did, decoding every word with ease and inflection. The other children nodded in satisfaction. Here was yet another friend who had reached the crowning moment, when reading had become, as we would say in our classroom, 'as smooth as butter.'*
*As I reflected on Beth's achievement, I marveled at the wonder of what she had achieved—Beth had 'cracked the code.' She knew, deep down, that she could read.*

Patti Connolly

Teaching a student to read literally changes her brain. Let's examine what happened in Beth's brain to understand how she reached this moment—and what needs to happen next.

This chapter covers the following topics:

1. Three Reading Stages
2. The Two Reading Routes
3. Word Recognition and the Brain
4. Myelin: Reinforcing Neural Pathways in the Brain through Practice
5. The Next Step in the Development of Beth's Brain
6. Parting Wisdom from Brain Research

## 1.    Three Reading Stages

Children learn to speak their language naturally through exposure and imitation; however, reading and writing require education. Because brains are set to decipher the spoken word, not the printed word, students have to rewire their brains in order to read. Like all students, Beth had to convert certain areas of her brain from their original tasks of handling spoken words and images to decoding written letters and words.

In 1985 British psychologist Ute Frith described three broad stages of learning to read: 1) the pictorial stage; 2) the phonological stage; and 3) the orthographic stage (Dehaene 2009, 199). This model of reading acquisition has become a classic and is useful for understanding the stages Beth passed through as she learned to read. These stages apply to all languages that are based on an alphabet.

**Pictorial Stage**

Beth's first attempts at reading were not real reading at all. Beth learned to "read" familiar signs and logos such as *McDonalds* and *Starbucks* as well as her name and a handful of other words, but she recognized these words the same way she recognized faces or pictures. She had no idea that the letters represented sounds. Instead she linked these written words directly to their meanings. At this point, Beth was in the very beginning stage of reading acquisition known as the pictorial stage.

In the pictorial stage a student learns to recognize a limited set of words using visual differences to identify them instead of sounding out each letter. For example, Beth might have focused on the word's length, shape, color, or the curvature of its form. However, she was not able to recognize that the letters in the word represented sounds and were part of a giant code. That is why reading experts call this kind of reading *artificial reading*.

In order to move beyond the pictorial stage, Beth had to stop treating each word as a picture. She had to learn to break a word into its component letters and link them to their speech sounds, or **phonemes**.

**Phonological Stage**

In the phonological stage, Beth approached reading in an entirely different way. Instead of seeing written words as pictures, she realized that they are made up of sounds that the letters represent. Reading is learning to decipher a giant code, or in other words, **decoding.**

Encouraged by this revelation, Beth began to decode (sound out) words, albeit slowly, letter by letter. In so doing, Beth used many regions of her brain in new ways. Beth had to recognize visual symbols (letters), match the symbol with its auditory sound (phoneme), blend the sounds together to create the word, and then find the word's meaning. She was really reading—just slowly and with much effort.

**Orthographic Stage**

Beth moved into the last stage when she could pick up an unknown text and read it with mastery. She no longer had to sound out words slowly because she could recognize chunks of words such as *-ind* in *bind* and *-tion* in *motion* as well as many whole words. Those words she did not recognize on sight she could decode quickly with little effort. Beth had cracked the code.

In the phonological stage, Beth's speed at decoding depended on the length of the word: the longer the word, the longer it would take her to decode it. As she progresses through the orthographic stage, this effect will slowly vanish until Beth is able to decode words instantaneously, regardless of length.

## 2. The Two Reading Routes

These three stages show the development of two reading routes in Beth's brain. Dehaene, a cognitive neuroscientist who studies the brain, refers to the first route as **letter to sound decoding** and the second as the **lexical route**. Both ways enable Beth to read written words.

The letter to sound decoding route develops in the phonological stage. Beth learned letters, became aware of phonemes, and then mapped sounds to the letters. She was then able to sound out words, but very slowly.

The lexical route develops in the orthographic stage. In this stage, Beth could take in all of the letters at once (for words with eight or fewer letters) and read automatically and fluently (Dehaene 2009, 204).

Regardless of which route Beth used to identify a word, her brain next shipped the information through a language circuit that developed when Beth practiced decoding. The language circuit connected different regions of her brain allowing Beth to create a **neural model** of the word, synthesizing visual, verbal, and meaning aspects courtesy of these various brain regions. In other words, every time Beth saw one of these words in print, she immediately connected to the neural model she had created of the word, including the word's pronunciation, spelling, and meaning.

When Beth read, she used both of these routes to identify the words she saw. She used the lexical route for regular reading when the words were familiar to her, and she used the letter to sound decoding route when she encountered new words. As she kept decoding these new words, they eventually become automatic and were processed through her lexical route. Reading creates a virtuous cycle: the more Beth read, the more words she was able to read automatically through her lexical route.

## 3. Word Recognition and the Brain

How Beth's brain identifies a word depends on which stage of reading she is in. The three stages of reading that Beth moved through correlated to her brain development. When it comes to reading, students in the orthographic stage literally have different brains than beginning readers. It is crucial to understand this progression because it will influence all aspects of early literacy education.

When Beth was in the pictorial stage of reading, her brain treated words like pictures. A region in her right hemisphere recognized words (the right occipito-temporal region) (Dehaene 2009, 207). Beth's brain linked whole written words directly to their meaning with no consideration for sound.

As she moved into the phonological stage, Beth learned to analyze the pieces of words, first very slowly through individual letters and then more quickly through patterns of letters. In so doing, she began linking visual memory with verbal memory using two regions of the brain located in the left hemisphere (Broca's area and the parieto-temporal area). One region is responsible for articulating spoken words. The other region pulls a word apart into individual sounds, or phonemes, and links letters to the sounds (Shaywitz 2003, 79). Note how Beth's brain changed. As she moved from the right side of her brain to the left, she stopped processing written words as pictures and began processing them as code.

When Beth entered the orthographic stage, her efforts in decoding enabled her brain to develop a faster way to recognize words. *The Roadmap to Literacy* refers to this area as the ***word identification hub***; Dehaene refers to it as the *letterbox*. (It is actually the *left* occipito-temporal region.) It recognizes a word instantaneously and sends it on to those regions of the brain responsible for speech sounds and meaning (Dehaene 2009, 53). However, the brain can only use the word identification hub to recognize a written word once the brain has processed the word many times through the letter to sound decoding route.

Beth's brain has come full circle. She has shifted word identification from one hemisphere to the other by developing the letter to sound decoding route in her left brain. In so doing, she has cracked the code and learned to read.

## 4. Myelin: Reinforcing Neural Pathways in the Brain through Practice

Neurologists have discovered that the brain develops certain capacities based on how it is used. When a person practices an action over and over, the brain creates a neural pathway. With each repetition of the behavior, a thin, waxy substance called *myelin* coats that particular neural pathway to reinforce it.

One way to think of neural pathways and myelination is to consider an urban legend about how one college figured out where to put its sidewalks (Medina 2008, 111–112). Over one summer, the college president had new grass planted in the campus's communal area, but he did not put in any plans for sidewalks. The grounds crew was aghast. How could he make no plans for sidewalks? Where should they go? The president told them to wait. He said that the best places for the sidewalks would just appear. The students returned in the fall and walked all over the commons, taking the shortest distance between buildings. Their feet soon created paths through the new grass, and that is where the sidewalks were placed. Repeated practice creates the neural pathway in the brain, and myelin is the cement that makes it firm so that it is not overtaken by mud and weeds.

Students must practice all aspects of reading, spelling, and writing over and over and over again, first to create and then myelinate both reading routes: letter to sound decoding route and lexical route. They then need to read often to build up a rich network of neural models of words. Repeated practice is the key to both.

## 5. The Next Step in the Development of Beth's Brain

Second-grader Beth has cracked the code. However, when it comes to learning to read, she is not done yet. From this point on, improvements in Beth's reading will coincide with further activation of the word identification hub in her brain. Further reading will create a rich bank of words in Beth's hub. Dehaene notes that the region referred to as the *word identification hub* (the letterbox) only reaches full maturity at the beginning of adolescence—provided, of course, that a student reads regularly enough to become an expert (Dehaene 2009, 207).

## 6. Parting Wisdom from Brain Research

Beth is an average student. What does brain research reveal about her peers?

Research has shown that leaving the pictorial stage is very easy for some students and very challenging for others. To move to the phonological stage, students have to realize the **alphabetic principle**, that letters represent sounds which form words. Students fall in three groups:

1. Up to 40% of students will discover the alphabetic principle for themselves quite easily—regardless of instruction. They make the connection between the letter and its sound, realize that writing is a code, and are ready to learn all of it. A few of them even teach themselves to read or learn to read from educational shows such as *Sesame Street*. These students will learn their letters and sounds quickly and effortlessly. They are the students who master each lesson on the alphabet in the first day or two and are bored with extra practice. They got it the first time and are ready to move on.

2. About 30–40% of students, like Beth, require extra practice to realize that writing is a code. In order for these students to learn the alphabetic principle they will need a number of opportunities to practice letter/sound relationships. However, with adequate classroom practice they will be able to move fully from the pictorial stage to the phonological stage.

3. About 20–30% of students will not learn the alphabetic principle unless they have intensive and appropriate direct teaching. In other words, the initial introduction and practice that was enough for Beth's group to learn the alphabetic principle will not be enough for this group. These students need additional instruction from their teacher. That instruction has to be very structured and sequential. The teacher has to lead them step by step through each skill and provide extra demonstrations, explanations, and practice sessions for them to get it. Furthermore, not all

reading programs include the step-by-step instruction this group needs. This group requires more effort from the teacher (or from a reading specialist if the school has one). However, if given intensive and direct teaching, these students will be able to realize the alphabetic principle (Hempenstall 2006, 18).

While the exact percentages vary by classroom, 1st Grade teachers should expect that they will have students in all three groups. Consequently, it will be necessary to **differentiate instruction** in the classroom by giving students different work, depending on their needs (see chapter 2.4 #3).

Why is it important that students who struggle receive the appropriate support? Students who do not successfully make the transition from the pictorial to orthographic stage lack the concomitant connections in their brains for efficient reading and are forced to use sub-par reading systems. While their peers can recognize words in 1/6 of a second, they will be forced to use slower, less accurate systems such as prediction from context, guessing from a picture, and guessing from the first letter (see chapter 1.6 #4) (Hempenstall 2006, 18). In other words, they will be stuck in a very early phase of reading: either *The Roadmap to Literacy's* Emergent Phase or beginning Phonemic Awareness Phase (see chapter 1.5).

As Hempenstall relates, new experiences literally cause the brain cells to form new connections. The brain has a quality called **plasticity**: it changes based on use. "It [the brain] responds to experiences that stimulate activity in particular areas of the brain, thereby facilitating the growth of neural connections in and between those active regions. That is why practice makes permanent" (Hempenstall 2006, 18). In other words, classroom instruction and practice help the student to develop the letter to sound decoding route and the lexical route, which result in the attainment of the orthographic stage. Furthermore, the path to developing the word identification hub for reading relies on the development of the letter to sound decoding route. In other words, a student only reaches the orthographic stage by going through the phonological stage. There are no shortcuts. All students go through the same process when learning to read. If a student has dyslexia, it is just more difficult (see chapter 6.6 #9).

Note: Although many students who have trouble moving into and through the phonological stage can be helped through direct, structured instruction, there are students who have learning challenges beyond what a teacher can address in the classroom. (See chapter 6.6 #4 and chapter 6.6 #9 for remedial suggestions.)

The difference between beginning readers in the pictorial and phonological stages and those in the orthographic stage is profound. In the book *Breakthrough in Beginning Reading and Writing*, Richard J. Gentry states: "Beginning readers are like tadpoles in metamorphosis….and as with tadpoles and frogs, little readers are not smaller, developing versions of the mature ones. They are *different* versions, needing special nurturing, alternative environments, and unique kinds of instructional support for growth" (Gentry 2007, 8). Beginning readers and mature ones are entirely different, as different as tadpoles and frogs.

Gentry's image points to a profound truth: reading instruction has to change to meet the students' level of brain development. However, do not overextend this analogy. Given time, tadpoles naturally mature into frogs, but beginning readers do not naturally mature into intermediate or advanced readers. The development of the two reading routes in the brain is the product of education, not a natural part of human development.

## Conclusion

Like Beth, students will go through three broad stages as they learn to read: pictorial (pre-reading), phonological (early reading), and orthographic (fluent reading). These stages reflect real changes in their brains, changes that are not a natural part of human development but are the products of education.

By the end of 3rd Grade, all Waldorf students without learning disabilities should be in the orthographic stage. They should be reading to learn, not learning to read. However, they still need years of practice to become expert readers and spellers. Their word identification hubs only reach full maturity in early adolescence, just in time for high school.

The information in chapter 1.2 applies to both English and German. Chapter 1.3 shows how a class's mother tongue will determine how easy or difficult it will be for that group of students to crack the code or reach the orthographic stage. The level of difficulty of a language's spelling system influences the organization of the brains of the people who become literate in that language. Differences in language literally create differences in the brains of the people who learn to read and write in those languages (Dehaene 2009, 117). English has a level of difficulty not present in many other languages. As you will see in the following chapters, this level of difficulty has ramifications for how to teach the mother tongue.

# 1.3 WHY IS ENGLISH SO COMPLICATED?

*Beware of heard, a dreadful word That looks like beard and sounds like bird.*
*And dead; it's said like bed, not bead! For goodness sake, don't call it deed!*
*So our English, I think you will agree,*
*Is the trickiest language you ever did see.*

—Anonymous, "The English Lesson"

This excerpt from "The English Lesson" just touches the tip of the iceberg: when it comes to reading, English truly is a tricky language. Just as it is important to understand how learning to read changes students' brains, it is necessary to understand how English evolved. This exploration will not only reveal why English is so challenging but will provide insight on how best to approach teaching it. It will also explain why Steiner's indications on teaching reading and language skills provide only the beginning of what you need in order to teach literacy and language arts skills.

This chapter covers the following topics:

1. The Three Broad Stages of English

2. Comparing Languages

3. The Historical Development of English

4. Recapitulating the Historical Development of English

## 1. The Three Broad Stages of English

Written languages can come in varying degrees of difficulty. While students who speak alphabetic languages have to move through all three of Frith's stages when they learn to read, the length of time it takes them to get to the orthographic stage varies by language. It is easier to learn to read and spell in some languages than in others. English is quite complex.

Bear et al. in *Words Their Way* show that English has three levels (Bear 2008, 5–6). *The Roadmap to Literacy* will use the analogy of making a layer cake to demonstrate these levels (i.e., the English layer cake).

Languages are a lot like cakes in that they can have a single layer or many layers. A phonetic language such as German or Italian only has one layer, the alphabetic layer. Languages with intricate spelling patterns like French have two layers: the alphabetic layer and a pattern layer. In contrast, English is a three-layered cake made up of an alphabetic layer, a pattern layer, and a meaning layer.

The **alphabetic layer** is the phonetic layer of English. It is the easiest to learn—one letter represents one sound and almost every word looks the way it sounds. This phonetic layer contains the three-letter words that students typically study after they know the alphabet: *cat, dog, man, bag, hop, tin,* etc. Learning the alphabet and its sounds is fundamental to mastering this layer.

**Figure 1.3.1 Layer One of the English Layer Cake: Alphabetic Layer**

**Figure 1.3.2 Layer Two of the English Layer Cake: Pattern Layer**

The **pattern layer** is the second layer of the English language cake. Letters still represent sounds, but instead of one letter representing one sound, *patterns*, or combinations of letters, represent a sound. For example take the long sound of *O*. This one vowel sound has at least six different spellings: open syllable (e.g., *no*), *OE* (e.g., *toe*), *O_E* (e.g., *home*), *OA* (e.g., *boat*), *OUGH* (e.g., *though*), and *OW* (e.g., *snow*). It is the teacher's task to know and then teach the most important of the spelling patterns for the 40+ sounds (depending on dialect) in English. It can take students one, two, or three years to master them because there are so many.

**Figure 1.3.3 Layer Three of the English Layer Cake: Meaning Layer**

The **meaning layer** is the final layer of the English language cake. In the first two layers, letters and combinations of letters represent sounds; in the meaning layer, students learn that words related in meaning are often related in spelling. In other words, rather than using patterns to spell the sounds heard, the student is taught to preserve the spelling of the **root word** or the **word root**.

Let's consider an example. *Music* and *musician* are related in meaning; consequently, they are also related in spelling. The word *musician* preserves the root word *music* in its spelling. Using the first two layers to determine the spelling of *musician* does not help much because common patterns of spelling render many possible incorrect spellings for this word such as *musishun, musition, musitian, musicion,* etc. Students must move into the third layer and consider meaning because the meaning is preserved in the spelling: *music + -an (a person who)*.

Similarly, word roots preserve a connection between meaning and spelling. The roots are word parts. They can go back to Latin and Greek. For example, the root *phil* or *philo* refers to *love*. Hence, words like *philosophy* are spelled with a *PH* rather than the letter *F* to preserve the root and reveal the word's meaning to those who know word roots.

## 2. Comparing Languages

Most languages do not have three layers. The most perfectly phonetic languages, such as German, the language of Rudolf Steiner and the first Waldorf school, have just one layer. More complex languages such as French have two layers. English, however, has all three.

Because of these three distinct layers of the English cake, it takes longer for English-speaking students to develop literacy skills than it does for students learning other languages. For example, at the end of 1st Grade, it has been found that German students read common German words with 98% accuracy, whereas, English students read common English words with 34% accuracy (Ziegler 2006, 430). Other studies show the same effect. "Even at the age of nine, a French child does not read as well as a seven-year-old German. British children only attain the reading proficiency of their French counterparts after close to two full years of additional teaching" (Dehaene 2009, 230–231). The more layers in the language cake, the more time it takes students to get to the Orthographic Stage.

English teachers have an obligation to teach students all three levels of their language. Understanding how this gap developed makes the task easier.

## 3. The Historical Development of English

Bear et al. describe how the three layers of English correspond to the three distinct periods in the history of the written language:

Old English

Middle English

Modern English

History explains why the additional layers developed.

### Old English Period (450 AD–1066 AD)

The Old English period dates back to the time of the epic poem *Beowulf*. The language is incomprehensible to modern speakers because it has changed so much over the years. In the following Old English excerpt, the words *we* and *in* are the only ones recognizable today: "Hwæt! We Gardena in geardagum, þeodcyninga, þrym gefrunon hu da æþelingas ellen fremedon" (Gummere 2007, prologue). (Translation: "Lo! We spear-Danes in days of old heard the glory of the tribal kings, how the princes did courageous deeds.")

English is a Germanic language, and Old English shared a number of traits with modern German: its nouns had both gender and case and its verbs were fully conjugated (see chapter 3.11.2). Despite these complexities, it was easy for people to learn to read and write in Old English. Like modern-day German, written Old English was very phonetic and had only one layer (see fig. 1.3.1).

Old English also had a limited vocabulary, only 30,000 or so words compared to Modern English's current 450,000. In his book *Mother Tongue*, Bill Bryson states, "Of the 30,000 words used in the Old English Period, 85% died out… that means that only about 4,500 Old English words have survived—about 1% of the total number of words in the *Oxford English Dictionary*. And yet those surviving words are among the most fundamental words in English: "*house, brother, live, love,* and so on" (Bryson 1990, 58).

Today, Old English words make up 1% of Modern English vocabulary, but they account for about half of the words in print in modern English. These words include the 100 most commonly used words (sight words): *the, I, is, you, to, for, but, and, at, in, on and*, etc. Ironically, these basic words are some of the hardest words for students to learn. English has changed so much over the centuries that many Old English words are no longer phonetic. Consider the words *no* and *do*. They look similar and should rhyme, but they do not.

### Middle English (1066–1500)

Middle English began precisely in 1066 AD. This date should stand in infamy for anyone who has struggled with English's spelling system. 1066 is the year that William the Conqueror and the Norman French conquered England. The effects of this event created the second layer of the English cake and ruined English's phonetically regular spelling system (see fig. 1.3.2).

Once the French established their court in England, the ruling elite began to speak French. As a result, a number of French words entered the English language: *pleasure, parliament, sergeant, lieutenant,* etc. During this period, roughly 10,000 new words were added to the language, and these words were spelled with French spelling patterns.

This mingling of French and English enriched the vocabulary, but it came at the expense of the structure of English. English lost most of its case system and the gender form of nouns. For example, the word *tongue* is no longer feminine or *foot* masculine. As a result of these changes, English became a simpler language to speak but a more complex one to spell (Bryson 1990, 54–55).

French had many patterns of letters for one sound, and by virtue of adopting so many French words with French spellings, English became one language with two spelling systems. Thus a new layer was added to the English language cake: the pattern layer.

Examples of the French pattern layer can be found in Chaucer's *The Canterbury Tales*. The language, while strange to modern ears, is comprehensible. For example, He coulde songes make, and well indite, joust, and eke dance, and well pourtray and write." (Chaucer 1392, prologue). The underlined words entered the English lexicon during this time, a gift from the French. (Oxford Dictionary 2017)

### Modern English (1500s to Present)

Modern English dates back to Shakespeare's time. Five major factors shaped the language to make it what it is today.

The First Factor: Scholarship: During the Classical Revival or Renaissance of the 16th and 17th centuries, scholars rediscovered Latin and Greek. As a result, English received an influx of secular Latin and Greek words, such as those ending with the suffix *-a*: *insomnia, area, formula*, etc. Rather than using the joint English-

French spelling conventions, these scholars insisted on preserving the foreign spelling as much as possible to show each word's connection to its original language (King 2000, 54).

The scholars did not limit their involvement to new words but retroactively "corrected" the spelling of many Latin-based words that had already entered the English language. Over the years, these words had come to be spelled phonetically, as if they were native English words. For example, *debt* in Middle English was spelled *det*. The scholars decided that these words must reflect their connection to Latin. Hence, they added the silent letter *B* into the word *debt* to show the word's connection to its origin word: *debitum* (King 2000, 55).

The Second Factor: Technology: In the year 1476, an Englishman by the name of William Caxton set up England's first printing press. Caxton brought over an experienced printing crew from Belgium. Masha Bell, researcher and vice chair of the English Spelling Society, discusses some of the consequences of this act in "The History of English Spelling." She says that the Belgian printers spoke little or no English and therefore made many spelling errors. As a result, the spellings for the words *eny*, *frend*, and *cittie* changed to *any*, *friend*, and *citie*. In addition early printers were paid by the line and therefore lengthened some words to earn more money or to make margins look neater. Many words became more complex and longer. The word *fondnes* became *fondness* and *shal* became *shall*, *etc.* (Bell 2017, 5–6).

To compound Caxton's printers' anomalies, copies of the English-language Bible were being printed abroad by people who spoke no English. The same word was found to be spelled several different ways on the same page.

The Third Factor: Johnson's Dictionary: By the 17th century, English spelling had become so chaotic hardly anyone knew what the rules were. For more than a century, spelling truly ran amuck. At the beginning of the 18th century, scholars began to standardize English spellings. In 1746 the English writer and poet Samuel Johnson began his monumental nine-year project: *A Dictionary of the English Language*. He began this herculean task of writing a dictionary as an attempt to bring some semblance of order to a language that he found to be, "copious without order, and energetick without rules: wherever I turned my view, there was perplexity to be disentangled and confusion to be regulated" (Johnson 1785, preface).

Other dictionary writers before Johnson had settled on one spelling for many words that had multiple variations. However, there were still several hundred words in common usage that had more than one spelling (Bell 2004, 56–57). Johnson was reluctant to lose these variations so he expanded on the idea of connecting different spellings to different meanings. He created a plethora of **homophones** (words that sound the same but are spelled differently) and added another layer of spelling difficulty to an already difficult language. In "Why English Spelling Should be Updated," Masha Bell writes: "Dr. Johnson stamped his authority on English spelling with his famous dictionary. In his day many words were still spelt differently by different writers. He chose his preferred versions, or linked different meanings to different spellings (e.g., *there-their*), paying very little heed to pronunciation. Many of our worst problems are due to him" (Bell 2005).

The Fourth Factor: Foreign Borrowings: The creation of modern English coincided with the rise of England as a world power. As the English built an empire around the globe, they encountered other languages and adopted a number of their words. From India (Hindi) came words such as *calico, bungalow, bandana, jungle,* and *veranda* (McCrum 2002, 357). From various Native American languages came *wigwam, hickory, pecan, chipmunk, igloo, and kayak* (ibid., 121–122).

English speakers love to use or borrow words from other languages. This borrowing is one reason why English has so many synonyms. Most languages have 100,000 or 200,000 words while English has over 450,000. Just think how many ways there are to express the concept *big*: gargantuan, immense, gigantic, monstrous, large, huge, behemoth, grand, enormous, vast, etc.

<u>The Fifth Factor: The Creation of New Words</u>: Besides borrowing words, English speakers loved to create them. Writers combine roots and affixes from multiple languages to create a multitude of new words. Shakespeare alone coined around 2000 words such as *excitement* and *courtship* (Bryson 1990, 64). The creation of new words continues to this day. The number of new words arising out of social media alone can be overwhelming. Recent additions include *selfie, phablet, twerking, facetime,* and *emoji.*

In conclusion, the history of English helps explain why English has three layers while German only has one. Waldorf's language arts curriculum is based on the indications Rudolf Steiner gave the German-speaking Waldorf school in Stuttgart in 1919. Fortunately, with a few minor tweaks, his indications can work very well for English's first layer, as it is a phonetic layer. However, it is necessary to go beyond Steiner's indications to teach the next two layers. Since these layers do not exist in German, Steiner did not offer any suggestions for them.

## 4.   Recapitulating the Historical Development of English

It is useful to know why English is so much more difficult to teach than German and to know that English-speaking teachers have to go beyond Steiner's indications to be able to teach reading and spelling. However, there is one more important fact that is critical to understand: proficient readers recapitulate the historical development of English when learning to spell and read.

Bear et al. in *Words Their Way* notes that students move through stages that mirror the history of English while they learn to spell and read (2008, 5–8). Let's view the three broad stages of English again through this lens.

The first stage is the alphabetic layer, where students read and spell phonetically—one letter per sound—just like the Old English did before the Norman invasion. This stage coincides with the Old English layer. A letter represents a sound, and a sound can be spelled with a letter. During this stage, students read easy phonetic readers that have simple **CVC Words** (Consonant-Vowel-Consonant words such as *cat, man, pig, hug, pop*) and spell these simple words in their writing.

The second stage is the pattern layer, where students begin to spell using silent letters and patterns of letters for one sound, just like the French. This stage includes **digraphs,** or two letters that represent one sound such as the letters *SH* in *ship* and the letters *AI* as in *sail.* (In *The Roadmap to Literacy* these digraphs will be referred to as **vowel teams** and **consonant teams.**) Students begin this phase by learning about the Silent *E*, as in the word *cake*, and proceed on to vowel teams such as Two Vowels Go Walking: the letters *OA* as in *coat*, the letters *AI* as in *mail*, and the letters *EA* as in *cream.* They learn **diphthongs** (when two vowel sounds are connected to make a "gliding" sound) such as the letters *OY* in *boy* and the letters *OW* in *cow.* They also learn words with **R-controlled vowels,** or words where there is a letter *R* after the vowel and the vowel sound changes, such as the letters *IR* as in *girl* and the letters *AR* as in *star.* This stage of reading and spelling recapitulates the Norman period when silent letters and patterns of letters to represent one sound began appearing in English under the Norman French.

The third stage is the meaning layer, where students focus on the meaning of the word root, prefix, and suffix, just like the Latin and Greek scholars. For example, when they learn that the root *phon* refers to *sound*, they gain a key to advanced spelling and vocabulary because they realize the connection between words such as *telephone* (across-sound) and *phonetic* (of or relating to spoken language or speech sounds). This stage mirrors the development of Modern English when Latin and Greek roots, prefixes, and suffixes were added into the language during the Renaissance.

This long journey to literacy may seem daunting for both students and teachers; however, it is well worth the effort. English may be more complex than other languages, but students who persevere and master its opaque reading and spelling are rewarded with access to the richest vocabulary on earth and the tools with which to spell it correctly.

## Conclusion

Chapter 1.3 shows that English is more complicated than German and other languages. Consequently, English-speaking students require more classroom instruction to advance to the orthographic stage than can be found in Steiner's indications. The next chapter considers how the historical recapitulation that students undergo is bigger than the history of English and its ramifications on how to teach it.

# 1.4 HOW STUDENTS RECAPITULATE THE HISTORY OF WRITTEN LANGUAGE

*When children are losing their baby teeth, they feel least connected with the kind of writing and reading prevalent in our present stage of civilization, because it represents the results of stylization and convention. Children, who have only recently come into the world, are suddenly expected to absorb the final results of all of the transformations that writing and reading have gone through.*

—Rudolf Steiner, *The Child's Changing Consciousness* (Trostli 2004, 100)

The last chapter demonstrated that students recapitulate the historical development of English as they learn to read and write. However, the recapitulation does not begin there: students also recapitulate the history of writing and reading that predates written English. Knowledge of how and why this recapitulation occurs is one of the keys to understanding how students learn to write and read.

This chapter covers the following topics:

1. The Development of Writing

2. Phonological Awareness

3. The First Alphabet

4. The Development of Written Conventions

5. The Development of Reading

6. Ramifications for Teaching

## 1.   The Development of Writing

Why did humans develop writing? (Hint: *Follow the money.*)

The earliest system of writing known is Sumerian cuneiform, and it was used to record business transactions as early as the fourth millennium BCE. It was a pictogram system, which means that a picture of an object represented the object itself. It was quite elegant to have a picture for every word; however, people had to memorize each word to become proficient—and there were 2,000 of them!

Over time, Sumerian pictograms gave way to Sumerian phonograms. Pictures began to represent sounds (syllables) instead of objects. Rather than an unwieldy 2000 pictograms, the Sumerians reduced the symbols needed for writing down to 200 phonograms—still a lot, but a definite improvement.

At the same time that the Sumerians simplified their writing system, the Egyptians had their own system, albeit a rather complex one. They had hieroglyphs, which are a form of pictogram, but they also had an alphabet.

The Egyptian alphabet consisted of 24 letters. Of particular note is the fact that all of the letters were consonants. (Note that Egyptians were not alone in creating alphabets that only contain consonants. Ancient Hebrew also omits vowel letters.) The combination of alphabet and pictograms created a writing system that was quite complex. Scribes had to memorize hundreds of separate signs.

**Figure 1.4.1 Ancient Egyptian Hieroglyph: Ankh (the word for *life*)**

The first system of writing that relied entirely on an alphabet was created by the Phoenicians before the first millennium BCE. Merchants in the Phoenician city of Byblos developed a writing system that used 26 letter symbols that were based on Egyptian hieroglyphs. Each of these 26 letters represented a sound. The genius of the Phoenicians lies in transforming the pictograms into a true alphabet. It is much easier to learn 26 letters than hundreds of separate signs (Florey 2009, 23–25).

Aspects of this brief history of writing recall aspects of Frith's pictorial stage and phonological stage (see chapter 1.2 #1). Early writing in the historical record was picture writing, and today early reading remains picture reading. Early writing then shifted to an alphabet, while today, the shift to the phonological stage still depends on learning the alphabet.

Human writing is a convention so why should this correlation exist between the historical record and the early stages of reading? The answer is simple. Both the development of writing and the brain changes that occur when students learn to read rest upon a developing consciousness of the archetypal foundation that underlies all human speech and writing: phonological awareness.

## 2. Phonological Awareness

All people who develop literacy have to become conscious of an archetypal reality that underlies human speech: **phonological awareness**, or an awareness that speech can be broken down into smaller units.

If you stop and think about it, people do not actually speak in separate words. Instead, "allofourwordsblendtogetherintoonesoundstream" (translation: all of our words blend together into one sound stream).

To be able to write and read, it is necessary to break this continuous stream of sound down into separate parts. There are three divisions of phonological awareness:

1. **Word:** The most basic break of the sound stream is into words. For example, a person needs to see that *Ilikejumpingrope* is really made of four words: *I, like, jumping, rope*. Being able to break the sound stream down into its separate words is called developing a **theory of word.**

20

2. **Syllable:** Each word can be broken down into beats, or syllables. For example, the word *like* is one syllable; *jumping* is two syllables. (It does not matter if a student hears the break as *jump-ing* or *jum-ping*. All that matters is that each syllable contains only one vowel sound and is logical. Therefore, no *j-umping* or *ju-mping*.)

3. **Phoneme or Sound:** The most difficult break to perceive is that of separating words into phonemes, or individual sounds. All words and syllables can be broken down into phonemes. For example, the word *cat* is made of one syllable but three phonemes: /k/ /ă/ /t/. The word *fish* also has three phonemes (/f/ /ĭ/ /sh/) but is spelled with four letters. In this case, the letters *SH* represent one phoneme, the sound /sh/. (To read phonemes, just pronounce the sound of the letter or letters in the forward slashes. For example, /sh/ is the sound the librarian makes when someone is being too noisy.) Becoming aware of individual phonemes and then being able to manipulate them is called developing **phonemic awareness.**

The development of phonological awareness is preserved in the early examples of writing. The Sumerian system reflects the first awareness that speech contains individual words as shown by a pictogram that represents an object (for the further development of theory of word, see chapter 1.4 #4). The Sumerians moved to phonograms that represent syllables, a more subtle breakdown of speech. The invention of the alphabet represents an awareness of the phoneme, or the most subtle of the archetypes in speech, and it often took a while before early peoples were able to work exclusively with a pure alphabetic code. The Egyptians used both pictograms and an alphabet concomitantly. Furthermore, early alphabets often omitted vowel letters (e.g ., Egyptian and Ancient Hebrew). This fact suggests that when people first started to develop phonemic awareness, awareness of consonant sounds came first.

Unlike some early scripts, modern English is based entirely on the alphabet. Past the pictorial stage, all exploration of phonological awareness is done based on the alphabet. It behooves us to explore the history of that first alphabet. It will have ramifications for how to teach.

## 3.  The First Alphabet

The genius of an alphabet is that it is a code where a written letter, or **grapheme**, represents a speech sound, or phoneme.

It would have been much easier for the Phoenicians to learn their alphabet because it was much more transparent than ours. When modern people learn the alphabet, they say, "*B*, /b/, baby," (i.e., "bee, bu, baby"), using the letter name, its sound (phoneme), and an anchor word to remember the connection. The Phoenicians used a system called *acrophony*, or uppermost sound. They would only have said, "Baby." In their system, the word *baby* would stand both as the name of the grapheme (i.e., the written letter *B*) as well as the **anchor word** that illustrates the grapheme's sound (i.e., *baby*). Instead of learning the *ABCs*, Kitty Burns Florey, author of *Script and Scribble: The Rise and Fall of Handwriting*, jokes that the Phoenicians would have had to learn their "Ax-Banana-Cats" (Florey 2009, 25).

Consider how much simpler the Phoenician alphabetic system is. Their letter came from a picture, the name of the picture was also the letter's name, and the letter's sound was embedded in its name. The connection between grapheme and phoneme is perfectly clear. What is the connection between the grapheme *B* and its name *bee*? There is none. The connection no longer exists.

In developing the written symbols, the Phoenicians looked to the Egyptian hieroglyphics; hence, the first true alphabet retained an association with the pictogram or picture. Steiner notes this fact, saying that Egyptian hieroglyphs "still retained some similarity to what they were intended to convey [and] ancient cuneiform writing also still had some resemblance to what the signs signified....The forms of these ancient writing... brought to mind the likeness of what they represented from the external world" (Trostli 2004, 85). This situation is no longer the case today.

When Waldorf teachers introduce the first consonants out of images (e.g., the letter *M* from the form of a mountain), they are re-enacting the historical development of letters for their students. This technique helps to forge a strong initial association between the grapheme and the phoneme for the students in the pictorial stage who are not yet aware of the connection between a letter, its phoneme, and its anchor word (see chapter 3.1 #7 and Figure 2.1.1 for an example).

The development of letters (graphemes) was a crucial step in developing literacy, but further development occurred later.

## 4. The Development of Written Conventions

Once people were using alphabets, it is natural to assume that their writing looked like writing from today, but it did not. Lowercase letters, mandatory spaces between words, and mandatory punctuation were all innovations that came during medieval times.

Lowercase letters came about with the development of a new script in the 9th century AD: minuscule. Prior to the development of minuscule, texts were written in capital letters, technically called majuscules (Netz 2007, 78).

Mandatory spaces between words also developed late. Greek was written without spaces between the words until the late Middle Ages (Netz 2007, 35). Plato, Archimedes, and other Greek philosophers all wrote words that blended together. They duplicated the speech they heard: one continuous stream of phonemes with no spaces between the separate words.

Standardized punctuation dates to around 800 AD. It came into existence with a particular type of minuscule handwriting known as Carolingian Minuscule, named after Charlemagne, the Holy Roman Emperor. Prior to Carolingian Minuscule, punctuation had been inconsistent, haphazard, or even nonexistent in texts. Now the quotation mark, comma, and question mark were used (Florey 2009, 34–35).

Why it may have taken so long to decide that it is mandatory to put spaces between words and to use punctuation will become clearer through examining the history of reading.

## 5. The Development of Reading

How did humans develop reading?

The answer is through writing. It may seem obvious in hindsight, but in order to read, someone first had to write. Writing preceded reading. So far, this chapter has considered how students recapitulate the history of writing as they develop phonological awareness. As it turns out, they also recapitulate the history of reading.

Beginning readers have some distinctive traits. When they first begin to read, they can only read familiar texts. When students first start to read unfamiliar texts, they invariably read out loud. Silent reading comes later. Looking at the historical record, it is possible to find some parallels.

Recall that the first writing was of business transactions. This material would have been familiar to both parties. The writing was a record of something already known. *Ipso facto*, the very first reading would have been of familiar texts.

There are also interesting hints in the historical record that people initially read aloud and that silent reading came later. One of the more interesting hints is from Saint Augustine, a professor of Latin rhetoric, who is most famous for his work *The Confessions of Saint Augustine*. (In it he has such choice phrases as "Make me chaste, Lord, but not yet.") He also has the distinction of recording the first definite instance of silent reading in Western literature.

In 384 AD, Augustine went to visit Ambrose, bishop of Milan, and there he encountered something extraordinary: the bishop was reading silently. Not only that, Augustine noted that he never read aloud. This situation was so unusual that Augustine, a professor himself, noted it in his writing and spent some time ruminating about it. The implication is that in his day, reading was typically done out loud (Manguel 1996, 41–42).

Prior to the 9th century, the monks working in the monastic scriptoriums used to read aloud as they copied their manuscripts. They would carefully enunciate each word and syllable as they transcribed. Not until the 10th century does silent reading become usual in the West (Manguel 1996, 50). Perhaps punctuation marks and spaces between words became standard to help readers make sense of the material when they were not reading aloud.

It seems likely that beginning students not only recapitulate the history of writing but also the history of reading. Reading began with familiar material. For a long period of time, reading was done aloud. Silent reading developed later. Students recapitulate this pattern as they learn to read, just as they recapitulate the development of phonological awareness as they learn to write.

## 6. Ramifications for Teaching

Through this history of writing and reading, it is possible to see correlations with the changes that education causes in students' brains during Frith's pictorial and phonological stages of reading presented in chapter 1.2 #1. Historically, the first writing and reading was picture writing and reading, and that situation holds true for beginning students as well—their first writing and reading is pictorial (i.e., Firth's first stage). This period was followed by a time when both pictograms and letters co-existed, just as they will for a student who is first entering the phonological stage. To switch to a purely alphabetic model that contains both vowels and consonant letters, people needed to develop full phonemic awareness for segmenting sounds, something the students will do as well during the phonological stage. It is unclear when early peoples entered the orthographic stage; however, it seems plausible that silent reading became common centuries after people first started to write and read. It will also take some time for students to reach that pinnacle. They will need to practice extensively to develop the lexical route in their brains.

Since students recapitulate the historical development of literacy, history can offer some guidance on optimal ways to teach literacy. For example, early people developed letters through pictures. Therefore, it is useful to teach the first letters of the alphabet through pictures, something Waldorf teachers already do. However, history also suggests additional things teachers could do:

- Early peoples developed phonemic awareness for consonant sounds before vowel sounds. Beginning students often do too. Therefore, it is logical to teach consonant letters before vowel letters. (This idea will be developed in chapter 3.1 Alphabet.)

- Ancient peoples experimented with words as pictures before they experimented with words as code. Therefore, it is logical to teach some words as pictures rather than code. The sight words that date back to Old English, particularly the phonetically irregular ones, are prime candidates for such treatment. (This idea will be developed in chapter 3.6 Sight Words.)

- Experimenting with writing spurred the development of phonological awareness in ancient peoples. Therefore, it is good to have beginning students write (i.e., compose, not copy) as much as possible so they, too, can develop phonological awareness. **Kid writing** is a type of writing that allows invented spellings and enables students to experiment with phonological awareness. (This idea will be developed in chapter 3.13 Kid Writing.)

- The first reading was always of familiar material. Therefore, it is logical that the first reading be **memory reading**, or the reading of familiar material. (This idea will be developed in chapter 3.15 Reading.)

Beginning student writers tend to omit the same conventions as the ancients; however, these errors are not all created equal. Some reflect archetypal realities such as the development of phonological awareness, while others merely reflect students' struggles with arbitrary human conventions. Either way, you can use your observations to assess informally and adjust classroom instruction accordingly.

- Beginning writers often omit the spaces between words. Just like the ancients, they write what they hear. Their written words all run together because that is how people speak. This error is archetypal and reflects the beginning stages of the development of theory of word, a critical part of phonological awareness. You can use samples of a student's kid writing to determine if more phonological awareness practice is needed for her to master theory of word.

- Students also develop phonemic awareness in stages. They typically follow the same pattern as the ancients and become aware of consonants before vowels. When children first learn to write, it is common for them to go through a phase of omitting vowels. You can track their development of phonemic awareness through their writing in much the same way you did with theory of word and work with this common spelling problem by working on phonemic awareness (see table 3.3.1).

- Young students also tend to use uppercase letters (or a mix of uppercase and lowercase letters). In their minds there is no difference between uppercase and lowercase letters; both capital $T$ and lowercase $t$ represent the same sound or phoneme /t/. The existence of uppercase and lowercase is pure human convention and does not relate to how students hear and experience language. In this case, beginning students are not recapitulating the development of writing when they mix up their uppercase and lowercase letters: they are merely trying to master this arbitrary convention. However, you can still use their writing to determine which letters they have yet to master and adjust your lessons accordingly.

- Finally, your students omit punctuation marks when they write. You can track their development of language mechanics through their writing in the same way you did with capitalization errors to provide more instruction and practice.

Note: Some readers might suggest that it would be logical to teach uppercase letters first and lowercase letters later on because ancient people developed uppercase letters first. Such reasoning would be faulty. Capital and lowercase letters are pure human convention. They do not reflect any archetypal reality such as the development of phonological awareness or any concomitant changes in the brain such as a shift from picture reading to working with a code. Students need to work with modern conventions to be able to read modern script, an idea that will be developed in chapter 3.1 when information is presented on how to teach the alphabet.

A good rule of thumb is to use the historical record to order aspects of your teaching that are archetypal in nature or that reflect the sequential nature of brain development as students develop literacy, but introduce human conventions as students need to know them regardless of when they show up in the historical record.

## Conclusion

Chapter 1.2 demonstrates that students learning alphabetic languages all move through the same stages. Chapter 1.3 shows that the history of English makes it harder to master literacy in English than in German and that students recapitulate the history of English when they learn to read and spell. This chapter discusses how students recapitulate the historical development of writing as they develop phonological awareness and the historical development of reading when they first start to read. In the next chapter, *The Roadmap to Literacy* will put it all together and present an overview of the five phases students move through as they learn to write and read in English. These phases will be the backbone of *The Roadmap to Literacy's* approach to teaching.

# 1.5 THE ROADMAP TO LITERACY: THE FIVE PHASES OF LEARNING TO READ AND SPELL

*Brain Development + Recapitulation of Development of English + Recapitulation of Development of Reading & Writing = The Roadmap to Literacy*

—Jennifer Militzer-Kopperl

The preceding chapters have examined both brain development and the fact that students recapitulate the historical development of reading and writing as well as the historical development of written English. This chapter will combine these truths to create a roadmap for teachers. This roadmap encompasses five key phases that English-speaking students progress through on the way to becoming expert readers and spellers: *The Roadmap to Literacy*. Working consciously with these phases is fundamental to teaching students how to read and spell in English.

This chapter covers the following topics:

1. An Introduction to the Phases
2. Points to Keep in Mind while Working with *The Roadmap to Literacy*
3. The Benefits of *The Roadmap to Literacy*

## 1.   An Introduction to the Phases

*The Roadmap to Literacy* is comprised of five key phases that are loosely based off of the work of Bear et al. in *Words Their Way*. Each phase has different tasks that the students must achieve before they move on to the next phase. These timelines will be indicated. However, the timing of this achievement will be determined by two factors: when you begin using *The Roadmap to Literacy* (i.e., 1st, 2nd, or 3rd Grade) and the needs of the students of your class. The five phases are:

1. Emergent
2. Phonemic Awareness
3. Pattern
4. Syllable
5. Latin/Greek

## The Emergent Phase

Description: The Emergent Phase represents the very beginning of learning to write and read.

In this phase, students work on phonological awareness, with an emphasis on developing: 1) theory of word; 2) an awareness of syllables; and 3) phonemic awareness for the first sound in a word. This basic level of phonemic awareness enables students to learn the sounds of letters, or the **sound/symbol correspondence**. To do so, they must recognize the alphabetic principle, that letters represent sounds. They also begin to learn **sight words**, the commonly used words in English that do not always 'play fair' because they cannot be sounded out or decoded. The reading approach that is used in this phase is **memory reading**, the "reading" of familiar material that students have memorized. Through memory reading, students practice theory of word, basic letter sound matching, and sight word recognition.

Brain Development: In the Emergent Phase, students are in Frith's pictorial stage (see chapter 1.2 #1). Their brains process whole words as pictures. To move forward, they must realize that words are not pictograms of the objects they represent but rather a code based on letters that represent individual phonemes (sounds). The key to this development is learning the alphabet, and the key to learning the alphabet is developing phonemic awareness for the first sound in words so the students can make the connection between Bear, /b/, B. The key to developing phonological awareness for word and phoneme is experimenting with writing systems. Just like ancient peoples, students will develop phonological awareness through experimenting with the alphabet. Once students have made these connections and know some letters, they are ready to move to the Phonemic Awareness Phase.

Students' Key Task: The students' key task in the Emergent Phase is to recognize the alphabetic principle in preparation for learning the sound/symbol correspondence for the entire alphabet. To recognize the alphabetic principle, they will first need to develop phonemic awareness for the initial sound in a word and learn some letters of the alphabet.

## The Phonemic Awareness Phase

Description: The Phonemic Awareness Phase represents the next step in learning to read and write.

Now that students realize that letters represent sounds, they can begin to encode using this new skill. Section 3.4 #1 will demonstrate that the key to teaching students to decode, or sound out words, is to first teach them to encode, or spell words sound by sound. Encoding will provide the necessary prerequisites in phonemic awareness for decoding.

By the middle of this phase, students' phonemic awareness will be strong enough for them to begin to decode. They begin with basic **CVC** words, the Consonant-Vowel-Consonant words such as *dog, hit, and man*. After mastering this decoding skill, they move on to the study of phonics rules (see chapter 4.1). Students continue with both memory reading and sight words. Once students have mastered basic decoding skills and a number of sight words, they are ready to begin reading simple decodable-texts.

Brain Development: In the Phonemic Awareness Phase, students are in Frith's phonological stage (see chapter 1.2 #1). They are switching word recognition from the right hemisphere to the left hemisphere. Their brains are developing the *letter to sound decoding route*. However, at the beginning of this phase, they are not ready yet to jump into decoding because their phonemic awareness is still underdeveloped. Writing spurs the development of their phonemic awareness, just as it did for ancient people. Learning to encode is the easiest way to create the *letter to sound decoding route*. After all encoding and decoding use the same skill set.

Next students learn to decode. In so doing, they work on developing the alphabetic layer of English (i.e., the simple CVC words that play fair and consonantal blends). When students have created the *letter to sound decoding route* in their brains and have developed full phonemic awareness for segmenting all of the sounds in words, they have completed the development of written languages in general. At this point students are ready to move into the aspects of the language that are specific to the historical development of English and will do so in the next phase: the Pattern Phase.

Students' Key Tasks: The students' key tasks in the Phonemic Awareness Phase are: 1) mastering the full sound/symbol correspondence (i.e., finish learning their letters and their sounds); 2) developing full phonemic awareness (i.e., when encoding, they represent each sound in a word with a logical letter choice, which demonstrates they have mastered segmenting sounds); and 3) developing the *letter to sound decoding route*.

Note: By using *The Roadmap to Literacy*, teachers and their students should be able to complete both the Emergent Phase and the Phonemic Awareness Phase by the end of 1st Grade.

**The Pattern Phase**

Description: The Pattern Phase represents the middle step in teaching students to read and write in English.

Now that students have full phonemic awareness and can segment all of the sounds in a word and use a letter to represent all of the sounds (e.g., *monstr* (sic) for the word *monster*), they need to learn English letter patterns that represent individual phonemes (e.g., the vowel teams such as the letters *OA* in *boat*). Students also begin to study **word families** (see below). Once students have mastered the various ways to spell the vowel patterns, they will begin to study **homophones**, or words that have the same pronunciation such as *blue* and *blew*. At some point in this phase, students crack the code and learn to read. Their fluency takes off.

The Pattern Phase refers to the two types of patterns students will use to develop fluency. The first type refers to the patterns of letters that represent a single phoneme. The second type refers to the use of chunks of words, such as onsets and rimes and syllables.

**Onsets** and **rimes** are a way to break down a syllable by splitting it at the vowel. They are best illustrated with **word families**, chains of words that have a common rime. Let's consider the *–all* word family in table 1.5.1.

**Table 1.5.1: The –all word family**

| The –all Family |
|:---:|
| tall |
| ball |
| call |
| small |
| stall |
| etc. |

The rime is the pattern of letters from the vowel to the end of a single-syllable word. The onset is any consonant or consonants that come before it. In the word *mall*, *m* is the onset and *–all* is the rime. In *stars*, *ST* is the onset and *–ars* is the rime. The dash preceding the rime refers to missing letters.

The use of onsets and rimes is the key to speeding up decoding. Rather than reading and spelling one sound or one letter at a time, students will start to recognize and use chunks of sound such as onsets and rimes in single-syllable words and syllables in longer words. Equipped with a large bank of sight words, knowledge of English's extensive collection of vowel patterns, and automatic decoding enhanced by the use of onset and rime and syllables, students will begin to read more and more, culminating in the moment when they crack the code.

Brain Development: At some point in the Pattern Phase, students will enter Frith's orthographic stage. Their brains begin to use the *word identification hub* and they begin to use the *lexical route* of reading. They begin to read fluently and silently. For less complex languages such as German, this point would be the end of the line; however, for English, it is only the middle of the journey. The students are only at the mid-point of the second of English's three layers: the pattern layer. They will take their first foray into the meaning layer when they consider homophones, but the bulk of the work occurs in the next two phases: the Syllable and Latin/Greek Phases.

Because students can read but have not yet mastered spelling all of the vowel patterns, a split usually opens between their reading and spelling skills. In the first two phases, encoding progresses faster than decoding. In other words, most students can encode (spell) words better than they can decode (read) words. In the Pattern Phase, this order reverses. By the end of the Pattern Phase, most students can decode words better than they can encode them because there are so many spelling variations for vowel sounds. As a result, it will be necessary to start teaching spelling as a separate subject. The students must learn to spell as well as they read.

Students' Key Tasks: The students' key tasks in the Pattern Phase are mastering patterns of letters and mastering the process of encoding and decoding using onsets and rimes. **Symbol Imagery**, a type of mental picturing for letters and numerals, will be critical for accomplishing these tasks (see chapter 1.6 #2 and chapter 3.5).

Note: If you are following the suggestions in this book, you should be able to complete the Pattern Phase by the end of 2nd Grade. (Students will continue to study spelling patterns based on the Pattern Phase in 3rd Grade as part of the spelling curriculum.)

## The Syllable Phase

Description: In the Syllable Phase, students transcend patterns such as onset and rime and learn to read and spell exclusively by syllables.

The study of affixes (prefixes and suffixes) is a key aspect of this phase. Students finish learning to decode by studying the rules for breaking words down into syllables. In addition, students will continue to study spelling as a separate subject with weekly spelling words, and the study of grammar will become paramount.

Brain Development: The Syllable Phase is the culmination of learning to read in English. Students have already reached the orthographic stage of reading, but they need the last bit of formal reading instruction: how to work with syllables, particularly affixes. By the middle of this phase, students will be able to decode just about any word in the language, and reading instruction (phonics rules) stops. However, spelling instruction will continue throughout this phase because it will take students longer to master encoding by syllable than it will for them to master decoding.

In the Syllable Phase, the students remain on the cusp of working with the meaning layer in English. While they get some additional work in this area when they consider the connection between spelling and grammar, particularly when they study the meaning of common affixes, the bulk of the work in the meaning layer lies ahead, in the Latin/Greek Phase (7th–8th Grade). In addition students in 4th Grade and beyond will have to learn how to handle increasingly advanced vocabulary and comprehension. They will also need to learn to read various nonfiction texts such as articles on animals or instructions on how to do something.

<u>Students' Key Tasks</u>: The students' key tasks in the Syllable Phase include mastering decoding all multisyllabic words and mastering encoding by syllable. It is imperative that students master the latter before they begin the Latin/Greek Phase.

Note: If you are following the suggestions in this book, you should be able to complete the <u>decoding</u> aspect of the Syllable Phase by the end of 3rd Grade. Work on the <u>encoding</u> aspect of this phase will continue on through the 6th Grade. (First teach the students to decode with phonics rules by the end of 3rd Grade, but reteach these rules as part of the spelling curriculum in Grades 4–6.)

## The Latin/Greek Phase

<u>Description</u>: The Latin/Greek Phase is dedicated to deciphering and spelling the <u>meaning</u> inherent in the Latin and Greek **roots** that found their way into English (see chapter 1.3 #3).

In the Syllable Phase, students mastered encoding and decoding by syllable. Now they must transcend spelling by syllable and learn to spell by **morphemes**, or the units of meaning inherent in a word. For example, if the word *philosopher* were spelled by syllables, it could be *fi-lo-so-fer, fi-lo-sa-fer, fi-lo-si-fer, fi-lo-se-fer,* etc. However, the word's spelling preserves its meaning: lover of wisdom. It is made up of two roots and one suffix: philo (love) + soph (wisdom—from Sophia) + -er (a person who). Hence the correct spelling is *philosopher*. Knowing the word roots is the key to spelling in this phase.

There is a secondary task in the final phase: vocabulary acquisition. In addition to mastering spelling, students can expand their vocabulary by studying word roots. For example, the word root *locut/loqu* means *speak* or *talk*. Note how many words are related: locution, eloquent, loquacious, loquacity, circumlocution (i.e., talking in circles—note the prefix *circ/circum*), etc. Once students learn word roots, they have a new tool for mastering vocabulary. When it comes to building up a sophisticated vocabulary, vocabulary lists are good, reading is better, but the systematic study of word roots is the best. Note how learning the root *locut/loqu* unlocked the meaning of five words that otherwise would have had to be memorized or gleaned from reading.

<u>Brain Development</u>: The Latin/Greek Phase represents the final layer of the English language: the meaning layer. Students entered the orthographic stage of reading in the Pattern Phase and mastered first decoding and later encoding in the Syllable Phase. The task of the students in the Latin/Greek Phase is to learn to consider meaning in spelling in addition to syllables, patterns of letters, and phonemes.

English has almost half a million words so the Latin/Greek Phase can provide a student of language enough material to last a lifetime. Spelling Bee champions spend years memorizing word roots to prepare for competition. Students in the junior high years need to master the process of spelling with word roots and be able to analyze words for meaning. This phase provides material for Grades 7–8.

<u>Students' Key Tasks</u>: The students' key tasks in this phase are learning to encode meaning through Latin/Greek roots and expanding vocabulary knowledge.

In summary, there are five phases that students need to master in order to become expert readers and spellers. Each phase has a key element to teach that will make it possible for students to achieve the tasks of each phase. *The Roadmap to Literacy* will use these phases as the basis for all of the recommendations in upcoming sections. See table 1.5.2 for a summary.

**Table 1.5.2: The Most Important Objective of Each Phase**

| Phase | Key Element Students Must Master |
|---|---|
| Emergent | Recognizing the alphabetic principle |
| Phonemic Awareness | Developing full phonemic awareness |
| Pattern | Developing symbol imagery* |
| Syllable | Working with syllables |
| Latin/Greek | Working with word roots |
| | *A form of mental picturing for letters in words. It will be covered in chapters 1.6 #2 and 3.5.* |

## 2. Points to Keep in Mind while Working with *The Roadmap to Literacy*

There are several important points to bear in mind.

First, the difference between readers in the phases is quite profound. Recall that J. Richard Gentry compares early readers to tadpoles and mature ones to frogs (see chapter 1.2 #6). His point is that the students in the early phases need different reading instruction than those in the middle and later phases. This difference in brain development between novice and advanced readers affects what students should read (familiar vs. new texts) and how they should read it (choral or class reading vs. silent independent reading). It affects which activities teachers do and why they do them. Knowing a student's phase allows teachers to choose the right activities to support the student and to lead her to the next phase.

Second, before going on to learn the skills taught in the last three phases, it is imperative that students move through each of the first two phases and develop theory of word and full phonemic awareness (i.e., when encoding, they represent each sound in a word with a logical letter choice, which demonstrates they have mastered segmenting sounds). If students do not develop the key element in each phase, they are at risk for developing predictable spelling and/or reading problems in the future. They then have to go back and master the underdeveloped skills either in class or in tutoring.

Third, it is common for some students to enter 1st Grade reading in the Phonemic Awareness Phase or even the Pattern Phase; however, it is prudent to make sure that their encoding (spelling) is at the same phase. A quick check can reveal if they have truly developed theory of word, phonemic awareness, and basic sight word spelling. If not, they will need instruction and/or practice in the lower phases despite the fact that they are reading in a higher phase. This work will allow their encoding skills to catch up with their decoding skills.

Fourth, if you follow the curriculum set out in this book, you may note some examples of grade-to-phase correlation (e.g., completion of the Pattern Phase by the end of 2nd Grade); however, this correlation is an anomaly. The phases do not coincide with the grades but rather with brain development and knowledge of how written English works. Always teach to your students' phases, not their grade level.

Fifth, the phases can be broken down into a beginning, middle, and end. This division will help with lesson planning and assessment (see chapter 6.2).

Note: If you are picking this book up in the 2nd or 3rd Grade, you must match your instruction to your students' phase(s). Assess first (see chapter 6.2) and begin wherever your students are in their journey, even if it means that you will not cover all of the material by the end of 3rd Grade. The early phases represent foundational brain development that must be in place for students to learn phonics rules. Teaching each of the phases to completion is more important than following the grade-level instruction laid out in this book.

## 3.    The Benefits of *The Roadmap to Literacy*

Once you understand the phases and learn to work consciously with *The Roadmap to Literacy*, you will be able to do the following:

- understand why teaching reading is a three-year process and teaching spelling instruction in English is an eight-year process
- see where Rudolf Steiner's indications are useful and know how to fill in the missing pieces that are specific to English
- determine which literacy skills to teach and in what order
- identify which stage a student is in by assessing her spelling (encoding) during writing assignments
- craft lessons to teach the very skills your students need to learn to move to the next phase
- recognize when and where students get stuck and how to get them moving forward again

These points are covered in greater depth in upcoming sections. For a breakdown of skills by phase, see chapter 6.2 #1.

## Conclusion

The five phases provide teachers with a roadmap that shows them which literacy skills to teach and when to teach them. They are based on the development of the brain and the fact that students recapitulate both the history of written languages and the history of English. The recommendations in *The Roadmap to Literacy* are organized around these five phases.

For practical purposes, only the first four phases are covered. (The Latin/Greek Phase is primarily for Grades 7–8.) Students are expected to master decoding by syllables by the end of 3rd Grade (i.e., phonics rules); they will continue to study encoding by syllables in 4th–6th Grades as part of spelling.

Sections 3–5 show you how to use the phases to develop effective main lessons and practice class lessons for your students; however, first, it is good to resolve an old argument concerning the three reading approaches most commonly used to teach literacy.

Note: If you start this program in 2nd or 3rd Grade, it is likely that some of your students will not be ready for the Syllable Phase in 3rd Grade. Teach to your students' phase(s) and plan to catch up in 4th Grade. Regardless of when you start this program, always teach to phase, not grade.

# 1.6 RESOLVING THE READING WARS

*The most damaging effects . . . are caused by one-sided illusions, by fixed ideas about how certain things should be taught. For example . . . the new phonetic method of teaching reading... superseded the old method of making words by adding single letters—a method that was again replaced by the whole-word method. . . . The ideas that underlie all three methods are good—there is no denying that each has its merits. It is bad, however, when these things become fads. (The order of the last two sentences has been switched by the author.)*

—Rudolf Steiner, *The Child's Changing Consciousness and Waldorf Education* (Trostli 2004, 181–182)

The last chapter introduced the five phases of *The Roadmap to Literacy* and showed how they unite both the development of the literary brain as well as mirror the historical development of English. This chapter will show you how to use the phases to determine which reading method to employee when teaching students: phonics, whole language, or the look-say method.

This chapter covers the following topics:

1. The Reading Wars
2. Sensory-Cognitive Functions
3. Sensory-Cognitive Functions and Reading Methodologies
4. Sensory-Cognitive Functions and Reading Skills
5. Using the Phases of *The Roadmap to Literacy* to End the Reading Wars

## 1.  The Reading Wars

When it comes to reading methodologies, there are several parallels between Steiner's time and the modern era. Today, just as in Steiner's time, there are three different reading methods: whole language, phonics, and look-say. Just as in Steiner's time, the ideas that underlie all three methods have their merits. Just as in Steiner's time, too many devotees of the methods have fixed ideas about how reading should be taught: the debate over the best method of reading instruction, after all, is referred to as *The Reading Wars*. Just as in Steiner's time, methods go in and out of fashion.

Every generation or so, the dominant method changes, but the war never ends for one simple reason: the opposing side is always able to point to a sizable minority of students who fail to learn to read under the method currently popular. The reason for the failure is simple: students need different approaches at different points along the journey to full literacy. The solution is also simple: use all three approaches, but apply the right approach at the right time. The phases show how to do so.

## 2. Sensory-Cognitive Functions

A prerequisite to understanding the wisdom behind each of the three reading approaches is a concept called sensory-cognitive functions.

Comprehension is the goal of reading, but how do students achieve it? Students need both reading skills and underlying capacities. **Skills** refer to academic skills taught in class such as phonics rules like the Silent *E* Rule and the ability to decode words. **Capacities** refer to the foundational abilities students should first develop before they learn specific skills. These capacities can include the ability to move the eyes freely from the board to the paper, to converge both eyes at the same point and move them across a line of print in tandem, to move from the end of one line of print down to the beginning of the next line, and to cross the midline, etc.

However, there are three important things that are both capacity and skill. They begin to develop on their own as part of human development, but they require education to develop to their full potential. Lindamood-Bell Learning Processes® (LBLP), a company that specializes in teaching remedial reading and other academics, has a useful framework for exploring these three transition skills and capacities called sensory-cognitive functions.

**Sensory-cognitive functions** lie at the intersection of a sense (seeing, hearing, or language) and the ability to think about and manipulate information provided by that sense. LBLP has identified three sensory-cognitive functions: phonemic awareness, symbol imagery, and concept imagery (Lindamood 1998, 4) (Bell 2001, 26–30). Let's explore each of these sensory-cognitive functions in this light and build upon what LBLP has identified.

**Phonemic awareness** is the first function, and it is related to the sense of hearing. Phonemic awareness is the ability to distinguish and manipulate the sounds, or phonemes, that make up individual words. To give one example, it is the ability to recognize that there are four phonemes in the word *breath*: /b/ /r/ /ĕ/ /th/ and that if you deleted the phoneme /r/ you would have a new word: *Beth*. This function is the ability to perceive and think about one aspect of the sense of hearing: individual phonemes. Education helps people develop full phonemic awareness (i.e., when encoding, they represent each sound in a word with a logical letter choice, which demonstrates they have mastered segmenting sounds).

Note: In many dyslexics, the brain is organized in such a way that the development of this function is compromised before the students even begin school. These students often require special training to rewire their brains to make phonemic awareness automatic (see chapter 6.6 #9).

**Symbol imagery** is the second function, and it is related to the sense of sight. It is the ability to visualize two-dimensional symbols such as letters and numerals. Close your eyes. Imagine the letters of your name. If you can do it, you are using symbol imagery. If you cannot, do not worry. In *The Science of Spelling*, Gentry speculates that approximately 20% of the population cannot (Gentry 2004, 22). Those who can imagine one or two letters can improve by doing exercises to develop symbol imagery. The goal is to visualize seven or more letters. Those who do not develop symbol imagery will have difficulty with learning spelling. (It can be done, but it does require additional work on the individual's part.)

**Concept imagery** is the third function, and it is related to the senses of sight and language. It involves the ability to visualize in three dimensions, not two, based on oral or written language. Close your eyes. Try to imagine a cat: pointy ears, whiskers, black and white fur, and collar. If you can see a cat (as opposed to the letters *C-A-T*) you are using concept imagery. Concept imagery is important for reading comprehension. When reading fiction, people with good concept imagery find that they are watching their own mental movie. This experience is one of the primary joys of reading. However, students who lack concept imagery often complain that reading is boring because they experience it as just words. Without the ability to picture the story, these students are right.

Note: Since this function makes use of the sense of language, those students who lack appropriate language skills will be unable to make use of concept imagery, even if they can visualize in three dimensions.

Note: There is some confusion in the Waldorf world about concept imagery and symbol imagery that needs to be cleared up. Many people lump them together under the umbrella term **mental picturing**. While both concept and symbol imagery are types of mental picturing, they are separate functions. It is possible to be strong in one but not the other. Developing concept imagery will not help with symbol imagery and vice versa.

## 3.   Sensory-Cognitive Functions and Reading Methodologies

Nanci Bell, author of *Seeing Stars*®: *Symbol Imagery for Phonemic Awareness, Sight Words and Spelling*, noted that sensory-cognitive functions correlate with specific reading methods and that their absence accounts for the failure of the reading methods. Consult Table 1.6.1.

**Table 1.6.1: Sensory-Cognitive Functions and Associated Reading Method**

| |
|---|
| Phonemic Awareness ..................…..... Phonics |
| Symbol Imagery ........................…...... Look-Say |
| Concept Imagery.........................…..... Whole Language |

*Source: Bell 2001, 22–26.*

**Phonics** is the method of instruction that emphasizes teaching students to decode, or sound out words. It teaches a series of rules called **phonics rules** to help students master encoding and decoding. However, if students lack phonemic awareness, phonics is ineffective.

**Look-say** is the method of instruction where students gain familiarity with words by seeing them in print over and over. It is the method used in the Dick and Jane readers. (See Spot run. Run, Spot, run.) However, if students lack symbol imagery, look-say is ineffective.

**Whole language** is the method that stresses putting quality literature (as opposed to the artificial texts favored by the other two methods) into student's hands so that they can use their language skills in real situations. However, if students lack concept imagery, whole language is ineffective. In addition, if students are given unfamiliar material to read and they have underdeveloped sight words and decoding skills, students can have excellent concept imagery and still fail to learn to read with this approach.

All three approaches have fatal weaknesses if taught in isolation. First, they are incomplete in and of themselves. Second, they depend on the development of sensory-cognitive functions, which in turn require varying degrees of formal education to mature. The solution to this paradox is found in the details.

## 4.   Sensory-Cognitive Functions and Reading Skills

In addition to underlying reading methodologies, sensory-cognitive functions underlie the development of three primary reading skills that all students must master as shown in Table 1.6.2.

**Table 1.6.2: Sensory-Cognitive Function and Corresponding Reading Skill**

| | |
|---|---|
| Phonemic Awareness...................... | Decoding |
| Symbol Imagery ........................... | Sight words |
| Concept Imagery .......................... | Using the context |

*Source: Adapted from Lindamood 1998, 4 Figure 1.1 The Reading Process.*

**Decoding** is the ability to sound out new words. Students say the sound (or syllable) in each word and then blend them together into a whole. This skill is most apparent when students are developing the *letter to sound decoding route* in the Phonemic Awareness Phase. After students have developed the *lexical route*, it shows up when they encounter an unfamiliar word and revert back to the *letter to sound decoding route*. It also shows up when authors make up new words. For example, even though the world had never seen the word *quidditch* before the Harry Potter series came out, people who had mastered decoding could read it effortlessly. However, not all words can be decoded.

**Sight words** are the commonly-used words in English that go back to the Germanic Old English words (see chapter 1.3 #3). These words are very common and many are highly irregular. The first 300 most commonly used words in English make up about 65% of the words in print (Fry 2006, 51). Many of these words have one or two irregularities. For example, *put* should be pronounced *putt*. A few are completely irregular. The word *of* should say *off*; a phonetic spelling for *of* would be *UV*. Given these factors, teach the students these words using the look-say method. The students memorize them as whole words.

**Using the context** refers to three distinct skills: 1) predicting; 2) self-correcting; and 3) vocabulary acquisition. Each of these skills is invaluable at a different stage of reading.

*Predicting* allows beginning readers to make educated guesses while they read. It helps make reading less of a chore. Beginning students use pictures and context to figure out words. Initially, beginners will not use print at all when guessing at a word from context, but as they move through the phases, they will use one or more letters of the word to refine their guess as shown below for Figure 1.6.1.

**Figure 1.6.1: "I play in the waves."**

*Painting by Francesca Lohmann*

36

*"I play in the___."*

Student's guess in the Emergent Phase: *"ocean?"* (Note: There is no match between the actual written word "waves" and the spoken word, "ocean.")

*"I play in the W_____."*

Student's guess in beginning Phonemic Awareness Phase: *"water"* (Note: The first letter matches.)

*"I play in the W_____S."*

Student's guess in middle of the Phonemic Awareness Phase: *"waves"* (Note: The student guessed the word correctly based on the first and last letter.)

Once students have developed decoding skills, they will use this strategy less and less. Instead, they will use *context* to alert them to when they have made a mistake. For example, a student is reading a book about a girl and her horse and comes across the following sentence: *She rode her horse.* However, she misreads the sentence and says, "She rode her house (sic)." When she hears what she has said or compares it with the picture on the page, she realizes she has made an error. She looks at the sentence again, particularly at the word *horse*. She then corrects herself, "She rode her horse."

Students who are using concept imagery will question many of their reading errors because they do not make any sense. When they go back and re-read the sentences, they will discover their errors.

The end stage of using the context is using it to learn new vocabulary words. Spoken English makes use of only a small fraction of its words. As students read, they will begin to discover an entirely new world of words that are only used in written texts. They will learn much of their vocabulary on their own, through their own independent reading. You can prime the pump by teaching them to use contextual clues to figure out new words from context as part of teaching vocabulary (see chapter 3.12 #6 and 7). Then their vocabularies will expand exponentially as they learn new vocabulary from reading. An example would be if a student read the following passage:

> As the children walked through the somber hall, their spirits fell. The dim bulbs barely gave out enough light for them to see the ancient, tattered remains of water-damaged rugs and moldy furniture. Was this to be their new home?

As the student reads this passage, she gets the impression that the word *somber* must have something to do with being dark or damaged. When she encounters this new word in other places, her understanding of its meaning and the correct usage will develop on its own.

Note that these three reading skills fall naturally into phases.

## 5. Using the Phases of *The Roadmap to Literacy* to End the Reading Wars

Determining which reading method is best is a fool's errand. All three are important, just at different times. They are broken down by phase and incorporated into *The Roadmap to Literacy* as shown in table 1.6.3.

**Table 1.6.3: Reading Methods by Phase**

| Reading Method | Emergent Phase | Phonemic Awareness Phase | Pattern Phase | Syllable Phase | Latin/Greek Phase |
|---|---|---|---|---|---|
| **Whole language** | Yes, but familiar texts only (memory reading and the student's kid writing passages). | Beginning: same as Emergent<br><br>Middle/End: Introduce some unfamiliar passages, but only under a teacher's guidance. | Yes | No | NA |
| **Look-say** | Yes, but familiar texts only (memory reading and the student's kid writing passages). | Yes | No | No | NA |
| **Phonics** | No | Beginning: No Middle: Begin End: Yes | Yes | Yes | NA |

Table 1.6.3 shows that you begin with look-say and whole language. Limit reading to memory reading with familiar texts such as poems and song lyrics. Wait to introduce phonics until you have taught the students enough phonemic awareness that they can make sense of it. Once the students have developed full phonemic awareness for segmenting sounds, phonics becomes the primary method of instruction.

Emphasize look-say when students first begin to learn sight words, but as the students' *word identification hub* develops, this approach will no longer be necessary.

Note: Keep in mind that you will be working with all three sensory-cognitive functions from the very beginning of 1st Grade. Only the reading skills taught will change. Section 3 shows you how to teach the sensory-cognitive functions along with reading skills.

This use of multiple modalities to teach reading is entirely in line with Steiner's indications. As mentioned in the epigraph, Steiner notes that German has three types of reading instruction and states, "The ideas that underlie all three methods are good—there is no denying that each has its merits." Right before that he states, "It is bad, however, when these things become fads" (Trostli 2004, 182). These words are profoundly true. In addition, just because Waldorf teaches from the *whole to the parts* does not mean that Waldorf only teaches using the *whole language* approach. This is a false tautology.

Let the reading wars be concluded, at least in Waldorf classrooms. Reading instruction should be balanced. All three methods of instruction point to a valuable piece of the reading puzzle. All three are needed, just at different phases.

## Conclusion

When you understand *The Roadmap to Literacy's* five phases, the answer to the question *"Which reading methodology should Waldorf teachers use?"* is simple: All of them, but in the appropriate phase.

# SECTION 2

Waldorf Methodologies

# 2.1 THE WISDOM OF THE WALDORF APPROACH TO TEACHING

Section 1 covers background information about literacy. Section 2 presents background information on Waldorf education.

All readers should read section 2, even those familiar with Waldorf education. The background information included in this section will be helpful in understanding how to use *The Roadmap to Literacy* curriculum in later sections. This section lays the groundwork for discussing what to teach in sections 3 and 4, how to teach it in section 5, and how to assess in section 6.

This chapter covers the following topics:

1. Teacher and Students as Authors
2. Developmental Approach: Hands, Heart, and Head
3. School Readiness
4. Teaching from the Image
5. Working with Stories
6. The Literature Curriculum
7. Inhale and Exhale: The Role of Breathing in a Lesson
8. From the Whole to the Parts
9. Using the Night: The Power of Sleep
10. Working with the Temperaments
11. The Four-Fold Human Being
12. Eurythmy and Form Drawing
13. Home Visits
14. Working with the Spiritual World

## 1. Teacher and Students as Authors

One of the most exciting and stimulating things about being a Waldorf teacher is the freedom to create lessons. In lieu of using standardized text books, Waldorf teachers create the lessons for their students out of their own research and creativity. Students create their own textbooks, called **main lesson books.** Hence, both teachers and students are authors.

Teachers have the freedom to choose the stories, images, and assignments they feel will best serve their students. This freedom can ignite an enthusiasm for learning that is palpable.

This freedom does have some healthy boundaries:

- the limitations of child development for each age
- the overall curriculum and story themes for the year as set out by Rudolf Steiner
- the school's **standards** (which will be referred to as **benchmarks**) for each grade

Furthermore, teachers must strive to meet the needs of their particular group of students. Teachers are responsible for educating every student in the class. Lesson plans must meet the needs of students who excel as well as those who struggle. Waldorf teachers have to take steps to differentiate instruction when they write their lesson plans (see chapter 2.4 #3).

## 2. Developmental Approach: Hands, Heart, and Head

Waldorf education honors child development. While children are capable of learning literacy skills earlier, Waldorf waits. In Waldorf schools, reading is not taught until the children are six or seven years old because the children should have time to complete key physical developments before they begin formal education.

There are three stages of development in the Waldorf curriculum:

1. Imitation/hands (birth–7 years)
2. Authority/heart (7 years–14 years)
3. Expertise/head (14 years–21 years)

Let's look at literacy through these stages of development.

### Hands

Pre-school children want to imitate the adults in their lives, usually by imitating what adults do with their hands, and that includes writing. However, children need time to complete their physical development before they use their energy on intellectual pursuits such as learning to read. It is developmentally appropriate for preschoolers and kindergarten students to engage in **pretend reading,** paraphrasing a story while engaging in pre-reading skills such as turning the pages in the right order. Such activities help foster the growth of book skills. It is also developmentally appropriate for them to engage in pretend writing where they make loops and squiggles and occasionally throw in some letter-like shapes. In kindergarten, they can be taught to write their names out of imitation. However, the work of learning to read is saved for 1st Grade.

### Heart

Students start 1st Grade when they are six or seven and are moving into the authority stage. Reading instruction takes place in Grades 1–3, at the beginning of the authority stage. In this stage, the children want to love, trust, and please the authority figures in their lives, and they will want to learn from a beloved teacher. This loving connection underlies the teaching of skills, and later on, content.

The students will be in this stage for their entire eight years in the grades. They benefit from the close relationships that form between the teacher and the students in her class.

Note: Since most pre-schools and kindergartens stress academic learning, the Waldorf philosophy of beginning formal academic training between the ages of six to seven years will cause Waldorf students to be out of sync with other schools. When parents put their child into a Waldorf kindergarten, they need to be prepared to make a commitment to have her continue with Waldorf through 3rd Grade. After that time, Waldorf students should be caught up with students who began academic work at a younger age (see chapter 1.1 #4).

**Head**

The students will enter this stage in high school. They will have mastered the literacy skills taught in the grades and will go on to get specialized instruction in different fields from teachers who are experts in those fields.

## 3.    School Readiness

Within the Waldorf philosophy, age is only one factor that determines whether a student is ready to learn to read and write. Another is **school readiness**, a state where students have mature capacities and are ready for formal instruction.

Here are some of the capacities that six- and seven-year-old children should have in place prior to entering 1st Grade:

- Ability to follow a three-step instruction. For example, "Please get out your main lesson book, your red and blue block crayons, and open your book to your picture of the mountain."
- Eye convergence. (As the bridge of their noses narrow, students' eyes can more easily focus on one single point on a page of text.)
- Integrated **midlines** (Young children have midline barriers that limit their movement. School-aged students should have overcome movement limitations that are characteristic of preschoolers. For example, they no longer use the right hand for tasks on their right side and the left hand for tasks on their left and no longer need to crouch down to pick up things on the floor. Integrated midlines are important in their own right for eye tracking, writing, and movement exercises, and they indicate appropriate brain/body maturity.)
- Fine motor skills for holding pencils
- Ability to sit and focus

All of these capacities play a role in learning to read and write.

Waldorf schools typically do a formal assessment of rising 1st Grade students to check these capacities among others. (A good 1st Grade readiness assessment can be found in Murphy-Lang's book *Developing the Observing Eye*.) This assessment can be done by the kindergarten teacher, the 1st Grade teacher, or another experienced teacher. Waldorf teachers consult the results before teaching 1st Grade and make plans to address their class's overall weak areas (if any) in class. If it is found that a particular student is struggling with one or more of the above-mentioned capacities, the teacher may ask the student's parents to address them outside of class because weaknesses in school readiness will affect a student's ability to learn literacy skills. (See chapter 6.6 on Working with Remedial Issues.)

## 4.    Teaching from the Image

Young students learn abstract concepts best when their teachers introduce these concepts through stories or images they can relate to. This process is referred to as *teaching out of the image* or *metaphorical speech* and is the basis for Steiner's advice to teachers: "Imbue thyself with the power of imagination" (Steiner 1998, 190).

The more teachers introduce abstract academic constructs in the guise of pictures, the more easily students are able to grasp the concepts. When creating these pictures for students, the most effective images are those that connect the subject matter to the students' own knowledge and/or experience of the world or that relate to a story told in class.

**Figure 2.1.1: The Mountain Picture for *Mm***

For example, it is possible to teach a letter from an image in a fairy tale. To introduce the uppercase letter *M* and lowercase letter *m*, use a fairy tale that mentions a tall mountain and a smaller mountain and then teach the letters out of the images of the mountains. Note that the picture of the mountains in figure 2.1.1 contains the forms of the letter *M* and *m* (see chapter 3.1.7).

You can also tell stories from your life to illustrate a concept. Patti Connolly often used stories about her dog. For example, she introduced the concept of silent letters as follows: She described how the dog sometimes likes to bark and be noisy while other times she likes to sit quietly in the sun and be petted. She then showed how the letter *B* is like the dog. In some words, it speaks its sound loud and clear: *bob, cab, tub, rib,* etc. In others words, it is silent: *lamb, comb, thumb,* etc.

You can also create stories that contain images. For example, in chapter 3.11 #6–8 the main parts of speech are brought to life through the characters of Queen Noun, King Verb, Princess Adjective, and Prince Adverb. The characters' personalities and activities personify their particular part of speech and provide the images. For example, King Verb is a very active fellow who is always doing things. Students have an easier time learning a new concept when there is an image they can relate to, and stories you make up can provide endless opportunities to teach from the image.

Teaching from the image makes it easier for students to relate to dry, abstract concepts. Sections 3 and 4 include many possible images to use.

## 5.   Working with Stories

Waldorf teachers work with four types of stories:

1. Academic Concept Stories

2. Literature Curriculum Stories

3. Pedagogical Stories

4. Home Surroundings Stories

**Academic Concept Stories** are stories that a Waldorf teacher creates to introduce a new academic concept. These stories contain one or more key images that the teacher will then highlight to teach a new academic concept. These teacher-created stories can stand alone or they can be serial in nature. Serial academic concept stories are called **umbrella stories**. (For an example, see *Englishland* in chapter 3.11 #6–8.)

**Literature Curriculum Stories** are the story recommendations Steiner gave for each grade (see chapter 2.1 #6). They form the basis for the literature curriculum. They are the most versatile of the stories. They can be used as *soul food* (stories that provide life wisdom and nurture the child's evolving spirit), pedagogical stories (see below), or as vehicles for providing images to introduce new concepts (i.e., just like an academic concept story).

**Pedagogical Stories** are stories that teachers tell to support a struggling student or address challenging behavior in the classroom. They work indirectly with the emotional or social needs of the class or individual students. Waldorf teachers usually make up these stories using images/characters from the natural or animal world to bring home the point. An excellent resource for the creation of such stories is *Healing Stories for Challenging Behaviour* by Perrow (see bibliography).

**Home surroundings Stories** are stories told to introduce the students to their local environment. They are told during the Home Surroundings Block in Grades 1–3. Grades one and two focus on nature stories; Grade three focuses on practical occupations. They are often created by the teacher, but they do not have to be. Many fine nature stories exist, such as *Paddy Beaver* by Thornton Burgess.

This topic is so important that there is an entire chapter dedicated to it: Working with Stories (see chapter 5.5).

## 6.   The Literature Curriculum

The **literature curriculum** refers to a canon of stories that Waldorf teachers tell to students in each grade. Steiner designed the curriculum to meet the students at different ages. He gave teachers ideas for stories to use at each stage of development. These indications form the basis for the language arts source material for each grade.

**First Grade**: The 1st Grade material is mainly made up of fairy tales. These stories are archetypal in nature and full of rich images. The tales told in 1st Grade are longer and more sophisticated than those told in Kindergarten. An example of an appropriate fairy tale for this grade would be the story "Snow White and Rose Red." It could serve as a vehicle for introducing the letter *B* with its image of the bear and provide practice for the sound /b/ with the story's many *B* words: bush, beard, bird, bag, bed, etc.

**Second Grade**: In the 2nd Grade, the story content reflects the fact that human beings have the capacity for the worst of behavior and the best of behavior. The stories are used to help the students come to terms with this dichotomy. They tell of the good deeds of saints and saintly people and the rascally or egotistical behaviors found in fables and some Native American animal tales. Fables and animal tales deal humorously and effectively with negative traits such as selfishness, lying, laziness, etc. Stories of saints illustrate the positive aspects of the human being.

**Third Grade**: The stories for the 3rd Grade come from the Old Testament. These stories are told more as soul food rather than as a source of images for academic instruction. It is at this time that the student leaves behind the magical world of the young child and focuses more on the physical world. (Waldorf refers to this process as the **nine-year change**.) The Bible stories are filled with situations where human beings have to overcome challenges, learn skills, and develop relationships to survive on the earth (e.g., Adam and Eve needing to find shelter upon being cast out of Paradise, Joseph using his knowledge of volume measurement to save the Egyptian people from famine, Esther saving her people because of her selflessness, etc.). Ethical lessons continue on through these stories.

The story curriculum continues in 4th–8th Grade and will be addressed in the sequel(s) to this book.

These stories are told for their own sake (soul food), but the literature curriculum for 1st and 2nd Grade can also double as academic concept stories. For example, Waldorf teachers use fairy tales to introduce letters (see chapter 3.1 #7).

## 7. Inhale and Exhale: The Role of Breathing in a Lesson

Lessons must **breathe**, or provide a balance between activities that require quiet and intense focus and those that allow the students to move, be noisy, or relax. The teacher should also be conscious of how long to keep the class focused on one subject before moving on to something different. As Steiner states in *Soul Economy*, "It is quite correct to say that children will tire if made to listen to the same subject too long" (Steiner 2003, 287). It is up to the teacher to choreograph the day to create this 'healthy breathing' in the lesson.

In main lesson and then continuing throughout the day, students need opportunities to use both their bodies and their brains. They need to be able to concentrate, then 'exhale' a bit during a transition from one focused activity to the next. They need to use their hands to create and then to sit quietly and receive. This breathing acknowledges that children learn with their whole being and that every aspect—intellectual, emotional, and physical (i.e., head, heart and hands)—needs to be involved during the educational process. Waldorf teachers who have mastered this dance seldom have any problem with classroom management, and their students have a greater opportunity for learning.

For an example of a main lesson rhythm that incorporates a healthy amount of inhale and exhale for 1st Grade, see chapter 5.2 #5–8.

## 8. From the Whole to the Parts

Steiner suggests that teachers teach from the whole to the parts. This can be done through two approaches.

One approach of teaching from the whole to the parts can be found in the very first language arts lesson when introducing a letter by first beginning with the whole sentence, then moving to the word, and finally focusing on the smallest part: the letter and phoneme. In *Renewal of Education*, Steiner states that "in the Waldorf School we always teach beginning not with letters, but with complete sentences. We analyze the sentences into words and the words into letters and then the letters into vowels. In this way we come to a proper inner understanding as the child grasps the meaning of what a sentence or word is. We awaken the child's consciousness by analyzing sentences and words" (Trostli 2004, 93).

Here is an example of how one teacher introduced the letter *M*. She began by writing the following sentence on the board: *They climbed up the mountain*. Then she continued as follows:

1. "When adults want to write the sentence *They climbed up the mountain*, this is how they would write it." (She read the sentence again and pointed to each word.)

2. She then underlined the word *mountain* and said, "This is how the word *mountain* is spelled."

3. She over-emphasized the initial /m/ sound in the word *mountain* and pronounced the word again: "MMMMMMMMMMMMMM. Mountain. *Mountain* starts with the sound /m/. When adults want to write the /m/ sound, they use the letter *M*."

By moving from the whole to the parts in this manner, teachers help students develop phonological awareness (see chapter 1.4 #2 and chapter 3.3).

The second approach that incorporates moving from the whole to the parts is to connect students with a broad look at what they already know about a subject before focusing in on specific aspects that are new to them (e.g., what they know about the role of fire in the world before delving into the chemical nature of fire in 7th Grade chemistry). This secondary approached is often used as an introduction to subjects taught in the 4th–8th Grades.

## 9. Using the Night: The Power of Sleep

Sleep is a critical aspect of education that Waldorf teachers strive to work with.

In *Study of Man*, Steiner talks about the importance of sleep in education. He says that in a physical sense, young children sleep well; however, during sleep, people process all of the experiences they had during the day, and children still have to master this process (Steiner 1998, 22).

Studies have shown that sleep consolidates new learning. When people are taught something, practice it, and then sleep on it, they perform the new skill up to 30% better the next day. Matthew Walker, PhD, Director of the Sleep and Neuroimaging Laboratory at Beth Israel Deaconess Hospital, says, "It seems to be that practice does not quite make perfect; it's practice with a night of sleep that makes perfect" ("The Science of Sleep," a segment on *60 Minutes*, a CBS television news magazine, that first aired on March 13, 2008).

Teachers can support the role of sleep by bringing a rich, meaningful curriculum that breathes (see chapter 2.1 #7). This rhythm makes it easier for the student to process everything they learned at school during the night, as well as accrue the benefits of sleep for the next day.

## 10. Working with the Temperaments

Steiner identified four personality types, or **temperaments.** Waldorf teachers work with these temperaments through pedagogical stories, games, and activities. The goal is to bring out the gifts and smooth out the rough edges.

**Cholerics** are the go-getters who love action. They thrive on doing things. They are natural leaders but can get pushy and bulldoze the other temperaments if they are not careful. Include action in stories and games in order to appeal to the choleric students. If needed, address the consequences of bossiness. These can include hurt feelings, misunderstanding, missing out on the good ideas of others, etc.

**Phlegmatics** are the easy-going people who are known for being able to stick with something and see it through. They love food, feel no need to rush, and thrive on routine. Phlegmatics are usually steadfast and reliable. They are slow to anger, but when they are roused, they can explode. It often takes phlegmatics longer to understand something, but once they do, their understanding has depth. Include references to food in stories and find some games with an element of repetition to appeal to the phlegmatic students. Address the consequences of phlegmatic behavior. These can include missing out on life experiences and allowing things to get out of hand because the phlegmatic person took too relaxed of an approach to a situation.

**Melancholics** are the sensitive people who perceive and remember everything—including every slight and injury. They seem to thrive on pain and misery, both their own and that of others. They can be very empathetic and kind when they are able to stop focusing on their own problems.Include references to suffering or great difficulties in stories, emphasize how characters overcome their struggles, and provide opportunities for melancholic students to experience setbacks that they have to overcome in games. Address the consequences of holding on to every perceived slight. These can include isolation for the melancholic person and annoyance for everyone else.

**Sanguines** are the sun-shiny people who have lots of enthusiasm but can struggle with follow through because they are easily distracted. They are highly social and love being with other people. They also have a tendency to be too talkative. Include lots of colorful, imaginative descriptions in stories to grab their attention and incorporate pauses when their attention wanders. The sudden silence will compel them to listen to you again. When possible, include lots of variety in class activities. Address the consequences of being too enthusiastic and social. These can include not finishing assigned work and bothering others, which can prevent them from completing their work as well.

In addition, a teacher must leave her own temperamental proclivities behind when teaching. The lesson must appeal to all temperaments.

Note: The topic of temperaments is very large and much of it falls outside the scope of this book. For more information, see Steiner's first lecture in *Discussions with Teachers*.

## 11. The Four-Fold Human Being

Steiner often referred to four aspects of the human being when talking about the developing child. Waldorf education is structured around the timeline of this 'four-fold' development. Teachers use this information to plan lessons and help remedial students. These four aspects are as follows:

1. **Physical body** refers to the part of the human that is perceptible to the eye. It provides a vehicle for interaction with the physical world through action and the senses and also through breathing and the digestion of food. (The growth of this body dominates the child from birth to seven years.)

2. **Etheric body** refers to the life body, or the element that provides the warmth, growth, and healing capacity in a living physical body. It is the blueprint for the physical body. Without it, the physical body is a corpse and returns to its natural elements. It also is the home for the habit body and responds to healthy or unhealthy life rhythms. (The growth of this body dominates the child from 7 to 14 years.)

3. **Astral body** refers to the emotional part of the human being and the aspect governed by desires, likes, and dislikes. (The growth of this body dominates the teenager from 14 to 21 years.)

4. **Ego** refers to the distinct individuality of each person. (The growth of this body dominates a young adult from 21 to 28 years.)

These elements dictate the organization of Waldorf schools. The education is based on an understanding of the four-fold human being. For example, students wait to begin formal academic instruction, including literacy, until they are seven years old (or until the academic year they turn seven).

Note: It is not that younger students cannot learn academic skills—they can: it is that they should not (see chapter 2.1 #2) unless there is a compelling reason (see chapter 6.6 #9).

## 12. Eurythmy and Form Drawing

Rudolf Steiner introduced two new subjects: Eurythmy and form drawing.

### Eurythmy

Eurythmy is a form of movement/dance that was invented by Rudolf Steiner. It makes speech visible by translating the sounds into gestures. It is always taught by someone with special training in Eurythmy.

There are many forms of Eurythmy. Performance Eurythmy is known as visible speech and visible music. A speaker recites a poem or tells a story while one or more Eurythmists perform the corresponding gestures. The same applies to a song. Therapeutic Eurythmy is a type of therapy prescribed by anthroposophical doctors. It involves specialized therapeutic movements given by a Eurythmist who has additional training in the therapeutic uses of Eurythmy. It is sometimes recommended when a student has learning challenges. The most important type for Waldorf education is Pedagogical Eurythmy. Waldorf students have classes that include imagery, music, poetry, and stories. The students imitate the Eurythmist and participate in movements that match the sounds. In so doing, they learn to coordinate their movements in a harmonious way and gain mastery of movement (Hoven 2012, 22–24).

**Form Drawing** is a type of drawing that educates the temperaments. Form drawing also educates judgement, will, balance, fine motor skills, and strengthens the etheric. It works with simple lines—straight and curved—to make increasingly more elaborate forms in each grade. Although it is an essential subject in its own right, it also helps with handwriting as shown in figure 2.1.2.

**Figure 2.1.2: Form Drawing Running Form**

**(Preparation for Lowercase Cursive Letters *i* and *c*)**

## 13. Home Visits

Perhaps unique to Waldorf schools is the custom of the **home visit**. In *The Child's Changing Consciousness*, Steiner tells the teachers:

> There should really be direct contact with the parental home—that is with what has happened before the child entered school… teachers should have a fairly clear picture of how the present situation of children was influenced by their social conditions and the milieu in which they grew up… For this to happen, however, knowledge of the child's home background, through contact with the parents, is of course absolutely essential. (Steiner 1996, 128)

A teacher conducts a home visit prior to the start of 1st Grade (or starting with a new class) and prior to accepting a new student into the class. By visiting a student's home, the teacher gains a lot of insight into the student and her circumstances. For instance, a home visit can provide the following:

- information about the trip to school: traffic, scenery, and how long it takes

- a chance to meet siblings and pets

- an opportunity to see the student's room and yard to get an idea of the play and home learning environment available to the student

- a time to do an initial (informal) assessment of the student's abilities in the areas of movement, following instructions, writing, reading, math, etc. through games and activities
- a chance to get to know more about both the parents and the student

Home visits also give the teacher an opportunity to spend one-on-one time with the student and to establish a close, personal relationship prior to the start of school.

## 14. Working with the Spiritual World

Designing and teaching a new curriculum every year can seem overwhelming. In addition, the classroom teacher is one of the most important and influential people in her students' lives—a humbling and sobering thought. How can anyone possibly rise to such a task?

Fortunately, help is available. Acknowledging and working consciously with the spiritual realm provides many benefits, including imagination, inspiration, and intuition. In addition, Steiner gave many meditations, including the **Six Basic Exercises**, a series of exercises that take only a few minutes each day (per exercise). These exercises help people take hold of their thinking, feeling, and willing and are very helpful for teachers. (For a good overview, go to http://tomvangelder.antrovista.com/pdf/basic.pdf.) Trained Waldorf teachers are encouraged to consult Steiner's book *How to Know Higher Worlds: A Modern Path of Initiation*.)

To undertake this journey without meditative support would be unbelievably draining. It is strongly recommended that it become a focus for personal study and/or discussion with a mentor.

## Conclusion

The Waldorf educational philosophy contains much wisdom. The reading approach outlined in this book can be used in any classroom, but the wisdom outlined here allows it to be brought in a way that is in alignment with the spirit of Steiner's indications.

The next chapter explores additions to the original Waldorf curriculum.

# 2.2 RESPONSIBLE INNOVATIONS AND SACRED NOTHINGS

*The spiritual world has no concern with things which have come into civilization only through external convention. For instance, the child naturally does not bring with him our conventional methods of reading and writing. . . Language and writing as we know them are conventions of our civilization.*

—Rudolf Steiner, *The Study of Man* (155)

Over the years, Waldorf education has benefited from the ideas of numerous talented teachers and other committed professionals. Many of these ideas have formed an integral part of Waldorf education as it is taught today. This development is appropriate and in alignment with Steiner's wish for teachers to strive to improve themselves and their teaching. It is the teacher's responsibility to present a curriculum that will prepare students to be successful in their time. The Waldorf curriculum is and always should be a changing, evolving approach to education. However, not all of the changes found today are of equal value, and a few are counterproductive.

This chapter covers the following topics:

1. Introduction to Sacred Nothings and Responsible Innovations
2. Distinguishing Sacred Nothings from Responsible Innovations

## 1.  Introduction to Sacred Nothings and Responsible Innovations

Changes to Waldorf education can be positive or negative.

Back in the early 2000s, Christof Wiechert, Director of the Pedagogical Section of the Anthroposophical Society, an international organization based in Switzerland that oversees the international Waldorf School movement, was visiting Waldorf schools in the United States. He was astounded at how many sacrosanct traditions had entered into US Waldorf classrooms. When he would ask teachers why they were doing these things (or having their students do them), the answer was usually, "Because that is what I was taught." In lectures Wiechert often refers to these traditions as *Sacred Nothings* or *Waldorf Myths* (i.e., questionable traditions which have evolved over the years with little consciousness around them). He has pointed out that most of these Sacred Nothings are of questionable value and some could even be counterproductive to the students and/or their education.

Wiechert wrote several articles about the practices that he has observed happening in US Waldorf classrooms that have little or no basis in the teachings of Rudolf Steiner and may even work against the aims of Waldorf pedagogy.

Here are some of these practices from "The Educational Practice of the Waldorf Schools," an article he published in the Pedagogical Journal:

- Borders in main lesson books: "One result of the use of the wax crayon blocks is that before use a page is framed first in colored borders. When this occurs for a definite and appropriate purpose and it is carried out carefully, there can be no objection. . . . However, when it happens automatically, as you will find in nearly all schools in the world (!), and when you hear, upon enquiring, it belongs to Waldorf schools, or else it is the way it was taught in the Seminar. . . then a habit has been established once again which shoots wide of its target. For as a rule these borders are anything but beautiful" (5).

- Form Drawing as the First Block of 1st Grade: "Painting and Form Drawing are activities that always take place once or more times a weeks . . . However, it ought never to be the content of an epoch [block]" (7).

- Building a Structure on Campus in 3rd Grade (e.g., as part of the Home Surroundings Block): "There is the danger that a class three that does not leave behind something they have built on the school grounds will easily be considered as not conforming to the curriculum. Yet, such an insinuation has no basis whatsoever" (8).

- Yearly Class Plays: "Is it pedagogically justifiable to put the whole timetable out of action for a class play in the lower or the middle school? How does it relate to the ethos of learning? When scarcely any lessons take place for weeks . . . so that rehearsals can take place?" (14). (see chapter 3.10 #8.)

Here are some of the practices Wiechert identifies in "On the Question of the Three-fold Structure of the Main Lesson":

- Circle in the lower grades: Wiechert states that dancing around in a circle, stamping and clapping makes the children tired, and they do these circle activities as if asleep. [Movement activities are done with the will, and people are asleep in their will.] He concludes, "Teachers will do well to lose no time in breaking this link of movement in sleep from knowledge gained through wakefulness" (9). (See chapter 2.3 #5.)

- The timing of stories: "What is the right moment, the "kairos" for storytelling? The story need not be at the end of the main lesson. It can fit elsewhere into the course of the day" (9–10) (see chapter 5.5 #9).

These questionable practices (or Sacred Nothings as Wiechert has often called them) as well as other such questionable practices that impact the teaching of literacy are addressed later in the book.

However, Wiechert and others have also observed innovative ideas in modern Waldorf classrooms. Many changes are wonderful additions that meet the needs of today's children. Elan Liebner, current head of the Pedagogical Council in the United States, calls these beneficial changes *Responsible Innovations*. He has been developing the idea in faculty development days and AWSNA summer conferences. Two examples of Responsible Innovations are:

- block crayons that can be used in lieu of paints for artwork across the grades
- free rendering: a form of story review created by Else Gottgens (see chapter 3.8 #2)

Both Responsible Innovations and Sacred Nothings exist in Waldorf classrooms and trainings.

## 2. Distinguishing Sacred Nothings from Responsible Innovations

It is helpful to distinguish Sacred Nothings from Responsible Innovations, particularly before you create your curriculum for the year.

First, look very consciously at what you are doing in the classroom and why. Always ask yourself why you are doing something. If the answer is *"That was how I was taught"* or *"I do not know,"* ask the following questions:

1. Does this approach further my students' skills? How?
2. Is this advice developmentally appropriate?
3. Does this suggestion feel like the right thing for my group of students at this time?
4. What are the advantages and disadvantages to what I have learned/ have been doing?
5. Is this activity or approach in alignment with Steiner's intent (i.e., is it in alignment with the four-fold development of the human being, etc.) (see chapter 2.1 #11)?

By following these steps, you should be able to separate the wheat from the chaff on your own and explain your decision if it differs from what has been considered customary at your school.

If you decide to deviate from your school's traditional path, it is advisable to have a conversation with your mentor. At this time you can lay out what you are going to change and why you think it is the best thing for you and your class. You also may want to explain what you will be doing with your parent body during a parent meeting. For example, if you determine that, unlike past 3rd Grade teachers at your school, you are not going to have your students spend their time drawing borders on every page of their main lesson books, you could share with the parents why you have made this decision and what you will be doing instead.

## Conclusion

As a Waldorf teacher, you have great autonomy and great responsibility for what you do in your classroom. When designing your curriculum, take into consideration what you were taught in your training, the advice of mentors, and the guidance found in texts such as *The Roadmap to Literacy*. Then create the curriculum that will best meet the needs of your students. By bringing this level of consciousness to your planning, you will be taking important steps toward fulfilling your responsibility as the architect of your students' education.

In upcoming chapters, those Sacred Nothings that could impede the teaching of literacy will be identified and alternatives suggested. It is up to you to decide how you incorporate this information into your lesson plans.

# 2.3 THE WALDORF SCHEDULE

Now that the philosophical underpinnings of Waldorf education have been presented, it is time to consider the Waldorf schedule and classes. These frameworks will provide the structure for the language arts skills presented in Sections 3 and 4 and curriculum planning in section 5.

This chapter covers the following topics:

1. Overview of the Waldorf Curriculum and Schedule
2. Main Lesson Block Rotation
3. Sacred Nothing: Practical Life Skills Blocks
4. Main Lesson Class Archetype
5. Sacred Nothing: Circle
6. Practice Class Archetype
7. Truncated Schedules

## 1.  Overview of the Waldorf Curriculum and Schedule

There are several unique aspects to the Waldorf schedule.

A Waldorf grades class is a class that goes from 1st Grade through 8th Grade. Ideally, the Waldorf grades class is taught by the same teacher from 1st through 8th Grade. In most cases this teacher is responsible for all of the academic instruction in all eight grades.

The Waldorf school year is divided into blocks of study that last three or four weeks. Each one is referred to as a **main lesson block.** During a main lesson block, students focus on one topic of study. These topics can be skills such as language arts and math or subjects such as geography or science. In Grades 1–3, students learn language arts and math skills; subjects such as science, history, and geography start in 4th Grade.

Each block is made up of **main lesson classes**. A main lesson class is a two-hour class that explores a specific topic of study. It is scheduled first thing in the day when the students are fresh. Main lesson includes auditory, visual, and kinesthetic activities, as well as one or more artistic activities such as drawing, painting, sculpting, singing, or drama. The goal of the main lesson class is for students to have multisensory learning experiences.

After the block is over, one of two things may happen. If the block is a *subject* block such as history, the material is put aside until the next time the block of study is taken up. (When teachers put a subject aside, they say it 'goes to sleep.') If it is a *skill* block such as math or language arts, students should continue to study the skill during daily **practice classes**.

Practice classes last 45–50 minutes on average. They are scheduled after main lesson. Most schools have a maximum of four practice classes each day: two in the morning and two in the afternoon. Practice classes include the practice of academic skills such as math and language arts. Other practice classes include foreign language, handwork, gardening, music, Eurythmy, form drawing, painting, movement (P.E.), etc. If these classes are taught by other teachers, they are often referred to as **special subject teachers**. In the lower grades, the Waldorf class teacher is responsible for all main lesson classes and all academic practice classes. She may be responsible for other classes as well, depending on the size of the school. (Smaller schools have fewer special subject teachers.)

There are nine main lesson blocks in an academic year. The way these blocks are laid out is called a **main lesson block rotation**. Waldorf teachers design their own curriculum and lay it out in blocks to create a main lesson block rotation for their class each year.

In addition, there should be nine practice blocks in an academic year. The way these blocks are laid out is called a **practice block rotation**. Waldorf teachers make their own block plans for both main lesson blocks and practice blocks. These **block plans** include a layout of the entire block which are used to create the daily lesson plans for main lesson classes and practice classes.

During main lesson blocks and practice blocks, Waldorf teachers cover the language arts **curriculum,** the skills, concepts, and/or content a teacher has to teach in each grade, as determined by each school's faculty. Students are then expected to meet the **standards** or **benchmarks,** a list of skills/content that students are to learn in each grade.

## 2.  Main Lesson Block Rotation

In Grades 1–3, students study three things: language arts (four blocks), math (four blocks), and **home surroundings** (one block). Language arts and math are skills blocks, but what is home surroundings?

### Home Surroundings

To get more information on home surroundings, it is necessary to turn to Stockmeyer's book *Rudolf Steiner's Curriculum for Waldorf Schools*, a compilation of all of Steiner's indications about Waldorf education. Home surroundings is a translation of the German word *Sachunterricht* and refers to "lessons given to the children from six to nine years old. In this subject the teacher is to interpret the child's surroundings in an imaginative way. Farming, housebuilding, and stories about plants and animals also belong to this subject" (Stockmeyer 1991, vi).

The Home Surroundings Block is often called *Nature Studies* in 1st and 2nd Grade and *Practical Occupations* in 3rd Grade. You will be given ideas on how to work with these stories in chapter 5.5.

In 3rd Grade, the emphasis of this block shifts from nature stories to the exploration of the natural environment of the area and the types of occupations it spawns. For example, if a school is located in farm country, the teacher may bring lessons about ploughing and the fruits of the field. If the school is near the sea, the teacher may bring lessons about fishing, boat building, etc. If a school is located in a forested area, lessons could be developed about logging, milling, and building. When this block is scheduled is up to the teacher. This block is usually scheduled when the class can experience a time of real activity for the given occupation(s) they will study (see chapter 5.5 #5–8).

**1st and 2nd Grade Block Rotation**

The block rotations for 1st and 2nd Grade alternate between language arts skills blocks and math skills blocks and include one Home Surroundings Block. *The Roadmap to Literacy* program will work most effectively if you start with language arts in 1st Grade and math in 2nd Grade while ending the year with Home Surroundings in both grades.

**3rd Grade Block Rotation**

In 3rd Grade, the Block rotation continues to alternate between language arts skills blocks and math skills blocks. *The Roadmap to Literacy* program will work most effectively if you begin with math. The single Practical Occupations Block can be woven into the 3rd Grade schedule whenever it is most convenient.

## 3. Sacred Nothing: Practical Life Skills Blocks

In 3rd Grade there is a Sacred Nothing that undermines the language arts curriculum: two or three main lesson blocks called *Practical Life Skills* or *Practical Activities*.

Practical life skills originated out of the home surroundings curriculum. Originally Steiner wanted the nine-year-old to gain an appreciation for the work of the practical occupations found in the local area. This block of study would then lead into the official introductions of history and geography in the 4th Grade.

In many places in the US, the topic of home surroundings has morphed into *Practical Life Skills Blocks* in the 3rd Grade. These blocks often include a study of natural fibers, various grains, cooking, carpentry, basketry, animal husbandry, farming, weaving, etc.

Even further afield is the current practice of teaching one or two blocks on *Shelters around the World* about the various types of houses built by indigenous peoples (e.g., the igloos of the Inuit, grass huts of the Masai, yurts of the Mongols, etc.). This block is entirely at odds with the initial impulse behind Home Surroundings: providing the students with an opportunity to learn about local occupations and handcrafts as a precursor to the study of local history and geography in 4th Grade.

In a private email to Janet Langley, Christof Wiechert wrote the following about home surroundings:

> Steiner indicated a Main Lesson block about the Handcrafts' professions found in the school's natural surroundings. That means NO farming if they live in the city, no grain identification if there is no farmland around you. But if your school is near the coast, we show them shipbuilding and fishery.
>
> It was not meant by Steiner to have a farm block with ploughing and manuring and all; Steiner's idea was that the children would look at all of the local crafts so they would learn to admire craftsmanship, not to do it–at that age!!-themselves.

Individual practical life skills can certainly be brought into the 3rd Grade curriculum in main lesson classes and in specialty classes. When reined in, they add value to the curriculum. For example, a cooking class in a 3rd Grade math block on measurement is an excellent way to practice math skills, and studying fibers in a handwork class makes good sense as does the study of grains in gardening class. Practical life skills can be part of many specialty classes such as handwork, gardening, and art classes, but they should not dominate entire blocks of main lesson.

Scheduled judiciously and consciously, practical life skills can enliven your curriculum rather than take it over. However, the singular Home Surroundings Block of 3rd Grade should reflect the occupations and industry of your locale (see chapter 5.5 #5 and #8).

## 4.   Main Lesson Class Archetype

A main lesson class lasts two hours and is organized around a flexible archetype of the ideal class. Table 2.3.1 contains the archetype of *The Roadmap to Literacy* main lesson schedule. You can use this archetype when preparing your daily language arts lesson plans or adapt it for the special needs of your class and school schedule.

**Table 2.3.1:** *The Roadmap to Literacy* **Main Lesson Schedule Archetype**

| **Main Lesson Archetype** |
|---|
| Opening (12–15 min.) |
| Skills Practice* (20–40 min.) |
| Introduction &/or Review* (~10–25 min.) |
| Bookwork* (~15–35 min.) |
| Story (~15–20 min.) |
| |
| *Can include one or two transition activities (3–5 min. total) |

Note: The archetype is very flexible. Feel free to adjust it to meet your needs. For example, it has been changed in 1st Grade to accommodate the fact that the story occurs in the Introduction &/or Review segment for the first three blocks when letters are being taught (rather than the Story segment). The change consists of two additional segments: **Speech/Song segment** for additional speech work and **Reading/Writing segment** for reading and writing. See table 5.2.7 for an example with the Speech/Song segment and Appendices 1A, 1C, and 1E for block plan templates that contain one or both segments.

### Opening

Opening refers to the beginning of the school day. Opening is a time to bring everyone together and prepare students for the work of the day. Meet your students at the door, shake each student's hand, take attendance, do a couple of activities, and conclude with Morning Verse. Opening should take no longer than 15 minutes.

There are three mandatory Opening activities: greeting each student, attendance, and Morning Verse. Greeting each student with a handshake allows you to check in with each child at the beginning of the day for a few seconds. (Ask them to look at you when saying "good morning.") Attendance can be elaborate or short (see chapter 3.10 #3). **Morning Verse** is a verse that Steiner gave for Grades 1–4. Just as students in public school systems often begin their day with the Pledge of Allegiance, students in Waldorf schools around the world say Morning Verse as part of their opening to main lesson.

Lower Grades Morning Verse

The Sun with loving light
Makes bright for me each day,
The soul with spirit power
Gives strength unto my limbs,
In sunlight shining clear
I revere, Oh God,
The strength of humankind,
Which Thou so graciously
Has planted in my soul, That
I with all my might, May
love to work and learn.
From Thee stream light and strength
To Thee rise love and thanks.

Rudolf Steiner

Below is a list of activities that often make up the Opening segment of main lesson:

- Singing: Singing is a great way to start the day. It enlivens the class, and songs can double as reading material in 1st Grade (see chapter 3.15 #2).

- Speech: Tongue twisters and poems warm up students' mouths and ears. They can also double as reading material in 1st Grade.

- Movement: Movement helps because most students have had a sedentary morning with a car ride to school. Examples of movement include a bean bag exercise, clapping game, reflex exercise, or midline exercise.

- Nature Observation: If your speech work or song is not seasonal, you can include a seasonal observation about nature (for example, you noticed that the maple tree's leaves are starting to change color).

- Riddle: You can include a riddle if you and your class enjoy them. Give it to the students at the end of the previous day and ask for their solutions that morning.

Remember to curtail your opening activities. Do not go beyond 12 to 15 minutes. As great as these activities are, they are only a warm up for the work that is to come, and there will be more opportunities for these activities during transitions.

## Skills Practice

Skills Practice is the first brush with academic work each day. It is used to consolidate language arts skills that were recently introduced by providing time for some much-needed practice during main lesson. It also helps to warm the students up for the more challenging lesson that is coming up.

In some Waldorf systems, Skills Practice is called Review. This segment is called Skills Practice to differentiate it from the review that you will do as part of the introduction to a new skill or concept.

Use Skills Practice time for ongoing practice such as:

- 1st Grade: phonemic awareness, memory reading, symbol imagery for letters, sight words, kid writing and other types of encoding (and later on, decoding)

- 2nd Grade: symbol imagery for words, kid writing, encoding and decoding to practice phonics rules, and sight words
- 3rd Grade: symbol imagery to practice phonics rules and spelling lists

It can also be used to practice grammar.

Skills Practice should take between 20 to 40 minutes each day.

Note: Many schools schedule **mental math practice** during the Skills Practice segment of main lesson. This practice is problematic. During a language arts block, students need skills practice time to warm up their literacy brains, not their math brains. In addition, they need follow-up practice with recently introduced literacy skills to myelinate their new neural pathways. Plan on reserving the Skills Practice segment of your language arts main lesson classes for language arts skill practice. Practice math skills in the math practice classes that are scheduled during a language arts block.

**Introduction &/or Review**

Introduction &/or Review is the time for the initial introduction of new concepts, content, or skills. It includes review because new learning takes place over two or three days. Recall that there is a benefit from working with the night and having students sleep on new learning (see chapter 2.1 #9). This segment includes **teaching rhythms**, or the initial introduction, the review of the newly introduced skill the next day, and related activities to reinforce the Introduction &/or Review. It should take between 10 to 25 minutes each day.

The Introduction is used to introduce new concepts, subject content, or skills:

1. New concepts are ideas that are unfamiliar to the students such as the initial introduction of the noun as a part of speech. On-going concepts include variations on a concept already introduced, such as proper and common nouns.

2. New subject content is the story or factual information you plan to work with in class such as information about a practical occupation in the 3rd Grade Home Surroundings Block (see chapter 5.5 #8). It will become more important in 4th Grade when students begin to study subjects.

3. New skills include phonics rules and language mechanics such as new capitalization protocols.

All new learning is taught through images and/or stories and activities that give students a multisensory learning experience.

The Review occurs the day after the introduction and provides students a chance to re-examine the new learning after having slept on it. It can include a review of the image and the rule or concept that goes with the image. See chapter 3.8 #2 for a full discussion on how to work with the review of stories.

Activities are activities that give students various multisensory opportunities to learn something new. They are included as part of the Introduction &/or Review. In the lower grades, introductory activities should be as kinesthetic or visual as possible. For example, as part of the introduction of the letter *M* in 1st Grade, have students look around the classroom for things that begin with the /m/ sound, practice the idea of verbs through a game of charades in 2nd Grade, or experience adverbs by playing an adverbial version of *Simon Says* (e.g., "*Simon says skip slowly.*") in 3rd Grade.

There are two types of activities. Some activities are best done as introduction and others as review.

- **Activity A:** any activity that follows the initial introduction and is geared more to the class as a group
- **Activity B:** any activity that follows the review the next day (This type of activity is geared towards smaller groups of the class.)

Many times Activities A and B will not be differentiated; however you can easily differentiate them by using a technique called **Drill Down**. For example, if the whole class did a movement activity together the first day (Activity A), ask a smaller segment to do the activity the second day (Activity B) (see chapter 2.4 #2).

After the Introduction &/or Review segment of main lesson is finished, students will continue to practice new skills during the Skills Practice segment of main lesson. For the most part, students will practice on their own rather than in groups during Skills Practice. Schedule daily practice until the class has mastered the new skill.

## Bookwork

Bookwork is the time for students to take what they have learned and put it down into concrete form through writing and/or drawing. Bookwork can be formal or informal in nature. It can include work in a main lesson book, a practice book, or a worksheet. Bookwork should take between 15 to 35 minutes.

**Main lesson books** are artistic expressions of the curriculum that students create during main lesson (see chapter 2.1 #1). The actual book the students use can be purchased or the teacher can bind the student's loose leaf work together at the end of the year. They include the students' very best writing and artwork. In 1st Grade most of the main lesson bookwork is copied; by 3rd Grade, most of the written content should be composed by the students themselves. The following are examples of main lesson book assignments:

- copying a poem the students have learned using their neatest handwriting
- drawing a picture under the teacher's guidance
- writing a final draft of a composition

**Practice books** are the notebooks that students use for practice. They include notebooks for rough drafts of writing assignments and pages where students can practice ongoing skills such as encoding and spelling words. They are for more informal assignments. The following are examples of practice book assignments:

- handwriting practice for a new letter
- a kid writing exercise (see chapter 3.13)
- a rough draft of a composition
- encoding practice and practice of weekly spelling words

A variation of the practice book is the **phonics rules book** where students will record their phonics rules and rules for mechanics in grammar (see chapter 4.1 Protocol).

In addition, students can do worksheets or other written assignments that are not in either book during the Bookwork segment of the lesson.

Note: Practice books can be used at any point during the main lesson class or the practice class, but main lesson books are normally worked on during the Bookwork segment of main lesson.

## Story

Stories are the key to Waldorf instruction. In Grades 1–3 the story should last between 10–20 minutes. The story can be told to introduce new learning or it can be told as soul food. Stories told to introduce new learning are always told during main lesson. They can occur in the Story segment or in the Introduction &/or Review segment. Stories told as soul food can be told during the Story segment or they can be told later in the day if more time is needed in main lesson. Snack time or the end of the day are good times to tell a soul food story if there is not enough time for a story in main lesson.

Note: Stories may also be told at other times of the day (e.g., during practice classes for handwork, form drawing, painting, modeling, etc.). Therefore, the Story segment of main lesson can be used to provide more time for practice activities, bookwork, etc. Flex the schedule to meet your needs or to avoid telling too many stories (see chapter 5.5 #9).

## Transitions

During transitions between the various segments of main lesson, students often need a brief break. This is the time for **Integrated Movement Activities** or IMAs. IMAs do the following:

- They help to meet the developmental needs of the class.
- They serve more than one function at a time.
- They provide a healthy breathing between **incarnating** and **excarnating activities,** the rhythm between quiet activities where the students' focus is on their work and the noisy activities where the students' attention is out in the environment.

Integrated Movement Activities should be integrated into the main lesson itself.

IMAs can include:

- singing or clapping games that feature movement
- speech exercises that feature movement
- developmental movements such as **Zoo Exercises**, **Brain Gym,** or **Bal-A-Vis-X** exercises (see chapter 6.6 #5)
- bean bag exercises (see chapter 6.6 #5)
- games such as *Simon Says*
- movement activities such as the **upside-down world,** an activity where the students drape themselves over their desk and hang their head and arms over the front so that they can see their dangling feet

Note: It is unwise to break the momentum of a lesson with an unrelated IMA. Therefore, the transition between Introduction &/or Review and Bookwork should be chosen with care. The other transitions can be random, unrelated activities, but Bookwork is a continuation of the Introduction &/or Review. Come up with some type of movement related to the concept or skill you are teaching or that is related to setting up for Bookwork.

## 5. Sacred Nothing: Circle

Readers familiar with Waldorf may have noticed a prominent omission of the main lesson archetype: **circle.**

This is by design.

Circle is an extended period of time (25–60 minutes depending on the teacher) that includes movement, speech, music, pedagogical exercises, etc. It is a prominent part of kindergarten, but it was not initially part of the grades education. It has since entered many main lessons and is part of some Waldorf teacher training programs. Circle is an example of a Sacred Nothing (see chapter 2.2).

Christof Wiechert challenges the pedagogical worth of *circle* in his article "On the Question of the Three-fold Structure of the Main Lesson." Because the Opening segment of the lesson sets the mood of the day, he suggests that teachers be flexible in what they present in the Opening. This will allow them to bring what their students need at that point in time. He suggests that Opening segment take no more than 15 minutes. He cautions against undertaking movement exercises that take a long time because the point of main lesson is new learning. He reminds teachers that the students will get movement during recess (Wiechert 2010, 5).

It is important to acknowledge that students often need help with movement challenges. If left unresolved, they can compromise learning. Students today need more help in this area than ever before. Many of the students need help integrating their physical and etheric bodies. Many students still have midline barriers and need help dissolving them. Many students have not fully established dominance yet. However, asking 1st-3rd graders to do a 25–60 minute circle at the beginning of the day and then having them sit for the next hour or more of academic work is counterproductive and does not work with a child's natural rhythm. Also, it makes it very difficult to cover the curriculum when a quarter to half of main lesson is used for purposes other than language arts instruction.

Fortunately, it is not necessary to choose between the curriculum and the developmental needs of the students. Instead of doing circle, do IMAs (Integrated Movement Activities). They can serve most of the purposes of circle activities while making more productive use of main lesson time.

Note: If most of the class needs extra movement activities to address remedial issues, see chapter 6.6 #4 and #5 for suggestions.

## 6. Practice Class Archetype

Recall that there are a maximum of four practice classes each day after main lesson. Each day, one of those practice classes should be devoted to the off-skill (e.g., during a math block it will cover language arts, and during a language arts block it will cover math). These classes are called **academic practice classes** or just **practice classes.** (Note: The practice classes in this book are referring to the one academic practice class that is scheduled each day in a math block that is reserved for language arts skill practice.)

An academic practice class lasts 45 or 50 minutes. There should be one every day. The ideal time for it is after main lesson but prior to lunch, when the students are still fresh. The academic practice class and main lesson class guarantees that students have daily practice in both math and language arts skills every day.

We have created a flexible archetype for language arts practice classes as shown in table 2.3.2. It was created to support *The Roadmap to Literacy's* curriculum and is offered for homeschool parents and Waldorf teachers to use as meets their needs and those of their students.

**Table 2.3.2:** *The Roadmap to Literacy* **Practice Class Archetype**

| Practice Class Archetype |
| --- |
| Skills Practice (15–20 min.) |
| Introduction &/or Review (10–15 min.) |
| Bookwork (15 min.) |
| Schedule a transition activity between segments if needed. |

The practice class is essentially an abbreviated main lesson class. There are some key differences as to what is scheduled in each of the three segments.

## Skills Practice

The Skills Practice segment in practice classes is similar to the Skills Practice segment in main lesson. Among the skills practiced during this segment are:

- letters of the alphabet
- phonemic awareness
- symbol imagery
- phonics rules (encoding and decoding)
- sight words (1st and 2nd Grades)
- spelling lists (3rd Grade only)

Schedule Skills Practice in every practice class.

## Introduction &/or Review

Introduction &/or Review is similar to main lesson, but it is much more limited in scope. Only introduce new content in the following categories:

- phonics rules
- mini-lessons from kid writing or composition
- sight words (1st and 2nd Grade) or spelling words (3rd Grade) on Mondays

Most of the time you will be practicing encoding and decoding with the current phonics rule when there is nothing new to introduce. On these days, Introduction &/or Review will be an extension of Skills Practice.

## Bookwork

Bookwork is the segment that most differs from main lesson. It alternates between the following:

- kid writing (1st and 2nd Grade)
- reading groups (includes memory reading in 1st Grade)
- grammar worksheet (3rd Grade)
- composition (3rd Grade)

Our use of practice classes represents quite a change. In the past, many Waldorf teachers have scheduled only two or three academic practice classes in the course of a week rather than one a day. Also, it is not uncommon for some Waldorf teachers to limit the introduction of new skills to main lesson only. They use their few academic practice classes solely for the practicing of previously introduced skills, even if the class has mastered those skills and is ready to move on. *The Roadmap to Literacy* is recommending a different approach for the following reasons:

- Mastering a new academic skill requires daily practice. Once the brain learns something new, it needs ongoing repetition to myelinate the newly formed neural pathways (see chapter 1.2 #4).

- Teachers need time to teach phonics skills if they are to cover the identified literacy curriculum by the end of 3rd Grade. This means that a rule is practiced as long as is needed for the class to master it (**80/80 rule**) and then the class moves on to the next rule. Working successfully and efficiently with phonics rules requires scheduling a continual flow of introduction and then practice regardless of whether you are teaching a language arts main lesson or practice block. (See Section 4 Phonics Rules.)

- The situation is similar with language mechanics and spelling. These skills also need ongoing practice.

Our changes improve student learning while honoring the Waldorf rhythm of main lesson blocks and practice class blocks.

Note: While there are three subsections in practice class, they do not need to be clearly delineated with transitions as in main lesson. It is desirable to mix the activities up so that more movement-based activities alternate with sedentary ones.

## 7. Truncated Schedules

In the United States it is fairly common for Waldorf 1st and even 2nd Grades to have truncated schedules. First graders are often dismissed shortly after lunch, just like kindergartners. Second graders are often dismissed an hour early. This truncated schedule is problematic because it makes finding time for daily academic practice classes a real challenge. If you only have ten practice classes per week, which is the case for many 1st Grades, there is little time left once you factor in music, form drawing, foreign language(s), games, gardening, handwork, Eurythmy, painting, etc.

We suggest that Waldorf faculties and school boards take up the topic of lengthening their school's 1st and 2nd Grade school days. Most European Waldorf schools moved to a full school day schedule (usually with one half day) a number of years ago. When discussing this with Janet, Christof Wiechert shared, "We could not adequately cover the curriculum if the students were only in school half days." His Waldorf School in The Hague adopted a full schedule for their 1st and 2nd graders over 25 years ago.

Both 1st and 2nd graders are able to be in school for the entire school day, especially if some attention is given to scheduling the less demanding classes after lunch. More and more Waldorf schools are making this change. If yours is not one of them, bring this proposal for consideration.

## Conclusion

The Waldorf school year is organized around blocks of study. Each block is made up of individual main lessons that last two hours each morning. Blocks of study rotate between language arts skills and math skills with one block of home surroundings. Students continue to practice academic skills during off blocks in their daily academic practice classes.

The next chapter will explore best teaching practices for the 15 aspects of language arts. This information, along with the phonics rules detailed in Section 4, will serve as the basis for the preparation of your language arts main lesson classes and practice classes.

# 2.4 TEACHING PRACTICES

This chapter highlights a few teaching practices that can be especially useful when teaching language arts.

This chapter covers the following topics:

1. Economy in Teaching
2. Drill Down
3. Differentiating Instruction
4. Classroom Management

## 1. Economy in Teaching

Economy in teaching refers to a common teaching practice of using one activity to meet two or more objectives.

For example, say your students need a break because they have been sitting for too long and are starting to get restless. They also need more practice on sight words. You can use economy in teaching by asking the students to stand up and do some sight word chants (see chapter 3.6 #6–8). They get to move and you work in an additional sight word practice at the same time.

Some aspects of language arts have a broader focus than others and can easily be made to serve more than one objective at a time. For example, kid writing (see chapter 3.13) has the following aspects built in: phonemic awareness, sight word spelling, handwriting, comprehension, etc. This activity has economy of teaching built into it.

## 2. Drill Down

Drill Down refers to a Waldorf teaching technique that is used to introduce and practice new material, skills, and movement. It is an example of a Responsible Innovation.

Drill Down starts with class activities, moves to small-group or partner activities, and ends with individual activities. It is typically done with movement activities such as **Take Time** bean bag activities (see chapter 6.6 #5) and music activities such as playing the flute or recorder. It can also be done with the initial introduction and/or review of language arts activities such as learning a new poem for speech. (See chapter 3.10 #6 for an example.)

By selecting a smaller group, or *drilling down* the number of students asked to do a practice activity, you make the students more conscious of their actions. When everyone in the class is doing an activity together, it is easy for students to be carried along by their peers or do an activity unconsciously. However, as you shift the focus from the whole class to a smaller group, the dynamic changes. Only a few students are active and the others are observing. This shift encourages those students performing the activity to be more conscious of their own participation, and it improves their learning.

Drilling down can be done in a variety of ways.

If you want everyone to have an equal chance to practice, use the following:

- Drilling down from class to row to desk partner
- alternating between boys and girls

If you want students to have more than one chance to practice, then choose:

- students who have brothers/sisters living at home
- students who are the oldest/youngest child in the family
- students who have dogs or cats
- students wearing a certain article of clothing (e.g., shorts or shoes with laces)

A variation is to use economy in teaching to review different academic skills. For example,

- students whose first names begin (or end) with a consonant/vowel
- students who were born in a winter month

If you have used random groups, end with "Those who have yet to do it" to make sure everyone has a chance to practice at least once.

You can also use Drill Down for other things such as introductions and informal assessments. You can ask several students who do an activity well to come up to the front of the class and demonstrate it for the others. Point out the specifics of what they did well so the rest of the class knows what you are looking for. Drill Down is also effective for informal assessments. It is hard to watch everyone in a large group. It is much easier to observe when students are drilling down and there are fewer students in a group.

Drill Down is an effective way to help students learn to do the work on their own. The class will carry individual students during the initial practice, but they will have to take more and more responsibility as you drill down the number of students doing the activity. By the time the initial introduction is over, students are expected to do all of the work on their own. Use it as you teach and practice new things.

## 3.   Differentiating Instruction

After the initial introduction is over, sometimes it will be necessary to provide the students with different classroom experiences and assignments to meet their needs (see chapter 1.2 #6). For example, you will most certainly have students in at least two different phases in 1st Grade. Some will need extensive practice to learn their letters; others will already be able to read. Therefore, it is necessary to **differentiate instruction** or give students different work, depending on their needs.

All students will hear the same story and do the same artwork, but their main lesson book content will look very different. Students in higher phases will have more extensive main lesson and practice books because they will be doing more independent kid writing entries or compositions. While they do more advanced work on their own, you can provide extra practice to small groups of students who are in a lower phase.

### Ways to Differentiate Instruction

How can you determine when to differentiate instruction, and if so, how? Let's contrast undifferentiated practice with differentiated practice.

Undifferentiated Individual Practice

This method works best when all of the students are at the same level. It is usually scheduled during Skills Practice, after the students have completed the initial Introduction &/or Review for new learning. Grammar is a good example. Students do not know about adjectives and adverbs until you introduce them; therefore, everyone is starting at the same place and should have the same assignment—at least initially.

For example, give each student in the class the same copy of a paragraph and ask them to underline all of the adjectives.

Differentiated Individual Practice

This method works best with written assignments students can do at their desk. This type of practice is usually reserved for the Skills Practice segment or Bookwork segment, after the students have finished the initial Introduction &/or Review for new learning.

For example, create two worksheets on adjectives. The first is for the majority of the class, and the second is for the advanced students. The first worksheet has sentences that have blanks where adjectives could be added. The second has harder sentences and asks the students to write a few sentences of their own using the most creative and interesting adjectives they can.

Small Groups

This method work best during the initial Introduction &/or Review segment or during the Skills Practice segment of main lesson or practice class. It works best when the class is covering the same content but the students are in different phases. It is possible to differentiate Activities A and B to meet everyone's needs.

For example, create a word sort activity for digraphs as shown in figure 2.4.1. (Two sources for pictures you can use in your word sorts are *Words Their Way* Appendix C and the card game "Blurble" created by Bernard Games of Portland, Or.)

**Figure 2.4.1: A Word Sort Activity for Digraphs using picture cards from the card game "Blurble"**

This word sort activity is part of the initial Introduction &/or Review of digraphs (see chapter 4.1 rule 2).

Divide the students into groups according to phase (see chapter 6.2 #1).

- Beginning Phonemic Awareness Phase: Provide a number of pictures of objects that <u>begin</u> or <u>end</u> with the digraph sounds /ch/, /wh/, /th/, and /sh/ (e.g., cherries, whisk, thimble, shell, or brush, bath, beach etc.). Students take turns sorting them into the right cups. This activity would only apply to the one or two students who are lagging behind the class. Note: There are no English words that end in *WH*.

- Intermediate Phonemic Awareness Phase: Provide pictures of objects that have the targeted sound embedded inside the word (e.g., bushes, flashlight, milkshake, crutches, ketchup, kitchen, matches, feather, father, finger, and hanger). Ask the students to sort them into the right cup.

- Advanced Phonemic Awareness Phase or Higher: Provide the same pictures of objects and include both those that begin or end with the targeted sound. Ask students to spell the words on a separate sheet of paper rather than sort the pictures into cups.

Each member of the class will be practicing the same content based on their level of phonemic awareness.

## Differentiating Instruction in Reading Groups

Some aspects of the lesson should be differentiated on principle. Reading and phonemic awareness are good examples of areas where students can vary in their competency. Students who are in different phases need practice geared towards their level. Small groups where the students need different lessons are best done in reading groups.

When the majority of the class is first learning to read, trying to work with a 'one size fits all' reader does not work. If the reader is too simple advanced students will be bored and if too difficult those who are just learning will get easily frustrated. It is better to work with separate groups.

Split the students into reading groups (see chapter 3.15 #10). Give each group reading material that matches its level. Meet with the lowest group more often than the highest to give those students extra practice on phonemic awareness and phonics rules so they can catch up with their classmates and not fall further behind. (Note: You can invite a student who is not a member of the reading group to come participate in an exercise with a different reading group if she needs extra practice in that area.)

For more information on differentiating instruction in reading groups, see chapter 3.15 #10.

## Differentiating Instruction for Outliers

You may have one or two students who will not need as much practice as their peers to learn to read (see chapter 1.2 #6). While the rest of the class is doing an activity or exercise to practice in the Skills Practice segment of the lesson, ask these students to do a writing exercise, catch up on other assignments, or work on weak areas (such as math facts or handwriting, etc.). Note: Just be careful to assess first to make sure the students have truly mastered the point of the lesson and are not contextual readers or accelerated readers who cannot encode. For example, students may be able to read words effortlessly (decoding) but still need further practice on spelling (encoding) or on phonemic awareness (see chapter 6.2 #4).

You may also have one or two students who need much more practice than everyone else. Modify expectations to provide extra practice in their weak areas. For example, while other students are copying an entry into a main lesson book, ask these students to do an activity that provides extra instruction or practice in their weak area. For example, you could ask a student to do a word sort targeted at any letters or sounds she is still struggling with (e.g., the sounds /ĕ/ and /ĭ/).

Strive to meet the needs of every student in the class by differentiating instruction.

## 4. Classroom Management

Classroom management is a big topic and is outside the scope of this book; however, it is always good to keep in mind the four legs of the chair of classroom management:

- the warm, respectful relationship between the teacher and the students
- creative, developmentally appropriate lessons
- a rhythmic flow between active times and quiet times (breathing)
- an environment where students feel safe to learn (no bullying or teasing)

When you have these four elements, classroom management is much easier.

Note: The second and third leg of classroom management are nothing more than solid lesson preparation based on a knowledge of the phases and best practices. If you spend the time necessary to make an appropriate curriculum, you will be on the way to good classroom management.

## Conclusion

Making use of your class time is essential for effective learning. You can achieve this objective by using the four techniques highlighted in this chapter. The next section will focus on the 15 aspects of language arts.

# SECTION 3

The 15 Aspects of Language Arts

# 3.1 THE ALPHABET

*Janet Langley's grandson taught her an invaluable lesson about the alphabet.*

*When Janet was giving her grandson his first lessons in reading, she brought him only the uppercase letters, as per local Waldorf tradition. He was excited to learn them, but he quickly became frustrated. He picked up a beloved book and went through the text looking for the letters he now knew. Capital letters were few and far between. Each sentence had one or sometimes two at the most. He picked them out, like peanut clusters in a box of Cracker Jacks. Then he wanted to know when she would teach him the letters that really mattered. He pointed to the lowercase letters that made up the vast majority of the writing on the page. "That's where the story is, Nana," he explained.*

The alphabet truly is the alpha of learning to read. There is a reason Rogers and Hammerstein wrote:

> Let's start at the very beginning
>
> A very good place to start
>
> When you read you begin with *ABC*
>
> > "Do-Re-Mi" from *The Sound of Music*

Without these 26 symbols, there is no learning to read or write.

Note: This chapter on the alphabet should always be read back to back with the chapter on handwriting as the two complement each other (see chapter 3.2).

This chapter covers the following topics:

1. Why the Alphabet Matters
2. Background Information
3. Sacred Nothings
4. Preparation
5. Scheduling
6. Initial Introduction
7. How to Teach the First Block: Consonant Letters
8. How to Teach the Second Block: The Remaining Consonant Letters
9. How to Teach the Third Block: Vowel Letters
10. Practice
11. Assessment
12. How to Help Struggling Students

# 1. Why the Alphabet Matters

As seen in section 1, the idea behind the first alphabet truly was a breakthrough: rather than using pictures to represent words, letters were used to represent phonemes, or sounds. Reading and writing in alphabetic languages is one giant code that rests upon phonemic awareness and knowledge of the alphabet. As students acquire these two skills, they learn to decode (or sound out) new words or encode (or spell by sound) words.

A perfect alphabetic language would be a perfect code. It would have one letter for every phoneme and one phoneme for every letter. As seen in chapter 1.3, English is an alphabetic language, but it is far from a perfect code because it has two extra layers on top of its alphabetic layer: pattern and meaning. Students have to master these two layers in addition to the alphabet to successfully handle encoding and decoding in English. These two extra layers are why learning to read and spell in English is so complicated. Once students learn the alphabet, they then need to learn **phonics rules** to handle the pattern layer. Phonics rules provide a way to stretch the 26 letters of the Latin alphabet to cover the 40+ sounds in English (see section 4).

However, despite English's complexity, learning the alphabet is still the starting point for learning to read and write. It is the beginning of rewiring the brain to develop the *letter to sound decoding route*. It is what spurs awareness of individual phonemes.

Learning the alphabet brings students' awareness to the pure phonemes in their language and thus makes it possible for them to build the neural network necessary for handling the code for reading and writing—not bad for 26 symbols made of straight and curved lines!

# 2. Background Information

The information in this subsection will provide a technical explanation of the alphabet and how it works. It is useful to know this information because it will help you plan your lessons and avoid some common pitfalls.

This subsection covers the following topics:

1. The Two Parts of a Letter
2. The Sound/Symbol Correspondence
3. Consonants and Vowels
4. Long and Short Vowel Sounds
5. Other Vowel Sounds
6. Point of Articulation
7. German and English Vowels
8. The Sound for the Letter A
9. Archetypal Vowels
10. Conclusion: Teach Vowels Last

## The Two Parts of a Letter

Every letter has two parts: the written symbol (**grapheme**) and the letter name. For example, the grapheme for the letter *T* is made up of two line segments that are perpendicular to each other while the name of this letter is the same as the word *tea*, or "a drink with jam and bread." Being able to name the letter, or **letter naming**, is a critical skill for students to master in its own right as well as for learning letter sounds.

As shown in table 3.1.1, the name of the consonant letter almost always includes the phoneme represented by the letter. For example, when pronouncing the name of the letter *T* (i.e., *tea*) you can hear that it is made up of two phonemes: /t/ and /ē/ (i.e., the long *E* sound). In some languages the vowel sound of a letter comes before the consonant sound, while in others the vowel sound comes after the consonant sound. In English the letters do both. For example, in the letter *T*, the consonant sound comes first (i.e., /t/ + /ē/). In the letter *S*, the vowel sound comes first (i.e., /ĕ/ + /s/).

**Table 3.1.1: Breakdown of Consonant Letter Names**

| Letter's Phoneme + Vowel | Vowel + Letter's Phoneme | Random | Partial Match |
|---|---|---|---|
| *B, D, J, K, P, T, V, Z* | *F, L, M, N, R, S* | *H, Q\*, W,* and *Y* <br> These letters have no relationship between the name of the letter and its sound. | *X, C,* and *G* <br> These letters have more than one sound. One of their sounds does contain a phoneme match, but not the other(s). |

*\*We classified the letter Q as random because QU is always taught as a unit with the sound /kw/; the letter Q (i.e.,/ k/ + /ū/) is not another way to spell the phoneme /k/.*

Vowels, however, are very different. In many languages, a vowel letter's name is identical to its phoneme. However, the five vowel letters in English do double duty. Each vowel letter has two vowel sounds: one that is identical to its name (long sound) and one that is random (short sound).

This information is useful for several reasons:

1. It offers guidance on the order in which to teach the letters. It is easier for students to match the letter and its sounds when the phoneme is embedded in the letter name. Teach these letters first. Doing so will help students in the Emergent Phase realize that letters represent sounds.

2. It shows which letters will need more practice. Plan to schedule extra practice for letters that are random or have partial matches between the letter name and its phoneme(s).

### The Sound/Symbol Correspondence

The **sound/symbol correspondence** refers to the connection between the grapheme (the written letter) and its phoneme (the letter's sound). Due to the oversized influence of the Roman Empire, many European languages make use of the Latin alphabet. Sometimes the letters represent the same sounds, and sometimes they do not. Table 3.1.2 reviews the sound/symbol correspondence in English for those readers who know multiple languages.

**Table 3.1.2: Sound/Symbol Correspondence in English (Alphabet Only)**

| |
|---|
| *Aa* /ā/ as in *angel* and /ă/ as in *apple* |
| *Bb* /b/ as in *boy* |
| *Cc* /k/ as in *cat* and /s/ as in *cent* |
| *Dd* /d/ as in *dog* |
| *Ee* /ē/ as in *eagle* and /ĕ/ as in *edge* |
| *Ff* /f/ as in *fig* |

| |
|---|
| Gg /g/ as in *goose* and /j/ as in *giraffe* |
| Hh /h/ as in *hand* |
| Ii /ī/ as in *ice cream* and /ĭ/ as in *igloo* |
| Jj /j/ as in *jack* |
| Kk /k/ as in *kite* |
| Ll /l/ as in *lion* |
| Mm /m/ as in *man* |
| Nn /n/ as in *nest* |
| Oo /ō/ as in *oak* and /ŏ/ as in *octopus* |
| Pp /p/ as in *pie* |
| Qq /kw/ as in *queen* |
| Rr /r/ as in *rabbit* |
| Ss /s/ as in *sun* |
| Tt /t/ as in *tiger* |
| Uu /ū/ as in *unicycle* and /ŭ/ as in *umbrella* |
| Vv /v/ as in *vine* |
| Ww /w/ as in *water* |
| Xx /ks/ as in *fox* |
| Yy /y/ as in *yellow* |
| Zz /z/ as in *zebra* |

Note: A phoneme is written between two forward slashes: /t/. When you encounter a letter so written, say its sound. This information is important for three reasons:

1. It shows you which English sound(s) is associated with each letter. (Different languages can pair different sounds with the letters.)

2. When you introduce the letter and its sound, mind your articulation. Make sure that you say the consonant sound as cleanly as possible. Avoid making the /ŭ/ after the phonemes when you can. (For example, /d/ not "duuuuh.") In some phonemes, this will not be possible (e.g., /p/). You will have to make an /ŭ/ sound after these phonemes, but make it short: /p/ as *puh* not *puuuuhh*. Hold the students to the same standard. When students add an extra vowel sound to the consonant, they struggle to decode words.

3. Some letters have more than one sound. It is necessary to teach both, but not during the initial introduction of the letter. See section 4 for more information on how to teach the other sounds.

**Consonants and Vowels**

The 26 letters of the English alphabet can be divided into vowels and consonants, but what exactly is a vowel and what exactly is a consonant?

**Vowels** are often described as singing sounds. To make a vowel sound, open your mouth and let your voice come out without shaping the sound in any way: uuuuuuuh, eeeeeeeee, ooooooooooooo, aaaaaaaah, etc. To make a different vowel sound, make your mouth wider or narrower and let your voice pour out. Play with putting your tongue further forward or back and try again. You have just created vowel sounds, all of them phonemes, but not necessarily phonemes used in the English language.

Unlike vowels, which are created by opening the mouth in various positions and sending forth sound, **consonants** are created by restricting the air passage with the tongue and lips. Try saying the phoneme for the letter *T*: /*t*/. Can you feel your tongue tapping the roof of your mouth just behind your teeth? That action restricts the air flow and makes the sound /*t*/ a consonant. Consonants can explode from out of your mouth, like the sound /*t*/, or they can be one long stream of air, like the sound /*s*/. Many consonants need to combine with vowels so that their sound can project out into the world. Try making the sound /*p*/ without adding the sound /*ŭ*/. How loud was the sound? Try one final experiment: Say the word "*help*" loudly enough to get someone's attention. Now try screaming this word without its vowel sound. It did not get much louder, did it? Without vowels, consonants do not carry far. They need the singing power of vowels to help them project.

In addition to the workings of the tongue, teeth, and palate, it is good to consider what Steiner had to say about vowels and consonants. In "A Lecture on Eurythmy," Steiner discusses vowels and consonants. About vowels, he says:

> True speech, however, is born from the whole human being. Let us take any one of the vowels. A vowel sound is always the expression of some aspect of the feeling life of the soul. The human being wishes to express what lives in his soul as wonder — Ah. Or the holding himself upright against opposition — A; or the assertion of self, the consciousness of ego-existence in the world — E. Or again he wishes to express wonder, but now with a more intimate, caressing shade of feeling–I.

> The character of the sounds is of course slightly different in the different languages, because each individual language proceeds from a differently constituted soul-life. (Steiner 1923)

About consonants, he says:

> The consonants are the imitation of what we find around us in external nature. The vowel is born out of man's inmost being; it is the channel through which this inner content of the soul streams outwards. The consonant is born out of the comprehension of external nature; the way in which we seize upon external things, even the way in which we perceive them with the eyes, all of this is built into the form of the consonants. The consonant represents, paints, as it were, the things of the external world. (ibid)

In other words, vowels convey the <u>speaker's</u> feeling life while consonants convey the outer world of material objects, but as the character of the sounds varies slightly across languages, what he identifies in German may not apply to English.

Between the physical creation of the sounds and the underlying meanings associated with them, you can get a complete picture of the difference between these two types of phonemes. This information will help you teach both vowels and consonants in 1st Grade.

## Long and Short Vowel Sounds

English has one long sound and one short sound for each vowel letter as shown in table 3.1.3. You will need to teach both long and short sounds for each vowel letter. In 1st Grade focus on the short vowel sounds. They will be critical in the Phonemic Awareness Phase. Focus on the long vowel sounds when you teach phonics rules. These long sounds will be critical in the Pattern Phase.

**Table 3.1.3: Long and Short Vowel Sounds in English**

| Letter | Short Sound | Long Sound |
|:------:|:-----------:|:----------:|
| *A* | /ă/ as in *apple* | /ā/ as in *angel* |
| *E* | /ĕ/ as in *edge* | /ē/ as in *eagle* |
| *I* | /ĭ/ as in *igloo* | /ī/ as in *ice cream* |
| *O* | /ŏ/ as in *octopus* | /ō/ as in *oak* |
| *U* | /ŭ/ as in *umbrella* | /ū/ as in *unicorn* and /oo/ as in *Luke* |

The terms *long* and *short* refer to how many movements the mouth makes to produce the vowel sound. The long sounds are made with two movements of the mouth while the short sounds are made with only one movement of the mouth. For example, try saying long *U* /ū/ (you), and then pronounce the short *U* (/ŭ/ as in *umbrella*.) Did you feel how your mouth slid from one position to another for long *U*? Vowel sounds that move from one position to another are called **diphthongs**. All long vowels are diphthongs, and some other vowel sounds are as well (e.g., /oi/ as in *boil*).

Notice that the long vowel sounds are obvious because they are identical to the letter's name while the short vowel sounds have no relationship to the name of the letter itself. For example, there is no connection between the short sound of *A* (i.e., /ă/ as in *apple*) and the name of the letter *A*. This fact makes teaching and learning short vowels difficult. Plan to spend extra time practicing the vowels when you introduce them.

**Other Vowel Sounds**

Long and short vowels are only some of the vowel sounds in English. The exact number of vowel sounds varies depending on dialect. *The Roadmap to Literacy* will cover the 16 basic vowel sounds: the ten long and short vowel sounds found in this chapter and the six additional sounds covered in section 4. These six additional vowel sounds are:

1. /oo/ as in *boo*
2. /oo/ as in *book*
3. /oi/ as in *boy* or *boil*
4. /au/ as in *awful* or *August*
5. /ou/ as in *owl* or *ouch*
6. /r/ as in *girl, myrrh, fur,* or *her*

That last one is not a typo. In English, the phoneme /r/ can be used either as a consonant or a vowel. When it is a vowel, it is always spelled as a **digraph** (two letters that represent one sound, also known as vowel teams or consonant teams). For example, the letters *ER, IR,* and *UR* all represent the sound /r/ when it is used as a vowel and are all vowel teams.

Note: These three *R*-controlled vowel teams are the ones that represent only one phoneme: /r/. The vowel teams *AR* and *OR* both contain a vowel sound in their own right. (Note: The letters *AR* contain the letter *A*'s broad sound: *AH* or /aw/.) (See *The Sound for the Letter A* below.)

It is important to realize that there are more vowel sounds than vowel letters. Learning the alphabet is only the first step in learning the code. It is also necessary to teach the students phonics rules (see section 4).

### Point of Articulation

When students first start encoding with short vowels, they will go through a phase where they will do so incorrectly by using **point of articulation**, which means students will use the pronunciation of the vowel letter's name to predict its short vowel sound. Consequently in the middle of the Phonemic Awareness Phase, they will make predictable errors as shown in table 3.1.4.

**Table 3.1.4: Student Errors Caused by Point of Articulation**

| Short Vowel Sound | Student Letter Substitution | Typical Encoding Mistakes Made by Students in the Mid-Phonemic Awareness Phase |
|---|---|---|
| /ă/ | None | NA |
| /ĕ/ | A | BAT for bet |
| /ĭ/ | E | PET for pit |
| /ŏ/ | I | LIT for lot |
| /ŭ/ | O | COT for cut |

*Source: Adapted from* Bear 2008, 138.

Do not panic if you teach the short vowel sounds and see your students mix them up when they try to spell words. It is normal. With repeated practice, students will make the correct association between the phoneme and the grapheme. (Make sure you schedule lots of practice when you make your block plans.)

### German and English Vowels

Steiner spoke German and referred to vowel sounds using German spelling conventions. Some vowel sounds that he referred to are the same in both languages; however, the spelling conventions do not align. This fact has created some confusion for English-speaking Waldorf teachers.

While English and German use the same five vowel letters, those letters do not represent the same sounds. Steiner used the German vowel conventions when discussing vowel sounds: "A as in *father*, E as in *eight*, I as in *me*, O as in *order*, and U as in *blue*" (Steiner 2000, 19 footnote 2). Note that these sounds are not the same as the vowel sounds given in table 3.1.3.

There are multiple ramifications to this difference:

1. In some Waldorf teacher trainings and in Eurythmy, the vowel sounds are taught using the German conventions. This situation has resulted in some confusion about which vowels sounds Waldorf teachers should teach and which vowel letters go with those sounds. The answer is simple: Teach the English sound/symbol relationships to the students when you are teaching the English language and save the German sound/symbol relationships for the German foreign language class.

   *The Roadmap to Literacy* recommends that you teach the English short vowel sounds first, when you introduce the vowel letters, and save the long vowel sounds for when you teach phonics rules.

2. Be aware of the differences in vowel spelling and vowel sounds when reading Steiner's indications on teaching vowels. In the original German, he is naming German sounds with German vowel spelling conventions. Sometimes the translator changes the spelling to the nearest English sound and sometimes not. Even when the translator changes the spelling to English spelling, the sounds referred to may not be exactly the same in the two languages (see Archetypal Vowels).

3. Also ask your school's Eurythmy teacher and/or speech teacher to refer to any sound by its English vowel letter's name rather than its German name. In other words, *AH* (/ŏ/) is the letter *O*'s sound.

4. It is necessary to screen your Waldorf teaching materials with care to make sure the vowel conventions use the English sound/symbol relationships and not the German, especially for the letter *A*.

## The Sound for the Letter A

The letter *A* has three sounds in English: short *A* (as in *apple*), long *A* (as in *angel*), and broad *A* (as in *father*).

By far the most common sound for the letter *A* is short *A* (i.e., /ă/ as in *apple*), followed by long *A* (i.e., /ā/ as in *angel*). The broad sound for *A (AH)* is not very common. It appears with certain spelling patterns such as the vowel teams *AW, AU,* and *AR*. These spelling patterns are taught when students learn phonics rules.

However, given the prominence of the sound AH in Steiner's German examples (see Archetypal Vowels, the next subsection) coupled with the fact that the sound AH does exist in a handful of very prominent English words such as *father*, some teachers have taught *A*'s sound as /aw/ (AH), just like in German.

This is a problem that expands exponentially. Teaching the incorrect sound for a vowel letter interferes with the students' ability to learn to decode and encode, which in turn undermines the formation of the *letter to sound decoding route*, which is the prerequisite for the *lexical route* (see chapter 1.2 #2), which in turn undermines the development of the *word identification hub* (see chapter 1.2 #3). It forces students to memorize easily decodable words as sight words (i.e., as whole units that do not play fair). It leads to some very interesting spelling errors such as students using the letters *G-A-D* to spell the word *god*.

Waldorf resources contribute to this sound/symbol confusion. In Waldorf resource material, it is common to see the letter *A* paired with the sound /aw/. For example, the book *A Journey through Time in Verse and Rhyme* (poems collected by Heather Thomas) has a poem that begins: "We say "ah" to all wonderful things that are" (Thomas 2009, 105). Waldorf teachers often use it to teach the letter *A*. However, its words for the letter *A* contain the broad sound, including seven words with the *R*-controlled vowel team *AR*. This poem would make a poor choice for teaching the vowel letter *A*; it would be an inspired choice for teaching the vowel team *AR* in phonics rules (see chapter 4.1 Rule 5: *R*-Controlled Vowels).

Be especially diligent in teaching the letter *A*. Make sure your initial introduction is of its short sound, not its broad sound. Choose reading material for the letter *A* with care too so you bring the right sound at the right time. Introduce the short sound. Save the broad sound for phonics rules.

## Archetypal Vowels

Steiner discusses inner soul moods relating to vowel sounds in *Practical Advice to Teachers* (lecture 2) and in *Eurythmy as Visible Speech*. The following information is offered for your information, not because you will teach it in the classroom *per se*.

Steiner identified soul gestures for a handful of vowel sounds. They are often referred to as **archetypal vowels.** The phonemes are universal, but the letters (graphemes) used to name them vary from language to language. In *Practical Advice to Teachers*, Steiner says that the soul gesture or inner soul mood arises from speaking the sound (or moving the sound in Eurythmy) not from listening to the sound (Steiner 2000, 21).

- /aw/ (AH) as in *awesome*
  - o German Spelling: *A*
  - o English Spelling: *O, AU, AW*, etc.
  - o Soul Gesture: wonder and awe (Big picture awe—at one's own existence)

- /ā/ as in *acorn*
  - o German Spelling: E
  - o English Spelling: *AI, A_E, EIGH*, etc.
  - o Soul Gesture: something has been done to me and I hold myself and confront it. (Note: It is the opposite of (AH) /aw/.)

- /German ō/ as in *order*.
  - o *Note:* This sound is not the English long O. English long *O* is a diphthong (sounds like O-wuh). The German *O* is not a diphthong. The lips stay extremely round.
  - o German Spelling: *O*
  - o English Spelling: *O* when it comes before the letter *R*
  - o Soul Gesture: something calls forth wonder and there is a wish to embrace it.

- /ē/ as in *eagle*
  - o German Spelling: *I*
  - o English Spelling: *EA, EE, E_E*, etc.
  - o Soul Gesture: self assertion

- /oo/ as in *boo*
  - o German Spelling: *U*
  - o English Spelling: *OO* (and sometimes *UE, EW*, etc.)
  - o Soul Gesture: drawing back into yourself; getting smaller, not asserting yourself

- /ī/ as in the pronoun *I*
  - o German Spelling: *EI*
  - o English Spelling: *IE, I_E, IGH*, etc.
  - o Soul Gesture: being intimate with something, an affectionate feeling such as towards a small child (Steiner 1984, 58–65)

However, in *Kingdom of Childhood*, Steiner indicates that the English sounds are somewhat differently connected with feelings and that the children should learn to develop the sounds from the way their own feelings are related to them (Steiner 1988, 120) (see tables 3.1.8 for more information).

In general, the students will experience the soul gestures of the vowels as they work with sounds in Eurythmy. As the teacher, your job is to teach them the sound/symbol correspondence in English so they can read and spell. However, you can consider soul gestures in preparation for teaching the very first lesson in vowel sounds (see chapter 3.1 #9).

# Conclusion: Teach Vowels Last

In conclusion, it is advisable to teach vowels last because of the difficulty students have in mastering short vowel sound/symbol relationships. This difficulty is due in part to the fact that there is no connection between the phoneme and the letter name for short vowels. It is also more difficult for students to learn vowels due to the difference between how vowels and consonants are produced in the mouth; consequently, students need to develop a higher level of phonemic awareness to handle vowel sounds than they do to work with consonants. (Note: This is a likely reason why many ancient peoples developed alphabets without vowel letters (see chapter 1.4 #1)). Finally, delaying the teaching of vowels forces you to wait to teach decoding until all of the students in your class are ready for it (see chapter 3.4 #2). Since you have to teach all of the letters of the alphabet anyway, it makes good sense to save the hardest letters for last thereby working with the sequential development of both phonemic awareness and the phases.

# 3. Sacred Nothings

Recall that Sacred Nothings are sacrosanct Waldorf traditions that have taken root in the curriculum and are of questionable value (see chapter 2.2). *The Roadmap to Literacy* has identified three Sacred Nothings regarding the teaching of the alphabet. They are: 1) when to introduce lowercase letters; 2) how and when to display the alphabet; and 3) vowel sounds.

## When to Introduce Lowercase Letters

The first sacred nothing centers on when to introduce lowercase letters.

Many Waldorf schools have a tradition of introducing uppercase and lowercase letters separately, sometimes even a year apart. In these schools, teachers wait until the spring of 1st Grade or the beginning of 2nd Grade to introduce lowercase letters, and a few do not teach lowercase handwriting at all but jump right into cursive. However, *The Roadmap to Literacy* recommends introducing uppercase and lowercase letters together from the very beginning for many reasons.

First, postponing lowercase letters retards student progress in multiple aspects of language arts. Mastering lowercase letters is a prerequisite for the following three aspects of language arts:

1. Grammar and mechanics: Students will not learn from the beginning to capitalize the first letter of people's names and the first letter of the first word in a sentence if they write every word in uppercase. Having to go back and reteach this correctly is time consuming and can be confusing for the student.

2. Sight words: Students must learn to recognize these frequently used words in lowercase letters as that is how they appear in books. Developing familiarity with these ubiquitous words is one of the keys to reading fluency.

3. Reading: Since more than 95% of the letters in books are lowercase, your students must know lowercase letters to be able to read books. They will naturally want to start trying once they have learned the alphabet and, as Janet Langley's grandson realized very quickly, learning only uppercase letters will not serve them at all.

Second, teaching uppercase and lowercase letters separately creates extra work for everyone in the class. Teachers who do so have to teach the alphabet twice, once for uppercase letters and once for lowercase letters. The time spent reteaching the alphabet in 2nd Grade cuts into the time needed to introduce, practice, and master phonics rules. In addition, students have to work harder to learn the graphemes when they are brought separately because they have to pair the uppercase and lowercase letters retroactively and recall which is which.

Third, learning uppercase and lowercase letters separately can compromise students' handwriting. When looking at handwriting samples from Waldorf students in the upper grades, it is not unusual to find three common mistakes:

1. Some students neglect to capitalize the first word in sentences and/or names (or have to waste time going back after writing a sentence to put in capitalization).

2. Some students write letters in various font sizes (e.g., they write some lowercase letters as tall as uppercase letters when they are supposed to be only half as tall).

3. Some students continue to mix uppercase and lowercase letters in the same word. Note the following sentence written by a 6th Grader: *"I have always Ignored My Fear of great heights. I Never paid much attention especially With No Peer pressure."* Mixing uppercase and lowercase letters is often a soft sign of dyslexia, but in the case of this 6th Grader, it was merely an unintended consequence of learning uppercase and lowercase letters separately.

**Figure 3.1.1: Uppercase/Lowercase *I***

*Source: Trostli 2004, 83.*

Finally, Steiner does not specify that teachers should introduce uppercase separate from lowercase. He does say that letters should be introduced through images. If you look closely at the illustrations he gives for the introduction of letters, you will find that Steiner himself sometimes brought lowercase letters from illustrations in an introductory lesson. In *Practical Advice to Teachers*, he draws both the uppercase and lowercase letter *I* together (Trostli 2004, 83). He shows how teachers could introduce the letter *I* and how the lowercase *i* emerges as a gesture of the uppercase as shown in figure 3.1.1. Furthermore, in *A Modern Art of Education*, Steiner brings uppercase *F* and lowercase *f* in the same introductory lesson for the letter *F* (Trostli 2004, 104) as shown in figure 3.1.2.

**Figure 3.1.2: Uppercase/Lowercase *F***

*Source: Trostli 2004, 104.*

For these four reasons, *The Roadmap to Literacy* recommends that you introduce uppercase and lowercase letters together from the beginning of 1st Grade.

## Alphabet Displays

A second Sacred Nothing centers on alphabet displays.

An alphabet display is an exhibit made up of each letter of the alphabet along with a corresponding **anchor picture** that begins with that letter such as a picture of a seal below the letter *Ss* or a king below the letter *Kk* (see figs. 3.1.3 and 3.1.4 for examples of anchor pictures). This display is usually placed above the blackboard in 1st, 2nd, and 3rd Grade classrooms. Initially, the alphabet display helps the students learn the letters of the alphabet and the sound/symbol correspondence. In later grades, it helps the students learn proper handwriting for printing and cursive letters.

Some schools ask that their 1st Grade teachers not display the alphabet at the beginning of the year. Instead, they ask that the teachers wait to display a letter until it has been formally introduced. As a result, the full alphabet is not available to the students until all 26 letters have been introduced, usually at some point in the early spring when the year is almost over. There is no evidence that this practice is something Steiner suggested. Furthermore, it is counterproductive.

Having the full alphabet on display from the first day of 1st Grade supports student learning for a number of reasons:

1. The alphabet display, in combination with "The *ABC* Song," helps students learn the graphemes of the alphabet quickly and with little effort.

2. An alphabet display enables many students to teach themselves the sound/symbol correspondence. Once the students enter the Phonemic Awareness Phase, they will realize that letters represent sounds. Between "The *ABC* Song" and the alphabet display, students will have all of the tools they need to teach themselves the sound/symbol relationship for the entire alphabet. (Recall that up to 40% of students can and will teach themselves.) (See chapter 1.2 #6.)

3. An alphabet display helps the rest of the class master the sound/symbol correspondence as well. Of the 26 letters of the alphabet, 14 letter names (or 54%) contain their primary phoneme (see table 3.1.1). The alphabet display both reinforces this connection as well as reminds students of the sounds for the tricky letters.

4. Each student has the letters of her/his name acknowledged from the beginning of the year, which they appreciate, especially those students whose names begin with vowels (see 3.1#9).

5. When it is time to accelerate the introduction of the rest of the consonants (second letter block), it is easy because students are already familiar with all of the letters since they see them every day.

6. Students will be doing a lot of composing when they begin kid writing (see chapter 3.13). When they cannot remember the letter or its sound, all they have to do is look up and use the alphabet display.

There are different philosophies about when to add anchor pictures for each letter in the alphabet display, including:

- displaying letters and anchor pictures from the first day of class

- only displaying an anchor picture and letter once a letter has been introduced

- a hybrid of the first two approaches

*The Roadmap to Literacy* recommends a hybrid approach that makes use of the phases. Here are the details:

1. At the beginning of the year, your alphabet display should contain just the letters (graphemes): *Aa, Bb, Cc …Zz*. You will refer to this display when you are working with "The *ABC* Song" (see chapter 3.15 #5) and when you are reviewing the letters of the alphabet that you have introduced.

2. After you introduce a letter in the first block, put up an anchor picture for that letter (i.e., the one your students drew in their main lesson books) (See fig. 3.1.3).

**Figure 3.1.3: Example of an Anchor Picture (Goose) for the Capital Letter *G***

***Courtesy of Ute Luebeck, teacher***

Note: The image of the goose contains the shape of the capital letter *G*, perfect for those students in the Emergent Phase who do not yet realize that letters represent sounds.

3. Just before the second consonant block, add anchor pictures for the remaining letters of the alphabet. It is not necessary for these anchor pictures to have the image of the letter embedded in them (see fig. 3.1.4).

**Figure 3.1.4 Example of an Anchor Picture for the Letter *Oo***

Note: This anchor picture does not have the image of the letter *O* within its form because all of the students should now be in the Phonemic Awareness Phase and realize that letters represent sounds. They no longer need the visual cue to make the connection between letter name, letter sound, and anchor word.

The hybrid approach allows you to create a sense of wonder when introducing the initial letters of the alphabet during the first block while allowing you to speed up the introduction of the alphabet in blocks two and three, in keeping with Steiner's indications (Trostli 2004, 76–77).

Note: Plan to use the main lesson book drawings from your first block as the anchor pictures for your alphabet display. Anchor pictures for the additional consonant letters can be of your choice as long as they reflect the phoneme clearly (e.g., do not use word with blends such as a picture of a tree for the letter *T* or a picture of a dragon for the letter *D*) (see chapter 3.1 #7).

For the vowels, choose anchor pictures that begin with the short vowel sound. The students will learn the long sound through the name of the letter.

### Vowel Sounds

The final Sacred Nothing centers on which vowel sounds to teach.

Some Waldorf teachers use the German sound/symbol correspondence for vowels rather than the English. For example, they teach that *A*'s sound is "AH" as in *father*. When Steiner presented the vowel sounds, he used the German vowel conventions (see chapter 3.1 #2), but as previously mentioned, English pairs different phonemes with the vowel letters. Teach the English conventions (i.e., long and short vowel sounds) (see table 3.1.3).

Discuss vowel sounds with your Eurythmy teacher and ask her if she plans on doing any work with the students that incorporates vowel sounds. If so, request that she refer to phonemes using the English letter correspondences rather than the German when she works with your students. This will prevent the students from getting confused. (Note: Eurythmy is traditionally taught using the German sound/symbol correspondence as the art form originated with German speakers.)

If the Eurythmy teacher can include short vowel sounds during your Vowel Block, so much the better. Moving the short vowel sounds while pairing them with the English letter name would help students make the association, (e.g., /ă/ as in *apple* is the letter *A*, etc.).

Note: Do not teach Eurythmy to the students unless you are fully trained in Eurythmy. The sound and movement are only the tip of the iceberg. It is better to forego Eurythmy than to do it incorrectly.

## 4.   Preparation

Do all of your preparation over the summer before 1st Grade begins. Consider the following steps:

1. Decide which font you will use for printing (see chapter 3.2 #4).

2. Set up your blocks. This work will include choosing which letters to teach in each block, which anchor pictures to use, etc. Use chapter 5.2 and chapter 3.1 #7–9.

3. Create and set up your alphabet display if you choose to make one (see chapter 3.1 #3). If you plan on adding the anchor pictures later, make sure you leave enough space for them when you put up the display.

4. If possible, ask your students' parents to teach them "The *ABC* Song" and how to print their first names prior to the beginning of the school year. (Be sure to specify that the parents use the standard convention of capitalizing the first letter and writing the rest in lowercase so that the students will use proper conventions from the beginning.)

5. If you can, plan a home visit with each student. While there, assess which reading phase the student is in (see chapter 6.2.). This will give you an idea of the phase the majority of your students will be in when beginning school. You could also use this opportunity to show the student how to write her name, if the parents have not done so.

## 5. Scheduling

When preparing your curriculum, you can use the block plan templates found in Appendix 1 or you can create your own. If you create your own, use the following points to lay out your blocks:

1. Begin instruction for the alphabet at the beginning of 1st Grade.

2. It will take students three main lesson blocks and three practice blocks to master the alphabet.

3. Teach the letters of the alphabet in the Introduction &/or Review segment and the Bookwork segment in main lesson. Practice the letters that were introduced in the practice block.

4. Use the 2½-day rhythm to introduce letters. (Note: Each block has a slightly different teaching rhythm which will be addressed in the following subsections.)

5. It will take ~30–45 minutes per lesson to introduce the letter(s).

6. Once students have mastered the alphabet, segue into phonics instruction.

## 6. Initial Introduction

The initial introduction to the alphabet is memory reading "The *ABC* Song." This introduction is also the first memory reading lesson (see chapter 3.15 #5).

**Prerequisite**: NA.

**Background Information:** It is easier to teach the alphabet if you work with these maxims:

1. Start from the whole (the displayed alphabet and "The *ABC* Song") and then move down to the parts (the letters).

2. Work with what the students already know to connect grapheme and letter name.

It is helpful if the parents of each rising 1st Grade student teach their child the song and how to write her first name over the summer. It guarantees that there will be a lowest common denominator of knowledge among your students when school begins. It is then very easy to introduce the entire alphabet by bringing the lyrics to "The *ABC* Song" and doing memory reading with the song. The students will sing the song while pointing to the matching letter/word and in so doing, learn to name the written letters of the alphabet. This introduction will occur the first full week of school, and practice will continue throughout the first block until the students have mastered it.

**When to Teach:** Teach this initial introduction to the alphabet the second week of school (i.e., the first week of your first language arts block).

**Sample Lesson:**

First sing "The *ABC* Song" together as a class. Then open up your chalkboard where the lyrics of "The *ABC* Song" are written as shown in table 3.1.5. Ask the students to watch what you do as you sing the song again. Use a long pointer (or yardstick) to point to each letter and the final words on the board as you sing. Students will literally see what they have sung. Then ask the students to read along with you as you <u>speak</u> each line. These lyrics will be their first memory reading lesson.

**Table 3.1.5: "The *ABC* Song" Written on the Board**

**The *ABC* Song**

A B C D E F G
H I J K
L M N O P
Q R S
T U V
W X
Y and Z
Now I know my ABCs
Next time won't you sing with me?

Note: when singing this song, add a break between K and L so that the students have enough breath left to clearly articulate LMNOP.

**Practice:** Continue to practice memory reading the lyrics to "The *ABC* Song" on a daily basis throughout the first block. First sing it and point to each letter; then say it and point to each letter. Vary your practice as follows:

1. Have a student point to the letters with the pointer while the class memory reads the lyrics.

2. Sing just one line of the song (e.g., *LMNOP*) and then ask the students to locate just that line.

3. Ask the students to find an individual letter such as *T*. (Show them how to find it by memory reading while pointing to each letter and stopping on the correct letter.)

4. Give each student a copy of the lyrics to read from and teach the students to touch each letter/word with their finger as they sing or say it.

Note: When you write out the lyrics, make sure to start a new line of print for each new line of the song. Put spaces between the letters and use upper and lower case letters for the words of the song as demonstrated in Table 3.1.5.

## 7. How to Teach the First Block: Consonant Letters

**Objective:** Teach 8–10 consonant letters.

**Prerequisites:** Students can sing "The *ABC* Song."

**Background Information:** Through memory reading "The *ABC* Song," students will be on their way to learning most of the letters. In teaching each letter individually, you help the students make the connection between the grapheme (printed letter) and the phoneme (its sound).

Begin by teaching consonants because they are easier to learn than vowels. There are three reasons why:

1. The tongue, lips, and/or teeth create friction for consonant sounds. This friction gives children something to 'bump up against' as they form the sounds in their mouth, making these sounds more noticeable.

2. For most consonants, there is a connection between the name of the consonant letter and its sound. There is no such connection with short vowels.

3. Consonants are more consistent. Most consonants have only one sound, but there are two sounds for each vowel letter.

As the students develop phonemic awareness, they will realize that the letter name usually contains the letter's sound and therefore they can teach themselves the sound/symbol relationship for many letters. This realization will be empowering for them, particularly as they begin to invent their own spellings during kid writing (see chapter 3.13).

**Steiner's Indications:** Steiner suggests bringing the initial letters from images (see chapter 2.1 #4 and figure 2.1.1).

There are two points to highlight. First, Steiner's technique of introducing letters from images recalls the historical development of the first alphabet (i.e., when graphemes emerged from pictograms) (see chapter 1.4 #1 and 3). In *Soul Economy*, Steiner says: "There is no need to limit ourselves to historical examples, and it is certainly appropriate to use our imagination. What matters is not that children recapitulate the evolution of letters, but that they find their way into writing through artistic activity of drawing pictures, which will finally lead to modern, abstract letter forms" (Steiner 2003, 143). Second, Steiner wanted the students' first experiences of a letter to be artistic. Therefore, show the students how to form the letter using modeling, drawing, or painting before you teach handwriting. It will help them learn the letter's form.

We suggest limiting the letter drawings to the consonants of the first language arts block in 1st Grade. These 8–10 letters will help the students realize that letters represent sounds, a goal of the Emergent Phase.

**Prep Work:** There are four things to consider: 1) which letters to introduce in this block and which image to use for each letter; 2) which stories to use that will provide the image; 3) how to introduce the uppercase and lowercase letters; and 4) scheduling the consonants in the block.

Step One: Which Letters and Which Images

You must determine which letters you will teach in this block. There are three guidelines for choosing the first letters:

1. Choose consonants that can easily be found within the form of an animal, person, or object.

2. Choose consonants where the phoneme is embedded in the letter name (e.g., *T*: /t/ + /ē/ or *S*: /ĕ/ + /s/) (see table 3.1.1).

3. Never choose words that begin with a **blend,** two or three consonants in a cluster.

Words like *snake, dragon,* and *tree,* while great images, begin with blends: *SN, DR,* and *TR.* The initial phoneme is wedded to another consonant sound, obscuring the phoneme. It is especially hard for students in the Emergent Phase or the beginning of the Phonemic Awareness Phase to separate out the /t/ from the /r/ in the blend *TR* in *tree.* They confuse it with the sound /ch/ as in *cheap.* The blend *DR* is just as challenging. They tend to confuse it with the sound /j/ as in *jeep.* Choose only words where the initial consonant is followed by a vowel.

Below are some possible images. These words are ideal because the letter naturally comes out of the image, the phoneme is found in the name of the letter, and the initial consonant sound is not part of a blend. Feel free to use any of these images or come up with your own.

*B*: bear, butterfly, bee

*S*: seal, seahorse

*M*: mountain, moth (outline of top of wings), mouth (top lip)

*D*: door

*T*: table (with one central support leg), toadstool, totem pole

*F*: fire, fish

*V*: valley, vine

*G*: goose (see fig. 3.1.3)

*L*: light (lit candle in a holder that has a base/handle to the right)

*K*: king (body as the straight line and an arm and leg extending out)*

*N*: needle (thread to form the right two lines of the letter *N*)

*Consider teaching the letter *K* in the first consonant block and the letter *C* in the second block. Because they share the phoneme /k/, it is less confusing for students if you do not teach them close together. Teaching *K* first makes sense because its phoneme is imbedded in the letter name and *K* only has one sound. Also, only teach the /g/ sound of *G* in this block and wait to introduce its /j/ sound when you are ready to teach Soft *C* and *G* (see section 4.1 rule 8).

<u>Step Two: Selecting the Story</u>

Once you have chosen the images you would like to use in the first Consonant Block, you will need to find a fairy tale to support each one. Here are some suggestions to consider:

1. The first prerequisite for every fairy tale selection is that you love the story! If it resonates in you, you will enjoy learning it and sharing it with your students, and they will love listening to it.

2. You do not have to tell each story verbatim. You can make lots of stories work for you by transforming or adding an element. For example, you can change a hill into a mountain so you can use the story to introduce the letter *M*.

3. When scheduling your stories, be sure to intersperse traditional, more serious fairy tales with a healthy dose of humorous tales. Try to bring a light-hearted story at least once every few weeks. An example would be Grimm's *The Golden Goose* for *G*.

4. Avoid fairy tales told in kindergarten.

<u>Step Three: Considerations on Introducing Uppercase and Lowercase Letters</u>

Decide if you will bring uppercase and lowercase letters together or separately and determine which terminology to use. Some teachers use the official terms (i.e., uppercase (or capital) and lowercase) as these terms are already descriptive in nature. Other teachers use *adult letters* and *child letters* or *big letters* and *little/small letters*. Even if you do not use the formal terms of uppercase and lowercase initially, you should begin using them by 3rd Grade at the latest.

Step Four: Scheduling the Consonants in the Block

Set up your first language arts block schedule using a series of 2½–day rhythms to fit in the introduction of two letters in one week. Table 3.1.6 shows how a teaching rhythm could be organized for block one. To fit in the second letter, start teaching it on Wednesday and finish it on Friday.

Note: Lesson segments that pertain to the first letter are in bold.

**Table 3.1.6 Teaching Rhythm for Block One: Two 2½–Day Rhythms**

|  | **Day One** | **Day Two** | **Day Three** | **Day Four** | **Day Five** |
|---|---|---|---|---|---|
| *Skills Practice* | *Practice Skills (see chapter 5.2#5)* | *Practice Skills (see chapter5.2 #5)* | 1. **Review letter #1.** 2. **Teach Activity B.** 3. **Teach handwriting for letter #1 (e.g., Bb).** | *Practice Skills (see chapter5.2 #5)* | *Practice Skills (see chapter5.2 #5)* |
| *Introduction &/or Review Note: Story is told here as it is used to introduce the letter.* | **Tell a literature curriculum story as a vehicle for introducing letter #1 (e.g., "Snow White and Rose Red").** | **Review the story. Write a sentence under the picture. Read the sentence, isolate the word (bear), and introduce the letter#1: B. Teach Activity A: phonemic awareness activity(s) for the letter's sound (e.g., /b/).** | Letter #2– day one: Tell a literature curriculum story as a vehicle for introducing letter #2. | Review story. Write a sentence under the picture. Read the sentence, isolate the word, and introduce the letter #2. Teach Activity A: phonemic awareness activity(s) for the sound of letter #2. | 1. Review letter #2. 2. Teach Activity B. 3. Teach handwriting for letter #2. |
| *Bookwork* | **Bookwork for Letter #1: Lead the students in a drawing from the story (e.g., a scene from the story with a bear in profile that looks like a B).** | **Teach students to form the uppercase and lowercase letter using art (i.e modelling, crayon, or painting the letters B and b).** | Bookwork for Letter #2: Lead the students in a drawing from the story in main lesson book, which includes the image for the letter being introduced tomorrow. | Teach students to form the uppercase and lowercase letter using art (i.e., modelling, crayon, or painting). | Go on a nature walk, act out one of the stories, or tell a story for soul food. |
| *Speech/Song* | **Teach a poem or song with the letter's sound (e.g., /b/).** | **Practice yesterday's poem or song.** | Practice yesterday's poem, song, or introduce a new tongue twister for the new letter. | Practice song, poem, and/or teach a tongue twister for letter #2. | Practice song, poem, and/or tongue twister |

Note: Immediately after telling the story, lead the students in a drawing based on the story. This picture will include the image you have chosen to help you introduce a specific letter (e.g., a bear for Bb). The students can then 'sleep on' the story and picture (an artistic adjunct to the story) before you teach the letter on day two.

Note: The schedule is compressed on Wednesday to fit in two teaching rhythms in one week. The introduction of two letters per week using a three day teaching rhythm was much easier for teachers in the original Waldorf School because the students went to school five days per week plus Saturday mornings.

**When to Teach:** Teach your two letters each week in the lesson segments noted in Table 3.1.6.

**How to Teach:** Follow your lesson plans based on the teaching rhythm outlined in table 3.1.6.

## 8. How to Teach the Second Block: The Remaining Consonant Letters

**Objective:** Teach the remaining consonant letters.

**Prerequisites:** NA; however, students should be in the Phonemic Awareness Phase (i.e., they realize that letters represent sounds and can encode the first sound in a word if it is a letter they have been taught). If they are not, teach the remaining consonant sounds anyway and do extra practice with phonemic awareness.

**Background Information:** The second block is similar to the first block but with a few key changes. The pace will increase and the introduction of letters will become simpler.

In the first consonant block, letters come from images. In the second, they are introduced through anchor words, concrete nouns that begin with a specific letter to help students remember the letter's sound, and **object words**, words that begin with the letter's sound that often come from the story. Bring the remaining consonants as a matter of course. At this point, the students will easily grasp that, for example, the letter *R*'s sound is /r/ as in *rock*.

Once the majority of your students realize that letters represent sounds (i.e., the marker that indicates they have entered the Phonemic Awareness Phase), they no longer need a letter picture that has the letter embedded in an anchor word. You can also begin to introduce more than one letter at a time. By using the phoneme embedded in each letter's name and the anchor word you connect to it, students will be able to learn two consonant letters in one teaching rhythm.

**Steiner's Indications:** Steiner suggests bringing some letters from an image but not all. He states, "If we were to base our teaching only on the process of drawing evolving toward reading and writing….we would have to keep the children in school until they were twenty" (Trostli 2004, 76). He suggests speeding up the introduction of the letters.

This advice is in keeping with the phases.

**Prep Work:** There are five things to consider: 1) which letters to introduce in this block and which anchor word to use for each letter; 2) which stories to use that will provide the image; 3) when to introduce two consonants at a time; 4) how to work with letters that need extra consideration; and 5) the 2½-day rhythm for the second block.

<u>Steps 1 and 2:</u> See first consonant block (section 3.1 #7).

<u>Step 3: Determine When You Can Introduce Two Consonants at a Time</u>

Bring two letters at a time if their phonemes are embedded in their names (e.g., *N*, *J*, *R*) and their phonemes are not too similar (e.g., *M* and *N* are similar sounds and should not be introduced in the same lesson). When a letter's phoneme is not embedded in its name (*H*, *W*, *Y*), introduce it by itself (see table 3.1.1).

<u>Step 4: Working with Letters that Need Extra Consideration</u>

Introduce the following letters in their own 2½–day rhythm: *H*, *W*, *Y*, *Q*, and *X*. Use the following considerations when introducing them:

1. Schedule extra practice during the initial introduction and review (i.e., Activity A and B) for these three letters: *H*, *W*, and *Y*. They are the only consonants whose letter names have no connection to their phonemes (*H* (A-ch), *W* (double you), *Y* (WI).

2. Teach the sound /y/ as in *yes* for the letter *Y*. The other sounds for the letter *Y* will be taught as a phonics rule (see chapter 4.2 rule 17).

3. Schedule the introduction of the letter *W* and *Y* far apart as some students mistakenly think that *Y*'s sound is /w/.

4. Always teach the letter *Q* with its companion letter *U* and the sound /kw/.

5. Teach the sound /ks/ as in *fox* for the letter *X*. The other sounds for the letter *X* will be taught as a phonics rule (see chapter 4.2 rule 16).

Schedule extra skills practice time for these letters after their 2½-day rhythm introduction.

Step Five: Working with the 2½-Day Rhythm for Block Two

Set up your second language arts block schedule using a series of 2½–day rhythms as shown in table 3.1.7.

Note: Lesson segments that pertain to the first letters are in bold.

**Table 3.1.7 Teaching Rhythm for Block Two**

| | **Day One** | **Day Two** | **Day Three** | **Day Four** | **Day Five** |
|---|---|---|---|---|---|
| *Skills Practice* | *Skills Practice (see Appendix 1C.)* | *Skills Practice (see Appendix 1C.)* | **Review letters #1 and #2. Do Activity B: phonemic awareness activity(s) for the letters. Introduce handwriting for letters #1 and #2.** | *Skills Practice (see Appendix 1C.)* | *Skills Practice (see Appendix 1C.)* |
| *Introduction &/or Review* | **Letters #1 and #2: Tell a literature curriculum story as a vehicle for introducing two letters. Include a number of object words for the letters.** | **Review the story. List object words as they come up in the review for letters #1 and #2. Focus on each letter's initial phoneme from the object words and teach that letter. Teach Activity A: phonemic awareness activities for the letters' sound.** | Letters #3 and #4 Day one: Tell a literature curriculum story as a vehicle for introducing two letters. Include a number of object words for the letters. | Review the story. List object words as they come up in the review for letters #3 and #4. Focus on each letter's initial phoneme from the object words and teach that letter. Teach Activity A: phonemic awareness activities for the letters' sound. | Review letters #3 and #4. Do Activity B: phonemic awareness activity(s) for the letters. |
| *Bookwork* | **Bookwork for Letters # 1 and# 2: Lead the students in a drawing from the story that has some of the object words you will focus on tomorrow in main lesson book.** | **Paint, draw, or sculpt letters #1 and #2 (uppercase and lowercase).** | Bookwork for Letters # 3 and # 4: Lead the students in a drawing from the story that has some of the object words you will focus on tomorrow in main lesson book. | Paint, draw, or sculpt the letters #3 and #4 (uppercase and lowercase). | Introduce handwriting for letters #3 and #4. Have students do a practice page of handwriting of letters #3 and #4, (uppercase and lowercase). |
| *Speech/ Song* | **Teach a poem, song, and/or tongue twister with either letter's sound.** | **Practice yesterday's poem, song, and/or tongue twister.** | Practice yesterday's poem, song, and/ or introduce a new tongue twister, | Practice yesterday's poems, songs, and/or tongue twisters. | Tell a story for soul food. |

Note: The schedule is compressed on Wednesday to fit in two teaching rhythms in one week.

**When to Teach:** Teach 2–4 letters each week in the lesson segments noted in table 3.1.7.

**How to Teach:** Follow your lesson plans based on table 3.1.7.

## 9.  How to Teach the Third Block: Vowel Letters

**Objective:** Teach the short vowel sounds for the letters *A, E, I, O,* and *U.*

**Prerequisites:** NA; however, students should be well into the Phonemic Awareness Phase. If they are not, teach the vowel sounds anyway and do extra practice with phonemic awareness.

**Background Information:** Vowels are the hardest letters for students to learn and thus are saved for last. In this subsection you will be shown how to bring the concept of vowels as well as how to teach the short vowel sounds.

**Steiner's Indications:** Steiner was clear that teachers should teach the vowels in a different way. He described the consonants as coming out of the physical world; therefore, they could be introduced through the world of concrete objects. However, as stated in chapter 3.1 #2, Steiner states that vowels come out of the soul life and therefore are best introduced through the gesture of feelings not objects.

This advice is wonderful for introducing vowels in German; however, it is inadequate for English. In the examples Steiner gave, the name of the vowel is identical to its sound: it is not necessary to use an anchor word or anchor picture for the vowels because their sounds are obvious. In English, there is no connection between the name of the letter and the short vowel sound, which is the sound that dominates early readers. For example, the short sound for the letter *A* (i.e., /a/ as in *apple*) has no connection to the name of the letter *A.* Therefore, anchor words and anchor pictures will be mandatory for vowel letters. That being said, *The Roadmap to Literacy* still recommends bringing the initial introduction of vowels in a way that is in alignment with Steiner's indications.

**Prep Work:** There are three things to consider when preparing to teach vowels: 1) the initial introduction of vowels; 2) the 2½-day rhythm for vowel letters; and 3) scheduling considerations.

Step One: Initial Introduction of Vowels

The initial introduction of vowels takes place over one or two days at the beginning of the block. During this time, have the students experience vowel sounds but do not connect them with any particular letters. There are two ways vowels can be introduced: discovering their singing nature or exploring their feeling nature. Use either or both introductions.

Discovering the Singing Nature of Vowels: An effective and entertaining way to introduce the singing nature of vowels is to speak to your class without them. Say, *"Gd mrnng frst grd. Hw r y? M lkng frwrd t ths d."* (Be forewarned, your students might think you have lost your mind!) After repeating this phrase one more time to more giggles and confused looks, explain that you had just said, *"Good morning, First Grade. How are you? I am looking forward to this day."* However, you had said those words without including some very special letters— the singing letters or the vowel letters *A, E, I, O,* and *U.* Without these five special vowel letters, language would sound rather awkward and certainly strange!

Next, have some fun saying the students' names without vowels. Say a student's name without any vowel sounds and see if the students can discover whose name it is. After students identify the name, be sure to put the "singing vowel sounds" back in. (e.g., *Smnth* becomes *Samantha.*) Through this activity, the students begin to understand that these vowels are needed for language to be beautiful and for it to sound right.

<u>Discovering the Feeling Nature of Vowels:</u> Another introductory activity is to explore the feeling nature of the vowel sounds (see chapter 3.1 #2).

In class, choose a few of the vowel sounds (not letters) found in Table 3.1.8 and discuss the emotions they evoke. Have the students say the vowel sounds and think about which emotion goes with each sound they make. Do not connect the vowel sounds to specific letters in this initial introduction. The objective is to experience the feeling nature of all the vowel sounds before introducing the five short vowel sounds for the letters *A, E, I, O,* and *U.*

Feel free to expand the feelings with your own examples. Recall that Steiner indicated the emotions associated with a vowel sound would vary across languages (see chapter 3.1 #2). They also can vary within the language. Regional differences certainly exist. For example, consider the Canadian use of "eh?" at the end of sentences.

**Table 3.1.8: American English Vowel Sounds and Corresponding Emotions**

| *Vowel Sounds* | *Emotion Conveyed by the Speaker* |
|---|---|
| /ă/ **as in** *apple* | Small expression of surprise and disgust (e.g., "/ă/, get that spider away from me.") |
| /ĕ/ **as in** *edge* | Ambivalence or lack of enthusiasm (e.g., "Do you want to go?" "/ĕ/.") |
| /ĭ/ **as in** *igloo* | Small expression of disgust (e.g., "/ĭ / That is icky.") |
| /ŏ/ **as in** *octopus* | Small feeling of illumination (e.g., "Ah, I get it now.") Note: This sound is closely related to the sound /aw/ for the letters *AU/AW.* |
| /ŭ/ **as in** *umbrella* | Larger expression of disgust (e.g., "Ugh!") |
| /ā/ **as in** *angel* | Anger that is directed outward (e.g., "/ā/, you get off my property!") |
| /ē/ **as in** *eagle* | Fear (e.g., "/ē/! Eek!") |
| /ī/ **as in** *ice* | Surprise (e.g., "I, yi, yi!") |
| /ō/ **as in** *oak* | Doubt or questioning (e.g., "Oh really?")<br>An intensifier of emotion (e.g., as in joy, disappointment, etc. ("Oh wow!", "Oh no!") |
| /ū/ **as in** *unicycle* | |
| /aw/ **as in** *paw* and *cause* | • Intensifier of negative emotion (e.g., "Ah, no.")<br>• Contentment (e.g., "AHHH, what a good meal.")<br>• Awe<br>• Fear |
| /oi/ **as in** *boy* and *coil* | Exasperation/frustration (e.g., "Oy vey.") |
| /ou/ **as in** *cow* and *pout* | Hurt/pain (e.g., "Ow!") |
| /oo/ **as in** *boom* | Admiration (e.g., /oo/, that's pretty.")<br>Fear (e.g., "/oo/, you scared me.") |
| /oo/ **as in** *foot* | Disgust (e.g., "Ugh, liver is so gross.") |
| /ur/ **as in** *her, fir, purr,* **and** *myrrh* | Anger (e.g., "Ergh, you make me so mad!")<br>Note: This phoneme is both a consonant sound and a vowel sound in English (see chapter 3.1 #2). |

When you introduce the vowels through emotions, first, make a vowel sound and really exaggerate the emotion/feeling. Have the students repeat it back. (Note: This step is crucial because the emotion in the vowel sound is the emotion experienced by the speaker, not the listener.) Have a short discussion about how this sound makes students feel when they say it or what it reminds them of. At the end of this activity, tell your students that all of these feeling sounds are called *vowel sounds.*

Note: During these initial introductions, do not teach the vowel letters with their vowel sounds. Instead, keep the introduction auditory. Focus on the singing and feeling nature of vowels. The sound/symbol relationships will be taught on subsequent days.

Step Two: The 2½-Day Rhythm for Vowel Letters

After you have spent 1–2 days exploring vowel sounds and how they differ from consonants, it is time to introduce the vowel letters themselves through anchor pictures. See fig. 3.1.4. Use the same 2½-day rhythm used for the second consonant block. You can use a fairy tale or create a story that has a number of object words for the vowel letter you will be introducing.

Note: Teaching the letter *E* is a challenge. It is hard to find an appropriate anchor picture. The letter *E*'s sound is /ĕ/, which is difficult to distinguish when there is the sound /f/, /l/, /m/, /n/, /s/, or /x/ right after it because the two sounds together are identical to the names of the letters *F* (i.e., *ef*), *L* (i.e., *el*), *M* (i.e., *em*), *N* (i.e., *en*), *S* (i.e., *es*), and *X* (i.e., *ex*) (see table 3.1.1). For example, *effort, elephant, empty, enter, escape,* and *excite* are all words where the following consonant masks the ĕ sound. Even the word *egg* is problematic because, while the initial sound is /ĕ/, it changes into a sound similar to /ā/ as the mouth moves into position to form the sound /g/. (You can hear it when you stretch out the sounds of a word such as when you do stretchable fabric phoneme exercise (see chapter 3.3 #2). A good object word for the letter *E* might be *edge* because it has a clearly pronounced /ĕ/.

Note: Schedule lots of extra practice as short vowels are irregular (i.e., their phoneme is not embedded in the name of the letter).

Step Three: Scheduling Considerations

As you prepare for this block, schedule the introduction of the vowel letters carefully. Space out the letters *E* and *I* and also space out the letters *O* and *U*. The short vowel sounds /ĕ/ as in *edge* and /ĭ/ as in *igloo* are very similar and hard for students to distinguish. Never introduce them back to back. Likewise, the vowel sound /ŭ/ as in *umbrella* and /ŏ/ as in *octopus* are also similar. Space them out as well.

**When to Teach:** Teach the initial introduction of vowels either through singing nature and/or feeling nature at the beginning of the block (see above). Then teach the vowels in the lesson segments noted in table 3.1.7. (Note: Use the same teaching rhythm as in the second consonant block. Just teach one vowel letter at a time rather than two consonant letters.)

**How to Teach:** Follow your lesson plans based on table 3.1.7.

**Curriculum Connection:** Start to teach phonics rules once your students have learned the vowel letters. Begin with CVC Words (see section 4.1 rule 1).

## 10.  Practice

Practice is critical. It forms part of your initial introduction in the Introduction &/or Review segment of main lesson (i.e., Activities A and B). It will be part of your ongoing practice in the Skills Practice segment of main lesson and practice classes (see chapter 2.3 #4). Finally, it can be used during classroom games.

**Activities A and B:** The following activities are good to use as part of the Introduction &/or Review of the letters of the alphabet:

- Students come up with words that begin with the letter they are learning. You write them on the board. Point out if the word has other letters they have learned. If the word is something some of your students might be able to spell, ask if a student would like to come spell it on the board. (This is a great activity for your more advanced spellers. Just make sure they write the word very neatly and clearly.)

- Students form the letters with their bodies. For example, three students on a team can form the capital letter *H*. (Note: This exercise works best with capital letters and straight lines. To determine the number of students needed, count the number of lines in the letter. For example, the letter *L* contains two lines.)

**Skills Practice:** During the Skills Practice segment be sure to include the following activities:

- Phonemic awareness exercises that include the alphabet—particularly **hand spelling** and then **finger spelling,** exercises to isolate sound in words, followed up with encoding sound(s) in the word (see chapter 3.3 #2 and chapter 3.4 #6 and #7).

- Symbol imagery exercises to aid the learning of sight words (see chapter 3.5 #3)

- Kid writing exercises to help develop phonemic awareness (see chapter 3.13)

- Memory reading "The *ABC* Song" (see chapter 3.15 #5)

- **Letter Practice:** Say a letter (grapheme) and have the students write it on their paper.

- **Sound Practice:** Say a phoneme (sound) and have the students write the letter on their paper.

Each activity is covered in depth in the noted chapter. These are your most important practice activities. Schedule them accordingly in the Skills Practice segment of main lesson once you have used a 2½-day rhythm to introduce the letter.

**Fun and Games:** Below are five fun practice activities that you can use to spice up your Skills Practice. Use them sparingly. A pinch of salt brings out the flavor; too much overwhelms the palate.

1. **Alphabet Clothesline:** Get 26 index cards and write an upper and lower case letter on each card (e.g., *Bb*). Get a long piece of yarn or clothesline and tie it between two trees. Get 26 clothespins. Hand out a card (or two depending on your class size) and a clothespin to each student. Sing the "The *ABC* Song" and then ask the students to pin the letters of the alphabet on the string in order. Have the students confirm the letters are in order by singing the song again. The next day before school starts, rearrange some of the letters and ask the students to put them back in the correct order.

2. **Matching Game:** Make a set of 52 alphabet cards: 26 uppercase cards and 26 lowercase cards (one letter per card). Pass out one card to each student. Have students find their matching letter (e.g., *A* finds *a*). You can lay out those cards that are not handed out to students on desktops, etc. They can look there if no one has their matching card.

3. **Symbol Imagery Game:** Students write a letter with their finger on a partner's back. The partner has to guess which letter it is. At first instruct them to just write upper case or just lower case letters. After awhile it can be their choice.

4. **Letter Bingo:** Create bingo squares that contain the letters of the alphabet. Pass them out to the students along with bingo chips. Call out the letters. The first student to get Bingo wins, but you can keep playing for longer if you want.

5. **Sound Bingo:** Create bingo squares that contain pictures that start with the letters you have taught. For example, a picture of a monkey for the letter *M*/ and a goose for the letter *G*, etc. (Use *Words Their Way* Appendix C as a source for pictures.) Pass them out to the students along with bingo chips. Call out the letters. The students have to figure out if any of their pictures begin with that letter's sound. The first student to complete a row (horizontal, vertical, or diagonal) wins, but you can keep playing for longer if you want.

## 11. Assessment

Assessment is a critical part of teaching. It is important to verify that students have mastered the skills they have been taught. See chapter 6.1 for background on assessment.

**Benchmarks** represent <u>minimum</u> levels of student achievement by the end of each grade for students to be on track to handle grade-level work in 4th Grade (see chapter 6.1 #9). Table 3.1.9 contains the benchmarks for sound/symbol (alphabet).

Note: The following benchmarks may not be exhaustive. Prerequisite skills for sound/symbol (alphabet) may be covered under other related language arts skills. For a full list of benchmarks, see table 6.1.4.

**Table 3.1.9: Benchmarks for Sound/Symbol Correspondence (Alphabet)**

|  | 1st Grade |
|---|---|
| **Sound/Symbol (Alphabet)** | Students can: <br> • Name all letters (uppercase and lowercase). <br> • Give each letter's sound(s) but only short vowel sounds are expected for vowel letters. |

There are three types of assessments. Recommendations for each type of assessment can be found in Sections 6.3, 6.4, and 6.5. You can use the following ideas as a starting point to set up an assessment program.

**Informal Assessments:**

1. Letter Practice: Say a letter name and ask the students to write the letter on a piece of paper. Note: Cover the alphabet display first or have the students turn and face the back of the room when writing.

2. Sound Practice: Say a sound and ask the student to write the letter (see chapter 3.1 #10).

**Teacher-Made Assessment:** Once a week, give a teacher-generated quiz that covers all the letters and sounds introduced to date. Model it off of letter practice and sound practice (see chapter 3.1 #10). Give it on Friday and use the results to tailor your instruction and practice in the upcoming week. For example, if most of the class knows the letter *T* but struggles with the letter *W*, curtail the practice of *T* in favor of more practice with *W*.

**Assessments Created by Educational Testing Groups:** If you choose to do this type of assessment, consider doing it three times a year. Use an assessment of the alphabet designed by an educational testing group such as DIBELS or AIMSweb (see chapter 6.1 #6). Otherwise use *CORE Phonics Survey: Alphabet Skills and Letter Sounds* found in Diamond's book *Assessing Reading Multiple Measures for Kindergarten through Twelfth Grade, 2nd edition. CORE* (Consortium on Reading Excellence, Inc.) Novato: Arena Press, 2008 (see chapter 6.3 #3).

See chapter 6.1 for more information about assessments and chapter 6.3 for more information about assessing in 1st Grade.

## 12. How to Help Struggling Students

**Assess:** When you see a student is struggling with learning the alphabet, do assessments (both formal and informal) to determine if the problem is with the grapheme, the phoneme, or both. Document your findings and place in student file (see chapter 6.3).

**Additional Instruction/Practice:** Next, provide this student with extra instruction and practice in the weak area(s). If the problem is in learning the grapheme, consider having the student walk the letter. Use chalk to write a giant letter on the pavement. Have the student stand facing the letter. Have her point to its lines. Next have her walk the lines. Then have her write the letter over and over on dotted midline paper. If the problem is with the phoneme, see that she has extra phonemic awareness practice (see chapter 3.3). Document what you try and the results.

**Remedial Solutions:** If you do not notice improvements in 3–4 weeks, it is time to contact your mentor for guidance and consult chapter 6.6 for additional information on remedial issues. Make sure you include recommendations for a vision screening and/or a hearing screening if you see signs of difficulty in these areas.

**Accommodations and Modifications:** Sometimes it takes a while for remedial issues to be resolved. Meanwhile, the student still needs support to function in class. Consider using the following as a temporary measure. Provide the student with a copy of the alphabet at her desk. You can buy a sticker that goes across the surface of the desk or you can provide a page with the alphabet written out. If you choose to laminate the page, make sure the student does not have Irlen Syndrome first (see chapter 6.6 #2).

If a student is struggling to differentiate the lowercase letters *b* and *d*, use the image of the <u>bed</u>. Have the student make a fist with both hands then stick up her thumbs. When brought together, the fists form the bed. The left fist makes the letter *b*; the right fist makes the letter *d*.

## Conclusion

The alphabet is the key to beginning to read and write. However, in the next chapter you will see that handwriting is the most efficient way to learn the letters of the alphabet and that it has an important role in a student's ability to learn to read and her ability to think and compose.

# 3.2 HANDWRITING

*The 1st Grade main lesson books looked wonderful, except for the handwriting. The writing was overlarge—possibly because it was in crayon—and each letter was a different height. Worse, the sentences resembled a rollercoaster, with words climbing up and plunging down across the page. In lieu of standard print on straight lines, each student's main lesson book writing was a unique blend of color, shape, and design. The result? The entries were almost impossible to read. When asked why the students had not been given pencils or lines, the teacher said that she wanted the students to approach the forming of their letters as drawings. Therefore, the students were "drawing" the words in color without lines. The teacher had been told that as the students practiced handwriting, their inner sense of judgment, schooled by form drawing classes, would guide them to the right form, size, and shape for each letter. The visiting teacher suggested that lined paper and graphite pencils would help the students' handwriting, but the teacher was not convinced these tools were needed.*

*Come 3rd Grade, the class's handwriting looked better: the letters were the right height, and the sentences were straight. The compositions were written in graphite pencil on lined paper. When asked about the change, the teacher related the following story:*

*After the visiting teacher's evaluation in 1st Grade, she had decided to experiment a little bit and let the students create their own lines using block crayons. Unfortunately, many students could not make these lines standard enough to be of much help. Then, in 2nd Grade, the situation came to a head. Students were ripping pages out of their main lesson books, striking out improperly written letters, and making derogatory comments about their own work. They wanted to do better, but they could not and were getting frustrated. She realized that something had to give.*

*The teacher decided to change her approach: She provided the students with lined paper, graphite pencils with erasers, and instructions on how to use the lines to make the letters the right size, as well as how to erase neatly when there was the inevitable mistake. The change in the class was palpable. Within a short period of time, the students regained their enthusiasm for writing and expressed pride in their work. She had given her students the materials and instructions they needed for proper handwriting, and all was well.*

When it comes to handwriting, students need both the proper tools and proper instruction to be successful. In this chapter you will discover how to teach handwriting and why it is an important skill to master, even in a digital age.

This chapter covers the following topics:

1. Why Handwriting Matters
2. Background Information: The Ergonomics of Handwriting
3. Sacred Nothings
4. Preparation
5. Scheduling
6. Initial Introduction
7. How to Teach Handwriting in 1st Grade
8. How to Teach Handwriting in 2nd Grade

## 1. Why Handwriting Matters

In the age of word processing, voice-to-text, and touch screens, why is it important to teach handwriting? Modern researchers, observation, and Steiner provide reasons why handwriting is still important.

In the New York Times article "What's Lost as Handwriting Fades," Maria Konnikova examines several studies that demonstrate the value of handwriting. Researchers have found that handwriting is important at various stages of education. Beginning students show differences in brain activity based on how they generate letters. Students who had not yet learned to read or write were asked to make letters three ways: trace the image, type the image, or write it freehand. When students formed a letter freehand, they exhibited increased activity in three of the areas of the brain that are activated in adults when they read and write. This effect was significantly weaker when they traced or typed.

Handwriting also affects composition in Grades 2–5. Virginia Berninger, a psychologist at the University of Washington, found that printing, cursive writing, and typing are all associated with distinct and separate brain patterns and that students with better handwriting had increased activation in the reading and writing networks of the brain. In addition, students wrote more when they used handwriting than when they used a keyboard, and they composed more quickly. Finally, the students expressed more ideas in their writing when they wrote by hand.

Handwriting remains important for high school and college students. Researchers have found that students learn better when they take notes by hand than when they type on a keyboard. Two psychologists, Pam A. Mueller of Princeton and Daniel M. Oppenheimer of the University of California, Los Angeles, have demonstrated this effect in the classroom and in the laboratory. It turns out that writing by hand allows the students to process the lecture's content and then reframe it. This process of reflecting and manipulating the information leads to better understanding and recall.

In addition to the gains reported by Konnikova, handwriting practice speeds up letter recognition. When Jennifer Militzer-Kopperl studied Russian in college, she had to learn the Cyrillic alphabet. For the first week of school, her only homework was handwriting practice: page after page of handwriting drill for each Cyrillic letter. Within a week or so, everyone in the class mastered the alphabet and began reading and writing exercises to learn grammar and vocabulary. Meanwhile, a friend in a different Russian program could not identify all of the Cyrillic letters after a month of classes and was contemplating dropping Russian as a result. She struggled to read the Russian words because she struggled with letter recognition. The students compared how they had been taught the alphabet and discovered one difference: Jennifer's class had extensive handwriting practice while her friend's class did not have any. Handwriting drill makes learning the alphabet easier.

Steiner brought one final reason why handwriting is important: It educates the will of the child. He indicates that handwriting is a physical activity and that students should write with an eye towards making their writing beautiful (i.e., that it should bring them aesthetic pleasure) (Trostli 2004, 137). He urges teachers to "accept no laziness in detail with the children" when it comes to handwriting (Trostli 2004, 142).

Handwriting is vital at every stage of a student's education. It helps students learn their letters, enables them to write better compositions, and improves learning in high school and college lecture classes. It also helps shape their will. If parents question Waldorf education's emphasis on handwriting over keyboarding, educate them on why handwriting is important. Handwriting makes learning language arts skills easier.

## 2. Background Information: The Ergonomics of Handwriting

Handwriting is vital, but students will be reluctant to engage in the process if it is uncomfortable. Enter ergonomics. Ergonomics refers to aligning the bodily aspects of physical work to the task at hand to make it easier to accomplish. As you introduce letters and practice handwriting, make sure students write correctly so they can enjoy many years of effortless writing free of sore wrists, arms, shoulders, and necks. Consider five points: 1) sitting position; 2) pencil grip; 3) paper position; 4) modifications for cursive; and 5) left-handed students.

### Sitting Position

Pay attention to the desks and chairs. Check that the students have the correct-sized chairs. Each student should sit with feet firmly on the floor with upper leg elevated just a little. The knee should be the highest point. This position ensures proper blood flow so that extremities do not fall asleep. The students' desks also need to be at the correct height so that the students' forearms rest comfortably on the surface. A good rule of thumb is this: a desk is at the correct height when the surface of the desk is even with the child's bottom rib when she is seated. Since children continue to grow throughout the year, check the desk height for each student. Good times are after winter break and after spring break.

### Pencil Grip

Make sure that your students use the proper (tripod) pencil grip while forming their letters. The tripod grip allows students to most effectively use their hand muscles. As a consequence, students' hands and arms will not tire easily when they hold the pencil, and they will be able to write with reasonable speed and accomplishment.

Here is a verse that Patti Connolly used to reinforce the correct grip:

> Thumb and Pointer work together
> to hold the pencil fast
> Pencil sits on fingers three
> With baby Pinkie last.

You can also emphasize that the middle finger is a pillow for the pencil to rest on. Just as a head depresses a pillow to form an indentation, so too can a pencil. (If you use a tripod grip, you can actually feel the bump that forms on your finger from years of holding a pencil.)

In addition, make sure that the students grip the pencil gently so as not to squeeze it too hard. (It hurts, you know!) Using an oversized pencil along with oversized lines can help students learn to relax their grip. You can also demonstrate that when you are holding a pencil correctly, someone can effortlessly pull it out of your fingers. If that person cannot, the pencil is being held too tightly.

Note: Go to the website http://www.ot-mom-learning-activities.com/pencil-grasp.html for guidance on teaching proper pencil grasp.

**Paper Position**

The paper should be directly in front of the student. Right-handed children place the upper right corner slightly higher. Left-handed children tilt the paper so that the upper left corner is higher, sometimes dramatically so. The left-handed students need to keep their wrists straight, their writing hand below the words they are writing, and their writing arm perpendicular with the bottom of the page. This keeps them from succumbing to the dreaded *hooked wrist* syndrome. In both lefties and righties, the non-dominant hand holds the paper steady. It can be anywhere along the margin of the side of the paper, from the top corner to the bottom corner.

**Modifications for Cursive**

When teaching cursive in 2nd Grade, teach the students to angle their paper or main lesson book even more than they do for printing. They should hold the paper with the non-dominant hand. The angle of the paper needs to follow the natural curve of the writing hand.

As students write, they should cross the midline freely. Their writing hand should be able to go into either side of the paper without the need to move the paper over. If they struggle, do exercises to address the midline such as Take Time, Brain Gym, or Bal-A-Vis-X (see chapter 6.6 #5).

**Left-Handed Students**

Left-handed students benefit from instruction from left-handed writers. If you are not one yourself, see if you have a left-handed colleague who can introduce pencil grip and paper position to this select group of students. Have this person demonstrate proper technique with scissors at the same time. The introduction will be more authentic and effective. Your students' wrists will thank you.

## 3.   Sacred Nothings

It is necessary to consider Sacred Nothings before discussing recommendations for the handwriting curriculum. There are several Sacred Nothings in the realm of handwriting. They fall into five categories: 1) supplies; 2) form drawing; 3) left-handed and ambidextrous students; 4.) the expectation that students use their best handwriting all of the time; and 5) borders.

**Supplies**

Many Waldorf schools use art supplies such as colored pencils, crayons, and blank white paper in lieu of writing supplies such as graphite pencils, erasers, and lined paper. This practice is a modern Waldorf tradition. Consider using some of the original supplies used in the original Waldorf classrooms: notebooks for practice, graphite pencils, erasers, and lined paper.

Many Waldorf teachers have their students write in crayon or colored pencil on white paper in a bound main lesson book. These traditions did not have their origins in Steiner's time. In an unpublished paper entitled "The Teaching of Handwriting," long-time Green Meadow Waldorf School teacher, Gisela O'Neil, writes: "If you look at the notebooks in use at the original Waldorf School during Rudolf Steiner's time, you will be amazed! They used small, thin, lined notebooks. . . Crayons for writing in the lower grades, and unlined paper for writing, are both later traditions" (O'Neil n.d.). Both the change of writing instrument and paper present their own set of problems.

Crayons and colored pencils make poor writing utensils. First, students cannot erase when they make a mistake when they are writing with crayons and colored pencils. Second, the act of writing is more difficult with art supplies. Both crayons and colored pencils have wider tips that make fine motor control more difficult and make it difficult to print in standard-sized letters. In addition, students have to use more pressure to get colored pencils to show up well on the page. Excess pressure contributes to writer's cramp and undermines the loose grip necessary for effortless, fluid writing. Graphite pencils resolve all three problems.

White paper is just as bad as crayons and colored pencils. In "The Educational Practice of the Waldorf Schools," Christof Wiechert writes: "For younger children the main lesson book [white pages bound together in a book format] can almost represent a threat on account of its defining character: every mistake is written permanently, is there for good, can no longer be put right. The white sheet can instill fear. In the first few years of school there should be main lesson books with removable pages or else a system consisting of loose leaves" (Wiechert 2010, 6)..

Many teachers ask, "Can't I have my students draw their own lines in their main lesson books with either pencils or block crayons?" *The Roadmap to Literacy* does not recommend it. Contrast pages of lines drawn by a student in 2nd and 3rd Grade with a page of handwriting paper used by the same student in 3rd Grade in figures 3.2.1–3.2.3. The handwriting paper is standard: It has lines and dotted midlines in perfect proportion. The student-drawn lines lack uniformity: they are of varying widths, tilt up or down, and/or wobble. For good or ill, the lines then go on to influence the form of the letters.

**Figure 3.2.1: 2nd Grader (self-drawn lines and crayon)**

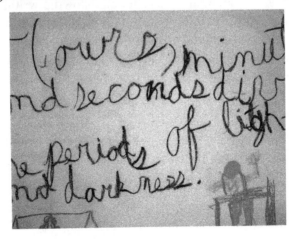

**Figure 3.2.2: Same Student 3rd Grade (no lines, colored pencil)**

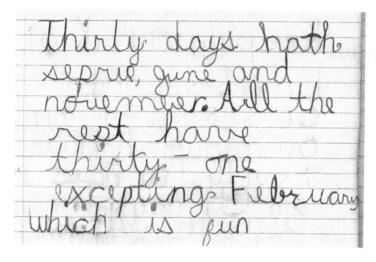

**Figure 3.2.3: Same Student Two Weeks Later (lines and graphite pencil)**

Figures 3.2.1–3.2.3 exemplify Gisela O'Neil's warning: "Sloppy writing is not helped by unlined paper" (O'Neil n.d.).

Some teachers think that having their students draw their own lines uses economy in teaching in that it forces the students to cross their horizontal midline, thus helping to erase the barrier to left/right brain integration. The goal is laudable, but this solution is seldom effective. Students who have retained a midline barrier use all kinds of avoidance techniques to keep from crossing the midline: they turn the book page vertical to draw lines from top to bottom, they turn themselves to face the side, or they move the paper under their crayon. If overcoming midlines is an issue for your class (and it is for most), there are more effective movement activities you could employ such as the bean bag exercises in Take Time, Brain Gym exercises, or Bal-A-Vis-X exercises (see chapter 6.6 #5).

Our recommendation: Use the right tool for the right job. Use art supplies for the initial artistic introduction of the letter in 1st Grade, but then use graphite pencils for all follow-up writing. Choose paper to match the task. For the initial artistic introduction of a letter (i.e., the very first experience of a letter that comes the day before students learn to print it), using unlined art paper and crayons makes sense; however, once students start printing the letters, use graphite pencils and handwriting paper with guide lines and dotted midlines. These supplies provide students the necessary guides to learn proper letter position and size, and they allow students to make corrections easily.

Main lesson books are not yet widely available in this format. Therefore, you could use practice notebooks with lines or use loose sheets of handwriting paper with lines for most of your writing work. When it comes time to write in the main lesson books, here are some recommendations:

1. If you have a small class, draw lines into the main lesson books. Get parents to help draw these lines.

2. If you have a large class, make liners for each student. Take a blank sheet from a main lesson book, draw the desired-size lines on the sheet with a thick, black marker, write the student's name in the corner, and then laminate it. This liner would then be placed behind the main lesson book page and used as a guide for letter placement.

3. Tape or paste the students' writing into their main lesson books.

**Form Drawing**

The second Sacred Nothing is starting 1st Grade with a form drawing block. According to Christof Wiechert, Rudolf Steiner never intended for form drawing to be taught as a block in the 1st Grade. In his article "The Educational Practice of the Waldorf Schools," he writes: "Painting and drawing are activities that always take place once or twice a week. . . . However, it ought never to be the content of an epoch [block]" (Wiechert 2010, 7). Wiechert shared with the authors that it was Steiner's intention that form drawing (the straight line and the curved line) be one of the focuses of "the first school lesson not the first school epoch [block]."

In his lecture series *Practical Advice to Teachers* (lecture 4), Steiner gives very clear instructions on how the very first lesson of 1st Grade should be conducted. In this lesson, teachers introduce the straight line and the curved line. Since all written letters, or graphemes, are made up of these two lines, learning how to form them prepares students for all subsequent writing and reading lessons.

Just because form drawing is not the subject for the first block does not mean that you should throw the baby out with the bathwater. This important art form should be an integral and ongoing part of your students' curriculum. Be sure to incorporate form drawing into your weekly practice class schedule as a class in its own right like painting or Eurythmy.

In 1st and 2nd Grade, use form drawing exercises to prepare the students for the handwriting instruction that is coming in the next week. For example, in 1st Grade, include an exercise in your weekly form drawing class where the students work with curved, sliding (diagonal), standing (vertical), and resting (horizontal) lines as needed to prepare them for the upcoming letters you will be teaching them. In 2nd Grade, practice running forms with loops and curves prior to introducing cursive letters. In this way, you can use fun and engaging form drawing exercises to prepare students for handwriting (see fig. 2.1.2).

Note: A good source for form drawing lessons is the book *Form Drawing* by Niederhauser and Frohlich published by Mercury Press.

**Left-Handed and Ambidextrous Students**

Another Sacred Nothing is that Steiner encouraged left-handed students to write with their right hand. Daniel Hindes explores this issue in "Rudolf Steiner on Teaching Left-Handed Children" in *Research Bulletin Autumn 2006 volume 12 #1*. In summary, he states that Steiner's indications are hard to document as they are buried in transcriptions of spoken advice which was specific to particular students and situations. Therefore, he suggests that the indication not be taken dogmatically. However, a few things are clear:

1. Steiner advises that ambidextrous children younger than nine should be encouraged to write with one dominant hand, preferably the right. (In this case, *ambidextrous* refers to those children who have not yet established a dominate hand.)

2. True left-handed students who are left-side dominant (i.e., dominant eye, ear, hand, and foot are all on the left) should remain left handed.

3. Any switching should never harm the student. A teacher must pay close attention to the student before, during, and after the intervention to properly evaluate the effects. (She should also be in communication with the student's parents about her plans in this area.)

Not only is it not necessary to switch left-handed students, it is often not desirable. Ambidextrous students who have yet to establish a dominant hand are another matter. Students need a dominant hand for writing. If you have ambidextrous children in your class and wish to learn more about supporting them, you could study the work of Dr. Michaela Gloeckler, head of the Medical Section of the Anthroposophical Society, and Audrey McAllen. They give helpful suggestions for working with these students' parents and the students themselves.

**The Expectation that Students Use Their Best Handwriting All of the Time**

There are teachers who have the expectation that their students give their best efforts at writing all of the time. In her article, Giselle O'Neil writes:

> To ask children every day to do 'their best' is a standard impossible to maintain. Once a week, perhaps on a Friday ("test day"), the class can be asked that each child do his very best. To confirm his utmost effort, after he has filled a page with writing, the student can put a star in the upper corner… [The teacher can then] give individual help by showing small steps, one letter at a time, towards improvement (O'Neil n.d.).

Giselle O'Neil also reminds readers that if teachers wish the children to write carefully, they must give them sufficient time. "If quality is the goal, then quantity must be limited" (ibid).

Most of the time, students should use legible handwriting. They will be doing a lot of writing, and their focus should be on spelling, punctuation, capitalization, etc., not on how beautiful their handwriting is. Save the expectation that students use their best handwriting for copying final drafts into their main lesson books and handwriting test day.

**Borders**

The use of borders has become almost ubiquitous in Waldorf main lesson books; however, they are a Sacred Nothing.

Borders in Grades 1–3 tend to be made with block crayons. Including such borders in all main lesson book work is a Sacred Nothing (see chapter 2.2 #1). In addition, it is good to question the use of the elaborate hand-drawn borders that are common in main lesson book entries in Grades 3–8 as well. Do they advance the objective(s) of the block? If so, how? Might the class time be better spent in other pursuits?

The following are three good rules of thumb for using borders:

1. Borders should be the exception, not the rule.
2. Include a border when it serves a purpose in addition to beautification of the page. For example, a border that is based on a recent form drawing, if done well, practices that skill in addition to beautification. A border that that illustrates the content of a student's main lesson book entry also would add value. For example, a drawing of a ruler could make a fine border for an entry in a Math main lesson book about measurement.
3. To be included, a border should serve more than one purpose, occupy only one side of the page (preferably opposite the fold), and not require too much class time.

If your border's only purpose is to beautify the page, skip the border and use the class time on an activity that furthers the development of literacy skills or that teaches new artistic skills.

## 4.  Preparation

Do your preparation over the summer. There are four things to consider:

1. Ordering handwriting supplies
2. Perfecting your own handwriting

3. Choosing a font

4. Ordering/creating handwriting workbooks

Note: There is additional summer preparation for Grades 2 and 3. See chapter 3.2 #8 and 9 for more information.

**Ordering Handwriting Supplies**

You will need the following supplies for each grade.

1st Grade:

- Oversized, graphite pencils such as *My First Ticonderoga* for all writing, including main lesson book work
- Giant erasers for the day the pencil's eraser inevitably is used up. (As all errors should be erased fully before students write in the correction, erasers get used up fast.)
- Pencil sharpeners. A dull pencil is more difficult to write with and produces less beautiful work than a sharp one.
- Lined paper with a dotted midline. The height should be just less than one inch for 1st Grade. First graders should use this paper for all writing.

2nd Grade:

- Regular graphite pencils
- Giant erasers
- Pencil sharpeners
- Lined paper with a dotted midline. The height should be about half an inch. Second graders should use this paper for learning cursive.

3rd Grade:

- Regular graphite pencils
- Giant erasers
- Pencil sharpeners
- Lined paper with a dotted midline. The height should be about one centimeter. Third graders should use this paper for practicing cursive.

You can order pages with dotted midlines from many handwriting companies.

**Perfecting Your Own Handwriting**

In *The Child's Changing Consciousness*, Steiner gives advice on teachers' handwriting. He states: "Whether [a letter, word or number] is written in an artistic, in a less-refined, or even in a slovenly way, makes a great difference. . . . It is not so much the outer actions that work on the child, but what lives behind them, whether unpleasant and ugly, or charming and pleasant" (Steiner 1996, 137).

Waldorf teachers need to model beautiful handwriting. A teacher can lose credibility in the eyes of her students and their parents if her own handwriting is poor. If you have any question about the quality of your handwriting (print and cursive), ask your mentor or other teacher for feedback. If changes or practice is suggested, work on handwriting each day until you are able to transform it.

**Choosing a Font**

The basic goal in teaching handwriting is to help the students learn to read other people's words and communicate their own thoughts through writing. Handwriting should not be an impediment.

When choosing a font, follow these guidelines. First, it must be easy to recognize, simple to form, and standard. There will be opportunities to learn a variety of stylistic fonts later on (e.g., Greek letters in 5th Grade and calligraphy in 6th, etc.), but in the early stages, simple is better. Second, it should be easy to transition to cursive. If you select a simple font in 1st Grade, the transition to cursive in 2nd Grade will go much more smoothly. Look for fonts that allow the lowercase letters to *hold hands* with each other. While not all of the letters will be able to connect easily (such as the lower-case letters *e, f, r*, etc.), most of them should.

The following two fonts fulfill the above criteria:

1. D'Nealian (Figures: 3.2.4 and 3.2.5)
2. Handwriting Without Tears (use internet search for examples)

**Figure 3.2.4: D'Nealian: Print    Figure 3.2.5: D'Nealian: Cursive**

*Source: www.dnealian.com*
Used with permission of Donald N. Thurber

Once you have selected your font, make sure you form each letter correctly. Your hand should mirror the direction traveled by the eye across the page. In English, people read from left to right, starting at the top of the page and working down to the bottom. For ease in reading and writing, the eye and hand should move in tandem not in opposition to each other. Make sure all of your printed letters are formed as shown in the guide. You will note that all uppercase letters and most lowercase letters are formed from top to bottom. There are a few lowercase letters (*s, e, d, f,* and *c*) that are not written top down; you will need to point this out when teaching these 'renegades.' If you find that you write some letters incorrectly, work on transforming your own handwriting prior to teaching handwriting to your students.

Note: Something as simple as forming a letter downward can help keep students on task. Students' eyes invariably follow the direction of the line being written. When the pencil stroke goes up, so do the eyes. If the eyes keep going, the student will look up—right off the page and into the environment.

**Ordering/Creating Handwriting Workbooks**

When it comes time to introduce print or cursive handwriting, either purchase a handwriting workbook or make your own practice book for each of your students. The workbook page shows the letter formation with arrows, which builds redundancy into the introduction. Students who are visual learners can see how to form the letters correctly. The workbook pages usually include a few warm-up letters that are traced, which is beneficial for students who are hesitant to try some on their own. Then they offer plenty of lines for students to form the letter by themselves over and over again.

Whether choosing a workbook or making your own practice pages, be sure the following are included:

- Both the uppercase and lowercase version of the letter are at the top of the page, preferably on a dotted midline. (This arrangement allows students to compare and contrast the height and width of the two versions of the letter.)
- There are arrows next to each letter to show which stroke to make first and second and in which direction.
- There are a couple of lightly drawn letters that the students can trace before they write some independently.
- There are at least two full lines for the student to write the letter over and over.
- There is a key word or two containing the letter at the bottom of the practice sheet for the student to copy as shown in figure 3.2.6.

**Figure 3.2.6: Example Handwriting Practice Page**

**Figure 3.2.7 Page with Dotted Midlines**

## 5. Scheduling

When preparing your curriculum, you can use the block plan templates in Appendices 1 and 2 or you can create your own. If you create your own, use the following points to lay out your blocks:

1. Begin instruction for handwriting at the beginning of 1st Grade. It will be part of teaching the alphabet (see chapter 3.1). Begin cursive instruction sometime during the first semester of 2nd Grade.

2. It will take 1st Grade students three main lesson blocks and three practice blocks to master printing the letters (uppercase and lowercase). Cursive is variable.

3. Teach handwriting in the Introduction &/or Review segment in main lesson. Practice the letters that were introduced in the practice blocks.

4. Teaching printing will be one day of the 2½-day rhythm to introduce the letter. Cursive is variable.

5. It will take ~10–15 minutes per lesson to introduce handwriting for the letter (both uppercase and lowercase version).

6. Once students have mastered cursive, segue into cursive copying for main lesson book and reading teacher's cursive handwriting on the board and in handouts.

7. Teach at least two letters a week (e.g., *Aa* and *Bb*). Use a standard consumable handwriting book or make your own pages.

## 6. Initial Introduction

The initial introduction to handwriting is spread out. It includes the straight line and curved line during the first week of school (see chapter 5.2 #4). It then includes the initial introduction to printing the first letter of the alphabet, which is part of learning the first letter (see chapter 3.1 #7).

**Prerequisite:** None for straight and curved line; however, students should have an artistic experience of the letter prior to learning to print it. For example, the students might paint the letter, draw the letter, or sculpt the letter out of clay or some other material.

**When to Teach:** Teach the straight and curved line the first day(s) of 1st Grade. Schedule the initial introduction of handwriting sometime during the first week of the first main lesson block as part of your introduction of the first letter.

**Sample Lesson:** Design your own introduction for straight and curved line. Follow the advice in your handwriting book if you are using one. If you are not, use the script in chapter 3.2 #7 *Englishland Introduction.*

With each lesson, remind students of the following points:

- sitting position
- how to hold a pencil
- how to position the paper and hold it
- modifications for left-handed students (if there are some in the class)

When you are teaching with a dotted midline, include the following instruction:

- How to print a letter from the top down and left to right. (Be aware a few lowercase letters such as *f* and *s* vary slightly from these guidelines. Only lowercase *e* begins in the middle.) Follow the guides given in a workbook, if you are using one.
- How to use the guidelines (i.e., the top and bottom lines and the dotted midline). They provide boundaries that show where to begin the stroke and where to end it.

For initial introduction of printing, see chapter 3.2 #7. For initial introduction of cursive, see chapter 3.2 #8.

## 7.   How to Teach Handwriting in 1st Grade

**Objective:** Teach students to print all letters (uppercase and lowercase).

**Prerequisites:** straight and curved line (introduced in week 1—See chapter 5.2 #4)

**Background Information:** In 1st Grade, teach the students to print each letter in uppercase and lowercase as part of your introduction of the letters. Finish handwriting introduction by the end of the third main lesson block, when you introduce your last letters. Use economy in teaching to practice handwriting as part of other assignments for the rest of the year.

**When to Teach:** Introduce printing as part of teaching the first letter of the alphabet. It will occur on day three of the teaching rhythm after you have introduced the letter and the students have had an opportunity to paint, model, or draw the letter artistically on day two (see chapter 3.1 #7 and table 3.1.6).

**How to Teach:** If you are using a handwriting book, follow its instructions for introducing a letter. If you are not, present the following image to introduce printing letters. It is the introduction to *The Roadmap to Literacy's* umbrella story, *Englishland,* which is used to teach letters, grammar, and mechanics.

### *Englishland* Introduction

*In the world of language there is a very special place called Englishland. Englishland is a vast country filled with all kinds of characters and letters who live together in villages scattered throughout the land. The letters of the alphabet live together in a place called Letter Village. In this village the capital (or uppercase) letters are the adults and the lowercase letters are the children (point to a letter in your alphabet display for an example). The wisest character in Letter Village is their Mayor. Whenever the letter citizens of the village encounter a problem, it is the Mayor who most often finds the solution.*

*We will get a chance over the next few years to hear about all of the challenges the letters of Letter Village run into and how the Mayor helps to solve them. But, before we can explore the adventures of the letter citizens, we first have to be introduced to them. Yesterday we met the letter M and today we are going to learn how the letter M would like to be written.*

*In Letter Village there is both an adult letter and a child letter for every letter in the alphabet. The child letters come in various heights. Some are very tall and some are very small. When the letters go on a page, the letter children are very careful to stand up straight and tall. Their feet always touch the earth* (Draw the base line on the board). *Their heads go up towards the sky.* (Draw the top line on the board.) *Some letter children are so tall their heads touch the sky. And some are so small that they only reach halfway up.* (Draw the dotted midline.)

*Because they are so tall, the adult letters' heads always touch the sky. There is an adult letter and a child letter for each letter of the alphabet.*

Model how to write an *M* using the following method: Put your piece of chalk on the top line and write an *M* as you say: *When we write the adult letter M, we start at the top of its first peak, which touches the sky and draw a line straight down to the earth. Then we draw its valley and finish by drawing the line from the top of its second peak down to the earth. That is how adults write the letter M.*

Pass out a handwriting practice page (complete with guidelines) and talk the students through writing the letter *M* using the description of peaks and valley. Have them try a few as you model writing it on the board for them. Then let them write several lines on their own. Once they have completed writing uppercase *M* on two or three lines, introduce the lowercase letter using the following dialogue:

*There is also a child letter for M. Instead of looking like two tall mountains, the child M is shaped like two round hills. It only reaches halfway to the sky.* Put your chalk on the dotted midline on the board and say: *The child M begins with a straight line that starts at the midline. It reaches down to the ground. Then the line travels back up the line and curves over to form two even hills side by side.*

Talk the students through writing a lowercase letter *m*. Have them try a few on their own with you modeling on the board. Then let them write several lines by themselves. See fig. 3.2.8 for an example.

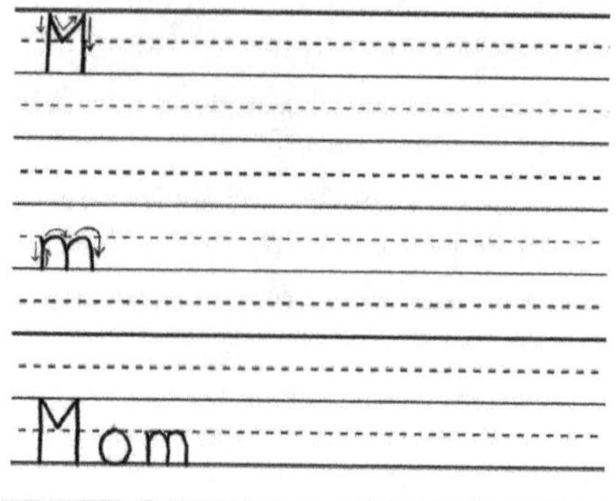

**Figure 3.2.8: Example Print Practice Page for *Mm***

Note: When you introduce a letter that goes below the base line, give the students an image such as, *"Some of the letter children have a root that lives underground just like a flower."*

**How to Practice**

There are two stages of handwriting practice: practice during the initial introduction of a letter (i.e., mastering how to form each individual letter) and application (i.e., practicing all letters in context).

Initial practice refers to the time students are learning to form each letter in isolation. This practice occurs during the third day you introduce the letter and is done in a handwriting workbook or on a practice page that you have made for the class (see table 3.1.6 and table 3.1.7). The students should put forth their very best effort to make each letter look like the model. A fun way to encourage this level of diligence is as follows: Write a line of the same letter on a dotted midline on the board. Make some letters the wrong height (e.g., they go over the line or they do not stand on the line), some the wrong shape (e.g., their circles are wobbly or not particularly round), and some with bad posture (e.g., they slouch forward or backward). Make one letter as close to perfect as you can. Then go through and critique each letter as a class. Award a star to the letter that is written in the best way. Now have the students fill a line on their paper with that letter. Once they have finished, they review each letter and put a star over their most perfect letter.

The second stage of handwriting practice is application. It occurs after the students have practiced letter formation in isolation and are now writing (copying, composing, or spelling). There are two types of application: best handwriting (artistic) and utilitarian/legible handwriting (composition/spelling). Best handwriting practice occurs naturally multiple times a week when students write in their main lesson books. After all, when students are writing in their main lesson book, the entire objective is beautiful handwriting. However, when they are spelling or composing, their handwriting should be legible, but necessarily beautiful. Their attention should be on the words they are communicating and how to spell them, not on how beautifully they can form the letters. Communicate your expectations for handwriting when you give the assignment. You might want to come up with two descriptive terms: one for best handwriting and one for utilitarian or legible only handwriting. Use the appropriate term to communicate the type of handwriting students are to use for a writing assignment. Continue to use handwriting paper with dotted midlines for most writing.

Note: During the first half of 1st Grade, students will write letters before they have a formal introduction into how to print these letters correctly as they will be copying words and sentences from the board and will be engaging in kid writing. Give them license to form these letters on their own until they have been taught how to write each letter.

If your students need extra practice in handwriting, here are a few ideas:

1. Have the students write their classmates' names beautifully.

2. At the end of the year, give the class seven letters (including at least two vowels) and challenge them to use the letters to write down as many words as they can. Then compile the list on the board and ask the students to copy the words using their neatest handwriting. This exercise is particularly useful if you want to focus on practicing a few particular letters.

3. Have students copy a riddle from the board. See if they can then figure it out and, if so, write the answer neatly below.

4. Have students copy a tongue twister from the board or make up their own.

5. Have students copy the following sentence from the board: *A quick brown fox jumped over the lazy dogs.* Then challenge them to discover its secret. (Answer: It contains all 26 letters of the alphabet.) This exercise doubles as an assessment of handwriting as it contains all 26 letters.

When you can, monitor the students as they practice handwriting. Walk around the classroom and observe. Correct any errors of letter formation and ergonomics.

## 8.  How to Teach Handwriting in 2nd Grade

**Objective:** Teach students to write in cursive. (Include both uppercase and lowercase letters.)

**Prerequisite:**

1. Students have mastered uppercase and lowercase printing. (Assess by asking students to write out the alphabet in their neatest handwriting (*Aa, Bb, Cc*, etc.) Walk around the room to observe letter formation. Cover any alphabet displays.)

2. Students are proficient with running forms in form drawing (see chapter 2.1 #12 and figure 2.1.2).

**Prep Work**

Continue to monitor your own handwriting. If you have not yet begun beautifying your cursive, do so the summer before by practicing every day. Keep in mind that your cursive must be worthy of emulation.

If you are not using a handwriting book, choose the order you intend to teach the letters and create handouts. Begin with those letters that are very similar to the lowercase print letters (e.g ., *d*, *c*, and, *i*). After introducing a few letters, show how they can hold hands. Possible first words include *hit, dip*, and, *cut*. Save the harder letters for last (i.e., the ones that need to change their shape such as the lowercase letters *r, f,* and *s*). Include handouts that show how they can hold hands. Possible practice words include *fur, sun,* and *far*.

**When to Teach:** Teach cursive letters during the first half of the year. The number of times per week is up to you.

**How to Teach:** Teach both uppercase and lowercase cursive in the same lesson, as you did in 1st Grade with printing. Schedule it in the Introduction &/or Review segment of main lesson. Practice can be in the Bookwork and/or Skills Practice segment.

**Formula for Introducing Cursive**

When first looking through Ute Luebeck's students' 2nd grade main lesson books, teachers jokingly accused her of doing the cursive writing for her students because each book's text was so neat. When asked what approach she took to achieve this remarkable feat, she shared this formula:

1. Conduct a number of *running form* exercises in form drawing prior to the introduction of cursive.

2. Introduce each letter individually.

3. Provide plenty of practice for each letter once introduced.

4. Walk around the classroom, monitoring and correcting handwriting.

**Practice Running Forms in Form Drawing**

Running forms are continuous form drawings where a pattern is initiated and repeated without ever breaking the line (see fig. 2.1.2).

In your form drawing class, be sure to include some running forms prior to and during the introduction of cursive. The practice will help with handwriting.

**How to Introduce Cursive: Imaginative Introduction and Initial Practice**

**Prerequisite:** Lesson on capitalization found in chapter 3.11 #6a.

Once the students have mastered running forms in form drawing, introduce cursive letters with an imaginative story such as the following:

*The Mayor of Letter Village was visiting a nearby town. While strolling about he came upon a group of the local letter children who were spelling words together, which is how letter children play. Lo and behold! The children in this town played in a most unusual way. They formed their words by holding hands. The first letter took its place at the beginning of the word and then each consecutive letter came over and held hands with its neighbor until the word was spelled. (Write the word "pot" on the board in print and then write it in cursive.)*

*The Mayor was so excited about this new way to spell words that he raced home and taught all of the letter people of his village how to spell words by holding hands. The adult letters continued to be the first letter in a sentence, but the child letters all held hands. They found that some of the time a few of the uppercase and lowercase letters had to change their shape a bit in order to be able to hold hands. But, they worked together to figure it out and after a time, all of the letters in the village had learned to do cursive.*

Then introduce your first cursive letter on the board. Use the dotted midline. Model the letter and a key word.

Pass out your handwriting page. It should have the same specifications as the page used to teach printing. Teach the students to angle their paper even more than they do for printing. They should hold the paper with the non-dominant hand. The angle of the paper needs to follow the natural curve of the writing hand and thus varies according to the child.

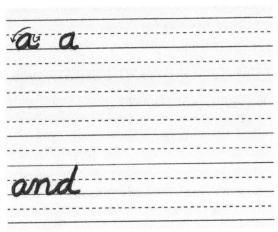

**Figure 3.2.9: Example Cursive Practice Page for Lowercase A (a)**

Demonstrate how to form the cursive letter on the board. Do one letter together as a class (uppercase and lowercase). Remind the class to use their very neatest handwriting. Then let the students do a page on their own, similar to Figure 3.2.9. (Note: The first practice page should include both the uppercase and lowercase letter, not just the lowercase as shown in figure 3.2.9.)

When each student is done with her practice sheet, ask her to raise her hand. When a student indicates she is finished, check her work and add a star beside the letter you want her to emulate and point out why you chose that letter.

## Cursive Practice

After practicing the letter in isolation, it is time to practice the letter in context. Have the students copy poems from the board into their main lesson books. Ask them to compose some of their kid writing in cursive or do some of their spelling practice (encoding) in cursive. As they show increasing proficiency, have students do some of their main lesson entries in cursive writing. First, begin by writing a title in cursive then move on to a sentence or two. By the spring, students should be able to take a rough draft of a short composition they have written in print and put it into their main lesson book in cursive.

If your students need more practice in forming the letters, use some of the same techniques that you used in 1st Grade for printing (see chapter 3.2 #7).

While your students are practicing their handwriting, be sure to walk around the class observing their letter formation, paper slant, and ergonomics. Provide direct instruction when needed. It is better to point out exactly what a student did well than it is to give a generalized compliment. For example, *"Look Ryder, see how the letters O and A are exactly the same height? That's what I'm looking for, nice work."* rather than *"Beautiful work, Ryder."*

## Teacher Transition from Print to Cursive on the Blackboard

Once you have introduced the cursive alphabet, you will need to help the students learn to read cursive. To make this transition, write on the board in cursive rather than print.

You can begin to transition your students to reading cursive by doing the following:

- writing the title or first line of a poem on the board in cursive
- giving students a copy of a poem or some sentences that you have written in cursive and having them write the text in print or vice versa
- always writing the day's schedule in cursive

Gradually write more and more in cursive as their ability to read it improves.

Note: A goal would be that by the end of 2nd Grade almost all of your handwritten text (on the board and in handouts) be done in cursive.

## Second Grade Printing Practice

In addition to practicing cursive, students should continue to practice printing. They must learn to reduce the size of their letters while maintaining the same standards in form. To reduce the size of their script, give the students lined paper with a dotted midline that is not as wide as the paper used in 1st Grade.

## Differentiate between Artistic Handwriting and Utilitarian Handwriting

Continue to give students guidance on what you expect for handwriting for their assignments. Differentiate between final products that need to have their most best handwriting and drafts where handwriting is secondary to spelling and composition. A good rule of thumb is that anything going into the main lesson book needs to be in their best handwriting. Any kid writing or composition assignment should be in utilitarian handwriting. The students should focus on spelling and writing down all of their ideas rather than on their handwriting.

## 9.   How to Teach Handwriting in 3rd Grade

**Objective:** Teach students to reduce the size of their handwriting (both print and cursive).

**Prerequisite:** NA

**Background Information:** There is nothing new to teach in 3rd Grade handwriting. Students will continue to use print and cursive writing for various assignments. However, by the end of 3rd Grade, students should be able to print and write cursive neatly on standard-sized lined paper (wide ruled).

**Prep Work:** Determine when you expect the students to print and when you want them to use cursive. One solution is to have the student print when composing rough drafts and use cursive for the final draft.

**When to Teach:** Use economy in teaching to work handwriting practice into the curriculum. For example, practice cursive through personal letter writing (e.g., to a beloved grandparent). Once the students have composed the letter, ask them to recopy it in their best cursive in letter format. This letter can then be mailed.

### How to Teach: Introduction to Standard-Sized Paper

Initially students will use paper that has lines that are around one centimeter with a dotted midline. However, by the end of the year, the students should be able to write on standard, wide-ruled lined paper. When you have students use wide-ruled paper for the first time, show them how to write neatly on it. Show that they can eyeball (i.e., visualize) the dotted midline and make each letter exactly the right height and shape in each of the three zones. In 3rd Grade, it is good to have them skip lines so the descending letters do not get entangled in other letters on the line below.

## 10.  Practice

Practice is critical. It forms part of your initial introduction in the Introduction &/or Review segment of main lesson (i.e., Activities A and B). It will be part of your ongoing practice in the Skills Practice segment of main lesson and practice classes (see chapter 2.3 #4). Finally, it can be used during classroom games.

**Skills Practice:** See the practice activities outlined in the subsections 3.2 #7–9 on how to teach handwriting in each grade. In addition, many aspects of language arts automatically provide handwriting practice. The following are included in Skills Practice after the initial introduction:

- encoding (see chapter 3.4)
- spelling (see chapter 3.9) (3rd Grade only)

Each is covered in depth in the noted chapter.

**Bookwork:** The following can be scheduled in the Bookwork segment:

- handwriting—copying poems, compositions, etc. into main lesson book
- grammar handouts/written exercises (see chapter 3.11)
- composition (see chapter 3.14) (2nd and 3rd Grade only)
- kid writing (see chapter 3.13) (1st and 2nd Grade only)

For additional activities to practice cursive handwriting revisit the ideas listed at the end of chapter 3.2 #7.

## 11. Assessment

Assessment is a critical part of teaching. It is important to verify that students have mastered the skills they have been taught. See chapter 6.1 for background on assessment.

**Benchmarks** represent <u>minimum</u> levels of student achievement by the end of each grade for students to be on track to handle grade-level work in 4th Grade (see chapter 6.1 #9). Table 3.2.1 contains the benchmarks for handwriting.

Note: The following benchmarks may not be exhaustive. Prerequisite skills for handwriting may be covered under other related language arts skills. For a full list of benchmarks, see table 6.1.4.

### Table 3.2.1: Benchmark for Handwriting

|  | **1st Grade** | **2nd Grade** | **3rd Grade** |
|---|---|---|---|
| **Handwriting** | Students can print all letters correctly (uppercase and lowercase). | Students can form all cursive letters correctly (uppercase and lowercase). | Students can write and read cursive script. |

There are three types of assessments. Recommendations for each type of assessment can be found in Sections 6.3, 6.4, and 6.5. You can use the following ideas as a starting point to set up an assessment program.

**Informal Assessments:** Watch your students as they write and observe both their handwriting and how they write. In addition, look at all of their assignments (main lesson book and practice book).

<u>When observing the student's handwriting note the following:</u>

- letter shape
- letter height
- letter size
- letter slant
- letters in relation to the bottom line
- letters in relation to the midline
- space between letters
- space between words

<u>When observing the student as she writes, consider the following questions:</u>

1. How does the student hold the pencil?
2. Does the student continue to mix uppercase and lowercase letters?
3. Does the student struggle to copy from the board?
4. Does the student have difficulty sitting correctly (e.g., kneeling on the chair, lying on the desk while writing, etc.)?
5. How much pencil pressure does the student use when writing?
6. How is the student's stamina?
7. Does the student cross the midline while writing?

**Teacher-Made Assessment:** Use dictations to assess handwriting

**Assessments Created by Educational Testing Groups:** NA

See chapter 6.3, 6.4, and 6.5 for more information about assessing in each grade.

## 12. How to Help Struggling Students

**Assess:** When you see a student is struggling with handwriting, do informal assessments to narrow down the area(s) of concern. Document your findings and place in student's file.

**Additional Instruction/Practice:** Next, use the results of your assessments to provide this student with extra instruction and practice in any weak areas. Document what you try and the results.

If a new student joins the class and does not know cursive, ask the parents to work on cursive at home using a program such as *Handwriting without Tears*. Summer vacation is an ideal time.

**Remedial Solutions:** If you do not notice improvements in 3–4 weeks, it is time to contact your mentor for guidance and consult chapter 6.6 for additional information on remedial issues. Use the following advice in combination with chapter 6.6.

Most Common Scenarios: There are two common remedial scenarios to be on the lookout for:

1. Students who continue to struggle to hold a pencil correctly despite repeated instruction and correction likely have a retained reflex in their hands. If they exhibit other signs of reflex difficulties such as difficulty sitting or participating in movement activities, refer them to an Occupational Therapist or an Extra Lesson practitioner who has training in reflex work. If many students in the class need extra work, consider doing a class program such as Sally Goddard Blythe's *Early Morning by the Pond*, a series of exercises designed for use in the classroom (Blythe 2005, 206–233).

2. Students whose handwriting is fine but who are slow at copying most likely have underlying vision problems. Refer appropriately (see chapter 6.6 #2).

Summary of Remedial Options: You can provide in-class work, modifications, accommodations, and referrals. Use the least restrictive measure(s) to deal with the problem. If that method does not work, continue down the list. Document everything you try. Include beginning date and end date, description of what you attempted, and the result. This information will prove invaluable in the event you need to make a referral.

- In-Class Remedial Work to Address Underlying Weakness:
    - Form drawing: Have the student practice some form drawing that would provide the stroke practice needed without the pressure of forming the letter.
    - Hand exercises: See below.
- Referrals
    - Occupational Therapist for severe reflex issues and core strength deficits
    - Extra Lesson for minor reflex issues
    - Optometrist/ophthalmologist for vision screening
    - Therapeutic Eurythmist if student appears to have dysgraphia, an extreme difficulty coordinating the limb and hands for writing tasks

- Irlen screener for **Irlen Syndrome** screening
- IEP at a public school if problem is severe (Note: Embark on this route only if you think the student would qualify for special services to address the issue, and the parents are willing to consider enrolling the student in the program recommended if she qualifies.)

See chapter 6.6 for more information about these therapies.

**Accommodations and Modifications:** Sometimes it takes a while for remedial issues to be resolved. Meanwhile, the student needs support to function in class. Consider using one or more of the following as a temporary measure:

- Adjust the size of the lined paper the student is using to accommodate her current script. (Reduce the size over time.)
- Provide a copy of the material on the board for her to use at her desk.
- Provide color-coded paper, such as the one in figure 3.2.10, to help the student stay in the proper space. (Image: The top area is in yellow for the sun, the middle area is in green for the grass and the lower area is brown for the ground/dirt under the grass. You could also use blue/sky, green/earth and brown/ underground.)

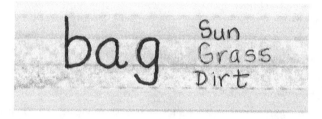

**Figure 3.2.10: Color-Coded Paper**

- Write the text in the student's main book lightly and then ask her to copy over your handwriting, making sure she does so slowly and carefully. Slowly phase out your participation as she develops more confidence and control.

**Hand Exercises**

There are many exercises you can do to strengthen the hands. Use the following exercises with the class or with small groups:

- Finger tapping (using both hands simultaneously tap the same finger of each hand on the desk, one after the other)
- Touching the tip of each finger with the thumb, first one hand at a time and then simultaneously
- Holding a long pencil, flute, dowel, etc. with the fingers of one hand and walking the fingers from the bottom of the object to the top and then back down again

Reflex issues often underlie hand problems, particularly handwriting challenges (see chapter 6.6 #4). If these exercises prove too challenging, students will often need to go back to work through hand reflexes. For an example of hand exercises in the form of a story, go to www.waldorfinspirations.com.

## Conclusion

As you have seen, handwriting provides numerous gifts for students. It strengthens the will and stimulates the neural capacities needed for reading and writing. It is a most efficient way to learn the letters of the alphabet. It is well worth the time to cultivate good handwriting in the early grades. However, knowing how to write the letters of the alphabet has little value without phonemic awareness. Without phonemic awareness, the students cannot learn to encode and decode. The next chapter will examine phonemic awareness in detail and consider ways to teach it. Learning the alphabet will jump start the development of this capacity, but most students require further instruction to develop full phonemic awareness for segmenting sounds.

# 3.3 PHONOLOGICAL AND PHONEMIC AWARENESS: THE KEY TO ENCODING AND DECODING

*Jennifer Militzer-Kopperl began kindergarten with minimal phonemic awareness: She could rhyme words but not hear that words were made up of sounds. She could print her name, but she did not know that letters represent sounds. She was at the beginning of the Emergent Phase.*

*At the start of the school year, Jennifer's teacher asked the class to play a classic phonemic awareness game: the students had to introduce themselves and say one thing that they liked that began with the same sound as their name. "Hi, I am Tina, and I like tigers." "Hi, I am Michael, and I like monkeys." When Jennifer had to introduce herself, she did not hesitate. "Hi, I am Jenny, and I like cats." Her teacher corrected her, "No, it has to be something that starts with the same sound as your name. You could say, for example, that you like jumping." Jennifer was puzzled. Cats were the thing she liked most in this world. As for jumping, she was rather indifferent to it. She would much rather play on the monkey bars, swing, or slide. She concluded that her teacher did not know anything about her.*

*However, as she learned the alphabet, Jennifer began to develop phonemic awareness. She realized that her name starts with the letter J, which stands for the sound /j/ as in jumping. With that knowledge, she now had an answer for the game: "Hi, I am Jenny, and I like jaguars."*

Students must develop phonemic awareness to make sense of the written code. Phonemic awareness underlies both decoding (sounding out words) and encoding (spelling words by sounds). Teachers must help their students develop full phonemic awareness because it is not a natural part of human development. Teaching the alphabet is the first step in building phonemic awareness, but there is much more to do.

This chapter covers the following topics:

1. Why Phonological and Phonemic Awareness Matter
2. Background Information
3. Preparation
4. Scheduling
5. Initial Introduction
6. How to Teach Phonological and Phonemic Awareness in the Emergent Phase
7. How to Teach Phonological and Phonemic Awareness in the Phonemic Awareness Phase
8. How to Teach Phonological and Phonemic Awareness in the Pattern Phase
9. How to Teach Phonological and Phonemic Awareness in the Syllable Phase
10. Practice

11. Assessment

12. How to Differentiate Instruction

13. How to Help Struggling Students

# 1. Why Phonological and Phonemic Awareness Matter

Phonological awareness is the ability to break speech down into three separate parts: words, syllables, and phonemes. Being able to break sentences down into separate words is called *theory of word* while being able to detect the individual phonemes, or sounds, in words and manipulate them is called phonemic awareness. All aspects of phonological awareness are important, but phonemic awareness is the most critical because phonemic awareness is fundamental to decoding, encoding, and phonics rules.

Aspects of phonological awareness are important for many reasons.

**Theory of Word:**

- prerequisite for finger pointing during memory reading in the Emergent and Phonemic Awareness Phases

**Syllable:**

- first awareness that words can be subdivided
- prerequisite for encoding and decoding by syllables (Syllable Phase)

**Phonemic Awareness:**

- prerequisite for encoding and decoding by sounds (Phonemic Awareness Phase and Pattern Phase)
- prerequisite for phonics rules (Phonemic Awareness, Pattern, and Syllable Phases)
- prerequisite for developing the *word identification hub* (see chapter 1.2 #3)

The development of full phonemic awareness requires education. Average children develop some phonemic awareness as part of child development, but not enough to support literacy.

In the book *Reading in the Brain: The New Science of How We Read*, Dehaene reports on research relating to the development of phonological and phonemic awareness. Researchers have explored which aspects of phonological awareness require formal education and which are a natural part of human development. One experiment involved Portuguese adults. Half of them were illiterate while the other half had just learned to read. The illiterate adults could hear that the syllables *ta* and *da* are different and could easily identify syllables and rhymes. They were only unable to pick up on the smallest division (i.e., phonemes). For example, they could not recognize that the sound /t/ appears in the words *tap, step,* and *rat*. In addition, they could not manipulate words by taking away a sound (e.g., they could not figure out that the word *cat* without the /k/ sound is the word *at).* The researchers showed that phonemic awareness is not a natural part of human development, but rather a product of formal education.

This conclusion was verified with literate Chinese adults. Chinese can be written two ways: with characters and with an alphabetic system known as Pinyin. It is a perfect experiment because Chinese who read characters are literate in a pictogram system while those who go on to learn Pinyin are literate in both pictograms and a system based on phonemes. Researchers found that the adults who could only read traditional Chinese characters failed on phonemic awareness tests just like the illiterate Portuguese, while those who had also learned the alphabetic Pinyin succeeded (Dehaene 2009, 201–202).

Students who are in the Emergent Phase are like the illiterate Portuguese adults and the Chinese who only read characters: they are not yet aware of phonemes. Teachers make them aware by teaching the alphabet and providing lots of activities to develop phonemic awareness. This education results in changes in the students' brains (see chapter 1.2).

The phases offer guideposts to show where students are in their journey of becoming literate. The development of phonemic awareness is critical to the first two phases. Students transition from the Emergent Phase to the PhonemicAwareness Phase when they realize that letters represent individual sounds. Students transition from the Phonemic Awareness Phase to the Pattern Phase once they can segment every sound in a word and represent it with an appropriate letter.

All students pass predictable signposts as you teach them phonemic awareness. **Signposts** refer to certain skills that are meaningful. In this case, they reflect changes in the students' brains that indicate which phase a student is in. In general, students will master things in the order shown in table 3.3.1.

**Table 3.3.1: Signposts for the Development of Phonemic Awareness**

| Phase | What Students Can Encode (Spell) | Examples of Student Spelling (Encoding or Kid Writing) |
|---|---|---|
| **End of the Emergent Phase** | First (or most prominent) sound in a word | *D* or *d* for dog |
| **Beginning of the Phonemic Awareness Phase** | First and last phoneme | *dg* for dog |
| **Intermediate Phonemic Awareness Phase** | Medial short vowel through point of articulation | *dig* for dog |
| | Medial short vowel—correct | *dog* for dog |
| | Blends: simple | *plan* for plan; *stopt* for stopped; but *jop* for drop and *jup* for jump |
| **Advanced Phonemic Awareness Phase** | Blends: complex (*TR* and *DR*) Blends: preconsonantal nasals | • *drop* for drop • *jump* for jump • *stopt* for stopped |

*Source: Material adapted from Bear 2008, 132.*

Note how this development in the Emergent Phase and the beginning of the Phonemic Awareness Phase mirrors key steps in the historical development of writing. Consonants come first, then vowels (see chapter 1.4 #1). (This is one reason why *The Roadmap to Literacy* strongly urges the teaching of consonant letters before vowel letters: it works with the development of phonemic awareness as reflected through the historical record.)

The phases represent real changes that occur in students' brains as the result of formal literacy education. The development of phonemic awareness determines where students are in the Emergent Phase and the Phonemic Awareness Phase. Students entering 1st Grade will be in different spots along the path to developing phonemic awareness. All of them need to be met where they are. Consequently, it will be necessary to differentiate instruction and practice in phonemic awareness.

Average students can master phonemic awareness easily if it is included in their education. However, dyslexic students have difficulty mastering phonemic awareness due to differences in the organization of their brains. It is much harder for them to make the *letter to sound decoding route*. Good instruction and follow-up practice in phonemic awareness will help all students, but moderately dyslexic students will likely need more than can be provided in the average classroom and severely dyslexic students may require separate and special instruction (see chapter 6.6 #9).

In conclusion, phonemic awareness is critical for literacy. Learning phonemic awareness has a symbiotic relationship with learning the alphabet: one spurs the development of the other. As will be demonstrated in later chapters, phonemic awareness enables students to begin to work with the code (i.e., encoding, decoding), which in turn creates the *letter to sound decoding route* in their brains, which is itself a prerequisite for developing the faster *lexical route* (see chapter 1.2 #2). Full phonemic awareness is the product of formal education; it is not a natural part of human development. Average students master phonemic awareness easily if they are taught properly; severely dyslexic students may require additional education. Teachers can use the milestones inherent in the Emergent Phase and the Phonemic Awareness Phase to determine which aspects of phonemic awareness their students have learned and which need further practice.

## 2. Background Information

There is a lot of background information for teaching phonemic awareness. This subsection will present this information along with crib notes to help you keep it straight:

- The Six Types of Phonemic Awareness
- Materialization Techniques (i.e., ways to practice phonemic awareness)
- Quick Reference for the Six Types of Phonemic Awareness and Materialization Techniques

Note: Recall that a lowercase letter written inside two forward slashes (e.g., /s/) indicates the letter's sound not the letter's name. For example, to read /s/, make the sound of a snake: sssssssssssssssssssss.

### The Six Types of Phonemic Awareness

There are six main categories of phonemic awareness for students to master, presented here in order of difficulty (easiest to hardest):

1. Phoneme Matching
2. Onset & Rime
3. Blending Phonemes
4. Sequencing Phonemes
5. Segmenting Phonemes
6. Manipulating Phonemes*

*Includes four types of manipulation: addition, deletion, substitution, and transposing. See below.

### Phoneme Matching

Phoneme matching refers to recognizing rhymes and alliteration. (**Alliteration** is a repetition of a first sound in a word as is common in tongue twisters such as *Peter Piper picked a peck of pickled peppers.*) Provided that children have exposure to Nursery Rhymes and language games in the home and/or preschool, they typically begin to develop recognition of rhymes on their own around age four. Students who have not had this experience are at a decided disadvantage.

Caveat: Children should already be familiar with rhymes upon entering 1st Grade. Should a student have difficulty learning to generate rhymes, consult a reading specialist. This difficulty is an early symptom of dyslexia. If present, a student should begin working with a specialist immediately in addition to all of the excellent work you will be doing in class.

## Onset and Rime

**Rime** refers to the vowel <u>sound</u> and any consonant sounds that come after it in a syllable or in a word that is only one syllable long. **Onset** refers to any consonant letter(s) that come before the rime. For example, c/at, cl/imb, and spl/ash. You can split a single-syllable word into its onset/rime ("*dog* is /d/… /og/") or blend the two together to create a word ("/d/…. /og/ make *dog*"). Onset and rime help prepare the way for blending phonemes and segmenting phonemes. They help students break spoken syllables down into smaller parts so the students can eventually hear the individual phonemes.

## Blending Phonemes

**Blending** refers to taking isolated sounds and combining them to form a word (e.g., "/p/… /ĭ/…. /n/ makes which word?" (pin). Blending is sometimes referred to as **synthesizing** or **oral synthesis**. It is great practice for decoding because it is decoding without the burden of letter recognition. Students practice it extensively in the Emergent Phase and the beginning half of the Phonemic Awareness Phase to get ready for decoding in the middle of the Phonemic Awareness Phase.

## Sequencing Phonemes

**Sequencing** refers to identifying the specific positions of sounds within a word. Initially it is identifying whether a sound appears in the beginning, middle, or end of a word (e.g., in the word *pan*, is the /n/ at the beginning, middle, or end of the word?). Then it is being able to identify which sound is at the beginning, middle, or end (e.g., in the word *pan*, which sound is at the end of the word? (/n/)). This stage helps students get ready to segment all of the sounds within words.

## Segmenting Phonemes

**Segmenting** is the opposite process of blending phonemes. It refers to breaking a word down into its phonemes. It has two parts. First, you say a word slowly and have the students count how many sounds it has. Once they can do this, have students identify the phonemes in the word (for example, *tin* /t/ /ĭ/ /n/).

## Manipulating Phonemes

**Manipulating** is the highest level of phonemic awareness. It is the only one to continue practicing past the Phonemic Awareness Phase. Here students change words by adding, subtracting, substituting, or transposing phonemes to form new words. You can work this skill as a reading skill or as a spelling skill.

- Addition: (two approaches)
  1. Ask students, "How do you change *pan* into *plan?*"

     Students reply, "Put an *L* after the *P.*"

  2. Tell students, "Add an *L* after the *P.* What does the word say now?"

     Students reply, "Plan."

- Deletion (two approaches for **elision** or subtraction):
    1. Ask students to say the word *cup*. (Students say, "Cup.")

        "Now say it without the /k/." (Students reply, "Up.")

    2. Ask students what sound they would need to delete or take away to change *cup* into *up*.

        Students reply, "Take away the /k/ sound."

- Substitution: (two approaches)
    1. Ask students, "If you take away the *C* in *cup*. Put a *P* in its place. Now what does the word say?

        Students answer, "Pup."

    2. Ask students what they would have to do to change *cup* into *pup*.

        Students reply, "Take away the *C* and add a *P*."

- Transposing:
    1. Ask students, " What would you need to do to the word *film* to change it into *flim?*"

        Students reply, "Move the *L* from after the letter *I* to before the letter *I*."

Note: Some aspects of phonemic awareness can be receptive or expressive. *Receptive* refers to recognition and *expressive* refers to self-generation. For example, "Do the words *dog* and *hog* rhyme?" (Receptive) "Find a word that rhymes with dog." "Log." (Expressive) Receptive is easier.

**Materialization Techniques**

The easiest way to introduce and practice most of the six aspects of phonemic awareness is through **materialization techniques**. Materialization techniques are ways to use tangible objects such as hands and fabric to make abstract elements of speech such as phonemes more concrete for beginning students (Gentry 2006, 51). This subsection of the chapter will discuss six of these techniques.

The techniques come from several sources. Numbers 1–5 come from Gentry's book *Breaking the Code* (Gentry 2006, 52–55). Word Sorting is from Bear et al's *Words Their Way* (Bear 2008, 51–68). Symbol imagery exercises are from chapters 11 and 12 of *Seeing Stars: Symbol Imagery for Phonemic Awareness, Sight Words and Spelling*® (Bell 2001, 73–103).

1. Shouting out rhyming words with a stomp or clap
2. Hand spelling
3. Stretching out the sounds in words with stretchable fabric
4. Finger spelling
5. Sound and letter boxes (Elkonin boxes)
6. Word sorting
7. Symbol imagery exercises

### Shouting Out the Rhyming Word with a Stomp or Clap

In this materialization technique, the class chants a nursery rhyme or verse. Once they get to a rhyming word, they stomp or clap and shout out the rhyme. For example,

The cock doth CROW… (shout and stomp) To let you KNOW, (shout and stomp)

If you be WISE, (shout and clap) 'Tis time to RISE. (shout and clap)

This technique is good for the easiest level of phonemic awareness: phoneme matching. Start it immediately in the Emergent Phase.

### Hand Spelling

Gentry invented this materialization technique to break a word down into onset and rime. To use hand spelling, follow these steps:

1.  Say the word and put out your fist (e.g., *bat)*

2.  Say just the onset, or the sound(s) that come before the vowel, and put up your thumb at the same time (e.g., /b/)

3.  Say the rime, or the vowel to the end of the word, and stick out the rest of your hand as if you were about to shake hands (e.g., *at)*

4.  Finally, put the onset and rime back together into a whole word and pull your hand back into a fist position (e.g., *bat)*

Hand spelling is a materialization technique that can be used in the following ways:

- to teach onset and rime

- to help students isolate the first phoneme in a word (Emergent Phase)

- to help students who struggle with the concept of rhyme and alliteration (rimes help with rhymes and onsets help with alliteration)

- to serve as a half step to segmenting phonemes

- to serve as an introduction to the concept of word families (end of the Phonemic Awareness Phase/beginning of the Pattern Phase) (see chapter 4.2 rule 9)

### Stretching Out the Sounds in Words with Stretchable Fabric

This is another technique from Gentry.

Get a large piece of stretchable fabric (i.e., fabric that visibly expands when pulled and then contracts back to its original size when the pressure is released). A yard of swim suit fabric purchased from a fabric store works well. Then say a word and hold up the fabric (e.g., sum). Next, say it slowly and stretch the fabric as you do so (sssssssssuuuuuuummmmmm). This example illustrates that you are *stretching* out the word. Then let the fabric return to its normal size and say the word again (sum) and repeat.

Stretchable fabric is useful in segmenting. It makes a great introduction as well as a fun way to practice. Students enjoy stretching the fabric and a word at the same time. (Note: Students who are off task lose their fabric and have to sit and watch. Using fabric is a privilege. They can try again the next day.)

### Finger Spelling

Finger spelling is a segmenting technique adapted from Orton-Gillingham reading programs. To finger spell, pronounce each consecutive phoneme at the same time you hold up a finger. You can start with your thumb or pinky finger. For example, in the word *scrape,* /s/ is said at the same time you hold up your thumb, /k/ goes with the index, /r/ goes with the middle, /ā/ goes with the ring, and /p/ goes with the pinky or vice versa.

This technique is useful for segmenting. It gives students the number of sounds in a word (not the number of letters—for example, no Silent *E*). It is used to help students identify all of the sounds in a word. Use it in the Phonemic Awareness Phase after hand spelling is mastered. It will help students master phonemic awareness. It will also help with their encoding as it is a useful technique to make sure there is a letter for each sound in a word.

### Sound and Letter Boxes (Elkonin Boxes)

This technique comes from Reading Recovery, another reading program, with a slight adaptation. Once the students have done their finger spelling, they make a box for each sound in the word. Then they go back and finger spell again and place a letter in the right box immediately after saying it. (The finger spelling is done with the non-dominant hand while the dominant hand writes down the letter.)

Note: It is good to do techniques 3–5 back to back to back as a way to master segmenting and apply it to encoding. Have the students stretch out the sounds in a word, finger spell the word, make the number of boxes indicated by the fingers, and finger spell the word again while writing each sound's letter down in its box as they say it.

### Word Sorting

This technique comes from multiple sources including *Words Their Way*. It is useful for all phases. Students have to sort words into categories by analyzing different features. For example, in the Emergent Phase, students are given ten pictures of common items and then asked to sort them into pre-arranged categories such as: words that start with the letter *P* or words that start with the letter *C*. (see fig. 2.4.1 for an example of a word sorting game.)

This technique can be used to practice multiple aspects of phonemic awareness. For example, when students are struggling to hear the difference between /ĕ/ and /ĭ/, you can have them sort pictures into the categories of *Words with E* and *Words with I*. For example, sorting pictures of a *bed, bread, thread, net, jet, sled, dress, vest, fish, chick, lid, bib, crib, gift, witch,* etc. Vet words carefully for pronunciation.

You can also continue to use this technique when students have mastered phonemic awareness. For example, in the Pattern Phase, you could ask students to sort a group of long *A* words into different spelling categories, thus finding the different spelling patterns on their own. For example, they would have to find the long *A* patterns in this group of words: play, neighbor, pale, steak, rail, grape, weigh, say, grail, mail, sake, sway, etc. (categories are: *AY, EIGH, A_E, EA,* and *AI*). Notice how the students are no longer working with pictures to develop phonemic awareness but are working with patterns of spelling to develop symbol imagery (see chapter 3.5).

This technique can be used as teach-led sorts, individual student sorts, buddy sorts, and speed sorts. Students can work with the same list of words in a multitude of ways for a variety of reasons (mastering phonemic awareness, introducing a spelling rule, practicing a spelling rule or spelling lists for the week, etc.). This technique offers a lot of versatility. It can be used also in spelling (see chapter 3.9).

- **Teacher-Led Sort**: The teacher models the sorting process in front of the class. She calls on students to help determine where a word goes and asks why it was placed in the category. She uses materialization techniques to check to see if students are right and to help correct errors.
- **Buddy Sort**: Students work together with their desk partner to sort words. They discuss their work and have to come to a consensus on which words belong in which categories.
- **Speed Sort**: Students work individually and sort their words as fast as they can.

You can ask students to turn in their work by having them either glue the pictures or words onto a page with categories or by having them write their sorted words in categories (either on a separate piece of paper or a practice notebook).

<u>Symbol Imagery Exercises</u>

Symbol imagery exercises come from Lindamood-Bell. They are an excellent tool for practicing transposing, but their primary purpose is to develop symbol imagery. For a full discussion on how to work with these exercises, see chapter 3.5 #3.

**Guidelines for Using Phonemic Awareness & Materialization Techniques**

Use table 3.3.2 to determine optimal ways to practice the different aspects of phonemic awareness.

**Table 3.3.2: Quick Reference for the Six Types of Phonemic Awareness and Materialization Techniques**

| | Matching | Onset & Rime | Blending Phonemes | Sequencing Phonemes | Segmenting Phonemes | Manipulating phonemes |
|---|---|---|---|---|---|---|
| **Shouting Rhyming Words** | X | | | | | |
| **Hand spelling** | | X | | | | |
| **Stretching Words** | | | X | X | X | |
| **Finger Spelling** | | | | | X | |
| **Sound & Letter Boxes** | | | | | X | |
| **Word Sorting\*** | X | X | | X | | |
| **Symbol Imagery Exercises\*** | | | | | | X |

\*Symbol imagery exercises include syllable cards and mystery word (see chapter 3.5 #3). These two exercises are also used in the Pattern Phase and the Syllable Phase as they can serve purposes other than the development of phonemic awareness. The other exercises are limited to the Emergent Phase and the Phonemic Awareness Phase.

## 3.  Preparation

It is important to prepare your phonemic awareness exercises over the summer. Prepare activities for the six different types of phonemic awareness and label them accordingly: Emergent Phase, Beginning Phonemic Awareness Phase, Intermediate Phonemic Awareness Phase, and Advanced Phonemic Awareness Phase.

**Theory of Word:** Choose poems and songs for speech and memory reading. Coordinate with speech chapter and reading chapter (see chapter 3.10 #4–8 and chapter 3.15 #3–7).

**Syllables:** No special preparation is needed.

**Phonemic Awareness:** Prepare material to use with the six types of phonemic awareness and materialization techniques.

<u>Six Types of Phonemic Awareness</u>

1. Phoneme Matching: Choose tongue twisters and rhyming poems. Coordinate with your speech curriculum (see chapter 3.10 #4–8) and use the summer preparation form to record your selections (see chapter 5.1 #4).

2. Onset and Rime: No special preparation is necessary.

3. Blending Phonemes: Ibid

4. Sequencing Phonemes: Ibid

5. Segmenting Phonemes: Ibid

6. Manipulating Phonemes: Coordinate with your symbol imagery curriculum (see chapter 3.5 #4).

<u>Materialization Techniques</u>

1. Shouting out Rhymes: Choose tongue twisters and rhyming poems. Coordinate with your speech curriculum (see chapter 3.10 #4–8) and use the summer preparation form to record your selections (see chapter 5.1 #4).

2. Hand Spelling: No special preparation is necessary.

3. Stretchable Fabric: Buy stretchable fabric at a fabric store. Swimsuit fabric works well. Generate a list of words that can be stretched using any of the three following methods. Pull out your fabric and start playing with short words to see if they can be stretched. (The word *sun* is an excellent choice. It is short and it can be stretched: sssuuunnn. However, the word *dog* is not. It is short, but two of its phonemes cannot be held because both the sounds /d/ and /g/ end abruptly.) Use the following sounds to make up words that can be stretched: /n/, /m/, /ng/, /l,/ /r/, /f/, /v/, /sh/, /th/, /s/, and /z/ plus all vowel sounds. Use the Rhyming Rime Machine to generate words (see table 3.15.2).

4. Finger Spelling: No special preparation is necessary.

5. Sound and Letter Boxes: Ibid

6. Word Sorting: Make lists of words to sort and get pictures of words for word sorting games (see fig. 2.4.1). Pictures can be found in *Words Their Way* Appendix C.

7. Symbol Imagery: See chapter 3.5 #4

## 4. Scheduling

When preparing your curriculum, you can use the block plan templates in Appendix 1–3 or you can create your own. If you create your own, use the following points about theory of word, syllables, and phonemic awareness to lay out your blocks.

**Theory of Word**

1. Begin instruction at the beginning of 1st Grade.

2. It will take students one or two months to master (complete by Thanksgiving of 1st Grade at the latest).

3. Teach it in the Skills Practice segment in both main lesson blocks and practice blocks.

4. Practice it daily for several minutes.

5. Once students have mastered theory of word, segue into more phonemic awareness practice.

**Syllables**

1. Begin instruction at the beginning of 1st Grade.

2. It will take students several months to master (complete by February of 1st Grade at the latest. You will reteach syllables in 3rd Grade, including accented syllables.)

3. Teach it in the Skills Practice segment in both main lesson blocks and practice blocks.

4. Practice it daily for several minutes.

5. Once students have mastered syllables, segue into more phonemic awareness practice.

**Phonemic Awareness**

1. Begin instruction at the beginning of 1st Grade.

2. It will take students the entire year to master, assuming they get sequential daily practice. (Mastery means they have mastered all aspects of phonemic awareness except for manipulating phonemes, which they will continue to practice indirectly in 2nd and 3rd Grade through symbol imagery.)

3. Teach it in the Skills Practice segment in both main lesson blocks and practice blocks.

4. Practice it daily for 10–15 minutes or longer. (Increase the practice time as you finish off theory of word and syllables practice.)

5. Once students have mastered phonemic awareness, segue into increased symbol imagery practice.

## 5.  Initial Introduction

There are three different aspects of phonological awareness to introduce: word, syllable, and phoneme. Remember to introduce all three during the <u>first</u> language arts block.

### Sentences into Words

Introduce theory of word in the first block as part of a memory reading activity (see chapter 3.15 #6 and #7).

Choose a simple sentence from a poem, verse, or song from class but do not choose an alliterative tongue twister where every word starts with the same letter. Have the students step, clap, or stomp this simple sentence. Next ask the students to do it again, but this time, count how many words there were. (One word = one step, clap, or stomp.) Then repeat the sentence slowly and distinctly, one word at a time, and write a line on the board for each word as you say it. Repeat the sentence slowly and point to each line. Finally, say each word and write it on its correct line.

Model read this sentence by using a pointer and pointing to each word as you go. Ask a student to come up and read the sentence, pointing to each word as she says it.

Finally, ask how they can find the word in the sentence. See if the students can figure out that they can repeat the sentence and point to each word, stopping at the targeted word. If not, demonstrate.

**Words into Syllables**

At the beginning of the phase, teach the students to count syllables three different ways: jaw drops, clapping, and finger counting. (Note: Initial introduction will be spread over many days.)

Jaw Drops: Have the students hold their hand under their chin, palm side down. Ask them to say the word *banana* slowly and count the number of times their jaw drops open and pushes their hand down. Practice counting lots of syllables in words this way. The students will see, hear, and feel the syllables in words.

Clapping: Next, show the students how to clap the syllables in their names. Demonstrate clapping the syllables of your name as you say it. For example, Jennifer: Je-ni-fer. (First names work better. *Ms. Militzer* is two words, but *Jennifer* is one.) Practice counting lots of syllables in names this way.

Any syllable break that is logical counts, even if it is not the dictionary break. Jen-i-fer or Je-ni-fer are equally good. A logical break is any break that sounds good and where a syllable contains only one vowel <u>sound</u>. (No Jenni-fer or Jen-iffer).

Say: "*There are three* (or whatever) *syllables, or beats, in my name.*" Then ask the students to do it with you this time. Repeat all of the steps as a class. Now practice with other names in the class.

Finger Counting: On a subsequent day after the class has mastered jaw drops and clapping syllables, demonstrate how to count syllables: tap one finger at a time against the palm of the other hand. Then hold up the number of fingers to show the number of syllables.

**Words into Phonemes**

Introduce phonemes when you introduce your first letter (see chapter 3.1 #7).

Note: The Waldorf maxim of starting from the whole and moving to the parts only applies to the <u>initial introduction</u> of reading (see chapter 2.1 #8). Whole to part does not apply to phonemic awareness practice. Segmenting practice is whole to parts (for example, the word *cat* can be broken down into its three sounds: /k/ /ă/ /t/). Blending practice is parts to whole (for example, the sounds /k/ /ă/ /t/ can be put together to make the word *cat*). The two types of practices mutually support each other. It is best to practice them together.

## 6. How to Teach Phonological and Phonemic Awareness in the Emergent Phase

**Objective:** Teach the three types of phonological awareness. Students are expected to develop theory of word and phonemic awareness for the first sound in a word.

**Prerequisites:** NA

**When to Teach:** Teach phonological and phonemic awareness daily in the Skills Practice segment of both main lesson and practice blocks.

**How to Teach**

Use materialization techniques to teach all three types of phonological awareness and include all three every day. The development of one aspect of phonological awareness will help the development of other areas. For example, phonemic awareness helps develop theory of word. Students use phonemic awareness for the first sound in a word coupled with letter knowledge to help distinguish where a word begins.

## Sentences into Words

The main materialization techniques are stepping, clapping, and stomping words in a sentence. In kindergarten, students should have had opportunities to step, clap, or stomp each word in a sentence. Start with a review of this skill (or teach it if it was not taught). It is also good for students to step, clap, or stomp <u>after</u> each word in a sentence. It is harder to do and brings more awareness of each word.

As the students start to gain proficiency, consider allowing them to take on more and more of the process. For example, a student could write the lines on the board while saying each word, and the other students could give a thumbs up/thumbs down to show if they agree. Just make sure that the students who already have proficiency in this area do not take over. This is a great time to differentiate instruction (see chapter 2.4 #3).

## Words into Syllables

The main materialization techniques are stepping, clapping, and stomping syllables in a word. In kindergarten, students may or may not have had the opportunity to step, clap, or stomp syllables. Start with a review of this skill (or teach it if it was not taught). **Do not differentiate instruction.** In the Syllable Phase, you will teach more about syllables. You will be grateful for the time you spent practicing syllables informally back in 1st Grade.

Once you have introduced syllables, practice clapping and counting syllables back to back. When the students have mastered clapping, drop it in favor of counting syllables. Move on to practicing any and all words. Pull select words from stories you tell or class experiences. It is easy to weave this practice in 10 seconds here, 20 seconds there. Have students count syllables while you are waiting for a special subject teacher to arrive or when you have an extra minute or two before snack or recess.

You can even demonstrate advanced techniques for counting on fingers once words go beyond five syllables. (6 = 5 +1, so to count six syllables on only one hand, you count five on thumb and fingers and then start over with the same thumb. 7 = 5 + 2. So to count seven on one hand, you count five on thumb and fingers and then start over with thumb and then index finger, etc.)

Note: Do not shy away from using technical vocabulary with students. They are sponges and will pick up your vocabulary effortlessly from context. They are here to learn. When teaching syllables, use the word *syllable*. When teaching homophones, use the word *homophone*. Children love new words, the more impressive sounding the better. Just be careful with the word *rime*. As a homophone, it can easily be confused with *rhyme*. This is one instance where a descriptive label might work better! Use your best judgment.

## Words into Phonemes

Students will get their first introduction to phonemes when you teach the first letter and its sound (see chapter 3.1 #7).

For Activity A and B, consider various materialization techniques, such as stretchable fabric and hand spelling. (Note: In the Emergent Phase, only use words where the onset is a single phoneme. Do not pick words with blends. For example, choose the word *dogs,* not *frogs*).

Students will need lots of practice after the initial introduction of phonemic awareness. This practice can include any letters the students have learned, but it will mostly use phonemes as the students are still learning the alphabet.

*Practice:* In the Emergent Phase, limit your materialization techniques to the first three:

- shouting out rhyming words
- hand spelling
- stretching out the sounds in words with stretchable fabric

In addition, play lots of games with rhymes:

- Which words rhyme? Give a list of three words and have the students identify which two rhyme (e.g., cat, horse, mat). Can you think of other words that rhyme with cat and mat? (rat, sat, fat, etc.)
- "What words rhyme with pig?" (big, twig, wig, dig, etc.)
- Big Pig: a game where you give the students clues for a pair of rhyming words. For example, "*These words refer to a large swine*" (big pig).

Also, have the students generate words:

- Beginning Sounds: "*How many words can you make that start with the /t/ sound?*" (tiger, terrible, town, etc.)
- Getting to Know You: This game uses alliteration. Everyone has to say one thing they like that shares the same initial sound in their name. For example, "*Hi, I'm Jenny, and I like jaguars.*" (Just make sure that the concept of sound is clear before beginning.) Do lots of materialization techniques such as hand spelling to help target the initial sounds in names first. If the student makes a mistake, do ***error handling*** as shown in table 3.3.3. Error handling is a process from Lindamood-Bell where the teacher responds to the error to help the student learn from it. It is a powerful teaching tool. It takes the sting out of being wrong and makes mistakes into beneficial teaching moments.

## Table 3.3.3: Process for Error Handling (modeled off of Jenny's mistake in Kindergarten)

1. **Student Error:** "Hi, I am Jenny, and I like cats."
2. Say something positive about the response. For example, "Cats are great, aren't they?"
3. Draw attention to the mistake.

   "But let's see what the first sound in the word cat is: /k/ /at/ (do hand spelling at the same time with the whole class). The first sound is /k/! Is that the same sound we hear in /j/ /enny/?" ("No.")
4. Help the student fix the mistake.

   "Jenny, what words can you think of that start with the sound /j/ like Jenny?" ("Jacks, jellybeans, juice, and jaguars.") "Which one do you like best?" ("Jaguars!")
5. You can also appeal to the class for help in generating an answer.

Use choice/contrast options if students need further help. "Which word starts with the /j/ sound: jam or potato?"

THE ROADMAP TO LITERACY

Practice in the Emergent Phase is to help students develop phonemic awareness for the first sound in words. You can use the script found in table 3.3.3 to help guide you.

## 7. How to Teach Phonological and Phonemic Awareness in the Phonemic Awareness Phase

**Objective:** Students achieve full phonemic awareness (i.e., all six aspects of phonemic awareness are to be mastered except for manipulating phonemes).

**Prerequisites:**

1. Students have developed phonemic awareness for the first sound in a word (as seen in their encoding practice).

2. Students realize they are off when they are pointing to an incorrect word when they Memory Read.

**When to Teach:** Teach daily during the Skills Practice segment of main lesson and practice classes.

**How to Teach:** Continue teaching phonological and phonemic awareness with the following added elements to help the students consolidate the skills they are working on and move on to the next set.

Sentences into Words

When students are pointing to the wrong word when they do memory reading, teach them to self-correct without having to start reading the passage from the beginning. Instead, they just need to use their knowledge of the alphabet coupled with their phonemic awareness for first sounds in words to find the right word in the current sentence they are reading.

Give the students opportunities to practice **elision** with words as well. Look for examples of compound words such as *butterfly* in your stories and poems. Then ask the students to take away the word *butter* in *butterfly* and see which word is left (*fly*). Introduce these exercises as a game. Compound words are an excellent source for material (see chapter 4.1 rule 7).

Words into Syllables

Continue to practice counting and clapping syllables.

Introducing elision with syllables: Drop one syllable from a two-syllable name. For example, what happens when we say *Jenny* without the /ee/? (Jen) A cautionary note: Make sure you vet the words at home. For example, the name *Peter* without the syllable *-ter* says *pee*.

Words into Phonemes

Continue to practice the same three phonemic awareness materialization techniques as in the Emergent Phase but add in these new ones:

1. Finger spelling

2. Sound and letter boxes (Elkonin boxes)

3. Word sorting

See chapter 3.3 #2 for a full description.

In the beginning of the Phonemic Awareness Phase, emphasize exercises such as these:

- Ending Sounds: "How many words can you say that end with the /t/ sound?" (cat, hat, mat, shut, etc.)
- Count Sounds: "How many sounds can you hear in the word pit?" (Say each sound to confirm.)
- Common Sounds: "What sound do all of these words have in common: snake, sun, slip?"
- Blending Sounds: "What word is made of these sounds: /h/ and /ŭ/ and /g/?

While the students are learning the letters of the alphabet, you can do some phonemic awareness exercises with sounds rather than letters. Here are some suggestions:

- Play with elision: Remove a sound from a spoken word to create a different word. For example, "Say Hannah's name without the /h/ sound. (Answer: Anna.)
- Create new rhyming words: "What word rhymes with *sat* but starts with the /v/ sound?" "The /k/ sound?" "The /m/ sound?
- Substitute sounds: "What happens when you change the /t/ in *Tom* to the /m/ sound?"

In the middle of the Phonemic Awareness Phase, start practicing symbol imagery exercises such as mystery word and syllable cards (see chapter 3.5 #3).

Throughout the Phonemic Awareness Phase, do lots of kid writing. Show the students how to expand from one or two words to a sentence and beyond. It is one of the best ways to practice phonemic awareness (see chapter 3.13).

**Figure 3.3.1: Final Draft of a Kid Writing Assignment (middle Phonemic Awareness Phase)**

Note: This student needs handwriting instruction for letters *t, l, f,* and *r*.

Practice phonemic awareness with the class <u>every</u> <u>day</u>. Keep in mind that by the end of the Phonemic Awareness Phase, students must develop full phonemic awareness (i.e., when encoding, they represent each sound in a word with a logical letter choice, which demonstrates they have mastered segmenting sounds). It is a necessary prerequisite for all of the phonics work in the Pattern Phase. The only aspect of phonemic awareness students will continue to practice in the Pattern Phase and Syllable Phase is manipulating. The other five aspects (i.e., phoneme matching, onset and rime, blending phonemes, sequencing phonemes, and segmenting phonemes) should be mastered by the end of the Phonemic Awareness Phase.

## 8.    How to Teach Phonological and Phonemic Awareness in the Pattern Phase

**Objective:** Teach students to expand their ability to manipulate phonemes for single-syllable words through symbol imagery.

**Prerequisite:** NA

**Background Information:** In the Pattern Phase, you will no longer teach phonological and phonemic awareness per se, but merely apply one aspect of phonemic awareness (manipulation) to increasingly more difficult words through exercises designed to develop symbol imagery such as syllable cards and mystery word (see chapter 3.5 #3).

**When to Teach:** Teach daily during the Skills Practice segment of both main lesson and practice blocks.

**How to Teach:** Do exercises involving manipulation with both syllable cards and mystery word (see chapter 3.5 #3).

## 9.    How to Teach Phonological and Phonemic Awareness in the Syllable Phase

**Objectives:** Reteach syllables, specifically syllable counting. Teach students to identify accented syllables.

**Prerequisite:** NA

**Background Information:** Students must learn to read and spell by syllables in the Syllable Phase. Therefore, it will be necessary to resume practicing syllables and teach accented syllables.

**When to Teach:** Teach daily during the Skills Practice segment of both main lesson and practice blocks.

**How to Teach:**

Re-introduction of Syllables

At the beginning of the phase, have the students re-explore syllables. Have them clap and tap syllables and count them as they did in 1st Grade. Then revisit jaw drops.

Have the students hold their hand under their jaws, palm side down. Ask them to say the word *banana* slowly and count the number of times their jaw drops open and touches their hands.

Ask the class why their jaw drops open for each syllable. Let them explore why it might be so and nudge them to the correct answer: each time a vowel sound sings, the jaw drops open. Tell the class that syllables are nothing more than the beats in a word created by the vowel sounds and whichever consonants they carry.

If you count the number of vowel <u>sounds</u> (not letters) in a written word, you automatically know how many syllables it has. If you count the number of beats (or chin drops) in a word, you automatically know how many syllables it has. Once the students have the process, teach them to decode and encode multisyllabic words (see chapter 3.4 #9).

Introduction of Accented Syllables

Introduce accented syllables just before you teach the schwa (see chapter 4.3 rule 31). Stand in front of the class and talk like a robot, giving each syllable in every word the same weight. When you speak this way, you will sound something like the Daleks in the television show *Dr. Who*.

For example, you could use your students' names. By saying "*Hello, Johnathan,*" or "*Hello, Francisco,*" without accenting any syllables you will sound very strange. Then say the same greeting in a normal voice, giving each word its proper accented syllable. Ask the class to figure out what was wrong with the first way you spoke and guide them to the correct answer: our voice rises and falls in words; not every syllable gets the same punch. The syllable where our voice rises is called the **accented syllable**.

It is possible to find the accented syllable by calling your pet. Just stand at the back door and call out in a loud voice: MOL-ly. Your voice will rise up and hold the accented syllable.

Practice calling pet names, but only use pets that have more than one syllable in their name. Be theatrical. Stand, cup your mouth, and really belt out the accented syllable and sustain it: FIIII-do, TIIII-ger, Sa-MAAN-tha, etc.

Then put the names up on the board and show how to write the accent mark over the syllable to show that it gets the accent.

Practice flexing the accent in various words by deliberately putting the accent on the wrong syllable. For example, SYL/la/ ble (right); syl /LA/ble (wrong) ; syl/la/ BLE (wrong).

## 10.  Practice

Practice is critical. Make sure you include practice activities in your initial introduction during the Introduction &/or Review segment of main lesson using Activities A and B. It will also be part of your ongoing practice in the Skills Practice segment of main lesson (see chapter 2.3 #4). Finally, it can be used during classroom games in your practice classes.

**Activities A and B:** See materialization techniques (chapter 3.3 #2) and advice on what to teach by phase (Sections 3.3 #6–9).

**Skills Practice:** The following are activities to include in Skills Practice after the initial introduction:

- materialization techniques (see chapter 3.3 #2)
- symbol imagery exercises (see chapter 3.5 #3)
- kid writing starting in the Phonemic Awareness Phase (see chapter 3.13)

Each is covered in depth in the noted chapter. These are your most important practice activities. Schedule them accordingly in the Skills Practice segment of main lesson during the Phonemic Awareness Phase.

**Fun and Games:** In addition, there are some fun practice activities that you can use to spice up your Skills Practice. Use them sparingly. Your main practice should be materialization techniques, but these games and songs are a delightful way to practice when you need a change of pace.

1. Sing the song "Down by the Bay." This song incorporates lots of silly rhymes that always show up in the same formula in the song. This song can be used in several ways: first, to work on identifying rhymes. ("*Who can find the word that rhymes with "fly"*? Or "*Which two words rhyme?*") Then students can be challenged to create their own rhymes (e.g., "*Did you ever see an ape wearing a cape ?*") Finally, it makes a great piece for pretend reading. You can choose the length (one stanza or the entire song).

2. Sing "The Name Game." This is an R&B hit from the 1960s that plays with rhymes. It is very catchy and fun to sing. Decide whether you will use the students' names or just random ones. Be sure to test all names before singing to avoid embarrassing rhymes that arise (for example with the name *Bart*). This is a good song to do once the children know some letters (especially *B*, *F*, and *M*) and need some practice with onsets and rimes.

3. Mystery Basket: After introducing three or four consonants, bring out a basket with a lid or silk over the top. Show your students one item for each of the letters they have learned (e.g., a nut for the letter *N*, a book for the letter *B*, etc.). After they have identified the object and the sound and letter associated with the item, place it into the basket. Each day bring out the basket and ask the students:

   - Which object in my basket begins with the sound /b/? Which one begins with the sound /l/, etc. (Add a new item for each letter you introduce.)

   - You can make the activity a bit more challenging by asking which item(s) ends with a sound such as /t/ (nut).

4. "I spy": Have students look around the room or outside and find objects that begin or end with a sound such as /p/ (e.g., pinecone, pebble, pot, pod, cap, and lamp).

5. Pick a letter you have introduced and ask the class to figure out whose name starts with that letter. (Do not allow a student to give her own name.) When the students are ready for a challenge, ask students to figure out whose name has the letter in the middle or at the end. Note: If you have a name display in the classroom, cover it up first so students have to use phonemic awareness.

6. First and Last: The first person says a word. The second person has to say a word beginning with its last sound, and so on (for example, task, kitten, nest). Note: Accept words that start with the letter *C* or *K* for the sound /k/. (This game is especially good for the beginning of the Phonemic Awareness Phase).

7. Mystery Tray: Get a tray and place 10–12 items on it that begin with the same sound (bell, ball, bark, etc.). Cover the items with a silk. Gather the students around you and tell them that when you remove the silk, they are to look at the items on the tray (in silence) for ten seconds. After the ten seconds, cover the tray and ask the students what sound all or most of the items begin with, then have them recall the various items. To increase the challenge, place a variety of items on the tray and ask, "Which item begins with the /n/ sound? Which one begins with /t/," etc.

8. Bring in a painting or drawing and have students identify those items in the picture that begin with a particular sound such as /g/ or /f/.

9. Practice long and short vowels through movement. The students curl up like a rock for words with a short *O* sound (pop, got, plod) and stretch up on tiptoes for the words with short *A* sound (sad, that, pal).

10. Heads Down Sound Game: Ask the class to close their eyes and put their heads on their desks. If you say a word that begins with a certain letter such as the letter *T*, raise their hand. Be sure to include words that begin with letters that have a similar sound (e.g., include some words that begin with *D* when asking students to identify words that begin with the letter *T*). Here are some other pairs that are similar: *K/G*; *F/V*; *M/N*; *L/R*; *H/W*, *P/B*, *Sh/Ch*, etc.). Variations of this game can be played with rhyming words and with words that end with or contain a letter as well.

11. Matching Game: Create bags or boxes of small items that start with two or more sounds along with six or more different letter cards. Distribute one set to each student or to pairs of students. Ask the students to lay the letter cards face up on the desk. Put each object on the letter that symbolizes the sound the item starts with (e.g., a bean on the *Bb* card). (If you make up one bag per student, each with different letters/items, you will be able to do an informal assessment to determine whether a particular student has grasped those sounds/letters.)

12. Advanced Matching Game: Include some cards and/or items that do not have a match. The students have to find out how many do not have a match. You could also switch so that the letters match the ending sound of the item.

## 11. Assessment

Assessment is a critical part of teaching. It is important to verify that students have mastered the skills they have been taught. See chapter 6.1 for background on assessment.

**Benchmarks** represent <u>minimum</u> levels of student achievement by the end of each grade for students to be on track to handle grade-level work in 4th Grade (see chapter 6.1 #9). Table 3.3.4 contains the benchmarks for phonological and phonemic awareness.

Note: The following benchmarks may not be exhaustive. Prerequisite skills for phonological and phonemic awareness may be covered under other related language arts skills. For a full list of benchmarks, see table 6.1.4.

**Table 3.3.4: Benchmarks for Phonological and Phonemic Awareness**

| | 1st Grade | 2nd Grade | 3rd Grade |
|---|---|---|---|
| **Phonological and Phonemic Awareness: Segmentation** | Students have mastered the following segmentation skills:<br>• sentences into words<br>• words into syllables<br>• single-syllable words into phonemes | NA<br>(Segmentation should have been mastered in 1st Grade. Assess to confirm.) | NA |
| **Phonemic Awareness: Deletion (Note: Deletion is a type of Manipulation.)** | Students have mastered the following deletion skills:<br>• initial sound<br>• end sound | Students have mastered the following deletion skills:<br>• initial sound<br>• end sound<br>• blends—initial sound | Students have mastered the following deletion skills:<br>• initial sound<br>• end sound<br>• blends—initial sound<br>• blends—embedded sound |

There are three types of assessments. Recommendations for each type of assessment can be found in Sections 6.3, 6.4, and 6.5. You can use the following ideas as a starting point to set up an assessment program.

**Informal Assessments:**

1. Kid writing for theory of word and phonemic awareness (see chapter 3.13)

2. Memory reading for theory of word (see chapter 3.15)

3. Encoding for phonemic awareness (see chapter 3.4)

4. Materialization Techniques (All six types of phonemic awareness can be practiced with real or nonsense words, but nonsense words are great in the Phonemic Awareness Phase for confirming that students have mastered a skill.) (See chapter 3.3 #2.)

**Teacher-Made Assessment:** Once a week, give a teacher-generated quiz on encoding. Use the results to tailor your instruction in the upcoming week. For example, if students have mastered encoding the first sound in a word, switch from hand spelling to finger spelling and work on encoding the first and last sounds in a word.

**Assessments Created by Educational Testing Groups:** If you choose to do this type of assessment, consider doing it three times a year. Use an assessment of the alphabet designed by an educational testing group such as DIBELS or AIMSweb (see chapter 6.1 #6). Otherwise use *CORE Phonics Survey: Alphabet Skills and Letter Sounds* found in Diamond's book *Assessing Reading Multiple Measures for Kindergarten through Twelfth Grade, 2nd Edition.* CORE (Consortium on Reading Excellence, Inc.) Novato: Arena Press, 2008 (see chapter 6.3 #3).

See chapters 6.3, 6.4, and 6.5 for more information about assessing in each grade.

## 12. How to Differentiate Instruction

It will often be necessary to differentiate instruction in order to meet the phonological and phonemic awareness needs of students in different phases.

The easiest way to differentiate instruction is to put students into groups by phase and make questions for each group. That way the entire class can participate in an exercise together and everyone will get her needs met. For example, if you are working with rhymes, you could hand spell the word *dog* together as a class. Then you could ask follow-up questions at different levels. *"Group one, who can tell me if these two words rhyme: dog and frog?"* *"Group two, who can tell me another word that rhymes with dog?"* *"Group three, what happens if I take away the letter D in dog and replace it with an F?"* (fog) Do not allow the more advanced students to answer the easier questions.

Sometimes you will want the students to do entirely different tasks. Give the advanced students a separate task to do such as writing out an entire line (or verse) on their own from memory using invented spelling for the words they do not know (see chapter 3.13 Kid Writing). You can use this time to do more work with the beginners.

If advanced students need a real challenge, you can set them the task of writing tongue twisters. When you find a spare minute during the day, you could invite them to come up and share their tongue twister(s) (once you have approved it.) This activity is a good one to do while waiting for a special subject teacher who is a minute or two late.

Finally, you can ask advanced students to get a book and read. Use this method sparingly in 1st Grade. It is better to give them their own task to accomplish and to hold them accountable for doing it.

## 13. How to Help Struggling Students

**Assess:** When you see a student is struggling with phonological and phonemic awareness, do assessments (both formal and informal) to narrow down the area(s) of concern. Document your findings and place in student's file. (see section 6).

**Additional Instruction/Practice:** Next, use the results of your assessments to provide this student with extra instruction and practice in any weak areas. You can differentiate instruction both in class and in reading groups. For example, you can modify your classroom instruction for each reading group or give an individual assignment to provide extra practice in a weak area. Decide which approach is best based on how many other students have similar struggles. (You can divide the class into groups before you begin formal reading groups if a subset of the class needs extra instruction or practice in one or more aspects of phonemic awareness. Just modify your main lesson schedule.) Document what you try and the results.

The rules of thumb for helping struggling students are as follows:

1. Use lots of speech exercises with proper articulation for warm ups.

2. Go back down to an easier aspect of phonemic or phonological awareness and build back up to the area the student struggles with.

3. Do lots of materialization techniques.

**Remedial Solutions:** If you do not notice improvements in a month, it is time to contact your mentor for guidance and consult chapter 6.6 for additional information on remedial issues. Make sure your remedial approach includes recommendations for a vision screening and/or a hearing screening if you see signs of difficulty as well as a reading program that deals with dyslexia.

**Accommodations and Modifications:** There are no good accommodation or modifications to offer this student. Any changes you make would undermine the development of phonological and phonemic awareness. Just keep providing extra practice at the student's level and make sure you get remedial support.

Do not wait for a student to outgrow difficulties with phonemic awareness. Its full development is not a natural part of child development. Always remember that students who struggle with phonemic awareness need more practice not more time. In addition, those who are dyslexic need special kinds of practice—and a lot of it, the younger the better. The brain is more plastic when a child is young (see chapter 1.2 #6). If you think you have a dyslexic student, refer the student to a specialist in 1st Grade. Talk to the kindergarten teachers about alerting faculty when a student struggles with rhyming games in kindergarten. It is worth considering early intervention in special cases (see chapter 6.6 #6).

## Conclusion

In this chapter you saw that phonological awareness has three components. The final component, phonemic awareness, is most critical for literacy. Its full development is not a natural part of child development but develops with education. If teachers know the signposts to look for as they are working with their class in the Emergent and Phonemic Awareness Phases, they will be able to adjust their curriculum to successfully support their students' progress (see table 3.3.1 and chapter 6.2). If a student struggles to learn phonemic awareness, it is a symptom of dyslexia and requires immediate remediation (see chapter 6.6 #9). Students who develop phonemic awareness will be able to learn phonics rules and go on to master encoding and decoding in English.

# 3.4 ENCODING AND DECODING

*The mastery of reading lies, above all, in our ability to decode new words.*

—Dehaene, *Reading in the Brain* (226)

*'Twas brillig, and the slithy toves*
*Did gyre and gimble in the wabe:*
*All mimsy were the borogoves,*
*And the mome raths outgrabe.*

*"Beware the Jabberwock, my son!*
*The jaws that bite, the claws that catch!*
*Beware the Jubjub bird, and shun*
*The frumious Bandersnatch!"*

—Lewis Carroll, "The Jabberwocky"

If you enjoyed this bit of lyrical nonsense, thank your teacher(s) for teaching you to decode. Decoding, or sounding out words, is the go-to strategy for figuring out unfamiliar words or nonsense words, such as the ones found in "The Jabberwocky." Encoding is the counterpoint of decoding. It means to spell a word by writing down, or encoding, the word's sounds. Initially encoding and decoding are limited to the 26 letters of the alphabet, but as students learn phonics rules, they expand the number of words they can decode and encode to include just about any word in the English language—including the nonsense words.

This chapter covers the following topics:

1. Why Encoding and Decoding Matter
2. Background Information
3. Preparation
4. Scheduling
5. Initial Introduction
6. How to Teach Encoding in the Emergent Phase
7. How to Teach Encoding and Decoding in the Phonemic Awareness Phase
8. How to Teach Decoding and Encoding in the Pattern Phase
9. How to Teach Decoding and Encoding in the Syllable Phase

Note: Much of this information will be covered in section 4 because phonics rules expand the number of words students can decode and encode.

# 1. Why Encoding and Decoding Matter

Mastery of encoding and decoding (and the concomitant phonics rules that go with them) opens up to students the entire world of literacy.

## The Shortcut to Mastering Reading and Spelling

Encoding and decoding are processes for reading and spelling.

Decoding enables students to read any unfamiliar word by translating a printed word into a spoken word. All they have to do is break the word down into manageable pieces. For example, say students were unfamiliar with the word *circumlocution*. If they know how to decode, they can figure it out easily by using specific rules to break the word down into syllables: cir/ cum/ lo/ cu/ tion. Each syllable has only a few letters and is much easier to read than the whole word.

Encoding allows students to spell just about any word by translating a spoken word into a written word. Can you visualize all 28 letters in the word *antidisestablishmentarianism?* Most people cannot. However, it is relatively easy to encode the word one syllable at a time: an/ ti/ dis/ es/ tab/ lish/ men/ tar/ i/ an/ ism.

Once students master encoding and decoding with phonics rules, they can read and spell just about anything.

## Clinical Proof of Decoding's Value

Dr. Bruce McCandliss, while a professor at the Sackler Institute in New York, proved the value of decoding (and helped determine when it is useful for students to learn words as whole entities) in a most ingenuous experiment.

McCandliss created a new alphabet. The letters of this alphabet formed words that looked more like pictures than words. He then presented two groups with an identical list of 30 words written in this unusual alphabet. The list contained both the words written in his new pictorial alphabet along with the English spelling of the word below. The first group was told to memorize each word as a picture (i.e., pictogram) and was not told that each word was really made up of letters. The second group was told that the words were made up of a new alphabet of letters.

The question was: which group would be able to learn the picture words better? Each day the two groups received an identical list of 30 words/pictures to memorize and had the same amount of time for practice.

After the first day, the first group performed better than the second group. They memorized the most words by memorizing words as pictures. However, on the second day, they began to lose ground. They forgot old pictures as they learned new ones. The words on the new lists supplanted the words they had learned on the old lists.

Meanwhile the second group was busily looking for the letters in the words. At first they were bad at it and did worse than the first group, but every day they got better. More strikingly, they did not forget their old lists—instead, their performance improved on all lists of words, both old and new. Soon they were starting to guess what the new words said (without looking at the English translation) on their own because they were looking at the words as a code and not as pictograms.

McCandliss's research demonstrates many things. First, when it comes to learning to read, it is much more efficient to learn to decode than it is to memorize individual words (Dehaene 2009, 226–227). Second, when people are <u>first</u> learning to read, it is initially easier to memorize words as pictures.

The ramifications of McCandliss's research are built into *The Roadmap to Literacy's* recommendations for both decoding and sight words. By assigning the right approach to the right phase, students have an easier time learning to read.

**Encoding's Secret**

How can you teach students to bridge the gap between recognizing words as pictures and decoding?

In the Emergent Phase and first half of the Phonemic Awareness Phase, encoding is the key to learning to decode. It can build the *letter to sound decoding route*. It works because encoding and decoding are mirror-image processes. Decoding is sounding out letters for reading while encoding is sounding out words for spelling. In decoding, students are given the letters and they must provide the sounds and blend them into a word. For example, the letters *DOG* have the sounds /d/ /ŏ/ /g/. When you blend the sounds together, they make the word *dog*. In encoding, students know the word they wish to write down and must segment it into its phonemes, or sounds, and write the appropriate letter(s) for each one. For example, the word *dog* has three sounds: /d/ /ŏ/ /g/. Match the letter to each sound to write down the word *DOG*. Note how the process for encoding and decoding is identical—just reversed.

It is much easier for beginning students to encode than decode. First, it is much easier for beginners to start from the whole rather than the part. Encoding starts with the whole (the word) and goes to the part (its individual phonemes) while decoding starts with the part (the phonemes) and goes to the whole (the word). Second, encoding is very forgiving of mistakes while decoding is a stickler for correctness. U kan red mi sentins, kant U? (i.e., You can read my sentence, can't you?) Even though every word is misspelled, the errors do not stand in the way of meaning.

However, watch how intolerant decoding is. See what happens when there is just one error in the following versions of the sentence: *The bad bug lived in the house.*

1. The <u>bed</u> bug lived in the house.
2. The bad <u>lug</u> lived in the house.
3. The bad bug lived in the <u>horse</u>.

Each sentence contains only one error; furthermore, each error is only off by one letter. However, the error completely compromises the meaning of the sentence in most cases. Instead of an imaginative story about a rascally bug, readers are left with emergency scenarios such as a bedbug infestation, a horrid houseguest who has taken up residency, and vet bills for an equine virus.

It is so much easier to create the initial neural pathways for the *letter to sound decoding route* through encoding than decoding. That is why *The Roadmap to Literacy* recommends teaching encoding first.

**To Review**

As you saw in chapter 1.4, alphabetic languages are nothing more than giant codes where a letter represents a sound. In contrast to pictogram languages such as Chinese where people have to memorize thousands of words, in alphabetic languages people only have to learn the alphabet and develop phonemic awareness to have the tools they need to *de-code* (i.e., sound out written words) and *en-code* (i.e., write down the sounds in spoken words) all of the words in a language.

Many languages have simple codes that just include the alphabetic layer, but as seen in chapter 1.3, English's code is quite complex because it has three layers (i.e., alphabet, pattern, and meaning). These layers create the need for phonics instruction because knowledge of the alphabet alone is not enough.

In addition, students' brains change as they learn to read (see chapter 1.2). First students must create the *letter to sound decoding route*. As they use this route, their brains create the faster, more automatic *lexical route*. But before the students can even start this process, they must learn baseline levels of phonemic awareness as well as the letters of the alphabet. For most students these achievements require formal education.

Teaching encoding and decoding in English is a balancing act between the demands of the language and a student's brain development. This brain development is the same for everyone. It is sequential and is represented by the phases (see chapter 1.5). (This statement is also true of dyslexics, although it is much more difficult for them due to differences in the organization of their brains.) (See chapter 6.6 #9.)

**Putting It All Together**

Dehaene is right: the mastery of reading lies, above all, in the ability to decode new words; however, that does not mean that students should start with decoding. Precisely the opposite is true.

Students are not ready for decoding until they are in the middle of the Phonemic Awareness Phase. First, they have to be taught the alphabet as well as phonemic awareness skills necessary to blend three sounds together (e.g., "The sounds /h/ /a/ /t/ make what word?").

Encoding instruction helps beginning students build the neural connections necessary for the *letter to sound decoding route* in a much more user-friendly way than decoding practice and phonics instruction. Therefore, in the Emergent Phase and the first half of the Phonemic Awareness Phase, students should only encode. Once they have developed the necessary neural connections, learning to decode and learning phonics rules is relatively easy for them. This fact forms the basis for the recommendation that beginning students do lots of kid writing (see chapter 3.13).

Be sure to match the instruction to the student's phase. There are consequences to bringing reading instruction out of order. Some students diagnosed with dyslexia are not truly dyslexic but merely undereducated. They did not get the instruction they needed to create the neural networks necessary for reading. When given explicit instruction in phonemic awareness and follow-up training in phonics, they quickly and effortlessly learn to read. Note: Contrast their ease in learning with the true dyslexic, a student who struggles through the entire process because her brain is not organized in a way to support the development of the *letter to sound decoding route* (see chapter 6.6 #9).

Finally, learning to read is greater than the sum of its parts. Instruction in phonemic awareness and the alphabet are critical to the success of encoding and decoding with phonics rules. There are, however, other language arts skills that are just as important, such as speech and grammar.

No matter how important encoding and decoding are, it is not optimal to teach them or any other language arts skill in isolation. While this chapter will focus exclusively on encoding and decoding to give you the information you need to plan an effective curriculum, always bring encoding and decoding as part of a larger language arts curriculum. The whole is truly greater than the sum of its parts.

## 2. Background Information

Teachers typically have a lot of questions about encoding and decoding. The information below will attempt to answer some of the more frequently-asked questions:

1. What is the encoding and decoding process?
2. Why do these three encoding and decoding processes work?
3. How do phonics rules relate to decoding?
4. Why does *The Roadmap to Literacy* wait to teach decoding skills until the middle of Phonemic Awareness Phase?
5. Won't encoding and decoding be out of sync?
6. How can you teach decoding through encoding?
7. What about nonsense words?
8. How long do I need to teach a phonics rule?

**What is the encoding and decoding process?**

There are actually three separate processes for encoding and decoding:

1. Encoding and decoding phonemes
2. Encoding and decoding onsets/rimes
3. Encoding and decoding syllables

These three processes align with the phases. Phoneme encoding and decoding is for the Phonemic Awareness Phase and is typically done in 1st Grade. Onset/rime is for the Pattern Phase and is typically done in 2nd Grade. Syllable is for the Syllable Phase and is typically done in 3rd Grade.

As students progress through the phases, they can decode larger and larger chunks of a word. In the Phonemic Awareness Phase, students sound out a single-syllable word one sound at a time. For example, *plan:* /p/ /l/ /ă/ /n/. In the Pattern Phase, students sound out a single-syllable word using onsets and rimes. For example, *plan* pl/+/an/. In the Syllable Phase, students sound out a multisyllabic word using syllables. For example, *plantation:* /plan/ /tā/ /shun/.

1. For more information about the process for encoding and decoding phonemes, see chapter 3.4 #7 and chapter 4.1 rule 1.
2. For more information about the process for encoding and decoding onset/rime, see chapter 3.4 #8 and chapter 4.2 rule 9.
3. For more information about encoding and decoding the process for syllables, see chapter 3.4 #9 and chapter 4.3 rule 22.

**Why do these three encoding and decoding processes work?**

The three processes work because vowels are necessary to carry the consonant sounds (see chapter 3.1 #2). As a result, every syllable has <u>one</u> vowel sound. Given that every word is at least one syllable long, people can use the vowels to figure out the syllables.

When a word has only one syllable, it can be decoded/encoded either by phonemes or onset/rime. Finding the vowel can be useful for both processes. The one complication is that the vowel sound can be spelled with more than one letter. Let's look at some one-syllable words (We have used all caps to make it easier to identify the letters that make the vowel sound.):

> CAT: 1 vowel sound represented by 1 letter
>
> KITE: 1 vowel sound represented by 2 letters
>
> TAIL: 1 vowel sound represented by 2 letters
>
> EIGHT: 1 vowel sound represented by 4 letters

**How do phonics rules relate to decoding?**

Phonics rules expand the number of words students can decode and encode. Teaching them allows students to have access to all of the ways sounds (phonemes) can be spelled.

Recall that English does not have one letter for every sound and one sound for every letter. As a result, digraphs (or consonant teams or vowel teams) are used to represent one sound. For example the long *E* sound can be spelled *EA* (bead), *EE* (reed), using a Silent *E* (cede), open syllable (be), *EI* when following the letter *C* (conceit), *EI* (field), and *EY* (key). Phonics rules teach these letter combinations.

**Why does *The Roadmap to Literacy* wait to teach decoding skills until the middle of Phonemic Awareness Phase?**

There are many reasons to wait. First, learning to decode is impossible for students in the Emergent Phase because they lack the necessary prerequisites for decoding: the awareness that letters represent sounds. In addition, they lack one or both of the following:

1. Full sound/symbol knowledge (e.g., the letter *A* is /ă/ like apple, the letter *B* is /b/ like bear, etc.)

2. Phonemic awareness (e.g., apple starts with the sound /ă/ and/or blending skills such as /ă/ /p/ /l/ is *apple*)

Through classroom instruction and practice in the above skills, students make the necessary connections in their brain to realize how the code works.

Second, students at the beginning of the Phonemic Awareness Phase struggle with decoding for many reasons. While they recognize that reading is a code, they are still learning the letters of the alphabet and phonemic awareness. Furthermore, decoding goes from the part (the sound), to the word, to the whole sentence; consequently, students have to wait until the end to get to the meaning. To further complicate things, a mistake can derail comprehension (see chapter 3.15 #14). As a result, decoding is very frustrating for these students.

Third, there is a better way to wire the brain: encoding. Encoding starts with the whole (i.e., the sentence or word the student wants to write) and moves to the parts (i.e., the words in the sentence or phonemes in the word) so it is grounded in meaning. It allows students to take the time necessary to isolate a phoneme and then find a letter match. Lastly, making mistakes in encoding does not derail comprehension. In most cases, the students can still read their misspelled words and with practice, so can you.

Since encoding uses the same neural pathways as decoding, it is much easier to build the *letter to sound decoding route* through encoding instruction than decoding instruction. That is why it is more effective to begin with encoding.

### Won't encoding and decoding skills be out of sync?

Yes, encoding and decoding skills will be out of sync; however, this situation does not occur because you wait to teach decoding. There is a natural variation in the timing of the <u>mastery</u> of these processes:

1. Emergent Phase: NA. Students can neither encode nor decode. Students are working on the prerequisite skills for encoding and decoding.

2. Phonemic Awareness Phase: Students usually encode better than they decode until the end of this phase, when decoding catches up.

3. Pattern and Syllable Phases: Students usually decode better than they encode.

This variation holds true even if the students are taught to decode early, as is done in most public schools.

### How do you go about teaching decoding through encoding?

From the beginning of the 1st Grade year, do exercises to stimulate the development of phonemic awareness as you teach the alphabet (see chapter 3.3). Once your students enter the Phonemic Awareness Phase, include daily practice in encoding (spelling first or most prominent sound in a word). Then when your students understand the process of encoding, begin kid writing (see chapter 3.13). Combining these practices will build the *letter to sound decoding route,* thus laying a good foundation for phonics rules.

### What about nonsense words?

Nonsense words (such as *sug* or *bim*) are useful and should be part of the encoding and decoding curriculum.

1. Nonsense words help prepare students to decode children's literature, which is filled with made-up language from Dr. Seuss to Harry Potter.

2. They help teachers assess students' encoding and decoding skills. Some students may already know how to read or spell commonly used words such as *hat, dog,* and *men*; none will be familiar with nonsense words such as *het, dag,* or *mon.*

3. They are a way for early readers to practice encoding and decoding. Many young students who are good readers have strong visual memories. They memorize many common words and use contextual clues to fill in the rest. If they do not go on to learn to decode, they hit a wall, typically around the end of 3rd Grade/beginning of 4th Grade when the words get more difficult and require decoding to sound out. Nonsense words help these students learn to decode and encode because they cannot just rely on their visual memory.

Some teachers worry that using nonsense words during encoding and decoding practice will compromise a student's ability to read by cluttering up their *word identification hub* with fake words. This concern is baseless. When it comes to decoding, the brain initially handles new words through the *letter to sound decoding route.*

The word only reaches the *word identification hub* if the student sounds it out over and over again (see chapter 1.2. #3 and #4).

Nonsense words are a powerful teaching tool. Include them in your encoding and decoding practice and assessment. The only rules are these:

1) Do not misspell a real word and use it as a nonsense word (e.g., *faik* for *fake).*

2) The words have to obey the rules of English. For example, you cannot use the letters *SR* as a blend (for example, *sreft*) because English does not have such a blend.

**How long do I need to teach a Phonics Rule?**

It is good to practice phonics rules until the majority of the class shows mastery the majority of the time. As a rule of thumb, follow the **80/80 Rule**: Begin to teach a new phonics rule when 80% of the class can successfully <u>decode</u> using the current rule 80% of the time. As you teach the new phonics rule, continue to practice both the old rule and the new rule for a time. Stop practicing the old rule once the class has mastered <u>decoding</u> it. (If a few students need to continue to practice the old rule, review it during their reading group.)

Note: The mastery of encoding with phonics rules comes later. The spelling curriculum will provide a chance to reteach the phonics rules and for students to continue to practice them.

## 3.  Preparation

Over the summer, make lists of words that you can use for all of the phonics rules you plan to teach in the upcoming year. Follow these steps:

1.  Make a separate page for each phonics rule and label each page clearly. (See chapter 4.1 for phonics rules for the Phonemic Awareness Phase, 4.2 for the Pattern Phase, and 4.3 for the Syllable Phase.)

2.  Generate words for each rule. Write down as many words as you can think of and then use the **Rhyming Rime Machine** to generate more (see chapter 3.15 #3). As you read over the summer, keep an eye out for words for each phonics rule and write them down on their appropriate list.

For example, say you want to prepare a list of words for the Silent *E* Rule (see chapter 4.1 rule 6). Your list could include: *lane, pine, rune, lone, poke, trike, cake, lake, like, spike, spine, swine, slake, grate, twine, wine, wane, wake, woke, spoke,* etc.

You could use the Rhyming Rime Machine for the word *lane* and generate the following words that share its rime *–ane*: bane, cane, Jane, lane, mane, pane, sane, wane, Zane.

3.  File these lists away for use when you make your lesson plans. You will use these words to introduce the various phonics rules and then practice encoding and decoding with them as well as practice symbol imagery exercises (see chapter 3.5 #3).

## 4.  Scheduling

When preparing your curriculum, you can use the block plan templates in Appendices 1–3 or you can create your own. If you create your own, use the following points to lay out your blocks:

**Encoding**

1.  Begin Instruction at the beginning of 1st Grade.

2.  It will take students until the end of 6th Grade to master <u>encoding</u> with all phonics rules. However, encoding instruction will end at the end of 3rd Grade after you finish teaching the last phonics rule. The spelling curriculum provides extra practice with spelling with phonics rules during Grades 4–6.

3.  Teach in the Introduction &/or Review segment and Skills Practice segment in both main lesson blocks and practice blocks.

4.  Teach daily. Schedule 10–15 minutes for the initial introduction of a new phonics rule and 5–7 minutes for daily practice.

**Decoding**

1. Begin Instruction during practice block three in 1st Grade.

2. It will take students three years to master <u>decoding</u> with all phonics rules.

3. Teach in the Introduction &/or Review segment and Skills Practice segment for both main lesson blocks and practice blocks.

4. Teach daily. Schedule 10–15 minutes for the initial introduction of a new phonics rule and 5–7 minutes for daily practice.

5. Once students have mastered decoding, segue into additional reading practice to improve fluency and comprehension.

## 5.  Initial Introduction

The initial introduction covers encoding because in *The Roadmap to Literacy,* students are taught to encode before they are taught to decode. The initial introduction covers encoding the first phoneme in a word.

**Prerequisites:**

1. The students know a few consonant letters.

2. Students can print the letters they know.

3. The students are familiar with isolating the first consonant sound in a word through hand spelling.

Note: Students do not yet need to realize that letters represent sounds; the encoding process will teach them that.

**Background Information:** Students learn to encode in the Emergent Phase and beginning of the Phonemic Awareness Phase to spur the development of phonemic awareness and to create the neural networks in their brains for decoding. They will learn to decode once they progress to the middle of the Phonemic Awareness Phase. Once they master encoding the first phoneme in a word, they are ready to learn to Kid Write.

**When to Teach:** Introduce encoding during the first main lesson block.

**How to Teach:** There are two lessons to present: familiar letters and unfamiliar letters.

<u>Sample Lesson 1 (Familiar Letters)</u>: Choose a simple CVC word from one of your stories that begins with a letter you have already introduced such as *B.* Then use the following script as a model:

Teacher: Let's hand spell the word bet.

Students: Bet, /b/ /et/, bet. (*Be sure the students answer with onset and rime. Watch your articulation and theirs.*)

Teacher: Which letter has the sound /b/? Johnny?

Johnny: T!

Teacher: T... Hmm.../t/ /ē/... Does the sound /t/ sound like /b/?"

Students: *NO!*

Teacher: Then T cannot be the right letter. Let's try another one. Suzy?

Suzy: *P!*

Teacher: *P. . .* Hmm. /p/ /ē/. Listen carefully. Are these sounds the same: /p/ /b/? *(Really overemphasize the difference as these two sounds are almost the same.)*

Students: NO!

Teacher: Then *P* cannot be the right letter. Which letter has the sound /b/ as in bet? Let me give you two choices: Is it the letter *B* (/b//ē/. /) or the letter *F* (/ĕ/ f/)? *(Note: This is an example of choice/contrast.)*

Students: *B!*

Teacher: *B. . .* Hmm. . . ./b/ /ē/. Does that sound like the first sound in the word bet?

Students: "YES!"

Teacher: I'm going to write that letter on the board. *B* for bet. That's the first letter in the word bet. That's the first letter adults write down when they want to spell the word bet. Let's do another word and see if we can figure out its first letter.

Sample Lesson 2: Unfamiliar Letters: Choose a simple CVC word from one of your stories that begins with a letter you have not yet introduced but that has its phoneme embedded in its name such as the letter *V* (see table 3.1.1). Then use the following script as a model:

Teacher: You are all getting so good at figuring out how to spell the first sound in a word. Do you know that there is a way that you can figure out letters I have not taught you yet? Here, I'll show you: Let's hand spell the word *van*.

Students: Van, /v/ /an/, van.

Teacher: Listen to the sound /v/. It sounds like one of the letters of the alphabet. Let's see if you can figure out which letter it sounds like. We will sing "The *ABC* Song." Listen carefully for the letter that has the /v/ sound.

Students and Teacher: *A B C D E F G*, etc.

Teacher: Which letter sounds like the sound /v/?

Entertain all answers. If students need a hint, direct them to the row that has the letter (i.e. *T U V*) and hand spell each consonant letter name to listen for the sound /v/. *(Note: Avoid using example words that begin with vowels.)*

Model this introduction daily until the students have the idea of how to figure out the first letter in a word. Then let the students try some on the board. Once they have the idea, have them do encoding on their slates or on pieces of paper. Correct all of the initial letters by modeling them as you did during the introduction.

## 6. How to Teach Encoding in the Emergent Phase

**Objective:** Teach students in the Emergent Phase to encode the first phoneme in a word.

**Prerequisites:** See chapter 3.4 #5.

**When to Teach:** Teach daily during the Skills Practice segment of both main lesson and practice classes.

**How to Teach Encoding:** Use the encoding process found in table 3.4.1 for both initial introduction and practice.

**Table 3.4.1: Process for Encoding the First Phoneme: Emergent Phase Only**

| Process for Encoding the First Phoneme | Example |
|---|---|
| 1. Say the word. | 1. "bun" |
| 2. Hand spell the word to isolate the first sound. | 2. "/b/…. /un/" (Note: This separates the onset and rime.) |
| 3. Identify the first sound. | 3. "/b/" |
| 4. Write the letter for the first sound. | 4. B ( Students can use the uppercase or lowercase letter.) |

Initially, students in this phase will not be able to find a matching letter. They are still developing phonemic awareness for the first sound in a word and are still learning the alphabet. Be very patient and very enthusiastic in trying all of their guesses. They will start joining in with you and discarding letters that do not work. If they need help, offer a **choice/contrast**, or two choices—one right letter and one wrong letter. Let them figure out which one would work.

When you are practicing, let the students in the Emergent Phase have several attempts to find the right letter. Make sure those students who are already in the Phonemic Awareness Phase or higher do not step in and offer it. (If necessary, differentiate instruction. Give advanced students a different task to do such as finding the last letter or the vowel.) This exercise will help the students in the Emergent Phase develop the neural network necessary to progress to the Phonemic Awareness Phase. As the students struggle to find the right letter, their brains are beginning to develop the *letter to sound decoding route* that they will eventually use to sound out new words. It is hard work. Give the students the time and space in which to do it.

**How to Teach Decoding:** NA. Students learn to decode in the middle of the Pattern Phase.

**Curriculum Connection:** Once roughly 80% of the class has mastered the encoding process for the first sound of a word, the class is now ready to move to the Phonemic Awareness Phase. Start kid writing (see chapter 3.13).

## 7. How to Teach Encoding and Decoding in the Phonemic Awareness Phase

**Objectives:**

1. Teach students in the Phonemic Awareness Phase to encode all of the sounds in a word (Note: They will not necessarily use the right letters, and that is fine.)

2. Teach students in the middle of the Phonemic Awareness Phase to decode. This introduction is the introduction to phonics rules. (The introduction to decoding is covered below and in chapter 4.1 rule 1.)

3. At the middle and end of the phase, teach the phonics rules for the Phonemic Awareness Phase (see chapter 4.1).

**Prerequisites:**

- Encoding: Students can encode the first (or most prominent sound) in a word. (Note: Students do not yet need to have the phonemic awareness skill of segmenting all of the sounds in a word. Encoding practice (coupled with finger spelling) will teach them that.)

- Decoding: At a minimum, most students (80%) should be in the intermediate Phonemic Awareness Phase or higher (see chapter 6.2). Make sure the students have the following prerequisites:

a.  Students can encode using vowel letters (the letter choice does not need to be correct).

b.  Students know all of the letters of the alphabet and are automatic at identifying both the letters and their sound. (This is the letter *B*. Its sound is /b/.)

c.  Students can blend phonemes together into a word (/d/…./ŏ/……/g/ is dog.). (See chapter 3.3 #2 Blending Phonemes.)

**When to Teach:** Teach encoding daily during the Skills Practice segment of both main lesson and practice classes. However, once the students begin phonics rules, teach during the Introduction &/or Review segment and the Skills Practice segment of main lesson and practice classes.

- Encoding: Start when most of the class can encode the first sound in a word on their own (as determined by their encoding practice). This point will vary by class. Plan to start by the end of November of 1st Grade at the latest. Plan to teach the Phonemic Awareness Phase by the end of 1st Grade. (Note: It is fine if you do not finish all of the phonics rules listed in 4.1 Phonics Rules for the Phonemic Awareness Phase. Teach the rules you do not finish at the beginning of 2nd Grade.)

- Decoding: Begin to teach decoding at the end of the third main lesson block (Vowels) or the beginning of the third language arts practice block. The majority of the class should be in the intermediate Phonemic Awareness Phase.

**How to Teach Encoding**

Continue to teach encoding as in the Emergent Phase, but change the process slightly.

There are two different processes to use for encoding as shown in tables 3.4.2 and 3.4.3. Use the one that matches the phase the majority of the class is currently in. Table 3.4.2 is for the beginning of the phase and table 3.4.3 is for the middle and end of the phase.

**Table 3.4.2: Process for Encoding by Phoneme: Beginning Phonemic Awareness Phase**

| Process for Encoding by Phoneme | Example |
|---|---|
| 1.  Say the word. | 1. "bun" |
| 2.  Finger spell the word to isolate each phoneme. | 2. "/b/ /ŭ/ /n/" |
| 3.  Say the phonemes again while writing a line for each letter. | 3. "/b/ /ŭ/ /n/" __ __ __ |
| 4.  Attempt to write a letter for each phoneme on its line. | 4. <u>b</u> ? <u>n</u> |
| | Encourage students to use lowercase letters. |

Until the students learn the vowel letters, accept made-up spellings. Let the students skip sounds they do not know.

**Table 3.4.3: Process for Encoding by Phoneme: Intermediate and Advanced Phonemic Awareness Phase**

| Process for Encoding by Phoneme | Example |
|---|---|
| 1. Say the word. | 1. "bun" |
| 2. Say each phoneme slowly and distinctly. | 2. "/b/ /ŭ/ /n/" |
| 3. Write the letter for each sound. | 3. bun (Encourage students to use lowercase letters.) |

Use the process in table 3.4.3 starting in third language arts practice block after you have taught the vowel letters in the third main lesson block (Vowels). Students will use this process to encode all phonics rules in the Phonemic Awareness Phase (see chapter 4.1).

Note: Always teach one step beyond what your students can do by themselves. If they can handle simple blends, model and practice complex blends together as a class and then have the students practice complex blends (see table 3.3.1: Signposts for the Development of Phonemic Awareness).

### How to Teach Decoding

Use the process found in table 3.4.4.

**Table 3.4.4: Process for Decoding by Phoneme**

| Process for Decoding by Phoneme | Example |
|---|---|
| 1. Underline the vowel letter or letters. | 1. b<u>a</u>g* |
| 2. Say the vowel sound. | 2. "/ă/" |
| 3. Say each sound from beginning to end. | 3. "/b/ /ă/ /g/" |
| 4. Blend the sounds together to form a word. | 4. "bag" (*Write the word in lowercase letters.) |

Note: This table is identical to table 4.1.1. (See chapter 4.1 rule 1 for more information on how to teach this process.)

Students will use this process for decoding the phonics rules for the Phonemic Awareness Phase. (See chapter 4.1 for more information on how to teach this rule.)

### How to Practice Encoding

Practice encoding every day during the Skills Practice segment of the lesson. There are two ways to practice.

<u>Encoding Practice: Words</u>

1. Preparation: Get out the lists of words you created over the summer for the various phonics rules. Use them to compile a list of words at your students' **instructional level**, or the zone where the student needs the support of the teacher to be able to apply a new skill and where the most learning occurs. Make sure you include both real and nonsense words on this list. (Start with more real words in the beginning and include more nonsense words as students approach mastery.) The list of words comes in three levels:

    a. Easy: **chains,** lists of words where one letter changes at a time (e.g., bet, bit, big, gig, gag, hag, hug)

    b. Medium: one shared consonant (e.g., bet, lab, bun, bog, rib)

    c. Hard: no shared letters (e.g., sob, tad, rig, vet)

2. Process: During the lesson read a word off your list. Have the students spell a word on their slates or on paper using the encoding process, then correct the words together.

3. Number: 3–10 words

4. Time: 5–7 minutes

Encoding Practice: Dictation: Start sentence dictation at the end of 1st Grade (see chapter 3.9 #8).

**How to Practice Decoding**

Practice decoding every day during the Skills Practice segment of the lesson. There are two ways to practice.

Decoding Practice: Words

1. Preparation: Same as encoding.

2. Process: Write a word on the board and call on a student to decode it using the decoding process in table 3.4.4. (If necessary, help the student or call on another student to help.)

3. Number: 5–10 words

4. Time: 5–7 minutes

Decoding Practice: Reading Passages with Simple Decodable-Text

1. Preparation: Put a short passage on the board that features the targeted phonics rule(s) the class is working on. For example, if you are working with digraphs such as consonant teams, you could use the following sentence: *The conch shell sat on the shelf.*

2. Process:

   a. Ask a student to point out sight words: *the, on.*

   b. Ask the class to find all of the consonant teams and underline them: *th, ch, sh, th, sh.*

   c. Call on a student to decode the first word that has a consonant team using the process in table 3.4.4.

   d. Repeat step three for the remaining words with consonant teams.

   e. Call on a student to read the entire sentence.

   f. Have the class read the entire sentence together (i.e., choral reading).

Note: It may be necessary to differentiate instruction for decoding so that students in higher phases do not undermine the lesson.

## 8.  How to Teach Decoding and Encoding in the Pattern Phase

**Objectives:**

1. Teach students in the Pattern Phase to use phonics rules to decode and encode vowel and consonant teams (i.e., digraphs) (see chapter 4.2).

2. Teach students to decode and encode using onsets and rimes.

**Prerequisites:**

- Encoding: Students use a letter to represent every sound in a word (Note: Their letter choice does not need to be correct, just logical.)

- Decoding: Students have mastered decoding by phonemes (see table 3.4.4).

- Phonemic Awareness: Students have full phonemic awareness (i.e., they have mastered all aspects of phonemic awareness except for manipulating phonemes).

Note: Teach word families only after students have developed full phonemic awareness. Never use this approach as a substitute for developing phonemic awareness. Students must be able to clearly decode each separate sound in CVC words and blends before moving to word families. If this initial step is not completed, students will drop sounds when they encode by syllables in the Syllable Phase. For example, *dependent* spelled as *de-pe-dent*.

## Background Information

There are two things to know before discussing how to teach decoding and encoding in this phase.

Reintroduction of Onsets and Rimes: Recall that a rime is the part of a single-syllable word that goes from the vowel to the end (e.g., *-at* in *cat*). The onset is any consonant(s) that comes before the rime (e.g., the letter *c* in *cat)*. Rather than sounding out each phoneme in a word (e.g., /k/ /ă/ /t/, cat), students can use the onset and rime to speed the process up (e.g., /k/ /at/, cat). Once they know the rime *–at*, they can quickly decode many words: *cat, hat, fat, sat, pat, rat, that*, etc. There are many common rimes as shown in table 3.4.5. These rimes are used in hundreds of words.

**Table 3.4.5: Rime Chart**

| A | E | I | O | U |
|---|---|---|---|---|
| –ad | –ed | –id | –od | –ug |
| –ag | –et | –ig | –og | –uck |
| –an | –en | –ill | –ot | –ut |
| –ap | | –in | –op | –un |
| –at | | –ip | | –ub |
| | | –it | | –up |

Word Families: Word families are chains of words that have the same rime (see table 1.5.1). They are the transition step from encoding and decoding with phonemes to encoding and decoding with onsets and rimes. Introduce the concept of word families at the beginning of the Pattern Phase. Use Table 3.4.5 to generate word families.

**When to Teach:** Teach daily during the Introduction &/or Review segment and the Skills Practice segment of main lesson and practice classes. If you started working with *The Roadmap to Literacy* in 1st Grade, plan to teach the entire Pattern Phase in 2nd Grade. Teach decoding and encoding skills together for each phonics rule.

## How to Teach Decoding

Continue to teach decoding skills, but change the process slightly. Teach the process for decoding by onset/rime as shown in table 3.4.6.

**Table 3.4.6: Process for Decoding by Onset/Rime**

| Process for Decoding by Onset/Rime | Example |
|---|---|
| 1.  Underline the rime. | 1.  Cl<u>ean</u> |
| 2.  Say the rime. | 2.  "/een/" |
| 3.  Say the onset + rime. | 3.  "/kl/ /een/" |
| 4.  Blend the onset and rime together. | 4.  "clean" |

Note: This table is similar to table 4.2.1. (See chapter 4.2 rule 9 for more information on how to teach this process.)

From here on out, teach using both decoding processes (i.e., phoneme and onset/rime). When you first teach a new phonics rule, practice the rule during the Introduction &/or Review segment using the process for decoding by phonemes (see table 3.4.4). Once students know the rule, begin practicing it in the Skills Practice segment using the process for decoding by onset/rime (see table 3.4.6). Using both processes will help the students master the rule. Students will use these processes with all phonics rules for the Pattern Phase (see chapter 4.2).

**How to Teach Encoding**

Continue to teach encoding, but modify the process so students encode by onset and rime rather than phoneme. See table 3.4.7.

**Table 3.4.7: Process for Encoding by Onset/Rime**

| Process for Encoding by Onset/Rime | Example |
|---|---|
| 1.  Say the word. | 1.  "clean" |
| 2.  Say the onset and spell it. | 2.  "/cl/" cl |
| 3.  Say the rime and spell it. | 3.  "/ean/" ean |
| 4.  Does it look right? | 4.  clean—"Yes, it looks right."* |

Note: This table is similar to table 4.2.1. (See chapter 4.2 rule 9 for more information on how to teach this process.)

Note: When students are encoding, there is no way to verify whether they are encoding by onset and rime or by phoneme except by watching a student's process while encoding. This scenario is not practical in a classroom of students but can be done if you are homeschooling.

**How to Practice Decoding**

Practice decoding every day during the Skills Practice segment of the lesson. There are two ways to practice.

<u>Decoding Practice: Words</u>

- Preparation: Make a list of words at your students' instructional level (i.e., neither too hard nor too easy). Use words from the list you compiled over the summer for each phonics rule. Make sure you include both real and nonsense words on this list. (Start with more real words in the beginning and include more nonsense words as students approach mastery.) For example,

- Easy: chains with rime (i.e., word families): trap, slap, zap, sap, lap, strap, etc.
- Hard: no shared rimes: strap, trum, slup, crat, twig, etc.
- Process: Write a word on the board and call on a student to decode it using the process for decoding by onset/rime (see table 3.4.6). If necessary, help the student or call on another student to help.
- Number: 5–10 words
- Time: Daily for 5–7 minutes

Decoding Practice: Passages

1. Preparation: Choose or compose a short passage that is unfamiliar to the students that features the targeted phonics rule(s) the class is working on. Write it on the board. For example "Oh no!" written by Jennifer Militzer-Kopperl for contrasting the two sounds for the letters *OW*: long *O* and /ow/:

April showers bring May flowers.

Rain makes the flowers grow.

When it rains a lot, the water will rise.

Water will flow over your toes.

If it goes too high, it will cover your nose!

Do not be slow.

Go to higher ground.

You will be safe and sound!

2. Process:

   a. Go through and identify the vowel teams (underline); determine which sound the *OW* is making.

   b. Call on students to locate various words in the passage.

   c. Call on a student to read each sentence.

   d. Have students read the passage together (i.e., choral reading).

Note: Do informal syllable breaking in this phase when you put passages up on the board. Model how to break words down into syllables; however, wait to teach formal syllable breaking until the Syllable Phase (see chapter 3.15 #8).

Curriculum Connection: You can use speech and song lyrics as part of your reading instruction (see chapter 3.15 #8).

**How to Practice Encoding**

Practice encoding every day during the Skills Practice segment of the lesson. There are two ways to practice.

Encoding Practice: Words

- Preparation: Same as decoding.
- Process: Have the students spell a word on their slates or on paper using the encoding process (either by phoneme or onset/rime). Then correct together.
- Number: 5–10 words
- Time: Daily for 5–7 minutes

Encoding Practice: Dictation of Sentences: (see chapter 3.9 #8)

## 9. How to Teach Decoding and Encoding in the Syllable Phase

**Objective:** Teach students in the Syllable Phase to use phonics rules to decode and encode by syllable (see chapter 4.3).

**Prerequisites:**

1. Students can decode and encode by onset and rime.

2. Students have mastered <u>decoding</u> phonics rules for the Pattern Phase. (Note: They will continue to practice encoding with these rules as part of the spelling curriculum in 3rd Grade.) (See chapter 3.9)

3. Students have developed symbol imagery for a minimum of seven letters. (Note: If students cannot visualize letters, waive this prerequisite. They can still learn the phonics rules, but it will be harder for them. Schedule extra phonics practice.)

**Background Information:** There are two common types of syllables that often carry meaning. They are referred to as **affixes**. Prefixes are common syllables that appear at the beginning of a word. For example, the prefix *re*-means to do something again. For example review means to view again. Suffixes are common syllables that appear at the end of a word. For example, the suffix "*-est*" refers to superlatives, such as *biggest*. Affixes are taught as a unit. They contain a dash before or after the letters to show they have to be added to something and cannot stand alone.

**When to Teach:** Teach daily during the Introduction &/or Review segment or the Skills Practice segment of main lesson and practice classes. If you have been following *The Roadmap to Literacy* program since 1st Grade, plan to teach the phonics rules for the Syllable Phase in 3rd Grade (see chapter 4.3). If you have started later, teach these rules when your class is ready for them.

Teach decoding and encoding at the same time, but mastery is expected at different times. Students are expected to master decoding with these phonics rules by the end of 3rd Grade, but they are not expected to master encoding with all of them until the end of 6rh Grade. (The spelling curriculum will provide them with additional instruction and practice so they can master these rules for encoding.) (See chapter 3.9.)

**How to Teach Decoding**

Start by teaching the process for decoding by syllable as shown in table 3.4.8.

**Table 3.4.8 Process for Decoding Multisyllabic Words**

| Process for Decoding Multisyllabic Words | Example |
|---|---|
| 1. Underline vowel sounds.<br>2. Break off prefixes and suffixes.<br>3. Try to start every syllable with a consonant. Make each vowel grab the letter before it if it is a consonant.<br>4. Read each syllable separately and then blend together. (When a syllable ends in a vowel (open syllable), try reading the vowel as long and short to see which one is right.) | 1. R e u n i f y<br>2. Re / u n i f y<br>3. Re / u / n i / f y<br><br>4. Re…YOU…nEYE….fy, re…. YOU… ni…fy: reunify" |

Note: This table is identical to table 4.3.2. (See chapter 4.3 rule 22 for more information on how to teach this process.)

You will use this process to teach decoding for all phonics rules that pertain to syllables. See chapter 4.3 for the phonics rules for the Syllable Phase.

**How to Teach Encoding**

Use Table 3.4.9 for the process for encoding by syllables.

**Table 3.4.9: Process for Encoding Multisyllabic Words**

| Process for Encoding Multisyllabic Words | Example |
|---|---|
| 1. Say the word out loud.<br>2. Say each syllable slowly and write a line as you say it.<br>3. Write down any prefixes or suffixes first.<br>4. Say the remaining syllables and write them down at the same time.<br>5. Put the word together and see if it looks right. | 1. "Comprehend"<br>2. "Com. . . pre*. . . hend"<br>3. Com<br>4. Com    pre    hend<br><br>5. Comprehend—"Looks right!"<br><br>* Open syllables can have long vowels (see chapter 4.3 rule 23). |

Note: This table is identical to table 4.3.3. (See chapter 4.3 rule 22 for more information on how to teach this process.)

You will use this process to teach encoding for all phonics rules that pertain to syllables. See chapter 4.3 for the phonics rules for the Syllable Phase.

**How to Practice Decoding**

Practice decoding every day during the Skills Practice segment of the lesson. There are two ways to practice.

Decoding Practice: Words

1. Preparation: Make a list of words at your students' instructional level (i.e., neither too hard nor too easy). Use words from the list you compiled over the summer for each phonics rule. Make sure you include both real and nonsense words on this list. (Start with more real words in the beginning and include more nonsense words as students approach mastery.) For example,

- Easy: chains with syllables (i.e., change one syllable at a time): motion, nation, native, nature, capture, caption, etc.
  - Hard: no shared syllables: moment, native, statement, etc.
2. Process: Write a word on the board and call on a student to decode it. If necessary, help the student or call on another student to help.
3. Number: 5–10 words
4. Time: 5–7 minutes

Decoding Practice: Passages

1. Preparation: Put a short but unfamiliar passage on the board that features the targeted phonics rule(s) the class is working on. Here is an example using the Big Four Prefixes: un-, dis-, re-, in- (see chapter 4.3 rule 24):

   Jason was afraid he would not remember what he needed to do so he made a list:

   1) Remember to disinfect the chicken coop.

   2) Inspect the classrooms.

   3) Unfurl the flag and place it on the flagpole.

2. Process:
   - Ask students to identify all of the prefixes and underline them.
   - Ask students to break each multisyllabic word into syllables. (Students use the process in table 3.4.8.)
   - Call on a student to read each sentence.
   - Have the class read the entire passage together (i.e., choral reading).

Curriculum Connection: You can use speech and song lyrics as part of your reading instruction (see chapter 3.15 #8).

**How to Practice Encoding**

Practice encoding every day during the Skills Practice segment of the lesson. There are two ways to practice.

Encoding Practice: Words

- Preparation: Same as decoding.
- Process: Have the students spell a word on their slates or on paper using the encoding process (see table 3.4.9). Then correct together.
- Number: 5–10 words
- Time: 5–7 minutes

Encoding Practice: Dictation: (see chapter 3.9 #8)

## 10. Practice

Practice is critical. It forms part of your initial introduction in the Introduction &/or Review segment of main lesson (i.e., Activities A and B). It will be part of your ongoing practice in the Skills Practice segment of main lesson and practice classes (see chapter 2.3 #4). Finally, it can be used during classroom games.

**Activities A and B:** NA. Continue to practice the decoding or encoding process that was just introduced.

**Skills Practice:** The following are activities to include in Skills Practice after the initial introduction of encoding and decoding:

- Encoding and decoding processes: Continue practicing—see above sections for instruction for each phase.

- Symbol imagery exercises: See chapter 3.5.

- Kid writing: See chapter 3.13.

- Dictations: See chapter 3.9 #8.

**Fun and Games:** In addition, there are some fun practice activities that you can use to spice up your Skills Practice. Use them sparingly.

The following activities do not practice encoding and decoding *per se,* but each one could be a good warm-up exercise to do prior to encoding and decoding.

- **Eagle Eye:** Use a memory reading passage that the students have in front of them or that is on the board. After memory reading the passage, ask the students to fly over the text as if they were eagles and spy a feature such as a word that begins with a featured sound such as the /b/ sound, a word that ends with the letter *T*, a word that has two *O*'s etc. Point to it with their finger. Ask a student to come up to the board, point out the word, and read it. Everyone else confirms they found the right word.

- **I Spy Phonics Rules** (late Phonemic Awareness Phase/Pattern Phase): Write a poem you have chosen on the board. Write the words that show the phonics element you wish to stress in a different color. Read the text. Ask the students what they notice about the text. Some may notice the highlighted words and be able to identify the similarities these words share. Note: You can also use this game to introduce a phonics rule.

- **Symbol Imagery with Memory Reading** (the Phonemic Awareness Phase only): Point to a word in a passage on the board, let the students look at it for one second per letter, then cover it and ask the students to write down or spell the word aloud. You could also do symbol imagery exercises with the word such as asking the students what the first letter was, the last, the vowel team, etc.

- **Eraser Gnome** (the Phonemic Awareness Phase only): The eraser gnome sometimes likes to come at night and erase a letter, a blend, a vowel combination and, at times, whole words in a familiar blackboard text. Have the students read the text without the missing element(s). Then ask for volunteers to write the missing letters or word(s) back in. Note: Erase a feature that you are targeting in class. For example, in the early Phonemic Awareness Phase, erase an entire sight word. Later in the phase, erase a consonant, vowel, blend, or one letter of a blend.

## 11. Assessment

Assessment is a critical part of teaching. It is important to verify that students have mastered the skills they have been taught. See chapter 6.1 for background on assessment.

**Benchmarks** represent <u>minimum</u> levels of student achievement by the end of each grade for students to be on track to handle grade-level work in 4th Grade (see chapter 6.1 #9). Table 3.4.10 contains the benchmarks for encoding and decoding.

Note: The following benchmarks may not be exhaustive. Prerequisite skills for encoding/decoding may be covered under other related language arts skills. For a full list of benchmarks, see table 6.1.4.

**Table 3.4.10: Benchmarks for Encoding and Decoding**

|  | 1st Grade | 2nd Grade | 3rd Grade |
|---|---|---|---|
| **Decoding** | Students demonstrate mastery decoding with the following phonics rules: <br>• CVC words<br>• Digraphs: *SH, CH, TH, WH, NG, OO*<br>• Simple blends | Students demonstrate mastery decoding with all phonics rules for single-syllable words. | Students demonstrate mastery decoding with all phonics rules. |
| **Encoding** | Students demonstrate mastery encoding with the following phonics rules:<br>• CVC words<br>• Digraphs: *SH, CH, TW, WH, NG, OO*<br>• Simple blends | Students demonstrate mastery encoding a <u>minimum</u> of the following phonics rules:<br>• Silent *E*<br>• Two Vowels Go Walking<br>• The Guardians<br>• Diphthongs | Students demonstrate mastery encoding:<br>• single-syllable words<br>• two-syllable words with common affixes |
| **Dictation** | NA—see encoding | Students can take dictation of simple sentences (i.e., subject/ predicate). Example: *The hare ran faster.* | Students can take dictation of sentences up to 7–10 words. Example: *In the forest the students found mushrooms and berries.* |

There are three types of assessments. Recommendations for each type of assessment can be found in Sections 6.3, 6.4, and 6.5. You can use the following ideas as a starting point to set up an assessment program.

**Informal Assessments:**

- Encoding: Give the students real and nonsense words that use the phonics rule(s) you are assessing.

- Dictations: Dictate sentences that contain words that use the phonics rule(s) you are assessing (see chapter 3.9 #8).

- Symbol imagery exercises (i.e., syllable cards and mystery word): Have the students do the exercises with their heads down on their desks. Ask them to give thumbs up or down to show whether they agree or disagree with the answer (see chapter 3.5 #3).

**Teacher-Made Assessment:** Once a week, give a teacher-generated encoding quiz that covers the phonics rule(s) you have been working on. Use the results to tailor your instruction in the upcoming week. For example, if 80% of the class shows mastery of one phonics rule, plan to introduce a new one the next week.

**Assessments Created by Educational Testing Groups:** If you choose to do this type of assessment, consider doing it three times a year. Use an assessment of encoding and one of decoding by an educational testing group such as DIBELS or AIMSweb (see chapter 6.1 #6). Otherwise use *CORE Phonics Survey* found in Diamond's book *Assessing Reading Multiple Measures for Kindergarten through Twelfth Grade, 2nd edition*. Also use an encoding assessment from *Words Their Way* such as *Primary Spelling Inventory* (see chapter 6.3 #3).

See chapters 6.3, 6.4, and 6.5 for more information about assessing in each grade.

## 12. How to Help Struggling Students

**Assess:** When you see a student is struggling with encoding or decoding with phonics rules, do assessments (both formal and informal) to narrow down the area(s) of concern. Document your findings and place in student's file. Success at encoding and decoding depends on the acquisition of the following four capacities and skills:

1. Phonemic awareness—particularly segmenting and blending (see chapter 3.3)
2. Alphabet knowledge—all letters (uppercase and lowercase) must be recognized automatically (see chapter 3.1)
3. Sound/Symbol knowledge—all sounds must be paired with letters and vice versa (see chapter 3.1)
4. Symbol imagery—particularly when students start to learn vowel team such as Silent *E* (see chapter 3.5)

Make sure all of these areas are strong. If students struggle, see section 6 for information on how to assess.

**Additional Instruction/Practice:** Next, use the results of your assessments to provide this student with extra instruction and practice in any weak areas. You can differentiate instruction both in class and in reading groups. For example, you can modify the instructions for each reading group, or give individual assignments to provide extra practice in a weak area. Decide which approach is best based on how many other students have similar struggles. Document what you try and the results.

If students struggle with a particular phonics rule, see the phonics rule in question in section 4.

**Remedial Solutions:** If you do not notice improvements in three or four weeks, it is time to contact your mentor for guidance and consult chapter 6.6 for additional information on remedial issues. Likely problems include weaknesses with the senses (e.g., vision or hearing problems), Irlen Syndrome, and/or problems with sensory-cognitive functions. For a full discussion, see chapter 6.6.

**Accommodations and Modifications:** There are no good accommodations or modifications to offer this student. Any changes you make would undermine the development of encoding and decoding. Just keep providing extra practice at the student's level and make sure you get remedial support.

## Conclusion

Decoding and encoding are important skills for students to master when working with an alphabetic language because the written language is a code. In English, decoding and encoding go hand in hand with phonics rules because phonics rules expand the number of sounds the 26 letters can represent so they can represent the 40+ sounds in the language.

It takes years for students to master the phonics rules for the English code, but by the end of 3rd Grade, students should have the tools they need to sound out, or decode, any word in the English language. Encoding proficiency takes longer. Students will go on to master encoding with phonics rules between Grades 4 and 6. Then they will expand their study of encoding to include Latin and Greek roots (i.e., the Latin/Greek Phase). Their success with learning phonics rules for encoding and decoding depends on symbol imagery, a topic that will be covered in the next section.

# 3.5 SYMBOL IMAGERY: THE KEY TO SIGHT WORDS

*Maria was a crackerjack speller. She could close her eyes and see the correct spelling for any word, no matter how long it was. This ability gave her a huge advantage when it came to learning spelling. She would read a list of spelling words and have it memorized for the test. She never missed one. Even better were her compositions. She used 25–cent words freely because she had full confidence in her ability to spell them correctly. Maria had a gift for spelling. It is one that more students could develop if they were taught differently.*

Symbol imagery is one of the three sensory-cognitive functions identified by Lindamood-Bell that students need to develop to become literate. The other two are phonemic awareness and concept imagery (see chapters 3.3 and 3.7).

In Waldorf education, *symbol imagery* often goes by the umbrella term **mental picturing**, a term that applies to both concept imagery and symbol imagery. This chapter uses the terms *symbol imagery* and *concept imagery* to avoid confusion.

**Figure 3.5.1: Symbol Imagery**

Close your eyes. Imagine the spelling of the word *cat*. If you can see the letters *CAT* or *cat*, you used symbol imagery as shown in figure 3.5.1.

This chapter covers the following topics:

1. Why Symbol Imagery Matters
2. Background Information
3. Symbol Imagery Exercises: Syllable Cards and Mystery Words
4. Preparation
5. Scheduling
6. Initial Introduction

## 1. Why Symbol Imagery Matters

Symbol imagery is important for two reasons: spelling and sight words.

Students need to be able to visualize a minimum of seven letters to be able to use symbol imagery to master spelling. This number is not arbitrary. Seven letters is the length of the longest single-syllable words, ex. *through* and *thought*. Students then learn to encode longer words syllable by syllable. There is no need to visualize the entire word.

The development of symbol imagery typically correlates with the development of phonemic awareness. This fact stands to reason: letters are symbols that represent phonemes. The development of symbol imagery supports the development of phonemic awareness and vice versa.

In *The Science of Spelling*, Gentry relates that 20% of the population has trouble with spelling (Gentry 2004, 22). He theorizes that the part of the brain that enables them to visualize the word is underactive or not functioning at all. These people either have no symbol imagery at all or weak symbol imagery. They may be able to see a few letters but not enough to handle single-syllable words.

A weakness in symbol imagery is not a problem in phonetic languages like Italian and German, but it is devastating in English. In phonetic languages, good phonemic awareness and knowledge of the alphabet are all that is needed for spelling because all words can then be encoded. Visualizing the spelling of a word is a perk, but it not necessary. In English, however, a weakness in symbol imagery is devastating for spelling. Is the correct spelling for *enough*: ENUFF, EANUF, EENUPH, etc.? Not being able to visualize a spelling in the mind's eye puts English spellers at a considerable disadvantage.

The second reason symbol imagery is important is it helps students learn sight words. Sight words are the short, highly irregular English words that come from Old English and that make up the majority of the words in print. They are taught as whole words since many of them cannot be decoded or encoded. Symbol imagery helps students read them and spell them correctly.

Fortunately, there are exercises to help develop symbol imagery. Most students can learn to visualize seven letters if they receive targeted instruction and practice, and some can learn to visualize extremely long words.

A small subset of students cannot visualize letters at all and will not be able to, even with instruction and practice. In subsequent subsections, you will find indications for how to help these students and instructions on how to teach symbol imagery to the rest.

## 2.    Background Information

There has been some confusion in the Waldorf movement about the roles of concept and symbol imagery exercises when it comes to improving students' spelling. Historically, the Waldorf movement has not differentiated between concept imagery and symbol imagery, referring to both as mental picturing. While both symbol imagery and concept imagery are forms of mental picturing, they are separate functions. Doing exercises to practice one does not improve the other.

An example of this confusion can be found in Else Gottgen's book *Waldorf Education in Practice*. In general, her chapter on spelling is very good. Gottgens correctly points out that both auditory discrimination (i.e., phonemic awareness) and visual memory (i.e., symbol imagery) are the underlying capacities for good spelling. However, her suggestion to have students recall 3D visual impressions such as the color of a classmate's shirt or how a student holds a pen in order to help them improve their spelling would not be effective. These exercises would improve concept imagery, but they would not improve symbol imagery, and by extension, spelling.

To help students develop the capacities to become good spellers you need to incorporate symbol imagery exercises into your daily curriculum.

## 3.    Symbol Imagery Exercises: Syllable Cards and Mystery Words

There are two primary symbol imagery exercises. They come from the Lindamood-Bell program *Seeing Stars®: Symbol Imagery for Phonological and Orthographic Processing in Reading and Spelling*. They are syllable cards and the mystery word game. (Note: The mystery word game is the Lindamood-Bell program's Syllable Board/Air Write®.)

The primary goal of symbol imagery exercises is to help students develop symbol imagery. The secondary goals are to practice encoding and decoding with phonics rules and to develop the aspect of phonemic awareness called *manipulating phonemes* (see chapter 3.3 #2). Manipulating phonemes is the only aspect of phonemic awareness you continue to teach after the Phonemic Awareness Phase.

Note: Plan to start both exercises in the middle of the Phonemic Awareness Phase when you introduce your first phonics rule (see chapter 4.1 rule 1).

### Syllable Cards

Syllable cards are cards that contain a word or syllable that can be decoded. The card can have a real word such as *hop* or a nonsense word such as *clusp*. Use these cards to teach the students to visualize letters and decode/encode. You can also use them to help the students practice manipulating phonemes.

Use the list of words you generated over the summer for each phonics rule to make your syllable cards. Write the word on a 5 x 7 index card in thick black Sharpie pen or write it on the board. For example,

# hop

**Table 3.5.1: The Process for Syllable Cards**

1. Show the card (or word on the board) to the class (one second per letter).

2. Take the card away or cover the word on the board.

3. Using their imaginary ink pens (i.e., their index finger), students write the word in lowercase letters on desk or in the air, saying the letter name as they write it.

4. Call on one student to say all of the letters back and then read the word; guide the student to the correct answer, if needed.

5. Make one change to the word involving manipulating phonemes (see chapter 3.3 #2). This change can be in decoding or encoding. For example, in decoding, you could: substitute a letter, delete a letter, add a letter, etc. and ask another student to read the new word. In encoding, you could ask the children how to change the spelling of one word to another (e.g., from hop to hip). Just limit your change to one phoneme.

6. Have another student spell the word backwards (e.g., P-O-H).

*Source: Adapted from Bell 2001, 77 Table: Lesson Summary: See and Image Syllables at the Simple Syllable Level.*

Hints:

- It is imperative that you do the exercises with lowercase printed letters. The goal is to have the students' symbol imagery match what they see in books.

- Build up to 10 words a day.

- This exercise will take 5–7 minutes.

- You do not need to do all six steps for each word. First, it is good to build up. Start with just a word. Then give a word and add a change. Then give a word, add a change, and spell it backward, etc. Second, adjust the exercise to the class. If it is challenging, do fewer words. If the students are energized, see how many changes they can make with one word.

- Include both nonsense and real words.

- Always align your syllable cards and mystery words with the phonics rule you are currently working on. 80% of the words should be with the current phonics rule. The remaining 20% are to review old phonics rules. The same formula applies to mystery word game.

**Mystery Word Game**

Mystery word game is played the same way as the syllable card game without the visual prompt of a syllable card. For the process, see table 3.5.2 It does not require any supplies.

**Table 3.5.2: Mystery Word**

| The Process for Mystery Word: Reading |
| --- |
| 1. Choose a word for a phonics rule the class is currently practicing and dictate one letter at a time (rate: one letter per second). |
| 2. Students write letters using their imaginary ink pens in air or on desk as you say them. |
| 3. Call on one student to spell the word out loud, letter by letter, and then say the word. |
| 4. Make one change and ask another student to say the new word. |

| The Process for Mystery Word: Spelling |
| --- |
| 1. Give the class a word to spell at the encoding level the class is currently practicing. |
| 2. Students write word using their imaginary ink pens in air or on desk. |
| 3. Call on one student to spell the word out loud. |

*Source: Adapted from Bell 2001, 129–130.*

Hints:

- Do 3–5 reading and 3–5 spelling words a day.
- This exercise will take 5–7 minutes.
- Lowercase letters are mandatory.

Manipulating Phonemes: you can work with phonemic awareness in the form of manipulation as part of a mystery word activity. You can manipulate phonemes in reading and in spelling. For example, say the word is *pig*. Ask the students to change the word to *prig*. (They have to add in the letter *R*.) Or ask the students to erase the letter *I* and write in a letter *U*. Now they have to read the new word (pug). You can add, delete, substitute, or transpose letters, thus working manipulating phonemes into your symbol imagery practice and further strengthening the connection between these two sensory-cognitive functions as well as motor planning (i.e., for air writing or desk writing). It is win-win-win.

Note: When manipulating phonemes during a symbol imagery activity, have the students erase a letter with their finger and write in a new letter <u>not</u> rewrite the whole word. This process or erasing a letter or adding a letter to a pre-existing word helps the students develop the ability to manipulate phonemes. The students must focus in on what is different and make the change with surgical precision.

## 4. Preparation

Over the summer, make lists of words that you can use for all of the phonics rules you plan to teach in the upcoming year. Follow these steps:

1. Make a separate page for each phonics rule and label each page clearly. (See chapter 4.1 for phonics rules for the Phonemic Awareness Phase, 4.2 for the Pattern Phase, and 4.3 for the Syllable Phase.)

2. Generate words for each rule. Write down as many words as you can think of and then use the Rhyming Rime Machine to generate more (see chapter 3.15 #3). As you read over the summer, keep an eye out for words for each phonics rule and write them down on their appropriate list.

For example, say you want to prepare a list of words for the Silent *E* Rule (see chapter 4.1 rule 6). Your list could include: *lane, pine, rune, lone, poke, trike, cake, lake, like, spike, spine, swine, slake, grate, twine, wine, wane, wake, woke, spoke,* etc.

You could use the Rhyming Rime Machine for the word *lane* and generate the following words that share its rime -*ane*: bane, cane, Jane, lane, mane, pane, sane, wane, Zane.

3. File these lists away for use when you make your lesson plans. You will use these words to get material for symbol imagery exercises as well as introduce the various phonics rules and practice encoding and decoding with them.

# 5. Scheduling

When preparing your curriculum, you can use the block plan templates in Appendices 1–3 or you can create your own. If you create your own, use the following points to lay out your blocks:

1. Begin instruction at the beginning of 1st Grade.

2. It will take the students two years to master visualizing seven letters. It will take them several additional years to master visualizing syllables within longer words.

3. Teach in the Skills Practice segment in both main lesson blocks and practice blocks.

4. Teach daily for 5–15 minutes per lesson.

# 6. Initial Introduction

The introduction of symbol imagery takes place over multiple lessons in the first language arts block in 1st Grade.

**Prerequisite:** Students have written their straight and curved line on the board (see chapter 5.2 #4).

**Background Information:** Teach students to visualize straight lines and curved lines and work up to visualizing letters so they can do exercises such as syllable cards or mystery word games.

Note: If you are reading this book for the first time and will be teaching 2nd or 3rd Grade, read the description for the Initial Introduction below but begin your symbol imagery class instruction with the CVC word exercises described in the middle Phonemic Awareness Phase instructions even if your students are beyond the Phonemic Awareness Phase. If these exercises are too difficult for your class, work your way backwards to one letter exercises or straight line/curved line.

**When to Teach:** Teach the second or third day of the first week of 1st Grade.

**Sample Lesson**

Tell the students that inside their index finger is hidden a magic ink pen (or chalk) that can write on their *inner blackboard.* You can write a line in the air (a *ghost line*), close your eyes, and then 'see' the line in your imagination.

Demonstrate how to write in the air:

1. Hold up your (dominant) index finger about 12 inches in front of your nose; your index finger should be pointed up to the sky.

2. Say, "I am going to watch my finger draw a line in the air."

3. Say "straight line" as you slowly and carefully draw a line in the air (top to bottom). (It should be about 9–12 inches long.) Follow your finger with your eyes as you draw the line.

4. Next ask the students to draw a straight line with you by using their magic ink pen. Tell them to watch their finger make the line. Do this together. *It is critical that students always watch their finger as they write.*

5. Tell the students that after you have drawn a line in the air you can close your eyes and see the line that you drew on your inner blackboard. Ask them to try it with you and see if they can see the line too.

6. Get everyone in the class to hold up their magic ink pens. Have them draw the line and say "straight line" at the same time watching their finger as it moves.

7. Then have the children immediately close their eyes and visualize it. Do this several times.

8. Afterwards discuss who could see the line. Tell them that sometimes this line is referred to as a *ghost line*. Ask if anyone could not see it (. Make note of which children struggle. Encourage those who struggle to keep trying.

9. Next do the same thing with a curved line.

Following this initial lesson, have the students use their magic ink pen to practice writing straight and curved lines on their desk as well as in the air. After practicing for a day or so, ask them how many can see the magic line better in their imagination when they write on their desk. Ask how many see it better in their imagination after writing in the air. Stress that some people find it easier to write on the desk and some find it easier to write in the air, but some people just cannot see the lines at all, and that is OK too.

Note: If any student struggles to see the line, use suggestions from How to Help Struggling Students.

## 7. How to Teach Symbol Imagery in the Emergent Phase

**Objective:** Teach students to visualize letters of the alphabet.

**Prerequisite:**

- Students know some letters.
- Students can visualize straight and curved lines.

**When to Teach:** Teach daily during the Skills Practice segment of main lesson and practice classes.

**How to Teach: Letter Drill**

Use the following process:

1. Show one letter for three seconds on the board or on a piece of paper (e.g., *B*).

2. Take it away and ask the students to air or desk write it with their finger while saying the name of the letter. Remind them to keep their eyes on their finger so they will be able to see the ghost letter when they close their eyes.

3. Have the students close their eyes and see the letter on their inner blackboard.

Once your students have practiced writing a letter enough times to know how to form it, have them practice air writing a letter without the visual cue. Just say the letter and have them write it in the air with their finger.

Remember:

- It is critical that students watch their finger as they write the letters.
- Students should always write the letter with their dominant hand and they should always form the letters correctly. Correct if you see anyone doing it wrong.
- Do not write the letter with the students. Instead, watch to make sure they are doing the exercise correctly.
- Do not spend more than five minutes a day on this exercise.

## 8.  How to Teach Symbol Imagery in the Phonemic Awareness Phase

**Objective:** Teach students to imagine words up to four letters long.

**Prerequisite:** Students can visualize two letters.

**When to Teach:** Teach daily during the Skills Practice segment of main lesson and practice classes.

**How to Teach**

How to teach symbol imagery varies.

<u>Beginning of Phonemic Awareness Phase</u>

A good way to move from one letter to two letters in symbol imagery is to practice writing the uppercase and lowercase letters together (e.g., *Bb*). This process is **advanced letter drill**.

1. Show the letters for three seconds on the board or on a piece of paper.
2. Take them away and ask the students to air or desk write the letters with their finger while saying the name of the letter (e.g., capital *B*, lowercase b). Remind them to keep their eyes on their finger so they will be able to see the ghost letter when they close their eyes.
3. Have the students close their eyes and see the letters.

Then switch to two different consonant letters (e.g ., *df* and *lp*). Use the same process as above just adapt for the name of two different letters.

Note: Do not spend more than five minutes a day on this exercise.

<u>Intermediate Phonemic Awareness Phase</u>

When students begin to decode and encode CVC words, introduce syllable cards and mystery words (see 3.5 #3).

Begin with all real words (e.g., bed). Use the syllable cards and/or CVC list you created over the summer (see chapter 3.5 #4).

Note: Each activity should take 5–7 minutes and be done daily.

Note: This is the spot to begin symbol imagery work, if you did not use *The Roadmap to Literacy* in the 1st Grade.

<u>Advanced Phonemic Awareness Phase</u>

Continue syllable card and mystery words, matching your words to the phonics rule your students are currently working on (with some review of the last phonics rule).

Switch to words with four letters when you begin blends. For example, *plan*.

Begin to include nonsense words. Tell the students that you will put in some nonsense, silly words. See if they can figure them out. For example, *teps*.

If your class can handle four letters, let them try five letters (i.e., two blends in one word). For example, *trust*.

See chapter 3.5 #3 for the process.

Note: Students will start by closing their eyes to visualize, but with practice, they will no longer need to. When they visualize with their eyes open, you will often see them looking up and to the side. This shows they are using their visual memory. A good rule of thumb is to have the class as a whole close their eyes until most of the students can visualize with their eyes open.

## 9.  How to Teach Symbol Imagery in the Pattern Phase

**Objective:** Teach student to visualize words up to seven letters long.

**Prerequisites:** Students can visualize four letters.

**When to Teach:** Teach daily during the Skills Practice segment of main lesson and practice classes.

### How to Teach

Continue syllable card and mystery word exercises. Start with four letters and work up to seven letters in single-syllable words. Match your words to the phonics rule you are currently teaching with some review of old rules. A good rule of thumb is to include mostly real words for the current rule and mostly fake words for the old rule(s). For example, *take, round, sprains* and *tump, sprot*.

Limit yourself to single-syllable words. There are only two exceptions: 1) words with inflectional endings such as –ed and –ing (e.g., *spotted* and *hopping*); and 2) compound words such as *cupcake*.

See chapter 3.5 #3 for the process.

## 10.  How to Teach Symbol Imagery in the Syllable Phase

**Objective:** Teach students to visualize separate syllables in a word (rather than more letters). By the end of 3rd Grade, they should be able to visualize words with two syllables. (They will learn to visualize longer words in 4th and 5th Grade.)

**Prerequisites:** Student can visualize seven letters, the longest amount for single-syllable words.

### Background Information

Only a few people can match Maria's visual memory for really long words such as *antidisestablishmentarianism*. Fortunately, anyone who has developed full phonemic awareness, knowledge of phonics rules, and symbol imagery up to seven letters can learn to match Maria's feat by spelling words by syllables. For example, an/ti/dis/es/tab/lish/men/tar/i/an/ism. There is no need to have a phenomenal visual memory. All students with average capacities can learn to accomplish the same spelling feats through other means.

**When to Teach:** Teach daily during the Skills Practice segment of main lesson and practice classes.

**How to Teach:** Continue syllable cards and mystery words, starting with words with two syllables and then progressing to three syllables. For example, you could use words such as *remain, unlikely, prediction, patience, and regional.* (In 4th through 6th Grade, students will focus on longer words.) (Note: Teach and practice words with three syllables, but mastery is not expected until a later grade.)

First teach the students how to break words into their syllables and discuss open and closed syllables (see chapter 4.3 rules 22 and 23). Demonstrate how to break a word into syllables for syllable cards and mystery word exercises. For example, progress: pro/gress. Do symbol imagery for each separate syllable: three letters in *pro* plus five letters in *gress*. It is much easier to remember each syllable separately than it is to remember the whole word.

**Curriculum Connection:** Teach the students to apply this technique to their weekly spelling words as well.

For example, let's spell the word *respectful.* It has 10 letters, well beyond many students' symbol imagery capacities. However, it is easy to spell if students divide and conquer the word. For example, in the word *respectful,* students already know the prefix *re-* and the suffix *–ful.* The only part they need to visualize is *spect,* which is only five letters, a feat that should fall within the capacity of most students, even those with weak symbol imagery. By breaking the words into syllables, there is less of a need to visualize.

## 11. Practice

Practice is critical. It forms part of your initial introduction in the Introduction &/or Review segment of main lesson (i.e., Activities A and B). It will be part of your ongoing practice in the Skills Practice segment of main lesson and practice classes (see chapter 2.3 #4). Finally, it can be used during classroom games.

**Activities A and B:** visualizing lines, letter drill, syllable cards, and mystery words

**Skills Practice:** Same as Activities A and B.

**Fun and Games:** In addition, there are some fun practice activities that you can use to spice up your Skills Practice. Use them sparingly.

- **Symbol imagery game:** Students write a letter with their finger on a partner's back. The partner has to guess which letter it is.
- **Symbol imagery with memory reading:** See chapter 3.4 #10.
- **Eraser gnome game:** See chapter 3.4 #10.

## 12. Assessment

Assessment is a critical part of teaching. It is important to verify that students have mastered the skills they have been taught. See chapter 6.1 for background on assessment.

**Benchmarks** represent <u>minimum</u> levels of student achievement by the end of each grade for students to be on track to handle grade-level work in 4th Grade (see chapter 6.1 #9). Table 3.5.3 contains the benchmarks for symbol imagery.

Note: The following benchmarks may not be exhaustive. Prerequisite skills for symbol imagery may be covered under other related language arts skills. For a full list of benchmarks, see table 6.1.4.

**Table 3.5.3: Benchmark for Symbol Imagery**

|  | 1st Grade | 2nd Grade | 3rd Grade |
|---|---|---|---|
| **Symbol Imagery** | Students can visualize three letters. | Students can visualize seven letters. | Students can visualize two syllables. |

There are three types of assessments. Recommendations for each type of assessment can be found in Sections 6.3, 6.4, and 6.5. You can use the following ideas as a starting point to set up an assessment program.

**Informal Assessments:** Modify the symbol imagery exercises (i.e., syllable cards and mystery word) by having the students do the exercises with their heads down on their desks. Ask them to give thumbs up or down to show whether they agree or disagree with the answer.

Curriculum Connection: Use syllable cards and mystery word as an informal assessment of decoding skills.

**Teacher-Made Assessment:** At the end of a block, prepare a symbol imagery quiz. Make up strings of letters consisting of three, four, or five random letters. (The total number of letters will depend on the length of words you are using for symbol imagery exercises.) Ask the students to write down the letters AFTER you have taken the card away. Show the letters for one second per letter. Take the letters away and ask the students to write down the letters on their paper. For example, *drtl*. (Note: It is better if the letters do not form a word—either real or nonsense. That way, students have to use symbol imagery to remember the letters.)

**Assessments Created by Educational Testing Groups:** NA

See chapter 6.3 for more information about assessing in each grade.

## 13.  How to Help Struggling Students

**Assess:** When you see a student is struggling with symbol imagery, do additional informal assessments with the student to narrow down the area(s) of concern. Document your findings and place in student's file.(see section 6).

**Additional Instruction/Practice:** Next, use the results of your assessments to provide this student with extra instruction and practice in any weak areas. You can differentiate instruction both in class and in reading groups. For example, you can modify the instructions for each reading group, or give individual assignments to provide extra practice in a weak area. Decide which approach is best based on how many other students have similar struggles. Document what you try and the results. In the case of symbol imagery, it is good to try some accommodations as part of your additional practice. Sometimes that will make all the difference (see below).

**Remedial Solution:** The decision to pursue a remedial solution is difficult and depends on the student and the resources available. Some people are incapable of learning symbol imagery (see chapter 1.6 #2). If you have such a student, modifications will be necessary, not remedial solutions. However, if a student can visualize one letter, she can be taught to visualize more. One option is to use the Lindamood-Bell program *Seeing Stars®: Symbol Imagery for Phonological and Orthographic Processing in Reading and Spelling* as part of your remedial program if and only if a student can visualize one or more letters (see chapter 6.6 #6). More research is needed in this area to determine if other therapies could help the most severe students.

**Accommodations and Modifications:** Sometimes it takes a while for remedial issues to be resolved. Meanwhile, the student needs support to function in class. Use the least restrictive accommodation that will make the student successful, and as remediation takes effect, move the student to a less restrictive accommodation.

1. Air Writing—not restrictive at all/no accommodation
2. Finger on desk (least restrictive accommodation)
3. Finger on slate
4. Carpet sample (experiment with various types to find the ones that work)

**Modifications:** If a student is incapable of learning symbol imagery, it is necessary to provide modifications. Here are two possible modifications:

1. Sand Tray
2. Slate and chalk

Neither one of these solutions will help the student learn to use symbol imagery. If you resort to either modification, be prepared to offer her alternative spelling strategies when you begin a formal study of spelling words in 3rd Grade (see 3.9 #7).

## Conclusion

Symbol imagery is the ability to visualize in two dimensions (e.g., letters and numerals). It is a sensory-cognitive function, and it needs explicit instruction to develop fully in most students. The development of symbol imagery and phonemic awareness should happen hand in hand in the first two phases. However, symbol imagery practice continues on past the end of phonemic awareness instruction because of English's highly irregular spelling.

Practice symbol imagery through all eight grades. Include daily symbol imagery exercises into your lesson plans in the Phonemic Awareness Phase, Pattern Phase, and Syllable Phase. Both syllable cards and mystery words can be done in 5–7 minutes. Scheduling 10–14 minutes a day on symbol imagery exercises will yield great results in reading and spelling proficiency. (Keep in mind these exercises do not have to be done at the same time. You can work in a few here and there, especially in transition times.)

When practiced faithfully, these exercises build students' capacity for symbol imagery, thus improving their phonemic awareness, decoding, encoding, sight words, and spelling skills.

# 3.6  SIGHT WORDS

*One morning, one of Janet's 1st graders came bursting through the door shouting out, "Mrs. Langley, I can read a whole bunch of words! Look!" He then proceeded to take out a copy of* <u>Mother West Wind's Children</u> *from beneath his jacket, open it up, and point to word after word, saying, "but, it, can, and, and, is, go, if, it, big, in, me, let, for, and, is" and so on until he had finished reading all of the sight words he knew on the entire page. Once he had finished, he looked up and beamed, "I know I still have to learn to read the other words, but, I'm on my way!"*

This chapter covers the following topics:

1. Why Sight Words Matter
2. Background Information: Sight Word Lists
3. Preparation
4. Scheduling
5. Initial Introduction
6. How to Teach Sight Words in the Emergent Phase
7. How to Teach Sight Words in the Phonemic Awareness Phase
8. How to Teach Sight Words in the Pattern Phase
9. Practice
10. Assessment
11. How to Help Struggling Students

## 1.  Why Sight Words Matter

It is necessary to differentiate words recognized on sight and sight words.

Students learn most of the words recognized on sight through decoding. Recall that as they encode and decode new words, they create the neural pathways for writing and reading. As they sound out words, they create the *letter to sound decoding route*, but when they sound out the same word over and over, they create a faster track known as the *lexical route*. They then use this route to recognize words on sight without having to sound them out (see chapter 1.2 #2).

It takes a lot of repeated attempts for a student to move a word into the *lexical route*. In *Breaking the Code*, Gentry reports that researchers have found that students in what *The Roadmap to Literacy* refers to as the Phonemic Awareness Phase need to sound out a new word at least seven times to recognize it on sight while students in the Pattern Phase will be able to learn the word after sounding it out three times (Gentry 2006, 26).

Sight words, however, are a different thing. Sight words are the common but highly irregular words that date back to Old English (see chapter 1.3 #3). Sight words come in three categories: phonetically regular, partially phonetic, and completely irregular. Here are some examples of each:

Phonetically regular (i.e., letters and sounds match completely):

- *and*
- *but*

Partially phonetic (i.e., partial match between letters and sounds):

- *put* (should be pronounced *putt* and spelled *poot* like *foot)*
- *the* (should be pronounced *thee* and spelled *thu)*
- *one* (should be pronounced *own* and spelled *wun)*

Completely irregular (i.e., no connection between letters and sounds)

- *who* (should be pronounced *woah* and spelled *hoo)*
- *of* (should be pronounced *off* and spelled *uv)*

In the *Instant Words List*, Fry reports that:

- The top 25 sight words make up about one third of all words in print.
- The top 100 words make up about half of all words in print.
- The top 300 make up about two thirds of all words in print (Fry 2006, 51).

A 'cocktail napkin' estimate of the top 300 words revealed that:

- 199 words or 66% of the words were phonetically regular.
- 102 words or 33% of the words were phonetically irregular.

To summarize, almost two thirds of all the words you read or write on a page can be found in a list of 300 words, and around one third of those words are irregular. These words are critical for reading fluency and correct spelling, but many of them violate the code. What is a teacher to do?

To get around these complications, many educators simply teach sight words as whole words through look-say. In other words, they treat sight words as units that students simply memorize. This approach is in line with students' brain development (see chapter 3.4 #1). Students in the Emergent Phase and beginning Phonemic Awareness Phase learn to recognize some sight words as pictograms just as readers of early writing systems did (see chapter 1.4 #1).

Prior to the middle of the Phonemic Awareness Phase, all sight words should be taught with the look-say method of instruction (i.e., teach students to memorize each word as a whole word or pictogram). Once students are in the intermediate Phonemic Awareness Phase, they begin decoding CVC words and will be able to use their budding encoding and decoding skills to sound out and spell those sight words that are regular. However given that one third of sight words are irregular, continue to teach sight words using the look-say method of instruction.

By helping your 1st and 2nd Grade students master common sight words, you will give them a huge boost in both reading fluency and in writing because they will already know more than half the words they see on the page or wish to write down. By teaching your 1st and 2nd Grade students both sight words and the code (phonics rules), you provide the instruction necessary to master English.

## 2. Background Information: Sight Word Lists

It is important to teach sight words, but there are many lists of sight words available. Which list to choose?

A popular list is the Dolch High Frequency Word List. It was created by Edward Dolch, a professor at the University of Illinois, and was first published as "A Basic Sight Word Vocabulary" in an educational journal in 1936. This list consists of the 220 most frequently used words or service words in print at the time. His list is in alphabetical order, and it omits nouns. He also published another list, the *Dolch Noun List*, which consists of 95 commonly used nouns.

Another popular list is the *Fry 1000 Instant Words*. Edward Fry, a Professor at Rutgers University, first published his list in 1957. (It was updated in 1980.) His words are listed in order of frequency and include nouns. It can be found at http://readsters.com/wp-content/uploads/comparingDolchandFryLists.pdf.

In addition, you could create your own list. Dolch encouraged teachers to select their sight words from the class readers their students were reading.

You could also use **The Roadmap to Literacy Sight Word List**. The list is an amalgam of the Dolch High Frequency Word List and the top 300 words on the Fry List. It is organized to support *The Roadmap to Literacy* curriculum. There are a total of 270 words in the list. The words are divided into two sets. The first covers the 20 most frequently used words. The second covers 250 additional common words.

*The Roadmap to Literacy* list is limited to 270 words because the students do not need to memorize every common word as a sight word. Once they develop the *letter to sound decoding route* and the *lexical route*, they will decode words on their own, and this independent reading will allow them to recognize common words on sight. However, many common words cannot be decoded because they are phonetically irregular. The study of sight words will help beginning students overcome this obstacle so they can focus on the words that can be decoded. As they then go on to independent reading, they will create more and more neural models of words on their own and will not need to learn every common word as a sight word. The study of sight words is only useful at the beginning phases of learning to read and should become obsolete once the *lexical route* is established.

To use *The Roadmap to Literacy Sight Word List*, see Appendix 4. Just as Dolch suggested, customize the order so that you teach the words that will appear in the memory reading material you have selected for your class (see chapter 3.15 #3).

## 3. Preparation

There are several things to do over the summer.

### Choose the Sight Words You Will Teach

First, select the sight words you want to introduce using the following guidelines:

1st Grade: Pick words from the sight word list that show up in your memory reading for the week. Once your students are starting to decode (last few blocks of 1st Grade), choose both sight words that follow the phonics rules you are teaching and one or more that break the rules. The class can have fun deciding which is which.

2nd Grade: Continue to compose your sight word lists of regular and irregular words. Introduce those sight words that reflect a specific phonics rule either right before or right after you teach that rule.

Curriculum Connection: Coordinate your sight words with your phonics curriculum. Locate any words on the list that are spelled with a specific phonics rule and include them on your sight word list either the week prior to or the week of the rule's introduction.

**Make Flash Cards**

Write your sight words on 5 x 7 cards. Print the words neatly in lowercase letters. Make sure the letters are large and clear enough to be seen by the students in the back row. You will put these words in the special sight word corner of your board. (Plan to use the words for various practice activities over the course of the week.)

**Create Sight Word Lists for Kid Writing Reference for 1st Grade**

Students will need a list of sight words once they begin kid writing at the beginning of the Phonemic Awareness Phase. They should get an updated list each main lesson block and each practice class block. Prepare these lists by following these steps:

1. Compile all of the sight words you plan for your students to know by the <u>end</u> of each block.

2. Make a final copy of these alphabetized words written neatly in <u>lowercase</u> letters. (When your students begin kid writing in the beginning of the Phonemic Awareness Phase, you will make copies of that block's sight words and distribute to the students at the <u>beginning</u> of the block. Students will put these word lists into their practice book for easy reference when kid writing.

3. You should have one list for each main lesson and practice block. The lists should be cumulative.

**Buy Consumable Spelling Dictionaries for 2nd Grade**

In 2nd Grade, use spelling dictionaries in lieu of sight word lists. These spelling dictionaries are longer, fuller versions of sight word lists. They contain a full page of common words for each letter. Each word has an example sentence that uses the word in context. The students will use the spelling dictionaries for their kid writing and get extra decoding practice reading the sample sentences.

It is good to purchase a consumable spelling dictionary rather than make one yourself. Unless you are willing to put in a lot of time and effort, the pre-made version will be the superior product. In addition, they are very inexpensive. You would spend more photocopying your version than it would cost to buy a set for the class. Your time is better spent creating effective lessons.

There are many varieties for sale on line. *The Roadmap to Literacy* recommends the following:

- For 2nd Grade (Pattern Phase): *The Quick-Word Handbook for Everyday Writers* from Curriculum Associates, Inc. This dictionary has 1,020 high-use writing words.

- For 3rd Grade (Syllable Phase): At the end of 2nd Grade, determine if you want your class (or select students) to continue using *The Quick-Word Handbook for Everyday Writers*. Purchase new copies accordingly. If your students are writing on a regular basis, the ones from 2nd Grade will be worn out.

## 4. Scheduling

When preparing your curriculum, you can use the block plan templates in Appendices 1–3 or you can create your own. If you create your own, use the following points to lay out your blocks:

1. Begin instruction during the first practice block of 1st Grade.

2. It will take students 1½-2 years to master sight words.

3. Teach in the Skills Practice segment in both main lesson blocks and practice blocks.

4. Teach daily for 5–10 minutes.

5. The number of sight words to teach per week varies by phase:

   a. Teach two in the Emergent Phase.

   b. Teach five in the Phonemic Awareness Phase and Pattern Phase.

6. Once you have completed sight words, segue into spelling in 3rd Grade.

## 5. Initial Introduction

**Prerequisites:** NA

**When to Teach:** You will need to introduce sight words twice. The first time is during the first practice block in 1st Grade when you begin to work with sight words. The second time is at the end of 1st Grade when students have enough decoding skills to realize that some sight words do not play fair.

### Sample Lesson for the Initial Introduction of Sight Words

Prep Work: Choose your first two sight words and a verse that the students already know that contains these words. Write the verse on the board in standard printing (a mix of uppercase and lowercase letters).

Introduction: Memory Read the verse together as a class (see chapter 3.15 #6). Then share an imagination such as the following:

*There are lots of people in the world, some you know and some you don't. It happens that sometimes we may meet someone once and then we don't see them again for a while. The next time we encounter this person, we have to ask their name because it has been so long since we last saw her that we don't remember her name. Then there are some people whose names we know right away because we see them all of the time, such as the names of our family and friends. When we see these people, we know them on sight. Just like our family and friends, there are some words that appear so often in books and verses that you will get to know them on sight, too. As soon as you see them, you won't have to stop and figure out the word, you will just know how to say it. These are called sight words because you recognize them the second you see them.*

After finishing the story about sight words, underline one sight word from the memory reading passage. Read the passage again, pointing to each word. Stop when you get to the sight word. Say: "*This word says_____.*"

Write the sight word on a 5 x 7 card in front of the class. Say each letter as you form it. Write in lowercase letters.

Hold the letter up in front of the class. Say: "*This word says__.*" Then spell it slowly, pointing to each letter as you say it.

Do the same for the second word.

Note: This initial introduction is the only time you will create the flash cards in front of the class. Next week, make the cards prior to class. Once you find the word in the passage, pull out the card, tell the students what the word says, spell each letter while pointing to it, and say the word again.

### Sample Lesson for the Second Introduction of Sight Words: Some Words Do Not Play Fair

Background Information: At some point, the class will realize that some of the sight words do not play fair (i.e., that they are irregular). This moment will likely happen when the class begins to decode words at the end of 1st Grade. When it happens, acknowledge that the students are right and relate the following story (or a similar imagination).

Introduction: Share an imagination such as the following:

*Have you ever gotten together with a group of kids to play and it turned into chaos because no one really knew what they were doing and the rules of the game kept being changed so no one really knew what was going on? Well, the same thing happened in the early days of Letter Village.*

*Before the Mayor of Letter Village came to live there, it was a time of chaos. When letters got together to play, they ended up spelling lots of words that didn't make much sense, or in some cases, any sense when you tried to sound them out. But, then again there were no rules to guide them. For example, P, U, and T got together and decided to spell the word* put. *Now it made sense for P and T to be the beginning and ending of the word* put, *but U's sound was /ŭ/. Yet the word they spelled was* put *not* putt! *And then there were words like* of. *O and F decided to get together and spell* of *and so they did. When U and V saw this new word, they just scratched their heads because* of *should have been spelled with their sounds /ŭ/ and /v/. It should have been spelled like this: UV (write on the board). Neither O nor F made the sounds found in* of. *But, they spelled it first so that was how it is spelled.*

*Finally, a few of the letters complained about this craziness and wrote to the Queen of Englishland and asked that she send someone to Letter Village to help them create rules for how words were to be spelled. Realizing the wisdom of this request, the Queen searched through the land until she found the wisest, most patient and organized person she could find. She appointed him the Mayor of Letter Village, telling him that it would be his task to help the letters figure out a way to spell words together that made sense.*

*Since the Mayor's arrival in Letter Village, the new words that the letters created made sense because they all follow the rules that he laid out, (give one or two examples of CVC words they could sound out). However, there still exist those words that were created before the Mayor and his rules came along. We have to learn them by sight because they do not follow the rules so we can't sound them out.*

## 6. How to Teach Sight Words in the Emergent Phase

Teach students their first sight words from *The Roadmap to Literacy Sight Word List* (Set One) (see Appendix 4).

**Objectives:**

1. Teach students to read the words through look-say.
2. Teach students to spell the words through chanting.

**Prerequisites:**

1. Students can identify the letters found in all of their first sight words.
2. Students can print the letters found in all of their first sight words.

**When to Teach:** Teach daily in the Skills Practice segment in main lesson block and practice blocks. Start in

The first language arts practice block in the 1st Grade.

**How to Teach Sight Words**

Once you have introduced the concept of sight words, continue to introduce two new words each week. Each word will need at least fourteen different exposures (i.e., practice opportunities) for students to master the word. Continue introducing two words per week until the list is completed or until the class moves into the Phonemic Awareness Phase, when you increase the number of new words per week to five.

There are many ways to introduce and practice these words. The best ways take into account the fact that students do not yet realize that letters represent sounds. They include sight word chants, memory reading, flash cards, etc.

## Sight Word Chants

Sight word chants involve movement and/or pantomime while students chant or sing the spelling of a sight word. They can be used to introduce and practice sight words. They are a particularly good way to work with sight words in the Emergent Phase and the first half of the Phonemic Awareness Phase because they allow students to learn sight words before symbol imagery is necessarily up and running.

Here are some ideas for creating sight word chants:

1. Arm Tapping: Stand up. Hold left arm in front, pointing down to make a 45 degree angle. Say the word. Chant each letter while simultaneously gently karate chopping the left arm from the shoulder to the wrist. Then say the word again while rubbing from the shoulder to the wrist in one sweep. Example: BUT: B (chop) U (chop) T (chop) BUT (Sweep).

2. Bunny Hop: Stand up. Say the word. Say each letter while hopping like a bunny in place or going forward. Example: IN: I (hop) N (hop) IN

3. Flamingo Hop: Same as bunny hop but on one leg.

4. Pat-A-Cake: Stand up. Face desk partner. Say the word while clapping your hands together. Say the first letter while right hand crosses to high-five partner's right hand. Clap your hands back together. Say the second letter while left hand crosses to high-five partner's left hand. Clap your hands back together. Repeat the word and clap Etc. For example, IT (clap): I (right high five), clap, T (left high five), clap, IT (clap). Variations include other versions of pat-a-cake or hand clapping games.

5. Character Voices: Introduce a character and her sound, For example, a baby (waaah), police (whistle), dog (woof), cat (meow), etc. Stand up. Say word in the character's voice. Say the first letter then make the character's sound. Say the second letter and make the character's sound. Then say the word again. For example, police: ON (Say it loudly): O (whistle with arm and hand held out as if trying to stop an unruly motorist) N (whistle with arm and hand held out) ON (Say it loudly).

The possibilities for chants are endless. Use economy in teaching to combine characters from stories with sight words for fun, customized chants. For example, do a character chant in the voice of a witch or other character from a fairy tale.

## Sight Words in Texts (Memory Reading)

Finding sight words in memory reading texts (see chapter 3.15 #6) can be excellent practice and a lot of fun. Have a hunt to find the sight word *without* pointing to each word and saying each word. You can take down the sight word card from the sight word corner and display it next to the text to help the students. When they become more proficient with that word, you can show the sight word briefly and take it away before asking them to find the word.

## Flash Cards

Write the sight words on oversized cards using lowercase letters. Show the cards to the class. On your signal, they have to say the word together. (Start with five or more seconds per word and gradually work down to one or two seconds per word.) Be sure to shuffle the flash cards so they are in a different order each time.

Additional Ways to Practice Sight Words

    1. Laser Pointer: Put a number of sight word cards up on the board in a random order. Use a laser pointer to indicate a word that the students have to read.

    2. Sight Word Shuffle: Do Flash Cards with all of the sight words the students have learned to date.

Mix up your sight word practice, but make sure that it is brief—no more than 5–7 minutes each day. Short daily practice will get you further than less frequent but longer practice sessions.

## 7. How to Teach Sight Words in the Phonemic Awareness Phase

Continue to teach students sight words from *The Roadmap to Literacy Sight Word List*. Finish the first set of words if you have not already done so. Then teach the second set (see Appendix 4).

**Objectives:**

    1. Continue to teach students to read the words through look-say, but switch to decoding once the students learn to decode (around the third language arts practice block).

    2. Continue to teach students to spell the words through chanting.

**Prerequisite:** When the vast majority of the class (80%) enters the Phonemic Awareness Phase (usually at or before November of 1st Grade).

**When to Teach:** Teach daily in the Skills Practice segment in both main lesson blocks and practice blocks.

**How to Teach Sight Words:** Continue to practice sight words using the same techniques as in the Emergent Phase. There will be a few changes to reflect the students' growing capacities:

- Increase the number of sight words to five a week.

- Once students learn to decode, draw students' attention to the fact that some sight words can be decoded but some cannot (see chapter 3.6 #5).

- Introduce two new ways of practicing sight words: symbol imagery and sight word lists or spelling dictionaries. For the remainder of the Phonemic Awareness Phase, use all of your sight word learning strategies (chants, cards, etc.), particularly those that work best for your class.

- Mastery will require 7 to 10+ exposures (i.e., practices). Schedule accordingly. You can continue to use the same methods in the Emergent Phase (see chapter 3.6 #6) and you can also begin using the following methods:

Using Symbol Imagery to Learn New Sight Words

In the middle of the Phonemic Awareness Phase, students should be able to handle three letters with symbol imagery. At this time, you can begin introducing and practicing sight words through symbol imagery.

Pick one or more words from your sight word list to practice that day. For example, let's say that you are practicing the word *the*.

    1. Clearly display the word card on the board (or write it on the board).

    2. Read the word (e.g., *the*), demonstrate how to air write or desk write the word while saying the letters aloud (e.g., "T-H-E").

    3. Finally close your eyes to visualize it in your imagination.

4. Ask the students do the same thing, either writing on their desk, their slate, or the air.

5. Next have them close their eyes and see it in the imagination on their mental blackboard.

6. Have students practice spelling it from their imagination and then reading it. (They close their eyes and visualize the letters: "T-H-E, the.")

Note that you have gone both ways—from the word to the letters and from the letters to the word.

Once the students have the idea, show the sight word card for just one second per letter and then turn it or cover it so no one can see it. As the students get more and more proficient, you then can ask the class to do some symbol imagery exercises. You can ask them to identify one of the letters (the first, the last, etc.). You can ask them to spell the word backwards (e.g., E-H-T for *the*). In this manner, you train the students to use symbol imagery to remember spelling. (In later grades, the same strategy is used to memorize spelling words.)

### Using Symbol Imagery to Review Old Sight Words

Select a few sight word display cards from the past. Do not let the students see these cards. See if the students can recall the visual image for these words. (*"Close your eyes. Look at the blackboard in your imagination. See the word the. "Who can spell* the?*"* (A student spells *T-H-E.*) *"What was the second letter?"* (A student says, *"E."*) *"Who can spell the word* the *backwards?"* (A student spells *E-H-T.*) Include a few minutes of review every so often.

### Using a Spelling List (or Spelling Dictionary) to Learn Sight Words

You can use the spelling lists (or spelling dictionaries) to practice sight words.

Ask the students to pull out their spelling list (or spelling dictionary). Ask them to find a sight word that they are working on such as *were*.

The students put their finger on the word once they find it and raise their hands. Once the majority of the class has the word, call on a volunteer to read off the spelling of the word.

Note: Make sure to give the class enough time for most students to find the word. If you make it a race, the slower ones will give up and not get any benefit from the exercise.

## 8.   How to Teach Sight Words in the Pattern Phase

Continue to teach students sight words from *The Roadmap to Literacy Sight Word List*. Finish Set Two (see Appendix 4).

**Objectives:**

1. Teach students to read the words through decoding unless they are irregular. If so, use look-say.

2. Teach students to spell the words through encoding unless they are irregular. If so, use symbol imagery if the word is short or chanting if it is long.

**When to Teach:** Teach daily in the Skills Practice segment of main lesson and practice blocks.

## How to Teach

Continue to teach and practice sight words as you did in the Phonemic Awareness Phase; however, as students progress through the Pattern Phase, the emphasis on sight word instruction shifts to reflect their growing capacities.

First, students in this phase usually require three, four, or five exposures to master the word (for reading). In addition, the students will require fewer repetitions in class to master reading new sight words because they will be reading more. Consequently, switch the emphasis to spelling practice. Students still require lots of practice to master spelling.

Second, practice in class shifts more and more to symbol imagery. If the students can visualize the word, they should not be chanting it. Save sight word chants for longer words that students cannot yet visualize.

When it comes to chants, you have three additional options in this phase:

1. Create your own rhythmic chant for the word. It includes a rhythm, but no melody. It can also include clapping or finger snapping. As an example, see the "Around Chant" in figure 3.6.1.

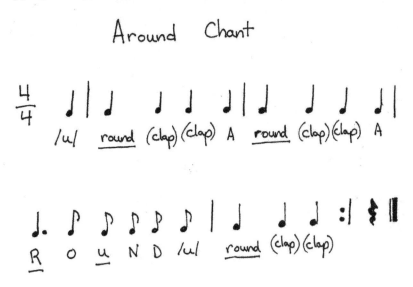

**Figure 3.6.1: Around Chant**

2. Put the spelling of a sight word into a popular song. An example would be singing/spelling the word *through* to the tune of "Kum-bah-ya:" *"T-H-R-OU-GH-through; T-H-R-OU-GH-through; T-H-R-OU-GH-through; Oh yes, that spells through."*

3. Create your own simple melody for a sight word song. The lyrics just need to include the letters and the word itself. It can also have gestures, if you are so inclined. See the "There Song" for an example in figure 3.6.2.

**Figure 3.6.2: There Song**

By the end of 2nd Grade, the students should be able to imagine seven letters and should not need chants any more.

## 9.    Practice

Practice is critical. It forms part of your initial introduction in the Introduction &/or Review segment of main lesson (i.e., Activities A and B). It will be part of your ongoing practice in the Skills Practice segment of main lesson and practice classes (see chapter 2.3.4). Finally, it can be used during classroom games.

**Activities A and B:** The following activities are good to use as part of the Introduction &/or Review of the week's sight words:

- sight word chants
- sight words in texts (memory reading)
- flash cards
- symbol imagery exercises
- spelling list/spelling dictionary

**Skills Practice:**

- same as Activities A and B
- laser pointer
- sight word shuffle

Schedule sight word practice in the Skills Practice segment of main lesson. You can use sight word chants as a transition activity as it can double as an IMA (integrated movement activity) (see chapter 2.3 #4).

**Fun and Games:** Below is an activity that you can use to spice up your Skills Practice.

Symbol imagery game: Students write a short sight word with their finger on a partner's back (one letter at a time). The letters should be large. In 1st Grade the writer should say whether she is going to use uppercase or lowercase letters. The partner has to guess which word it is and spell it out loud or write it down. (Note: This is good for words with 2–4 letters only.)

# 10. Assessment

Assessment is a critical part of teaching. It is important to verify that students have mastered the skills they have been taught. See chapter 6.1 for background on assessment.

**Benchmarks** represent <u>minimum</u> levels of student achievement by the end of each grade for students to be on track to handle grade-level work in 4th Grade (see chapter 6.1 #9). Table 3.6.1 contains the benchmarks for sight words.

Note: The following benchmarks may not be exhaustive. Prerequisite skills for sight words may be covered under other related language arts skills. For a full list of benchmarks, see table 6.1.4.

**Table 3.6.1: Benchmarks for Sight Words**

|  | 1st Grade | 2nd Grade | 3rd Grade |
|---|---|---|---|
| **Sight Words: Reading** | Students can read 70+ sight words. | Students can read all sight words from *The Roadmap to Literacy* list (i.e., set 1 and set 2). | NA |
| **Sight Words: Spelling** | Students can spell 20+ sight words. | Students can spell 150+ sight words. | NA |

There are three types of assessments. Recommendations for each type of assessment can be found in Sections 6.3, 6.4, and 6.5. You can use the following ideas as a starting point to set up an assessment program.

**Informal Assessments:** You can assess informally by observing the following practice exercises:

- Oral reading: See chapter 3.15 #7 simple decodable-text.
- Kid writing: See chapter 3.13.
- Dictations: See chapter 3.9 #8.

**Teacher-Made Assessments:**

- Once a week, give a teacher-generated spelling quiz of all the sight words practiced that week.
- At the end of the block, give the class an informal spelling test of all the block's sight words.
- At the end of the school year, make your own assessment using the words you taught that year. Include 25–30 of the more challenging sight words. Give the assessment to each student individually.

**Assessments Created by Educational Testing Groups**: If your school has an assessment tool, consider using it. If not, NA. (We do not recommend using the *CORE* sight words assessment.)

See chapters 6.3, 6.4, and 6.5 for more information about assessing in each grade.

## 11.  How to Help Struggling Students

**Assess:** When you see a student is struggling with sight words, do assessments (both formal and informal) to narrow down the area(s) of concern and to document your findings. Sight words depend on the acquisition of many skills including:

- Alphabet knowledge: See chapter 3.1.
- Symbol imagery: See chapter 3.5.

Make sure both of these areas are strong if students struggle. See Section 6 for information on how to assess.

**Additional Instruction/Practice:** Next, use the results of your assessments to provide this student with extra instruction and practice in any weak areas. You can differentiate instruction both in class and in reading groups. For example, you can modify the instructions for each reading group or give individual assignments to provide extra practice in a weak area. Decide which approach is best based on how many other students have similar struggles. Document what you try and the results.

**Remedial Solutions:** If you do not notice improvements in three or four weeks, it is time to contact your mentor for guidance and consult chapter 6.6 for additional information on remedial issues. Be sure to check for eye issues such as a need for prescription glasses, vision therapy, Irlen colored overlays, etc. (see chapter 6.6 #2). Also check for movement issues including weak balance.

**Accommodations and Modifications:** Sometimes it takes a while for remedial issues to be resolved. Meanwhile, the student needs support to function in class. Once students begin kid writing (early Phonemic Awareness Phase), they are expected to use their sight word list to spell familiar sight words correctly. If they routinely misspell these words, first remind them to use their list during kid writing. You can provide a special list of commonly misspelled words for students to be on the lookout for.

Students who struggle with symbol imagery can continue to use chants to learn the spelling of all their sight words in the Pattern Phase. Put the students into a small group to practice chanting with words with five or fewer letters. Giving this modification to the rest of the class will undermine their development of sight words through symbol imagery. The whole class should only use chants to spell sight words if the word is longer than five letters.

### Extra Practice: Sight Word Box

Some students will need extra practice to learn to read sight words. An effective way is with a sight word box. It can be done in school or at home.

First, collect the words that a student is struggling with (or that a small group is struggling with). Use *The Roadmap to Literacy* sight word list if you are not sure and have the student read each word. Any word that is not said automatically needs more practice. Print each word on a 3x5 card in lowercase letters with a black pen. Initially include no more than 10 sight words.

Have the student practice reading each of these words until some are automatic (i.e., the student can say them instantaneously with no sounding out or hesitation). Then move the quicker words up a level and add in new slow words to replace them. That way there will always be a core group of 10 words that need the most instruction and a larger group of words to practice. Do the sight word box daily.

The number of times a student needs to read the word automatically before it is retired from the box varies. In the Phonemic Awareness Phase, plan on 10–14 repetitions. By the Pattern Phase, plan on 7. You can use tally marks on the back of the card to keep track.

## Conclusion

Being able to recognize words automatically is a very important part of reading. Students will learn to recognize most words through decoding, but the most common words in the English language are highly irregular. They are called sight words and are taught as whole words. Instruction begins in the Emergent Phase, well before students are ready to learn to decode. Begin teaching sight words as soon as you put your first memory reading passage up on the board. Your students will reap the benefits of reading and writing faster and more confidently.

# 3.7 CONCEPT IMAGERY: THE KEY TO COMPREHENSION

*During the 3rd Grade year, Ms. Lynn read* <u>The Secret Garden</u> *to her class. The book had beautiful illustrations, and the students wanted to see them as she read. In order to strengthen her students' mental picturing (i.e., concept imagery), Ms. Lynn told the class that first she wanted them to see the pictures of the story in their mind and then once she had finished, she would show them the pictures.*

*When she had finished the book, Ms. Lynn let her students see the illustrations. The students exclaimed, "That's not what he looks like!" or "In my garden the wall was covered with roses," and so on. The students were actually disappointed with the story's illustrations, each declaring that their characters, house, and garden were better.*

Concept imagery is one of the three sensory-cognitive functions identified by Lindamood-Bell that students need to develop to become literate. The other two are phonemic awareness and symbol imagery (see chapter 1.6 #2).

In Waldorf education, the term *concept imagery* often goes by the umbrella term *mental picturing*, a term that applies to both concept imagery and symbol imagery. This chapter uses the term *concept imagery* to avoid confusion.

Close your eyes. Imagine a cat. If you see a furry mammal with whiskers, you are using concept imagery as shown in in figure 3.7.1. If you imagine the letters *C-A-T*, you are using symbol imagery (see fig. 3.5.1).

**Figure 3.7.1: Concept Imagery**

This chapter covers the following topics:

1. Why Concept Imagery Matters

2. Preparation

3. Scheduling

4. Initial Introduction: Grades 1, 2, and 3

5. Exercises to Develop Concept Imagery (Verbal Language)

6. Exercises to Develop Concept Imagery (Reading)

7. Practice

8. Assessment

9. How to Help Struggling Students

## 1. Why Concept Imagery Matters

Concept imagery's main job is to enable comprehension.

When students read or listen to a story, they need to imagine what is going on. If they cannot, they think the story is just words and is thus boring. In contrast, students who do not have problems with concept imagery create an entire mental movie when they read or hear a story. They see all of the details and action in their mind's eye. This imagination is what makes reading pleasurable.

Concept imagery develops when young children get plenty of language experience with loving and attentive caregivers. This experience includes conversation, listening to stories, and language play (e.g., nursery rhymes, guessing games, etc.).

Children can have weaknesses with concept imagery for various reasons, but exposure to media can be a big factor. Screen time (TV, computers, iPads, and cell phones) derails the development of concept imagery because screens provide the pictures for the children. Thus, in the current environment where the visual media is often replacing live language, you cannot assume that rising 1st graders have adequately developed concept imagery skills.

Note: This weakness in concept imagery is detrimental in any educational setting, but it is worse in a Waldorf classroom because concepts are introduced through stories and images (see chapter 2.1 #4). Students who cannot use concept imagery are at a serious disadvantage.

## 2. Preparation

No special preparation is necessary over the summer.

During the school year, prepare your concept imagery curriculum as part of preparing your first story(s) in Grades 1–3. Choose the story you will use to model concept imagery. Prepare your concept imagery introduction and include it in your lesson plans (see chapter 3.7 #4).

## 3. Scheduling

When preparing your curriculum, you can use the block plan templates in Appendices 1–3 or you can create your own. If you create your own, use the following points to lay out your blocks:

1. Begin instruction the first week of 1st Grade as a prelude to story review.

2. Teach during the Introduction &/or Review segment in main lesson for stories. When you teach concept imagery for reading will vary based on your schedule.

3. Make sure you schedule time to review concept imagery during these times:

   - 1st Grade: Introduce concept imagery the day after the first two or three fairy tales.

- 2nd Grade: Review when students switch to chapter books with reduced or no illustrations in reading groups.

- 3rd Grade: Ibid and when students begin reading nonfiction.

4. Teach for 5–7 minutes per lesson, but only the lessons noted in point 3.

5. Note: Always move into listening comprehension immediately after each concept imagery review.

## 4. Initial Introduction: Grades 1, 2, and 3

It is necessary to check concept imagery skills in each grade.

**Prerequisites:** NA

**Background Information:** First graders have a big transition to make. In Waldorf kindergartens they have scaffolding to support language comprehension: Stories are repeated verbatim for days, and often they have corresponding puppet shows. In 1st Grade, students should be able to do all of the picturing on their own without the aid of puppet shows or listening to the story a second or third time. Most students make this transition seamlessly, but it is incumbent to teach concept imagery at least initially to make sure that all of your students have the necessary prerequisites for good comprehension. It is then necessary to check in 2nd and 3rd Grade to make sure students continue to use concept imagery for both listening and reading comprehension.

**When to Teach:** The times to teach these initial introductions will vary by grade.

**How to Teach:** In the beginning of 1st Grade, model concept imagery skills to your students, practice some together, and then let the students try some on their own.

There are three areas to introduce:

- 1st Grade: Oral Language

- 2nd Grade: Reading fiction books with chapters and few illustrations

- 3rd Grade: Ibid and reading nonfiction

### Sample Lesson for First Grade

Right after you have told a story, discuss with the class what you pictured for one of the scenes from the story. You can use the Lindamood-Bell Structure Words to help frame your description as shown in table 3.7.1.

**Table 3.7.1: Lindamood-Bell Structure Words®**

| What | Number | Movement | Perspective |
|------|--------|----------|-------------|
| Size | Shapes | Mood | When |
| Color | Where | Background | Sound |

*Source: Bell 2007, 87.*

For an example, consider the scene in Grimm's "Hansel and Gretel" where the two children first discover the witch's house. The house was made of bread, the roof of cakes, and the windows of transparent sugar. You could say:

"I imagine a boy and a girl walking up a path towards a house (i.e., what). The children are little—maybe four and six years old (i.e., size). They both have blond hair. The boy is wearing brown shorts and a green shirt; the girl is wearing a red dress (i.e., color). The house is in the forest (i.e., where). There are trees behind it (i.e., background). The house is a golden brown because it is made with loaves of bread (i.e., color). The roof is covered in little white cakes and the two round window panes by the door are made of thin layers of transparent sugar (i.e., number and shape). I see Hansel and Gretel reach out and pull off a piece of bread (i.e., movement). They are smiling and look very happy because they have something to eat and are very hungry (i.e., mood). Then from inside the house, I hear a thin voice call out, "Nibble, nibble, like a mouse, Who is nibbling at my house? (i.e., sound).

Next, ask the students how they pictured different elements of the scene. For example, ask if someone pictured Hansel differently, or Gretel. Affirm all right responses and share that each of us makes our own movie in our imaginations when we listen to stories. Then discuss other aspects, such as the house.

Finally, choose a different scene, such as the one where Hansel puts a bone through the window for the witch to feel. This time, let the students share their images first. Ask the students how they pictured it. For example, ask how students pictured the witch. Affirm all right responses and correct all wrong responses. Students may not add foreign elements to the story, but they are free to imagine any element as they like as long as it does not contradict the story. For example, if the story says the heroine has black hair, it is wrong to say it is blond. However, if the story does not say what color the heroine's hair is, students may imagine it any color they like. Then share how you pictured it and conclude that we all make our own pictures. Some parts will be the same and some will be different.

Lastly, when you review your story the next day, prompt the students to use their mental movie from the day before to remember all of the parts. Ask comprehension questions to make sure they understand the story (see chapter 3.8 #2).

### Second Grade/Third Grade: Reading Fiction Books with Chapters

The second big transition is when students begin to read chapter books with few to no illustrations. This point will occur at different times for different reading groups.

Many students rely on the illustrations in early readers to help them create their own mental pictures. The transition to chapter books with few to no illustrations in 2nd and 3rd grade is a critical time to review mental picturing. Use the same process to model good concept imagery while reading. Then pay particular attention to the written comprehension questions you give the students about a book to confirm that each one is able to use concept imagery in the absence of illustrations. Continue to practice together as a class as long as necessary.

### Third Grade: Reading Nonfiction

The final transition is when students begin to read nonfiction. Picturing nonfiction is more difficult than imagining a story. There is no strong emotion, dramatic tension, or plot to hook students' interest. Help the class make the transition.

In 3rd Grade, give the class nonfiction reading assignments. A good time to introduce this work is during the Practical Occupations Block (see chapter 2.3 #2). Give the class short, grade-appropriate passages on relevant topics (see chapter 5.5 #8). Model how to use concept imagery with the class as they read the passage. Follow-up with written comprehension questions as an informal assessment to confirm that the students are able to comprehend what they have read.

## 5. Exercises to Develop Concept Imagery (Verbal Language)

You should not need to teach concept imagery after the initial introduction; however, sometimes a class (or a group of students) needs help developing concept imagery. Listening games are another way you can help strengthen your class's capacity for concept imagery. They can be done with a class or with a small group of students. Below are a few favorites.

**Grandmother's Suitcase:** The following is a variation of the classic recall game that can be played forward or backward. Say: *"Grandma is going on a trip, and the class is going to help her pack. I put in the suitcase…"* (Say one item such as *sunscreen*. The next person has to remember your item and add a new one. For example, person two would say, *"I put in sunscreen and a bathing suit."* (If going backwards, reverse the order: *"I put in a bathing suit and sunscreen."*) If a student gets the order wrong or cannot remember an item, she is out.

Before beginning the game, introduce how to use concept imagery to remember the items. (We brought in a suitcase and acted it out by putting in imaginary items.) Share how you imagine the first item. For example, *"The first item I am putting in is a bottle of sunscreen. When I imagine this bottle in my mind, it is yellow with a picture of a red and blue beach ball on its label."* Ask students to close their eyes and see if they can picture that sunscreen bottle. Now move on to the second item. *"I packed in Grandmother's suitcase a bottle of sunscreen and a bathing suit."* Ask students to close their eyes and imagine a bathing suit. What kind is it? What color? Call on a few students to share what theirs looks like. Then discuss how we all see slightly different mental movies and that is OK.

Each time you play this game, you can provide a theme such as packing for a trip to the beach or turning the suitcase into a keepsake trunk. Before they start playing the game, remind students to make mental pictures of each object as it is being added to the suitcase/trunk.

Note: This game can be modified to include the students who are out. At the beginning of the game, tell the class that everyone will have to write the entire list at the end of the game so those students who are sitting down had better pay attention. Let the students use invented spellings (kid writing) to generate their lists. At the end, write the entire list in order on the board and have the students correct their own work.

**The Directions Game** is from Lindamood-Bell. To introduce the game, tell the class, *"I am going to give you three directions (or fewer if the class is really struggling). While I am giving you the directions, I want you to close your eyes and imagine yourself doing what I am saying. When I am done, I will clap my hands, and you can open your eyes."* Then give them three directions with a one-second pause between each. For example, *"Take out your green crayon. (pause) Take out your phonics rules book. (pause) Write a lowercase B on the last page."* (Clap) Then ask, *"Who imagined what I said?"* (Observe who raises their hands.) *"Who can tell me all three things?"* Call on one student and say, *"Begin with I see myself getting…."*). If the student is wrong, acknowledge what she got right and ask if someone else would like to try to recall all three directions. Then let the students do the three directions.

Observe the students as they follow your directions and note any who are not able to remember them. You can then model the correct order or bring up one of the students who followed the directions to model it.

As you are forming your class, work this game into your routine. You can train the entire class to pay attention to your directions and to follow them precisely.

Note: This game makes an excellent transition between lesson segments. It is particularly good to use when setting up for the Bookwork segment (see chapter 2.3 #4). For an example, see table 5.2.10.

**Simon (or "Teacher") Says** is a great way to play the Directions Game at a faster tempo. Have the class stand up and explain the rules. If you say "Simon says," they must do what you say. If you do not, they must not. If they do, they will be out and will have to sit down. Let one of the winners be the new Simon for the next round if you are so inclined.

**Body Geography** is a Waldorf variation of "Simon Says." It comes from *The Extra Lesson* by Audrey McAllen. It helps the children become aware of their bodies and of right and left. It also helps to practice following directions. Once the children have adequate concept imagery skills in the games listed above, step it up a bit and start doing Body Geography exercises. They can be done from 1st through 8th Grade.

1st Grade and 2nd Grade: Introduce the concept of right having different meanings (correct vs. right side). Then play the Directions Game but only with directions that relate to touching different parts of their body. Start by giving one direction (e.g., right hand touches right big toe). Then build up giving two directions at a time and then three.

2nd and 3rd Grade: Continue to do the exercises. Expand to four and five directions when the class is ready to do so. Be creative: knees, toes, and noses can be used to touch body parts.

Note: "Simon Says" and Body Geography are both good IMAs during a transition (see chapter 2.3 #4). In addition, Body Geography has value in and of itself, beyond practicing concept imagery or transitioning.

If students need additional instruction, consider doing exercises from the Lindamood-Bell program *Visualizing and Verbalizing® Program for Cognitive Development, Comprehension, and Thinking* (see chapter 6.6 #6).

## 6. Exercises to Develop Concept Imagery (Reading)

You should not need to teach concept imagery after the initial introduction; however, sometimes a class (or a group of students) needs help developing concept imagery. Here is an exercise you can do with the class or a small group of students.

Ask the students to draw selected scenes from a class reader from memory. When you first begin these practice exercises, hold a discussion first for student to share how they pictured the scene. You can even have a student read aloud selections and share mental movies. Then ask each student to draw her own picture of what she saw. As the students progress, drop the rereading, then the class discussion. Students should be able to imagine what they read without any scaffolding or additional help.

Note: Start with broader scenes. For example, how did you imagine the farm in *Charlotte's Web*? (The drawings might include an overview of animals in the farm or a barn scene.) Progress to more specific scenes. For example, what did Templeton the rat look like when he was eating Wilbur's food at the end of the story? (The drawings would include Templeton at the trough, eating the best of Wilbur's food, and he would be obese.) These drawings can also be used to assess students' concept imagery.

If students need additional practice for reading, consider doing exercises from the Lindamood-Bell program *Visualizing and Verbalizing® Program for Cognitive Development, Comprehension, and Thinking* (see chapter 6.6 #6).

## 7. Practice

Because students should enter 1st Grade with adequate concept imagery, practice is less critical. Some aspects are optional.

**Activities A and B:** See chapter 3.7 #4.

**Skills Practice:** Only if a small group of students needs extra practice (see chapter 3.7 #5 and #6).

**Fun and Games:** In addition, there are some fun practice activities/games in Sections 3.7 #5 and #6 that you can use to practice concept imagery.

## 8.   Assessment

Assessment is a critical part of teaching. It is important to verify that students have mastered the skills they have been taught. See chapter 6.1 for background on assessment.

**Benchmarks** represent <u>minimum</u> levels of student achievement by the end of each grade for students to be on track to handle grade-level work in 4th Grade (see chapter 6.1 #9). There is no benchmark for concept imagery *per se*. Students should be proficient at using concept imagery when they start 1st Grade. Instead, assess concept imagery through comprehension (see table 3.8.2).

There are three types of assessments. Recommendations for each type of assessment can be found in Sections 6.3, 6.4, and 6.5. You can use the following ideas as a starting point to set up an assessment program.

**Informal Assessments:** Assess concept imagery informally by using reviews from stories (see chapter 3.8 #2). If you see difficulties, pull the student aside to do a teacher-made assessment for concept imagery.

**Teacher-Made Assessment:** (Only include if you see a student is struggling with comprehension.) In a quiet environment, meet with the student one on one and ask the student to:

- Follow several sets of directions (three directions for 1st Grade; four directions for 2nd and 3rd Grade).

- Listen to two or three short grade-level passages and answer questions about them.*

- Read two or three different short grade-level passages and answer questions about them (if student can read independently).*

*Probe the student's responses to discover if the student is visualizing and if so, how thoroughly. For example, if the question asked how many eggs were in a basket, and the student answered *"five,"* ask what she imagined (e.g., *what color was the basket, where was it, what color eggs were in it, etc.*). Do these exercises in a non-threatening, friendly manner. This discussion will provide a window into a student's concept imagery, or lack thereof.

**Assessments Created by Educational Testing Groups:** NA

See chapters 6.3, 6.4, and 6.5 for more information about assessing in each grade.

## 9.   How to Help Struggling Students

**Assess:** When you see a student is struggling with concept imagery, do assessments (both formal and informal) to gather information about the weakness and to document your findings (see chapter 6.3 #2; 6.4 #2; 6.5 #2).

**Additional Instruction/Practice:** Next, provide this student with extra instruction and practice in the weak area(s). Document what you try and the results. Ask the student's parents to read to the student every night from simple chapter books with minimal to no pictures. Have them discuss the story pictures they imagined together. They can even draw pictures if so inclined so that the story has some illustrations.

**Remedial Solutions:** If you do not notice improvements in three or four weeks, it is time to contact your mentor for guidance and consult chapter 6.6 for additional information on remedial issues. If the situation is severe, the student may need the Lindamood-Bell program *Visualizing and Verbalizing® Program for Cognitive Development, Comprehension, & Thinking* (see chapter 6.6 #6).

**Accommodations and Modifications:** Sometimes it takes a while for remedial issues to be resolved. Meanwhile, the student needs support to function in class. Consider using the following accommodation as a temporary measure. For class work, repeat the instructions to the student privately after giving them to the whole class and have the student repeat them back in her own words or write them down.

## Conclusion

Given the oral nature of Waldorf methodology, Waldorf students often develop phenomenal listening skills and memories, but these accomplishments depend on the full development of concept imagery. It used to be that teachers could take concept imagery for granted, but given the modern world, the development of concept imagery is under assault. Even students who attended Waldorf preschools and kindergartens may be affected. There is much you can do in class to help students develop concept imagery, but some students may need more assistance. Be proactive. Students do not outgrow weaknesses in concept imagery; they only become more pronounced as the language demands increase in the classroom with each passing year.

# 3.8 LANGUAGE AND READING COMPREHENSION

*Jennifer Militzer-Kopperl was teaching a boy with poor language and reading comprehension. He had learned to use concept imagery and was practicing with grade-level reading passages. The text they were working with said:*

> *The word 'highway' has a very old history. In England, over a thousand years ago, roads were higher than the ground around them. Workers threw up earth from ditches to form a raised or high way of travel. Because they were higher, they were called 'highways.' These first highways were built by the Romans, who had invaded England. (Boning 1976, 6.1)*

*The student summarized the passage. Then Jennifer asked him to share his mental pictures. The student blushed and stammered, "I know this is wrong, but I see the workers getting sick on the road—throwing up dirt." Suppressing a smile, Jennifer nodded, "You are correct—that is wrong. Watch me." She grabbed a Kleenex and deliberately threw it up in the air. The boy exclaimed, "Oh! They threw <u>dirt</u> up on the road! That's how they raised the road!"*

Concept imagery underlies good reading comprehension and good language comprehension; however, comprehension requires more than visualization; it also requires knowledge of the varieties and nuances of the language. After all, in the vignette above, the student's initial mental picture technically matched the text yet his inability to comprehend how the term *threw up earth*'was being used prevented him from understanding the passage.

This chapter covers the following topics:

1. Why Comprehension Matters
2. Background Information: Four Types of Review
3. Preparation
4. Scheduling
5. How to Teach Comprehension in 1st Grade
6. How to Teach Comprehension in 2nd Grade
7. How to Teach Comprehension in 3rd Grade
8. Practice
9. Assessment
10. How to Help Struggling Students

## 1.  Why Comprehension Matters

There are two kinds of comprehension: language comprehension and reading comprehension. Both type of comprehension have two sides: expressive and receptive. When students understand language (spoken or written), it is called **receptive language**. When they express themselves (spoken or written), it is called **expressive language**. Both are critical skills.

Expressive and receptive language are important for many reasons. Language is how people make sense of the world they encounter. They can step away from the percept, the thing that is perceived, and examine it through concepts thanks to language. Those with rich vocabularies can think in greater depth because they can examine nuances in concepts that are not apparent to others. In addition, language helps people express themselves and understand others. Finally, language is the foundation for reading and writing. If students have weak language skills, it will show up as a reading problem even if they crack the code.

Language comprehension is a capacity that should be well formed when students enter 1st Grade. They should be able to speak in complete sentences, follow three-step directions automatically, and be able to comprehend oral stories through their own concept imagery. Students will make use of all of these language comprehension skills from the beginning of 1st Grade and will build upon them. By 3rd Grade students are expected to transform their comprehension of the material presented in class into their own compositions for their main lesson books. In addition to good literacy skills, they need good language comprehension to be able to make this leap.

Reading comprehension is just as critical as language comprehension. If a student struggles with reading comprehension, it often creates a vicious circle. Students need lots of practice to create and then myelinate the reading pathways in the brain. Students who do not comprehend well do not read for pleasure; consequently, their reading pathways do not always get the repetition they need. Their reading often remains slow and halting, which further undermines their reading comprehension. These students then need remediation in both reading skills and in concept imagery to catch up with their peers.

Students need good expressive and receptive skills in both spoken language and written language. Waldorf relies heavily on oral imaginations and stories when it comes to introducing new concepts in Grades 1–3. Consequently, if a Waldorf student struggles with listening comprehension, it can undermine the student's education.

## 2. Background Information: Four Types of Review

The primary way Waldorf teaches comprehension is through review of stories and materials presented in class. This review is done during the Introduction &/or Review segment of main lesson. There are four types of review:

1. Sequential Retelling
2. Factual Recall Questions
3. Higher Order Thinking Skill Questions (HOTS)
4. Free Renderings

Use these four types of reviews as appropriate for the developmental phase of your class and as dictated by the story's purpose (i.e., providing an image for the next day's lesson; generating a list of words that could be used in a composition; preparing students to write a story summary, etc.). Each approach will develop different aspects of comprehension. Below is a description of each type of review.

### Sequential Retelling

Sequential retelling, or story retelling, is where the students retell a story in order (e.g., what happened first, second, etc.). The goal is the development of sequential memory. It is often the main type of review used in 1st Grade and is largely confined to that grade; however, you can use it in later grades to review a story or material that is told over several days in preparation for the next installment. You can also use it as a way to review a chapter in a book the students were assigned to read on their own.

**Factual Recall Questions**

Factual Recall Questions are questions you pose to the class. There are three possible goals: 1) To focus the students' attention on a particular aspect of a story or lesson to introduce a new concept or skill; 2) To assess comprehension of a reading assignment; 3) To review an oral presentation before writing about it.

Here are some examples of factual recall questions for the story of "Hansel and Gretel":

- Who: Who abandoned Hansel and Gretel in the wood?
- What: What did Hansel use to find the way back home?
- Where: Where did the witch put Hansel?
- When: When did the witch leave?
- Why: Why did Hansel stick the bone out of the window?
- How: How did Hansel and Gretel escape?
- How (duration of time): How many days were they gone?

**Higher Order Thinking Skills Questions (HOTS questions)**

HOTS questions go beyond factual recall questions because they require additional thought. Their goal is to develop five important thinking skills:

1. Identify the main idea
2. Make inferences
3. Predict outcomes
4. Draw a conclusion
5. Evaluate the material

The following examples are based on the story "Hansel and Gretel" to show how they might be incorporated into an end-of-year 1st Grade story. These questions can be very simple or rather complex. Make sure that you use the type of question and level of sophistication that fits your class (see chapter 3.8 #5). You can begin including these questions once your class is proficient at factual recall questions.

Main Idea is when the students isolate the theme, moral, or most important element of the story. For example, "*What is the main idea of the story?*" (Hansel and Gretel get trapped by a witch but escape.) In 3rd Grade answers to this type of question could be used for a title or topic sentence of a paragraph.

Inference occurs when students must read between the lines to deduce a fact that is not stated directly. It can be a *why* or *how* question that considers cause-and-effect relationships that are implied in the text. For example, "*Why did Gretel stay at the witch's house rather than escape?* (She did not want to leave Hansel.)

Prediction occurs when students consider what might happen next in the story. They draw upon both what has happened so far and their own experiences to make this prediction. For example, "*The story ended with Hansel and Gretel scattering their gems and pearls around the cottage. What do you suppose they did with them the next day?*" (Hansel and Gretel might have picked them up and put them in a chest for safe keeping or their father might have taken some of them to town to sell.)

Note: It is important that students do a few HOTS questions that take them beyond the confines of the story. It is important that students develop the skill to infer or predict even though "the story did not say." As they get older, these skills will become more and more important. The prediction questions they do in the early grades introduce them to the concept of thinking outside the box of the author's words. Thinking goes beyond recall.

Conclusion refers to when students use the material to arrive at their own unique thought. If inference is when the author states a fact indirectly that the students then must infer, conclusion is when the students go beyond what the author says and bring their own new thought that builds directly off of what the author said. For example, "*Gretel gave her brother a chicken bone to use to fool the witch. What does this tell us about Gretel?*" (Gretel is clever. She thinks of a way to trick the witch and save her brother's life.)

Evaluation occurs when the students make a judgment about the material based on prior experience or information. For example, "*What do you think about Hansel and Gretel's decision to go back home to their father?*" (They knew he cared about them and thought that their gift of the pearls would make their step-mother accept them.)

## Free Rendering

Free rendering is an alternative way to review a story brought by Else Gottgens, a Dutch Waldorf teacher and mentor. There are three types:

- written
- dramatic arts
- visual arts

For this type of review, the students choose an artistic medium and quickly create something from the story: a picture, a little skit, a beeswax model, etc. Free rendering has a number of benefits in the creative, imaginative realm of student development, but is not as effective of a tool for developing language comprehension as the other methods already mentioned.

Introduce free rendering once your students' comprehension is good and you want to enliven the Introduction &/or Review segment of the main lesson.

Written renderings: Students compose a written response to some aspect of the story. For example, it could be a poem or tongue twister or they could describe the most vivid scene using either adjectives or adverbs.

Dramatic arts renderings: Students use pantomime or drama to create a brief play to act out a scene in front of the class. (Provide sacks with various props and costumes they could use.) Some students write the script, some assemble the costumes and props.

Visual arts renderings: Students create something from the story using various art supplies: construction paper, yarn, colored Popsicle sticks, beeswax, scissors and/or glue. Students can also draw a quick sketch from the story or model something with beeswax, clay, or plasticine clay.

Note: Make free renderings brief. The point is review, not the creation of artistic masterpieces. Free rendering should be limited to 10 minutes and never go beyond 15 minutes from start to finish. The students can take home their unfinished work if they would like to complete it. At first there may be some frustration around not being able to finish—especially with melancholic and phlegmatic students. If you hold firm to the time limit, they will adjust their endeavors and/or their expectations. If you do not, this type of review will eat up too large of a chunk of time to be worthwhile.

## 3.  Preparation

During the summer and/or over the school year, there are a few things you need to do:

- Oral Language Comprehension: In Grades 1–3, decide what kinds of review you will use and write review questions for the stories you plan to tell. Use these guidelines:

  - 1st Grade: Decide which types of review you plan to use for each story and assemble any needed supplies. Write review questions.

  - 2nd Grade: Ibid.

    Note: Include factual recall questions, HOTS questions, and free renderings. Only use sequential retelling when you need to review a story that goes over several days or if a lot of students were absent the day before and you need a more thorough review to bring them up to speed.

  - 3rd Grade: Ibid.

    Note: Include factual recall questions and HOTS questions. Only use sequential retelling when you need to review a story that goes over several days or if students were absent the day before and you need a more thorough review to bring them up to speed.

- Reading Comprehension: In the 2nd half of 2nd Grade and in 3rd Grade, write questions for the material students read in reading group. Include at least four factual recall questions and at least one HOTS question.

Make sure you highlight the pertinent information for stories that will introduce a new concept.

## 4.  Scheduling

When preparing your curriculum, you can use the block plan templates in Appendices 1–3 or you can create your own. If you create your own, use the following points to lay out your blocks:

1. Begin instruction the first practice block of 1st Grade.

2. It will take students until the end of 8th Grade to master comprehension because students will have to master increasingly more difficult levels of comprehension with each academic year.

3. Teach listening comprehension in the Introduction &/or Review segment in main lesson. Teach reading comprehension whenever you schedule it.

4. Teach using a two-day rhythm for listening comprehension and a one-day rhythm for teaching reading comprehension as shown in table 3.8.1.

5. Schedule 5–15 minutes per lesson, depending on the type of review you choose to do.

6. In 2nd and 3rd Grade, segue into written comprehension questions and alternate with oral comprehension questions from then on.

**Table 3.8.1: Teaching Rhythms**

| Two-Day Rhythm |
| --- |
| • Day One: Tell the Story. <br> • Day Two: Do the review of the story. |
| **One-Day Rhythm** |
| • Students read the story. <br> • Students answer review questions (oral or written). |

## 5. How to Teach Comprehension in 1st Grade

Comprehension in 1st Grade mainly focuses on language comprehension because students do not start reading unfamiliar stories until the end of the school year.

**Objectives:**

1. Confirm that students have good receptive language comprehension skills and that they comprehend the stories you tell in class.

2. Teach student to use good expressive language (e.g., to answer in complete sentences and to provide listeners with the right amount of information to understand what they are saying).

**Prerequisite:** Students can use concept imagery for spoken language.

**When to Teach:** Teach in the Introduction &/or Review segment in main lesson blocks only.

**How to Teach:** In 1st Grade, use all four types of review as appropriate. The first three build off of each other logically, and free renderings can be added in as an alternative to the others.

Sequential retelling is the type of review to begin with. Once students become proficient with it, you can use this type of review in many ways:

- Student retell: Have the class retell the story in their own words. Go around the class and ask each student to add a sentence or two in chronological order. If the next person does not have the next part, just move on and come back to that person later. After the class has completed the story, ask the students if any important parts were missing. (The important element is that the story is sequential and contains all of the essential points.) Note: You can also ask for volunteers to tell the story in sequence. Mix both approaches.

- Do a chronology of emotions (e.g., *"How do you think the hero/ine felt at the beginning of the story, after this event and that event, and at the end?"*)

- Bring in objects that were mentioned in the story, have the students discuss the role of each one. Which one appeared first, second, third?

- Name the various people/characters that appeared in chronological order and what each one did.

- For 1st Grade: Write out a very simple summary of the story on the board leaving blanks and have the students fill in the blanks. (Choose ahead of time whether or not to provide possible answers in a list.) This summary could then go in the main lesson books.

- Choose a specific subject such as animals and identify which one appeared first, next, etc. When did each come in to the story? What was their role? Or you could choose one animal and chronicle its journey through the story.

Factual Recall Questions come right on the heels of sequential retelling reviews. They are used to introduce or review a new concept. Use factual recall questions to guide your students' recall to the pertinent part(s) of the story as a review of the important facts that you will highlight in your introduction of the new concept.

Note: The students are to answer all of the questions in complete sentences. Model answers in complete sentences and make students repeat the answer to help them correct their answers.

HOTS Questions can be included after spring break once your students demonstrate proficiency with factual recall questions. Build them into your factual recall questions. For example,

- Factual recall: "What did Hansel drop on the ground to make a trail home?" (Hansel dropped breadcrumbs.)

- HOTS: "What could Hansel have used to make a better trail?" (He could have used red maple leaves.)

- HOTS: "Why would red maple leaves have made a better trail?" (They would make a better trail because no animals would eat them.)

You can easily determine whether your group is ready for a particular type of HOTS question by asking one and listening to the answers. If your class understands the question and eagerly engages in answering it, they are ready. If they seem puzzled or miss the point, wait until they are more mature in their thinking and try again. When doing main idea, ask for other possible titles for the story. Students have a hard time formulating the main idea in a simple sentence, but they can invent new titles that reflect an aspect of the main idea.

Free renderings should be included once the students demonstrate solid comprehension skills, are familiar with the routine of main lesson, and can be trusted to stay on task when the structure is relaxed. Begin with the visual arts (drawing, modeling, making creations with various materials, etc.). Towards the end of the year, when the students have basic kid writing skills, expand into the dramatic arts and script writing. (Remember to watch the time. Limit this activity to 10–15 minutes.)

Note: It is not necessary to do much work with reading comprehension in 1st Grade. Once the students begin reading decodable-text, you can include a few HOTS questions. You will find that factual recall questions are ineffective because the texts are simple and the illustrations give away the answers.

## 6.  How to Teach Comprehension in 2nd Grade

Comprehension in 2nd Grade will include both language comprehension and reading comprehension. Reading comprehension will pick up as students begin to read decodable-text without as many illustrations.

**Objectives:**

1. Confirm that students have good receptive language comprehension skills and that they comprehend the stories you tell in class and the stories they read.

2. Teach student to use good expressive language (e.g., to answer in complete sentences and to provide listeners with the right amount of information to understand what they are saying) for both listening comprehension and reading comprehension.

**Prerequisite:** Students can use concept imagery for spoken language and written language.

**When to Teach:** Teach in the Introduction &/or Review segment in main lesson blocks only for listening comprehension and teach in whichever segment you schedule reading in for reading comprehension.

**How to Teach: Language Comprehension**

There are some changes in the types of review to use in 2nd Grade.

Sequential Retelling is largely phased out. It is only used to review a story that is told over two or more days (e.g., the story of St. Francis of Assisi) or if you are introducing a composition and need to review a story sequentially as preparation to compose a summary.

Factual Recall Questions are still used to introduce or review a new concept. Continue to use factual recall questions to guide your students' recall to the pertinent part(s) of the story as a review of the important facts that you will highlight in your introduction of the new concept.

HOTS Questions become more common. Mix them in with your factual recall questions so there is an even mix.

For main idea questions, phase out questions that ask for alternative titles for the story in favor of asking the students what the main idea of the story is. For example you could ask, *"What is the main idea of the story of St. Francis and the Wolf of Gubbio?"* (The main idea is that St. Francis tamed the mean wolf.) Help the students figure out how to say their main idea in one complete sentence. Stress that this does not mean they should tell the whole story but rather the main idea or the most important idea in the story. This concept takes lots of practice to develop. Model it by asking the class to help you create main ideas before asking the students to come up with ideas on their own.

Do not do main idea questions with fables because they are told as soul food stories. The moral is best left for the students to work with inwardly.

It is possible to use HOTS questions to work on social skills or on emotional development. One way to do so is to discuss what would have happened if a particular character had made a different choice.

Free Renderings should be included on days when the lesson needs some enlivening. If a lesson feels heavy or pedantic, consider switching the Introduction &/or Review segment to free rendering.

In 2nd Grade, you can give the students more free rein to choose their type of free rendering if you provide some choices. For example, students can choose to draw a picture, make a beeswax character, or write a dialogue with some friends that they will then perform in front of the class.

**How to Teach Reading Comprehension**

As students begin to read books without pictures, begin to monitor reading comprehension by including factual recall questions and HOTS questions. The questions can be oral or written. The majority should be factual recall questions, but include at least one HOTS question.

If you have not done so already, teach students to use the language of the question in their answer. For example, if the question said, *"When Cori saw the kitten for the first time, what did she think of him?"* the students would have to include part of the question in the answer for their answer to make sense. For example, they could say, *"When Cori saw the kitten for the first time, she thought he was pretty."* or *"Cori thought the kitten was pretty when she saw him for the first time."* If they just said, *"She thought he was pretty,"* the reader would not know what they were talking about.

It is good to get students in the habit of using the language of the question in the answer. It will serve them well as they write their own compositions based on a written prompt.

## 7.   How to Teach Comprehension in 3rd Grade

Students will have an even mix of language and reading comprehension in 3rd Grade.

**Objectives:**

1. Confirm that students have good receptive language comprehension skills and that they comprehend the stories you tell in class and the stories they read.

2. Teach student to use good expressive language (e.g., to answer in complete sentences and to provide listeners with the right amount of information to understand what they are saying) for both listening comprehension and reading comprehension.

**Prerequisite:** Students can use concept imagery for spoken language and written language.

**When to Teach:** Teach in the Introduction &/or Review segment in main lesson blocks only for listening comprehension and teach in whichever segment you schedule reading in for reading comprehension.

### How to Teach Language Comprehension

In 3rd Grade, use factual recall questions and HOTS questions to review Old Testament stories.

Factual recall questions are useful when reviewing a story that the students will be writing about for their main lesson book entry. The questions and ensuing discussions in your review should help students focus in on the important aspects and give them language that they can use to write their summaries.

HOTS questions can be used to initiate class discussions about the Old Testament stories, especially regarding the actions of a story's characters and the consequences of those actions.

Curriculum Connection: Review main ideas when doing composition writing, particularly when introducing paragraphs and practicing writing paragraphs (see chapter 3.14 #7).

Teach students a new way to answer main idea HOTS questions. Shift away from including the language of the question in the answer in favor of stating the main idea as a possible topic sentence of a paragraph or composition. For example, if you discussed sheep farming as part of the Practical Occupations Block (see chapter 5.5 #8), you could ask, *"What is the main idea of the presentation we heard yesterday about sheep husbandry?"* You would then guide students towards a possible topic sentence (e.g., *"Farmers who take care of sheep have to do a lot of work to make sure the sheep stay healthy and safe,"* rather than "The main idea is that *farmers who take care of sheep have to do a lot of work to make sure the sheep stay healthy and safe."*). This practice will help the students prepare to write their own compositions. They can then back up this topic sentence with lots of supporting details such as how the farmer has to shear the sheep and make sure the sheep's hooves do not get infected, etc.

Phase out free renderings in order to provide more time for composition work.

### How to Teach Reading Comprehension

Continue to use factual recall questions in reading groups as you did in 2nd Grade. All of the questions should be answered in complete sentences. Build up to short answer essay questions in 3rd Grade starting with two sentences and building up to a paragraph once students learn to write paragraphs.

Some advanced students may be reading an assigned book silently on their own rather than participating in reading groups. If so, give them their own written questions to answer after they finish the reading assignment for the day.

## 8. Practice

Practice is critical. It forms part of your initial introduction in the Introduction &/or Review segment of main lesson (i.e., Activities A and B). It will be part of your ongoing practice in the Skills Practice segment of main lesson and practice classes (see chapter 2.3 #4).

**Activities A and B:** The following activities are good to use:

- sequential retelling
- factual recall questions
- HOTS (Higher Order Thinking Skill) questions
- free renderings

(See chapter 3.8 #2 and 3.8 #5-6 for advice by grade.)

**Skills Practice:** NA

**Fun and Games:** NA

## 9. Assessment

Assessment is a critical part of teaching. It is important to verify that students have mastered the skills they have been taught. See chapter 6.1 for background on assessment.

**Benchmarks** represent <u>minimum</u> levels of student achievement by the end of each grade for students to be on track to handle grade-level work in 4th Grade (see chapter 6.1 #9). Table 3.8.2 contains the benchmarks for comprehension.

Note: The following benchmarks may not be exhaustive. Prerequisite skills for comprehension may be covered under other related language arts skills. For a full list of benchmarks, see table 6.1.4.

**Table 3.8.2: Benchmark for Comprehension**

|  | **1st Grade** | **2nd Grade** | **3rd Grade** |
|---|---|---|---|
| **Comprehension** | Students can answer factual review questions for stories told in class. | Students can answer factual review questions and HOTS questions for stories told in class and for stories they have read. | Students can answer factual review questions and HOTS questions for stories told in class, factual presentations, and material they have read. |

There are three types of assessments. Recommendations for each type of assessment can be found in Sections 6.3, 6.4, and 6.5. You can use the following ideas as a starting point to set up an assessment program.

**Type of Assessment:** Assess comprehension formally and informally.

- Informal Assessments: You can assess informally by using any type of review done in class.
- Teacher-Made Assessment: Create a teacher-made assessment for any story or reading assignment you wish to assess. It is even possible to do these formal assessments in the latter part of 1st Grade when the students' kid writing is advanced enough that you can decode their answers. Read a question with the students and then ask them to write their answer in the space provided.

- Assessments Created by Educational Testing Groups: If you choose to do this type of assessment, consider doing it three times a year. Use an assessment of the alphabet designed by an educational testing group such as DIBELS or AIMSweb (see chapter 6.1 #6).

See chapters 6.1, 6.3, 6.4 and 6.5 for more information about assessments.

## 10. How to Help Struggling Students

**Assess:** When you see a student is struggling with comprehension, do assessments (both formal and informal) to narrow down the area(s) of concern and to document your findings. Pay particular attention to concept imagery for both listening and reading comprehension. Pay attention to weak reading fluency (and/or weak accuracy) for reading comprehension and address any weaknesses found (see chapter 3.7, chapter 3.15, and section 6).

Note: Some students do not participate in story review because they are shy or unsure of themselves. In 1st Grade, give these students 8–12 weeks before you start to assess, but in 2nd and 3rd Grade, assess after one month. Pull the student aside and check story comprehension informally. If everything checks out, no further action is necessary.

**Additional Instruction/Practice:** Next, use the results of your assessments to provide this student with extra instruction and practice in any weak areas. You can differentiate instruction both in class and in reading groups. For example, you can modify the instructions for each reading group, or give individual assignments to provide extra practice in a weak area. Decide which approach is best based on how many other students have similar struggles. Document what you try and the results.

Some students can make mental pictures but have difficulty answering HOTS questions. To provide targeted instruction in particular aspects of comprehension, consider using the *Specific Skills Series* by Richard A. Boning. This series has grade-level books that target one aspect of comprehension such as main idea or inference. The passages are short—typically around one paragraph. They can be done with the entire class, small groups, or individuals. Books can be purchased in sets or individually off the internet. They are a good resource if students need more practice with one or two types of HOTS questions.

**Remedial Solutions:** If you do not notice improvements in a month, it is time to contact your mentor for guidance and consult chapter 6.6 for additional information on remedial issues. However, if students' comprehension skills are extremely mismatched (i.e., listening comprehension is much better than reading or vice versa), keep the following points in mind:

- When a student has good listening comprehension but poor reading comprehension, check the student's reading fluency and accuracy. Fluency is crucial because slow, halting reading undermines comprehension. The student's attention is directed towards decoding and word recognition, rather than meaning. If the student reads particularly slowly, the student may even forget the beginning of the sentence before reaching the end. Accuracy is crucial because students need to read at least 95% of the words correctly to comprehend what they are reading (see chapter 3.15 #14). In fact, good readers' accuracy is above 97% (Howell 2008, A19). If students fail fluency and/or accuracy screenings, assess basic reading skills: decoding skills and sight word recognition (see section 6). If the student can read fine, then provide *Visualizing and Verbalizing*® (see chapter 6.6 #6).

- When a student has good reading comprehension but poor listening comprehension, consult the remedial chapter (chapter 6.6) to make sure that capacities are well developed. Then provide the Lindamood-Bell program *Visualizing and Verbalizing*® *Program for Cognitive Development, Comprehension, and Thinking* (see chapter 6.6 #6).

**Accommodations and Modifications:** Sometimes it takes a while for remedial issues to be resolved. Meanwhile, the student needs support to function in class. Consider using the following modification as a temporary measure. Give the student a question in advance. If the student is also shy or lacks confidence, you can check in with her before class to make sure she knows the answer so that when you call on her she will be able to answer. Start off with easy questions until she is ready to enter into reviews.

## Conclusion

Comprehension is the goal of both written and spoken language. Concept imagery is the foundation for good comprehension skills (see chapter 3.7). With it in place, students can develop exemplary skills in comprehension for both written and oral language. The various types of review discussed in this chapter will help you develop your students' comprehension skills. They can also help you assess your students' comprehension. Help any student who struggles with comprehension. Waldorf relies heavily on the element of verbal images (stories) when it comes to introducing new concepts in Grades 1–3. Consequently it is imperative that Waldorf students have appropriate comprehension skills.

# 3.9  SPELLING

*A colleague had given her 5th Grade class a written assignment and had asked the students to have a parent proofread the assignment before they handed it in. One girl with divorced parents anxiously approached the teacher after class. She said she would do the assignment, but it would not get proofread. She shared that her mother's spelling was so bad that spell check did not help her very much. This situation brought up the question: just how effective is spell check?*

This chapter covers the following topics:

1.  Why Spelling Matters
2.  Background Information
3.  Preparation
4.  Scheduling
5.  Initial Introduction
6.  How to Teach Spelling in 1st and 2nd Grade
7.  How to Teach Spelling in 3rd Grade
8.  Dictation
9.  Practice
10. Assessment
11. How to Help Struggling Students

## 1.   Why Spelling Matters

Spelling is a vitally important part of language arts education. Being able to spell is just as critical as being able to read. Some people argue that in the age of spell check, good spelling skills are no longer important. This thinking is flawed. There are three key reasons why it is critical for all students to master spelling.

First, not all writing is done on a computer. The SAT, ACT, Catholic High School entrance exam, and job applications all require students to generate their own spelling. Spelling mistakes in these situations reflect poorly on the student and result in lower scores, fewer admissions, and possibly lost job opportunities.

Second, poor spelling skills continue to reflect poorly on the writer once schooling is done. Adults who cannot spell proficiently appear unintelligent and/or uneducated and are judged accordingly.

Finally, spell checkers have limitations. Spell checkers generate a list of possible correct spellings for each misspelled word. The misspelling has to be reasonably close or else the spell checker will not generate the correct spelling in its list. Also a person has to be able to recognize the correct spelling from the given list. In other words, to use spell checkers, a person has to be a reasonably good speller already. The International

Dyslexia Association (IDA) recommends waiting until a child is spelling at a 5th-Grade level before using spell check (https://dyslexia.org.spelling/).

Good spelling suggests that basic academic skills are well developed. Good spelling gives students confidence in themselves and in their work. It also gives other people confidence in the writer, her abilities, and the message. Spelling is a critical skill for students to master.

## 2. Background Information

We have been in many upper-grades Waldorf classrooms where spelling instruction has been abandoned all together. Teachers relate that they have accepted the fact that they have some good spellers and some that struggle. They state that they have no idea how to help the latter at this point. If teachers follow *The Roadmap to Literacy*, the number of struggling spellers would be greatly reduced because students would have the foundational knowledge they need to spell correctly: encoding (chapter 3.4) sight words (chapter 3.6), and phonics rules (section 4). Upper-grades teachers would then be free to focus on upper-level spelling (i.e., the Latin/Greek Phase, something that will be addressed in a future book).

### Prerequisites for Good Spelling

Good spelling has several prerequisites. The first is phonemic awareness. To be able to spell all of the sounds in a word a student must first be able to segment each sound. The second is symbol imagery. Students who can imagine the correct spelling of a word can then determine which pattern of letters is correct when there is more than one way to spell a word. The third prerequisite is meaning. Students need to consider the meaning of a word when they spell it. They begin to work with meaning as early as 1st Grade when they learn to use –s at the end of the word to make the word mean more than one. For example, even though they can hear the sound /z/ at the end of the word, the correct spelling is *dogs* not *dogz*.

These three prerequisites correspond to the three layers of the English layer cake. Phonemic awareness corresponds to the first layer. Symbol imagery corresponds to the second layer. Meaning corresponds to the final layer.

In addition, handwriting can contribute to good spelling. When students form the words and letters correctly, it reinforces symbol imagery and an eye for which spelling looks right. Writing words also helps some students recall their spelling through motor memory.

### A Prominent Spelling Myth

A prominent spelling myth is that students can become good spellers through reading (i.e., if students read a lot they will automatically develop good spelling). The reality is more complicated.

If a student has exemplary symbol imagery, good spelling can be the result of copious reading. Seeing words in print once or twice is enough for these students to remember how to spell them. The visual patterns of words get stored in the spelling lexicon in their brains as they read.

If a student has average symbol imagery, lots of reading can create good receptive spelling skills but not necessarily cross over to good expressive spelling skills. In other words, this student may know if a word looks right when she sees it but not be able to generate the word's spelling. This student can recognize the correct word if it appears on a spell check list.

However, if a student has poor symbol imagery skills lots of reading does not carry over into good spelling. This type of student is unable to generate the spelling from visual memory and cannot pick out the right spelling from a lineup.

It is good to have struggling spellers read more. The majority of students will get some spelling benefit from it. However, it may not be enough. Working consciously with the four types of spelling will insure that your students have the best chance to become good spellers.

**The Four Types of Spelling**

There are four main types of spelling, and they correspond with the phases. The four main types of spelling are:

- Chanting
- Encoding Sounds (phonemes)
- Visualizing (symbol imagery)
- Encoding Meaning (morphemes)

Chanting is used by children who do not have access to the higher three strategies. Recall kindergartners who proudly state that they can spell *Mississippi* and then proceed to chant: MISS–ISS–IPP-I. They do not necessarily know that letters represent sounds. Instead, they are using a chant to recall the letters. Or recall the beloved Mickey Mouse Club theme song: *Who's the leader of a club that's made for you and me? MIC-KEY-MO-US-E.* The most important musical elements are pitch and rhythm. Knowledge of the code is secondary to the chant. Chanting can be the training wheels students use while they are learning the other spelling strategies.

Encoding Sounds (phonemes) is used by students who know that letters represent sounds and who have partial to full phonemic awareness. This strategy is more advanced than chanting. Here students listen to the phonemes and come up with appropriate letter matches. Rather than chanting *MIC-KEY-MO-US-E*, students break words down into syllables and phonemes to figure out appropriate ways to clothe the sounds they hear in written letters. For example, the word *mouse* is segmented as follows: /m/ /ou/ /s/. It clearly starts with an *M*, has a vowel that could be spelled with the letters *OU* or *OW*, and ends with a /s/ which could be spelled with an *S*, *SS*, *SE*, or *CE*. All of these spellings are appropriate encodings for *mouse:* mouse, mowse, mous, mows, mouss, mowss, mouce, mowce.

Visualizing (symbol imagery) is the next development of spelling. It has two stages: receptive and expressive. Receptive visualizing enables students to recognize that most of the encodings they generate look wrong. As you looked at the eight possible spellings for *mouse,* some of them looked worse than others. For example, it is clear that the spelling *mowss* is flat-out wrong whereas *mouse* looks quite reasonable. Expressive spelling allows students to visualize the letters for a word in their own imagination. They do not have to encode all of the spellings to then recognize the right one. Instead, they use symbol imagery (i.e., they can close their eyes and visualize the right spelling). It is much more efficient.

Encoding Meaning (Morphemes) is the icing on the cake. In addition to phonemic awareness and symbol imagery, students can consider the meaning of a word and determine which units of meaning (**morphemes**) they need to use. This analysis can range from beginning to advanced skills. For example, students can begin to use it as early as the Phonemic Awareness Phase when they want to spell a word like *boys* (root word: boy; plural marker: –s). As the phases progress, they use it more and more. By the Latin/Greek Phase (not covered in this book), morphemes become the primary units for learning the spelling of new words. Rather than encoding sounds, students encode meaning. Mixed in with the spelling of the word *philosopher* is an awareness of how the word is constructed. Philosopher: phil *(love)* + Sophia *(wisdom)* + -er *(suffix denoting person who);* **cognates**, or related words: philosophy. Inherent to the spelling of *philosopher* is the meaning of the word: a person who loves wisdom.

These four types of spelling each have their place and time. The strategies used depend on a student's phase as shown in table 3.9.1.

**Table 3.9.1: How to Teach Spelling by Phase**

| Spelling Technique | Emergent | Phonemic Awareness | Pattern | Syllable | Latin/Greek |
|---|---|---|---|---|---|
| **Chanting** | yes | yes | beginning of phase only | no | no |
| **Encoding Sounds** | no | yes* | yes | yes | yes |
| **Visualizing (symbol imagery)** | no | yes* | yes | yes | yes |
| **Encoding Meaning (Morphemes)** | no | inflectional endings only (–s,–ed ,–ing) | Ibid and homophones | Ibid and affixes that have meaning | Latin and Greek roots |

*Students will have limited ability. Augment with other methods.

Students in the Emergent Phase primarily use chanting and work on developing encoding. Students in the Phonemic Awareness Phase still rely on chanting for sight words, but they use it less and less as their major focus is on encoding and symbol imagery. Students in the Pattern Phase have full phonemic awareness and need to rely more and more on symbol imagery to handle the myriad vowel patterns in English. Students in the Syllable Phase need all three: encoding, visualizing, and meaning to encode multisyllabic words. By the Latin/Greek Phase, students have perfected the lower spelling systems and encoding morphemes, or meaning, takes center stage to enable vocabulary development and advanced spelling skills.

In your spelling curriculum, wait to study formal spelling lists until after you have taught both sets of words on *The Roadmap to Literacy's* sight word list (or the equivalent). This will place your students at the end of the Pattern Phase or beginning of the Syllable Phase (3rd Grade). By then the students should have developed the necessary prerequisites for good spelling and be ready to study specific word lists.

### Jump Rope Spelling

Some teachers like to pair jumping rope and spelling as a form of economy in teaching. It is worth reconsidering whether this is the best use of your Skills Practice time. First, jump rope spelling is a form of chant spelling and should thus have a short shelf life (the Emergent Phase and the beginning of the Phonemic Awareness Phase when students are not yet up and running with phonemic awareness and symbol imagery and the beginning of the Pattern Phase for words with five or more letters). Second, it is inefficient. Only one student at a time gets to spell. A better choice is sight word chants (see chapter 3.6 #6). An entire class can practice them together, and it takes less than 30 seconds per word.

### Spelling Lists: Reteaching Phonics Rules

Recall that students' ability to decode outpaces their ability to encode during the Pattern Phase (see chapter 3.4 #2). As a consequence, it is necessary to teach phonics rules twice. The first time is when you teach encoding and decoding. The second time is when you teach spelling in 3rd Grade. Your spelling program should be comprised of weekly spelling lists. Each spelling list should consist of grade-appropriate words that are organized around phonics principles (rules). The words illustrate the principle(s) of the week and contain a few notable exceptions. When teaching your weekly spelling words, review the applicable phonics principles and ask students to determine which words utilize which principles. This will help them master grade-level spelling.

### 3. Preparation

Spelling preparation only applies in 3rd Grade because that is the year students begin to study spelling as a separate entity (i.e. not part of encoding or sight words).

**Background Information:** Over the summer, decide whether you will buy a spelling program or make your own weekly lists of words. Buying a quality spelling program is the most fail-safe option. In good programs, the words have been carefully selected and sorted by experts. Each lesson is a unit. You can rearrange the order of the lessons as needed to fit in with your curriculum. However, you must vet the program. Many companies throw together lists of words as an afterthought to a reading program. If the creators of the spelling program are unaware of the phases students move through in developing spelling skills, these lists of words can be worse than words selected randomly.

**Four Items in a Good Spelling Program:** If you are considering a program, there are guidelines you can follow to determine a spelling program's quality. They are the same techniques you would follow if you wanted to make up your own lists of words. They are as follows:

1. Each list should be organized around studying a spelling concept and/or contrasting various spelling concepts. For example,

   - Spelling Rules (e.g., contractions or the rule *I Before E except after C*)
   - Phonics Rules (e.g., a review that compares ways to spell Long *A: AY, AI,* and *A_E)*
   - Encoding that the class still struggles with (e.g., spelling patterns for a vowel sound such as Long *E*)

2. The most common concepts should be phonics rules the class has mastered in decoding but not encoding. Keep in mind the primary objective of spelling tests is helping students' encoding skills catch up with their decoding skills.

3. While good spelling lists are organized around a principle, they should not be 100% predictable. Instead, they should have a few examples of common words (or derivatives of common words) that do not follow the rule or they should focus on reviewing two or more spelling patterns for one sound. This variety serves two purposes: 1) It helps the students learn irregular words; and 2) It encourages students to engage with the lesson. If every word is predictable, students tune out.

4. The words are ones often used (and misspelled) at the grade in question. For example, *breakfast* is a word used by 2nd and 3rd graders while *exhaust* is not. This principle would include common sight words that many students continue to misspell such as *because*.

If you chose to make up your own lists, consider the encoding and decoding rules you taught and apply the guidelines above to hone your list down. You can also split the difference between the two approaches for generating spelling lists by using *Words Their Way* as a resource for finding ready-made lists of words that have spelling features.

Note: If you choose to begin spelling in late 2nd Grade, start with 10–12 words initially. In 3rd Grade select 15–20 words per week. Homophones make a logical choice (see chapter 4.2 rule 21).

**Recommendations for Spelling Programs:** Below are three commercial spelling programs worth considering: (You would use these programs as the source for your weekly spelling words.)

1. Zaner-Bloser spelling program has a spelling program with pre-made lists and workbooks. It can be found https://www.zaner-bloser.com/products/spelling-connections.php. It is the easiest to implement in a classroom. No background knowledge is necessary.

2. *All about Spelling* by Marie Rippel is an Orton-Gillingham approach. It has scripted lessons at different levels.

3. *How to Teach Spelling* by Laura Rudginsky has workbooks but is not scripted.

You can decide if you want to purchase workbooks for each student or just use the list of words and create your own practice exercises.

**Spelling Lists are Separate from Vocabulary Lists:** Vocabulary and spelling are separate subjects. In too many 3rd-8th Grade Waldorf classrooms the vocabulary list has become the spelling list or vice versa. This approach shortchanges both spelling and vocabulary. Spelling is developed systematically through the phases. A good spelling curriculum reviews the phonics rules students have mastered for decoding. It includes important, grade-level words that students need to learn to spell. *The Roadmap to Literacy* does not recommend the formal study of vocabulary until the 4th Grade (see chapter 3.12 #2). However, if you do choose to teach vocabulary in 3rd Grade, make sure your spelling list and vocabulary list are separate.

## 4. Scheduling

When preparing your curriculum, you can use the block plan templates in Appendices 1–3 or you can create your own. If you create your own, use the following points to lay out your blocks:

1. Begin instruction at the beginning of 3rd Grade.

2. It will take students until the end of 8th Grade to master spelling. Students will have to master increasingly more difficult levels of spelling with each academic year. However, the formal study of spelling often ends at the end of 6th Grade, and students study vocabulary and spelling together in 7th and 8th Grade as part of the Latin/Greek Phase.

3. Teach spelling daily in the Skills Practice segment in both main lesson blocks and practice blocks.

4. Schedule about 15 minutes for a spelling lesson and a little longer for a test if you plan to have the students correct it.

## 5. Initial Introduction

This is the initial introduction to the weekly spelling lists for 3rd Grade. For information on teaching spelling in 1st and 2nd Grade, see chapter 3.6 Sight Words, chapter 3.4 Encoding, and chapters 4.1 and 4.2 Phonics Rules.

**Prerequisites:** NA

**When to Teach:** Teach at the beginning of 3rd Grade.

**How to Teach:** Introduce the concept of spelling words and the weekly test. If you are using spelling workbooks, pass them out and explain their use and your expectations (e.g., whether you want students to rip out pages and hand them in or submit the entire book, etc.). Then give a pretest using the week's list of words and have the students correct it. The next day, introduce the first lesson, which will be a chance to teach or reteach a phonics rule or a spelling rule.

## 6. How to Teach Spelling in 1st and 2nd Grade

There is no separate spelling program in 1st and 2nd Grade. Instead, spelling is taught through sight words and encoding (see chapter 3.6 Sight Words, chapter 3.4 Encoding and Decoding, and chapters 4.1 and 4.2 Phonics

Rules for information on what to teach). Your instruction should make use of the four spelling strategies: chanting, encoding, visualizing, and meaning. Chanting should only be used for long words that students cannot visualize. Phase out chanting over 2nd Grade. Discontinue it once students can visualize seven letters.

You can incorporate some dictation into your language arts curriculum in the 2nd Grade as an exercise for developing listening skills in combination with encoding. If you do this, make sure the sentences you are asking the students to write are short and include words that use the phonics rules and sight words they know (or should know). Follow the guidelines in chapter 3.9 #8 for how to do a dictation.

## 7.   How to Teach Spelling in 3rd Grade

In 3rd Grade, continue with encoding. Begin weekly spelling tests in place of sight words.

**Objective:** Reteach phonics rules and/or spelling rules so that students' encoding skills can catch up with their decoding skills.

**Background Information**: A well-chosen list of spelling words allows you to reteach a rule that students have already mastered in decoding but still need to master in encoding. Students in the Pattern Phase and the Syllable Phase learn to decode faster than they learn to encode (see chapter 3.4 #2). Weekly spelling tests build redundancy into the system. It also allows you to focus on words that do not follow the rules as well as commonly used words in each grade that students should know how to spell.

In addition the spelling tests lay the foundation for good study (and homework) habits in the middle and upper grades. They give students the opportunity to practice the techniques you have taught in class at home and provide them with weekly feedback on how they are doing. Success is determined most often by how well students practice—an invaluable life lesson. (Also, some have to practice more than others to achieve the same goal. Life is not fair—another valuable lesson.)

Testing is vital. The pre-test confirms that the list is at the instructional level for your class, and the test confirms that what you are doing in class is effective. If a majority of your students are spelling 80% or more of the pre-test list correctly, the list is too easy and needs to be more challenging. Conversely, if a majority of your students are misspelling most of the words on both pre-test and test, what you are doing is not effective. You will need to figure out why and make adjustments. Tests allow you to see clearly and navigate effectively.

**When to Teach:** Teach at the beginning of 3rd Grade during the Skills Practice segment of both main lesson blocks and practice blocks. Do the pretest on Monday, the final test on Friday, and spend the days in between reviewing the phonics rule or spelling rule for the week and practicing the words.

### How to Teach: The Weekly Spelling Test Process in Class

Pre-Testing (Monday): Give the words to the class sight unseen. Say the word, use it in a sentence, and repeat the word. Then each student writes it down on a sheet of paper (or half sheet). If a student does not know how to spell the word, she takes a best guess. Each student does her own work. No copying from a neighbor. No helping. Pre-tests can be corrected in class. Either have students swap with a neighbor or put away their graphite pencils (verify they have) and use a colored pencil to correct so there is no possibility of changing an answer. Collect the test so that you can assess whether the test is too easy, too hard, or at the instructional level.

Note: Some teachers ask their students to put an X next to the word if it is right and a check if it is wrong. This can be problematic. Consider: A class of 25 students with a spelling test of 20 words would require a teacher to scan 500 marks for just one test. Instead, teach the students to mark on the test only if the answer is wrong. This process will simplify your life. You can estimate how a student did in one glance: the cleaner the page, the better the performance. It will also save your wrist if you ever have to correct the tests.

Teaching (Monday or Tuesday): If the pre-test indicates that the words are at the instructional level, proceed to reteach the principle covered by the word list. First, review the phonics rule or teach the spelling rule and then apply it to the list of words by analyzing the words to see if they follow the rule.

Analyzing (Tuesday): Students analyze the spelling words individually and mark the tricky letters with a colored pencil. This process includes writing the misspelled words correctly and then tracing over or underling in color those letters that do not play fair. The process shown in table 3.9.2 comes from Lindamood-Bell.

**Table 3.9.2: How to Analyze a Spelling Word**

| Instructions | Example of a Multisyllabic Word |
|---|---|
| Analyze a word to see if it plays fair or if it cheats. Use the decoding process for single-syllable or multisyllable words (see chapter 3.4 #7, #8, and #9). | Word: Wednesday<br>Wed/nes/day |
| Mark any letters that cheat by going over them with a colored pencil or pen. | Wed/nes/day |
| Say the word the way it should be pronounced if it were to play fair. Say it slowly and pronounce each sound clearly. | "Wed....ness....day" |
| Close your eyes and visualize the whole word syllable by syllable. | Wed nes day |
| Open your eyes and repeat the word as if it played fair (i.e., pronouncing it the way it is spelled). As you say each syllable, write the letters in the air or on the table. | "Wed....ness....day"<br>Wed nes day |

*Source: Adapted from Bell 2001, 161.*

Practicing (Tuesday through Thursday): Once students have learned/reviewed the spelling principle and analyzed the words, it is necessary for most students to practice. Here is a list of activities that have been found to be effective:

- Study words with desk partners.
- Practice spelling quizzes with desk partners.
- Perform word sorts (see chapter 3.3 #2).
- Write sentences using the spelling words.
- Write a paragraph using as many spelling words as possible. (Be sure to have students underline the words.)

Do one or more of these activities each day. (Note: Include spelling practice activities from your spelling workbook, if you are using one.)

Testing (Friday): Give the initial spelling test again. Give the words in random order. Say the word, use it in a sentence, and repeat the word. Students write down the word on their paper. Ask them to keep their eyes on their own paper and put a question mark next to a word if they are unsure of its spelling. Students can exchange papers or correct their own paper but first have the students clear their desks so that the only objects on their desks are the test and the colored pencil for correcting. Have the students record those words they missed and need to practice. For instance:

1. Students can put their misspelled words into a spelling journal or make their own spelling cards for more practice. Have the students record the words they misspelled on the test into a special journal or stack of 3 x 5 cards. Ask them to review the spelling of these words periodically. Note: Spelling cards can be kept on a ring or in a box so they do not get misplaced.

2. Spelling words that are misspelled can be written ten times each or can be used in creative sentences. Emphasize the aspect of the word that is misspelled by highlighting it.

3. If the class as a whole is still struggling with a word, add it to your next spelling list.

**Differentiating Instruction**

Everyone in class should get the same list of spelling words; however, if you have some advanced spellers in your class, you can add in a few challenge words or extra credit words for them. Do not spend classroom time practicing or reviewing these words.

If you have students who are not capable of doing the list with the class, it is imperative that they receive intervention either in class or out of it to work on weaknesses that are preventing them from learning their spelling words. You can temporarily reduce their number of spelling words while they receive this instruction.

## 8. Dictation

The encoding assessment in 1st and 2nd Grade and the weekly spelling tests in 3rd Grade are a useful way to reinforce spelling and phonics rules as they provide the students many opportunities for practice. They are, however, an inefficient way to assess spelling because they only show whether the students can spell a word in isolation. To assess the efficacy of your spelling program, it is necessary to look at spelling in context. An effective way to do this is by using spelling assessment dictations.

**Background: Dictation** is a practice exercise where students write down the sentence or sentences that the teacher says. It can focus on spelling (encoding, sight words, and/or spelling words) and/or mechanics (capitalization and punctuation).

A spelling assessment dictation is a dictation that is used for assessment rather than practice. It focuses on spelling words (or sight words in 2nd Grade) the class has studied and allows you to see if students have internalized the spelling words they have learned. They are similar to regular dictations but with a few key differences. A spelling assessment dictation should be done every four, five, or six weeks at the end of a particular spelling focus. You would not have an official spelling list that week because the students should already be familiar with the words in the dictation from the previous weeks. (Use this freed up time in your Skills Practice segment to work on the current phonics rule your class is learning.)

Note: If you are using a spelling program such as Zaner-Bloser, it may contain a spelling review lesson that reviews all of the spelling words taught over the last 4–6 weeks. You could use that in lieu of a spelling assessment dictation.

**Preparation:** Create a series of sentences (i.e., two or three sentences in 2nd Grade) or a paragraph that incorporates a selection of the spelling test words you have taught over the block. (In 3rd Grade, incorporate previous sight words, as well.)

Note: Select the words for this dictation with care. All of the words should be words the students can spell or encode. You will have covered too many words in weekly spelling tests to include them all in one dictation. You can also include sample words from the phonics rules you have covered.

**The steps for a dictation are:**

1. <u>Teacher dictates</u>: Stand up in front of the class and say, "*I will say each sentence once. Then you will repeat it and write it on your paper.*" Read the sentence slowly, clearly, and distinctly. Do not dictate punctuation marks but let your voice convey them.

Note: Some teachers go so far as to repeat each phrase or sentence anywhere from 3–5 times. This is an inefficient use of class time and promotes lazy listening skills. Avoid repeating yourself. Expect the class to listen the first time.

2. <u>Students repeat</u>: Immediately after you say the sentence, your students repeat the phrase or sentence in unison. Do not repeat the sentence with them. If the students struggle to repeat the sentence, break the next sentence into phrases and write shorter sentences next time.

Note: By the end of 3rd Grade, students should be able to remember the sentence on their own and this oral repetition will not be necessary. You can experiment with deleting this step and see how they do.

3. <u>Students write</u>: After repeating the sentence the students write the phrase or sentence. Do not offer help. Do not repeat the sentence.

4. <u>Teacher reads dictation and students proofread</u>: After the last sentence of the dictation has been written, say, "*I will read each sentence one more time. As I read, fill in any punctuation you missed and underline any words you think you might have misspelled and wish to double check.*" Then read the entire passage again, slowly. Again, use your voice to indicate where punctuation should go. Students should return to words that are underlined and do their best to spell them correctly. This process allows students the opportunity to proofread their own work and gives them the chance to make corrections. (If a student is missing a word(s) or phrase, you have to decide whether you will restate the word/phrase or tell them to proof what they were able to write.)

5. <u>Teacher corrects</u>: Ask students to turn in their papers. After class, correct the dictations. Flag the words you would like the students to continue to practice on their own (e.g., words from previous spelling tests or sight words). If a number of students misspelled words that use a common phonics rule, have the class or small groups continue to practice the rule during the upcoming practice or main lesson block.

6. <u>Students review and practice misspelled words</u>: Pass the papers back the next day. Have the students note which words they missed. Have students use spelling journal and spelling cards to practice misspelled words (see chapter 3. 9 #7). Ask the students to return the dictations to you to be placed in their spelling folder or wherever you keep their assessment work.

**Afterwards:** For spelling assessment dictations, analyze the students' mistakes to determine which words need more practice. If >50% of the students misspelled a spelling word, reteach that word in your next block. File all dictations into the students' spelling folder or file. They will be useful as informal assessments when you do report writing and Parent Teacher Conferences.

## 9. Practice

Practice is critical. It forms part of your initial introduction in the Introduction &/or Review segment of main lesson (i.e., Activities A and B). It will be part of your ongoing practice in the Skills Practice segment of main lesson (see chapter 2.3 #4). Finally, it can be used during classroom games.

**Activities A and B:** See chapter 3.9 #7 Analyzing.

**Skills Practice:** See chapter 3.9 #7 for activities to include in the Skills Practice segment after the initial introduction.

**Fun and Games:** In addition, below are two practice activities that you can use to spice up your Skills Practice. Use them sparingly.

- Dismiss the class for recess by asking each student to spell one of the weekly spelling words. If she misses, she gets to look at her list while you go on to others. After everyone else has had a turn, return to her for the correct spelling.
- Hold a spelling bee using weekly spelling words (pick words from a hat).

## 10. Assessment

Assessment is a critical part of teaching. It is important to verify that students have mastered the skills they have been taught. See chapter 6.1 for background on assessment.

**Benchmarks** represent <u>minimum</u> levels of student achievement by the end of each grade for students to be on track to handle grade-level work in 4th Grade (see chapter 6.1 #9). Table 3.9.3 contains the benchmarks for spelling.

Note: The following benchmarks may not be exhaustive. Prerequisite skills for spelling may be covered under other related language arts skills. For a full list of benchmarks, see table 6.1.4.

**Table 3.9.3: Benchmarks for Spelling**

|  | **1st Grade** | **2nd Grade** | **3rd Grade** |
|---|---|---|---|
| **Spelling** | NA—see sight words and encoding. | NA—see sight words and encoding. | Students can spell 3rd Grade level words in context. |
| **Dictation** | NA—see encoding. | Students can take dictation of simple sentences (i.e., subject/ predicate). Example: *The hare ran faster.* | Students can take dictation of sentences up to 7–10 words. Example: *In the forest the students found mushrooms and berries.* |

There are three types of assessments. Recommendations for each type of assessment can be found in Sections 6.3, 6.4, and 6.5. You can use the following ideas as a starting point to set up an assessment program.

**Informal Assessments:** Observe students' compositions and dictations.

**Teacher-Made Assessment:** Use a weekly spelling test (either teacher-generated or from a published spelling program if you are using one).

**Assessments Created by Educational Testing Groups:** Ibid.

See chapters 6.3, 6.4, and 6.5 for more information about assessing in each grade. See also encoding and decoding (chapter 3.4 #11) and sight words (chapter 3.6 #10).

## 11. How to Help Struggling Students

**Assess:** When you see a student is struggling with spelling, do assessments (both formal and informal) to narrow down the area(s) of concern and to document your findings. Spelling problems often stem from weak phonemic awareness, weak symbol imagery, and/or weak encoding and phonics (see chapter 3.3, 3.4, 3.5, as well as section 4 and section 6).

In addition to assessing the student, assess your spelling curriculum. Check the following:

- Are the spelling words at your students' instructional level?
- Are the students getting enough practice at school and at home?
- Is the practice effective?
- Has each student developed full phonemic awareness and symbol imagery to seven letters?

Take steps to address any imbalances you discover.

**Additional Instruction/Practice:** Next, use the results of your assessments to provide this student with extra instruction and practice in any weak areas. You can differentiate instruction in class. For example, you can modify your classroom instruction, skills practice, or an individual assignment to include extra practice in the weak area. Decide which approach is best based on how many other students have similar struggles. Document what you try and the results.

Try using spelling tricks. The first two are part of The Weekly Spelling Test Process in Class/Analyzing that was introduced in 3rd Grade (see chapter 3.9 #7).

1. **Highlight the Irregularities:** First, draw attention to irregularities in the words. The overwhelming majority of letters in most words play fair. If you can focus on the letters that do not, it is easier to memorize words. For example, let's highlight the irregularities and/or unusual spelling patterns in the following words:

    Often (the *T* is silent)

    Wednesday (both *D* and *E* are silent)

    Principal (the *A* is part of an unfamiliar suffix, –al)

Having the students highlight the tricky letter with a colored pencil can be enough to stimulate their symbol imagery for the part that does not play fair. This trick is made even more effective when used in combination with the next trick: deliberate mispronunciation.

2. **Deliberate Mispronunciation:** Another way to remember the spelling is to deliberately mispronounce a word by saying it the way it is spelled. For example, *often* becomes off-TEN and *Wednesday* becomes *WED-NESS-day*. (Emphasize the syllable(s) that is mispronounced.) All of the silent letters are heard loud and clear when you say a word the way it is spelled. Students can then use their fully developed phonemic awareness to encode the tricky parts of words.

3. **Mnemonic Devices:** A third trick is the use of mnemonics. Mnemonics are memory devices. To use a mnemonic device, isolate the tricky part of a word and create a trick to remember it. For example, *The princi**pal** is my* <u>pal</u> or <u>Ron</u> *is interested in the envi**ron**ment.* Note: These mnemonics will not play a huge role in spelling in 3rd Grade, but they are worth knowing. They will become more important in spelling in 4th –8th Grade.

While students will be familiar with the first two tricks from the spelling process, they may need reminders to make use of these tricks when memorizing words. Stress that many adults still make use of the tricks they learned in school to help them with words that do not play fair.

**Remedial Issues:** If you do not notice improvements in 3–4 weeks, it is time to contact your mentor for guidance and consult chapter 6.6 for additional information on remedial issues. If students appear to be doing their best but still misspell words in context, check for one or more underlying weaknesses. First, have vision checked fully. They may need glasses, vision therapy, or **Irlen overlays**. Second, there may be a timing issue between their sub-vocalization of the word's spelling and what their hands are writing. If this is the case, they may need to do exercises to help with timing such as Take Time and/or Bal-A-Vis-X (see chapter 6.6).

**Accommodations and Modifications:** Sometimes it takes a while for remedial issues to be resolved. Meanwhile, the student needs support to function in class. Consider using the following modifications as a temporary measure.

1. Adjust the level of spelling words for a small group of students or suspend spelling tests and have the students practice phonemic awareness drills and symbol imagery drills at school and home until their skills are better established.

2. If all else fails, chanting can be used. Chanting is truly the option of last resort. It has no connection to symbol imagery or phonemic awareness, the twin pillars of good spelling. Worse, unless the word is spelled often after the spelling test, it is really easy to forget the chant. However, if a student truly cannot visualize any letters at all despite your work on symbol imagery, chanting is an acceptable modification.

Keep in mind that after 2nd Grade, chanting is a modification. Before then, students are still working on developing symbol imagery to seven letters and chanting is encouraged for words they cannot visualize.

**Great Spelling Tests; Lousy Spelling:** Sometimes students do a great job on their spelling tests but continue to misspell the words while writing. If that happens, do some sleuthing to discover the source of the problem.

- Spelling errors in rough drafts are to be expected. The students are concentrating on the content not the spelling. Teach your students how to proofread their work and expect them to do so (see chapter 3.14 #7).

- If students miss words after proofreading, ask them to write the misspelled words 10–20 times each. After a few weeks, this practice will weed out *laissez faire* attitudes in many students—particularly if you keep increasing the number of times the misspelled word must be written.

- If a student continues to struggle, check out remedial issues. Pay particular attention to weaknesses in symbol imagery, eye tracking/glasses, and Irlen Syndrome.

## Conclusion

Mastering spelling is as important as learning to read. Teach your students the four spelling strategies and provide plenty of practice. It is not possible to augment truly poor spelling with technology. Therefore, build spelling instruction into your class schedule.

# 3.10 SPEECH

*Mindy was an imaginative student in the Phonemic Awareness Phase who had poor articulation. One day she wrote an exciting story for a kid writing assignment. It featured bike thieves and action heroes (i.e., Mindy and her stuffed rabbit). It also featured bagis. Jennifer Militzer-Kopperl puzzled over Mindy's draft. Who or what were bagis?*

*Jennifer asked Mindy to read her story, and as she read, things began to make more sense. "Mindy saw people taking bikes. She ran home to get Bun-Bun. When she got back, the* ba' guys *were gone." Bagis were bad guys.*

*Mindy's poor articulation affected her phonological awareness and her spelling. Because she dropped the final consonant in the word* bad *(ba'), she inadvertently created a contraction: ba'guys. She did not realize that her word* bagis *was really two separate words:* bad guys. *She encoded the word exactly as she articulated it:* bagis.

When it comes to encoding, beginning students will write down words as they pronounce them—dropped letters and all. Their speech and articulation thus become very important because students with good articulation and speech habits have a leg up on their classmates.

This chapter covers the following topics:

1. Why Speech Matters
2. Background Information: A Note About Singing
3. Sacred Nothings: Birthday Verses and Attendance Rituals
4. Preparation
5. Scheduling
6. How to Teach a Poem: Grades 1–3
7. How to Use Speech to Cultivate Phonemic Awareness: Grade One
8. How to Work with Speech in a Class Play: Grades 1–3
9. Sharing (Show and Tell): Grade One
10. Practice
11. Assessment
12. How to Help Struggling Students

## 1.  Why Speech Matters

Speech is a critical but often overlooked aspect of language arts. It is important for many reasons.

First, speech is crucial because Waldorf education is primarily an oral education, and speech is ubiquitous in main lesson. In the article "Living Language and Waldorf Education" Waldorf speech instructor Helen Lubin states:

Main lesson embraces different kinds of attention to speech: greeting, morning verse, activities of the rhythmic part of a main lesson—which includes daily speech practice per se—presentation of subject content, the way speech informs writing and reading, and a teacher's over-all human presence through the spoken word. The connection between cultivation of the spoken word and classroom management is striking. (Lubin 2007, 27)

Second, as Lubin notes, speech supports classroom management, but only when it is used consciously. Teachers' voices (especially women's) often become shrill when they are trying to get their students' attention. Instead of achieving this purpose, shrill voices just add to the din and make things worse. It is better to take a moment to ground yourself and then consciously drop your voice down into its lower register. This change of tone catches the students' attention because it is a new and commanding sound.

Third, a teacher's speech serves as a role model for the students' speech. It is important that you speak correctly and properly so that your students have a good model to follow. In listening to well-formed speech from authorities, students develop a feeling of the rise and fall of tones, rhythm, and meter. This advice does not mean that you need to speak in an artificial, sing-song way or develop an affectation such as over-pronouncing every letter in a word. After all, English has a multitude of silent letters as well as ancient pronunciations embedded in its spelling such as the *GH* in *night*. It does mean that you aim to speak calmly and articulate properly.

Fourth, speech supports the development of phonological and phonemic awareness. In *The Renewal of Education*, Steiner states:

> In school we need to work so that the children learn how to bring their speech into a peaceful regularity. We need to require that the children speak syllable for syllable, that they speak slowly and that they properly form the syllables so that nothing of the word is left out. … The children need to grow accustomed to proper speech and verse, to well-formed speech, and develop a feeling rather than a conscious understanding of the rise and fall of the tones in verses. We need to speak to the children in the proper way so that they learn to hear. (Trostli 2004, 252)

Students will demonstrate whether or not they are learning to hear (i.e., developing phonological and phonemic awareness) as they invent spellings that match their speech and articulation as shown in the story about Mindy and her *ba'guys (bagis)*. They model their speech on the speech they hear around them. Difficulty with articulation can then affect the development of literacy skills. Students use their own articulation to invent spellings in kid writing (see chapter 3.13); consequently, if they struggle to pronounce a word, they struggle to encode it.

Speech is important as the foundation for literacy skills and as an art in its own right. It is an integral part of the Waldorf curriculum. Imitation is the best way for students to learn speech. Articulate clearly during speech exercises so you are a good model and have students articulate each word and syllable correctly too so they reap the full benefits of speech instruction. Work consciously with your own speech and you will develop a powerful tool for classroom management.

## 2.   Background Information: A Note about Singing

Although singing is not speech *per se*, they do have similarities and can be taught in a similar manner.

Singing gives students the opportunity to experience language naturally and spontaneously. Students at this age think through their feelings, and songs are soul food for the feeling realm.

When it comes to instruction, treat singing as another speech exercise. Introduce and practice songs the same way you would introduce and practice verses, poems, and tongue twisters. Select songs that have an aspect of the language arts skill(s) you are working with (e.g., grammar, sight words, letters/phoneme(s), etc.).

That way, you can use song lyrics for memory reading too, along with poems and tongue twisters (see chapter 3.15 #2).

## 3. Sacred Nothings: Birthday Verses and Attendance Rituals

There are two Sacred Nothings to consider: birthday verses and elaborate attendance rituals.

### Birthday Verses

Birthday verses are a custom that has sprung up over the years. Some Waldorf teachers write verses for their students and hand them out at the beginning of the school year or on the students' birthdays. The questionable aspect is when teachers then have the students come up to the front of the class and recite these verses every week on the day they were born as part of main lesson. The use of birthday verses in Waldorf classrooms, especially in the lower grades, has become ubiquitous in parts of the United States.

This idea appears to have originated from what Steiner referred to as *report verses*. In *The Kingdom of Childhood*, Steiner encourages teachers to write a student report where "each child receives in his report a motto or verse for his own life, which can be a word of guidance for him in the year to come" (Steiner 1988, 141). There is no mention that this verse should be said by the student every week in the classroom, recited on the day of the week she was born, or that she should say it at school at all.

In his article "Rethinking the Threefold division of the Main Lesson," Christof Wiechert discusses birthday verses as part of main lesson. He points out that this is not necessarily a bad custom, but he states: "It can easily become something that has little meaning, especially if the verse was written by the teacher months before and is no longer relevant for the student. Then we see a totally unengaged pupil reciting his verse in front of his bored classmates. The procedure is of no value to anyone and… truly precious time has been lost" (Wiechert 2010, 14).

If you feel a student needs some inner support to move through a particular challenge, there are numerous ways to help such as:

- telling a pedagogical story (see chapter 2.1 #5);
- choosing a literature story for main lesson that has a character or event that speaks to the issue;
- teaching the class a poem or song that could help;
- asking the student to assist with a special project.

If you want to write pedagogical verses for each student, ask parents to incorporate them into the child's home life instead of using main lesson time.

### Attendance Rituals

The second sacred nothing involves attendance rituals. They have become a part of some Waldorf classrooms. Some teachers sing a question to each student and each student has to sing a response back. For example, "*Good morning Michael, are you here?*" "*Yes, Mrs. Langley, I am here.*" This practice has a short shelf life. It is useful as a tool for teacher and students to learn the names of each student in the class in 1st Grade. However, after those first few weeks, the time spent on singing attendance could be better spent on one or two additional opening activities in main lesson.

Our recommendation: Sing attendance only at the very beginning of 1st Grade. Sing attendance for two weeks if the students already know each other from kindergarten. Sing attendance for three or four weeks if they do not. After this introductory period is over, take attendance quickly and quietly. You could also ask the students if anyone is missing, briefly acknowledge their absence, and move on.

Spending time in main lesson on birthday verses and/or elaborate attendance rituals can seriously undermine the amount of time available to you for teaching your lessons.

## 4. Preparation

Prepare much of your speech curriculum over the summer and align it with other aspects of your curriculum. In addition, work on your own speech and singing.

**Background Information:** Recall a time when you listened to a speaker whose voice or manner was unpleasant (e.g., the speaker spoke too fast or had a shrill or nasally voice). It was only after the speaker stopped talking that you realized how clenched your body was. Imagine what happens to students faced with such a teacher day after day.

Since you will be with the same group of students for up to eight years, it is important that you work on your voice. This work includes articulation, enunciation, modulation, pacing, and tone. Teaching is a marathon for the larynx. It is best to train for it so your vocal instrument is as fit as possible.

**Speech Curriculum:** In all three grades, look for poems, tongue twisters, and songs that are seasonal or topical. Pick speech exercises that will allow your students to practice one or more aspects of language arts:

- alphabet: 1st Grade
- phonemic awareness: 1st Grade
- sight words: 1st and 2nd Grade
- decoding (phonics rules): 1st– 3rd Grade (note: start at the end of 1st Grade)

Curriculum Connection: You can use these exercises for memory reading (see chapter 3.15 #2) and dictation (see chapter 3.9 #8).

**How to Improve Your Speech:** Make sure you have speech exercises to practice. If you are still in teacher training, make sure your course of study includes speech education with a regular regimen of speech exercises. If you are not, there are many exercises you can explore on your own. In *Teaching Language Arts in the Waldorf School*, Roberto Trostli shares a number of Steiner's suggested speech exercises (262–270). They include articulation exercises for individual phonemes and syllables and for regulating the breath. An easy but fun exercise to do on your own is to practice putting the emphasis on the wrong syllable (such as: *the emphasis on the wrong syllable*).

As you practice your poems and tongue twisters, shift your focus to these three particular areas: 1) how you recite poetry, 2) staying present in your speech, and 3) modulation.

The first is how you recite poetry. Avoid reciting poetry in a routine way or by using a singsong voice. Instead, work on enlivened recitation, speaking the rhythm of the words while simultaneously imbuing the recitation with the meaning behind the words through concept imagery.

The second is setting aside unrelated thoughts and emotions. Often times, thoughts and speech are unrelated. For example, you may be saying the morning verse while thinking about what to make for dinner or feeling annoyed about something. As much as possible, your inner mood should match the words of your lesson. One way to work on this objective is to practice Rudolf Steiner's Six Basic Exercises (see chapter 2.1 #14).

The third is learning to use voice modulation effectively to support classroom management. Inexperienced teachers often try to gain control of an unruly group of students by raising their voices over the din to get the students' attention. As mentioned above, this strategy seldom works, and it just adds to the cacophony of sounds in the room. It is more effective to speak in a slightly lower register. Work on developing this lower register over the summer so you can use it during the school year.

While these suggestions may seem like a lot of extra work, they will pay off in spades over the school year, particularly when it comes time to teach your speech exercises.

**How to Improve Your Singing:** Advice on how to improve singing is outside the scope of this book. Find a singing teacher and/or join a choir to get additional practice.

## 5.   Scheduling

When preparing your curriculum, you can use the block plan templates in Appendices 1–3 or you can create your own. If you create your own, use the following points to lay out your blocks:

1. Begin instruction at the beginning of 1st Grade.
2. Practice speech until the end of 8th Grade.
3. Teach speech in the Opening segment of main lesson and during Transition. (Note: In *The Roadmap to Literacy*, 1st Grade has an additional segment that can be used, the Speech/Song segment at the end of main lesson.)
4. Teach daily for around 10–15 minutes.

## 6.   How to Teach a Poem: Grades 1–3

Teaching a poem involves both introduction and practice. Both stages make use of a process called *Drill Down* (see chapter 2.4 #2).

Below is a description of how to teach a poem in the 1st Grade.

**Preparatory Work**

If needed, edit the poem to support your teaching objectives. For example, there is a poem by George Cooper called "Twenty Froggies." You could change it from twenty to ten froggies so that students could use their hands/fingers to represent the frogs.

Note: It is recommended that teachers use gestures when teaching most poetry and songs in Grades 1–3. Active poems and songs make good transition activities.

**Introduction: Day One**

1. If you were going to use the poem about the ten froggies, you should introduce the poem through a brief story or imagination to connect the students to the subject of the poem. For example, you could share an experience of having observed a group of frogs croaking loudly as they took turns sitting on a log and jumping into the cool water. After this imaginative introduction, ask if anyone in the class has ever watched frogs in a pond. Allow a few students to share their observations, then tell the students that thinking about those frogs reminded you of a poem about ten special froggies.

2. Next, while they are still sitting, recite the poem in its entirety to the class using the gestures you will teach with the poem.

3. Ask the class to stand.

4. Teach them the poem using the following steps:

   a. Model line #1 with the gestures you made for that line.

   b. Students repeat the line and gestures with you.

   c. Students repeat the line and gestures on their own. If needed, you can say the first word or two to get them started in unison.

   d. Listen to their speech. Are they articulating all of the sounds fully? Is their pacing right?

   e. If it is not right, restate the word or portion that needs more work and have the students first repeat just that word/phrase and then the entire line again. Have high standards when teaching a poem. Do not move on until they have it.

   f. Repeat steps 1–5 for the second line.

   g. Now recite lines one and two together using the gestures and repeat steps 2–5.

   h. If their recitation is clean and clear, move on to the third and fourth lines using the same process.

   i. End this practice by saying all the lines together.

**Introduction: Day Two**

Review: The second day, recite the portion of the poem learned yesterday with the class joining you (all use gestures). Then use Drill Down so that smaller groups of students can practice it (see chapter 2.4 #2). Split the class in half and have the first half recite the first line or stanza while the second half watches. Then switch for the second line or stanza, etc.

New: After practicing the poem, teach the next set of lines or verse using the same process as on day one.

**Introduction: Day Three and Beyond**

Review: Recite the portion of the poem taught yesterday with the whole class. Use gestures. Then repeat it again but drill down to a smaller group of students who say the line or stanza. For example, row one recites line one, row two recites line two, etc.

New: After practicing the poem, teach the next set of lines or verse as on day one.

Continue to introduce the poem day by day until the entire poem has been taught. Periodically have the class recite the poem from beginning to end. After the poem has been taught, you can use it for memory reading, have the students copy it for handwriting practice, perform it at an assembly, etc.

Note: Come prepared with lots of speech material. Young students learn songs and poems very quickly. What may take you days to learn they can memorize after one or two recitations!

**Practice**

Once all of the students have learned the poem, continue to practice it. Enliven the practice using these tips:

- Vary the volume. Have the students whisper the poem, say it in a tiny voice, a giant voice, etc.

- Teach the students to alternate between outer and inner voicing of the poem. Teach them that when you snap your fingers, they are to say the words inside their own heads where no one else can hear. Then at some point in the silent poem, clap your hands as a signal for them to continue saying the poem out loud. Alternate, back and forth. If you have been diligent about teaching them the pacing and breathing of the poem, they should all be very close together when they begin to speak it out loud again.
- Popcorn Drill Down: Ask desk partners or rows to recite a specific line or verse. Be unpredictable so no one knows who will get called on next.
- Popcorn Drill Down with Individual Students: Ask individual students to recite a specific line or verse. Note: In 1st Grade, only call on volunteers.

Even though this process can be cumbersome at first, the students will catch on quickly. Drill Down helps students memorize a poem and holds them accountable for learning it fully. It is important that all students know all of the words to all of the poems because you will use these poems for memory reading (see chapter 3.15 #2).

## 7.   How to Use Speech to Cultivate Phonemic Awareness: Grade One

In addition to learning poems and verses for their own sake, speech work can help students in 1st Grade develop phonemic awareness.

Beginning students use the position of their mouths when forming a sound to help them gain phonemic awareness. Choose poems and tongue twisters with useful elements. Then insist upon proper enunciation. Playing with **alliteration** (repeating consonant sounds) and assonance (repeating vowel sounds) delights young students, allows them to feel how to form the sound, and strengthens their long-term memory of the sound.

Note: When using speech to cultivate phonemic awareness, articulation is everything, but the articulation that matters most is the students' own.

### The Emergent Phase

In the beginning of 1st Grade when you are introducing the alphabet, choose poems and tongue twisters that repeat the sound of the letter you are teaching. Teach the material as noted above. Make sure that the students fully articulate every sound. For example, you could use some of the following tongue twisters written by a class of 6th graders for their 1st grader buddies:

*On his jungle journey, Jolly Jody jingled, juggled, and jumped.*

*The vicious vultures' victims veered away to avoid becoming vittles!*

*Yanni, the yellow yard dog yelped and yanked his chain.*

*Zulu, the zany zebra, zipped about the zoo.*

Tongue twisters will help warm the students' mouths up so they can feel the sounds of the letters and become conscious of the phonemes that make up individual words, particularly the preconsonantal nasals of /mp/ and /nk/ in the words *jumped* and *yanked* (see chapter 4.1 rule 3: Blends).

233

Note: Although tongue twisters and alliterative poems are great for stressing a certain phoneme, they are not a good choice for memory reading in the Emergent and early Phonemic Awareness Phases. It is difficult for students at this level to isolate and read a word beginning with a specific phoneme if there are a number of words beginning with that phoneme on each line. Use this material for memory reading in the later Phonemic Awareness Phase when your students need to develop phonemic awareness for the end sound in a word.

**Phonemic Awareness Phase**

When the students are in the Phonemic Awareness Phase, help them develop phonemic awareness for end sounds, vowels, and blends by choosing poems and tongue twisters that contain the element your students are currently working on.

When teaching vowels, include works that feature assonance. Make sure they have the sound you want for each vowel letter. The following verse features the short vowel sound of *A* and would be excellent to include in the Vowel Block:

> *Pam and Stan ate a ham*
> *With candied yams and grape jam.*

When your students progress to digraphs and blends, choose verses or tongue twisters that feature those sounds such as the following:

*For the digraph /th/: Thirty thrilled thoroughbreds thundered through the throes of the storm.*

*For the blends /sl/, /sn/, and /sw/: Slithering snakes slowly swallowed slimy, slippery snails.*

Articulating the blends clearly will help the students learn to hear the separate phonemes in the blends.

## 8. How to Work with Speech in a Class Play: Grades 1–3

Working with a class play is well outside the scope of this book; however, below are a few guidelines you might wish to consider when it comes to incorporating a play into your main lesson and practice classes. By incorporating play line practice into your Opening and Transition segments of main lesson and practice classes you can avoid having it take over your schedule.

Whether or not you decide to have your students perform a play should be a personal decision. Consider the traditions of your school and/or the needs and character of your class. Recall that doing a play every year is a Sacred Nothing (see chapter 2.2 #1). Furthermore, many 1st Grades are not ready for a play. In 1st Grade, many teachers choose to have the class perform a poem and a few songs at a school assembly or present a little skit in the classroom for their parents at the end of the year.

If you do choose to perform a play, you can either write your own or choose one found on the AWSNA website (*https://waldorfeducation.org/awsna*) or from a book of Waldorf plays. If you select a published play, feel free to change the number of characters or some of the dialogue to fit the needs of your class. (Note: Writing your own class play can be an excellent pedagogical exercise. However, if you are not experienced at playwriting seek out the help of a mentor teacher.)

Practicing lines over a two- or three-month period allows the students to learn the play without the pressure of jamming a lot of practice into a short amount of time. The schedule that follows avoids numerous stressful situations for teacher and students.

Note: The following is for a longer play. (Half this timeline for 1st Grade.)

**Ten Weeks Out**

- First tell the story the play is based on during your Story segment of main lesson.

- A day or so later, read the entire play to the class.

- Teach all of the students all of the lines. (The plays Waldorf teachers typically use are written in verse with accompanying actions and therefore fairly easy to memorize.)

- Incorporate play lines and songs into the Opening segment of your main lesson in lieu of other speech and music activities. (Use part of your games class(es) to practice any dances you might wish to incorporate. Ask your school Eurythmist (if you have one) to work on the dance/ Eurythmy aspects during her class.

- Read the play as part of your class reading in both main lesson and practice classes. (In 1st and 2nd Grade, use memory reading.)

**One Month Out**

- Begin to act out the play in the classroom.

- Individual students say their lines, if applicable.

**One Week Out**

- Practice the play on the stage.

- Use one practice period per day for play practice.

## 9. Sharing (Show and Tell): Grade One

This aspect of speech is truly the icing on the cake; however, teachers with truncated schedules will not have time for it. If you have full school days in 1st Grade and have a free practice period available in your weekly class schedule, you might wish to have a sharing or *Show and Tell* class.

In *Practical Advice to Teachers*, Steiner recommends that 1st Grade teachers "cultivate as much simple speaking and conversation with the children as possible" (Trostli 2004, 258). This time was used to teach the students to use proper German rather than the vernacular, a dialect that differs radically from educated speech. It is a concern in German, but it is not as large a problem in English, unless you are teaching students who speak a non-standard version of English. However, sharing or Show and Tell does have some additional benefits. It gives the students practice in articulation and in the social aspects of language. Sharing time also gives students the opportunity to practice reading social cues and adjust their conversation accordingly. It is a nice thing to include, if time allows.

Friday afternoons are a particularly good time to schedule sharing. A few students each week can bring an item from nature or a book to share with the class. (Limit the items to be shared to those of the literary or natural world.) The students learn to tell a little bit about their special item and then give others time to ask questions or share a comment. Limit the amount of time talkative students speak so that others get a chance.

## 10. Practice

Speech practice is critical. It forms part of your initial introduction in main lesson (i.e., Activities A and B). It will be part of your ongoing practice in the Opening segment of main lesson (see chapter 2.3 #4).

**Activities A and B:** Drill Down—See How to Teach a Poem/Introduction (see chapter 3.10 #6)

**Skills Practice:** See How to Teach a Poem/Practice (see chapter 3.10 #6)

**Fun and Games:** NA

## 11. Assessment

Assessment is a critical part of teaching. It is important to verify that students have mastered the skills they have been taught. See chapter 6.1 for background on assessment.

**Background Information:** Speech should be well formed when students enter 1st Grade. There should be no problem with the following:

- voice: how people engage the breath and vocal cords to produce sound

- articulation: how the mouth forms speech sounds

- fluency: the ability to speak in a natural flow without stuttering or hesitating

Students should have no difficulties with the mechanics of speech other than articulation errors secondary to the loss of teeth.

Common articulation errors include difficulty pronouncing /l/, /r/, /th/, /sh/, /s/, and /w/. For example, *wabbit* for *rabbit*, *Mithith* for *Mrs.*, *stway* for *stray*. If one of your students cannot pronounce a phoneme correctly, refer the student for a screening with a speech therapist.

**Benchmarks** represent <u>minimum</u> levels of student achievement by the end of each grade for students to be on track to handle grade-level work in 4th Grade (see chapter 6.1 #9). There is no formal benchmark for speech. Students should demonstrate proper speech and articulation when they enter 1st Grade.

There are three types of assessments. Recommendations for each type of assessment can be found in Sections 6.3, 6.4, and 6.5. You can use the following ideas as a starting point to set up an assessment program.

**Informal Assessments:** Observe the mechanics of speech as students talk.

**Teacher-Made:** Pull a student aside and have her repeat words and/or sentences after you. Note any problems with voice, articulation, or fluency.

**Assessments Created by Educational Testing Groups:** NA

## 12. How to Help Struggling Students

**Assess:** When you see a student is struggling with speech, it is necessary to consider your observations:

- If the student has articulation errors or a speech impediment, refer her to a speech-language pathologist (speech therapist) immediately. Practicing errors sets them in, like a stain in cloth. Students with poor articulation can have difficulty communicating because their speech is difficult to understand. Those with speech deficits are more likely to be teased or bullied, particularly as they get older. Remediation will take time. Refer students as soon as you recognize a speech problem. A screening can be done privately through the child's pediatrician.

- If the student has difficulty learning the words to a poem, assess her comprehension, concept imagery, and hearing. Address any weaknesses you find (see chapter 3.7, 3.8, and 6.6).

**Additional Instruction/Practice:** If the assessment checks out, provide more speech practice. Make sure the student is doing the exercises consciously. See Drill Down (chapter 2.4 #2).

**Remedial Solutions:** There is no remedial solution for speech issues *per se*. See above (Assess) for how to help.

**Accommodations and Modifications:** It is not advisable to offer accommodations or modifications in speech unless recommended by a specialist.

## Conclusion

Speech exercises are important in their own right as well as serving as a vehicle for memory reading. Include speech exercises in your lesson plans and practice your own speech exercises. Proper speech makes your job as a teacher much easier.

# 3.11 GRAMMAR

*Jennifer Militzer-Kopperl was frustrated. For the past semester, she had been trying to teach her 7th Grade tutee to spell past tense verbs correctly, but his essay contained another spelling error: skipt (i.e., skipped). They reviewed the spelling rules for past tense verbs, but by this time, he could recite them with her. Jennifer then asked him what a verb was, and he rattled off a definition glibly. She was stumped. He knew the rule so why couldn't he apply it? Then she had an idea. Jennifer turned to her student and said, "Underline all of the verbs in your essay." As she watched him underline words, the source of his problem began to come into focus. He underlined nouns, adjectives, and adverbs but skipped most of the verbs. The source of his problem was now clear: he could not learn to spell past tense verbs because he could not identify verbs.*

This chapter does double duty. In addition to introducing grammar, it provides a model of how to work with umbrella stories, the serial stories the teacher invents to bring a concept through an image. *The Roadmap to Literacy's* umbrella story is called *Englishland*. *Englishland* is found in subsections 6–8 under the subtitle *Introductory Image from Englishland*.

This chapter covers the following topics:

1. Why Grammar Matters
2. Background Information: Going beyond Steiner's Indications
3. Preparation
4. Scheduling
5. Initial Introduction
6. How to Teach Grammar in 1st Grade
7. How to Teach Grammar in 2nd Grade
8. How to Teach Grammar in 3rd Grade
9. Practice
10. Assessment
11. How to Help Struggling Students

## 1. Why Grammar Matters

Grammar is the skeleton of language. It gives language its form. All languages share certain elements of grammar. For example, they all have parts of speech such as nouns and verbs and follow grammatical rules. However, different languages use different rules for grammar. To give just one example, some languages put adjectives before nouns while others put them after.

The study of grammar has largely gone out of fashion, but it is a critical skill for students to develop for many reasons.

- Knowledge of grammar gives the students the freedom to express the same thought in different ways; therefore, students who learn grammar have more flexibility in their speech and writing.

- Students can use grammar to master spelling and written conventions in their own language.

- Students can apply their knowledge of grammar to help them learn foreign languages.

Young children absorb their grammar unconsciously through imitation; however, students undergo a major change in their relationship to grammar around the start of 1st Grade (i.e., age seven). Steiner encourages teachers to help students with this change. He says that the students must leave off developing language at random through imitation and begin to develop the grammatical side of language. This requires education. Teachers impart power and firmness to language by introducing writing and reading (Steiner 1998, 185–186).

In learning writing and reading, students become aware that language is made up of words, and words are made up of phonemes. The study of grammar expands upon the development of phonological awareness. For example, students realize that not only is speech made up of separate words and groups of words, but these words and groups can perform different tasks in a sentence. Some words are nouns; others are verbs. Nouns can have different jobs in a sentence, as either subjects or objects (direct, indirect, or object of a preposition). This realization changes their relationship to speech and writing. Students who know grammar can engage with language consciously. As a result, their thinking becomes more focused and their use of language more effective.

This chapter will point out some of the information Steiner brought about the subject of grammar. It will also focus on some of the differences between German and English and discuss how these differences complicate the teaching of grammar in English if a teacher tries to follow the German model. Finally, this chapter will offer advice on how to teach English grammar using Steiner's indications when they are applicable to English.

## 2. Background Information: Going beyond Steiner's Indications

Steiner states, "We do not need to teach grammar in a way other than by bringing what already exists as a *completely developed language structure* (italics added by author) into consciousness" (Trostli 2004, 280–281). This advice is an inspiring guide for an inflected language such as German, but what happens when you have to teach a language that no longer has a completely developed language structure such as English?

Recall that English once had a completely developed grammar that contained case endings for nouns and verbs that conjugate, but it lost its inflections during the years after the Norman Conquest (see chapter 1.3 #3). German, however, retained the inflections. Steiner is right to say to German speakers that "we do not need to teach grammar in a way other than by bringing what already exists as a completely developed language structure (i.e., an inflected language. Words added by author) into consciousness" (Trostli 2004, 280–281). However, English is different. Steiner even commented unfavorably on its difference when he noted that word order in French and English is more fixed than it is in German (Trostli 2004, 285).

You must respect the differences between English and German when planning your grammar instruction. It is necessary to review Steiner's indications about grammar and identify which ones can apply to English and which ones cannot. In many instances, English speakers cannot use Steiner's indications because the structure of the two languages varies too much. In these instances, it is necessary to look at the spirit of Steiner's indications rather than the letter. In other words, look to the genius of the English language.

## Differences between English and German Grammar

When speaking about grammar instruction to the first Waldorf teachers, Steiner says: "When the child speaks, the grammar is already there. You should allow the children to speak sentences in the way they are used to speaking so that they feel the inner connection and inner flexibility of the language. You can then begin to draw the child's attention and make them aware of what they do unconsciously... .You can develop the entirety of grammar by simply making the children more aware of the life of the grammar that is already there when the child has learned to speak" (Trostli 2004, 279).

It is good to teach grammar in the context of a sentence, but it is no *simple* thing to make an English speaker aware of the grammar that is already there. When it comes to grammar, English and German have opposing gestures. German proudly wears its grammar on its sleeve whereas English conceals its grammar.

German has a case system and verbs that conjugate. However, as can be seen, English lost most of its case system after the Norman Conquest, as well as most of its verb conjugation system. As a result, English shows grammatical relationships in a different way.

Let's examine how a case system works. Here are four sentences in English. Note that the words *the man* never change even though the same article and noun serve different functions in the sentence.

1. The man likes ice cream. (subject)
2. They saw the man. (direct object)
3. The hat of the man is blue. (object of a preposition)
4. She gave a gift to the man. (indirect object)

In German, the words *the man* (i.e., *der Mann*) would have a case ending to show the grammar. For example,

1. Der Mann likes ice cream. (subject in the nominative case)
2. They saw den Mann. (direct object in the accusative case)
3. The hat of des Mannes is blue. (object of a preposition in the genitive case)
4. She gave a gift to dem Mann. (indirect object in the dative case)

Observe how the case system gives each word its own unique form, making its grammar obvious.

German verb conjugation makes verb forms unique too. Conjugation is when the verb changes to reflect the subject (i.e., 1st person, 2nd person, 3rd person and whether the subject is singular (for example, *I*) or plural (for example, *we*)). Let's look at the conjugation of the verb *to speak* in both languages.

| Conjugation of the Verb *To Speak* in English and German ||
|---|---|
| I speak | *Ich spreche* |
| You speak | *Du sprichst* |
| He/she/it speaks | *Er/sie/es spricht* |
| We speak | *Wir sprechen* |
| You speak | *Ihr sprecht* |
| They speak | *Sie sprechen* |

Note how in English the verb *speak* only changes in the third person singular. The conjugation is almost entirely lacking.

Verbs conjugate in German. Just like with nouns, German verbs wear their grammar on their sleeves. The grammar is literally tacked on to the end of each word.

In contrast to German, English goes out of its way to conceal the grammatical identity of its words. Consider these two words: *bites* and *weekly*. Out of the context of a sentence, it is impossible to determine their parts of speech with any certainty. Is *bites* a plural noun or a 3rd person singular verb? ("*I will just take little* bites." or "*The dog* bites *him every time.*") Is *weekly* an adjective or an adverb? (*She gives a* weekly *report. The magazine comes out* weekly.) One word can serve as multiple parts of speech. This situation seldom happens in German because of the case system and verb conjugation.

Consider how different English is from German. In English, the same word can be used as multiple parts of speech. In German, it cannot; each part of speech has its own form. Therefore, when teaching German-speaking students, the focus would be on a student's inner knowledge of her language— how each word has its own unique form, its part of speech identity tag. English-speaking students cannot learn grammar this way. The question then becomes how to teach grammar in English in a Waldorf way?

Note: Students of language know that there are a few remnants of a case system in English pronouns. However, since students routinely misuse pronouns, teachers cannot rely on their speech to guide their understanding of a pronoun's proper usage. For example, it is not uncommon for teachers to hear students mangle grammar by making statements such as: "*Me* (sic) *and Joey are going to play together.*" When it comes to pronouns, English-speaking students learn grammar to correct their pronoun usage rather than use their spoken language to learn grammar!

### How to Teach Grammar in English

When teaching English grammar, look to two things: 1) the genius of the language; and 2) how students learn. English grammar resides in word order and the resulting relationships of words in sentences. *The dog bit the man* Vs. *The man bit the dog.* Subjects come before verbs. Verbs come before direct objects. Word order, not case, is the way to determine who did the biting. Therefore, a solid teaching methodology has to draw out the importance of word order, and all grammar must start from the sentence, not the word.

In addition to the genius of English, consider how students learn. When it comes to language, they frequently learn to do something before they fully understand what it is they are doing and why. They learn best if you reteach the material from different angles when they are at different ages.

Therefore it is recommended that you:

1. Correct student speech errors as they come up.

2. Have the students apply basic written mechanics correctly before they learn the grammar behind the mechanics. (For example, teach basic language mechanics such as punctuation and capitalization as you teach kid writing in 1st Grade (see chapter 3.13).

3. Teach the students to apply basic inflectional spelling endings before you study grammar and then again afterward.

4. Introduce grammar gradually over many years.

5. Always analyze words in the context of a sentence.

Begin teaching grammar by correcting students' speech, starting in 1st Grade. For example, a student says, "*Jimmy and me want to go to the library.*" You can correct the error by saying, "*You mean, Jimmy and I want to go to the library.*" Have the student repeat the corrected sentence back to you. If students never receive correction, they will continue to misuse grammar. (How many adults do you know who still do not use personal pronouns correctly?)

You can also begin to teach spelling rules that pertain to grammar on a need-to-know basis before students learn the formal grammar behind them. Then, reteach the same concept with the grammatical explanation once the students learn grammar. For example, when composing simple sentences in their kid writing, students in 1st Grade can learn to use –s to show that there is more than one of something (e.g., dogs) and –ed to show that something already happened (e.g., jumped). Students in 2nd Grade can learn about plural nouns and discover why to put the suffix –s on the end of nouns, and students in 3rd Grade can learn about tense and discover why to put the suffix –ed on the ends of verbs. They will have been using the convention for some time before they realize *why*.

Grammar is an abstract concept, and English provides students very few clues. Therefore, begin to teach the parts of speech in 2nd Grade, but limit the discussion to nouns and verbs. As Steiner suggests in *Faculty Meetings with Rudolf Steiner*: "A child of seven and a half can certainly differentiate between an activity and a thing. You do not need to emphasize the terminology. You could begin with stories and make the difference between a thing and an activity clear. That is something a child at that age can grasp" (Trostli 2004, 303).

Teach adjective and adverb in 3rd Grade and the rest of the parts of speech in 4th Grade. By spacing the introduction and practice of parts of speech over several years, students have an easier time mastering grammar.

When you teach the parts of speech in 2nd and 3rd Grade, always consider the grammar of the word in the context of a sentence. For example, the word <u>swimming</u> is not a verb; it is a verb, noun (gerund), or adjective.

1. He <u>is swimming</u>. (verb)

2. I like <u>swimming</u>. (gerund, a verb form used as a noun)

3. His <u>swimming</u> trunks are blue. (adjective)

The word <u>swimming</u> only settles on its part of speech once it is used in a sentence. Therefore, always provide context when you teach and practice parts of speech.

In summary, English and German differ very much in grammar. It is necessary to respect those differences when planning your grammar curriculum.

## 3.  Preparation

There are three things to do over the summer to prepare to teach grammar:

1. Study grammar.

2. Choose or create an umbrella story to use to teach grammar.

3. Sketch out main lesson book pages for the parts of speech: noun, verb, adjective, and adverb (2nd and 3rd Grade only).

Note: It is not recommended that you put all of the mechanics (i.e., capitalization and punctuation rules, etc.) in the main lesson book. Save main lesson book pages for parts of speech: noun, verb, adjective, and adverb. The goal is for the students to learn to apply mechanics, not create their own grammar book to use as a reference. If your students would benefit from recording a rule for an element of mechanics, have them use their phonics rules book (see Section 4 Protocol).

## Study Grammar

In the last couple of decades, many schools have dropped the instruction of grammar; consequently, many otherwise well-educated adults did not get an adequate education in the subject. If you have reservations about your own grammar skills, use the summer to remediate them.

Although you would not share Steiner's thoughts on grammar with your students directly, meditating on them during your preparation may help you develop a different relationship to the subject of grammar:

- Noun: "By learning to name things with nouns, we distinguish ourselves from the world around us. By calling a thing a table or a chair, we separate ourselves from the table or chair; we are here, and the table or chair is there" (Trostli 2004, 274).

- Verb: "The development of our consciousness takes place in our relationship to things when we address them . . . If I say a verb— for example, "A woman writes"— I not only unite with the being in relation to whom I used the verb, I also do with her what she is doing with her physical body [I simply suppress the activity]. I unite my I with the physical body of the other when I use a verb" (Trostli 2004, 274).

- Nine-Year Change: "You will realize that by making grammar conscious in a living way, you work on the creation of an I-consciousness in the child. You must orient everything toward that knowledge that exists in the body around the age of nine, when a consciousness of the I normally awakens" (Steiner 2001, 111–112).

- Adjective: "By naming an object with a noun, I dissociated myself from it; when I describe it with an adjective I become one with it again….When I say, 'The chair is blue,' I am expressing a quality that unites me with the chair (sentence order changed by author)" (Trostli 2004, 274).

- Grammar/Mechanics: "You should teach the children punctuation to give them some feeling for logic" (Trostli 2004, 307).

If you know a foreign language, consider comparing how that language works with nouns, verbs, adjectives, and adverbs as another way to refresh your knowledge of grammar.

If necessary, get an elementary grammar book and review the concepts you will need to teach in the upcoming year(s). A common resource teachers use is *The Blue Book of Grammar and Punctuation; Eleventh Edition* by Jane Straus. The website http://www.grammarbook.com is based on this book and offers basic definitions with examples of most grammar rules and parts of speech.

Once you have a good understanding of grammar, then you can consider your umbrella story.

## Umbrella Story

An umbrella story is a serial story that is used to introduce related concepts to young students through an imagination. The umbrella story that the authors created for this chapter is called *Englishland*. It is used as a model for how to introduce grammar to students in Grades 1–3.

There are other umbrella stories as well. One can be found in *Grammar-land* by M.L. Nesbitt, a book that was first published in 1878 and can be downloaded from the Internet.

You can use umbrella stories like Nesbitt's or *Englishland* in whole or part or make up one of your own. Just make sure that you understand the grammar concepts in full and that whatever imagination you bring resonates with you.

## 4. Scheduling

When preparing your curriculum, you can use the block plan templates in Appendices 1–3 or you can create your own. If you create your own, use the following points to lay out your blocks:

1. Begin instruction during the middle of 1st Grade for mechanics and the middle of 2nd Grade for formal grammar (i.e., parts of speech).

2. Teach grammar until the end of 8th Grade. Students will have to master increasingly more difficult levels of grammar in each academic year. They will have to know all of the parts of speech by the end of 4th Grade in order to be ready for formal grammar study of a foreign language in 5th Grade.

3. Teach grammar in the Introduction &/or Review segment of both main lesson blocks and practice blocks for mechanics and the Introduction &/or Review segment of main lesson for formal grammar. Use the Bookwork segment for written work when you are introducing a new concept; use the Skills Practice segment for additional practice. Mechanics do not need to go into a book *per se*; however, if you think a rule would benefit from being written down, use the main lesson book for mechanics that are taught in main lesson and the phonics rules book for mechanics taught in practice blocks.

4. Use a two-day grammar rhythm to teach the parts of speech. Introduce mechanics when they come up.

5. The number of minutes per lesson: varies. It can be five minutes for a mini-lesson in mechanics or 20–30 minutes for formal grammar (i.e., 10–15 minutes for Introduction &/or Review and 10–15 minutes for Bookwork).

**Teaching Rhythm**

Use a two-day rhythm to teach grammar concepts and then continue to practice them in the Skills Practice segment until the students have mastered them. Teach grammar only in main lesson blocks, with the exception of the review block taught during practice classes in the beginning of 3rd Grade. Use a two-day rhythm as shown in table 3.11.1.

**Table 3.11.1: Two-Day Rhythm for Grammar**

| Day One | Day Two |
|---|---|
| • Tell an umbrella story to introduce the concept. <br> • Teach the concept from the image. <br> • Do practice Activity A. <br> • Assign any related bookwork.* | • Review the story, image, and concept. <br> • Do practice Activity B. <br> • Assign any related bookwork.* |

*When it comes to bookwork, Steiner was adamant that students should only write the rule and not include any teacher-generated examples. He says: "If they [the students] are allowed to write down the examples, they absorb the form of the example too strongly. In terms of teaching grammar, the examples ought to be dispensable… for only the rule should finally remain" (Trostli 2004, 292). With this in mind, the bookwork suggestions are of two types:

- Put the parts of speech into the main lesson book with a beautiful drawing (e.g., nouns and verbs.). Include a definition of the part of speech but not an example. Work with specific examples in the students' practice books and/or worksheets.

- Practice mechanics in practice books. Most of the time, there is no need to write down the rule; however, if you think that writing down the rule would benefit your students, put the rule in their phonics rules book.

## 5. Initial Introduction

There are two initial introductions to grammar. The first happens in 1st Grade when you teach capitalization (see chapter 3.11 #6). The second happens in 2nd Grade when you begin to teach parts of speech (see chapter 3.11 #7).

## 6. How to Teach Grammar in 1st Grade

The 1st Grade grammar curriculum comes directly out of the students' excitement for learning to write and read.

**Objective:** Teach students to apply basic mechanics (i.e. punctuation and capitalization) as soon as they learn to write.

**Prerequisite:** The students should know how to use kid writing and most of the class should be able to compose their own sentence(s).

**Background Information:** Students learn to apply basic language mechanics correctly before they understand the grammar behind them. They will be doing a considerable amount of kid writing where their writing habits are being formed (see chapter 3.13). Each point will be retaught in upcoming years from the point of view of grammar and/or decoding/encoding rules.

**When to Teach:** Teach the initial introduction during the Introduction &/or Review segment. Reteach the concepts during class mini-lessons for kid writing.

### How to Teach

In 1st Grade, the grammar curriculum covers the following mechanics and spelling conventions:

1. Capitalization: first words in sentences, people's names, and the pronoun *I*
2. Punctuation: periods at end of sentences
3. Spelling: encoding inflectional endings (–s for more than one; –ed for actions that have already happened) (see chapter 4.1 rule 4)

Use the teaching rhythm to schedule these lessons (see table 3.11.1). For each lesson, *The Roadmap to Literacy* will offer:

- an introductory image from the umbrella story, *Englishland.*
- activities (i.e., the multisensory learning opportunities for the whole class or groups that are part of the Introduction &/or Review segment of the lesson) (see Activities in chapter 2.3 #4 and Drill Down in chapter 2.4 #2).
- ideas for bookwork (i.e., the individual work students do in their main lesson book or practice book).

Note: All grammar bookwork for 1st Grade should be done in practice books or in conjunction with their kid writing.

These ideas are merely a starting point. Feel free to add your own ideas to the list.

## 6a. Capitalization: First Words in Sentences, People's Names, and the Pronoun *I*

This introduction has three parts.

### Introduction Part One: Capitalizing the First Word in a Sentence

<u>Objective</u>: Teach students that the first word in a sentence is capitalized.

<u>Prerequisites</u>: Students have echo read or memory read a passage on the board that is written in sentences.

<u>Curriculum Connection</u>: Introduction to *Englishland* (see chapter 3.2 #7).

<u>Introductory Image from Englishland</u>

*In the world of Language there is a very special place called Englishland. Englishland is a vast country filled with all kinds of characters and letters who live together in villages scattered throughout the land. The letters of the alphabet that we are learning about live together in a place called Letter Village. In this village the capital (or uppercase) letters are the adults and the lowercase letters are the children. The wisest character in Letter Village is their Mayor. Whenever the letter citizens of the village encounter a problem, it is the Mayor who finds a solution.*

*The letter children of Letter Village are a lot like regular children—they love to play together. When letter children play together, however, they spell words…. lots and lots of words. After a time, the Mayor of the Village saw that he could arrange the words in such a way that when they were read from left to right they expressed an idea such as, "we like pizza" or "it is raining" (Write one on board without capitalizing the first word or using a period.). This was a very exciting invention, and when asked what he called these word groups, the Mayor quipped, "I am going to call them* <u>sentences</u> *because each one makes sense!"*

*From that day on, the Mayor and the child letters were so busy forming words and sentences that they didn't even notice that the uppercase/adult letters had become quiet bored, for they had nothing to do.*

*Finally one day, the adult letter A went to the Mayor to complain about this dilemma. It told the mayor that although the uppercase letters enjoyed watching the little ones play as they formed words and sentences, the adult letters were feeling, well, rather useless. The Mayor said that he would think about this problem and see if he couldn't come up with a solution.*

*After a little while, the Mayor came up with an idea that not only would solve the adult letters' problem but would help him solve one of his own. For some time now, the Mayor had been trying to figure out how to show where one sentence ends and the next begins. He would separate the ending letter of one sentence from the beginning of the next, but this solution did not work very well. The nature of child letters is just like that of regular children: they liked to play together. It was quite difficult to keep the ending and beginning child letters apart!*

*And what was the solution the Mayor came up with to solve these two problems? He decided he would place a big letter at the beginning of every sentence. It would be the big letter's job to signal that a new sentence was beginning. He also decided to rename these letters* <u>capital </u>*letters rather than adult or uppercase. He felt that they needed a special name for this special job.*

*This turned out to be an ingenious solution to both problems. The capital letters liked being important, and they liked the idea of being responsible for announcing to the world that a new sentence was beginning.*

Activities:

- Ask the students to count the number of capital letters in your memory reading passage on the blackboard.

- Before class, create a brief summary of a story you have recently told your class that includes proper names (capitalized) and make copies for everyone. Have the students read the summary with you (as best they can) then ask them to circle each capital letter that begins a sentence.

Note: When you do either activity to identify the first words of sentences that get capitalized, the students will notice that there are other words that begin with adult letters that do not begin the sentence. That realization can lead in to the next lesson: a Letter Village story about why people's names are always capitalized.

Bookwork: Give a kid writing assignment and ask the students to make sure they use capital letters (adult letters) to show when they begin a thought.

**Introduction Part Two: Capitalizing People's Names**

Objective: Teach students to capitalize people's names.

Prerequisites: Students have echo read or memory read a passage on the board that has names.

Introductory Image from Englishland: Write an add-on to the *Englishland* story where the Mayor realizes that capital letters should also be used at the beginning of someone's name: *"For a person's name is very special and deserves to be honored."*

Activity: Create a short paragraph based on a story you have recently told that has a number of proper nouns in it OR use a familiar poem or nursery rhyme that has a number of proper nouns in it. Give the students a copy of the passage. Read the passage using echo reading (see chapter 3.15 #2 ). Once students know the passage, have them stand up every time a proper name is spoken.

Bookwork: Give a kid writing assignment about their families and ask the students to make sure they use capital letters to honor a person when they write the person's name.

**Introduction Part Three: Capitalizing the word I**

Objective: Teach students to capitalize the pronoun *I*.

Introductory Image from Englishland: Write a final segment for the *Englishland* story where the Mayor realizes when we present or speak of ourselves as *I*, we also should be honored.

Activities

- Give every student a book from your classroom library, have them turn to a page with lots of words on it, and count the number of times a capital letter is used to announce the beginning of a sentence and the number of times it is used to begin a name (or for the word *I*).

- Give the students a passage that has all three types of capital letters in it. Have them select three different colored pencils. Use one of the colored pencils to highlight the capital letters found at the beginning of each sentence, use the second colored pencil to highlight those used at the beginning of proper names, and the third to highlight the word *I*.

<u>Bookwork</u>: Give a kid writing assignment asking students to introduce themselves. Start with *My name is___*. Include one or two things they like or information about themselves. Ask the students to make sure they capitalize the word *I* when they use it.

## 6b. Punctuation: Periods at End of Sentences

<u>Objective</u>: Teach students to put periods at the ends of sentences.

<u>Prerequisites</u>: Students begin to notice periods at the ends of sentences.

<u>Introductory Image from Englishland</u>:

*One day, capital A came to the Mayor of Letter Village with a dilemma. It told the Mayor that as the spokesperson for the other capital letters, it wanted the Mayor to know that they were having a bit of a problem with the ending letter of the sentence before them. Even though the capital letters' presence alerted the readers of a story that a new sentence was beginning, the little letters at the end of sentences kept bumping into them. Capital A asked the Mayor to come up with some way to keep the little ones in place.*

*The Mayor soon came up with an idea. When the little i and j were created, he had lots and lots of dots made to put on top of them. But as it turned out, the small **j** did not turn up in words very often so he had a large surplus of lowercase **j** dots in his warehouse. His idea was to place those spare dots at the end of each sentence to remind the little ones that they were to stay connected to their sentence and not wander off! This solution worked very well. The little ones, who did not really want to cause trouble, now knew where they were to stop, and the capital letters no longer had bruises from being bumped into!*

*The Mayor also added an additional rule for the use of periods. He informed anyone who read a sentence that when they got to a period, they were to take a breath. The period was like a stop sign for the reader.*

*Period is my name.*

*Stopping a sentence is my game.*

<u>Activity</u>: Read a passage from a story and ask the class to figure out how many sentences you read. (Hint: *"How many times do I stop talking and pause before I go on speaking?"*) Also, it can be fun for them to hear you read a passage without stopping at the periods. Soon it becomes one breathless jumble of sounds!

<u>Bookwork</u>

- Day One: Give students a copy of a summary of a story you have told. Leave out all of the capital letters and periods. Read the story together as a class several times and then discuss how hard it is to tell where one sentence ends and the next one begins. Then read it to the class (with pauses for punctuation) and ask them to put in all of the punctuation marks (periods) and capital letters. (Collect and correct.)
- Day Two: The students could copy the summary into their main lesson book.

<u>Curriculum Connection</u>: Give the students many opportunities to practice stopping the flow of their memory reading when they come to a period.

## 6c. Inflectional Endings Lesson #1

Inflectional endings for the plural –s and past tense –ed are covered in section 4 as part of the phonics rules curriculum of 1st Grade (see chapter 4.1 rule 4). Teach them as mini-lessons from kid writing (see chapter 3.13 #5).

Note: Plan to reteach this lesson many times throughout the year. It will take some time for the students to learn it.

Grammar instruction in 1st Grade is limited to mechanics. If students raise questions about other punctuation marks or capital letter usages, it is fine to describe their role briefly. Let the students know that they will learn more about them later.

## 7. How to Teach Grammar in 2nd Grade

In the 2nd Grade, students begin the formal study of grammar.

**Objectives:**

1. Teach students the first parts of speech: noun and verb.
2. Continue to teach mechanics.

**Prerequisite:** NA

**When to Teach:** Teach the initial introduction of your first part of speech during the Introduction &/or Review segment of main lesson during the second half of 2nd Grade. Use the Bookwork segment for follow-up work that is part of the initial introduction. Reteach mechanics during class mini-lessons for kid writing and composition as needed.

**How to Teach**

The 2nd Grade grammar curriculum contains the following topics:

a. The Three Grammatical Rules for a Sentence

b. Three Types of Sentences and Their Punctuation

c. Nouns: Initial Introduction

d. Nouns: Proper and Common Nouns

e. Nouns: Emphasizing Place Nouns

f. Plural Nouns

g. Verbs

Use the two-day teaching rhythm to schedule these lessons (see chapter 3.11 #4). Each lesson includes:

- an introductory image from the umbrella story, *Englishland*;
- Activities (i.e., the multisensory learning opportunities for the whole class or groups that are part of the Introduction &/or Review segment of the lesson) (see Activities in chapter 2.3 #4 and Drill Down in chapter 2.4 #2);
- Ideas for bookwork (i.e., the individual work students do in their main lesson book or practice book). Use both books for the parts of speech but focus on practice books for mechanics. The goal is not for the students to make a beautiful grammar textbook that contains the rules for mechanics but to practice applying those mechanics in their writing. Note: If students need to write down a rule for mechanics, use the main lesson book in main lesson blocks and the phonics rules book in practice blocks.

These ideas are merely a starting point. Feel free to add your own ideas to the list.

## 7a. The Three Grammatical Rules for a Sentence

<u>Objective</u>: Lay the foundation for subjects and predicates in 3rd Grade by teaching the three grammatical rules for a sentence. Present these rules in an imaginative way so that the students can apply the rules in their writing.

<u>Background Information</u>: A sentence expresses a complete thought. Sentences follow three grammatical rules:

1. They are about someone or something. (i.e., Each sentence has a noun.*)
2. They tell its action or more about it. (i.e., Each sentence has a verb.)
3. They make sense.

*Just allow students to use pronouns as nouns in 3rd Grade. You will differentiate between noun and pronoun next year.

<u>Introductory Image from Englishland</u>

*At first, only the Mayor of Letter Village composed the sentences made from the words the letters created. After a while the Letter Villagers wanted to try to make some sentences by themselves. The Mayor thought this a grand idea since he could not always stop what he was doing to help them make sentences. However, just like people make mistakes when they are first learning something new, the letters made mistakes, too. When this happened, they would call for the Mayor to help them fix the problem.*

*After being called over time after time, the Mayor realized that he needed to give the letters some sentence guidelines or laws to help them check whether they had made a proper sentence. So he instructed them thus:*

*"If you are to live in Letter Village and make your own sentences, you must follow the laws of our country, Englishland. The first law is this: All sentences must be about something or someone. The second law: All sentences must tell what that someone or something did, or tell more about it or him or her. The third law: Every sentence must make sense."* (Write these laws on the board.)

*"Let's consider the sentences that you have just brought to me. I will pass out citations to each sentence that doesn't follow the sentence laws. Each citation will tell you which law it is breaking. Then, I trust you to fix the sentence yourselves. When you have fixed it, come show me what you have done."*

*The first sentence said: <u>Licked the spoon.</u> The mayor put a citation on it: #1) This sentence does not say who or what licked the spoon. Please fix.* (Write the sentence on the board and its citation.)

*The second sentence said: <u>My fuzzy rabbit.</u> The mayor put a citation on it: #2) This sentence does not say what my fuzzy rabbit did or more about it. Please fix.* (Write the sentence on the board and its citation.)

*The third sentence said: <u>Dan sneezed a rubber ball.</u> The mayor put a citation on it: #3) This sentence does not make any sense. Please fix.* (Write the sentence on the board and its citation.)

*The villagers got to work fixing each sentence. As soon as they had finished, they stood in front of the mayor so he could inspect their efforts. Here is what they did.* (Add in the missing words to the sentences.)

1) *Tina licked the spoon. The mayor said, "Now we know who licked the spoon—Tina!"*
2) *My fuzzy rabbit is nice. The mayor said, "Now we know that the rabbit is nice."*
3) *Dan squeezed a rubber ball. The mayor said, "Ah, it makes much more sense to say that Dan squeezed a ball rather than he sneezed a ball!"*

*Then the mayor exclaimed, "Well done!" And with that encouragement, the villagers rushed off to make more sentences.*

Activity: You can ask the students to give out citations, just like the Mayor. Have them work in pairs. One student has the partial sentence cards and the other copies of the three different citations. Together they decide which citation to give each partial sentence and they fix the sentence so that it is complete. You can model this task by saying a sentence that contains an error such as, "*The black cat.*" Ask: "*Who is the sentence about?*" (black cat) "*What is the cat doing?*" (We do not know—the action is missing.) "*Which citation is that?*" (#2) "*What do we need to do to fix the sentence?*" (Add an action. For example, *The black cat hissed.*)

Bookwork: Give the students a handout where each sentence needs to be fixed. Ask them to fix the sentences.

## 7b. Three Types of Sentences and Their Punctuation

Objectives: Teach the students the three types of sentences and their corresponding punctuation marks. (The fourth type, the Imperative, is covered in 3rd Grade.)

Background Information: Here are three of the four types of sentences along with their punctuation:

1. A declarative sentence or statement ends in a period.
2. An interrogative sentence or question ends in a question mark.
3. An exclamatory sentence or exclamation ends in an exclamation point.

Introduce the sentences using their formal or informal names (*interrogative* or *question*). If you choose the latter, switch over to the formal names in 4th Grade.

Prerequisite: Students understand what a sentence is.

Introductory Image from Englishland

*Words on the page just lie there, lifeless, until we read them and bring them to life again. However, we have to figure out how the author wanted the words to be said. For instance, when an author writes a sentence such as the following, "You ate all of your dinner," (Write the sentence on the board.), the author could be saying it several ways. For instance:*

- *"You ate all of your dinner." (Say as a statement.)*
- *"You ate all of your dinner!" (Say with excitement.)*
- *"You ate all of your dinner?" (Say as a question.)*

*The author tells us which one is right by placing one of three symbols at the end of each sentence. These symbols are called punctuation marks. They tell us how the author wants us to read or say her words.*

*To learn about punctuation marks and how they help us read, we need to get to know some very special characters: Period Pete, Question Quinn, and Exclamation Esther, the Town Crier. Each of these characters was called upon by the Mayor of Letter Village to help him bring the right voice to each written sentence.*

*At first, all of the sentences created in Letter Village were just descriptions of things that the villagers saw or did such as, The ball is blue. or We went to the beach. Everyone knew that these sentences were just sharing information and were meant to be read with a normal voice. As we learned earlier, to let the reader know when a sentence had ended, the Mayor had ordered that the final word of every sentence be followed by a dot, which served as a little stop sign.*

*What I forgot to tell you was that these dots were put there by the Mayor's nephew, Period Pete. In fact, the mayor was so grateful that his nephew was willing to do this important task that he changed the name of the dot to "period" in his honor. But, there was a problem with ending every sentence with a period. The Mayor noticed that when someone asked a question the speaker's voice would change at the end by going up a little bit. Yet, when the question would be written down and someone would read it like an information sentence, it sounded funny. (Give an example…speak a bit "robot-ish" at the end.) Just as the Mayor was trying to figure out what to do about this dilemma, a friend of his nephew's, Question Quinn, came to town.*

*Now Question Quinn was about the most curious character the Mayor had ever met. She spent most of her time asking questions or looking for questions to answer. When she heard about the Mayor's dilemma, she jumped at the chance to help.*

*"First of all," she declared, "We must make a new ending mark for sentences that are questions. That way, when someone reads a question, it will be clear how to say it properly."*

*The Mayor, seeing the wisdom in this idea, gave Question Quinn permission to create a special ending mark to be used at the end of every question. Quinn thought long and hard about how to form a question mark. Then it came to her. Since asking questions always included listening for the answer, she would create a mark that looked something like an ear. (Draw a question mark on the board and point out the ear shape formed by the curve of the question mark.)*

This imagination could continue on with the introduction of Exclamatory Esther. Make up your own description for this character and her important job.

Here are some other ideas for possible characters:

- Declarative sentence: a reporter
- Interrogative sentence: a detective
- Exclamatory sentence: a court jester, town crier, etc.

Just make sure they fit into your overall umbrella story for grammar.

<u>Activities</u>

- Have students practice reading sentences using the punctuation to inform them as to how they should say (voice) the sentence.
- Write a sentence on the board that could be an exclamation, a question, or a statement. (Do not put in the punctuation.) Read the sentence in such a way that it is clear which punctuation mark it should have. Ask a student to come up and add the proper punctuation (e.g., *You fell down.*).

<u>Bookwork</u>

- Dictate sentences and have the students figure out the punctuation.
- Design writing assignments where students have to write using only one type of sentence. For example, be a person who just won a prize and is telling everyone about it using exclamatory sentences.

## 7c. Nouns: Initial Introduction

Objective: Teach students their first part of speech: nouns.

Prerequisites: Students understand what a sentence is.

Steiner's Indications: Steiner recommends starting with the verb (Trostli 2004, 303); however, *The Roadmap to Literacy* recommends starting with the noun because word order is critical in English sentences, and in English the subject/noun leads the verb.

Background Information: Nouns are people, places, things, and ideas (e.g., freedom). However, when it comes to 2nd Grade instruction, it is best to limit nouns to the first three. (The concept of an idea as a noun fits better once the students have gone through the nine-year change and can better entertain abstract concepts (e.g., liberty, association, government, etc.) Idea nouns will be touched upon in the 3rd Grade curriculum through the –ness suffix (e.g., kindness, fondness, etc.) and further developed during the study of the meanings of the Big Four Suffixes in the 4th Grade. A creative way to introduce nouns is through the imagination of Queen Noun, the mother of all things.

Introductory Image from Englishland

*In the beginning, long before Letter Village was founded, Englishland was nothing but a barren wasteland with a King and a Queen. Queen Noun thought, "How boring! I want a kingdom that is filled with all kinds of wonderful people, places, and things." So Queen Noun went about creating a land filled with numerous people, places, and things.*

*She created all kinds of* people: *Americans, Canadians, Iranians, and Chinese. (Be sure to include the origin of the students in your class.) She made butchers, bakers, and candlestick makers. She made babies and students and grandmothers and uncles and cousins.*

*She made all kinds of* places: *the forest, the field, the desert. She made towns and theme parks. She made offices and classrooms. She made playgrounds and parking lots. She made _____. (Insert the name of your city, state, or country and other proper noun places your students might be familiar with.)*

*She also made all kinds of* things: *toys, books, games. She made dogs, cats, pigeons. She made cards and jump ropes and swings. She made monster trucks and factories and clouds. In honor of all of the wonderful things Queen Noun created, King Verb wrote the following poem:*

Bunnies, bubbles, and berries, too

Waterfalls, flowers, and sky so blue

Gardens, rainbows, stars and sun

Queen Noun created every one.

Curriculum Connection: Teach the students this little poem about nouns or a similar poem in speech.

Activity: Have students go outside and write down ten nouns. Afterwards, have each student share one or more items on his or her list. Ask the class to determine what kind of noun it is: person, place, or thing. Write three columns on the board and put each word into its correct column. Then ask small groups of students to classify the rest of the nouns on their lists together and make a list in columns to show their work.

Bookwork

- Take a number of the nouns the students found in the activity above and put them together to create a poem or add some of them to King Verb's poem, which concludes the story above. Have the students write the poem in their main lesson books.
- Have the students do a teacher-led drawing of Queen Noun in their main lesson books and write the definition of noun as a caption: *A noun is a person, place, or thing.*
- Teach the students a poem such as "The Rainbow" by Christina Rossetti and have them underline the nouns (https://www.familyfriendpoems.com/poem/the-rainbow-by-christina-rossetti). For example, *Boats sail on the rivers.*

## 7d Nouns: Proper and Common Nouns

Objectives: Teach students to capitalize proper nouns and to identify which nouns are proper and which common.

Prerequisite: Students have mastered basic nouns (people, places, things).

Background Information: Proper nouns name specific people, places, and things and are capitalized: John, Canada, Empire State Building. Common nouns name generic people, places, and things and are written with a lowercase letter: boy, country, sky scraper.

Introductory Image from Englishland

*The Mayor of Letter Village was coming to visit the King and Queen of Englishland and he was bringing all of his letter citizens. Queen Noun was anxious to be the perfect host. She wanted to make sure there were things for all of the letters to do. So she went out among her noun subjects and told them that the letter people were coming to make signs for every noun in the kingdom. But Queen Noun was worried. What would the capital letters do? There would be no sentences so they could not be the first letter in the sentence. How could she make them feel special?*

*Queen Noun went for a walk among her subjects to ponder her problem. She saw a little girl playing with a litter of puppies. She knew the girl by name: Alice. So she called out, "Good morning, Alice. What cute puppies you are playing with." After visiting with Alice for a few moments, the Queen continued on her walk. Soon she saw a group of children playing in the meadow. At that moment she realized that if the letter citizens made a sign for Alice, it would look like this: (Write Alice on the board). But, if they made a sign for the children, it would be spelled like this: children. Individual people's names should be capitalized because each person is unique! What about places? And things? Are some places and things unique too? Could capital letters be used to honor each noun that names a unique place or thing?*

*Queen Noun thought about this idea as she strolled through her garden. As she looked about, she saw lots of common roses. But, then her gaze landed on the special yellow and pink roses called Rainbow's End. "I could capitalize Rainbow's End because it names a particular type of rose!" she exclaimed. Then she hurried to the center of town. There were lots of office buildings without names, but one was special. It was called Market Tower. "I could have Market Tower capitalized because it names a particular office building," she thought. Finally, she reflected on her own beloved kingdom. "Englishland is the name of this particular kingdom; it certainly should be capitalized!"*

*When the Mayor and the letter citizens arrived, Queen Noun explained their task. The letter children would spell the words for common nouns, the generic nouns that named any person, place, or thing. But the capital letters would be used for the first letter of any proper noun that named a specific person, place, or thing.*

*The letter people got right to work and had a marvelous time making the signs for the nouns of Englishland.*

Activities

- Ask the students about the places they were born and have lived, favorite places to go on vacation, etc. As you write down their place names, have them help you decide whether the name should be capitalized as a proper noun or written in lowercase as a common noun.

- *Stand up, Sit down*: Have students stand up if you say a proper noun and sit down if you say a common noun. On day one, have the whole class do the activity together; then on following days, drill down and have smaller groups (including rows or desk partners) do the activity while the others watch.

Bookwork

- Give each student a paper and ask them to divide it into two columns. At the top of the first column, have them write *Common Nouns* and at the top of the second column write *Proper Nouns*. On the board write the words in the left-hand column (add more examples if you have time). Discuss why these words are examples of common nouns. Then ask them to come up with their own examples of a proper noun equivalent. You might want to do the first one together. Remind them about the need for capitalization.

| Common Nouns | Proper Nouns |
| --- | --- |
| bridge | Golden Gate |
| city | |
| boy | |
| man | |
| etc. | |

- On a subsequent day, have the students look through a book to find common and proper nouns. First, they compile them into lists and then share with the class.

**7e. Nouns: Emphasizing Place Nouns**

Objective: Provide extra instruction for nouns that are places if the students need it.

Introductory Image from Englishland

*Queen Noun often wanted to send a note to a friend who lived on Birch Street. She needed a way to let the messenger know how to identify which street was Birch Street. Queen Noun invited the letter people to come and help her make signs for each location. They made signs for each street. They made signs for special places such as (Insert the name of your town.) and the North Pole where their friend Santa lived. They made signs for common places like living rooms and kitchens and playgrounds and classrooms; anywhere you could go was a place and was given a name. The Queen and the letter people made each place a name tag or sign. You can still see some of these signs today when you enter the city limits of a town or drive down a street. For example when driving into Placerville, you will see a sign that says: "Welcome to Placerville." Or you might attend a parade that is being held on Main Street.*

Activity: See chapter 3.11 #7d.

Bookwork: Have the students divide a piece of paper into three equal columns. At the top of each column have them write one of three words: *Person, Place,* or *Thing*. Then give them a list of nouns and ask the students to write each noun in its proper column. For example, the word *bird* would go in the things column, the word *Chris* in the person column, and the word *beach* in the places column.

## 7f. Plural Nouns

<u>Objective</u>: Students have been working with plural nouns since 1st Grade (see chapter 4.1 rule 4). Now introduce the concept of singular and plural nouns and help students learn to identify them.

<u>Introductory Image from Englishland</u>

*Queen Noun was happy with all of the people, places, and things found in her Kingdom. She gave every one a unique name. But one day, she saw something that surprised her.*

*Queen Noun was walking through the park when she saw a new animal scurrying away. It had a mask and a striped tail. She smiled and gave it a name: raccoon. Then two more little animals scurried out behind her. They, too, had a mask and a striped tail. "Oh my!" gasped Queen Noun, "What is this?"*

*She thought and thought about what to do. First she wanted to give each animal a different name. She decided that the second one would be called a* <u>jacoogalee</u> *and the third one would be a* <u>mystonosap</u>. *Just as she was getting up, a flock of pigeons flew past. There were dozens of them! She tried to figure out which one was* pigeon *and what to call the rest. "Come back!" cried Queen Noun. "I have to give you all names!" But the birds kept flying.*

*Queen Noun sat down and sighed. It was hopeless! How could she even think about naming every single different noun in the kingdom when so many nouns were so similar? Exhausted from her efforts, Queen Noun fell asleep on the grass.*

*When she woke up, she had an idea. What if she called the similar nouns by the same name but added a little something to the end to show when there was more than one of them?*

*Queen Noun ran off to find the raccoon, the* <u>jacoogalee</u>, *and the* <u>mystonsap</u>. *She found them washing their faces in the river. She snuck up and said softly, "You are all raccoons."* (Emphasize the /z/ sound at the end: raccoonsssssss.)

*From that day forth, Queen Noun named every noun in the kingdom. When there was only one, it was a singular noun, like raccoon. When there was more than one, it was a plural noun, like raccoons. She just added an S to the end, to show that there was more than one of something, that the noun was plural.* (Write singular noun: raccoon; plural noun: raccoons on the board.)

Note: *The Roadmap to Literacy* recommends that you teach irregular nouns in 4th Grade during the Human Being and Animal Blocks (e.g., child/children, mouse/mice, and goose/geese).

<u>Activities</u>

- Have students go outside and write down ten nouns. Ask them to find singular nouns and plural nouns. Afterwards, have each student share one or more items on his or her list. Ask the class to determine what kind of noun it is: singular or plural. Write columns on the board and put each word into its correct column. Then ask small groups of students to classify the rest of the nouns on their lists together and make a list in columns to show their work. Note: If students find irregular nouns such as *children*, point out that these nouns are special.

- Have students empty the contents of their desk. Divide these items into two broad categories—items they only have one of (e.g., consumable spelling dictionary, pencil sharpener, etc.) and items they have two or more of (e.g., pencils, erasers, etc.) Have the students make a list of these items in two columns—singular and plural.

Bookwork: Have the students write a rule for singular and plural nouns in their main lesson books. Illustrate the rule by leading a drawing of things that have a singular gesture and a plural gesture (e.g., a single tulip and a rose bush filled with roses).

## 7g. Verbs

Objective: Teach students about action verbs as their initial introduction to verbs.

Prerequisites: Students know what a sentence is and are proficient at identifying basic nouns.

Background Information: The study of verbs fits into the 2nd Grade curriculum particularly well. Verbs feature prominently in the literature curriculum stories of the year because students are contemplating actions when they learn about saintly people and see examples of the worst excesses in human behavior in the fables (see chapter 2.1 #6).

To avoid confusion, the initial introduction of verbs in 2nd Grade is limited to action verbs. You will teach helping (auxiliary) verbs and being (linking) verbs in 3rd Grade (see chapter 3.11 #8e and #8f).

For example, *Jane and Peter are* <u>baking</u> *cookies.* The action verb is *baking.* The word *are* is the helping verb.

## Introductory Image from Englishland

*After Queen Noun made her kingdom, there were so many interesting people, places, and things that the King could not wait to engage in the world around him. He played in the mud, harvested and ate the strawberries growing in the garden, slept on a bed, and was perfectly happy. Queen Noun loved to see him being so active that she went from calling him just plain King to King Verb, the King of Actions.*

I am King Verb, I like to act,

To walk, to run, to dance–It's a fact.

To plough, to build, to work, to strive,

I like to feel that I'm alive!

Curriculum Connection: Teach the students this little poem about verbs or a similar poem in speech.

## Activities

Once you have introduced the concept of *doing* or *action* words as the purview of King Verb, there are many practice activities you can include as part of the initial introduction of verbs. Just remember that in every practice activity, the students must always use the verb in the context of a sentence.

- *Charades in Sentences*: Give each student a verb to act out. For example, jump, swim, dance, skate, eat, etc. Have the students come up one at a time and act out the verb in their sentence. Ask the class to guess which verb the student is acting out. The answer should be stated as a sentence. Write the complete sentence on the board and ask the students to find the verb. Underline the verb.

Note: At this point accept both the progressive and simple past tense (e.g., "*Jim was jumping.*" or "*Jim jumped.*").

Ideas for actions: eat, wash, dress, shave, dance, ski, swim, etc.

Note: Limit the action verbs in the initial introduction to intransitive verbs, (i.e., verbs that do not take a direct object). For example, "*Jim* <u>swims</u>." rather than "*Jim* <u>makes</u> *a basket.*"

- *Supply the Verb:* Make a list of animal names on the board and ask the students to come up and add an action word for each kind of animal (e.g., *Dogs* <u>bark</u>. *Cats* <u>purr</u>. *Wolves* <u>howl</u>.).

- *Copycat:* The students form a circle, and the first student (you select) does one simple action (For example, touches her nose with her thumb) and all of the students copy her action and say, "I touched my nose." Then the student to her left touches her nose with her thumb and adds a new action, for example, jumping one time. All of the students copy the first and second action saying, "I touched my nose and jumped." The third child touches her nose, jumps, and adds a new action such as nodding her head. All of the students copy her action and say, "I touched my nose, jumped, and nodded." …and so on. (Limit the number of rounds. Once the students get silly because they can no longer remember, it is already past time to stop.) Then have the students write down the list of actions they performed and underline all of the verbs.

- *Newspaper Reporter:* Take the students outside with their *reporter* notebooks and pencils. Each student sits apart from the others. First have the students observe their area and then write as many sentences as they can about what is happening around them (e.g., *The bird flies.*). Next, have the students close their eyes and <u>listen</u> to the world around them. After a minute, ask them to open their eyes and write down what they heard in sentences (e.g., *The wind is blowing. The leaves are rustling. The car horn is honking. A child is laughing,* etc.). Once back in the classroom, have each student underline the action verb in each of her sentences. Then ask each student to share one sentence. Ask the class to identify the action verb.

<u>Bookwork</u>

- Have the students do a teacher-led drawing of King Verb in their main lesson books and write the definition of verb as a caption: *A verb is an action word.*

- Take some of the verbs the students found in the activity above and use them to create a poem or add some of them to the poem written in the story. Have the students write the poem in their main lesson books.

<u>Error Handling</u>: At some point, a student will use a gerund form in a sentence. A gerund is a verb ending in the suffix –ing that is used as a noun. For example, *Playing* is fun. Ignore the mistake in 2nd Grade. Wait to discuss gerunds until a later grade.

<u>Curriculum Connection</u>: Once the concept of verbs has been introduced, teach the following phonics rule: Inflectional Endings #2: –s, –es, –ed, and –ing (see chapter 4.2 rule 13).

**2nd Grade Conclusion**

Verbs conclude the official grammar instruction in 2nd Grade. Schedule regular grammar practice in the Skills Practice segment of main lesson. In addition, utilize economy in teaching to review nouns and verbs. For example, have students read a poem on the board and locate sight words, nouns, and verbs.

## 8. How to Teach Grammar in 3rd Grade

In the 3rd Grade, students continue to learn parts of speech and mechanics.

**Objectives:**

1. Teach students two more parts of speech: adjective and adverb.

2. Continue to teach mechanics.

**Prerequisite:** Students must be able to identify basic nouns and action verbs in sentences.

**Background Information:** The grammar curriculum in the 3rd Grade ramps up as students enter the nine-year change. They are leaving the dreaminess of young childhood and are ready to handle more grammar.

**When to Teach:** Introduce new grammar concepts during the Introduction &/or Review segment of main lesson blocks and teach language mechanics in the Skills Practice segment of both main lesson and practice blocks. Reteach mechanics during class mini-lessons for composition.

### How to Teach

You will have two grammar blocks in 3rd Grade. Introduce the following grammar concepts in your two grammar blocks in the following order:

- a. Review of 2nd Grade Grammar
- b. Introduction to Adjectives
- c. Introduction to Adverbs
- d. Verb Tense
- e. Being Verbs
- f. Helping Verbs
- g. Possessive Nouns and Apostrophes

Introduce these aspects during any main lesson block or practice block at any point during the year on a need-to-know basis.

- h. Capitalization Rules
- i. Synonyms and Antonyms
- j. Contractions
- k. Commas
- l. Quotation Marks

Use the two-day teaching rhythm to schedule these lessons (see chapter 3.11#4). Each lesson includes:

- an introductory image from the umbrella story, *Englishland*
- Activities (i.e., the multisensory learning opportunities for the whole class or groups that are part of the Introduction &/or Review segment of the lesson) (see Activities in chapter 2.3 #4 and Drill Down in chapter 2.4 #2)
- ideas for Bookwork (i.e., the work students do in their main lesson book or practice book). (Use both books for the parts of speech but focus on practice books for mechanics. The goal is not for the students to make a beautiful grammar textbook that contains the rules for mechanics but to practice applying those mechanics to their writing. If students need to write down a rule for mechanics, use the main lesson book in main lesson blocks and the phonics rules book in practice blocks.)

These ideas are merely a starting point. Feel free to add your own ideas to the list.

**8a. Review of 2nd Grade Grammar**

<u>Objectives</u>: Review 2nd Grade grammar and teach subject and predicate and imperative sentences.

<u>Background Information</u>

This review has four parts. During the first practice block, spend two weeks reviewing grammar. Review the sentence rules, nouns, and verbs. To keep the students engaged, bring a few new points as part of the review: subject/predicate and imperative sentences. There are four parts to this review. You can spend as many days per part as you need for the class to be ready to go to the next lesson. Use activities for each day to help the students grasp the concept. Use Drill Down for practice activities on subsequent days (see chapter 2.4 #2) and also include individual work.

<u>When to Teach</u>: If you begin with a math block in 3rd Grade as recommended, schedule this review during the first practice block of the year.

**Introduction Part One: Review Nouns and Verbs**

<u>Prerequisites</u>: NA

<u>Introductory Image from Englishland</u>

*Queen Noun decided to take a census, a list, of the people, places, and things in Englishland.*

*As you may recall, nouns are people, places, and things, and Queen Noun wanted to find out all she could about which people, places, and things were part of her kingdom. She set forth with a pad of paper and wrote down the name of every person she met: Lisa, Fred, Annika, Jay, Shondra, Jose, the secretary, policeman, fireman, and pilot. She wrote down the names of places such as Sacramento, Australia, Canada, Europe, hospital, and airport. She wrote down the names of things such as cats, dogs, flowers, bees, rocks, shoes, and umbrellas.*

*As she went around the kingdom, her husband, King Verb, accompanied her. But instead of working on the census, he ran, jumped, laughed, sang, played, and danced and then disappeared.*

*Queen Noun got very annoyed. "King Verb, where are you and what are you doing now?" she asked. "Why aren't you helping me take a census of all of the nouns in our kingdom?"*

*King Verb crawled out from behind a rock. "I was hiding," he said. "Nouns are your thing. I like to take action!"*

*Queen Noun said, "If you want action, you can help me with the census. Here," she said, handing him the pad of paper and pen. "You can write down the nouns while I say them. Writing is action."*

*King Verb followed behind Queen Noun, dutifully writing down each noun: butterfly, truck, trashcan, baby, and park. Then he began to fidget.*

*"Queen Noun," he said. "See that tree? I think there are probably some nouns in it. I had better climb it to see. Just to be sure." And before she could say a word, King Verb handed her the pad of paper and pen and climbed the tree as fast as he could. Leaves rained down as he shook the branches. Then King Verb's head popped out.*

*"Look!" he cried gleefully, "Squirrels!"*

*Queen Noun picked up the pad of paper, shook her head, and smiled to herself as she wrote down all of the nouns King Verb found in the tree: nest, eggs, centipedes, sap, acorns, birds (blue jays and magpies)… and so on.*

*From then on, Queen Noun added names to the census while King Verb ferreted out every noun he could find. He dug, he climbed, and he crawled around. He looked everywhere. At the end of the day, Queen Noun smiled to herself. Thanks to King Verb's thorough searching, the census was quite complete.*

<u>Activities</u>

- Have the class work together to help Queen Noun find all of the nouns in the sentences you have written on the board. Review that a noun is a person, place, or thing.
- Have the class also find the action words (verbs) in the sentences once verbs are introduced.
- Hand out various simple sentences. Ask the students who received one of the sentences to take turns pantomiming the action in the sentence for the class.

<u>Bookwork</u>: Give the students a handout and ask them to underline all of the nouns and circle all of the verbs. (Bonus: identify if the noun is a person, place, or thing.)

**Introduction Part Two: Subject and Predicate**

<u>Prerequisites</u>: Students can identify nouns and verbs.

<u>Background Information</u>: The **subject** (or **complete subject**) is who or what the sentence is about. The **predicate** (or **complete predicate**) is what the subject does. For example, *The little boy swam in the pond.* The complete subject is *the little boy.* The complete predicate is *swam in the pond.*

<u>Introductory Image from Englishland</u>

*The next day, the royal couple set out to find more nouns for Queen Noun's census.*

*Soon, the royal couple came upon some letter children. As you recall, letter children play by forming words. Once they form words, they join together to form sentences. The mayor was checking their sentences to make sure they were still forming them correctly. He made sure they followed the rules:*

1. *They are about someone or something.*
2. *They tell its action or more about it.*
3. *They make sense.*

*Queen Noun added the words* letter children, mayor, *and* sentences *to her census list. She added the word* rules *to her census sheet. She was about to continue on with her census when the mayor started acting peculiar. What was he doing? She had to find out!*

*The mayor went up to a sentence. It said: "The brown puppies play in the grass."*

*The mayor said, "All of the words that tell who or what the sentence is about stand to my left."*

*Then the mayor said, "All of the words that tell the action or more about who or what the sentence is about, stand to my right."*

*The sentence split into two groups: "The brown puppies" and "play in the grass."*

*Queen Noun was flabbergasted. What was this? How could she add it to her census sheet? She went to the mayor for an explanation.*

*"Mayor, would you please tell me what you are doing to that sentence? It is not a sentence any more. What are these groups of words? What have you done?"*

*The Mayor smiled and said, "Queen Noun, may I introduce you to the two parts of a sentence? They are called* <u>subject</u> *and* <u>predicate</u>. *The subject tells you who or what the sentence is about. The predicate tells you more about the subject or what it does."*

*Queen Noun went over the subject. It said, "The brown puppies." It was what the sentence was about. "Greetings, subject," she said. She wrote* <u>subject</u> *down on her census.*

*She went over to the predicate. It said,* <u>play in the grass</u>. *It was what the subject does. "Greetings, predicate," she said. She wrote* <u>predicate</u> *down on her census.*

*Queen Noun smiled and called King Verb over to meet the new nouns: subject and predicate.*

*Then King Verb ambled over. He looked at the subject with little interest but when he came to the predicate, he leapt up and ran to the grass and began to play in it.*

*"Dear, what are you doing?" asked Queen Noun.*

*"I'm playing in the grass!" yelled King Verb. He ran and jumped and crawled through the grass. He rolled over and over and did summersaults.*

*"Dear, why on earth are you playing in the grass?" asked Queen Noun.*

*"Because the predicate said to!" shrieked King Verb joyfully.*

*Queen Noun and the mayor started to laugh. So did all of the letter children. Their king was trying to do headstands in the grass. In place of a crown, King Verb had hundreds of pieces of grass sticking to his head.*

<u>Activity</u>: Have the class split sentences into complete subject and complete predicate.

<u>Bookwork</u>: Write simple statement sentences on the board and ask the students to copy them on their paper and split them into subject and predicate. (Note: Avoid auxiliary verbs.)

## Introduction Part Three: Simple Subject & Simple Predicate

<u>Objective</u>: Teach students to identify simple subjects and predicates.

<u>Background Information</u>: The **simple subject** is the noun or pronoun in the complete subject. The **simple predicate** is the verb in the complete predicate. For example, *The little boy swam in the pond*. The simple subject is *boy*. The simple predicate is *swam*.

<u>Prerequisites</u>: Students can identify (complete) subject and predicate.

<u>Introductory Image from Englishland</u>

*The next day Queen Noun and King Verb went out again to work on their census. They saw the letter children playing again. Only this time, the letter children had constructed a stage in the park. They were getting ready to have a contest, and they needed judges. Would the Queen and King be willing to help them?*

*Queen Noun and King Verb walked over. They saw there was a special place for the judges. The Mayor, who was hosting the contest, was already there. He indicated two seats for the royal couple. Queen Noun and King Verb sat down.*

*"Let the contest begin," said the Mayor.*

*A subject of a sentence walked out on the stage. It said, "The fastest horse."*

*"Distinguished judges," said the Mayor, "Which word is the most important word in the subject?"*

*Queen Noun and King Verb walked over to the subject of the sentence. They looked at each word: "The fastest horse." They began to deliberate to figure out which word was the most important.*

*Queen Noun said, "The word <u>the</u> cannot be the most important word. Subjects have to tell who or what a sentence is about. The word <u>the</u> does not tell us anything."*

*King Verb said, "The word <u>fastest</u> cannot be the most important word. Subjects have to tell us who or what a sentence is about. The word <u>fastest</u> could be about anything… .like a car, or a runner, or a song, or even me! I'm the fastest King!" and King Verb ran around the stage three times to prove it.*

*Queen Noun and King Verb went to the last word: <u>horse</u>. They nodded their heads. This word was most important! It told that the sentence was about a horse.*

*Queen Noun announced, "It is the opinion of the judges that <u>horse</u> is the most important word in the subject. It tells us what the sentence will be about: a horse!"*

*The Mayor brought out a special ribbon. It said, "Simple Subject." In this case <u>horse</u> was the most important word in the subject part of the sentence so he pinned it to the word <u>horse</u>. All of the letter children clapped, and the word <u>horse</u> took a bow.*

*Then the predicate came on stage. It said, "galloped around the track."*

*"Distinguished judges," said the Mayor, "Which word is the most important word in the predicate part of the sentence?"*

*Queen Noun and King Verb walked over to the predicate of the sentence. They looked at each word "galloped around the track." They began to deliberate to figure out which word was the most important.*

*King Verb said, "The word <u>track</u> cannot be the most important word. Predicates have to tell us what the subject did. The subject did not track anybody. Track is the field. It is a noun, not a verb!"*

*Queen Noun said, "Yes, and the word <u>around</u> cannot be the most important word in the predicate. It does not tell us what the subject did. And the word <u>the</u> does not tell us anything."*

*Queen Noun and King Verb went to the word: <u>galloped</u>. They nodded their heads. This word was most important! It told what the horse did: galloped!*

*King Verb said, "It is the opinion of the judges that the word <u>galloped</u> is the most important word. It tells us what the subject did. The horse galloped!"*

The Mayor *brought out a special ribbon. It said, "Simple Predicate" on it. He pinned it to the word <u>galloped</u>. Then the simple subject and simple predicate came out, joined hands, and took a bow. Everyone cheered as the curtain came down on the stage.*

*The mayor jumped up from his seat. He read what the words sad. "Goodness gracious!" exclaimed the Mayor. "Look everyone! We have a new sentence. "The sentence says: <u>Horse galloped</u>. It has a subject that tells what the sentence is about: horse. It has a predicate that tells what the subject did: galloped. It makes sense: Horse galloped." It is smaller than the initial sentence, but it is still a sentence!"*

*"Letter children," the Mayor boomed. "Let's have a special round of applause for our distinguished judges, Queen Noun and King Verb. They have selected the most important words in the subject and predicate! How do I know? Because their simple subject and simple predicate make a simple sentence!"*

*All the letter children cheered. King Verb took a bow.*

<u>Activity</u>: Ask the class to judge which is the most important word in subjects and predicates. Check the answers by seeing if they form simple sentences.

<u>Bookwork</u>

- Write simple statement sentences on the board and ask the students to copy them on their paper and split them into subject and predicate. Then ask them to underline the simple subject and circle the simple predicate. Finally, rewrite the simple subject and simple predicate into a simple sentence.

- Challenge the students to find all of the nouns in a sentence and then determine which one is the subject. For example, *Jane eats macaroni at the table with Frank.* The nouns are: *Jane, macaroni, table, Frank*; however, only *Jane* is the subject of the sentence because she is the one who does the action: *eats*.

**Introduction Part Four: Imperative Sentences**

<u>Objective</u>: Review the three sentence types taught in 2nd Grade (i.e., statement, question, exclamation) and teach the final sentence type: commands (imperative).

<u>Prerequisite</u>: Students can identify the subject of a sentence.

<u>Background Information</u>: An imperative sentence (command) is one where the subject is often implied. For example, *Eat your dinner.* The subject (you) is implied. Seldom would you hear someone say, *"You eat your dinner."* or *"You clean your room."* An imperative sentence can end in a period or an exclamation mark, depending on the forcefulness of the command. Help the students hear the difference in tone and emotion behind the words.

Examples of a normal command:

> *Please clean your room.*
>
> *Go to the shed and get out a rake.*
>
> *Meet me in the garden.*

Examples of a forceful command:

> *Watch out!*
>
> *Do not open that door!*

<u>Introductory Image from Englishland</u>

*Queen Noun was finishing off her census. She had every type of person, place, and thing she could think of. She just needed a few more items for her census: the names of the sentences.*

*She saw sentences that made statements such as* <u>John likes fish</u>. *and* <u>The weather was warm</u>. *They always ended in a period. She wrote down* <u>Statements</u> *on her census.*

*She saw sentences that asked questions such as "Are you sleepy?" and "Who wants ice cream?" They always ended in a question mark. She wrote down Questions on her census.*

*She saw sentences that showed strong emotion such as "I burned my finger!" and "There is a mouse in the house!" They always ended in an exclamation mark. She wrote down Exclamations on her census.*

*Queen Noun was about to close the book on her official census of the nouns in Englishland when she saw the letter children making a horrible mistake. One of their sentences had no subject!*

*"Mayor, Mayor, come quick!" she yelled.*

*The Mayor ran as fast as he could to Queen Noun. "Whatever is the matter, your majesty?" he panted.*

*"The letter children are disobeying the law! They need your help to fix their sentence!" exclaimed the Queen.*

*Queen Noun brought him over to the sentence. It said: "Wash the dishes."*

*"Mayor, look at that! This sentence has no subject. You must give the letter children a citation for disobeying the laws of sentences."*

*Queen Noun wrote Citation down in her census. When she looked up, the Mayor was smiling.*

*"Queen Noun," he agreed, "You are right that this sentence has no subject. And yet you are wrong. This sentence is still a sentence."*

*Queen Noun was so flabbergasted, she dropped her census book. "Mayor, how can that be?" she asked. In answer, the Mayor whistled, and a word came running up. The word said, "You."*

*The word "you" hopped into the beginning of the sentence. It now said, "You wash the dishes." Then it hopped back out.*

*"Greetings, Queen Noun," said the word You. "Let me introduce you to a new type of sentence. It is called a command. When you give a command, you almost always drop the word you. But rest assured, if it is needed, I am ready and willing to jump back into the sentence to make it clear that the sentence has a subject and is not breaking the law."*

*"Please get back into the sentence," said Queen Noun to the word You. It happily complied. Queen Noun read: "You wash the dishes." The subject was You. The predicate was "wash the dishes."*

*"What do you know?" Queen Noun thought to herself. "You do not need to say the word You when you give a command!"*

*The Mayor came up and said, "Let me show you the best feature of commands. You can use periods or exclamation points at the end. When you are upset or need the job done now, put an exclamation point on the end to show people you mean business."*

*An exclamation point took the place of the period at the end of the sentence. Now it said, "Wash the dishes!"*

*"I show people you mean what you said," piped in the exclamation point. "You can use me when you are upset, excited, frightened, or your command is very important."*

*Queen Noun wrote Command into her census. Now there were four types of sentences. "Thank you, Mayor and letter children. I apologize for implying you had broken the law."*

*"That's OK, your majesty," said the letter children. "Our sentence did look like it had no subject after all!"*

*"Now, if you'll excuse me," said Queen Noun with a smile, "I need to find King Verb and teach him about commands. I have a huge list of chores for him to do about the castle, and commands will be just the thing. If he does not listen, I will use some exclamation marks!"*

*And Queen Noun walked away, busily making a new list. In place of her noun census, she had a Honey Do list, a list of chores for her King to do that weekend.*

<u>Activities</u>

- Say commands as statements and as exclamations. Have the class determine the right form of punctuation.

- Have the class make up commands. Test them to see if they are commands by putting the subject *you* back into the sentence.

- Have the class make up the *Honey Do list* for King Verb based on chores they have to do around their house.

<u>Bookwork</u>: Ask the students to compose their own commands. (You can give them scenarios such as: traffic cop, parent, boss, teacher, etc.)

## 8b. Introduction to Adjectives

<u>Objectives</u>: Teach the students to identify adjectives in sentences and to use them in their writing.

<u>Prerequisite</u>: Students can identify nouns in sentences.

<u>When to Teach</u>: Teach adjectives in your first grammar main lesson block.

<u>Introductory Image from Englishland</u>

*King Verb was quite content to do something new every day in his kingdom, but Queen Noun felt something was missing. She wandered alone among her gardens, looked at the flowers, observed the animals, and went to all of her favorite places, but she could not figure out what was wrong. Although full of energy and purpose, the kingdom seemed drab. The sky had no color. The flowers were all the same washed-out color. Each tree was exactly the same as the one before it. Even the rabbits all looked exactly the same.*

*Although the Queen sensed that something was missing, she didn't really know what it was until she gave birth to a baby girl named Princess Adjective. Unlike everything else in the kingdom, Princess Adjective had been born in full, vibrant color. She had curly red hair, rosy red cheeks, and sparkling blue eyes. (Customize her description to reflect your community.)*

*The King and Queen knew that once they had a child their life would change, but little did they know how much! For their daughter was born with a very special gift. Every time the Princess looked at something, her loving gaze changed it. In her presence, the sky turned a bright, vibrant blue. Every flower in the garden took on a particular hue: ruby red roses, sunshine yellow daffodils, and baby pink hyacinths. Some trees grew taller, some thicker. Some animals had smooth, soft fur like the mink while others were covered with hard scales like the armadillo. Princess Adjective even gave animals different personalities. For example some rabbits were curious and bold while others were shy and timid. Through the gaze of Princess Adjective, everything in the kingdom was transformed and took on its own unique qualities.*

*Thanks to the gifts of her dear daughter, Queen Noun's world was no longer drab but full of every kind of color, shape, and, texture. When the Princess was old enough to walk, she and her mother could be seen strolling through the land hand in hand, making each person, place, or thing special. In fact, the words that helped describe nouns became known as adjectives in honor of the Princess.*

Activities

- Gather a group of items and place them in a basket. Take one out at a time and have the students write the name of the item on the right side of their paper. Then ask them to come up with as many *describing words* or adjectives as they can for the item. After they have done this for each item, go around and have them share some of their adjectives.

- Play 20 questions with adjectives. Choose something in the room and have the students use adjective questions to identify it. Ex. *"Is it* one *color?" "Is it* yellow*?" "Is it* larger *than the door?"* Have another student point out which word was the adjective.

- Give each student a sentence with a line before its noun. For example, Mary likes_____dogs. Have the students come up with as many words as they can to describe the noun. Have them share with the class. Point out that all of the words they come up with are Princess Adjective's words. These adjectives make the dogs unique.

- Using the adjectives the students came up with in one of the previous activities; help them learn about adjective categories. You can provide the categories or help the students generate them. They could include:

    - number (e.g., ten, many, few)

    - demonstrative (e.g., this, that, those)

    - sense: color (e.g., blue, red, pale), taste (e.g., bitter, sweet), sound (e.g., noisy, quiet), touch (e.g., soft, rough), smell (e.g., stinky, soapy), etc.,

    - superlative (e.g., good, better, best, smaller, smallest)

Have your students take turns sorting their adjectives into the correct category.

Bookwork

- Have the students do a teacher-led drawing of Princess Adjective in their main lesson books and write the definition of adjective as a caption: An adjective describes a noun.

- Have the students write one of the poems about adjectives in their main lesson book.

- Give the students a handout and ask them to underline all of the adjectives and draw an arrow from the adjective to the noun to show which noun it describes.

**8c. Introduction to Adverbs**

Objective: Teach the students to identify adverbs in sentences and use them in their writing.

Prerequisites: Students can identify verbs in sentences.

Background Information: Adverbs describe verbs. They can be derived from adjectives. They frequently end with the suffix –ly. The introduction to adverbs has four parts.

**Introduction Part One: Adverbs**

<u>Introductory Image from Englishland</u>

*For a long time, King Verb had delighted in watching the world about him change as Princess Adjective brought her gifts such as color, size, number, and texture to the people, places, and things she encountered. However, after a while he noticed something. Although the bunnies were all different colors and personalities, they always hopped the same way. Likewise, when people walked around the town, they all walked the same, and every time it rained, the rain fell in exactly the same way. Every action that happened in the Kingdom was done the same way.*

*The King mentioned this situation to the Queen. She agreed that this was rather boring but really had no idea what to do about it. So in order to cheer him up, she suggested that King Verb take their three-year-old son, Prince Adverb, for a walk in the woods. "I so enjoy my walks with Princess Adjective, and it is time for dear little Adverb to see more of the world."*

*"You are right," agreed the King. "He has never been outside of the castle walls. I will take him with me tomorrow."*

*The next day, the King fetched young Prince Adverb from the nursery, and the two ventured out beyond the castle. King Verb was accustomed to doing every action exactly the same way every time, but Prince Adverb was so excited about exploring a new place that he made each action unique. Instead of walking on the path just so, he sometimes walked <u>slowly</u> looking at the flowers, then <u>quickly</u> as he followed a lizard through the grasses. He also began to sing. But instead of singing the same way every time as King Verb did, he sang <u>loudly</u> and <u>joyfully</u> when seeing a large oak tree and yet <u>very softly</u> when he came across a baby bird looking out of its nest. Whatever the little Prince did, he did it <u>uniquely</u>, in his own way, according to how he felt.*

*As he watched his young son do things in such a varied and delightful way, the King knew that he had found his answer. He would issue a proclamation that every person and creature in the kingdom should look for ways to do things differently and that the words that would describe how their actions would be done would be known as <u>Adverbs</u> in honor of the little prince who had started it all. To help spread this proclamation, the King decided that he would journey about Englishland with his young son and have Prince Adverb demonstrate that just because a verb or an action was happening does not mean it always has to happen the same way every time.*

*The citizens of Englishland had great fun coming up with new ways to act. They worked <u>hard</u> and they <u>hardly</u> worked; they dressed <u>neatly</u> and <u>sloppily</u>; they walked <u>fast</u> and <u>slow</u>; they drew <u>carefully</u> and <u>haphazardly</u>; they ate <u>quickly</u> and <u>slowly</u>; the wind blew <u>gently</u> or howled <u>loudly</u>. Following Prince Adverb's example, the citizens of Englishland made all of their actions unique.*

<u>Activities</u>

- Give each student a sentence with a line before its verb. For example, *Mary____eats pizza.* Have the students come up with as many words as they can to describe the verb: noisily, quietly, happily, messily, loudly, obnoxiously, etc. Have them share with the class. Point out that all of the words they came up with are Prince Adverb's words. They make the way Mary eats unique.

- The next day, put all of the words the students came up with on the board. Challenge them to find what is the same about many (or all) of the words. (Adverbs usually end in –ly.) Once the class has this revelation, then tell the students the following ending of the story:

*King Verb noticed the same thing you did: adverbs often end with the letters LY (the sound "lee"). So that his son would have this sound whenever he needed it, King Verb decided to hire the letters LY to follow the Prince around. As it turned out, this was a very good idea for Prince Adverb used this duo a lot because he practiced making adverbs every day.*

Bookwork

- Have the students do a teacher-led drawing of Prince Adverb in their main lesson books and write the definition of adverb as a caption: an adverb describes a verb.

- Have the students copy a poem about adverbs in their main lesson book.

- Give the students a handout. Ask them to underline all of the adverbs and draw an arrow from the adverb to the verb it describes. (Note: Limit your adverbs to those that modify verbs rather than adjectives (e.g., Tom runs <u>quickly</u>, not Tom is <u>very</u> fast.)

Curriculum Connections:

1. Here is a possible speech activity and/or main lesson book entry:

"Adverbs" by Janet Langley

Verbs like to move to and fro

But we tell them **how** to go

And **when** they should move about;

That's why ADVERBS have such clout.

Quickly, swiftly, quietly

Loudly, boldly, suddenly,

Without us, verbs are boring

Readers soon would be snoring!

2. After the introduction of adverbs, teach Phonics Rule 27: Suffixes Beginning with Consonants: –ful, –less, –ness, –ly (see chapter 4.3 #27).

## Introduction Part Two: The Relationship between Adjectives and Adverbs

Introductory Image from Englishland

*Princess Adjective invented hundreds and hundreds of words. Words like:* beautiful, graceful, noisy, quiet, sleepy, hearty, *and so many more I cannot name them all. She kept all of these delightful words on shelves in her bedroom. Every morning she would dust her words and choose the ones she would need to describe the things she thought she would see that day when she went out to play.*

*While she was playing with her adjectives, she heard her brother crying. "Mother!" she called. "I think Prince Adverb has hurt himself in the garden."*

*Queen Noun rushed out to see what was making her son cry. Following the sound of his sobbing, she discovered him under a lilac bush. Since he didn't seem injured, she sat on a bench beside the bush and asked him why he was crying. "Does your tummy hurt?"*

*Prince Adverb shook his head. He took a deep breath and blurted out, "Everyone is better than me at making words. You, King Noun, Princess Adjective. It's not fair."*

*Queen Noun smiled. "I am sure it seems that way now," she said. "However, you are still very young. You will get better at it as you get older. You just need some practice."*

*Queen Noun thought for a minute. Then she said, "I know how we can help you practice. I will lend you some nouns that you can change into adverbs." Queen Noun handed him the following nouns:* lilac *and* park. *"Here, Prince Adverb, use my words and add your* ly *to the end to make some adverbs."*

*Prince Adverb smiled and wrote his –ly at the end of the first word:* lilacly. *"That word sounds wrong," he said. Casting* lilacly *aside, he placed his –ly at the end of park:* parkly. *Both the Queen and Prince looked at each other and shook their heads. Queen Noun's words did not make good adverbs. Prince Adverb started to tear up again.*

*Queen Noun thought for a minute. Then she smiled. "It is silly to expect nouns to turn into adverbs. What we need are some verbs!" Then she called out, "King Verb, will you help us?"*

*King Verb ran over, and Queen Noun explained the problem. She said that she and Prince Adverb wanted to borrow some verbs so he could practice making adverbs. King Verb gave them the words* cry *and* run. *Prince Adverb eagerly wrote his –ly on both of them:* cryly *and* runly. *King Verb, Queen Noun, and Prince Adverb couldn't help but laugh at how silly they sounded. But, it didn't take long before the Prince's eyes began to fill with tears once more.*

*Having arrived in the garden just in time to witness this last scene, Princess Adjective walked over. "Here, try these," she said. She handed over the adjectives* loud *and* joyful. *Prince Adverb wiped away his tears and tried one last time. He wrote his –ly on the end of both words:* loudly *and* joyfully.

*"They sound right," acknowledged Queen Noun. "Let's try them out in a sentence."*

*Prince Adverb, reflecting on his earlier behavior, declared, "I cried loudly!" And he smiled. The Queen then observed, "Look, Prince Adverb smiled joyfully!"*

*"It works!" exclaimed Prince Adverb. He hugged his sister. "I can practice making adverbs with adjectives!"*

*"Yes, you can," replied the Princess. "But I must warn you: you will not be able to use all of my adjectives to make adverbs. You will have to experiment with each adjective to see if you can make an adverb out of it." And she left Prince Adverb with a big stack of her words, including these adjectives here." (Open chalkboard to reveal a list of adjectives and go right into Activity A.)*

Activity A: Making Adverbs out of Adjectives. Write a list of adjectives on the board and have the students add –ly to the end to see which words can be made into adverbs and which cannot. For example, *happy, red, more, excited, angry, better, some,* etc.

Curriculum Connection for Spelling: *Sometimes Princess Adjective's words ended in two L's like the word* frill. *When Prince Adverb tried to add his –ly onto the end of these words, it looked pretty silly.* (Write the word *frilly* with three L's on the board.) *Seeing his dilemma, Queen Noun pointed out that two L's were quite enough for any word, and it would be OK for Prince Adverb just to add a Y.*

Activity: Work with the students to come up with other shared words: (e.g., *slow: slowly; bad: badly; quick: quickly; sweet: sweetly; rapid: rapidly*).

Bookwork: Write a list of adjectives on the board before class. Include words that become adverbs by adding –ly and some that do not (e.g., *small, shy, sad, quick, blue, rough, little, etc.*). Have the students divide a paper in half. At the top of the left half write the word adjective, and at the top of the right half write the word adverb. Ask them to write the list of adjectives in Princess Adjective's column. Ask students to determine which of the adjectives could be turned into adverbs by adding Prince Adverb's special –ly ending and then write those words in his column. Leave the other spaces blank.

**Introduction Part Three: Good vs. Well**

<u>Background Information</u>: One of the most misused words in the English language is *good*.

<u>How to Teach</u>: Tell your students that *good* is an adjective describing something that is pleasing, but *well* is an adverb meaning that something is done in a pleasing or acceptable manner. For example,

You had a *good* race. Here *good* describes the race. You ran the race *well*. Here *well* tells how you ran.

<u>Activities</u>

- Create a number of sentences that use either *good* or *well*. Read one of the sentences to the class but leave off the word *good* or *well*. Ask the students to discuss if the word should be an adjective or adverb before deciding which word to put in the blank.
- Give the students a worksheet with a number of sentences that use either *good* or *well* (e.g., *You drew that good/well.*). Have them circle the correct word for the sentence. You can put the rule on the board for them to refer to.

<u>Bookwork</u>

Make a handout. Draw a few sketches of positive scenarios such as a person winning a horse show (or cat show, dog show, 4H competition, state fair, etc.), an actor accepting an award, a student holding up a paper with a smiley face on it, etc. Ask the students to write two related sentences for each picture, one using the word *good* and the other using the word *well*. For example, *Stacy has a good horse. He trots well.*

Note: Grammar usage is constantly evolving. It is acceptable to say *good* or *well* to answer the question *How are you?* When used in this context, *well* refers to one's health, and *good* refers to one's overall state of affairs. Do not correct the students on this point. Either response is now considered acceptable usage.

**Introduction Part Four: Ambiguous Words**

<u>Background Information</u>: There are some words that can be either an adjective or an adverb (e.g., early, fast, hard, high, late, near, straight, and wrong).

<u>How to Teach</u>: Point this fact out as these words appear in your adverb work with the students. Does the word describe a noun or does it tell how something is done? For example,

- It is a <u>fast</u> motorcycle. He rides his bike very <u>fast</u>.
- This is a <u>hard</u> task. He works very <u>hard</u>.
- We saw many <u>high</u> trees. The plane flew <u>high</u> in the sky.

<u>Activities</u>: NA

<u>Bookwork</u>: Provide sentences that use ambiguous words and underline the words. Have the students figure out if the word is an adjective or adverb and then compose another sentence that uses the word as the opposite part of speech. For example, if the sentence said *He drove straight,* the students could write *I drew a straight line.* You will continue to work with ambiguous words in the 4th Grade.

**8d. Verb Tense**

<u>Objective</u>: Teach your students past, present, and future tense.

<u>Prerequisites</u>: Students can identify verbs.

<u>Background Information</u>: This lesson has two parts.

Students need to learn basic verb tense before they can advance to helping verbs because helping verbs often carry tense. The way to bring tense is to show students what they are doing when they add –ed to the ends of words.

<u>When to Teach</u>: Teach in the middle or end of 3rd Grade.

Some Waldorf teachers postpone tense work until the 4th Grade and use the images of the three Norns from Norse Mythology to bring this concept to life. Because 3rd Grade students struggle with using the proper tense in their writing, they need instruction now. You can easily use the Three Norns to review and then expand upon tenses when you introduce the perfect tense in 4th Grade.

**Introduction Part One: Past and Present Tense**

<u>Introductory Image from Englishland</u>

*King Verb is a very active person. He loves to do things. One day, he did all of his normal activities and then decided to begin a diary of all of the things he did each day. After assembling his writing tools, King Verb sat down and began. Since King Verb started every day in the same way, he wrote that thing down on a scrap of paper to help him remember. He wrote down, "Every day I jump in the creek."* (Write this sentence on the board.).

*Then King Verb opened his notebook to the first page and wrote down his first sentence, "This morning I jumped in the creek."* (Write this sentence on the board.).

*"Wait a second," said King Verb. "This can't be right. Something is wrong with the verb." He looked at his list. The verb clearly said, "Jump."* (Underline the word on the board.) *Then he looked at his sentence in his notebook. The verb clearly said "Jumped."* (Underline the word on the board.) *"What are those letters E and D doing at the end of my verb?" he wondered.*

*King Verb was so frustrated he ran to his meditation tree to think. "What is the difference between* jump *and* jumped?*" he asked himself. He thought and thought, but he could not figure it out. Finally, he said to himself, "King Verb, you must actually do the sentences to see what the difference is."*

*King Verb took his scrap of paper and notebook to the creek. He looked at his first sentence. It said, "Every day I jump in the creek." In he went with a giant SPLASH! He stepped out. He looked at the second sentence. It said, "This morning I jumped in the creek." King Verb stood at the edge of the creek. He prepared to jump. He tried to jump. But he just could not jump. Something was wrong. "This sentence means I already jumped!" he exclaimed. "I can't do it. It is already done! Finished! Over!"*

*King Verb went back to his tree and sat down. "The letters E and D when together at the end of a word are very powerful," he said aloud. "They show something has already happened. They show something is in the* <u>past</u>, *not happening now in the* <u>present</u>."

<u>Activity</u>: Ask the class to clap if you read a sentence in the past tense and to stomp if it is in present tense.

<u>Bookwork</u>: Give students a list of verbs and ask them to use each verb to write an original sentence in the past and in the present tense (e.g., the verb *to walk*. Students could write: *I walk to the door. I walked to the playground.*) Note: Make sure that you do not include any irregular verbs (e.g., *draw/drew, eat/ate, run/ran,* etc.).

## Introduction Part Two: Future Tense

<u>Introductory Image from Englishland</u>

*The next day, King Verb was very excited. He said, "When I do actions, I am doing them in the present. When I write about things that I have already done, I write about what I did in the past. I wonder what happens when I think about things that I plan to do?"*

*King Verb thought about what he planned to do that day. He had the following items on his list: Eat cherries, catch a fish, sew a patch. King Verb sat down under his tree and said, "Today I <u>will</u> eat cherries. I <u>will</u> catch a fish. I <u>will</u> sew a patch on my clothes."*

*He jumped up. "I haven't done any of these things yet so they are not in the past. I am not doing them right now so they aren't happening in the present. So what kind of actions or verbs are they?"*

*King Verb ran up to his wife, Queen Noun. "Queen Noun, you must help me name something," he said. "I know there is the present for what you are doing right now. I know there is the past for things you have finished doing. But what should we call it when we want to think about what we are going to do?"*

*Queen Noun smiled. "Why not call it future?" she suggested. Then the Queen paused and said, "I also think you should give each of these types of sentences a special title that shows when the action happens. Do you know the Old French word for time is <u>tens</u>? Why not call something that happened sometime in the past, <u>past tense</u>, something that is happening right now in the present, <u>present tense</u>, and something that will happen sometime in the future, <u>future tense</u>?"*

*"That's it!" exclaimed the King. "From now on every verb will either be past, present, or future tense depending on when in time it happens."*

<u>Activity</u>: Ask the class to help you classify sentences: past, present, future.

<u>Bookwork</u>:

- Ask students to make up a sentence in each tense using a particular verb tense (e.g., the verb *to play* in past, present, and future tenses).

  Past: They played in the park.

  Present: We play in the basement.

  Future: Susan will play with her friend.

- Have the students write the same paragraph in present tense, past tense, and future tense. Generate the contents of the paragraph ahead of time by doing an activity as a class. Then ask the students to tell you just the verbs for the things the class did (e.g., walked, saw, jumped, sang). Write those verbs on the board. Then ask the class to write the paragraph in only the past tense. The next day, ask them to rewrite their paragraph only in the future tense.

- Have students write three different paragraphs:

  1. Compose a paragraph about something that happened to them when they were young.

  2. Compose a paragraph about their present year (i.e., 3rd Grade).

  3. Compose a paragraph about what they want to be when they grow up or some other future topic.

Note: When writing about present tense, it can be about that moment in time or about a current section of time: the current year, age, grade, week, day, etc. These are sometimes easier to write about once the concept of present moment is explored.

## 8e. Being Verbs

Objective: Teach students to identify being verbs in sentences and introduce their basic uses.

Prerequisites: Students can identify verbs in sentences and can identify the verb's tense.

This concept is introduced in three lessons.

### Introduction Part One: Being Verbs

Background Information: Being verbs are verbs that show a state of being or that rename the subject. They are also called *linking verbs*. These examples all show a state of being or of linking:

- I <u>am</u>.
- He <u>is</u> happy.
- They <u>are</u> hungry.
- He <u>is</u> a teacher.

Introductory Image from Englishland

*King Verb was always busy doing things. He ate, washed, dressed, helped in the garden, and played. But one day, something new happened. After a long night of dancing and singing, King Verb took a nap. When he woke up, he realized that napping was different from the things he usually did. This action had no action. It was just sleep. But he still had done it so it must be a verb!*

*This realization sobered King Verb. When he went outside, instead of climbing a tree, he decided to sit under it and meditate. While he was sitting, he realized something: I <u>am</u>. Even when I am not doing anything, I <u>am</u> here!*

*When King Verb got up from his meditation, he was very excited indeed. "I do not have to be in action all of the time. I can also just be!" He shared his realization with Queen Noun after he got home. She said, "I think we should call these new verbs <u>being verbs</u>." And that is their name to this day.*

Activity: Write sentences on the board that contain either a being verb or an action verb. Underline each verb. Have the students discuss whether the verb is being or action and how they can tell. Here you will introduce some of the other being verbs besides *am* (i.e., *is, are, was, were*). The three being verbs *be, being, been* require helping verbs and will be covered in the next section.

Bookwork

- Main lesson book: Compose a poem about being verbs. Have the students copy it into their main lesson book.
- Practice book: Give the students sentences that contain action verbs or being verbs. Have them underline the verb and identify which kind it is.

### Introduction Part Two: Being Verbs Can Help Nouns Rename the Subject

Objective: Teach students that being verbs can help nouns rename the subject (i.e., predicate nouns or predicate nominative).

<u>Prerequisites</u>: Students can recognize being verbs and nouns in sentences.

<u>Background Information</u>: Being verbs help nouns rename the subject of the sentence. Action verbs take direct objects, but being verbs take predicate nominatives.

- Action Verb: I <u>play</u> ball. The word *ball* is the direct object. It receives the action of the verb.
- Being Verb: I <u>am</u> a teacher. The word *teacher* renames the subject.

Direct objects and predicate nominatives are concepts the students will learn in later grades. However, you can build the foundation for these lessons through an imaginative introduction.

<u>Introductory Image from Englishland</u>

*King Verb had learned an important lesson when he meditated under the tree. Verbs could have action or being. He wanted to share this news with his wife, so the next day, King Verb invited Queen Noun to go with him into the woods.*

*Queen Noun did not want to go. "You are so active," she responded, "The last time I went with you, we climbed, jumped, swam, and ran all day long. I was so exhausted, I almost didn't make it home! I prefer to go around and admire the people, places, and things about our castle. You go on without me."*

*However, King Verb begged her to come. He told her that this time it would be different. "We do not have to do anything really, we can just sit and be." Puzzled, the Queen agreed to go with him into the woods.*

*As soon as they got to the King's favorite climbing tree, King Verb sat under the tree, closed his eyes, and said, "I am." The Queen watched him tenderly. When he said, "I am" the second time, she finished his thought by adding the noun "a king." He then repeated, "I am," and Queen Noun finished his sentence with the noun "a husband." The third time King Verb said, "I am," the Queen said, "a father."*

*After a while the King smiled, opened his eyes and said, "Thank you, Queen Noun, for your help. We make a good team."*

<u>Activities</u>

- Play the Renaming Game. Pick a person (real or fictitious) and ask the students to rename him/her with as many nouns as they can. They can work in teams or partners. Then have them share their answers with the class. (Sharon is a student, sister, daughter, friend, runner, artist, singer...)
- Then have each student do this activity for themselves. Have them write five sentences each beginning with "*I am...*"
- Give the students a list of sentences where nouns come after the verbs. Use a good mix of action verbs and being verbs. Have the students identify the verbs and whether they are action verbs or being verbs. For the being verbs, ask them to underline the subject and the noun that rename the subject (i.e., that are predicate nominatives). For example, <u>King Verb</u> is a <u>husband</u>.

**Introduction Part Three: Being Verbs Can Help Adjectives Describe the Subject**

<u>Objectives</u>: Teach students that being verbs can help adjectives describe the subject.

<u>Prerequisites</u>: Students can identify nouns, adjectives, and being verbs.

<u>Background Information</u>: Adjectives do not need to be next to the nouns they describe. Being verbs can help adjectives describe the subject of a sentence (i.e., predicate adjectives). These are concepts the students will learn in later grades. However, you can build the foundation for these lessons through an imaginative introduction.

<u>Introductory Image from Englishland</u>

*King Verb had discovered that verbs can have actions or just show being. He wondered what would happen if he invited Princess Adjective to come mediate with him. Would she have any insights to share?*

*Princess Adjective walked with her father to his favorite tree. When King Verb sat down, he closed his eyes and said, "I am. I am. I am." Princess Adjective watched him and then finished his thoughts with three adjectives:*

*"I am…… .quiet."*

*"I am…….happy."*

*"I am…….handsome."*

*When King Verb finished his meditation, he got up quietly and hugged Princess Adjective. "I never realized I could <u>be</u> so many things," he declared. "I was just too busy doing things to notice. Thank you, Princess Adjective!"*

*And from that day forth, King Verb divided his time between doing and being, and the kingdom flourished.*

<u>Activity</u>: Choose a character from one of the Old Testament stories you have told. Ask the students to find as many words as they can that could go in the blank: David was\_\_\_\_\_ (*a King, wise, a good flute player, etc.*). Then have the class separate them into nouns and adjectives.

<u>Bookwork</u>: Ask students to pick a favorite person or character and make a list of her personal attributes. Start each sentence with the name of the person, then write *is* and an adjective (e.g., *My father is tall. My father is kind.*).

## 8f. Helping Verbs

<u>Objective</u>: Teach students to identify helping verbs in sentences and their basic functions.

<u>Prerequisites</u>: Students can identify action verbs and being verbs.

<u>Background Information</u>: Helping Verbs help both action verbs and being verbs. They show tense. For example,

- I <u>will be</u> good. (*Will* shows future tense and *be* shows being.)
- I <u>am eating</u>. (*Am* shows present tense and *eating* shows action.)
- I <u>was hunting</u>. (*Was* shows past tense and *hunting* shows action.)

<u>Introductory Image from Englishland</u>

*King Verb had discovered that he could do or just be. One day as he was meditating under his favorite tree, he tried to just be in the present moment, but his mind kept wandering to what he would be doing tomorrow. "First, I <u>will</u> eat breakfast, then I <u>will</u> play with Prince Adverb. I will walk in the woods. I will be happy. I will… ," Then it hit him: "Will, will, will. Will is a verb too! But is it an action verb or a being verb?"*

*He wrote each sentence down in the dirt with his finger: (Write on board.)*

- *I will eat breakfast: Eat is an action verb. So what is will?*
- *I will play with Prince Adverb: Play is an action verb. So what is will?*
- *I will be happy: Be is a being verb. So what is will?*

*King Verb was mystified. He had absolutely no idea what the word* will *could be since it could be used with both action and being verbs. He decided to figure it out by playing his favorite game: detective. He put on his detective hat and got out his pencil and notebook.* "What clues should I look for?" *he asked himself.*

*First, King Verb interviewed himself.* "King Verb, what were you doing when you found the word will?" "I was trying to meditate, but I kept thinking about tomorrow," *he answered himself. Then he wrote* <u>tomorrow</u> *down in his notebook.*

*Then the King decided to see what would happen if he got rid of the word* <u>will</u> *(Erase* will*). Now his sentences said:*

- *I eat breakfast.*
- *I play with Prince Adverb.*
- *I be happy.*

"Wait a second," *said King Verb.* "Without the word will, these sentences are about right now, the present, not tomorrow." *He wrote down* <u>present</u>' *in his notebook.*

*Then it hit him:* "I think the word <u>will</u> helps make a sentence be about tomorrow or the future!" *Excited about this new idea, King Verb decided to try out two sentences to see if he was right.*

"Today I <u>dance</u>, but tomorrow I <u>will dance</u>." (Write this sentence on board.) The word <u>will</u> helps the action verb, dance. It lets us know that the action will happen tomorrow.

"I am happy, but next week when I go to the beach, I <u>will be</u> happier." (Write this sentence on board.) The word <u>am</u> tells us how I am feeling in the present moment (I am happy.), but when <u>will</u> comes before <u>be</u>, it **helps** us know that the being verb will happen in the future.

*Delighted that he had solved the mystery, King Verb raced home to tell Queen Noun about this new verb.*

*It was obvious to the Queen that this new type of verb should be called a* <u>helping verb</u> *because it helps action and being verbs tell that something will happen.*

<u>Activity</u>: Put sentences up on the board that contain simple helping verbs such as *will, am, is, are, was, were.* Read the sentences and discuss whether the sentence happened in the past, present, or future.

I am playing a game.

Tina will be a fireman.

I was sleeping.

Jason is eating pizza.

They are going quickly.

They were being quiet.

First ask the class to underline the main action or being verb. Then identify the helping verb. Discuss whether this helping verb shows past, present, or future action. For example,

1. I *am* <u>playing</u> a game.

   playing = action verb; am = helping (present tense)

2. Tina *will* <u>be</u> a fireman.

    be = being verb; will = helping (future tense)

<u>Bookwork</u>: Give students a handout. Ask them to identify the main verb and the helping verb. Then identify if the sentence is in the past, present, or future tense.

### 8g. Possessive Nouns and Apostrophes

<u>Objective</u>: Teach students to use apostrophes to show possession.

<u>Prerequisites</u>: Students can identify nouns.

<u>Background Information</u>: One of the hardest things for students to learn is possessive nouns. They sound identical to plural nouns. Worse, the students have to consider whether the possessive noun is singular or plural to determine where the apostrophe needs to go (e.g., *the girl's horse or the girls' horse*). Working with possessives means students have to consider the meaning layer of the English layer cake (see chapter 1.3 #1), and not just once, but twice. It is a lesson that will take years to master. This introduction is only the beginning.

<u>How to Teach</u>: Schedule extra practice for this concept and be prepared to reteach it as needed in mini-lessons throughout the year.

This lesson has two parts.

### Introduction Part One: Possessive Nouns

<u>Introductory Image from Englishland</u>

*One day in Letter Village, the letter children were playing. They made sentences as they always did. But today, there was a problem: some of the noun words were grabbing other noun words to help make some sentences. This resulted in some very peculiar-looking sentences, such as* <u>Tinabike is red</u>. (Write this sentence on the board.) *or* <u>I played with Joeyfriend</u>. *The letter children did not like being grabbed, and they started complaining loudly.*

*Hearing the noise, the Mayor of Letter Village came over and asked, "What's this? What seems to be the problem?" He then read the sentences and started laughing.*

*"It's not funny," complained the letter children who had formed the words* <u>bike</u> *and* <u>friend</u>. *"Make those words Tina and Joey leave us alone!"*

*"But we need to show that you belong to us!" cried the words Tina and Joey.*

*"It is not good to grab others," said the Mayor. Then he turned to the Tina and Joey words and admonished them, "You must keep your hands to yourself."*

*The Tina and Joey words let go, looking a bit embarrassed.*

*"Now," said the Mayor. "Let's solve the problem. How else can we show ownership other than grabbing?"*

*"Let's make a sign!" said one of the letter children. "We'll put the letter S on the sign and place it at the end of the word to show that it owns the noun that comes after it!"*

*The letter children quickly made a letter S sign. Now the sentences said:* Tinas bike is red. I played with Joeys friend. (Write the sentences on the board.)

*"Hmm," said the Mayor. "I like the idea, but there is a little problem. Who can see it?"* (Ask if anyone can help the Mayor. Entertain all ideas. Then continue the story.)

*The letter S found the problem. "Sir, he said, "When I am at the end of words, I show that a noun is plural. I show that there is more than one. These sentences mean that there is more than one Tina! That there is more than one Joey!"*

*"Very good," said the Mayor. "We need to add something so no one gets confused." And he called on the apostrophe.*

*The apostrophe is a tiny floating comma. It flew up in front of the letter S. The Mayor said, "When you see the apostrophe in front of the S, it means that the word owns the noun that comes after it. There is no need to grab on to something or someone to show it belongs to you."*

Activity: Write several nouns on the board. Have students help you come up with something that each noun might possess (e.g., *dogs ball; trees leaves; chickens eggs, etc.*). Then turn the first one into a sentence (e.g., *The dogs ball is blue.*). Using the Mayor's idea of adding an apostrophe to show ownership, have a student come up and place it correctly. Point out how this floating comma tells us that there is one dog and the ball is his. Do one or two more together and then have students come up with five of their own sentences that show that one noun owns another noun by using an apostrophe.

Bookwork

- Main lesson book: Have the students write the rule in their books (main lesson if taught during main lesson block or phonics rules book if taught during a practice block).
- Make a handout that contains sentences with missing words that are either a plural noun or a singular possessive word. Ask the students to fill in the missing word and decide if it should have an apostrophe S or just an S. Example, *This is_____car (Mike). There are two____in the line (girl).*

**Introduction Part Two: Plural Possessives**

Background Information: The location of the apostrophe determines whether a possessive noun is singular or plural. Use an apostrophe S for singular nouns and use an S apostrophe for plural nouns.

- The girl's horse is tan (i.e., girl's = singular possessive—one girl owns one tan horse).
- The girls' horse is tan (i.e., girls' = plural possessive—two or more girls own one tan horse).

Introductory Image from Englishland

*Now that apostrophe S was here to show possession, the letter children did a better job of keeping their hands to themselves. But soon after the invention of the apostrophe, they ran into another problem. It happened the day that Queen Noun put out a bunch of Prince Adverb's old toys that he had outgrown. There were bikes, scooters, trucks, cars, toy soldiers, teddy bears, board games, and a tea set that he used for his cookies and milk. She meant for all of the boys in the area to play with them. She wrote a note for them that said, "These are the boy's toys." (Write the sentence on the board.) Then she left to attend to other matters in the castle.*

*The first boy there saw the note and claimed all of the toys as his. But when the other boys got there, they claimed that Queen Noun meant for them all to share the toys. Soon the boys were grabbing the toys and arguing so loudly that the Mayor of Letter Village came over.*

*"Boys!" he cried. "What is the meaning of this? Keep your hands to yourself. What is the problem?"*

*"They are trying to take my toys!" cried the first boy.*

*"They aren't his toys—they are for all of the boys!" exclaimed the others.*

*"What does the sign say?" asked the Mayor. He read the sign: These are the boy's toys.*

*"They are mine!" claimed the first boy. "They are for all of the boys!" responded the rest.*

*"Silence!" demanded the Mayor. Once the boys settled down, he scratched his head and said, "I cannot believe that Queen Noun would mean for one boy to have all of the toys. We must ask Queen Noun what she intended."*

*Queen Noun was asked to come settle the dispute. "Prince Adverb's toys are for all of the boys," she said. "I meant for them to be shared."*

*"See, they were to be shared," declared one of the boys.*

*"Wait a second," said the Mayor. "I think perhaps I was the one at fault here. I think this was an honest mistake. It sure looked like only one boy owned all of the toys."* (Ask the class how many of them agree that it looks like only one boy owns the toys.)

*"We have to come up with some way to show if one person owns the toys or if lots do," said the Mayor. "Does anyone have any suggestions?"*

*The children thought and thought about it. One child wanted to put an apostrophe S at the end of boys to show that all of the boys owned the toys: boys's. But everyone agreed that it sounded silly when it was spoken aloud: "boyz-z."*

*Another child raised his hand. "Mr. Mayor," he said, "I have a suggestion. Why don't we just put the apostrophe after the S? When a noun is plural, it ends in S anyway. Just put the apostrophe at the end: boys'." Now the sign said: "These are the boys' toys."*(Fix the sentence on the board.) *Everyone agreed this was a good idea.*

*News of the Queen's generosity quickly spread and though all of the boys were happy, the girls were not. "I don't think it's fair," said one girl. "Why should the boys get all of the toys?"*

*Hearing this, Queen Noun laughed. "I think you have a good point," she said. "If you girls can fix my sign, you can play with the toys too." She held out her black pen. One of the girls took it. She marched over to the sign and wrote "and girls'" so it now read: "These are the boys' and girls' toys."*(Write the sentence on the board.)

*Queen Noun read the new sign out loud, and all of the children cheered and began to play with the toys. Now it was clear that the toys belonged to all of the boys and girls, not just one boy and one girl.*

<u>Activity</u>: Act out this rule. Write a sentence on the board: *The student's pencils are on the desk.* Ask the class whether the sentence is about one or more students. Once determined, have a student come up and put her pencils on the desk. Then change the sentence to: "*The students' pencils are on the desk.*" Have the class determine how to act out the change. Do a number of these reenactments.

<u>Bookwork</u>

- Main lesson book: Help your students come up with a rule for showing possession that they can put into their book (main lesson if you teach in a main lesson block; otherwise phonics rules book). The rule could be very simple (e.g., *If the word is a single noun, use -'s. If the word is a plural noun, use –s'*).

- Practice book: Ask the students to compose their own possessive noun sentences. Give them a list of words to mix and match. Include two lists, one of people and the other of things. Ask the students to make possessive nouns and put them in complete sentences (e.g., People: *Mom, Gary, sister, brothers, teacher, painters, pirates, baker, etc.*; Things: *horses, bedroom, gold, car, toothbrush, etc.* Sentence: *The pirates' gold is buried in a treasure chest.*). Make these lists relevant for your class and area.

Error Handling

Students sometimes think that just because a sentence shows possession, they can use an apostrophe (e.g., *I have cats'*(sic).). Remind them that the possessive noun owns whatever word comes next. In the sentence, the cats do not own anything. There is no word after it. Therefore, it has no apostrophe. (Fortunately, elementary students rarely write sentences such as *That book is Jen's*, so this rule will suffice for the time being.)

Note: The following lessons are brought throughout the year on a need-to-know basis. Work them into your lessons during any main lesson block or practice block, including math blocks.

**8h Capitalization Rules**

Prerequisite: Students can identify proper nouns.

Background Information: Students need to learn basic capitalization rules, but the rules should be presented over many years. Begin the process in 3rd Grade, but be prepared to add to this list each passing school year.

Capitalize the first letter of:

1. Streets, rivers, lakes (e.g., Lotus Lane, Rio Grande River, Lake Michigan)

2. Names of special holidays (e.g., Kwanzaa, Hanukkah, Christmas)

3. Names of months and days of the week (e.g., June and Monday)

4. All titles of respect when they proceed a name (e.g., Dr. Johnson, Mr. Smith, Mrs. Jones, Judge Ginsberg, Governor Brown, etc.)

5. Names of special structures and buildings (e.g., Golden Gate Bridge, Tower of Babel, etc.)

6. Thank you notes: capitalize the first letter of each word in the salutation. (Dear Friend,) and the first word in the closing (e.g., Sincerely yours,)

When to Teach: Present capitalization rules throughout the year on an as-needed basis. For example, you would bring the idea of capitalizing the days of the weeks and months during your study of time in a math block.

Note: Do not try to teach all of these rules at once.

Introductory Image: NA

Activities: NA

Bookwork: NA

Note: If you have not done it already, use the term *lowercase letters* rather than *little letters* or *child letters* because that is what grown-ups call them.

**8i Synonyms and Antonyms**

Background Information: Synonyms are words that mean the same thing; antonyms are words that mean the opposite of each other. Ex. *angry* and *mad* are synonyms; the words *happy* and *sad* are antonyms. A study of synonyms will enrich the students' vocabularies by providing a selection of words from which to choose in conversation. They also provide students with options for replacing what many refer to as *tired* or *worn out* words with more interesting, less common words when writing compositions. A knowledge of antonyms can also enliven compositions by introducing elements of contrast.

<u>When to Teach</u>: Teach synonyms and antonyms at any point during the year on an as-needed basis.

## Introduction for Synonyms

<u>Introductory Image from Englishland</u>

*One day, the Royal family of Englishland decided to play a game. Each person would choose one word and then try to find as many words as they could that meant the same thing. They decided to call these words that had similar meanings synonyms. When they gathered back together at the day's end, they shared their discoveries.*

*Princess Adjective, who was looking for synonyms for the adjective <u>small</u> found 15 of them! They were: little, microscopic, teensy, wee, petite, minute, paltry, miniature, meager, runty, puny, pint-sized, tiny, infinitesimal, and minor.*

*Queen Noun chose the noun <u>road</u>. Besides street, she found: path, lane, boulevard, thoroughfare, avenue, drive, highway, route, trail, parkway, and turnpike. Twelve in all!*

*King Verb chose the verb <u>walked</u>. He found his synonyms by doing the following: He ambled, strolled, lumbered, sauntered, paced, shuffled, stepped, meandered, strutted, trudged, slogged, plodded, tramped, and wandered. Fourteen synonyms, almost as many as Princess Adjective.*

*When young Prince Adverb returned with his synonyms he looked a bit sheepish. "I know I was supposed to be collecting synonyms for the adverb <u>always</u>, and I did find a few: continuously constantly, permanently, forever, repeatedly, eternally, and consistently. But, those were all such big words that by the time I finished writing them down I was exhausted and fell asleep. So I only found seven synonyms."*

*Queen Noun stepped forward and gave her young son a pat on the head and grinned, "That is okay, Prince Adverb. You did well finding such challenging words."*

*And with that, the family concluded their game. However, they have left a challenge for others to try the game for themselves.*

<u>Activities</u>

- Give the students several words that have many synonyms such as *big, small, bad, good, etc.* Have the students work together in teams to see which team can come up with the most synonyms in ten minutes. Which word ended up having the most synonyms?

- Buddy Cards: Make a number of cards, each with a pair of synonyms on it. (Make one set of cards for every two students.) On the first day, show the cards to the students and discuss the synonyms. It will be helpful if one of the words is fairly common and the other not as common. For example, *noise* and *clamor* or *danger* and *hazard*.

The next day, cut each card so that the words are now separated and mix them all up. Distribute the cards one per student and ask the students to find their buddy or synonym. Once the pairs are united, you can put them up on the board and review them. The first time you make a set of these *buddy cards*, it is best to use only two synonyms, but later you could make *buddy cards* that have three synonyms (e.g., *divide, separate, split*).

<u>Bookwork</u>: Put a poem or song lyrics on the board. Then give a synonym for selected words and see if the students can locate its mate in the poem. For example in the line: *"The goblet of gold was dazzling to behold,"* you could say the words *cup, glittering, and see,* and the students would have to give you the words *goblet, dazzling, and behold.*

**Introduction to Antonyms**

Introductory Image from Englishland

*Princess Adjective was playing with her collection of adjectives when she noticed something. Many words had similar meanings, but others had opposite meanings. For example,* good/bad; nice/mean; hungry/full. *(Write words on the board.)*

*"Mother!" she called, "What is the name of these opposite words? If synonyms mean* same, *which word means opposite?"*

*Queen Noun came over and looked at the pairs of opposite words. "They are antonyms," she declared, "Opposites are antonyms."*

Activities

- Get a book for toddlers that features opposite words such as Sandra Boynton's *Opposites*. Read the book and have your students compile lists of antonyms.
- Have a number of words written on the board, each that has an antonym. Have students come up with each word's opposite. See if they can think of even more than one word with the opposite meaning (e.g., antonyms for the word *energetic* include: *lazy, sleepy, sluggish, lethargic, and inactive*). Later point out that those multiple antonyms become synonyms when they are paired together.

Bookwork: Put a poem or song lyrics on the board. Then give an antonym for selected words and see if the students can locate its mate in the poem.

**8j. Contractions**

Background Information: Contractions are two words that are put together into one. For most contractions, a vowel sound is dropped from one word, resulting in a dropped syllable. People use apostrophes to point to the spot where the sound used to be. See table 3.11.2 for a list.

**Table 3.11.2: Contractions**

| am | are | us | is | would/had | have | will/shall | not |
|---|---|---|---|---|---|---|---|
| I'm | you're<br>we're<br>they're<br>who're | let's | he's<br>she's<br>it's<br>what's<br>that's<br>who's | I'd<br>you'd<br>he'd<br>she'd<br>we'd<br>they'd<br>it'd | I've<br>you've<br>we've<br>they've<br>could've<br>would've<br>should've | I'll<br>you'll<br>she'll<br>he'll<br>it'll<br>we'll<br>they'll | can't<br>isn't<br>shouldn't<br>couldn't<br>wouldn't<br>aren't<br>doesn't<br>wasn't<br>weren't<br>hasn't<br>haven't<br>hadn't<br>didn't<br>won't*<br>don't* |

\* Note: Most contractions sound like their original two words (e.g., you are = you're; is not = isn't). However, there are two that sound significantly different: *do not = don't* and *will not = won't*. Teach the words *don't* and *won't* as sight words.

<u>When to Teach</u>: Introduce contractions at any point during the 3rd Grade.

<u>Curriculum Connection</u>: Add contractions to your weekly spelling tests if they are not included in your spelling program.

<u>How to Teach</u>: Teach the contractions by groups. The same letter or letters will be dropped every time. Teach them all in 1–2 weeks.

Note: Do not teach students the grammatical difference between the words *it's* and *its* because they do not yet know pronouns. Instead, tell them that people decided that the –'s only belongs to the contraction form. When you proofread, always read *it's* as *it is*. If you can, you used it right. If you cannot, use the word *its*.

<u>Introductory Image from Englishland</u>

First ask your students, *"Have you ever joined the play of a group of children and in the process been shoved around—even if it wasn't on purpose?"* (Take a few comments.) *"Did it ever get so uncomfortable that you left and went off somewhere else to play?"* Once a few students have shared experiences, tell them that shoving sometimes happens in Letter Village when the letter children get together to spell words.

*The first time this happened in Englishland, the letter children were being very energetic when trying to spell,* <u>I am a boy.</u> (Write the sentence on the board.) *Finally, the letter* <u>A</u> *got so fed up being smushed between* <u>I</u> *and* <u>m</u> *that it left the group and went home.* (Erase the letter A.) *So when the Mayor came by, this is what he saw:* (Point to the board: <u>I m a boy</u>.). *"Hmm," said the Mayor, "What happened to the letter* <u>A</u>*?"*

*When he heard about the roughhousing, he decided to place an apostrophe in the letter* <u>A</u>*'s place to hold the spot for the missing vowel.* (Write the apostrophe in on the board.) *And since that day, whenever the letter children get a little too rambunctious and one or more letters leave, an apostrophe is put in their place to hold it for them so that when they are ready to come back, they will know where to stand. .*

<u>Activities</u>:

- *Contraction Game* (Easy Version): Have students cut a piece of 8½ x 11 paper in long strips with each about 1" wide. On each strip have them write two words that can be contracted. Have them fold the paper in such a way that only the contraction is showing and the missing letter(s) are hidden beneath the fold. Students ask their partners to read their contraction and then write down which two words were combined to make the new word (e.g., the word *don't* is made up of the words *do not*).

- *Contraction Game* (Hard Version): Students use the same strips of paper but ask their partners to figure out how to spell the contracted version of the words.

<u>Bookwork</u>: Give students a passage that contains contractions in all of the sentences. Have students find the contractions and write out the expanded version of the words. Conversely, give students a passage that contains expanded versions and ask the students to write out all of the contractions.

## 8k. Commas

<u>Background Information</u>: Commas indicate a brief pause; they are not as final as periods. They show where the author wants the reader to pause in a longer sentence. For example, *In all of her vast travels, she only found one new plant.* Commas also keep material organized.

Teach the following comma rules:

1. Listing or series commas: Use a comma in a series or list of three or more names or items. Include the Oxford comma, (i.e., the last comma in a series before *and* or *or*).

2. Use a comma to separate the day of the month from the year (e.g., November 8, 2005).

3. Use a comma to separate a city name from its state name (e.g., Tucson, Arizona).

Additional uses of commas will be part of the 4th Grade curriculum and beyond.

When to Teach: Teach commas throughout the year on a need-to-know basis.

Curriculum Connection: Introduce the use of the comma to separate city and state when you teach thank you notes. Have the students write the addresses on their envelopes.

How to Teach: Teach students to pause when they come to a comma in their reading and use the above three comma rules in their writing. Do not try to teach all of the comma rules at once. This subject does not really need a trip to Letter Village to introduce it. Rather you could introduce commas by looking at how you have written the date on the board and ask the students why they think adults put a comma between the date and year (i.e., as an additional way to separate the numbers of the date from the numbers in the year).

Activities:

- Have the students add in the comma to the date each morning for the remainder of the current block.

- Dictate some dates and have the students write them down with proper comma usage.

- Put together two bags of items. For example you could have a rose soap, vanilla coffee, and an orange pencil in one bag and a rose, soap, vanilla (flavoring), coffee, orange, and pencil in the other. Hand out a worksheet with two sentences that say: *In sack #1 we found rose soap vanilla coffee orange pencil. In sack #2 we found rose soap vanilla coffee orange pencil.* Open sack #1 and take out each object. Ask your students to add commas to the first sentence to make the sentence true. Then do the same with sack #2. Write the same sentences on the board and have the students come up and add in the appropriate commas.

- Have students take their practice book and a pencil outside and write sentences about what they see. Each sentence should include 3–5 things and use the listing comma (e.g., *In the garden I see a wooden gnome, a butterfly, and lots of flowers.*). Once they return to the classroom, they can share some of their sentences with the class.

## 81. Quotation Marks

When to Teach: Teach quotation marks at any point in 3rd Grade.

How to Teach: Present a scenario with no quotation marks and no reference(s) to the speaker(s).

One possible approach would be to write a passage on the board from a book that uses quotations but when you read it, delete any reference to who said what. For example, this extrapolated passage between Pig, Turtle, Iguana and Rooster from *Cook-a-doodle-doo* by Stevens and Crummel: *"No, no, no. Don't cut the butter with scissors. Use these two table knives, like this. Looks mighty dry in there, perhaps I should taste it. Not yet. Now the recipe says to beat one egg. I can do that!"*

Next, give students a handout with the full quotations:

*"No, no, no,"* said Rooster. *"Don't cut the butter with scissors. Use these two table knives, like this."*

*"Looks mighty dry in there,"* said Pig. *"Perhaps I should taste it."*

*"Not yet, Pig,"* said Turtle. *"Now the recipe says to beat one egg."*

*"I can do that!"* cried Iguana (Stevens 1999, 25–26).

This presentation is a graphic way to demonstrate that quotations provide a way for the author to tell the reader that a conversation is happening and to indicate who is saying what.

A second possible approach would be to have the Mayor of Letter Village figure out how to show who said what so conversational sentences do not get all mixed up. (You could have some fun showing what it could look like without the words *she said.... he replied.)*

After this introduction, hold a conversation with the students to determine which elements would be needed for a quotation to be helpful to the reader. Be sure to draw out the following points and interject the following images:

1.  A way to know which words are someone's direct speech: Quotation marks indicate the beginning and ending of a quotation. They are like little arms that hold the speaker's words together. Show how they are written as if to embrace the sentence. *"I can do that!"* cried Iguana.

2.  A way to know who is doing the speaking: Authors identify the person doing the talking by beginning or ending the quotation with the name of the speaker. It does not matter whether the identification of the speaker is at the beginning or the end (e.g., *"No, no, no,"* said Rooster. Rooster said, *"No, no, no."*).

3.  A way to know what kind of emotion is behind the quotation: The reporting verb along with the quotation's ending punctuation are two clues to how the author wants a person to read the quotation. For example consider these two sentences: *"I can do that!"* <u>cried</u> Iguana. Or *"I can do that,"* <u>said</u> Iguana. It is easy to hear the emotion in the first example.

Next, teach your students the two basic formats for simple quotations:

1.  Quotation before speaker:

    -   Statement quotations: 1) Place quotation marks around the quotation; 2) Turn the quotation's period into a comma; 3) Add the reporting verb and identify the speaker; 4) Put a period at the end (e.g., *"I will,"* offered Rooster.).

    -   Question or exclamatory quotations: 1) Place quotation marks around the quotation and keep the end punctuation mark; 2) Add the reporting verb and identify the speaker; 3) Put a period at the end (e.g., *"I will!"* crowed Rooster.).

2.  Speaker before quotation: 1) Identify the speaker and add the reporting verb; 2) Add a comma; 3) Put quotation marks around the quotation; 4) Keep the capitalization and end punctuation the same as if writing a simple sentence (e.g., Rooster crowed, *"Cock-a-doodle-do!"*).

Note: Wait until a later grade to introduce broken quotations such as *"I wonder,"* inquired Dan, *"whether I can ask a favor?"*

Activities: Make up sentences such as *Mom said, "Do your homework."* Put each word of the sentence and each punctuation mark on a separate card. Put all of these cards into an envelope and write the number of cards inside. For example, the example above would have nine cards. Divide the students into small teams based on the number on the envelope (i.e., there is one card for each member of the team). Give each team an envelope, ask each student to take one card, and have the students assemble themselves into the right order so that the sentence with a quotation makes sense and is punctuated correctly.

Bookwork: Give students dictation sentences where they have to add in the quotation marks. For example, *Mom announced, "I will pick you up after school today."*

Note: As much as possible, avoid using the word *said* when teaching quotations. Encourage students from the very beginning to use more interesting, informative verbs.

## 9.  Practice

Practice is critical. It forms part of your initial introduction in the Introduction &/or Review segment of main lesson (i.e., Activities A and B). It will be part of your ongoing practice in the Skills Practice segment of main lesson and practice classes (see chapter 2.3 #4).

**Activities A and B:** See suggestions in subsections for Grades 1–3. Use Drill Down when appropriate (see chapter 2.4 #2).

**Skills Practice:** The following are activities to include in Skills Practice after the initial introduction:

- Worksheets where students must identify one or more parts of speech.
- Note: For 3rd Grade and beyond there is a great resource for providing your class with a short, but effective daily grammar practice: *Caught 'ya! Grammar with a Giggle* by Jane Bell Kiester. This book includes a sentence filled with errors for each day of the schoolyear. (Each sentence also includes a featured vocabulary word.) If you have your students write their corrected version in a composition book, they will realize that each sentence is the next installment in a humorous story. Kiester gives the teacher many opportunities to personalize the story, which makes it even more enjoyable. (Read the instructional information at the beginning of the book first.)

**Fun and Games:** In addition, you could do some *Mad Libs* with your class. *Mad Libs* are paragraphs where key words have been left out. Students have to contribute words for various parts of speech without knowing the context. You read the completed paragraph back to them, filling in the missing key words. The paragraph tends to be quite funny. Write your own or buy a book.

## 10.  Assessment

Assessment is a critical part of teaching. It is important to verify that students have mastered the skills they have been taught. See chapter 6.1 for background on assessment.

**Benchmarks** represent <u>minimum</u> levels of student achievement by the end of each grade for students to be on track to handle grade-level work in 4th Grade (see chapter 6.1 #9). Table 3.11.3 contains the benchmarks for grammar.

Note: The following benchmarks may not be exhaustive. Prerequisite skills for grammar may be covered under other related language arts skills. For a full list of benchmarks, see table 6.1.4.

**Table 3.11.3: Benchmarks for Grammar**

| | 1st Grade | 2nd Grade | 3rd Grade |
|---|---|---|---|
| **Grammar: Parts of Speech** | NA | Students can identify the following parts of speech in sentences:<br>• nouns<br>• verbs | Students can identify the following parts of speech in sentences:<br>• nouns<br>• verbs<br>• adjectives<br>• adverbs<br>In addition, they can identify:<br>• possessive nouns<br>• verb tense<br>• being verbs<br>• helping verbs |
| **Grammar: Mechanics** | When writing, students capitalize the first word in a sentence, names, and use periods at the end of sentences. | When writing, students use end punctuation correctly (period, exclamation point, and question mark). | When writing, students use the following correctly:<br>• commas in a list and with quotation marks<br>• apostrophes in possessive nouns and contractions<br>• capitalization of proper nouns<br>• quotation marks |

There are three types of assessments. Recommendations for each type of assessment can be found in Sections 6.3, 6.4, and 6.5. You can use the following ideas as a starting point to set up an assessment program.

**Informal Assessments:** You can assess informally by using any written practice exercise where students have to identify parts of speech.

**Teacher-Made Assessment:**

- Once a week, in 2nd and 3rd Grade, give a teacher-generated quiz that covers the grammar you taught that past week. Model it off of the written practice activities you did over the week. Give it on Friday and use the results to tailor your lessons in the upcoming week. For example, if the class still needs more practice identifying verbs, continue to practice that skill the following week.

- At the end of a block, give an assessment activity or quiz that covers all of the grammar taught in the block. Use the results to determine if additional practice will be needed in the future, and if so, how much.

**Assessments Created by Educational Testing Groups**: NA (unless your school has one) See chapters 6.4 and 6.5 for more information about assessing in 2nd and 3rd Grade.

## 11. How to Help Struggling Students

**Assess:** When you see a student is struggling with grammar, do assessments (both formal and informal) to narrow down the area(s) of concern. Document your findings and place in student's file. Students who struggle with grammar may have difficulties with concept imagery and/or comprehension (see chapter 3.7, chapter 3.8, and section 6).

**Additional Instruction/Practice:** Next, use the results of your assessments to provide this student with extra instruction and practice in any weak areas. You can differentiate instruction both in class and in reading groups. For example, you can modify the instructions for each reading group or give individual assignments to provide extra practice in a weak area. Decide which approach is best based on how many other students have similar struggles. Document what you try and the results.

If you have a group of students who are struggling and they are in 3rd Grade, consider providing instruction in basic sentence diagraming. Use an image to introduce the concept such as building a sentence house.

Here is an example for the following sentence: *The tall man ate quickly.*

Note: Only put the parts of speech that you have taught into the sentence diagram. In this case do not include the article *the*.

**Teacher:** "*We can make a house for a sentence to live in. The base floor looks like this.*"

_____(Draw a base line.)

"*And we put in rooms for the subject and the verb.*"

_____|_____ (Put in a perpendicular line through the horizontal line to create two rooms.)

"*The subject (that the sentence is about) lives in the first room* (on left). *The verb lives in the second room* (on right). *Let's put the subject in its room and the verb in its room.*"

"*If we did our job right, we have a cave man sentence:* man ate."

_____man_____|_____ate_____

"*To show where the adjectives and adverbs live, just put them on the staircases that lead down into the basement. Adjectives live below the nouns; adverbs below the verbs.*"

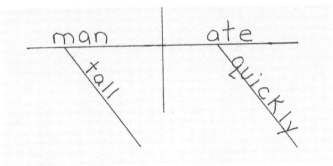

**Figure 3.11.1: Diagram House**

Students in 4th Grade should begin to learn simple sentence diagramming, but you can introduce the basics in 3rd Grade to help students if needed (see fig. 3.11.1).

**Remedial Solutions:** Do not pursue a remedial solution if the student's only weakness is grammar. Grammar will be reviewed extensively in subsequent grades. Furthermore, maturity does help with the acquisition of grammar. If there is no other concern, the student will likely have an easier time learning grammar as she gets older. However, confirm that the student does not have any language comprehension issues first.

**Accommodations and Modifications:** Do not provide accommodations or modifications for grammar.

## Conclusion

As you can see from the examples given in this chapter, grammar does not have to be a boring, lifeless drill of rule after rule. It can be brought through imaginations and characters that delight and inform the students. However, grammar does need to be practiced. Students must master every aspect of English, including grammar. Have fun teaching grammar with the umbrella story you choose or create!

# 3.12 VOCABULARY

*While teaching 3rd Grade a teacher gave a writing assignment that focused on the story of David and Goliath. She encouraged her students to find another adjective other than <u>giant</u> to describe Goliath. Her plan was to combine these words into a list to show them how rich our language could be. After the students were finished with their rough draft, she asked them each to read their description of Goliath. She was delighted and impressed when she heard the following synonyms for giant: monstrous, huge, hulking, immense, gigantic, massive, gargantuan, mighty, enormous, and even the hybrid ginormous. After she wrote each of these descriptive words on the board, the students asked if they couldn't use all of them in their composition to describe Goliath. (Of course, the answer was, "Yes.") From then on every time they were assigned a composition, the students wanted to know what words were the <u>giant</u> words for that assignment. They delighted in finding as many synonyms as they could and in sharing them with the class.*

This chapter covers the following topics:

1. Why Vocabulary Matters
2. Background Information: Vocabulary vs. Spelling
3. Preparation
4. Scheduling
5. Initial Introduction
6. How to Teach Vocabulary in 1st Grade
7. How to Teach Vocabulary in 2nd Grade
8. How to Teach Vocabulary in 3rd Grade
9. Practice
10. Assessment
11. How to Help Struggling Students

## 1. Why Vocabulary Matters

English has approximately 500,000 words, about three to five times the vocabulary of other common languages, however, most of these words are not used in everyday speech. While every native speaker becomes familiar with the oral vocabulary of English through conversation, television, and common culture, only those who are well read are familiar with English's rich written vocabulary. Vocabulary is a badge that identifies those who are well versed in language and those who are not.

One of the ways society determines who goes on to college and graduate school is through tests that include vocabulary. Some examples include the ACT, SAT, and GRE. This decision is not random. For students who are well read, the words are usually well known or at least familiar. For those who are not, the words might as well be in a foreign language. Without extensive study and reading, students do not score well. The tests serve as literacy gatekeepers.

Once students graduate and enter the professions, having a good vocabulary continues to matter. Those who use language well are perceived to be more intelligent and often find more doors for advancement open to them.

Even if some students choose life paths other than those that require a college degree, command of the English language will serve them well. Having the vocabulary to succinctly and clearly express one's thoughts and ideas has advantages in all realms of life.

For these reasons, it is imperative that students develop a good expressive and receptive vocabulary (i.e., they understand many vocabulary words and are able to use them correctly in their speech). However, there are no shortcuts to developing a good vocabulary.

Good vocabulary comes from extensive and engaged language exposure. It starts with parent/child interactions, grows with teacher/student interactions, and continues with student/book interactions. Teachers help students make the transition from spoken to written vocabulary. They build upon what students have received from their families by adding their personal vocabulary to the vocabulary found in the poems, songs, and stories they share with their students. Finally, they must make sure that their students go on to become extensive readers. These steps will help students develop stellar vocabularies.

Methods used to teach vocabulary change as children grow. The individual students who enter 1st Grade will have varying foundational skills in English vocabulary based on their own biographies.

In the early years, vocabulary growth comes through spoken language. All young children get basic language exposure when caregivers spend time engaging with them. However, some children get something extra: caregivers who read to them. Books provide a warm and nurturing language experience that is top notch in sentence structure, grammar, and vocabulary. Books transcend the typical daily language experience. Children who have books read to them have better language skills than those who have not had this exposure.

Once children start preschool or kindergarten, they continue to learn new vocabulary primarily through imitation. Schools such as Waldorf expose students to a rich vocabulary early on through songs, verses, and fairy tales. (Programs where teachers frequently read to students or tell them lots of stories provide a similar benefit.) Good early childhood education is a great equalizer. It provides the experience of stories and good language that many students lack prior to coming to school.

You will build upon your students' language experience when they start school. Your tools include stories, speech work, and reading. In Grades 1–3, the emphasis is on spoken vocabulary. In Grades 4–8, the emphasis will switch to written vocabulary.

## 2.  Background Information: Spelling vs. Vocabulary

There is one point to emphasize: vocabulary and spelling are separate subjects.

In too many classrooms, the vocabulary list has become the spelling list or vice versa. This approach shortchanges both spelling and vocabulary. Spelling is developed systematically through the phases. A good spelling curriculum reviews the phonics rules students have mastered for decoding. It includes important, grade-level words that students need to learn to spell (see chapter 3.9 #2). Vocabulary, however, comes directly out of the curriculum. The stories you tell and the speech work you bring are the source of your vocabulary instruction.

## 3.  Preparation

The preparation that you do for vocabulary in Grades 1–3 occurs when you are selecting stories, poems, and songs for your curriculum. As you are selecting stories for your curriculum, choose them with an eye towards enriching your students' vocabulary (see chapter 5.5). Make note of vocabulary words you plan to teach.

## 4.  Scheduling

Teach new vocabulary words as they come up. Formal vocabulary instruction begins in 4th Grade.

## 5.  Initial Introduction

Teach vocabulary as it comes up. The introduction will vary based on the grade (see chapter 3.12 #6, #7, and #8).

## 6.  How to Teach Vocabulary in 1st Grade

In 1st Grade teach students new vocabulary through stories, poems and songs as they come up.

**Objective:** Teach the students to figure out new vocabulary words through modeling using the context.

**When to Teach:** Teach when new vocabulary words come up in the Opening segment or the Speech/Song segment.

**How to Teach:**

Some of the time you will just use the word in context and allow students to figure out its meaning. At other times you can follow the vocabulary word with an appositive to help the students understand its meaning. For example, *he was ascending, or going up, the stairs.* Use a mixture of both approaches.

When you are choosing poems for speech and memory reading, look for poems that have new vocabulary words in addition to sight words. For example the following tongue twister has the sight words: *does, from, his.* It also has three new vocabulary words: *dustman, dangling,* and *dislodges.*

> *Dustman daily does his duty.*
> *From his dusty, dangling dust pans*
> *He dislodges dirty dust.*

To teach vocabulary from this tongue twister, begin by teaching your students the tongue twister in its entirety. After reciting the tongue twister a few times, you can begin to discuss what the poem is about as in this sample lesson:

*"This poem is about a dustman. Does anyone know what a dustman is?"* (Entertain a brief discussion. The answer here should not be difficult to reach.)

*"In our poem, it says that he uses dusty, dangling dust pans. Does anyone know what the word dangling means?"* (Again, briefly discuss the meaning of the word. If the students do not get the definition, pull out a ring of keys and let the keys dangle. Tell the students that when adults want to describe something that is loosely hanging down, we call it dangling.)

*"So if the dustman has some dangling dustpans, what could that look like? Where could they be dangling?"* (Let them discuss briefly.)

*"Another unusual word in our poem is dislodges. If you have a bunch of dust in your dustpan, what are you supposed to do with it?"* (Dump it in the trashcan). *"So you will want to get rid of it. That is what the dustman does in this poem, but instead of saying he dumps it, this poem uses the word dislodges, which means to loosen and get rid of. He wants to make sure that none of the dust takes up lodging in his dustpans!"*

**Curriculum Connection: Memory Reading:** In the Emergent Phase and at the very beginning of the Phonemic Awareness Phase, use only poems and songs for memory reading, not tongue twisters. Students in these phases need to learn to use the first letter of a word to keep their place while memory reading, something that is impossible to do when all of the words start with the same letter. (See chapter 3.10 #7 for more about using speech to cultivate phonemic awareness.) However, in the middle of the Phonemic Awareness Phase, start to include tongue twisters for memory reading. It will force students to focus on the end of the word as well as the beginning, and would help them move through the phase. (See chapter 3.15 #6 for more information about memory reading.)

Use economy of teaching to include vocabulary work as part of reading instruction by choosing poems, sentences, and song lyrics with a rich vocabulary.

## 7.    How to Teach Vocabulary in 2nd Grade

The vocabulary curriculum expands in 2nd Grade.

**Objective:**

1. Continue to teach new vocabulary words in speech.
2. Teach the students to figure out new vocabulary words through modeling using the context for reading.
3. Teach students to use vocabulary words in composition.

**When to Teach:** Teach when new vocabulary words come up in reading passages or during composition writing.

**How to Teach**

In 2nd Grade, there are several more ways to teach vocabulary. They include:

- reading speech and song lyrics from the board
- composition writing for main lesson books (in the spring)
- teaching synonyms: the solution to worn-out words

### Reading Speech and Song Lyrics from the Board

In most of 2nd Grade the students will no longer be memory reading; however, they will be reading speech and song lyrics from the board before they learn them (see chapter 3.15 #8). You can continue to bring new vocabulary from speech exercises by putting new poems, lyrics, or short passages on the board. After the class has read the poem, teach how to use the context of the poem to determine the definition of unknown words. For example, put this excerpt from a new poem written by Janet Langley on the board:

> *He stands so straight and bold*
>
> *As sunlight around him flows;*
>
> *His feathers are burnished gold;*
>
> *And then he elegantly crows.*

Ask a student to read the entry aloud. Then ask the class what character they think this passage is about. (Rooster). What word points to this conclusion? (crows) Then ask the students to identify those words unfamiliar to them (i.e burnished and elegantly). Underline each word. Demonstrate how to use context to try to figure out a word's meaning. Ask students to guess the meaning and explain their reasoning. One approach is to write all of the guesses on the board, then put a star by the correct definition or write it up if no guesses were correct and explain why it is correct. Another way to help them find the definition is to present them with some questions. For example, ask what word *burnished* is describing (gold). Then have a brief discussion about the color of gold (Is it dull, shiny?). Given that roosters crow in the morning sunlight do they think that the rooster's feathers would be a dull or shiny gold color? (Yes, the sun would cause the golden color of the feathers to shine so burnished must mean polished or shiny.) Then ask the students to try to figure out the meaning of the word *elegantly*.

Note: You can use this same approach for a song you plan to teach in music class.

Curriculum Connection: You can teach reading from speech and song lyrics on the board (see chapter 3.15 #8).

### Composition Writing for Main Lesson Books

During the second half of 2nd Grade, students begin writing short compositions for their main lesson books. When asking the students to write their own main lesson book compositions discuss possible vocabulary words ahead of time and put them on the board. Ask students to use these words in their writing.

### Teaching Synonyms: The Solution to Worn-Out Words

While students will study synonyms formally in 3rd Grade (see chapter 3.11 #8i), begin teaching students to use synonyms as soon as you start teaching them how to write compositions. The goal is to help the students avoid using worn-out words such as *walked, went, said,* etc. in their writing from the beginning.

One teacher kept a wall-hanging of pockets that had a worn-out word pinned to each of the pockets. Inside of each pocket was a list of synonyms for that specific word. These alternatives were words that the students had come up with as a class. Whenever a student was writing and needed an alternative to the worn-out word she was about to use, she could come to the word pocket, look at the list, and select another word to use. Each time a student found an alternative for a worn-out word in a book that she was reading, she showed it to her teacher. At the appropriate time, the student would share the new word with the class and then add it to the appropriate 'pocket list.'

## 8. How to Teach Vocabulary in 3rd Grade

The vocabulary curriculum further expands in 3rd Grade.

**Objectives:**

1. Continue to teach the objectives from 1st and 2nd Grade.
2. Teach the students synonyms as part of grammar (see chapter 3.11 #8i).
3. Teach the students common idioms.

**When to Teach:** There is a lot of flexibility in when to teach idioms. Teach them throughout 3rd Grade. You will determine the best time in your curriculum to teach idioms. They are usually taught in the Introduction &/or Review segment on days when you need a filler lesson. They can also be taught in math blocks.

**How to Teach Idioms**

Introduce **idioms** to your 3rd graders. These cultural sayings can be a source of confusion to children, yet students often delight in the pictures the words create. For example, "*Becky said that she would be glad to be the guinea pig.*"

Begin by showing your students how idioms are really a type of synonym, albeit often very funny ones. In the sentence above, the term *guinea pig* serves as a synonym for *test subject* or *the first one*. Idioms use picture descriptions to communicate their meaning rather than a word definition. Hence, rather than say, "*Becky would be glad to be the first to try the mystery drink,*" people often say, "*Becky has offered to be our guinea pig for trying out the mystery drink.*"

You could feature an idiom of the week. (A good source is *The Cambridge Dictionary of American Idioms* by Heacock.) Write the idiom on the board and then use it in several sentences, and see if the students can guess what it means.

With just a little effort you can find idioms that have a connection to what you are studying. For example when studying money, you could introduce, *He is worth his weight in gold* and share its origin with the class: "*This saying has been used for a very long time. The meaning behind the phrase is that the person who is 'worth his weight in gold' is very valuable to the endeavor or task at hand*" (Hendrickson 2000, 727).

Other possible idioms are: It's as easy as pie; hot potato; best thing since sliced bread; don't cry over spilt milk; don't count your chickens before they've hatched; you hit the nail on the head; hit the hay; that's the last straw; once in a blue moon; at the eleventh hour; a piece of cake; pull the wool over his eyes; sit on the fence; take it with a grain of salt; straight from the horse's mouth, whole nine yards; nest egg; an arm and a leg; a New York Minute; a penny for your thoughts.

## 9. Practice

It is not necessary to schedule in practice around vocabulary in Grades 1–3. However, do make a point to use the new vocabulary words in your review questions for stories (see chapter 3.8 #2). Insist that the students use the new vocabulary word when they provide the answer. For example, if you asked, "*Why did James* <u>ascend</u> *the stairs of the monastery?*" the student would answer, "*James ascended the stairs so he could ring the monastery's bell.*"

## 10. Assessment

We do not recommend that you assess vocabulary *per se* in Grades 1–3.

## 11. How to Help Struggling Students

**Assess:** While you will not assess vocabulary directly, you may see a student is struggling with finding the right words to use while speaking. This problem may be limited to new vocabulary word or words in general. In either case, do informal assessments to narrow down the area(s) of concern and to document your findings. This student may have trouble with concept imagery and/or comprehension. Address any weaknesses that come up (see section 6, chapter 3.7, and chapter 3.8).

**Addition Instruction/Practice:** Next, use the results of your assessments to provide this student with extra instruction and practice in any weak areas. You can differentiate instruction both in class and in reading groups. For example, you can modify the instructions for each reading group, or give individual assignments to provide extra practice in a weak area. Decide which approach is best based on how many other students have similar struggles. Document what you try and the results.

**Remedial:** Do not pursue a remedial solution for a weakness in vocabulary *per se*. However, be sure to include a request that the student have her hearing evaluated if you see other symptoms of difficulty with her hearing (see chapter 6.6 #2).

**Accommodations and Modifications:** In Grades 1–3 there is no appropriate accommodation or modification for weak vocabulary.

## Conclusion

A good vocabulary curriculum includes all aspects of vocabulary development. Fortunately, it is relatively easy to build vocabulary instruction into the rest of your language arts curriculum. Draw vocabulary out of your speech work, stories, and reading material. You can also emphasize vocabulary in your Home Surroundings Blocks (see chapter 5.5 #5 –#8). With just a bit of pre-planning, it is possible to help your students develop a rich vocabulary.

# 3.13  KID WRITING: THE KEY TO EARLY LITERACY

*Would you believe that the most effective way to teach reading is through writing?*

In this case, the word *writing* does not refer to the traditional Waldorf practice of students copying the teacher's sentences, words, or letters from the board; instead, it refers to a lesser-known Waldorf practice called *Talking on Paper,* where the students themselves compose their own simple missives and write down their best guesses at spelling by themselves. This process is found in both Waldorf and mainstream education and goes by many names: talking on paper, kid writing, phonics-based spelling, invented spelling, temporary spelling, and developmental spelling.

*The Roadmap to Literacy* uses the term *kid writing* rather than *talking on paper* to emphasize that the students are doing all of the writing themselves, from composing the words to inventing the spelling to writing the letters down on paper. Using the term *kid writing* helps remind both teachers and students that the students are doing the writing themselves—using whatever they know of phonological and phonemic awareness, phonics skills, and sight words and making tons of glorious mistakes in the process.

This chapter covers the following topics:

1.   Why Kid Writing Matters
2.   Preparation
3.   Scheduling
4.   Initial Introduction of Kid Writing
5.   The Kid Writing Process
6.   How to Differentiate Instruction
7.   Classroom Management
8.   Practice
9.   Assessment
10.  How to Help Struggling Students

## 1.   Why Kid Writing Matters

Kid writing is important for many reasons.

First, it helps beginning students master key literacy skills. It is much easier for students to learn the alphabet (the letter names, sounds, and how to write them) when they are using them to compose their own messages. Kid writing gives students practice separating the sound stream down into individual words (see chapter 1.4 #2). It also promotes the development of phonological and phonemic awareness.

Kid writing is in alignment with child development. It works from the whole to the parts (see chapter 2.1 #8). It begins with comprehension and helps students lay the foundation for decoding skills by having them encode (see chapter 3.4 #1). It is a child-friendly way for students to make the specific neural connections between various regions of the brain in order to learn to read (see chapter 1.2 #2).

In addition, kid writing is in alignment with Waldorf practices. In *Discussions with Teachers*, Steiner states: "If we proceed rationally we will get far enough in the first grade so that the children will be able to write simple things that we say to them or that they compose themselves. If we stick to simple things, the children will also be able to read them" (Trostli 2004, 10).

In other words, Steiner is recommending that students in 1st Grade do kid writing. This idea already exists in germ form in some Waldorf classrooms in the guise of *Talking on Paper*. Else Gottgens, an international Waldorf mentor teacher, describes a Waldorf version of kid writing in her book *Waldorf Education in Practice*. She calls it *Talking on Paper* and dedicates an entire chapter to the practice. She states:

> We grant the children the joy of unrestrainedly tossing down their thoughts on paper by means of the newly learned letters. And–if we then perform the miracle of reading that back to them–we have really made it. It does ask for some effort on our part to decode their masterpieces…., but we shall find that we learn quite quickly. If–in spite of our efforts–we still cannot make head or tail of it, we need not tell them so, but we can always ask: "Please, would you read it to me?" …Wrong Spelling does not come into it. It is a right spelling, the children's spelling, and it should be called by that name. (Gottgens 2011, 27)

Gottgens suggests starting Talking on Paper no later than April of 1st Grade after all of the letters have been introduced; however, due to its important role in developing the neural pathways for reading, *The Roadmap to Literacy* recommends that it be introduced as soon as the students realize that reading and writing are a code (i.e., as soon as they realize that letters represent sounds and enter the Phonemic Awareness Phase). Kid writing helps students:

- learn their letters and sounds more quickly
- develop phonemic and phonological awareness
- lay the neural foundation for decoding skills

Beginning earlier has the added benefit of keeping students who can read engaged and learning while their classmates master the alphabet and basic sight words. It can also shore up their phonemic awareness skills if they are contextual readers or accelerated readers who cannot encode (see chapter 6.2 #4).

If you start kid writing once most of your students enter the Phonemic Awareness Phase and follow through with the recommendations in this book (including practice), more than 85% of the class should be writing and reading their compositions by the end of 1st Grade as well as reading simple decodable-texts. By the middle of 2nd Grade, the class should have basic spelling skills and be ready to learn how to write simple compositions.

## 2.  Preparation

When preparing your kid writing curriculum, there are some things you can do over the summer and other considerations that will need to be done during the school year.

**Summer Preparation**

Your summer preparation will include making decisions about several items:

- Format for Kid Writing Books
- Sight Word List and Consumable Spelling Dictionary
- Kid Writing Topics

Format for Kid Writing Books

Create pages for kid writing.

The top page would consist of a frame (about half the page) in which the student could draw a picture, an area for student writing (with dotted midlines), and an area for adult underwriting. Figure 3.13.1 is an example of a blank kid writing page suitable for the beginning Phonemic Awareness Phase, when students will only write a title for their picture. Create an additional page that just has lines (with midlines) and no picture frame for those students who need more space to write. In 2nd Grade, revise your form so the lines are smaller. (There is a full page example that you can download on www.waldorfinspirations.com.)

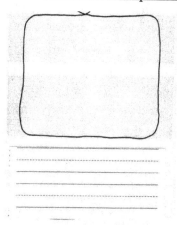

**Figure 3.13.1: Kid Writing Template for Beginners**

These pages can then be stored in many ways. If your school has a binding machine, you could bind a number of these pages into books—either before or after the students write. If you do not have access to a binding machine, get a three-ring binder for each student's kid writing assignments. (Make sure the students put a date on each assignment so you can monitor progress.) All of these formats keep the students' writing organized and in chronological order, perfect for use in Parent Teacher Conferences and for informal assessments when you want to document student progress.

Note: Do not put kid writing into main lesson books. Kid writing is for practicing phonological and phonemic awareness, encoding, and sight words. In general, it is better for the class to do a new kid writing assignment and get more practice than it is to copy an old kid writing assignment into a final draft. This approach is in contrast with composition writing, which is revised and is often copied into main lesson books.

<u>Sight Word Lists and Consumable Spelling Dictionary</u>

Create your sight word lists for 1st Grade and order your spelling dictionaries for 2nd Grade (see chapter 3.6 #3).

<u>Kid Writing Topics</u>

Make a list of possible topics for students to write about. During the school year, flesh it out with topics that are more relevant to recent class experiences (e.g., field trips, nature walks, assemblies, etc.). Some possible topics include:

- Pets
    - Write about your pet (or friend's pet).
    - Describe your pet.
    - Tell about a funny thing your pet once did.
- Family
    - Describe or write about a family member.
    - Describe activities your family likes to do.
    - Tell a funny story about something that happened to you or a family member.
- Vacation
    - Describe what you did or where you went.
    - Tell about something that happened to you (or your family) over vacation.
    - Tell about something interesting you saw on vacation.
- Recess:
    - Tell about what you like to do at recess.
    - Describe your favorite game and who you play with.
- Thank you notes: At some point during the school year, give a special kid writing assignment where the students make thank you notes for the parent helpers on a day the helpers are not there.
- Miscellaneous:
    - Describe one of the chores you have to do at home.
    - Tell about your favorite place to go and what you do there.
    - Tell about your favorite scene from yesterday's story.
    - Tell about the toy you liked the most when you were little.

Keep all topics factual and neutral. Do not assign creative writing or imaginative topics to students in 1st and 2nd Grade. These topics will come later in the Waldorf curriculum.

**Other Considerations**

During the school year, it will be necessary to do some additional preparation:

- Bringing Kid Writing to the Class Parents
- Training Parent Helpers
- Plans for Publishing Kid Writing Assignments

<u>Bringing Kid Writing to the Class Parents</u>

Schedule a presentation about kid writing for the class parents several weeks prior to your plan to introduce kid writing in class.

At this presentation, share what you will be doing (and why) with your class parents. Be sure to cover these points:

- Introduce what kid writing is and why you will be doing it. (It is always good to keep the class parents abreast of what you will be doing in the classroom, particularly when it seems counterintuitive.)

- Explain how to support their child when she tries to do kid writing at home, which she likely will. For example, they must be careful not to point out misspellings. They can, however, show enthusiasm for her efforts. If they cannot read the writing, just ask the child to read it to them.

- Ask for parent volunteers to help with kid writing in the classroom. Lead a follow-up workshop for those parents who volunteer.

<u>Training Parent Helpers</u>

At the training meeting, go over the follow points:

- Explain the job of parent helper: to empower the students rather than give the students the answer.
  - They can assist students who are stuck with drawing a picture or writing by asking them to tell about what they are considering drawing and/or writing about. Putting their ideas into words will help students gather their thoughts about what they want to put on their paper.
  - They should help students isolate sounds by hand spelling or finger spelling with them (see chapter 3.3 #2).
  - If a student is stuck, they can offer a choice/contrast option. For example, is the sound /t/ in the word *cat* the letter *M* or the letter *T*?
- Model how a parent volunteer can help a student.
- Train the volunteers to:
  - tell which phase a student is in (see table 3.13.1)
  - conduct a mini-lesson for each phase
  - acknowledge a phase-specific element that is good in a student's writing
  - choose a mistake for a mini-lesson that is at the student's instructional level (neither too easy nor too hard)
  - do adult writ**ing** while explaining what they are doing and why to the student
- Have the parent volunteers do some role-playing exercises and offer constructive criticism to help them improve.

Give them examples of kid writing at various phases for these exercises as shown in table 3.13.1.

**Table 3.13.1: Samples of Kid Writing by Phase with Signposts and a Suggested Mini-Lesson**

| Phase | Sentence(s): | Signpost(s) | What to Teach in a Mini-Lesson |
|---|---|---|---|
| **Phase** | *I made big frozen waffles. Mom wanted me to eat oatmeal. I skipped that.* | | |
| **Intermediate Emergent Phase** | xgPT | There are no letter sound matches nor is there a letter or magic line for each word. | Do hand spelling to identify the first letter in any word and have the student write it down. |
| **Beginning Phonemic Awareness Phase** | I m b f ___ | There is a letter sound match for most words and each word is represented by a letter or line. | Do finger spelling to identify the last letter in any word and have the student include it. |
| **Intermediate Phonemic Awareness Phase** | I md bg fn wfls. | There are end sounds but no vowels. | Do finger spelling to identify the medial vowel in the word big or made. |
| | I mad beg frn wfls. Mom watid me to et otmel. I skt tat. | There are vowel letters and some blends. There is an error caused by point of articulation: beg for big (see table 3.1.4). The digraph *TH* is missing the letter *H*. There is no preconsonantal nasal in the word wanted (see 4.1 rule 3). | Pick One: Review the letters *E* and *I* to correct the word big. Do finger spelling to add in the preconsonantal nasal in the word want. Review the digraph *TH* for that. |
| **Advanced Phonemic Awareness Phase** | I mad big frozin wofls. Mom wantid me to eat otmel. I skipt that. | The student exhibits full phonemic awareness (i.e., student has segmented the word and has a letter for every sound). Short vowel represented by correct letter. Preconsonantal nasal is right. | Review the Final *E* Rule (see chapter 4.1 rule 6) to correct the word made. |
| **Beginning Pattern Phase** | I made big frozin wofls. Mom wantid me to eat otmel. I skipt that. | Note the addition of the Silent *E* rule in the word made. | Review Two Vowels Go Walking (See chapter 4.2 rule 10) to fix either oat or meal. |
| **Intermediate Pattern Phase** | I made big frozin wofls. Mom wantid me to eat otemeal. I skipt that. Etc. | There are some attempts at using vowel teams/vowel patterns such as *O_E* and *EA*. The student consistently misspells the suffix –ed. | Review the spelling for the suffix –ed (see chapter 4.2 rule 13). |
| **Advanced Pattern Phase** | I made big frozin wofls. Mom wanted me to eat oatmeal. I skipt that. Etc. | Note the correct spelling for all vowel teams such as *O_E* and *EA*. The student is inconsistent at spelling the suffix –ed. | Review the spelling for the suffix –ed (see chapter 4.2 rule 13). |

<u>Publishing Kid Writing Assignments</u>

Decide if you want students to publish some of their kid writing pieces for the class library.

There are many ways you can work with publishing kid writing assignments.

- Select one assignment to be put into a final draft. All students would redraw their picture and write the corrected text (the adult writing) using their neatest handwriting.
- Select individual kid writing assignments that would be good for other students to read. Ask the authors to create a final draft. (Put these pieces into the class library.)
- Have the most advanced students write a final draft while you lead exercises in the Skills Practice segment that are too easy for them. This gives the advanced students something exciting to do while you work with the rest of the class. This system keeps everyone engaged and guarantees fresh reading material for the classroom library.

If you decide to publish kid writing assignments, decide upon a format. You can put these entries into a special notebook or bind them into a spiral bound book. Assemble any supplies you will need.

## 3.   Scheduling

When preparing your curriculum, you can use the block plan templates in Appendices 1–3 or you can create your own. If you create your own, use the following points to lay out your blocks:

1. Begin instruction when most of the class has entered the Phonemic Awareness Phase. They now understand that a letter represents a sound and they can identify the first (or the most prominent) sound in a word. (For most classes it will be at or before November of 1st Grade.)
2. Teach kid writing until the middle/end of 2nd Grade.
3. Teach kid writing in the Reading/Writing (this segment found in 1st Grade only), Skills Practice, and/or Bookwork segments in both main lesson blocks and practice blocks. You can schedule kid writing with the whole class or with small groups.
4. Schedule kid writing 2–3 times per week.
5. The number of minutes needed per lesson varies. Schedule 15 –30 minutes if you split up the lessons; 30–40+ minutes if you do an entire lesson in one day.
6. At the end of 2nd Grade, discontinue kid writing in favor of composition writing.

## 4.   Initial Introduction of Kid Writing

Kid writing is one of the most important skills you will teach.

**Prerequisites:**

1. 80% of the class is in the beginning Phonemic Awareness Phase (or higher).
2. Students know some letters, but not necessarily all, and they can print the letters they know.
3. Students know how to use the alphabet display to find a potential letter-sound match (see chapter 3.4 #5).

4. Students can hand spell (see chapter 3.3 #2).

5. Students can encode the first sound of a word (see chapter 3.4 #6).

Note: It is OK if some students are still in the Emergent Phase as long as the majority of your students are in the Phonemic Awareness Phase. It is also fine if students do not know all of the letters of the alphabet as long as there is an alphabet display (see chapter 3.1 #3). Kid writing will help the students learn their letters.

**Introduction:** This introduction is a variation of one given by Feldgus in *Kid Writing: A Systematic Approach to Phonics, Journals, and Writing Workshop* (Feldgus 1999, 33).

TEACHER: First graders, you already know some letters and how to write your names. Today you are going to learn how to write even more. You are going to learn to Kid Write. When you do kid writing, you write down your own words and sentences using sight words and any letters you hear when you think of the word you want to write. Whatever you write will be just right for you. That's why it is called 'kid writing.' So let's first do some kid writing together. In this case you are going to help me write about our story from yesterday, "Goldilocks and the Three Bears." *(Lead a discussion on memorable moments in the story. Accept all correct answers with enthusiasm.)*

Now I am going to choose the scene where Goldilocks is eating some porridge and do a quick drawing of that scene. *(Do a quick rough sketch on the board. Finish in one minute or less.)*

Now I have to think about what I would like to write about this scene. *(Pause for a second to "think" and then continue.)* Since this is a picture of when Goldilocks ate the porridge, I am going to write, *A girl ate the porridge.* But, instead of writing our story sentence in adult writing, you are going to help me do it in kid writing. I will say each word in the sentence and you will listen to the word and tell me what letter sounds you hear. And if you do not know any letters in the word, we will use a magic line to hold a spot for the word. Let's do this sentence together: *A girl ate the porridge.*

My first word is <u>A.</u> Does anyone hear any letters when I say the word *A*?

1ST GRADERS: A!

TEACHER: Good, I'll write that letter first and since it is the first word in the sentence, I will capitalize it using its adult letter. *(Write the letter A on the board under your drawing.)*

TEACHER: *(Point to the word on the board.)* It says, <u>A.</u>

TEACHER: A girl ate the porridge. The next word is <u>girl.</u> Let's hand spell the word together." *(Class and teacher hand spell the word girl: "/g/ /irl/.)* What letters do you hear in the word girl? Raise your hand if you hear a letter. Lucy?

Lucy: R.

Note: For the initial introduction, accept any letter given, even if it is wrong.

TEACHER: Yes, R. is in the word girl. I'll write that letter next. *(Write the letter R on the board.)*

TEACHER: *(Read each "word" by pointing to the letter written on the board.)* It says "<u>A girl.</u>" Our next word is <u>ate.</u> Do you hear any letters in the word ate?"

1ST GRADERS: 8!

TEACHER: Yes, it does sound like the number 8. Let's write the number 8 down for that word. *(Write the number 8.)*

TEACHER: *(Read each "word" by pointing to the letters/numerals written on the board.)* It says, <u>A girl ate</u>. Our next word is <u>the</u>. That is one of our sight words this week! Who can remember how to spell the word the? Raise your hands. Misha?

MISHA: T….H… .E!

TEACHER: Yes! Very good! That does spell the word *the. (Write the word* the *on the board.)*

TEACHER: *(Read what is now written on the board and point to each letter/numeral/word.)* Our sentence now says, <u>A girl ate the</u>. Our last word is <u>porridge</u>. That's a long one. Does anyone hear any letters in porridge?

1ST GRADERS: Silence.

TEACHER: With kid writing if you do not know any of the letters in the word, you use a magic line to take the word's place. Since no one hears any letters they know, I will use a magic line to stand in for the word porridge. *(Draw a line for the word porridge.)*

Note: For the initial introduction, make sure to include at least one magic line.

TEACHER: Look! You have just helped me write this sentence in kid writing. See, we have something for every word: a letter, a number, or a magic line. It says, <u>A girl ate the porridge</u>. *(Point to each letter, numeral, and line as you say its word.)*

TEACHER: Now I'll show you how this sentence would look in adult writing. *(Write the sentence directly under the first one, saying each word slowly and distinctly and writing the letter as you say its phoneme.)*

A r 8 the_____.

A girl ate the porridge.

TEACHER: Look what a good job you did with kid writing. You have the same letter I do in my adult writing for the first word *A*. You heard one of the letters in the word *girl: R*. You got a number for the word *ate*. You spelled our sight word *the* correctly. And you used a magic line when you didn't know any letters for *porridge*. That's great!

Do this type of introduction once or twice for the whole class. Students in the Phonemic Awareness Phase and Pattern Phase who have the idea can then begin to Kid Write.

## 5.   Kid Writing Process

**Objective:** Students build the *letter to sound decoding route* through kid writing. They practice phonemic awareness, theory of word, encoding, and sight word spelling in the process.

**Prerequisites:** See Section 3.13 #4.

**Background Information:** The following approach to kid writing is a combination of ideas from *Kid Writing: A Systematic Approach to Phonics, Journals, and Writing Workshop* by Feldgus, various books by Gentry, and *Waldorf Education in Practice* by Else Gottgens.

**When to Teach:** *The Roadmap to Literacy's* kid writing curriculum is versatile and can be scheduled easily in 1st and 2nd Grade Waldorf classrooms during multiple lessons segments such as Reading/Writing (this segment found in1st Grade only), Skills Practice, and Bookwork.

**How to Teach:** The kid writing process has seven steps that can be done in one day or spread out over several days:

1. Phonemic Awareness Warm-up Exercises (5–7 minutes)

2. Kid Writing Guidelines (Topic and Assignment) (2–5 minutes)

3. Drawing the Sketch (5–7 minutes)

4. Kid Writing (5–10+ minutes)

5. Proofing (Later Phonemic Awareness and Pattern Phases)

6. Adult Writing

7. Class Mini-Lesson (optional) (5–7 minutes at end of class)

Total Time: 30–40+ minutes.

<u>Phonemic Awareness Warm-up Exercises</u>: Always do phonemic awareness warm up exercises prior to kid writing to model the skills you want the students to use when they Kid Write. The exercises you choose will depend on the majority of your students' current phase (see chapter 3.3 #2).

- Emergent Phase: stepping/clapping/jumping words in a sentence, hand spelling (emphasize onsets), and/or stretching words

- Beginning Phonemic Awareness Phase: hand spelling (emphasize onsets) and/or stretching words

- Intermediate and Advanced Phonemic Awareness Phase: finger spelling and sound and letter boxes (Elkonin boxes)

- Pattern Phase: hand spelling (emphasize rime) and/or encoding with onset and rime

<u>Kid Writing Guidelines (Topic and Assignment)</u>: Begin with a short review or introduction about the topic so that the students begin to create some inner pictures. The topic could be about a factual topic of your choosing such as their pets or an element from a story you recently told--such as their favorite scene. (If you are doing kid writing on a story you have told, you can do your story review at this time.) This will help the students determine what they want to draw and write about. Once your students are comfortable with kid writing, you could give them the opportunity to write about a topic you suggest or give them a choice of topics.

The length of the writing will depend on the students' phases.

- Emergent Phase: 1–2 word titles (Students think of a word or title that tells what their drawing is about.)

- Beginning Phonemic Awareness Phase: 2–5 word titles

- Intermediate Phonemic Awareness Phase: 2+ sentences

- Advanced Phonemic Awareness Phase: ½ page or 1 page about the picture

- Pattern Phase: 1–2 pages about the picture

Remind students to use magic lines if they are unsure about a word.

<u>Drawing the Sketch</u>: The picture students draw is a sketch to anchor their writing. These kid writing sketches are similar to free rendering: They serve an academic purpose and are not done for artistic development. A sketch should take no more than 5–7 minutes.

Note: Waldorf teachers are often taught that drawings and paintings through 5th Grade should be led by the teacher with the goal that each lesson will teach the students something new artistically (e.g., a different way to draw a tree, how to draw a face, etc.). This advice holds true for art lessons and for artistic work that goes into the main lesson book, however, it does not hold true for kid writing. The point of kid writing is the writing, not the picture. The picture is only an anchor for the writing.

<u>Kid Writing</u>: After they have completed their drawings, the students then write about their picture, using whatever knowledge of letters, phonological/phonemic awareness, encoding, and sight words they have. Expectations and time will vary based on which phase each student is in. Teacher and parent volunteers go around the classroom and offer support.

- Emergent Phase: Help these students isolate the first phoneme in the word. Use hand spelling to help the students break off the first sound and then help the student figure out which letter goes with the sound.

- Phonemic Awareness Phase: Help these students isolate all of the sounds in a word by using finger spelling.

- Pattern Phase: Remind students to use their spelling dictionaries (2nd Grade only). You can answer questions about words not found in their dictionary.

<u>Proofing (optional)</u>: At some point during the Phonemic Awareness Phase give the class their sight word list and teach them how to use it (see chapter 3.6 #3). Then teach the class to check the spelling of all of their sight words before coming to you for adult writing. If they have misspelled a sight word, send them back to their desk to fix the error before coming back to you for adult writing. (Note: Underline the misspelled sight word for students who need this accommodation; do not for those who are capable of finding the error on their own.) Doing so will make the students accountable and will allow you to spend more time teaching mini-lessons on phonemic awareness and encoding.

At the beginning of the Pattern Phase (usually 2nd Grade) give each student a spelling dictionary (see chapter 3.6 #3). Students underline any words they want to check and then look them up in their dictionary. Answer spelling questions for words not in students' spelling dictionaries.

<u>Adult Writing</u>: During the first few months of kid writing, it is best to have adult writing during the lesson itself. It gives the students immediate feedback, and the volume of their writing is small so it does not take long per student. Once the student is done with the writing, she would come to an adult for feedback. Ideally, you would have a classroom aide to help you or one or two parent volunteers. You will likely have a small crowd of students around you as you are doing the adult writing with an individual student. Use this situation to your advantage and conduct a mini-lesson. Let the other students see what you are doing and learn from it. Here is the process:

- Have the student read her kid writing to you, pointing to each word as she goes.

- Acknowledge something that the student did well (e.g., *"You used a magic line for every word!"*).

- Pull one element out for a mini-lesson. The element you choose will depend on the student's instructional level.

- Emergent Phase: Try to help the student get a letter match for the first sound in a word. If the student is not sure, ask the other students who are standing around to help. You can give a **choice/contrast** if no one knows. *"Is it the letter T or the letter M?"* Have the student write in the correct letter.

- Phonemic Awareness Phase: As the students progress encourage them to find letter matches for all of the sounds in a word, including utilizing any phonics rules that you have taught (e.g., blends or digraphs).

- Then write in the adult writing directly under the kid writing. Print neatly and talk through your process as you go. Model and explain anything you think the student needs explained (e.g., for someone in the Emergent Phase you might show them how you begin on the left and move to the right as you write or point out how you left a space between each word).

It will only take a few minutes per student to do the adult writing, but every student who is gathered around can benefit from seeing you model how to write like an adult. It is not necessary to get to every student during every lesson. You can do your adult writing on the rest of the papers after class.

Note: If you prefer to move around the classroom assisting students, rather than remaining stationary where they come to you, you can still do mini-lessons for the student you are helping. If you assign seating during a language arts main lesson block according to like phases, the student's neighbors will also benefit from the mini-lesson.

Once the students no longer need this immediate feedback, you can do your adult writing during prep classes or after school. Have the students review what you have written and look for matches between their kid writing and your adult writing the next time you have a kid writing session.

Class Mini-Lesson (optional): At the very end of the lesson or at the beginning of the next lesson, conduct a **mini-lesson** with the class (or group) as a chance to reteach something most of the students are struggling with. Choose 1–3 examples of their kid writing which have errors that the majority of the class could learn from. (The number will vary on the time available.) Put the work up anonymously. Write the sentence with the error up on the board as the content of your mini-lesson, then teach the lesson to your students' current phase.

- Beginning Phonemic Awareness Phase: Acknowledge something the student did well and then pull out one teaching element. For example, *"See how the author has a letter for the beginning of every word. That shows real progress. Let's see if we can figure out one more letter for the word* pig. *Let's finger spell* pig *together: /p/ /ĭ/ /g/. Who can tell what the last letter is: the letter that makes the /g/ sound?"*

- Intermediate and Advanced Phonemic Awareness Phase: Acknowledge something the student did well and then pull out one teaching element. For example, *"This author has both a beginning and ending letter for the word pig. Let's see if we can figure out one more letter for the word pig. Let's Finger Spell pig together: /p/ /ĭ/ /g/. Who can tell what the middle letter is, the letter that makes the /i/ sound?"*

- In the Pattern Phase: Acknowledge something the student did well and then pull out one teaching element. For example, *"The author used a final E to show that the vowel is long in the word grain (i.e., grane). Let's see if we can figure out another way to spell the long A sound."*

Note: The mini-lessons are your chance to reteach phonemic awareness and phonics elements. You should choose elements that will benefit most of the students. You will know what they need by looking at all of their kid writing during prep periods. As you do adult writing with the students, make a mental note as to whose writing has an element that would be useful for the class mini-lesson. (See table 3.3.1 for examples of spelling mistakes that show where students are in the process of developing encoding and phonemic awareness. Also see also Table 6.2.2 for encoding.)

## 6.  How to Differentiate Instruction

There are two ways to differentiate instruction: kid writing groups and story frames.

### Kid Writing Groups

There are many ways to work with groups.

- For the first few months of kid writing, all of the students in the class will be kid writing at the same time. However, by the end of 1st Grade or beginning of 2nd Grade, you can differentiate instruction by pulling students for reading group while the rest of the class is kid writing. See chapter 3.15 #10 for instructions on how to schedule reading groups.

- If your beginning 1st Grade students have a wide range of phases, you may want to conduct your mini-lessons with small groups rather than the whole class.

- If you have just one or two students whose phase levels are higher than the rest, you can ask them to make final drafts of selected pieces of their kid writing rather than participate in warm-up exercises and mini-lessons. These final drafts can then serve as additional material for your class library.

### Story Frames

Use story frames to differentiate the assignment. Everyone will write about the same topic, but the length and format will differ by phase.

**Story frames** are templates Gentry created that help students begin to write and then expand the volume of their writing. They act as templates to help students organize their writing. (Despite the name, students will be using story frames to tell about events in their lives and possibly to retell stories you have told the class, not write their own fiction.) These story frames come from the book *Breakthrough in Beginning Reading and Writing* (Gentry 2007, 30–32), but they have been adapted to the phases.

- Titles

- Sentence

- Beginning, Middle, End

- First, Then, Next, Last, (Finally)

Titles: Ask students in the Emergent Phase to write a title for their picture. For example, Goldilocks and the Three Bears. The goal would be for the students to get something for each word: a letter, a numeral, or a magic line.

Sentence: Use this frame at the beginning of the Phonemic Awareness Phase to help the students expand from a title to a complete thought. For example, let's take the title *Goldilocks and the Three Bears*. You would like the student to expand it into a sentence. Ask the student to find who or what is in her picture and then tell what is happening. For example, Goldilocks went into the house. (Note: The student's writing will look like gibberish at the beginning of this phase. You will need to ask her to read it.)

Beginning, Middle, End: Use this frame for intermediate Phonemic Awareness Phase to help the students expand one sentence into multiple sentences. The student just writes one sentence for the beginning of the story, one for the middle, and one for the end of the story. For example, Goldilocks went into the house. She slept on the bed. Goldilocks ran away. (Note: The writing will be full of errors, but you will be able to decipher the words.)

<u>First, Then, Next, Last, (Finally): Easy Version</u>: Use this frame for advanced Phonemic Awareness Phase to help the students expand their writing up to a half a page. This frame can be used to generate one sentence per frame. It is good for expanding a one to three sentence response into a simple paragraph. For example, First, Goldilocks went into the house. Then she ate the porridge. Next she sat on the chairs. Last she slept on the beds. Finally the bears came home and Goldilocks ran away. (Note: The writing will contain misspellings.)

Note: This frame would work well for walks and other experiences the class had. For example, First we saw blue jays. They made a lot of noise. Then we walked to the park. I wore my new coat. Next, we collected acorns. Etc.

<u>First, Then, Next, Last, (Finally): Advanced Version</u>: Use this frame for the Pattern Phase to help the students expand their writing up to one page and beyond. Ask the students to write two or more sentences per frame. For example, First, Goldilocks went into the house. She saw a table with breakfast on it. Then she ate the porridge. She did not like the porridge that was too hot. She did not like the porridge that was too cold. She only liked the kind that was just right. Next she sat on their chairs. One chair was too soft. One chair was too hard. She sat on the chair that was just right. Last she slept on the beds. She picked the one that was just right. Finally the bears came home and Goldilocks ran away.

<u>Day 1, Day 2, Day 3, Day 4, End of Vacation</u>: Use this frame for the intermediate and advanced Pattern Phase. This frame is a way to generate multiple simple paragraphs. The students write multiple sentences for each frame, and each frame is its own paragraph. It is the students' first exposure to paragraph writing. For example,

On day one we went to Lake Tahoe. I went swimming. I got sunburned. I played in the inner tube. I wore my swim fins and my goggles.

On day two my cousins came. We made hotdogs and played. I built a sandcastle. But my cousin smashed it. Then he made a sandcastle. I put a stick on top for a flag.

On day three we drove out to visit my aunt and uncle. They have a white house. They have a dog. I ate lasagna. I slept on the floor.

On day four we drove home. I fell asleep in the car. My brother poked me. I told him to stop but he did not. I told mom to tell him to stop. He stopped.

The end of vacation was not fun. The ride home was too long. I am glad to be home. I missed my dog and my cat. They were glad to see me!

Feel free to generate your own story frames and put them up on your board as a guide for students to use to expand their writing.

## 7. Classroom Management

Expect a steady hum of noise when students are doing kid writing. Students in the Phonemic Awareness Phase have to subvocalize to write and read. Encourage students to help each other—just as long as they do not plagiarize from other writers or dictate the spellings to less capable classmates. (Teach helpful aid and unhelpful aid. It is never too early to learn that everyone must do his or her own work.)

It is especially good for students to try to figure out how to spell words together. Consider having the students work in small groups with others in their phase or with a desk partner who is at the same level rather than pairing a strong student with a weak student. You will have an easier time teaching mini-lessons to the group or the pair of students in question and you will prevent weak students from growing dependent on strong spellers to help them. During a literacy block, consider seating students with a desk partner at her same level.

Set the expectation that students are working the entire duration of kid writing. Provide acceptable activities for students to do after they finish their work for the day: reading, making a final draft of their writing for the class library, etc. Without a task, they will distract the students who are still working.

## 8. Practice

Kid writing is both the culmination and application of literacy skills. Rather than scheduling extra kid writing, schedule extra practice of the skills that make up kid writing:

- phonological/phonemic awareness
- alphabet
- encoding
- sight words
- grammar: mechanics

## 9. Assessment

Assessment is a critical part of teaching. It is important to verify that students have mastered the skills they have been taught. See chapter 6.1 for background on assessment.

**Benchmarks** represent <u>minimum</u> levels of student achievement by the end of each grade for students to be on track to handle grade-level work in 4th Grade (see chapter 6.1 #9). Table 3.13.2 contains the benchmarks that pertain to kid writing.

Note: The following benchmarks may not be exhaustive. Prerequisite skills for the benchmarks that pertain to kid writing may be covered under other related language arts skills. For a full list of benchmarks, see table 6.1.4.

### Table 3.13.2: Benchmarks that Pertain to Kid Writing

|  | 1st Grade | 2nd Grade |
|---|---|---|
| **Sound/Symbol (Alphabet)** | Students can: <br>• Name all letters (uppercase and lowercase). <br>• Give each letter's sound(s) but only short vowel sounds are expected for vowel letters | NA |
| **Handwriting** | Students can print all uppercase and lowercase letters correctly. | Students can form all uppercase and lowercase cursive letters correctly. |
| **Phonological and Phonemic Awareness: Segmentation** | Students have mastered the following segmentation skills: <br>• sentences into words <br>• words into syllables <br>• single-syllable words into phonemes | NA <br>(Segmentation should have been mastered in 1st Grade. Assess to confirm.) |

| | | |
|---|---|---|
| **Phonemic Awareness: Deletion** (Note: Deletion is a type of Manipulation) | Students have mastered the following deletion skills:<br><br>• initial sound<br>• end sound | Students have mastered the following deletion skills:<br><br>• initial sound<br>• end sound<br>• blends—initial sound |
| **Encoding** | Students demonstrate mastery encoding with the following phonics rules:<br><br>• CVC words<br>• Digraphs: *SH, CH, TH, WH, NG, OO*<br>• Simple blends | Students demonstrate mastery encoding a <u>minimum</u> of the following phonics rules:<br><br>• Silent *E*<br>• Two Vowels Go Walking<br>• The Guardians<br>• Diphthongs |
| **Sight Words: Reading** | Students can read 70+ sight words. | Students can read all sight words from *The Roadmap to Literacy* list (i.e., set 1 and set 2). |
| **Sight Words: Spelling** | Students can spell 20+ sight words. | Students can spell 150+ sight words. |
| **Grammar: Mechanics** | When writing, students capitalize the first word in a sentence, names, and use periods at the end of sentences. | When writing, students use end punctuation correctly (period, exclamation point, and question mark). |

There are three types of assessments. Recommendations for each type of assessment can be found in Sections 6.3, 6.4, and 6.5. You can use the following ideas as a starting point to set up an assessment program.

**Informal Assessments:** NA. You will not be able to assess the students' work informally as students will routinely get help with their kid writing.

**Teacher-Made Assessment:** Once a month , give a kid writing assignment for assessment purposes. Explain that this is a special kid writing assignment that they will do by themselves without help to see what they are able to do on their own. Store these drafts in student files (see chapter 6.1 #8) and use them to monitor each student's progress. Use table 3.3.1 to monitor progress in the Phonemic Awareness Phase. Observe the students' use of phonics rules and sight words in the Pattern Phase.

**Assessments Created by Educational Testing Groups:** NA

See chapters 6.3 and 6.4 for more information about assessing in each grade.

## 10. How to Help Struggling Students

**Assess:** First, when you see a student is struggling with kid writing, do assessments to narrow down the area(s) of concern. Document your findings and place in student's file. For kid writing to be successful, it is necessary to teach students how to encode and how to spell common sight words. In addition, students need good concept imagery. If students struggle to Kid Write, check these three areas and provide support in those areas that are weak.

**Additional Instruction/Practice:** Next, use the results of your assessments to provide this student with extra instruction and practice in any weak areas. You can differentiate instruction in class. For example, you can modify your classroom instruction or an individual assignment to include extra practice in the weak area. Decide which approach is best based on how many other students have similar struggles. Document what you try and the results.

**Remedial Solutions:** Kid writing is the culmination of many different skills. Provide remedial solutions for whichever skill(s) tested weak when you assessed.

**Accommodations and Modifications:** Do not provide accommodations or modifications for kid writing. Unlike when helping a student with a composition, telling the student how to spell words or taking dictation for the student would undermine the point of the lesson. However, sometimes students struggle with kid writing because they are not comfortable making mistakes. For kid writing to work, students have to be OK with making mistakes and improving. Make sure your attitude towards kid writing and its mistakes is positive. Then help your students to celebrate mistakes and the growth of their skills. See Carol Dweck's book *Mindsets* for more information.

## Conclusion

Kid writing is a process of teaching students reading skills through writing (i.e., decoding skills through encoding). In kid writing, students invent their own spellings to write down their own words. Teachers with knowledge of the phases can identify the progress of their class as well as individual students, create lessons to reinforce the skills the students are currently working on, and teach the skills students need to go to the next phase.

Teach kid writing to the class as soon as the majority of students are in the Phonemic Awareness Phase (i.e., once students realize that letters represent sounds). This realization will occur while the students are still learning the alphabet. By teaching kid writing at this time, you get a record of how students' skills are progressing in the following areas: sound/symbol knowledge, phonological and phonemic awareness, sight words, phonics skills, and mechanics. You can use this information to monitor progress in all of your students, plan better lessons, show parents at Parent Teacher Conferences, and write reports at the end of the school year. Kid writing is worth its weight in gold. It is a best practice for the Waldorf classroom, and it is at the heart of *The Roadmap to Literacy*.

# 3.14 COMPOSITION

*A 5th grade teacher was being evaluated. She was asked for examples of her students' work, including several sets of main lesson books. When the evaluator opened up the first book and read the student's compositions. She nodded approvingly to herself. They were all very nicely written. Then she went to the second book. These too were nicely written, but there was a problem: they were identical to the essays in the first book—as were the essays in the third and fourth books she examined. What was going on in this classroom?*

*The evaluator asked the teacher for an explanation. Why did all of the students have identical work in their books? As it turned out, the teacher thought that by modeling good composition for her students, they would pick up on how to write well. She had composed all of the essays, and the students had been copying her work from the board for five years! Only one entry in each book was composed by the students themselves. These singular compositions, unsurprisingly, did not reflect the level of competency one would expect to find in 5th Grade work.*

*As you would expect, the teacher-generated entries were very well written, but they had little value to her students outside of handwriting practice. In 2nd Grade, students should start composing short main lesson book entries on their own with teacher guidance. By 4th Grade, they should be composing all of the content themselves, with the possible exception of copying a poem or two. The teacher of this class had a lot of work ahead of her to bring her students up to speed in this very important area.*

This chapter covers the following topics:

1. Why Composition Matters
2. Background Information
3. Preparation
4. Scheduling
5. Initial Introduction: The Four Steps to Teaching Composition
6. How to Teach Composition in 2nd Grade
7. How to Teach Composition in 3rd Grade
8. Book Reports
9. Practice
10. Assessment

11.   How to Help Struggling Students

# 1.   Why Composition Matters

Composition is a critical skill for all students to learn.

Mastering composition can open many doors since writing is a major component of communication in today's world. Many tests for colleges and advanced training require students to demonstrate that they can write essays under time constraints. When it comes to professional careers, writing skills are a key to getting into trainings and for advancing. Written communication is central to educational and professional life.

Learning to write well takes years of instruction and practice. Writing effective compositions requires that students master three things: 1) use of language; 2) thinking; and 3) structure. They need to have a good vocabulary as well as proficiency with sentence structure and the rules of written language (capitalization, punctuation, and spelling). In addition, the process of writing compositions requires students to think. They need to consider their audience to figure out what is important to include and what is better to leave out. They need to think about how ideas relate to each other. Finally, students need to make decisions about the structure and form they will employ. They have to decide which point of view they will take, how long the finished product will be, if they will use an outline, etc. Composition writing is the culmination of many aspects of language arts.

For Waldorf students, many of their compositions will also include one additional element: mastery of curriculum content. Since Waldorf students do not have textbooks, their main lesson book compositions serve as the content of a textbook. It is therefore important that they begin to learn the basics of composition writing before beginning to study subjects in 4th Grade. They will need composition skills to record the curriculum content.

These goals are quite lofty. How do students get there?

Students begin to work with composition when they do kid writing. Recall that in the book *Discussions with Teachers*, Steiner suggests that 1st Grade students write simple things that they compose themselves (Trostli 2004, 10). Steiner goes on to say:

> At the beginning of the second grade, we will continue with the telling and retelling of stories and... . the children can be brought gradually to the point of writing down the stories we tell them. After they have had some space to digest the stories, have them write short descriptions of what we've told them about the animals, plants, meadows, and woods in the surroundings.... The third grade is essentially a continuation of the second....We will continue to increase the children's ability to write about what they see and read. (Trostli 2004, 11)

In other words, in the 2nd Grade, students begin to write compositions about the stories they have learned in class, including Home Surroundings stories. In the 3rd Grade, students not only continue to write about curriculum content and the stories they hear in class, but they begin to learn to write about something they have read. These steps form the basis of the composition curriculum and lay the foundation for the writing students will learn to do in Grades 4–8.

It is as critical for Waldorf students to learn basic composition by the end of 3rd Grade as it is for them to learn to read.

## 2. Background Information

When it comes to teaching composition, there are several points to consider:

1. The role of the main lesson book
2. How composition differs from kid writing
3. The four steps to teaching composition

### The Role of the Main Lesson Book

One of the things that sets Waldorf apart from other methodologies is the main lesson book.

Rather than use a textbook, Waldorf students are responsible for creating their own book which reflects what they have learned. This process requires students to be more engaged with the material they are studying. When students write their own compositions and get honest feedback from their teacher, they both learn the material as well as how to write.

Mastering composition writing takes education and practice since writing is a craft as well as an art. Students are apprentices and need to be taught the tricks of the trade. They do most of their writing in practice books (or loose sheets of paper). Not all of their compositions will be edited, revised, and recopied into their main lesson books. Much of their writing will be for practice.

Working with main lesson books requires that teachers accept imperfections as students learn. The main lesson book was never supposed to be an artistic masterpiece (see chapter 3.2 #3). It provides students a place to record what they are learning.

### How Composition Writing Differs from Kid Writing

Composition writing differs from kid writing in a few key ways.

In kid writing, the students *talk on paper*. They write in a stream-of-consciousness style with invented spellings to practice phonics. The goal is for students to master sound/symbol relationship (alphabet), phonological and phonemic awareness, encoding/decoding skills, and sight words. Content, grammar, and mechanics are secondary to spelling (i.e., phonetic spelling). Kid writing is about the creation and myelination of the neural pathways that underlie encoding (and thus decoding) and sight words (see chapter 1.2 #2).

In composition writing, however, content and mechanics are the heart of the lesson. Students learn to develop their ideas into appropriate content and then put them into proper written structure. Over the years, they learn to consider word choice, sentence structure, paragraph structure, report structure, and/or essay structure. Mechanics play an important role as well; spelling, capitalization, and punctuation are all equally important, and grammar usage comes to the forefront.

Table 3.14.1 contains an example of how a teacher would handle a sentence if it were written as part of a kid writing lesson as opposed to a composition lesson. It uses the sentence: *Me and my brothr lik choclit cake.*

**Table 3.14.1 An Example of the Difference between Teaching Kid Writing and Composition Writing**

**Using the Sentence:** *Me and my brothr lik choclit cake.*

| Individual Student Kid Writing Mini-Lesson (1st or 2nd Grade) | Group Composition Writing Lesson (3rd Grade) |
|---|---|
| "Nice job getting a letter out for each sound in the word *chocolate*!<br><br>"Let's look at that word *like*. Your word says *lick*. What could we do to change *lick* to *like*? (Or "How could we make the *I* say its name?")<br><br>"Let me show you how this would look in adult writing: Me and my brother like chocolate cake!<br><br>"Nice job with your kid writing, Danny. You are done!"<br><br>Note: If a student said this sentence in a conversation, you would address the grammar mistake and insist that she say the sentence correctly after you: *My brother and I like chocolate cake.* However, in the case of kid writing, you let it go because the point of the lesson is developing phonemic awareness and encoding skills not correcting the content. | "Adults do not start sentences with the word *me*. Instead of *me*, we must use the word *I* to start a sentence when we are referring to ourselves. For example, instead of saying, "'Me like chocolate cake,' you would say what?" (acknowledge correct answer) "Yes, we would say, 'I like chocolate cake.'" "Also, when we are writing about something we did with another person, we are polite and put the other person's name first. So in this case, we would write, 'My brother and I like chocolate cake.'" "Third graders, how could we expand on this sentence? Could we say more about why you and your brother like chocolate cake? What is it about the cake that makes it good?" (A student offers, "Because Mom makes the icing out of real fudge.")" Then let's add 'because Mom makes the icing out of real fudge.'" (Insert the extra words into the sentence on the board.)<br><br>"There are several spelling mistakes in this sentence. I'll underline them." (Underline errors.) "Now each of you write this sentence after correcting the spelling errors." |

In this example, you can see how the emphasis shifts. In kid writing, the emphasis was always on encoding and the teacher ignored grammatical mistakes. In composition writing, the teacher worked with the students to fix the grammar and expand the content to make the sentence stronger. The spelling of the sentence was relegated to the end as something the students fixed before writing their second draft.

**The Four Steps to Teaching Composition**

Whenever you teach a new type of composition, follow these four steps:

- modeled writing
- shared writing
- guided writing
- independent writing

**Modeled Writing** features the teacher standing in front of the class, demonstrating the process for writing a new type of writing.

**Shared Writing** is when the teacher and students in the class compose the new type of writing together or when two or more students compose one piece of writing together.

**Guided Writing** is when the students write their own compositions by themselves but with the teacher's assistance, as needed.

**Independent Writing** is when the students write their compositions without the help of their teacher.

Once the students can write independently, it is time to begin the process anew by introducing a different type of composition. These steps will be modeled as part of the initial introduction of composition (see chapter 3.14 #5).

## 3. Preparation

Over the summer, when you are planning your year for 2nd and 3rd Grade, consider how and when you will teach composition.

In 2nd Grade, composition is limited to summaries and is taught during the second half of the year (i.e., towards the middle or end of the Pattern Phase). As you plan your year, consider possible topics for summary, including literature curriculum stories about saints and/or saintly people, field trips, nature walks, etc.

In 3rd Grade, there are five types of composition to teach. As you plan your year, consider when you could teach these types of composition. For example,

1. Paragraphs: Write about field trip experiences using adjectives.
2. Summaries: Write about Old Testament stories, class/individual readers, field trips, nature walks, etc.
3. Why and how HOTS question paragraphs: Have students write a paragraph that answers a particular (HOTS) question about an aspect of a book they are reading, an Old Testament story, etc.
4. Thank you notes: Have students write thank you notes to parent volunteers.
5. Reports: Write a book report (see chapter 3.14 #8).

Determine possible composition topics as you plan your main lesson blocks.

## 4. Scheduling

When preparing your curriculum, you can use the block plan templates in Appendices 1–3 or you can create your own. If you create your own, use the following points to lay out your blocks:

1. Begin instruction in the second half of 2nd Grade.
2. Mastery of this skill will not happen until the end of 8th Grade. Students will have to learn increasingly more difficult composition skills in each academic year.
3. Teach composition during the main lesson Bookwork segment in 2nd Grade and during the main lesson and practice Bookwork segment in 3rd Grade.
4. Use a two-day teaching rhythm for informal writing and a three-day rhythm for formal writing.
5. Each lesson should last between 20 –25 minutes.

**Teaching Rhythms**

Use a two-day or three-day rhythm to teach writing. Both can be used for all of the steps of teaching writing.

A two-day rhythm is suitable for writing practice. Use practice books. See table 3.14.2.

**Table 3.14.2: Two-Day Rhythm for Composition**

| Day One | Day Two |
|---|---|
| • Lead prewriting activities (review, discussion, assignment, and/or brainstorming).<br>• Students write rough draft.<br>• Students proofread.<br>• Teacher corrects compositions after class with an emphasis on mechanics (including spelling). | • Teach 1–2 mini-lesson(s) around common error(s).<br>• Pass back compositions.<br>• Students make corrections. |

A three-day rhythm is suitable for compositions that are going to be copied into a main lesson book. Use both practice books and the main lesson books. See table 3.14.3.

**Table 3.14.3: Three-Day Teaching Rhythm**

| Day One | Day Two | Day Three |
|---|---|---|
| • Teacher does prewriting with class (review, discussion, assignment, and/or brainstorming activities).<br>• Students write rough draft.<br>• Students proofread.<br>• Teacher corrects compositions after class with emphasis on content and mechanics. | • Teacher conducts 1–2 mini-lesson(s) around common error(s).<br>• Teacher returns compositions.<br>• Students revise their writing and fix errors in mechanics.<br>• Teacher corrects compositions after class with emphasis on mechanics. | • Teacher returns compositions.<br>• Students rewrite composition into main lesson book using neatest handwriting. |

It is possible to do a variation on the three-day rhythm for book reports. Break the report down into smaller sections or paragraphs. Have the students do one section per day until the report is done. Then correct the compositions. You can have the students revise the content one or two times as needed before they write the final draft in their neatest handwriting (see chapter 3.14 #8).

## 5. Initial Introduction: The Four Steps to Teaching Composition

Although the following examples are for the initial introduction of summaries in the 2nd Grade, you should return to these four steps every time you introduce a new style or type of composition:

- modeled writing
- shared writing
- guided writing
- independent writing

## Modeled Writing

Modeled writing is when you, the teacher, do all of the writing in front of the students and model the steps of the writing process, including verbalizing the inner speech writers do in their heads while they write. The objective is to show students that even adults think about and edit what they write; they do not automatically compose perfect sentences. *The Roadmap to Literacy* recommends that the first time you use modeling is when you teach the students to write a summary. Topics include a summary of a story, a field trip, or a nature walk. As you write on the blackboard, share your inner dialogue aloud. Follow these steps to demonstrate what to do when writing and why:

1. Tell your students that you are going to write a short summary of yesterday's story or experience on the chalkboard. For example, you might start with, "I want to write about how we explored the river yesterday."

2. Say, "First I want to think about what I saw, then what I smelled. Describe both and write a few key words down. For example, caterpillar, pipevine swallowtail butterfly, thistles, etc. These words form a **word bank**, a list of words that should be used in a composition. This process is an early brainstorming technique.

3. Next, say, "How do I want to begin?" For example, "Yesterday, the 2nd Grade went for a walk by the American River."

4. Then ask, "Which detail do I want to describe first? I think I will start with the first thing we saw—the caterpillar." Write a sentence about the caterpillar.

5. Continue writing sentences for the other details. Model how to deal with spelling. Say, "Hmm, I am not sure if I spelled that word correctly. I will spell it the best I can and underline it so I can come back and check it at the end." This demonstration will teach the class not to interrupt their writing each time they do not know how to spell a word. (Note: Deliberately misspell at least one underlined word.)

6. Keep reading the paragraph over as you write, showing how to read with expression and how a writer changes her mind along the way. Change your mind about a word or phrase. Show one or two self-edits, such as adding a descriptive word with a carat or crossing out a line or phrase if you change your mind about what you want to say or how you want to say it.

7. Keep your summary to a few simple sentences so that most of your students can read it and feel that they could have written it.

8. Model how to look up words that are underlined in a dictionary or the consumable spelling dictionary (see chapter 3.6 #3). Fix your spelling error(s).

You will use modeled writing each time you introduce a new type of writing to your students.

## Shared Writing

After a few modeled writing sessions, students yearn to compose the summary with you. When they start offering suggestions, invite them into the process by doing shared writing.

Follow the modeled writing steps above, giving the prompts for each step but letting the students offer suggestions for content. This process is usually quite lively! Let go of your unrealistic expectations for polish and perfection and keep these summaries short and simple at the beginning.

Here are some important tips to make your shared writing activities successful:

1. Begin the process for the class by setting the tone of the lesson. Introduce the activity and the topic. Remind the students that they must raise their hands. (Note: Only call on the students who raise their hands and correct the behavior of those who shout out answers. Otherwise shared writing gets too chaotic.)

2. Once you have identified the topic for the summary, ask a student to offer a sentence that tells the reader what the composition is going to be about. Tell the class that you are going to use the offered sentence as a place to start writing.

3. Guide the process (see steps in Modeled Writing) making sure that it is moving along at a good pace as the students offer their suggestions for improvements and additional sentences.

4. Engage in lots of thinking aloud. Show how the students might change sentences along the way.

5. Be careful—there are usually a few children who unconsciously try to monopolize this activity. Ask the quiet ones for their suggestions.

6. If students share an inappropriate or silly sentence, let them know with a look that that type of contribution will not do. Do not allow these students to derail the lesson.

## Guided Writing

Usually after engaging in shared writing for several assignments, most of the students are ready to move on to writing on their own or with a partner. You will be walking around, helping the students as needed.

Here are the instructions for guided writing:

1. Discuss the topic ahead of time as a class to prime the pump before the students begin to write. Write the word bank words on the blackboard. Ask the students to make a point to use as many of the words from the word bank as they can when writing their compositions.

2. Write the first sentence of the summary on the blackboard. Ask them to copy the sentence and then finish the summary in their own words. Be explicit on the content you want the students to cover in their summary. Keep it very simple at the beginning.

3. Let the students work alone or with a partner.

4. Tell the students that if they choose to work together, their collaboration has to be in a whisper so that all of the groups can concentrate. They both need to sign their names to the finished draft to show that they are co-authors.

5. Move around the room giving suggestions, helping struggling students, and helping those who have finished their writing to read over their work and edit it. Make sure that you encourage your students who are working together to help each other and build off of one another's strengths.

## Independent Writing

Independent Writing is the type of composition that students can do on their own. Some of these compositions will go into their main lesson books, others will remain rough drafts.

Here are the instructions for independent writing:

1. Put the topic on the board. Make sure the topic and your expectations are clear. For example, write 4–8 sentences about Saint Francis. Include as many of the word bank words as you can in your composition.

2. Give the students a set amount of time to write.

3. Include a few minutes at the end for them to share their writing with each other.

4. After class, correct the compositions. It is good to make your corrections in a red, green, or orange pen so they stand out clearly.

5. The next day conduct one or more mini-lesson(s) around common student errors in content, mechanics, or structure. However, you can share examples of good vocabulary or interesting sentence structure. You could also select a few compositions for student feedback. They can share what they like about the composition and make suggestions on how a composition might be improved. (Let the authors remain anonymous.)

6. Return the corrected compositions to the students. You can have the students look over their corrections, revise their composition, or copy the corrected draft into their main lesson books.

## 6. How to Teach Composition in 2nd Grade

**Objective:** Teach students to write short summaries of what they have learned to go into their main lesson books.

**Prerequisites:**

1. Spelling: The students can spell most sight words and encode phonetically.

2. The students are able to write 1–2 pages of kid writing on their own.

**When to Teach:** Begin to teach composition the second half of 2nd Grade. Teach it in the Bookwork segment of main lesson.

**How to Teach**

Summaries

Use the four steps to teaching composition to teach summaries (see chapter 3.14 #5). These summaries usually go into the students' main lesson books. If you build up their summary composition skills, by the final main lesson block of the school year, students should be able to compose up to 30% of their main lesson book entries; the rest will be poems, illustrations, etc.

You can use a two-day or a three-day rhythm depending on whether you want the students to copy their compositions into their main lesson books (see chapter 3.14 #4).

Proofreading

Students in 2nd Grade should read through their draft and look for mistakes in the following areas:

- Punctuation: Do all sentences end with a punctuation mark?

- Capitalization: Do all sentences and proper nouns begin with a capital letter?

- Spelling: Are all words spelled correctly? If a student is not sure about a spelling, she should consult her consumable spelling dictionary. If she is unable to find the word, she should underline it to indicate that she does not know how to spell it.

## 7.  How to Teach Composition in 3rd Grade

**Objective:** Teach students to write paragraphs, summaries, thank you notes, and book reports.

**Prerequisites:** Students can compose a summary on their own.

**When to Teach:** Teach composition in the Bookwork segment of main lesson and practice block.

**How to Teach:** In 3rd Grade, you will present explicit instruction on many different types of composition:

- paragraphs
- summaries in paragraph form
- HOTS questions in paragraphs: why and how
- thank you notes
- book reports (see chapter 3.14 #8)

In addition, you will expand upon proofreading skills.

Remember to use the four steps to teaching composition for each type of composition during a main lesson (see chapter 3.14 #5). You can use a two-day or a three-day rhythm depending on whether you want the students to copy their composition into their main lesson book.

<u>Paragraphs</u>

Students in 2nd Grade learned to start a new paragraph when they changed topics as part of using story frames (see chapter 3.13 #6). In 3rd Grade, students need to learn proper paragraph structure:

- topic sentence (main idea of the paragraph or introduction to paragraph)
- detail one
- detail two
- detail three
- conclusion sentence

This structure will be their introduction to paragraph form. It will undergo several evolutions in later grades, but it will always have the big three: topic sentence, body (i.e., detail sentences), and conclusion.

There are two good images to use to introduce paragraphs: Sandwich and Hand.

*Imagination Idea #1: The Sandwich*

One way to introduce a paragraph is to tell students that a paragraph is like a sandwich. Just as a sandwich has to have some things to make it be a sandwich, so too does a paragraph. Ask the students, *"What are the things that need to be in a sandwich to make it a sandwich?"* (Take all answers and draw the picture on the board as you go: bread, cheese, meat, vegetables, lettuce, tomatoes, etc.) Stop when you get three ingredients in between two slices of bread.)

Then ask, *"Why do we need to have two slices of bread for our sandwich?"* (It falls apart otherwise. If they do not get the answer, describe a sandwich that fell apart.)

Then tell the class, *"A paragraph is just like the sandwich I drew on the board. It has a topic sentence that tells what the paragraph will be about… .its topic. Then it has three detail sentences that tell about the topic of the paragraph. It ends with a conclusion sentence that signals the paragraph is ending. The topic sentence and conclusion sentence hold the three details together, just as bread holds a sandwich together."*

*"When we write a paragraph, it helps to set out everything that will go inside it, just as we would pull food out of the refrigerator before we begin to make a sandwich. We can put a few words into our sandwich picture here to remind us of our ideas when we write. Let's plan a paragraph about the story of Noah and the Flood from yesterday. What is the topic of our paragraph?"* (Noah and the Flood). *"I will write that in my top slice of bread to remember to write a sentence introducing the topic of the paragraph. Let's pick three details to put in the sandwich."* (Take all answers and then pick three: God warned Noah, Noah made an ark, he took many animals on board, Noah sent out a dove, the ark landed and everyone got off, there was a rainbow, etc.). Put a few key words into each part of the sandwich to remember your three details. *"All we need now is a concluding sentence to tell that our paragraph is done. How could we conclude the story?"* (Take all answers and pick one: God promised not to destroy the world again, Noah and his family were happy to get to land again, etc.)

Using the above exercise as an example, explain that just as each person likes different things on her sandwich, so too will each writer choose different things for her paragraph. As long as it has a topic sentence, three supporting details, and a conclusion, it is still a paragraph. (If you are so inclined, you can make another sandwich—this time with different ingredients (for example, veggie patty, lettuce, and cheese) and with different supporting details and conclusion.)

*Imagination Idea #2: The Hand*

Another way to introduce the paragraph format is the hand. Hold up your hand and tell the students it is their guide to writing a paragraph. Show them that the thumb is the topic, the middle three fingers are tell-tell-tell (supporting ideas), and the pinky is the closing or conclusion. You can have them trace their hand and write some key words on each finger to help them remember. (Use the same language and key words as in the sandwich image.)

You can also present a little chant: *"Topic, Tell, Tell, Tell, the Closing."* Have the students point to their fingers while they chant. Have them do it with you a few times and then continue to refer to it as long as needed to remind them that they always have the format for a paragraph *in hand.*

Once students understand paragraph structure, it is time to practice before they try writing one on their own. Here are some activities:

*Activities*

1. Take a paragraph that has a clear structure (topic sentence, three supporting sentences, and a closing sentence) and cut each sentence into separate strips. Divide students into groups of five and hand each a sentence. Let them work together to figure out the order of the sentences to form a good paragraph. Variation: Write a paragraph on the blackboard but mix up the sentences. The students have to figure out the correct order of the sentences.

2. Make a handout with three examples of paragraphs on it. One of the paragraphs is written correctly, one has a topic sentence, but the following sentences do not support the topic, and one does not have a conclusion sentence. Have the students get together in groups and see if they can find the well-written paragraph and discover what is wrong with the other two.

3. Give the students the topic and closing sentences and have them come up with the three supporting sentences. Variation: Give the three supporting sentences and have the students come up with the topic sentence and/or conclusion sentence.

Now students are ready to try writing paragraphs on their own. Here are different formats to use in 3rd Grade: summaries in paragraph form, HOTS questions (why and how), and thank you notes.

<u>Summaries in Paragraph Form</u>

The students have been summarizing stories and nature walks since 2nd Grade. Now they have to put their summaries into proper paragraph format. Their paragraph must have a topic sentence, body sentences, and conclusion sentence. They may include three, four, or five detail sentences in their paragraph.

*Introduction One: Revising to cut back on details*

Students often try to include too much detail. You can choose a student paragraph for a lesson for the whole class or make up one yourself. Show how one long description can be summarized by finding the main concepts in order to simplify the text. For example,

> On our nature walk, we saw many interesting things. The butterflies in the meadow were in the flowers. They had black piping on their wings. Then they flew over John's head. Then they disappeared in the trees. The acorns had lots of holes in them. They were scattered on the ground. I think a squirrel ate them. The river was low. There were no rapids. Everything was dry because of the drought.

There are three main concepts underlying all of the details: butterflies, acorns, and river. Each of those things should be its own rich sentence. Model how to revise this paragraph's body into three key details. It could look something like this:

> On our nature walk, we saw many interesting things. The <u>butterflies</u> with black piping on their wings flew over our path. On the ground a squirrel was feasting on <u>acorns,</u> which had lots of holes in them. There were no rapids because the <u>river</u> was low. Everything was dry because of the drought.

Then give the students another paragraph and let them revise it themselves. *Introduction Two: Making a topic sentence by finding the concept*

Students often need help crafting a topic sentence for their summary. Select a passage from a story and ask the students to summarize it in one concise sentence by figuring out the most important thing and leaving out the rest of the details. Let's try an example.

> The woman dragged the net out of the sea and over the beach. She opened the net to reveal a mound of glittering, silver fish. One fish shone brighter than the rest. It said, *"If you free me, I will grant you three wishes."* The woman lifted the fish from the net and released him into the sandy surf.

Once the students have determined the most important thing (i.e., a woman caught a magic fish), they can add in pertinent supporting details and a conclusion to wrap up the paragraph.

*Introduction Three: Judicious Use of Modifiers*

Teach students to use an adjective or adverb to embellish the sentence and to judge the result.

For example, An <u>old</u> woman caught a fish but released it when it promised her three wishes. A woman caught a <u>silvery</u> fish but released it when it promised her three wishes. A woman caught a fish but released it when it <u>desperately</u> promised her three wishes.

Note: This exercise is good to do to practice adjectives and adverbs. Have the class vote on which version of the sentence they like best. Be silly, and try to put all of the adjectives and adverbs together and discuss the judicious use of language and when less is more. Also discuss the fact that sometimes it is best not to use any modifiers at all. It depends on why you are writing the paragraph. It is good to add modifiers when you are being descriptive, but you should avoid them when you need to be concise such as when you are focusing on the plot or action of the story or are giving instructions. They then are a distraction.

*Introduction Four: Conclusion or How to Wrap Up a Paragraph*

Teach students multiple ways to conclude their summary by adding in a good sentence to wrap up the paragraph. There are several possibilities:

- Restate the topic sentence in different words (e.g., The old woman released the fish in exchange for wishes.).

- Make a conclusion (e.g., The old woman's wishes were foolish.).

- Tell readers why they should care (e.g., If you get magic wishes, be careful what you wish for.).

- Tell a moral (e.g., The old woman learned to be content with what she had.).

*Activities*

After each introduction, give the students activities to do to practice the idea. It is good to ask students to work as desk partners initially and then to follow up with individual writing in the Bookwork segment of the lesson.

## HOTS Questions in Paragraphs: Why and How Questions

Students now are reading chapter books on their own and are reading some assignments together as a class (or in a reading group). They have been answering Higher Order Thinking Skills (HOTS) questions in class (see chapter 3.8 #2). Now teach them to write a one-paragraph response around a *why* or *how* question. Follow the four steps to teaching composition (see chapter 3.14 #5).

An example of a HOTS question for the book *Charlotte's Web* would be, "*Why are Charlotte and Wilbur friends?*"

Note: *The Roadmap to Literacy* recommends that you wait until most of your class has moved through the nine-year change before asking them to do this type of composition.

## Thank You Notes

Use a truncated version of the four steps to teaching composition (see chapter 3.14 #5).

Suzanne-Marie English, author of *The Etiquette of Kindness*, offers the following advice on how to say thank you. By modeling this approach, you can teach your students how to express gratitude in an exemplary manner.

1. First discuss when it would be appropriate to write thank you notes and why they are meaningful. Stress that writing a thank you note should be about more than just saying those words.

2. When you write your topic sentence, do not begin with the word *I*. Instead look for a way to shift the focus to the person you are thanking and use either *you* or *your*. Also, include the gift by name. (For example, "Thank you for your kindness in sending me the sweater…" or "Your handwork class is one of my favorite classes…" or "The sweater you gave me was such a….")

3. When you write detail sentences, include what the gift or deed means to you and/or how you will use it.

4. When you conclude your paragraph, inquire into how the recipient is doing or include some other gesture of interest in him or her personally.

5. Always use your nicest handwriting.

6. When writing, use proper grammar, punctuation, and correct spelling.

Curriculum Connection: It is good to ask the students to write thank you notes to parent volunteers (e.g., drivers for field trips, etc.). It will teach them gratitude for the adults who make it possible for the class to do these activities and will show the parents appreciation in a very meaningful way. (Parents who feel appreciated are more likely to volunteer again and to get other parents to join them.)

Proofreading

For each type of writing, students should proofread their work before handing it in.

Students should read through their draft and look for mistakes in the following areas: punctuation, capitalization, and spelling. Here are the things to proofread for in 3rd Grade:

- Punctuation:
  - o Do all sentences end with a punctuation mark?
  - o If you have any lists within a sentence, did you use commas?
  - o Do all quotations have the quotation marks and other punctuation in the right places?
  - o Did you use apostrophes for possessive nouns?
- Capitalization:
  - o Do all sentences begin with a capital letter?
  - o Do all proper nouns begin with a capital letter?
- Spelling: Are all words spelled correctly? Use your consumable spelling dictionary to check. Underline any words that you are still not sure about.

Insist that students proofread before they hand in their work. You can ask them to do so with a red pencil so you can confirm that it has been done if you wish. Be sure to set aside enough class time for them to proofread their work.

## 8. Book Reports

**Objective:** Teach students to write a series of related paragraphs that they can put together into a short book report.

**Prerequisites:**

1. Students can read Level M books or higher independently (see chapter 3.15 #3).

2. Students can compose a proper paragraph (see chapter 3.14 #7).

**When to Teach:** Teach in 3rd Grade in the Introduction &/or Review segment and the Bookwork segment of main lesson. It will take about three or four weeks to teach the entire process. (Note: This introduction is optional. If your class is not ready, wait until 4th Grade to teach book reports.)

**How to Teach:** Teach the students to write a series of three paragraphs, each one about a different aspect of the story (e.g., plot, main character, and setting). Have the students put these three paragraphs together into a short report and include an artistic element such as a drawing, painting, or diorama to create a book report.

Teaching the book report will be like teaching three different composition lessons. Each of the three paragraphs will be its own lesson. Teach each one using the four steps to teaching composition (see chapter 3.14 #5). Use a book you have read aloud to the class for modeled writing and shared writing, a book from reading group for guided writing, and have students use one of their independent readers as the basis for independent writing. The independent writing will become the first book report the students compose on their own. Teach mini-lessons around common writing problems.

Three modeled writing lessons are presented using the book *Charlotte's Web*. Each lesson covers one paragraph. They can be taught on Mondays. Do the shared writing, guided writing, and independent writing the rest of the week. Then start a new lesson the following Monday.

Before you begin teaching your students how to write a book report, talk about when adults and children read a good book how they like to tell others about it. This is one of the ways that people find good books to read. Ask if they have ever told a friend or family member about a book they enjoyed reading. After a few comments, segue this conversation into discussing another way that people can share about books they have read and that is to write about them. The advantage to written book reports (or *book sharing*, if you prefer) is that it is a way you can tell people about a book without having to repeat yourself over and over. But, in order to share about a book in writing it helps if you think about what it is people would like to know. . .

At this point you can transition into the three main parts of a book/story using the following guidelines.

Lesson 1: Plot

Tell the students they are going to learn to write a book report. The report will have three paragraphs. The first paragraph will be about plot. Plot is the action of the story. You will model how to write a paragraph about the plot for the book report.

Brainstorm things to write about using these questions:

- What was the problem or challenge the main character faced?
- How did the problem start?
- What was the most exciting or interesting part of the book?
- How or why did the main character get involved in the challenge?
- What did the main character do to overcome or help solve the challenge?

Do all your thinking out loud and write your answers to the questions on the board.

Next choose 3–5 details that would go well together that could be put into a paragraph. Do all your thinking out loud and decide upon the related details to include. Then write a topic sentence for them. Use the details to write the detail sentences for the paragraph. For example,

> *Charlotte's Web is a story about how a spider named Charlotte saves her friend Wilbur's life. The farmer is planning on killing Wilbur because he is a pig. Wilbur does not want to die. His friend Charlotte comes up with a plan to save him. She tricks people into thinking that Wilbur is a special pig. She writes messages about him in her web like "Some Pig." Lots of people come to see the messages in the spider web. Wilbur wins a prize at the State Fair because he is famous. The farmer decides to spare Wilbur's life.*

The next day, repeat the lesson but write about another story's plot using the shared writing approach.

<u>Lesson 2: Main Character</u>

The next week, use modeled writing as you emphasize the main character of a book. Teach the students that there are many different characters, but the main character is the one the story is about or the most important character.

Brainstorm things to write about using these questions:

- Who was the main character of the book?
- What did the main character look like?
- How old was the main character?
- Find 5–7 adjectives to describe the main character. Back these adjectives up with an example from the book.

Here are some sample answers:

- Who was the main character of the book? (Wilbur the pig.)
- What did the main character look like? (He started off a tiny runt but grew into a large white pig.)
- How old was the main character? (At the beginning he was a baby. By the end he was one year old.)
- Find 4–7 adjectives to describe the main character. Back these adjectives up with an example from the book.
  - Not very smart—He did not realize the farmer was going to kill him.
  - Lazy—He likes to sleep.
  - Trusting—He broke out of his pen when the other animals told him it was okay. It wasn't.
  - Impatient—He had a hard time waiting for morning so he could discover who had talked to him in the night.
  - Lonely—He really wanted a friend. He was lonely before Charlotte came.
  - Humble—Wilbur fainted when he won an award for being famous.

As you begin to compose your paragraph, make sure you share your thought process out loud. This will help your students understand the inner dialogue that writers engage in as they decide what to write.

Choose 3–5 details from the bolded points above that would go well together in a paragraph. Then write a topic sentence for them. For example, *Wilbur was a pig who wanted a friend.*

Use the details to write the detail sentences for the paragraph. For example,

*Wilbur was a pig who wanted a friend. He was born a tiny white runt who lived with a girl named Fern. When he grew too big to stay with Fern, he moved to a new farm. At first he was very lonely. Then one night he heard a soft voice say that she would be his friend. Wilbur was impatient for morning to come so he could meet this new friend. The voice came from a spider named Charlotte. Charlotte became Wilbur's best friend. When she died, Charlotte's daughters became his friends. Wilbur was no longer lonely.*

The next day, repeat the lesson but choose a different character (Charlotte) or choose a different character from another story using the shared writing approach.

<u>Lesson 3: Setting</u>

The third week, teach the students to write a paragraph about setting. Tell them that setting is where the story takes place.

Brainstorm things to write about using these questions:

- When did this story take place (modern day, ancient times, etc.)?
- Where did the main part of the story take place (in a house, on a farm, in a forest)?
- Describe the setting.
    - o See: What did it look like?
    - o Hear: What noises could be heard there?
    - o Smell: What did it smell like?
    - o Touch: What did it feel like there?
    - o Taste: What could be tasted there?

Choose 3–5 details that would go well together that could be put into a paragraph. Then write a topic sentence for them. Use the details to write the detail sentences for the paragraph. For example,

*Wilbur lives in the pig pen in a barn. It smells of hay and of manure. Wilbur chose a warm manure pile for his bed. He has a trough for his food. The hired man brings Wilbur leftover food like potato skins, skim milk, and crusts of bread. Geese, lambs, and a rat also live in the barn with Wilbur. It is a nice place for a pig to live, but sometimes he finds it boring.*

The next day, repeat the lesson but using shared writing. By the end of three weeks, students will have three paragraphs that together comprise a book report. The following week, have the students rewrite the three paragraphs into a final draft. Have them do their related art either in class or at home. The book report is done and students will know how to write the next book report on their own.

<u>Mini-Lessons</u>

When the students start writing guided and Independent writing reports, conduct mini-lessons around common writing problems. If students are repeating the same subject over and over again in each sentence, demonstrate ways to combine the sentences or change the subjects. For example, Tom is a boy. Tom is brave. Tom fights evil.

To revise these sentences, students could:

- Combine these sentences into one sentence (e.g., Tom is a brave boy who fights evil.).
- Flesh out each sentence (e.g., Tom is a nine-year-old boy with black hair. Tom is very brave because he defends people. Tom fights evil after school.).
- Change the subjects of some of the sentences so that each sentence does not begin with the word *Tom* (e.g., Tom is a boy. He is brave. He fights evil.).

Show the students options for revising the sentences (including mixing options) and let the students determine which rewrite they like best.

<u>Creative Alternatives to Standard Book Report Paragraphs</u>

Once students can write a book report on their own, alternate standard book reports with other, more creative approaches so that your students do not get burned out on this format. Some ideas for these alternatives include:

- Write a different ending to the book (What would have happened if _____ didn't happen but _____ happened instead?)

- Choose a scene from the book and create a diorama of the scene. Write a paragraph about the scene (Where is it located, who lives there, etc.)

- Choose a character and draw a picture of the character based solely on the author's descriptive passages.

- Choose a favorite character (perhaps not the main character) and write a paragraph or two about the character's role in the book and why you liked that character.

- Choose a part of the book that includes dialogue between two or more characters. Make either paper puppets or clay models of these characters. Write out the dialogue from the book and present a short play using the characters and dialogue created. (Do this type of report only after you have introduced quotations.)

- Write and then present a short verbal presentation about your book to the class. (Optional: dress as one of the book's characters.)

- Choose a favorite scene from the book and make it the centerpiece for a poster designed to advertise the book.

Book reports require the students to comprehend what was written and find a way to communicate both the author's words and their own thoughts about a book. These skills will be honed for years to come. They will learn how to write a full book report in 4th Grade (i.e., one that includes a proper introduction and a concluding paragraph with possible recommendations).

## 9. Practice

Practice is critical. It forms part of your initial introduction in the Introduction &/or Review segment of main lesson (i.e., Activities A and B). However, it is not included in your ongoing practice in the Skills Practice segment of main lesson or as a classroom game. Instead, composition practice is always part of Bookwork in both main lesson and practice blocks. See chapter 3.14 #6 and #7 for more information for 2nd and 3rd Grade composition practice.

## 10. Assessment

Assessment is a critical part of teaching. It is important to verify that students have mastered the skills they have been taught. See chapter 6.1 for background on assessment.

**Benchmarks** represent <u>minimum</u> levels of student achievement by the end of each grade for students to be on track to handle grade-level work in 4th Grade (see chapter 6.1 #9). Table 3.14.4 contains the benchmarks for composition.

Note: The following benchmarks may not be exhaustive. Prerequisite skills for composition may be covered under other related language arts skills. For a full list of benchmarks, see table 6.1.4.

**Table 3.14.4: Benchmarks for Composition**

|  | 1st Grade | 2nd Grade | 3rd Grade |
|---|---|---|---|
| **Composition** | NA (see kid writing) | Students can write brief summaries (3–4 sentences) of stories they have heard or about something they have done. | Students can write:<br>• a paragraph<br>• 1–3 paragraph summaries for their main lesson books<br>• a thank you note |

There are three types of assessments. Recommendations for each type of assessment can be found in Sections 6.3, 6.4, and 6.5. You can use the following ideas as a starting point to set up an assessment program.

**Informal Assessments:** All compositions are informal assessments since you assess the students' actual work rather than use a separate test. Always use the students' rough drafts for assessment purposes as main lesson book compositions reflect your corrections.

Pay attention to the following areas:

- mechanics: capitalization and punctuation
- spelling: sight words, encoding, and weekly spelling words (if applicable)
- sentence structure: no fragments or run-on sentences
- paragraph structure: topic sentence, supporting sentences, and conclusion
- vocabulary: appropriate word choice
- content: Does the composition make sense? Did she understand the story?

Give students appropriate feedback to help them correct their mistakes. Some feedback will be given as class mini-lessons so that everyone can benefit.

**Teacher-Made Assessment:** NA

**Assessments Created by Educational Testing Groups:** NA

See chapters 6.3, 6.4, and 6.5 for more information about assessing in each grade.

## 11. How to Help Struggling Students

**Assess:** When you see a student is struggling with composition, do assessments to narrow down the area(s) of concern. Document your findings and place them in the student's file. Pay particular attention to comprehension, handwriting, and spelling (see chapter 3.2, 3.8, and 3.9).

**Additional Instruction/Practice:** Next, use the results of your assessments to provide this student with extra instruction and practice in any weak areas. You can differentiate instruction both in class and in reading groups. For example, you can modify the instructions for each reading group, or give individual assignments to provide extra practice in a weak area. Decide which approach is best based on how many other students have similar struggles. Document what you try and the results.

**Remedial Solutions:** Composition is the culmination of different skills. Provide remedial solutions for whichever skill(s) tested weak.

**Accommodations and Modifications:** Sometimes it takes a while for remedial issues to be resolved. Meanwhile, the student needs support to function in class. Consider modifications as a temporary measure. Here are some possibilities:

1. Take turns writing. Take the student's pencil and say, "*Go ahead, tell me what you want to say.*" Stop her after one sentence and write it down, modeling whatever phase of writing they are at in the process. Then ask what she wants to say next. Hand the pencil back and say, "*You go ahead and write that down.*" If the student says, "*I do not know what to write about,*" give her an idea for a sentence. You can take the playful approach by initiating a "*let's go back and forth*" discourse. This trick will often get the reluctant students going.

2. Provide a sparse outline of events in the story for the student to use to help jog her memory about other events.

3. Take dictation from the student for part of the assignment.

Whenever you give a student a modification, make sure you take steps to address the underlying problem. Used as a long-term fix, accommodation can cripple an otherwise capable student.

## Conclusion

Composition writing is quite different from kid writing. In its step-by-step deliberate process, it is more akin to building than to talking. It takes careful pre-planning before words are committed to paper. It can go through several revisions in order to perfect it. Composition writing depends on its form for its beauty and its usefulness. Teach the students the form and how to create it, and they will have a solid foundation for the reports and compositions in the years ahead.

# 3.15 READING

*Heidi, a bright, capable student who has just graduated from the 8th Grade, is a slow reader who has been accepted into honors English her freshman year. Is her slow reading speed a problem?*

In this chapter that question will be answered. This chapter examines how you can teach reading through the phases so that all of your students can become proficient at this vitally important skill.

This chapter covers the following topics:

1. Why Reading Matters
2. Background Information
3. Preparation
4. Scheduling
5. Initial Introduction
6. How to Teach Reading in the Emergent Phase
7. How to Teach Reading in the Phonemic Awareness Phase
8. How to Teach Reading in the Pattern Phase
9. How to Teach Reading in the Syllable Phase
10. How to Differentiate Instruction Reading Groups
11. How to Create an Independent Reading Program
12. Book Reports
13. Practice
14. Assessment
15. How to Help Struggling Students

## 1. Why Reading Matters

In today's world, the answer to the question *"Why does reading matter?"* seems self-evident. From the decline of manual labor to the rise of information technology, the world is a tough place for those who are illiterate. However, there are two lesser-known conditions that matter just as much as illiteracy: partial literacy and lack of fluency. There is also a common Waldorf misperception about reading that needs to be addressed. Information on these three areas is described below.

### Partial Literacy

Literate people have rewired their brains to decode, developed the *word identification hub,* and read extensively to create a rich lexicon of words they recognize instantaneously (see chapter 1.2 #3). The best of the bunch have also developed a vast vocabulary and are exceptional spellers. However, there are many people who began the journey to full literacy but never completed it. These people are partially literate.

The skills of the partially literate coincide with the phases they have developed. For example, those who have mastered the Phonemic Awareness Phase can sound out simple words but struggle with vowel patterns, and those who have mastered the Pattern Phase can decode single-syllable words but still struggle with longer words. As a result, the partially literate have problems reading texts at different levels. Up to a certain level, they can read fine, but beyond it, their skills prove inadequate, and they no longer can manage.

To avoid partial literacy, make sure your students are progressing through the phases properly and do not get stuck.

## Lack of Fluency

People with weak reading fluency also have a reading problem. Let's consider the scenario of Heidi, the slow reader who is going into Honors English in 9th Grade. On an oral reading fluency test, Heidi is found to read 80 correct words per minute at an 8th Grade level; however, average readers can read 150 correct words per minute aloud and over 200 correct words per minute when they read silently. Heidi can manage less than half that speed.

In high school, a student might well spend three or four hours on homework each night; however, that time assumes an average reading speed, something Heidi does not have. A reading assignment that will take an average reader 45 minutes to complete will take Heidi over an hour and a half. Unfortunately, Heidi will have homework in her other classes—and her English reading will be both longer and harder than the homework in regular English. If it takes the honors English student one hour to read the assignment, it will take Heidi more than two hours—on top of her other homework.

Some would argue that Heidi could get the book on tape. This solution is a devil's bargain. While it would cut her English homework time down, it would make her reading fluency problem worse over the long run. Every year, the reading will get harder. Those students who read the text themselves will have concomitant growth in their reading fluency, but Heidi will not. Consequently, she would become increasingly dependent on books on tape. When Heidi joins the professional world, the true price of the devil's bargain will become clear: courtroom briefs do not come on tape, and neither do business reports at a board meeting. She will have to read those on her own, very slowly.

Weak reading fluency is an academic and professional handicap. Work will always take longer to complete. Accommodations do not exist outside of school—unless a person can afford a personal assistant. Make sure all of your students develop adequate reading fluency to avoid this problem.

## Readers and Nonreaders

There is a common misperception among some Waldorf teachers that there are readers and nonreaders. This dichotomy is too simple. It implies that the ability to read is an either/or phenomenon rather than a process that spans years. There are two common errors that can grow out of this false dichotomy.

When teachers say their students are readers, they are usually referring to the change that occurs when students move from Frith's phonological stage to the orthographic stage, a shift that should occur at some point during Grades 1–3 (see chapter 1.2 #1). This change is dramatic; however, it did not come out of the blue. Learning to read is a process. Students are nonreaders in the pictorial stage, beginning readers in the phonological stage, and readers in the orthographic stage. The transition time should be acknowledged because the work of the phonological stage is a prerequisite for entering the orthographic stage. Saying that there are readers and nonreaders glosses over it and contributes to a common teaching error: advising parents to give a late reader more time rather than assessing development in the phonological stage to see if there is a problem that should be addressed (see chapter 6.6 #1).

There is a second problem: teachers often stop assessing reading once their students become readers because they assume that their work is done. In reality, having students enter the orthographic stage does not mark the end of the teacher's job in this area. Students need to master harder and harder levels of text with each passing school year. The texts, sentence structure, ideas, and vocabulary will become more demanding, and students need additional instruction and practice each year to handle the complexities in language that they will encounter. In addition, students need to develop reading fluency. That bar goes higher with each passing school year until around 5th Grade when students' oral reading fluency is expected to reach around 150 words per minute (silent reading is even higher). Even when students do reach this level, they will have to continue to work to maintain it. A teacher's job does not stop once students enter the orthographic stage; it merely changes.

Rather than thinking of reading as a switch (off: nonreader/on: reader), think of it as a marathon. Make sure the students are ready to run at the start of the race (i.e., they are developmentally ready to learn to read when they are in the pictorial stage), monitor their progress closely at the beginning of the race to make sure they hit their stride (i.e., assess during the phonological stage to make sure they hit the expected signposts at the expected time), and continue to monitor and offer instruction and support in the orthographic stage to make sure that all students are continuing to make the expected progress in fluency, vocabulary, comprehension, etc. to finish the marathon by the end of 8th Grade.

Reading is fundamental for today's world. Any form of weakness puts a person at a considerable disadvantage academically, personally, and professionally. Address common reading problems when students are young. Once they have cracked the code, strive to get all of your students reading fluently using more advanced levels of texts each school year.

## 2. Background Information

There are several types of reading and different ways to teach them.

### Types of Reading

Students will use five types of reading, with the last four pertaining to the classroom:

Pretend Reading (preschool)

Memory Reading

Echo Reading

Decodable-Text Reading

Independent Reading

Pretend Reading consists of paraphrasing the content of a well-known story without word-to-word matching. Many a preschooler has delighted relatives by pretending to read a favorite book. The child uses the pictures as a guide and tells the part of the story that goes along with each illustration. The child's language does not match the written words on the paper (that will come later in memory reading). This type of reading is suitable for children who are not yet in school.

<u>Memory reading</u> consists of making word-to-word matches of spoken word to written word with a text that the student has already memorized such as morning verse, song lyrics, etc. The student points to each word while reciting it. The student is not reading *per se*, but she is learning many things, including aspects of phonological awareness such as letter/phoneme matching and theory of word. This type of reading is the first type of reading a student will do in school. It is suitable for the Emergent Phase and beginning to intermediate Phonemic Awareness Phase.

<u>Echo Reading</u> is a variation of memory reading with an unfamiliar text. It is a call-and-response reading where the teacher reads a line for the students and they 'read' it back, pointing to each word as they go or following along as the teacher points to each word on the blackboard. It is useful for waking up dreamy students who are just going through the motions with familiar material.

<u>Decodable-Text Reading</u> refers to the reading students do with simple texts that they can decode. Students use the three reading strategies that they have learned (i.e., sight words, decoding, and contextual clues) to read an unfamiliar but simple text. This text can be a passage on the board or a **leveled reader**, a beginning reader with controlled vocabulary used for practicing beginning reading skills. The class begins this stage under the guidance of the teacher as guided reading (see below). When students are at different reading levels, the teacher often splits them into reading groups. This type of reading is suitable for the intermediate Phonemic Awareness Phase, Pattern Phase, and Syllable Phase.

<u>Independent Reading</u> consists of students reading without support. They start with basic decodable-text, progress through harder and harder leveled readers, and finally advance into chapter books, first with illustrations and then without. When students make their first attempts at independent reading in the mid to late Phonemic Awareness Phase, they pass through a stage where they use **subvocalization**, where they must say the words aloud, whisper to themselves, and/or mouth the words silently. They become capable of silent reading in the Pattern Phase. This type of reading is suitable for the intermediate Phonemic Awareness Phase through the Latin/Greek Phase.

## Ways to Teach Reading

When teaching reading, use three types of reading instruction:

> choral reading
>
> guided reading (used in reading groups)
>
> class reading

The type used depends on the students' phases.

<u>Choral Reading</u> consists of people reading aloud in unison. It can be used for memory reading, echo reading, and decodable-text reading. Choral Reading is suitable for the Emergent Phase, Phonemic Awareness Phase, Pattern Phase, and Syllable Phase.

<u>Guided Reading</u> consists of any type of reading done by an individual student with the support of an adult. It is used whenever the reading material is too challenging for the student to do independently, but that is at her instructional level. However, the main type of guided reading in a classroom is reading-group reading, reading done in a group with one teacher and several students who are at the same level. Students take turns reading aloud and the teacher provides support while the other students use their finger and then just their eyes to follow along in their books. It is suitable for the Phonemic Awareness Phase, Pattern Phase, Syllable Phase, and Latin/Greek Phase.

Class Reading is reading done from a book selected by the teacher for the entire class. Reading can be done: 1) silently in class or as homework; or 2) aloud with one student reading at a time and the rest of the class following along in their books. The class then discusses the reading together under the guidance of the teacher. Both formats (silent and aloud) should be used. To do class reading, the entire class (or >85% of it) should be able to do independent silent reading at the level of the selected book. While class reading can begin in 3rd Grade, it must be done from 4th through 8th Grade. Class reading is suitable for the Syllable Phase and Latin/Greek Phase.

**Putting It All Together**

Students will use different types of reading based on their phase. Consequently, classroom instruction must change as students advance through the phases. Fortunately, these transitions are smooth, overlapping from one phase to the next. Table 3.15.1 illustrates how the types of reading and ways to teach reading change across the phases.

**Table 3.15.1: Quick Reference for Teaching Reading by Phase**

| Type of Reading | Emergent Phase | Phonemic Awareness Phase | Pattern Phase | Syllable Phase | Latin/Greek Phase |
|---|---|---|---|---|---|
| Memory Reading | X | X | | | |
| Echo Reading | X | X | | | |
| Decodable-Text | | X | X | X | |
| Independent Reading | | X | X | X | X |
| **Teaching Method** | | | | | |
| Choral Reading | X | X | X | X | |
| Guided-Reading | | X | X | X | X |
| Class Reading | | | | X | X |

Use your students' phases to determine the best ways to teach reading and to decide what kind of reading your students should do.

## 3. Preparation

There are many things to prepare over the summer:

- Select/Create reading material for your students.
- Create a classroom library.
- Choose read-aloud books.
- Write questions for reading groups.

**Select/Create Reading Material**

First it is necessary to obtain suitable reading material for your class. It is relatively easy to compile suitable reading material for the Pattern and Syllable Phases, but it can be a challenge to find good reading material for the Phonemic Awareness Phase. Therefore, *The Roadmap to Literacy* recommends that you make your own readers in 1st Grade and choose suitable material for 2nd and 3rd Grade.

<u>Steiner's Indications</u>: This advice is in keeping with Waldorf tradition. Steiner was fine with teachers using primers (Trostli 2004, 190). However, he was critical of some published reading anthologies because he thought the texts were so inane that they created philistines. Consequently, he asked teachers to compile their own anthologies (Trostli 2004, 167).

Note: While Steiner was referring to German readers from 100 years ago, it is possible that the situation is even worse in English today because the words in the first layer of the English layer cake are the concrete nouns of everyday existence: cat, dog, sit, jump, etc. Books in English that are limited to decodable words are by definition limited in content.

<u>Text Levels</u>

When choosing or creating decodable-text material, independent reading material, or books for class reading, consider its text level and match it to the students' phases. (When choosing material for memory reading or echo reading, the text level does not matter. Choose material at any level.)

We have taken a description of text levels which is adapted by Sachem Literacy Coaches from the books *The Continuum of Literacy Learning Grades K–2* and *The Continuum of Literacy Learning Grades 3–5* by Pinnell and Fountas and paired it with the phases in *The Roadmap to Literacy*.

- Emergent Phase: NA—use memory reading
- Phonemic Awareness Phase: Levels A–D
- Pattern Phase: Levels E–M
- Syllable Phase: Level M and higher

Here is a description of each level:

- Level A: One simple sentence per page. Sentence falls on one line. Illustrations predominate. Word usage: predominantly sight words with nouns that match the illustrations.

- Level B: One sentence that falls over two lines of text. Illustrations predominate. Word usage: predominantly sight words with nouns that match the illustrations.

- Level C: 2–6 lines of text per page with lots of repeated lines and phrases. Illustrations predominate. Word usage: predominantly sight words with nouns that match the illustrations.

- Level D: 2–6 lines of text per page with fewer repeated words/phrases. Illustrations predominate. Word usage: mix of sight words, simple decodable words, compound words, and words ending in –ing.

- Level E: 3–8 lines of text per page. Illustrations predominate. Word usage: mix of sight words, simple decodable words, compound words, and words ending in –ing.

- Level F: Multisyllable decoding (e.g., unhappy). Text and illustrations are coming into balance. Word usage: all of the above plus contractions and possessives.

- Level G: 3–8 lines of text per page. Text is smaller and may contain a few challenging vocabulary words. Text and illustrations are coming into balance. Word usage: same as level F.

- Level H: Text contains more challenging vocabulary. Text and illustration are roughly balanced. Students often begin reading these books silently to themselves.

- Level I: Short texts (8–16 pages) and easy chapter books (40–60 pages). Books often contain illustrations although not necessarily on every page. Sentences get longer (i.e., some go longer than ten words). Students often can read these books fluently with expression.

- Level J: Wide variety of texts (simple biographies, short chapter books, informational text). Sentences get longer. Illustrations tend to be smaller or less frequent.

- Level K: Expanded variety of texts (all of the above plus realistic fiction, fantasy, and traditional literature). Number of characters increases. Illustrations tend to be smaller or less frequent.

- Level L: Number of illustrations decreases; Student is learning new concepts through reading; consequently, student needs to vary reading pace. Use of words includes technical words and content-specific words. Example: *Amelia Bedelia*.

- Level M: Fiction chapter books such as series books or mysteries; Characters undergo change in the story. Examples: *The Littles,* some books in The Magic Tree House series, and *Flat Stanley*.

- Level N: Examples: *Amber Brown* and some books in The Magic Tree House series.

- Level O: Examples: *The Boxcar Children, Pippi Longstockings,* and Beverly Cleary books *(Ramona,* etc.).

The text levels go up to Z, but this information will get you started for planning materials for Waldorf Grades 1–3.

Creating 1st Grade Reading Material

There are two types of readers you will need: Memory Readers and decodable-text. **Memory Readers** are collections of the speech material that your class will memory read together. **Decodable-texts** are leveled readers that use simplified text suited for beginners. They feature common sight words, decodable words, and illustrations that match.

When compiling material for your Memory Readers, include lots of verses and poems that contain vocabulary of a higher order. To a certain extent, this type of reader can offset the banality of decodable-texts.

When compiling material for decodable-texts, first research the kinds of decodable-texts that are available to you. Many schools have a collection of easy phonics readers. You can determine their text level by using the chart.

You can also fill in missing pieces by purchasing phonics readers on line. However, it is often easier and quicker to create material for the Phonemic Awareness Phase yourself, particularly if you are dissatisfied with your options.

How to Create Memory Readers

It is not hard to create a physical book to accompany the memory reading you will do in 1st Grade. Just follow these steps:

1. After you have selected your speech material and scheduled your memory reading for your block plans, type or handwrite the words to each piece in a large font. Each piece will be one page of your Memory Reader. It is good to have both typed and handwritten entries so students get used to seeing both types of print.

   Note: You may want to make two books. The first features material from September through December. The second features material from January on. As an added bonus, you can send the first book home with each student over the holiday so they can continue to practice at home.

2. Add an illustration or two to each page if you are so inclined.

   Note: Unless you want to spend a fortune on color copying, it is best if the illustration is a simple black-and-white drawing that is easily reproducible on a copier. A simple drawing in the corner of the page will suffice. It can help the students identify the piece.

3. Make a table of contents with page numbers for each entry.

4. Make a fancy cover if you are so inclined.

   Note: A beautiful color drawing would be very appropriate, and it would not cost very much to make one color copy per book.

5. Bind the material together with a staple or several staples. You could also create these books using the school binding machine or have it done at a copy center.

How to Create Decodable-Texts

It is remarkably easy to create your own decodable-texts for beginners. Jennifer Militzer-Kopperl made an (unpublished) series for a struggling student (see chapter 6.6 #10). Once she perfected her process, it only took 45 minutes to an hour to compose the story and make the book (including simple illustrations).

We suggest that you write most of your stories over the summer but plan on making a few others during the school year as needed. Students love stories about themselves and their experiences. You can write a class story about a trip or a walk the students experienced; however, as a teacher, it is best not to write about individual students to avoid jealousy. (If you are homeschooling, it would be a good idea.)

Here are the steps:

1. Schedule your block plan. Pay particular attention to phonics rules, sight words, etc.

2. Look at the phonics rule(s) and the sight words the class already knows or will be working on. For example, the Silent *E* Rule and related sight words that end in *E* such as *these, come,* etc.

3. Generate a list of content words that could go in a story by using onsets and rimes.

   a. Find common rimes for the phonics rule in question (e.g., *–ape* and *–one* for the Silent *E* rule).

   b. Plug these rimes into The Rhyming Rime Machine in table 3.15.2 to generate a list of words (cross out any words that are undesirable). Some examples of *–ape* and *–one* words include: *cape, gape, nape, tape, grape, scrape, drape, bone, cone, hone, zone, crone, drone, clone, scone,* and *stone*.

**Table 3.15.2: The Rhyming Rime Machine**

| Onsets: One Consonant | | Onsets: R-Blends | Onsets: L-Blends | Onsets: S-Blends | Onsets: W-Blends |
|---|---|---|---|---|---|
| B | P | Br | Bl | Sc | Sw |
| C | Qu | Cr | Cl | Sk | Tw |
| D | R | Dr | Fl | Sl | |
| F | S | Fr | Gl | Sm | |
| G | T | Gr | Pl | Sn | |
| H | V | Pr | Sl | Sp | |
| J | W | Tr | | Squ | |
| K | X | | | St | |
| L | Y | | | | |
| M | Z | | | | |
| N | | | | | |

Use these words to brainstorm scenarios for plots. For example, someone got a lime cone and a grape scone or someone drove a car in the red zone and hit a cone, etc. (If you do not like the words you generated, merely generate more through The Rhyming Rime Machine.)

4. Mock up one of the plots by following these guidelines:

    a.    Add a character (a person whose name illustrates the phonics rule or a recurring character you make up). For example, Eve, Steve, Gabe, and Jane.

    b.    Take a scenario for a plot and run with it. Say "*yes*" to whatever happens—like in improvisational theatre—to create funny twists. For example, Eve buys one lime cone and one grape scone. Which should she eat first? Both! (Draw a funny picture of Eve puzzled as to how to open her mouth wide enough to eat them). Another example: Steve hit the cone in the zone. The police chased him and gave him a fine.

5. Write a rough draft around your scenario.

    a.    Length: Strive for an even numbers of pages. (It is easier to make the physical book if the pages are even.)

        i.    Easy decodable-text readers should be 6 or 8 pages with one or two short sentences on each page and an illustration.

        ii.    Intermediate decodable-text readers can expand up to 10 or 12 pages with two or three sentences on each page and an illustration.

        iii.    Advanced decodable-text readers can be 12–20 pages with two, three, or four sentences on each page and an illustration.

    b.    Ideas for fleshing out the plot to expand the length of the book:

        i.    Add descriptions for sanguine students (e.g., green, sweet lime cone).

        ii.    Add emotions for melancholic students (e.g., Eve felt good, bad, fine, etc.).

        iii.    Add action and suspense for choleric students (e.g., Steve hit the cone and the police chased him.).

        iv.    Add repetitions and food for phlegmatic students (e.g., Steve hit one cone. Steve hit two cones. Steve hit three cones. Steve had grape pop in the car.).

    c.    Additional Suggestions:

        i.    If the students do not know blends yet or past tense, add the words do or did to verbs. For example, Steve did stop vs. Steve stops or Steve stopped.

        ii.    Use illustrations to help carry the story. For example, draw a picture of the police car behind Steve's car when he is hitting the cones. Have the students predict what will happen next when the reading group works with the story.

        iii.    Make a cover page with the title of the story and the author's name. For example, Steve and the Cone Zone by Jennifer Militzer-Kopperl.

      iv.    Optional: Add a final page that says The End and that has a humorous sketch implying what will happen next. For example, Eve holding her stomach because she ate too much.

6. Make the Master Copy

    a.    Figure out how many pages your story will be. Jigger the text to make the page numbers even.

    b.    Take half that many sheets of white paper.

    c.    Fold the stack of pages in half.

    d.    Number your pages. Do not number the backside. Leave it blank. That way, nothing will bleed through when you make copies.

    e.    Write your text and draw your picture on its correct page.

        i.    Write the text at the bottom of the page in heavy black Sharpie using your neatest printing.

        ii.    Draw a simple black and white picture above the text to illustrate the story.

    f.    When done, make a cover page with the title of your story and your name. (Fold another page in half and add it to the stack of numbered pages.)

7. Copy your book

    a.    Use your school's photocopier to make copies of the book. You can make enough for your largest reading group (6 students + 1 for the teacher) and plan on reusing the book for the different reading groups or you can make enough to give each student a copy to take home to read if it is an extra special book. Note: Two-sided copies are not recommended. It is difficult to get the pages to line up and the Sharpie tends to bleed through.

    b.    Optional step: Use a different colored piece of paper for the cover.

    c.    Take one complete set of copies (including front cover). Fold them in half to make the book. Use an extra-long stapler to put two staples through the center fold to hold the book together.

Note: Waldorf teachers are taught to make beautiful illustrations using crayons and paint rather than draw with lines. However, when making decodable-text, use simple black and white line drawings. Beautiful color illustrations will not copy well on a photocopier, they cost more, and they take too long to make. Instead, use your time to perfect the story so it is a worthwhile text for early decoding practice.

## Compiling 2nd and 3rd Grade Reading Material

In 2nd and 3rd Grade, when your students are in the Pattern and Syllable Phases, you can use pre-made readers such as *Fee Fi Fo Fum* by Arthur Pittis. You can also choose suitable reading material by following the text level guidelines. *The Roadmap to Literacy* does not recommend creating your own reading material. The students should no longer need to memory read and there are many suitable books available on the market for students in the Pattern and Syllable Phases.

**Class Library**

The second thing to do is set up a class library over the summer.

Work with your mentor and colleagues to develop a list of recommended books for each level of reading. Know the level of each book on your list so you can recommend more challenging books and easier books as needed. Ann Grandin, librarian for the San Francisco Waldorf School, has created lists of books organized by grade level, genres, and subjects. They include a brief description of each book. Go to http://sfwaldorf_org/grade-school/academics/student-support/library to find these summer reading lists.

Use these lists and other books to create a library for your class. Stock your classroom library with lots of these books for students to check out and have at their desk. You can get these books from many sources. Used bookstores and recycled goods stores such as Goodwill are great for finding quality yet inexpensive literature. In addition, ask parents to donate their children's used books to the classroom library. Finally, library book sales and garage sales can be good sources for used books. Divide the books into three categories: beginning readers, intermediate, and advanced. (We used three different colors of stick-on circles to indicate a book's level.) In 1st Grade, include copies of memory reading material, echo reading material, and published kid writing stories (see chapter 3.13 #2).

During the school year, set the expectation that students who are finished with their work are to read quietly at their desks. If they do not have a book, they are to go to the library and check one out (see chapter 3.15 #11).

**Choose Read-Aloud Books**

The final thing to do over the summer is to choose books to read to your class (often referred to as *read-aloud* books). Be sure to ask your mentor and other teachers for ideas, but ultimately you need to select the books that will best meet the needs of your students. One rule of thumb is to choose stories that are about children close to the age of your class.

Because read-aloud books are usually read in 5–15 minute spans of time, it will take you 1–3 months to read one book. You can schedule read-aloud time during the first 5–10 minutes of snack/lunch time, during the beginning of handwork while the teacher is getting the students set up, when a special subject teacher is running late or is absent, etc. Use this reading time to model how to read well. The only academic instruction you will do with these books is in 3rd Grade, when you use one of them to model how to write a book report (see chapter 3.14 #8) and as an opportunity to ask prediction HOTS questions (see chapter 3.8 #2).

**Write Questions for Reading Groups**

In 2nd and 3rd Grade, prepare questions for reading groups. Read each book you plan to assign to the students and write comprehension questions over the summer. Include one or more group discussion questions and written comprehension questions. Use a mix of factual recall questions and HOTS questions (see chapter 3.8 #2).

Doing this work over the summer will give you the materials you need for the school year.

## 4. Scheduling

When preparing your curriculum, you can use the block plan templates in Appendices 1–3 or you can create your own. If you create your own, use the following points to lay out your blocks:

1. Begin instruction:
    a.  Memory reading: Start at the beginning of 1st Grade.
    b.  Decodable-text/leveled reading/reading group: Start after students can decode CVC words (by the end of the third language arts practice block in 1st Grade at the latest).
    c.  Independent reading: Start in the middle of 1st Grade (Use old memory reading texts and students' kid writing).
2. It will take students years to master reading fluency because the texts will get harder each year.
3. Teach in the following lesson segments:
    a.  Memory reading: Teach in the Reading/Writing segment or Speech/Song segment, two segments added to a few blocks in 1st Grade to provide extra time for these skills (see chapter 2.3 #4 and Appendix 1A, 1C, and 1E).
    b.  Decodable-text/leveled reading/reading group: Teach as follows:
        •   1st Grade: Reading/Writing segment
        •   2nd Grade: Bookwork segment
        •   3rd Grade: Scheduled ongoing reading groups during practice blocks (three practice classses per week).
    c.  Independent reading: Practice daily whenever students finish their work.
4. Use the following teaching rhythm:
    a.  Memory reading: Daily until the students start decodable-text, then less often.
    b.  Decodable-text/leveled reading/reading group: 2–3 times a week per group (1/week for advanced groups).
    c.  Independent reading: Daily when students finish work (either using memory reading text or decodable-text as appropriate).
5. Number of minutes needed per lesson:
    a.  Memory reading: 10 minutes
    b.  Decodable-text/leveled reading/reading group: 15–20 minutes per group
    c.  Independent reading: Variable: when the students are done with their work, they read independently throughout the entire school day.
6. Number of minutes of reading per grade:
    a.  1st Grade: 5 –15 minutes daily
    b.  2nd Grade: 20 –30 minutes daily
    c.  3rd Grade; 30+ minutes daily (including reading at home)
7. Once you have finished teaching reading in Grades 1–3, segue into additional time for reading groups and/or class readers and individual readers beginning in 4th Grade.

## 5.   Initial Introduction

**Prerequisites:** The students can sing "The *ABC* Song."

**Background Information:** Young children usually learn the alphabet by singing "The *ABC* Song." Thus their first experience of letters is through speech. It is easy to transition them into graphemes, the written letters, by teaching the students to memory read the lyrics to the song.

**When to Teach:** The initial introduction of reading occurs the first day of the first full week of school (i.e., the first day of the first language arts main lesson block).

**Sample Lesson:** The introduction to memory reading is also the introduction of the alphabet. (This information is also presented in chapter 3.1 #6.)

First Memory Reading Lesson (Introduction to the Alphabet)

Sing "The *ABC* Song" together as a class. Then open up your chalkboard where the lyrics of "The *ABC* Song" have already been written (see table 3.15.3). Ask the students to watch what you do as you sing the song again. Use a long pointer (or yardstick) to point to each letter (and the final words) on the board as you sing. Students will literally see what they have sung. Then ask the students to read along with you as you <u>speak</u> each line. These lyrics will be their first practice in memory reading.

**Table 3.15.3:**

```
The ABC Song

A B C D E F G
H I J K
L M N O P
Q R S
T U V
W X
Y and Z
Now I know my ABCs
Next time won't you sing with me?
```

Note: when singing this song, add a break between K and L so that the students have enough breath left to clearly articulate LMNOP.

**Practice:** Continue to practice memory reading the lyrics to the "The *ABC* Song" on a daily basis throughout the first block. First sing it and point to each letter; then say it and point to each letter. Vary your practice:

- Have a student point to the letters with the pointer while the class memory reads the lyrics.
- Sing just one line of the song (e.g., *LMNOP*) and then ask the students to locate just that line.
- Ask the students to find an individual letter such as *T*. (Show them how to find it by memory reading while pointing to each letter and stopping on the correct letter.)
- Give each student a copy of the lyrics to read. Teach the students to touch each letter/word with their finger as they sing or say it.

Note: When you write out the lyrics, make sure to start a new line of print for each new line of the song. Also leave spaces between the letters.

## 6. How to Teach Reading in the Emergent Phase

**Objective:** Teach students to memory read.

**Prerequisite:** Students can sing "The *ABC* Song."

**Prep Work:** Use this advice to choose appropriate memory reading material.

1. Choose pieces that have long and short English vowel sounds. Recall that many Waldorf resources use the broad sound for *A* (/ah/ as in *all*) rather than the short sound (/ă/ as in *at*). Avoid using these pieces with beginners (see chapter 3.1 #2 *The Sound for the Letter A*).

2. Avoid tongue twisters and other alliterative text for memory reading. When each word begins with the same letter, the students in the Emergent Phase lose a primary means to determine which word is which.

**When to Teach:** Teach daily in the Skills Practice segment or the Reading/Writing segment in 1st Grade.

**How to Teach:** Use choral reading to do both memory reading and echo reading.

<u>Memory Reading Format</u>

Use speech activities that students have memorized including song lyrics. Write the words on the board. Follow this format:

1. Day One: choral reading as a whole class

2. Day Two: choral reading in groups (e.g., row one reads the first line, row two the second, etc.)

3. Days Three and on: pick and choose from these options:

    a. Have a student point to the letters and ending words with the pointer while the class memory reads them.

    b. Say just one line of the verse and ask the students to locate that line.

    c. If your class is ready, consider giving each student their own copy of the lyrics to read from. Teach the students to finger point while they read. Their finger serves as the pointer.

Plan to work with the same text for at least a week and maybe more depending on the length of the poem or song. Once the students seem to be comfortable working with the piece in different ways, it is time to move on to a new poem or song lyrics. Put a copy of the lyrics in the class library for students to memory read on their own when they finish their work. Add a little sketch on the side so students have a picture to help them identify the piece.

<u>Echo Reading Format</u>

Pick an unfamiliar <u>short</u> passage with words that begin with the letters you have introduced. Follow this format:

1. Day One

    a. Read the entire piece to the students.

    b. Read the first line and point to each word with a pointer.

c. Have class *echo read*. Point to each word as the class says the line together with you.

d. Repeat for each subsequent line.

e. End by reading the entire piece together as you point to each word.

2. Day Two

    a. Read the entire piece to the students.

    b. Read the first line and point to each word with a pointer.

    c. Have the first row *echo read*. Point to each word as they say the line together with you. Repeat this process with each row. Then proceed to the next line and repeat.

    d. End by reading the entire piece together as you point to each word.

3. Day Three (echo reading has become memory reading)

    a. Pass out a copy of the text.

    b. Have the entire class read the passage with you as you say it. Point to each word on the board as the students point to each word on their copy (no echoing). Then observe their process, as you move about the room. Help those students who are struggling to follow along.

    c. Have each row take one of the lines and read it together as you point to each word on the board. (The rest of the class follows along pointing to each word on their paper-no echoing.)

    d. Ask if there are any students that would like to read the entire passage. Those who would like to do so can do it together as you point to each word. The others follow along on their paper, pointing to each word.

Plan to work with the same text for at least a week. Once the students seem to be comfortable working with the piece in different ways, it is time to move on to a new piece. Put a copy in the class library for students to memory read on their own when they finish their work. Add a little sketch on the side so students have a picture to help them identify the piece.

## Practice: Reading Games to Play with the Emergent Phase Reading

With both memory reading and echo reading, play phonemic awareness games such as *Find My Word*. To play *Find My Word*, ask the children to find one of the words in the text. One of the ways they can do this is to recite the poem and point to each word until they say the word in question. Another game is to ask students to find the word in the second line that begins, for example, with the /b/ sound, etc. Have the students discuss how they found the word, thus nudging everyone towards using their developing phonemic awareness skills and knowledge of letters.

## 7. How to Teach Reading in the Phonemic Awareness Phase

**Objectives:** Finish teaching memory reading and echo reading. Introduce simple decodable-text and independent reading. Teach the following reading strategy: predicting.

**Prerequisites:**

1. Students realize letters represent sounds.

2. Students are able to find the letters they know in a passage.

**Prep Work: Choosing Memory Reading Material**

Follow the same protocol for memory reading as outlined in the Emergent Phase but be sure to include tongue twisters and pieces that are alliterative. These force the students to consider the end sound of words, not just the beginning sound.

**Background Information:** A lot is going on in the Phonemic Awareness Phase. In this phase, students must transition from memory reading to the beginning of independent reading. Guided reading using decodable-text is the means for helping the students make this transition.

**When to Teach:** Teach daily in the Reading/Writing segment of main lesson.

**How to Teach:** Use choral reading to do memory reading and echo reading for the first half of the Phonemic Awareness Phase. In the second half, add in guided reading for simple decodable-text reading. Throughout the phase, have the students do independent reading.

Memory Reading Format: Follow the same advice as from the Emergent Phase, but give each student their own copy of the lyrics to read from rather than doing all of the work on the board. Teach the students to finger point while they read. Their fingers serve as the pointer.

Echo Reading Format: Choose longer pieces and follow the same format as in the Emergent Phase.

Simple Decodable-Text Reading: Starting in the middle of the Phonemic Awareness Phase, begin simple decodable-text in reading groups. (Eighty percent or more of the class should be there by the third language arts practice block or the fourth language arts main lesson block of the year.) For a period of time, you will do both memory reading as a class and simple decodable-text in reading groups (see chapter 3.15 #10).

Here are the prerequisites that show the majority of the students are ready for simple decodable-text:

a. Students are proficient at memory reading (i.e., they can point to words as they read them and self-correct when they are off).

b. Students are automatic with identifying all of the letters of the alphabet and their sounds.

c. Students are capable of decoding CVC words (both real and nonsense).

d. Students know all 20 sight words on *The Roadmap to Literacy's* Sight Word list–Set 1 (see Appendix 4).

Note: For that small group of students who are not ready for decodable-text, continue memory reading. Also, when working with their reading groups, focus on improving those areas that are preventing the students from beginning decodable-text. In addition to the prerequisites listed above, include more practice in phonemic awareness if necessary.

Independent Reading: The first forays towards independent reading are when students practice reading the adult writing in their kid writing assignments and when they go back over the various memory reading texts they have worked with in class. The third foray occurs when they reread the leveled readers they have read in reading group on their own or to a classmate. By the end of the Phonemic Awareness Phase, students will begin true independent reading as they pick up unfamiliar leveled readers and attempt to read on their own. They will read slowly and haltingly, they will make mistakes, and they will subvocalize. All of these traits are hallmarks of the Phonemic Awareness Phase and will improve with practice.

Set the expectation that whenever students finish an assignment, they can either read or write. Their reading material can be memory reading, kid writing, familiar leveled readers, and new leveled readers. They can read to themselves using sub-vocalization or they can read with a classmate who is also done.

<u>Predicting</u>: Predicting is a useful reading strategy in the Phonemic Awareness Phase as a shortcut for underdeveloped decoding skills however, it is necessary to help the students transform this strategy into a better strategy: self-correcting (see chapter 1.6 #4).

Instead of decoding every unfamiliar word, students in the Phonemic Awareness Phase will use their concept imagery plus rudimentary phonological awareness to make educated guesses about words, especially if there is an illustration available.

For example, say a student is reading a text that says "*I have a dog.*" There is a picture of a child standing next to a small dog. The student may use predicting to guess the word "*dog*" without sounding it out. The student might also say "*puppy*" instead of dog because it would also match the picture.

You can help students develop the ability to predict by modeling good book skills. You can show the students the pictures and talk about what the story will likely be about. By talking about it ahead of time, the students are primed to use the pictures to help them figure out unfamiliar words.

Note: This strategy is only appropriate at the very beginning of learning to read. It has a short shelf life. Do not let it go much beyond the 1st Grade Phonemic Awareness Phase. What is beneficial quickly becomes detrimental when applied at the wrong time.

In the Phonemic Awareness Phase, help students grow beyond their guessing by showing them how to fix the error when their guess is off. (Refer to error handling in table 3.3.3).

1. Acknowledge what the student did well: "Puppy sure would make sense."
2. Then draw her attention to what is wrong: "But *puppy* begins with the /p/ sound, and I see that this word starts with the letter *D*, not *P*."
3. Show her how to fix it: "Let's sound out this word and see what it says: /d/ /ŏ/ /g/... .dog! It says 'I have a <u>dog</u>.'"

As students begin to decode more and more on their own, this strategy can be transformed into a related skill: <u>Self-Correcting</u>. It will be discussed in the Pattern Phase.

**Practice: Reading Games for Choral Reading in the Phonemic Awareness Phase**

Use the same games as in the Emergent Phase but include Eraser Gnome and Punctuation Tap

<u>Eraser Gnome Game</u>: On one of the days following the introduction of a memory reading passage, erase at least one word from each lines of text you are using. Do this before school begins. (Make sure the word begins with a letter you have introduced or is a sight word you have taught.) Have the students identify the missing words using their developing phonemic awareness skills and sight word knowledge. If a sight word is missing, have someone come up and write in the missing word. For other missing words, ask if anyone knows how to spell that word. (This suggestion gives more advanced spellers an opportunity to use their skills.) Choose a student to come up and fill in the missing word.

<u>Punctuation Tap</u> is a game to teach the students to pause for punctuation marks even before you formally introduce them. You can have the class tap or clap twice for a stop sign (i.e., a period, question mark, or exclamation mark) and once for pause (i.e., a comma). Then you can assign one row of students the job of clapping the punctuation while the rest of the students have to read and pause appropriately. Finally, you can

have the students read and pause appropriately. You can use the pointer to tap on the board if the class blows through the punctuation traffic signs.

## 8.   How to Teach Reading in the Pattern Phase

**Objective:** Continue decodable-text and independent reading. Teach students to read unfamiliar speech and song lyrics from the board and to self-correct when they make an error.

**Prerequisite:** Students can read simple decodable-texts that contain the sight words and all phonics rules taught in 1st Grade.

**Background Information:** In the Pattern Phase, students make the transition from slow, halting decoding to smooth and silent reading—albeit when decoding at a grade-appropriate level.

**When to Teach:** Teach reading in the Bookwork segment, the Skills Practice segment, and/or the Opening segment. The number of times per week will vary.

**How to Teach:** Use guided reading for simple decodable-text reading. Throughout the phase, have the students do independent reading. Use speech and song lyrics for guided reading.

Simple Decodable-Text Reading: It is necessary to assess the students and put them into appropriate reading groups (see chapter 3.15 #10).

Independent Reading: Create an independent reading program for each student (see chapter 3.15 #11).

Guided Reading: Speech and Song Lyrics from the Board: Even though you will no longer be using memory reading as your reading curriculum, you still will have the students read poems—the difference is that you will put the poems up on the board to read before the students learn them rather than after. Use this opportunity to teach guided reading and demonstrate how to sound out multisyllabic words. An example follows:

*Quiet ferns with curling heads*
*Are resting in their garden beds.*
*Fuzzy fiddleheads unfurl*
*Emerald kirtles spin and twirl.*
*Excerpt from "My Garden" by Elliot Drake-Maurer, 5th Grade student*

Ask a student to read the entry aloud. When she gets to a multisyllabic word that she cannot read, model how to sound it out by breaking the word down into syllables. Cover up all but one syllable at a time and read each syllable as you go: fid/dle/heads, un/furl, em/er/alds, kir/tles. (Note: You are modeling a variation on the process students will learn in the Syllable Phase when they learn to break the words into syllables to decode them. You are not modeling the dictionary breaks for syllables.) Then have the student(s) repeat after you. This practice will allow them to begin to use the same strategy when they encounter longer words in their independent reading. They will learn the rules for decoding with syllables in the next phase.

Curriculum Connections: You can teach vocabulary from speech lyrics on the board (see chapter 3.12 #7). You can also practice decoding with phonics rules with speech lyrics on the board (see chapter 3.4 #8).

Self-Correcting: Self-Correcting is a reading skill that students in the Pattern Phase need to master.

Students use concept imagery to alert them to mistakes they have made because what they read did not make sense. Let's say that the text says, "*She rides a horse,*" but the student reads it as, "*She rides a* house." The student realizes her mistake because of concept imagery: the mental picture is of a girl sitting on top of a house, riding it. By going back to re-read the sentence, she can use her skills in sound/symbol awareness and decoding to realize that the word was *horse* not *house* because the vowel was *OR*, not *OU* (see chapter 1.6 #4). Students should be self-correcting in the Pattern Phase, when they start to build up some fluency.

You can help students develop this skill by modeling it in class. Teach it by reading a passage from the board to the class and making a deliberate mistake that could be detected from concept imagery. Then model finding the error.

For example, the text says, "*David is afraid of snakes; he thinks they will bite him*," but you read it as, "*David is afraid of* snacks; *he thinks they will bite him.*" Say, "*Hmm…that didn't make any sense*," and explore your error through concept imagery. ("*I imagined David getting bitten by potato chips and veggie sticks. That doesn't make any sense.*") Then model looking at the word in question and discovering your error using symbol imagery. ("*SNAKES—the E would make the A say its name.*" Sound out the word slowly. "*That says snakes! David is afraid of* snakes; *he thinks they will bite him. That makes more sense.*") Just make sure that you have taught the rule in question first.

Note: You can use economy in teaching and address the melancholic temperament at the same time by being delighted that you were able to find your mistake. You can change the tenor of your class around mistakes by making it fun and interesting to find them and fix them. Hold the attitude that mistakes are not something to hide—they are opportunities to learn from! "*Smart people acknowledge their mistakes and fix them.*" If you model lightness around your own errors, intended and otherwise, your class will benefit.

Once the tenor is set, you can develop a class habit. If someone is reading aloud and makes a mistake that is detectable from concept imagery, ask, "*Did that make sense?*" and then explore the error. If it is safe to make mistakes in your class, students will quickly get the idea and will learn how to monitor themselves (see chapter 6.1 #11). This good habit will carry over into their independent reading, and they will monitor themselves.

## 9.   How to Teach Reading in the Syllable Phase

**Objectives:** Continue to use reading groups with decodable-text at each group's level. Throughout the phase, have the students do independent reading. Teach students to read nonfiction (optional).

**Prerequisite:** Students are proficient at decoding with digraphs (i.e., vowel and consonant teams). (Note: Encoding proficiency is not expected at this time.)

**When to Teach:** Teach reading in the Bookwork segment and the Opening segment. The number of times per week will vary.

**How to Teach:**

Guided Reading: Speech and Song Lyrics from the Board: Continue having students read poems or song lyrics before they learn them (see chapter 3.15 #8). Use this opportunity to practice decoding by syllable with phonics rules (see chapter 3.4 #9).

Decodable-Text Reading: It is necessary to assess the students and put them into appropriate reading groups (see chapter 3.15 #10).

Independent Reading: Create an independent reading program for each student (see chapter 3.15 #11).

Nonfiction: Optional—It can be taught in 3rd or 4th Grade.

It is good to teach students to read nonfiction. It is an entirely different type of reading. Reading fiction involves getting carried away by the story—the plot, the emotions, the suspense. Reading nonfiction involves engaging with the text through the head, and it involves a slow, analytical process. However, mastering it will serve the students well when they go on to research and write reports and when they study subjects such as history, geography, and zoology beginning in 4th Grade.

Give the class a short passage that is nonfiction. It could be about a local occupation during the Home Surroundings Block. Tell the class that this work is nonfiction and explain what that means. When you read nonfiction, there is a process you should follow:

1. Before you begin reading, you:

   • Look over the title, author, pictures, and subheadings.

   • Ask 1–3 factual questions that you hope to find the answers for while reading.

For example, if your passage is about building a house using timber frames, one of your questions could be "*What is a timber frame?*"

2. As you are reading:

   • Check at the end of each paragraph to see if one or more of your questions have been answered. If so, write down a brief answer (key words, phrases).

   • Write new questions if new questions come up.

For example, Timber frame = building with heavy timbers, not 2 x 4s. New question: Why is it used?

3. After you finish reading:

   • Review your questions. Answer them if you can. Write in full sentences.

   • Briefly summarize the text in one sentence (main idea).

For example, Timber framing is building with heavy timbers, not 2 x 4s, to make a very sturdy building.

Practice reading nonfiction together two or three times as a class. Then have desk partners work together to read nonfiction. Give the students a copy of the steps to remind them what to do. Then have students read nonfiction on their own.

## 10. How to Differentiate Instruction: Reading Groups

Begin Reading groups in the middle of the Phonemic Awareness Phase as soon as the majority of your students can decode simple CVC words. Continue in the Pattern Phase and Syllable Phase.

### Background Information

The benefit of using reading groups to differentiate instruction is that you can match the text to the level of the students. The students in a class are usually at different reading levels. To be effective, the text level must match the students' levels. If the text is too hard, the students will guess; if it is too easy, they will not be practicing their reading strategies: sight words, decoding, and using the context. Both practices undermine the lesson; the former also undermines the confidence of the least-able readers. Leveled texts in reading groups allow you to meet everyone's needs.

**How to Organize Reading Groups in the Phonemic Awareness Phase and the Pattern Phase (1st and 2nd Grade)**

For reading groups to be successful, they need to be set up appropriately.

Put the students into appropriate reading groups using both formal and informal screening assessment (see chapter 6.2). Once you have an idea of which reading group a student should be in, do a final screening using the actual reader that the group will be using. Have each student read a page to you. (Note: This step can be done during the reading group.) If a student struggles to read the text, consider moving her to a group that will use an easier reader. Try to keep your groups to a maximum of six students. More than that and it is hard to give adequate attention to each student. If you have a big class and a teaching assistant, have the assistant teach some of the groups.

During the first week or so, monitor the students' placements and the level of the text you have selected for each group. Make sure the level of the text is at the instructional level of the students. If a student stumbles over only one word in twenty, the level is too easy and she can read it independently. If the student stumbles over half of the words, the level is too hard and she will become frustrated. You are looking for something in between: the instructional level, the zone where the student needs your help to read and benefits from your guidance. If you have placed a student in the wrong group, move the student to a more appropriate group. If you have selected material that is too easy or too hard for the group, adjust accordingly (see chapter 3.15 #3).

When it comes time to meet with your reading groups, give an assignment to the rest of the class that each can work on independently and quietly. Set the expectation that no one is to interrupt a reading group. See *Classroom Management during Reading Groups* below.

When working with a reading group, pass out a copy of the book to each student. Explain that the students will be taking turns reading and that while another student is reading, they are to follow along quietly in their books. Each student is to use her finger to point at each word as it is being read. (Enforce this rule. A student who is not following along is a student who is getting minimal benefit from the experience.) Let the students know that you will help them if they get stuck. If a student pauses for 3–5 seconds, either provide the word or help the student sound it out. Make sure students honor punctuation, especially periods and commas. Correct mistakes as the students make them. Make sure that every student gets an equal chance to read during every reading group session. Determine how much reading each student should do based on how long the book is and the average student's attention span. For example, in the Phonemic Awareness Phase, have each student start with a sentence and expand to several sentences up to a short page. In the Pattern Phase, have each student read a paragraph or a page if the pages are short.

As you guide the students' reading, make appropriate changes in the group. Advance their reading level as they improve. Move students to different groups if their reading takes off or lags behind.

**How to Organize Reading Groups in the Syllable Phase (3rd Grade)**

It is advisable to schedule reading groups outside of main lesson in 3rd Grade. Set aside two or three practice classes each week for reading groups (see chapter 2.3 #1). These classes will be ongoing and meet throughout the entire school year. Note: These classes will be in addition to the five practice classes set aside for the off block (math in language arts main lessons and language arts in math main lessons). Use parent volunteers to lead some of the reading groups. It is good to schedule these classes at the end of the day or before or after lunch to make it easier for parents to volunteer.

At the beginning of the school year, assess your students and divide them into groups based on ability. You can use fluency testing or mastery of reading skills to group your students (see chapter 3.15 #14). Aim to have no more than six students in a group if possible.

Schedule your reading classes as follows:

1. If the students are reading at or above a 3rd Grade level, have the students take turns reading out loud from a book at their level for the first half of the class (roughly 20–25 minutes). Follow up with a group discussion about the reading (5–7 minutes). For the remainder of the class, have written comprehension questions for the students to answer. These questions should be a mix of factual questions and/or HOTS questions, or give your students one question that is used as the basis for writing a short paragraph (see chapter 3.8 #2 and chapter 3.14 #7). If not writing a paragraph, the students should answer all of the questions in complete sentences.

2. If the students are reading below a 3rd Grade level, spend the first half of the class working on weak reading skills such as sight words, phonemic awareness, phonics rules, decoding, encoding, etc. During the second half, the students should take turns reading out loud from a book at their level. Discuss the material as you read to check comprehension and to model good reading skills.

Before the school year starts, ask for parent volunteers to lead some of your reading groups. Provide a brief training on how to work with the students during reading group time. Give the parents the students who are at or above the class's average reading level while you work with the students who are at the lower level. Be sure to highlight the following points during training:

1. Do not discuss student performance with other parents.

2. How and when to correct students if they make a mistake reading.

3. Your expectations for discipline and how to maintain it.

4. How to work with the questions you prepared over the summer (see chapter 3.15 #3).

Note: It is best if parents do not assist the same reading group that their child is in.

## Classroom Management during Reading Groups

Classroom management is critical to the success of your reading groups.

In 1st Grade and 2nd Grade, teach students to work independently and quietly for short periods of time while you work with reading groups. To be successful, you will need three things:

- well-planned lessons
- clear expectations and consequences
- Integrated Movement Activities (IMAs) during transitions

First, you must create well-planned lessons ahead of time and be clear on what you want the students to do. By matching the activities to the various groups of students and to the class as a whole, you will meet the students' needs. As a result, they will be much more likely to stay on task while you work with a reading group.

Second, you must determine your classroom expectations and consequences ahead of time. The students will live up or down to your expectations. If you tolerate noise, they will learn that it is OK to be noisy. If you insist upon quiet (and hold the line), they will learn that they must be quiet. Be consistent in what you expect and what happens when students do not behave. They will relax into the consistency and then stay on task.

Third, it helps if there are clear times when noise is expected and clear times when quiet is expected and the times are rhythmical. Rhythm replaces strength. The students will get used to the routine and do it automatically.

In 3rd Grade, most of the students will be with a parent volunteer for the entire period. Set out your expectations at the beginning of the year and ask parent volunteers to maintain them. Advise the volunteers on how to handle discipline problems ahead of time. If the students encounter the same expectations in reading group that you use in class, there will be few problems.

## 11. How to Create an Independent Reading Program

Besides participating in reading groups, students should be engaged in an individualized independent reading program. Starting around the middle of 1st Grade, set the expectation that students are to read quietly at their desks when their work is done. Over the years, students will log hours of extra reading practice.

During the school year, each student can pick books at her level. Help students explore a variety of genres and authors. Beginning readers can be somewhat formulaic and contain a repetitive vocabulary and style. If a student wants to read all three titles in a limited series back to back, that is understandable. However, if she is preparing to read her 4th Magic Tree House Book, ask her to alternate genres. (Note: If students really want to read a book that is too advanced for them, encourage their parents to read it to them.)

Some teachers schedule short book talks with students where a student tells the teacher about the book she is reading. This practice is good to use while students in the class are doing independent reading. Use these talks to check in to make sure the student comprehends what she is reading and that the book is at her level. Be sure each student gets a turn before starting over with the first student. Try to schedule one talk with each student over the course of a month.

## 12. Book Reports

See chapter 3.14 #8 for how to teach book reports.

## 13. Practice

Practice is critical. Most of your students' practice will come during their independent reading time. There are many spare minutes in the school day that students can use to practice reading. Make sure your students are reading when they finish their work. In addition, expect the students to read at home. The following are the recommendations for reading practice:

- 1st Grade: 5–15 minutes a day
- 2nd Grade: 20–30 minutes a day
- 3rd Grade on up: 30+ minutes a day

## 14. Assessment

Assessment is a critical part of teaching. It is important to verify that students have mastered the skills they have been taught. See chapter 6.1 for background on assessment.

**Background Information: Fluency**

The best way to assess reading is through **fluency**.

Fluency refers to how quickly and accurately a student can read starting at the end of 2nd Grade. Research has shown that assessing fluency is a good way to measure reading comprehension (Hall 2006, 249). Students who read quickly and accurately almost always understand what they read. It can be a better way to check comprehension than asking them questions about the text when they are done. This fact may seem counterintuitive, but it stands to reason. Students who read easily put all of their attention on comprehension while those who are struggling with word recognition and decoding have to split their attention. In addition, they are less likely to make mistakes, which would also undermine comprehension.

Weak reading fluency undermines comprehension. The student's attention is directed towards decoding and word recognition, rather than meaning. If the student reads particularly slowly, the student may even forget the beginning of the sentence before reaching the end.

Accuracy is crucial because students need to read <u>at least</u> 95% of the words correctly to comprehend what they are reading. In fact, Ken Howell notes in "Performance Criteria for Fluency and Fluency Scores: A Discussion" included in *CORE* that good readers' accuracy is above 97% (Howell 2008, A18).

Let's explore why accuracy is so critical. The first sentence is right; the following are off by just one letter in one word.

Right: There is a bad bug. He lives in the house.

Wrong: There is a <u>bed</u> bug. He lives in the house.

Wrong: There is a bad bug. He lives in the <u>horse</u>.

Misreading just one word in a sentence results in accuracy scores of 90%, which looks good on paper but results in seriously misconstrued mental pictures—in this case, *bed bug infestations or horse diseases.*

If students fail fluency and/or accuracy screenings, go back and assess basic reading skills including decoding skills, sight word recognition, and phonemic awareness.

**Benchmarks** represent <u>minimum</u> levels of student achievement by the end of each grade for students to be on track to handle grade-level work in 4th Grade (see chapter 6.1 #9). Table 3.15.4 contains the benchmarks for reading.

Note: The following benchmarks may not be exhaustive. Prerequisite skills for reading may be covered under other related language arts skills. For a full list of benchmarks, see table 6.1.4.

**Table 3.15.4: Benchmarks for Reading**

|  | 1st Grade | 2nd Grade | 3rd Grade |
|---|---|---|---|
| **Reading Fluency** | NA—Students can read simple decodable-text that contains sight words and all phonics rules taught in 1st Grade, but hold off on formal fluency testing.) | Students can read 2nd Grade passages from any formal reading fluency program. Reading fluency should be a <u>minimum</u> of 61 correct words per minute with >95% accuracy. This fluency score is at or above the 25th percentile for public school students at the end of 2nd Grade.* | Students can read 3rd Grade passages from any formal reading fluency program. Reading fluency should be a <u>minimum</u> of 95 correct words per minute with >95% accuracy. This fluency score is at or above the 40th percentile for public school students at the end of 3rd Grade.* |

*Note: These scores come from the Hasbrouck and Tindal *Oral Reading Fluency Norms Grades 1–8 2005* reprinted in *Assessing Reading Multiple Measures* (Diamond 2008, 80). (See table 6.1.1 for information on interpreting percentiles.)

There are three types of assessments. Recommendations for each type of assessment can be found in chapters 6.3, 6.4, and 6.5. You can use the following ideas as a starting point to set up an assessment program.

**Informal Assessments:** Observe students' reading during reading group.

**Teacher-Made Assessment:** Pick a passage and ask each student to read it aloud to you. Observe how fluently they read and/or count how many words they read per minute and note their errors. (Note: Do not let the other students hear or else they will have memorized the passage after hearing it a number of times.)

**Assessments Created by Educational Testing Groups:** If you choose to do this type of assessment, consider doing it three times a year. Use an assessment of fluency designed by an educational testing group such as DIBELS or AIMSweb (see chapter 6.1 #6). Otherwise use *MASI-R Oral Reading Fluency Measures* found in Diamond's book *Assessing Reading Multiple Measures for Kindergarten through Twelfth Grade, 2nd edition*. *CORE* (Consortium on Reading Excellence, Inc.) Novato: Arena Press, 2008 (see chapter 6.4 #3 and 6.5 #3).

See chapters 6.4 and 6.5 for more information about assessing in 2nd and 3rd Grade.

## 15. How to Help Struggling Students

**Assess:** When you see a student is struggling with reading, do further assessments (both formal and informal) to narrow down the area(s) of concern. Document your findings and place in student's file. Many things can contribute to weak reading skills (see section 6 for more information).

**Additional Instruction/Practice:** Next, use the results of your assessments to provide this student with extra instruction and practice in any weak areas. You can differentiate instruction both in class and in reading groups. For example, give individual assignments to provide extra practice in a weak area or modify what you teach in reading group to provide more practice. Decide which approach is best based on how many other students have similar struggles. Document what you try and the results.

**Remedial Solutions:** Reading is the culmination of different skills. Provide remedial solutions for whichever skill(s) tested weak. If you do not notice improvements in three or four weeks, it is time to contact your mentor for guidance and consult chapter 6.6 for additional information on remedial issues.

**Accommodations and Modifications:** Sometimes it takes a while for remedial issues to be resolved. Meanwhile, the student needs support to function in class. In the case of tracking and eye problems, consider using accommodations and modifications as a temporary measure. There are four good possibilities:

- Give students a copy of material written on the board to use at their desks.

- Use a window card. Get a 3 x 5 card and cut a small window in the center that is big enough to frame one word at a time. The students use it to block out the other words on the page so they can see just one word at a time.

- Use a tracking device that goes under the line of print so students can keep their place. Use a short ruler or 3 x 5 card.

- Use a magnifying bar to enlarge the words on one line (see http://irlen.mybigcommerce.com/educational-aids/).

These accommodations and modifications should be used as temporary measures while students get remedial help with their underlying challenges. They are like casts—when used properly, they provide short-term support that helps facilitate healing; however, when used too long, they can exacerbate the underlying problem and cause further disability. Do not allow accommodations and modifications to take the place of any necessary remediation.

## Conclusion

Reading is truly the culmination of language arts instruction in Grades 1–3. It makes use of almost all of the skills taught in these three grades. It is the key to developing language arts skills in future grades. It is the key to higher education, a prerequisite to success in many professions, and a life-long pleasure. Reading instruction ends at the end of 3rd Grade. In 4th Grade students are no longer learning to read; instead, they will be reading to learn. Make sure your students have mastered this necessary skill so they can move confidently into the 4th Grade curriculum and begin to study subjects. Be prepared to continue to assess reading fluency in each passing grade to make sure students' reading continues to develop appropriately. Recall that students' *word identification hubs* only reach maturity at adolescence and that they need lots of practice to become expert readers (see chapter 1.2 #5).

# 3.16 CURRICULUM CHART ONE: THE 15 ASPECTS OF LANGUAGE ARTS

A curriculum is a list of the skills, concepts, and/or content taught in each grade. This first curriculum chart provides an overview of all the material covered in Section 3.

Note: The 15 language arts skills are either taught by grade and/or phase. **Skills that must be taught by phase are in bold type.**

**Curriculum Chart One: The 15 Language Arts Skills**

| Language Art Skill | 1st Grade | | 2nd Grade | 3rd Grade |
|---|---|---|---|---|
| | **Emergent Phase** | **Phonemic Awareness Phase** | **Pattern Phase** | **Syllable Phase** |
| **Chapter 3.1 Alphabet** | "The *ABC* Song" <br><br> **The first 8–10 letters of the alphabet (uppercase and lowercase)** | **The remaining letters of the alphabet (uppercase and lowercase)** | NA | NA |
| Chapter 3.2 Handwriting | Form drawing (straight and curved lines); <br><br> Uppercase & lowercase printing | Uppercase & lowercase printing | Form drawing (running forms); <br><br> Uppercase & lowercase cursive | Handwriting practice for printing and cursive (smaller lines) |
| **Chapter 3.3 Phonological and Phonemic Awareness** | **1. Sentences into words** <br><br> **2. Words into syllables** <br><br> **3. Beginning phonemic awareness:** <br> • **phoneme matching** <br> • **onset & rime** <br> • **blending phonemes** | **All aspects of phonemic awareness:** <br> • **phoneme matching** <br> • **onset/rime** <br> • **blending** <br> • **sequencing** <br> • **segmenting** <br> • **manipulating** | **Phonemic awareness: manipulating** | **Phonemic awareness: manipulating** <br><br> **Syllable: accented syllables** |

| Language Art Skill | 1st Grade | | 2nd Grade | 3rd Grade |
|---|---|---|---|---|
| | **Emergent Phase** | **Phonemic Awareness Phase** | **Pattern Phase** | **Syllable Phase** |
| **Chapter 3.4 Encoding and Decoding**<br><br>**See Section 4 Phonics Rules** | **Encoding: first phoneme in a word**<br><br>**Decoding: NA** | **Encoding and decoding by phonemes**<br><br>**Encoding: all sounds in a word**<br><br>**Decoding: begin only after alphabet is introduced and teach phonics rules in section 4.** | **Encoding and decoding by onset/rime**<br><br>**Continue teaching phonics rules in section 4.** | **Encoding and decoding by syllable**<br><br>**Continue teaching phonics rules in section 4.** |
| Chapter 3.5 Symbol Imagery | 1. Visualizing straight and curved lines<br><br>2. Visualizing 1–2 letters | Visualizing words with 3–5 letters | Visualizing words with 6–7 letters | Visualizing syllables in words with 2–3 syllables |
| Chapter 3.6 Sight Words | *The Roadmap to Literacy* Sight Word Set 1 | *The Roadmap to Literacy* Sight Word Set 2 | *The Roadmap to Literacy* Sight Word Set 2 | NA |
| Chapter 3.7 Concept Imagery | Practice games and activities to strengthen visualization skills. | Practice games and activities to strengthen visualization skills. | Review and model concept imagery as students begin to read books without illustrations. | Review and model concept imagery as students begin to read books without illustrations. |
| Chapter 3.8 Comprehension | Review stories using sequential retell | Review stories using the following:<br><br>• sequential retell<br>• factual recall questions<br>• free renderings<br>• HOTS questions (after Spring Break only) | Review stories (including books) using the following:<br><br>• sequential retell (only for stories that span several days)<br>• factual recall questions<br>• HOTS questions<br>• free renderings | Review stories (including books) using the following:<br><br>• factual recall questions<br>Location: Chapter 3.8 Comprehension/ 3rd Grade first bullet point.<br>• HOTS questions |
| Chapter 3.9 Spelling | NA—<br><br>See encoding and sight words. | NA—<br><br>See encoding, sight words. | Teach homophones at end of phase. | Teach weekly spelling words. Include dictations. |
| Chapter 3.10 Speech | Teach poems, songs, and tongue twisters. | Ibid | Ibid | Ibid |

| Language Art Skill | 1st Grade | | 2nd Grade | 3rd Grade |
|---|---|---|---|---|
| | Emergent Phase | Phonemic Awareness Phase | Pattern Phase | Syllable Phase |
| Chapter 3.11 Grammar | Parts of speech: NA<br><br>Mechanics: NA<br><br>Sentences: Insist students answer questions in complete sentences. | Parts of speech: NA<br><br>Mechanics: Capitalize first word in a sentence and people's names; use periods at end of a sentence.<br><br>Sentences: Insist students answer questions in complete sentences. | Parts of speech: nouns and verbs (action only)<br><br>Mechanics: capitalize proper nouns and use periods, question marks, and exclamation points<br><br>Sentences: Teach the three sentence types: declarative, interrogative, exclamatory. | Parts of speech: adjectives, adverbs, verbs (being and helping verbs, verb tense), possessive nouns<br><br>Mechanics: contractions, commas, and quotation marks<br><br>Sentences: Teach imperative sentences.<br><br>Other: synonyms and antonyms |
| Chapter 3.12 Vocabulary | Teach words as they come up in memory reading, stories, poems, and songs. | Teach words as they come up in memory reading, stories, poems, and songs. | Teach words as they come up in stories, poems, songs, and literature you read to the class. | Teach words as they come up in stories, poems, songs, and literature you read to the class. |
| Chapter 3.13 Kid Writing | 1–2 word titles | Expected length:<br>• beginning: 2–5 word titles<br>• intermediate: two or more short sentences<br>• advanced: 1/2–1 page | Expected length:<br><br>1–2 pages | NA—See Composition. |
| Chapter 3.14 Composition | NA | NA | Teach students to compose short summaries for their main lesson book using:<br><br>1. Modeled writing<br>2. Shared writing<br>3. Guided writing<br>4. Independent writing | Teach the following:<br><br>1. paragraphs<br>2. summaries in paragraph form<br>3. HOTS questions paragraphs: why and how<br>4. thank you notes<br>5. book reports |

| Language Art Skill | 1st Grade | | 2nd Grade | 3rd Grade |
|---|---|---|---|---|
| | Emergent Phase | Phonemic Awareness Phase | Pattern Phase | Syllable Phase |
| Chapter 3.15 Reading | Teach memory reading and echo reading. Use choral reading for both. | Teach memory reading and echo reading through choral reading.<br><br>Start decodable-text through guided reading once students can decode.<br><br>Encourage independent reading of familiar texts. | Teach decodable-text reading through guided reading and choral reading.<br><br>Encourage independent reading when students finish work. | Teach decodable-text reading through guided reading and choral reading.<br><br>Encourage independent reading when students finish work.<br><br>Class reading: optional. |

# SECTION 4

Phonics Rules

# SECTION 4 PROTOCOL

Phonics rules are taught using the same protocol. This information applies to chapters 4.1, 4.2, and 4.3.

**Scheduling:** Use block plan templates found in Appendix 1–3 (depending on your grade) or create your own (see chapter 3.4 #4).

**Pacing:** If you begin *The Roadmap to Literacy* at the beginning of 1st Grade, plan to finish the Phonemic Awareness Phonics Rules in 1st Grade, the Pattern Phase Rules in 2nd, and the Syllable Phase Rules for <u>decoding</u> in 3rd Grade. If you begin later, try to avoid having to teach phonics rules in 4th Grade. However, if you need to, use your 4th Grade language skills practice classes to do so.

## Introduction: Two-Day Teaching Rhythm

| Lesson Segment | Day One | Day Two |
|---|---|---|
| **Introduction &/or Review** <br><br> **or** <br><br> **Skills Practice segment** | Introduce phonics rule. <br><br> Bookwork: students record rule in phonics rules book. <br><br> Activity A | Review phonics rule. <br><br> Bookwork: finish any follow-up written activities. <br><br> Activity B |

Do not use the main lesson book for phonics rules. Use a special phonics rules book, a small composition book with lines just for phonics rules. Have the students write down the rule and an (optional} image. Rather than giving students examples of words that follow the rule, let them discover them on their own. One way is to encourage your students to be on the lookout for words that follow these rules when they are reading independently. Ask them to record these words in their phonics rules book on that rule's page or the adjacent page. Give them time in class to look for examples of words using these rules, if needed.

**Practice:** Practice in the Skills Practice segment of main lesson and/or practice class until 80% of the class can <u>decode</u> with the rule 80% of the time (i.e., **80/80 Rule**). Once this goal has been reached, introduce a new phonics rule. Continue to practice the old one until all have mastered it. (Note: If there are just a few students who need more practice, differentiate instruction.)

**Differentiated Instruction:** If students master the rule early, ask them to read independently. If they need additional practice, schedule it in their reading group.

**Benchmark:** It is expected that students will be able to <u>decode</u> correctly using all phonics rules by the end of 3rd Grade and be able to <u>encode</u> correctly using all phonics rules by the end of 6th Grade.

**Curriculum Connection:** Related language arts skills will be noted with each phonics rule as they come up.

**Note**: Go back and read chapter 3.4 Encoding and Decoding before working with phonics rules.

# 4.1 PHONICS RULES FOR THE PHONEMIC AWARENESS PHASE

**Phonics rules** are the rules that expand the number of words students can decode and encode. They cover the letter combinations that stretch the 26 letters of the Latin alphabet to represent the 40+ sounds in English (see chapter 3.1 #1). The three chapters in section 4 cover 33 phonics rules for you to teach. They are divided into three phases: Phonemic Awareness Phase, Pattern Phase, and Syllable Phase. Mastering these 33 rules will help students develop the pattern layer of the English layer cake (see chapter 1.3 #1). This chapter covers the phonics rules for the Phonemic Awareness Phase.

Prerequisites for Teaching Phonics Rules for the Phonemic Awareness Phase:

- Students should be in the intermediate Phonemic Awareness Phase (see chapter 6.2 #1).
- Student should have full sound/symbol knowledge (see chapter 3.1 #2).
- Students should be able to encode CVC words (Consonant-Vowel-Consonant words such as *hip, man, dog).*
- Students should be able to segment and blend phonemes (see chapter 3.3 #2).

Most students enter the intermediate Phonemic Awareness Phase at some point either before or during the third and final Alphabet Main Lesson Block or the third practice block of 1st Grade. By this time, they will know all of the letters of the alphabet and will have had plenty of experience with phonemic awareness, encoding, and kid writing.

This chapter covers the following phonics rules:

- Rule 1: Decoding by Phoneme (CVC Words)
- Rule 2: Beginning Digraphs: Consonant Teams *SH, CH, TH, WH, NG,* and the Vowel Team *OO*
- Rule 3: Blends
- Rule 4: Inflectional Endings #1: –s and –ed
- Rule 5: *R*-Controlled Vowels: *AR, ER, IR, OR,* and *UR*\*
- Rule 6: Silent *E*\*
- Rule 7: Compound Words #1\*
- Rule 8: Soft *C* and *G*\*

\*Phonics rules 5–8 can be taught at the end of the Phonemic Awareness Phase or the beginning of the Pattern Phase, but aim to finish phonics rules 1–4 by the end of 1st Grade at a minimum.

## Rule 1: Decoding by Phoneme (CVC Words)

**Phase:** Middle of Phonemic Awareness Phase

**Prerequisites:**

- Phonemic Awareness: Students can blend and segment CVC words using phonemes (sounds) not letters

- Encoding: A prerequisite to learning to <u>decode</u> CVC words is that students include a vowel letter (not necessarily the right one) when <u>encoding</u> CVC words (see table 3.3.1).

- Alphabet: Students are automatic at letter naming, sound/symbol correspondence, and identifying vowel letters.

- Memory reading

**Expected time for students to achieve the 80/80 Rule:** 2–3 weeks with daily practice after introduction

**Background Information**

This is not really a phonics rule. Instead, it is a decoding process, specifically encoding and decoding by phoneme. It is used to teach all phonics rules that cover single-syllable words. You might be tempted to teach these words as word families (e.g., bug, hug, rug, jug, etc.). Do not do it. The purpose of working with CVC words is so that students in this phase get the opportunity to decode each separate phoneme and then learn to blend them all together. The appropriate time to introduce word families is during the Pattern Phase. See chapter 3.4 #7 and 8 for more information.

Begin decoding with three-letter words rather than two letter (VC or CV) words because CVC words overwhelmingly 'play fair' (i.e., the words follow the phonics rules) whereas two-letter words do not. CVC words using the short vowel sounds such as *cat, bid, met, bun, hot,* etc. are very predictable because each letter has only one possible sound. Words such as *so, do, go, no,* and *to* are not predictable. Logically, all of those words should rhyme, but they do not. Two-letter words are better taught as sight words.

**The Rule:** Teach the process for decoding by phoneme as shown in table 4.1.1. Students will use this process to decode all of the words for subsequent phonics rules in the Phonemic Awareness Phase.

**Table 4.1.1: Process for Decoding by Phoneme**

| Process for Decoding by Phoneme | Example |
|---|---|
| 1. Underline the vowel letter or letters. | 1. ba̲g* |
| 2. Say the vowel sound. | 2. "/ă/" |
| 3. Say each sound from beginning to end. | 3. /b/ /ă/ /g/" |
| 4. Blend the sounds together to form a word. | 4. "bag"<br>*Write the word in lowercase letters. |

Note: This table is identical to table 3.4.4.

Note: Students should already know the process for encoding words by phoneme and be proficient at using it. See chapter 3.4 #7 table 3.4.2 and table 3.4.3 for the process.

**Introductory Image:** A choir master warming up each letter's voice. He starts with the singing sound (the vowel), has each letter say its sound in turn, then blends them all together into a word.

**Activities:** Introduce syllable cards and mystery words (see chapter 3.5 #3).

**Bookwork:**

- Phonics rule book: Do not put this rule in the phonics rules book. This rule is merely the process for encoding and decoding, not a rule *per se*. Jump right into encoding and decoding practice with CVC words.

- The bookwork activities for day two are the same as above.

**How to Help Struggling Students:** Make sure the prerequisites are automatic, particularly sound/symbol knowledge and blending. If students struggle in any area(s), do extra practice as a warm-up before encoding and decoding CVC words AND pull struggling students aside for additional practice during class. If a student struggles with distinguishing the lowercase letters *b* and *d*, see chapter 3.1 #12.

## Rule 2: Beginning Digraphs: Consonant Teams *SH, CH, TH, WH, NG,* and Vowel Team *OO*

**Phase:** Middle of Phonemic Awareness Phase

**Prerequisites:** Decoding CVC Words at 80% mastery

**Expected time for students to achieve the 80/80 Rule:** 2–3 weeks with daily practice after introduction

**Background Information:** Digraphs are two letters that work together to represent one sound. They are also called *consonant teams* or *vowel teams* since two letters have teamed up to make one sound. They exist because English has more sounds than it has letters to represent them. Teaching these letter teams is just like teaching additional letters of the alphabet. With the exception of *WH*, the consonant and vowel teams represent unique phonemes.

**The Rule:** The letters in consonant and vowel teams cannot be sounded out individually; instead they work together as a unit.

**Introductory Image for SH, CH, and WH:** Would you like to have a friend who is so kind and polite that she lets others choose what to play? When the letter *H* plays with the following letters, it allows the other letter to go first, and *H* also lets the other letter choose what to play.

- *S* likes to play spies or librarian: "sh, sh, sh."

- *C* likes to play trains: "ch-ch-choo-choo."

- *W* likes to play detectives or newspaper reporters and asks the /wh/ questions: "What happened? When? Where? Why?" (Suggestion: Try creating a little play around this scenario.)

**Introductory Image for TH:** *TH* lisps because it lost its two front teeth. Sometimes it lisps loudly like in the word *then*. Other times it lisps quietly like in the word *thin*. Experiment with lisping quietly (i.e., unvoiced consonant sound for *TH*) and loudly (i.e., voiced consonant sound for *TH*) by saying the two sounds of *TH*.

Note: After this initial introduction, the student's knowledge of how the word is pronounced will normally supply her with the proper pronunciation of *TH*.

**Introductory Image for NG:** (Pronounced /ng/ with no vowel sound; as opposed to –*ing*.) *NG* is a musician who likes to make beautiful sounds: ring, sing, song, gong, sang, rang. The letters *NG* like to go last so their sound can float out to create fairy music: /ng/. (Note: The sound /ng/ should be very quiet. The only way to make it loud is to add a vowel such as the letter *I* as in –*ing*. When introducing this sound, make sure you pronounce it correctly. Do not add a vowel sound.)

**Introductory Image for *OO*:** The letters *OO* have two sounds: /oo/ as in *boo* and /oo/ as in book. They are sets of twins. The first pair of twins is excited to try new foods and says, "/oo/, that looks delicious;" the second pair is disgusted by new food and says, "/oo/, that looks disgusting."

**Bookwork:**

- Phonics rule book: Make a page for each digraph. For example, *CH* make the /ch/ sound as in "Choo-choo." (Students can draw an illustration of a train with the words "choo-choo" coming out of the smokestack if they wish.) Have the students leave space to write in words that use this rule. In figure 4.1.1 you can see an example of the *OO* vowel team entry.

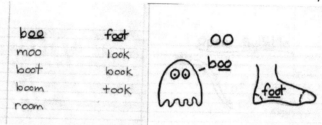

**Figure 4.1.1: Example of an OO Vowel Team Phonics Book Entry**

- **Other written activities for day two:** Make a worksheet where students have to circle pictures that feature the targeted vowel or consonant team and write the word next to each picture. Note: You can use worksheets from phonics programs or get pictures from the book *Words Their Way* Appendix C.

**Additional Ways to Practice:**

- Practice book: Include short dictations with sight words
- Word sorting (see chapter 3.3 #2)

Note: When searching for items for the /ng/ sound, avoid verbs that have an –ing suffix ending (e.g., fishing). Look for words where /ng/ is part of the root word. Some /ng/ words to use: king, ring, song, wing, lung, string, swing, ping pong, gong, and long.

**How to Help Struggling Students:** If students have trouble with digraphs, there are two areas you should pay attention to.

1. If students have difficulty learning to spot the vowel or consonant teams in a word, they need more symbol imagery practice. They have to be able to remember more than one letter at a time to be able to see the vowel or consonant teams embedded in a word.

2. You will notice that some students misspell words with consonant and vowel teams despite knowing how to spell the digraph. This error often stems from timing difficulties. Students have to coordinate segmenting phonemes and writing letters. If the mouth, hand, or eye is off by a fraction of a second, they will frequently drop a letter—and it is often one of the letters in a digraph. These students need practice with movement exercises that require timing of hand/ear/eye/mouth. Bean bag exercises from Take Time and then Bal-A-Vis-X can be effective <u>if</u> the students do them consciously with perfect timing (see chapter 6.6 #5). If they cannot, refer them to a remedial teacher. If your school does not have one, see if there are any occupational therapists in the community who would be able to help. In the meantime, teach the students to hold the sound of the consonant or vowel team for a longer period of time when encoding its letters whenever possible. For example, shhhhhip or ringgggg.

# Rule 3: Blends

**Phase:** Mid to late Phonemic Awareness Phase

**Prerequisites:** decoding consonant teams at 80% mastery, ability to segment and blend phonemes in single-syllable words with four sounds

**Expected time for students to achieve the 80/80 Rule:** 3–4 weeks with daily practice after introduction

**Background Information:** Two consonant sounds together with no vowel between them are called **blends**. For example, in the word *clamp,* the letters *CL* and *MP* are blends. Blends and consonant teams are made up of more than one letter, but in consonant teams, the letters represent one sound while in blends, each letter has its own sound. For example, the word *chip* has three sounds /ch/ /ĭ/ /p/ while the word *clip* has four sounds /c/ /l/ /ĭ/ /p/. *CH* is a consonant team because the two letters represent one sound, and *CL* is a blend because the letters represent two sounds.

Blends are classified based on where they appear in a syllable: beginning or end. Beginning blends come before a vowel in a single-syllable word; end blends come after the vowel. Include the following in your lessons:

Beginning Blends

- *S* blends: SC, SK, SL, SN, SM, SP, SPH, ST, SW
- *R* blends: BR, CR, DR, FR, GR, PR, TR
- *L* blends: BL, CL, FL, GL, PL, SL
- trigraph blends: SPL, STR, SCR, SPR

End Blends

- plural CVC words: too many to list (for example, *PS* in *cups*)
- *R*-controlled vowels with a consonant after: too many to list (for example, *RL* in *girl*)
- preconsonantal nasals: ND, MP, NT, NK,NGTH
- miscellaneous: ST, SP, SK, FT, PT, LT, LF, LP
- trigraph blends: plural words that end in a blend: too many to list (For example, *NDS* in *bonds*)

Blends are extensive. Do not try to teach each blend as a separate unit as you would with consonant teams. It would take too long and it is not necessary. The consonant teams represent unique phonemes and have to be learned as if they were separate letters, but the students already know all of the letters and sounds in blends. There is a shortcut that will help students master most blends in a very short time: phonemic awareness.

**The Introduction for Most Blends:** No image is included for this introduction. Instead, modify the encoding and decoding processes to teach the majority of blends. First, practice segmenting and blending sounds in phonemic awareness until the students are automatic up to four sounds (see chapter 3.3 #2). Then, show the students how to use their knowledge of the code to match letters and sounds to encode and decode blends.

To teach encoding, begin with a simple CVC word and then change it into a word with a blend. For example, change *pan* into *plan* as shown in table 4.1.2.

## Encoding Blends

Some students will not need the process for transitioning into blends (shown in table 4.1.2) because they will have taught themselves blends as part of kid writing. Use it for the ones who are still struggling to encode blends.

**Table 4.1.2: Process for Transitioning into Encoding Blends**

| Process for Transitioning into Encoding Blends | Example |
|---|---|
| 1. Say the word quickly and then slowly. Put one finger up for each sound, tapping the palm of your other hand as you do say it slowly. | "Pan, /p/ /ă/ /n/." (Three fingers) |
| 2. Write lines on your paper to hold the space for the sounds. | ___  ___  ___ |
| 3. Say the word slowly again and write the letter for each sound on its line. | p a n |
| 4. Ask the students which extra sound or letter would be needed if you wanted to spell "plan". | "/l/ or the letter L" |
| 5. Ask them to squeeze the letter in where they hear it. | p l a n |

There was no need to teach the *PL* blend at all. Phonemic awareness told the students which letters to use.

## Decoding Blends

Similarly, the process for decoding with blends is just as easy.

**Table 4.1.3: Process for Decoding Blends**

| Process for Decoding Blends | Example |
|---|---|
| 1. Underline the vowel letter. | sp<u>o</u>t |
| 2. Say the vowel sound. | /ŏ/ |
| 3. Say each sound from beginning to end. | "/s/ /p/ /ŏ/ /t/" |
| 4. Blend the sounds together. | "spot" |

In the process outlined in table 4.1.3, there was no need to teach the *SP* blend at all. Knowledge of the alphabet coupled with phonemic awareness (blending) enabled the students to decode it without additional instruction. Consequently, students master almost all of the blends practically overnight. When you teach phonemic awareness first, you take a gigantic shortcut and save both you and your students hours of work covering each blend.

**The Introduction for *TR* and *DR*:** Once students are approaching mastery of most blends, begin to introduce these two difficult blends. The blend *TR* sounds similar to *CH* and *DR* sounds similar to *J*; consequently, students often confuse them. Listen to how similar the following words sound: *truck* and *chuck; drum* and *chum*. Initially teach these two blends as units by using the names of students and/or faculty: Tracy, Drake, Drew, KaTRina, ShanDRa, Tristan, Dre, etc. Then transition into the following formula: excellent articulation + finger spelling + targeted practice = student mastery (see chapter 3.3 #2 and 3.10 #7).

**The Introduction for Preconsonantal Nasals:** When the letters *N, M,* or *NG* appear <u>before</u> another consonant, they are called **preconsonantal nasals,** and they make up the most difficult blends to encode. For example, li<u>nt</u>, ju<u>mp</u>, and le<u>ngt</u>h. Students will need to practice encoding blends with preconsonantal nasals more than the other blends. Use the formula: excellent articulation + finger spelling + targeted practice = student mastery (see chapter 3.3 #2 and 3.10 #7).

Do not worry if your students are coming along nicely with blends in general but are still struggling with encoding preconsonantal nasals. When students demonstrate mastery encoding them in their kid writing, it is a sign that they have full phonemic awareness for segmenting sounds and are ready to go to the Pattern Phase.

Note: *NG* is a digraph but when it comes before a consonant, it forms a preconsonantal-nasal blend. Example: lo<u>ng</u> (digraph); le<u>ngt</u>h (preconsonantal-nasal blend).

**Activities:**

1. Do <u>picture</u> sorts around the difficult blends *TR* and *DR.* Have students sort /tr/ and /ch/ words such as *truck, chuck, train, chain,* etc. (see chapter 3.3 #2).

2. Do brainstorming exercises with the class around *TR/CH* and *DR/J* words where the students generate words for these sounds and determine how to spell them.

**Bookwork:**

- Phonics rule book: NA—jump right into practice.
- Other written activities for day two: NA—jump right into practice.

**Practice:** Begin to use nonsense words as part of your practice if you have not already done so. Tell your students that you will use nonsense, silly words like *hickory, dickory* or any other nonsense words they know from nursery rhymes. Then begin to include nonsense words in their encoding, decoding, syllable cards, and mystery word exercises.

**Curriculum Connection:** In the Speech/Song segment, include tongue twisters that feature *TR/CH* and *DR/J* words. (Note: *The Roadmap to Literacy's* 1st Grade main lesson archetype includes the possibility of additional lesson segments such as the Speech/Song segment See chapter 2.3 #4).

**How to Help Struggling Students:** If students struggle with decoding blends, it is most likely one of three things.

1. First, make sure that code knowledge is automatic. If students have to think about which sound a letter has, it makes decoding much more difficult. Practice letter/sound and sound/letter matching (see chapter 3.1 #10 and chapter 3.3 #10).

2. Second, students may need more practice with phonemic awareness in blending sounds together. Give them lots of oral practice with blending blends. For example, can you figure out my word? /s/… /k/… /ă/ … /m/… Put them all together, and what do you get? (scam) (see chapter 3.3 #2 for more information).

3. Third, check students' pronunciation for consonant phonemes. Students will often add the sound /ŭ/ at the end of a consonant (e.g., making the letter *P*'s sound *puh* rather than /p/). When they try to sound out a word with a blend, they get a word with an extra syllable or two. For example, *spot* can become *su-pot* or even *su-pu-ot*. Do not let this situation develop. From day one, insist that students pronounce each phoneme clearly and cleanly: /s/ not /su/ and /p/ not /pu/ (see chapter 3.10). If a student has developed this bad habit, model saying each sound clearly and

insist the student do as well. If necessary, do some warm-up drills where the student has to say just the sound of a letter without any extra /ŭ/ at the end. Practice until the student can say phonemes cleanly. Then work on decoding blends.

If a student still struggles with decoding blends, pull him or her aside and try one final trick: starting with the rime as shown in table 4.1.4. This is a variation on decoding and should only be used as a last resort.

**Table 4.1.4: Last-Resort Process for Decoding Blends**

| Last-Resort Process for Decoding Blends | Example |
|---|---|
| 1. Underline the vowel and say its sound.<br>2. Read the rime (i.e., the vowel to the end of the word).<br>3. Add on one letter at a time from the initial blend, moving from right to left. | 1. sp<u>o</u>t<br>2. "ot"<br>3. "pot"… "spot" |

# Rule 4: Inflectional Endings #1: –s and –ed

**Phase:** Middle to late Phonemic Awareness Phase

**Prerequisites:** Ability to segment and blend phonemes in single-syllable words with four sounds. Students have begun kid writing.

**Expected time for students to achieve the 80/80 Rule:** NA: This is an introduction and guide for the students. Full mastery will come as a result of lessons covered in the next two phases (see chapter 4.2 rule 13 and chapter 4.3 rule 28).

**Background Information**

This rule is different from the other rules in several ways.

This rule will be taught multiple times: the first in the Phonemic Awareness Phase, the second in the Pattern Phase, and the final time in the Syllable Phase. Students are not expected to master it at this time.

In addition, the introduction of these two inflectional endings is the very beginning of working with the meaning layer of the English layer cake (see chapter 1.3 #1). Recall that in addition to making letter/sound matches, students have to think about the meaning of the words they are encoding. In fact, when encoding with these two common endings, they have to ignore letter/sound matches and encode meaning.

For this phonics rule, decoding is secondary to encoding. Teach this rule when these inflectional endings begin to show up in your students' kid writing, and then reteach it periodically as a mini-lesson (see chapter 3.13 #5). This rule has a very narrow focus: encoding common inflectional endings with the correct letters, *S* and *ED*. The objective is to prevent the students from developing the habit of spelling past tense words with the letter *T*. It will take students a couple of years before they master every nuance of encoding with these two suffixes. *The Roadmap to Literacy* postpones the teaching of the more sophisticated aspects of inflectional endings until later phases.

- When to double the final consonant will occur in both the Pattern and Syllable Phases (see chapter 4.2 rule 13 and chapter 4.3 rule 28 for the 1–1–1 Rule).

- The grammar behind the inflectional endings will occur in 2nd and 3rd Grade.

**The Encoding Rule for Plural Nouns:** When a word means more than one (plural), put the letter *S* at the end. Sometimes the letter *S* sounds like the letter *Z*, but it is still spelled with an *S* to show that the word is plural.

For example, *cats* and *dogs*. In both words, the *S* shows that the word is plural, but in *cats* the *S* sounds like /s/ while in *dogs* the *S* sounds like /z/.

**Introductory Image:** Use images from the umbrella story <u>Englishland</u> (see chapter 3.2 #7):

*The letter children were using their letters to make words. They wrote down exactly what they heard: BUGZ for bugs, CATS for cats, DOGZ for dogs, HATS for hats, etc. The Mayor noticed that all of these words were special: they showed that there was more than one of something. However, he thought that having two letters show that there was more than one was too confusing so he decided that there should be only one letter to show that something was plural. But, which one should it be, the letter S or the letter Z? The mayor chose the letter S because it was always about whereas Z was often somewhere asleep... hence the saying taking a 'Z'. To this day, whenever you want to show that there is more than one, you write the letter S, even when it sounds like the letter Z.*

**The Encoding Rule for Past Tense Verbs:** The suffix –ed shows that an action has already happened. For example, *Yesterday, I jumped.* The suffix –ed can make the sound /d/, /t/, or /ed/ (/id/ in some areas). For example, *rained, baked,* and *sledded.*

**Introductory Image:** *The letter children loved to spell words. They wrote down exactly what they heard: HANDID for handed, CALLD for called, and POKT for poked.* (Write these words and their misspellings up on the board.)

*This was all well and good in that everyone could read the words and knew what the letter children meant. However, the Mayor was not satisfied. Something was wrong.*

*"All of these words show that something has already happened,"* said the mayor. *"LaKeesha handed Sam his sandwich* <u>yesterday</u>. *Juan called his grandmother* <u>last week</u>. *Sammy poked his brother when they rode to school* <u>this morning</u>. *All of these things have already happened. We must put something on the ends of all of these words to show that they describe something that has already been done. We will use the letters ED on the ends of words to show they already happened."* (Correct the words on the board: handed, called, poked.)

*The Mayor sent out a decree telling the letter children to use the letters ED on the end of a word to show it already happened instead of the letters D, T, or ID. And from that day forth, the letter children started using ED to show a word already happened. They even reminded each other when they made an inevitable mistake. Whenever the citizens of Letter Village saw a word, they could tell at one glance which ones have already happened.*

**Note:** Leave the explanation for doubling a consonant before the suffix –ed (e.g., begged) for the Pattern Phase (see chapter 4.2 rule 13). Leave the irregular verbs such as leap/leapt and keep/kept for 4th Grade. This introduction is just a foretaste of things to come.

**Bookwork:**

- Phonics rule book: Do not draw a picture or put this rule in the phonics rules book. These rules will be written up formally in later phases.

- On day two go right into practice.

**Additional Ways to Practice:**

Follow up practice can include:

- Spelling plural words with the letter *S* regardless of the sound (e.g., *beds, hats, books, dogs, etc.*).

- Spelling past tense words with the letters *ED* regardless of the sound (e.g., *sledded, biked, rained, etc.*).

- Follow up with lots of practice decoding words with *ED*. When students first decode words with an –ed suffix, focus on decoding the root word and then making it already have happened. If the word is *jumped,* ask the students to find the root word (jump) and then say it like it happened yesterday. You can even put it in a sentence: Today I jump; Yesterday, I_(jumped).

- Include decoding with plural nouns as part of working with blends. Students' knowledge of English will provide them with the correct pronunciation for plural nouns most of the time.

**Note:** Do not have the students figure out which sound the letter *S* or *ED* is making in plural and past tense words. There is no educational value in having the students consider the sounds. Instead, the students must consider the meaning. For example, when encoding and decoding, draw attention to the meaning of the words. Instead of asking the students which sound the letter *S* has in the word *dogs,* ask them if the word means one or more than one and prompt them to use the right letter to show that the word is plural when they spell.

**Curriculum Connection:** A good time to introduce (and reintroduce) these two inflectional endings is in mini-lessons in kid writing since that is when students will need to use this information (see chapter 3.13 #5). Expect to reteach this lesson on a regular basis.

## Rule 5: *R*-Controlled Vowels: *AR, ER, IR, OR,* and *UR*

**Phase**: End of Phonemic Awareness Phase/beginning Pattern Phase

**Prerequisites:** Symbol imagery up to four letters, automaticity on blends with the letter *R: BR, CR, TR,* etc.

**Expected time for students to achieve the 80/80 Rule:** 1–2 weeks with daily practice after introduction

**Background Information**

The sound /r/ sometimes acts as a vowel in English.

The word *girl* really only has three sounds: /g/ /r/ /l/. In English, the phoneme /r/ can be a consonant sound or a vowel sound. (Note: Expect students to spell the word *girl GRL* in their kid writing when they first begin to spell.)

The word *grip* has four sounds: /g/ /r/ /ĭ/ /p/. Note that it has a vowel sound: /ĭ/. The letter *R* is part of a blend: *GR* and is acting as a consonant.

When you spell, you have to be conscious of the whole word or syllable. Is the /r/ sound acting as a vowel or a consonant? Here is the rule: if there is already a vowel sound, it is a consonant. If not, it is a vowel.

Note: *R*-controlled vowels include long vowels (see chapter 4.2 rule 12).

**The Rule:** When the letter *R* comes after a vowel letter, the vowel sound changes. (The sounds vary by region. Modify to match yours.)

**Introductory Images:** 'Bossy *R*' or 'the Director *R*' tells vowel letters what to say when it comes up behind them in a word:

- *AR* = argh, similar to the sound made by pirates (e.g., *arch, bar, card*)

- *OR* = or, just like the word (e.g., *orange*)

- *ER/IR/UR* = /r/, the sound of the letter *R* (e.g., *her, girl, fur*)

**Bookwork:**

- Phonics rule book: Have the students put these pictures and the rule into their phonics rules book. Have them leave space to write in words they will find that follow this rule. Note: You can put more than one consonant or vowel team on a page, just as you did when introducing the alphabet (see chapter 3.1 #8).

- Other written activities for day two: Make a worksheet that includes pictures of words that follow this rule. Have the students circle the pictures and write the spellings next to the pictures.

Note: You can get pictures from sources such as Appendix C from *Words Their Way* or the picture cards from the game *Blurble Volume 1*. Do not try to trick the students by including words that feature both blends with the letter *R* (ex *GR, TR, PR*, etc.) and words with *R*-controlled vowels that make the sound /r/ (e.g., girl, monster, burr, etc.).

**How to Help Struggling Students**

Students will often encode words without the vowel letter (e.g., *GRL* for *girl*). Tell the students to make sure each word contains a vowel letter. For the letters *ER/IR/UR*, they will need to write the word out three ways and use their symbol imagery to see which looks right. If they cannot tell, they should take their best guess and then ask the teacher or look it up in their consumable dictionary if they are in 2nd Grade (see chapter 3.6 #3 and chapter 3.13 #2).

# Rule 6: Silent *E*

**Phase:** End of Phonemic Awareness Phase/beginning Pattern Phase

**Prerequisite:** symbol imagery up to 4–5 letters, otherwise students will have trouble spotting the Silent *E* at the end of the word.

**Expected time for students to achieve the 80/80 Rule:** 1–2 weeks with daily practice after introduction

**Background Information:** Silent *E* is the first foray into long vowels. When you see your students begin to experiment with Silent *E* in their invented spellings, you will know they are entering the end of the Phonemic Awareness Phase and will soon be ready for the Pattern Phase curriculum.

**The Rule:** When Silent *E* comes after a vowel (e.g., tie) or a consonant preceded by a vowel (e.g., bake), the vowel becomes long and the *E* is silent.

**Introductory Images:** Silent *E* as a super hero or word wizard

- As a super hero, Silent *E* jumps over a single sound in a single bound and makes the vowel say its name. But *E* does this so silently that no one can hear him. (This image comes from Lindamood-Bell.)

- As a word wizard, Silent *E* transforms one word into another by writing the letter *E* on the end of a word such as *pin*, and then whispering, "Letter *I*, say your name and I'll be silent in this game." *Pin* becomes *pine*.

**Activities**

1. Silent *E* Practice Riddles: Write several riddles you have made up on the board. Then ask your students to answer the riddles by writing the answer on a slate or in their practice book. For example, *What can I do with my hand that is found in the ocean? (wave)*

2. Silent *E* hunts using poems with lots of Silent *E*: For example, this poem by Patti Connolly.

*Una, sad and pale,*

*Tells a shocking tale*

*Of a dragon with a flame*

*That someone brave must tame.*

The students copy down the poem and then find all of the words that have a Silent *E*.

**Bookwork:**

- Phonics rule book: Have the students put this picture and rule into their phonics rules book. Have them leave space to write in words that follow this rule.

- Other bookwork for day two: Make a worksheet that includes pictures of words that use Silent *E* such as *cape, lake*, etc. Have your students circle the pictures where they can hear the long vowel sound and write the spelling next to the picture. Note: Do not try to trick the students by including words that feature long vowel spellings other than Silent *E*. Only include pictures that feature short vowel words and long vowel words with Silent *E* (e.g., *lap* and *lake*). You can use pictures from sources such as Appendix C from *Words Their Way* or the picture cards from the Bernard games version of *Blurble Volume 1*.

**How to Help Struggling Students:**

- If students have trouble learning to decode with Silent *E*, check their symbol imagery. If students are processing words one letter at a time, they will not see the Silent *E* and realize its role until it is too late. Do extra symbol imagery exercises so students can process four or more letters at a time.

- If students have trouble learning to encode, have them check their words by decoding them. If they cannot do it alone, have them work with partners or go around and point out words for them to check.

## Rule 7: Compound Words #1

**Phase:** Late Phonemic Awareness Phase/beginning Pattern Phase

**Prerequisites:** CVC words, consonant digraphs, consonantal blends, *R*-controlled vowels, Silent *E*, and symbol imagery up to 4–5 letters

**Expected time for students to achieve the 80/80 Rule:** 1 week with daily practice after initial introduction

**Background Information:** Words that are made up of two words are called compound words. Examples include *bedbug, baseball, homerun*, etc. They have a long tradition in English. In the Anglo-Saxon days, kennings were common. A kenning is a metaphorical phrase or a compound word that is used to name a person, place, or thing indirectly. For example, in the epic poem *Beowulf*, the sea is called a *whale road*.

Breaking compound words down into two separate words is the very beginning of learning to work with multisyllabic words.

**The Rule:** Two unrelated words can be combined into one to create an entirely new word. For example, bed + bug = bedbug.

**Introductory Image:** Continue the umbrella story *Englishland* by having a *name committee* travel the land to come up with names for things. They did not have the authority to create new words by themselves so they combined two existing words to create a new name. For example, hotdog, goldfish, hilltop, suntan, windmill, turnpike, sagebrush, sandpaper, etc.

**Teaching Process for Decoding:** Look for each word in the compound word and put a break line between them. Example: *homerun home / run.*

**Teaching Process for Encoding:** Have the students spell each word as a separate word and then put the two words together to make the compound.

**Activities:**

1. Say three simple compound words (e.g., baseball, handshake, bedbug) and see if the class can discover what is unusual about these three words. After they have figured it out (with or without your guidance), write the words on the board and ask the students to figure out how the sport *baseball* got its name. Then discuss the other two words. Introduce the new vocabulary word *compound*, the combining of two or more parts. Thus compound words describe words that are made up of more than one word.

2. Practice compound words the next day. Before class, write down a number of simple, familiar compound words on separate pieces of paper. Cut each word in half. Distribute the halves to your students so that each student gets part of a compound word. The students then need to find their other half. (Remind them that they may have the beginning or the end of the word.) Once all of the students have found a match, have each pair show their word and read it to the class. (Make the words large enough that they can be read from the back of the classroom.)

Variation: You could also do the second activity with pictures (photos or drawn). When the students come up to show their word, they would first write the two halves on the board to create the compound word and then show their two pictures. See fig. 4.1.2 for an example.

 +  = **Dollhouse**

**Figure 4.1.2: Compound Words**

**Bookwork:**

- Phonics rule book: Have the students put this rule into their phonics rules book and have them include a drawing similar to fig. 4.1.2 to illustrate compound words. Have them leave space to record compound words they will find during independent reading.

- Other written activities for day two: Create a worksheet which has the first part of compound words listed on the left side and the second part of each word randomly listed on the right side. The students draw a line connecting the two halves of each compound word. Ask them to write the new compound word. Note: Have the students do the work with graphite pencils so they can erase if they make a mistake. (If students are not making any mistakes, the worksheet was too easy. Try to make your exercises challenging without becoming frustrating.)

**How to Help Struggling Students:** Make sure symbol imagery is well developed.

## Rule 8: Soft *C* and *G*

**Phase:** End of the Phonemic Awareness Phase and beginning of the Pattern Phase

**Prerequisites:** Silent *E*, symbol imagery up to 4–5 letters

**Expected time for students to achieve the 80/80 Rule:** 2–3 weeks (to master both) with daily practice after introduction

**Background Information:** The letters *C* and *G* have two sounds. Their primary sound is referred to as their hard sound (i.e., /k/ as in *cat* and /g/ as in *gate*). Their secondary sound is their soft sound (i.e., /s/ as in *cent* and /j/ as in *giant*).

The soft *G* sound can also be made by the letters *DGE* on the end of a word. These letters appear at the end of words that have a <u>short</u> vowel followed by the sound /j/ (e.g., *judge, ridge, ledge)*. This rule will be taught later (see chapter 4.2 rule 14).

**The Rule:** To make *C* or *G* soft, follow it with the letters *E, I,* or *Y.* For example, <u>c</u>ent, ra<u>c</u>ing, and <u>c</u>ycle; <u>g</u>em, pa<u>g</u>ing, and <u>g</u>ym. *C* will always be soft, but *G* can be hard or soft. For example, <u>g</u>ynecology.

**Introductory Image for Hard and Soft *C*:** When the *C* truck goes down the highway, it makes the sound /k/ /k/ /k/. When it comes to a sign that says "*I, E, Y,*" the road goes DOWN to the right. As the *C* Truck goes down the incline, it makes the sound /s/ /s/ /s/ as if applying its airbrakes (see fig. 4.1.3).

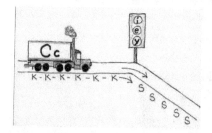

**Figure 4.1.3 Truck Image to Show Two Sounds of *C***

**Introductory Image for Hard and Soft *G*:** When the *G* truck goes down the highway, it makes the sound /g/ /g/ /g/. When it comes to a sign that says "*I, E, Y,*" the *G* truck has to choose whether to continue going straight ahead making the sound /g/ /g/ /g/ or go DOWN to the right and make the sound /j/ /j/ /j/.

**Activities:** Have the students pretend to be the letter *C* or *G*. Then show them a word that has a signal letter in it such as *cent* or *gym* or that does not such as *cup* or *gum*. The students have to decide which way the truck goes and then decode the word.

**Bookwork:**

- Phonics rule book: Have the students draw a picture of the truck similar to Figure 4.1.3 and write the *C* and *G* rules into their phonics rules book. Have them leave space to write in words that follow these rules. (During their independent reading, challenge them to find words that follow these rules and add them to their book.)

- Other written activities for day two: Make a worksheet with pictures of words that follow these rules. For example, *spice, ace, ice, cent, race,* etc. Have the students provide the spelling for each word. Note: Use pictures from sources such as Appendix C from *Words Their Way,* other phonics books, or the picture cards from the Bernard games edition of *Blurble Volume 1.*

**How to Help Struggling Students:**

1. Make sure students' symbol imagery is solid.

2. Demonstrate that the letter *E* can make a vowel long as well as change the hard sound to a soft sound. For example, *stage.*

## Conclusion

In contrast to students in other languages, English-speaking students take longer to learn to read and spell because they have to master phonics rules (see chapter 1.3 #2). Phonics rules expand the students' encoding and decoding beyond the 26 letters of the alphabet.

In order to be on track to finish all phonics rules by the end of 3rd Grade, make sure your 1st Grade students have completed a <u>minimum</u> of phonics rules 1–4. They should have full phonemic awareness by the end of 1st Grade (i.e., they should be able to encode a letter for every sound in a word, including preconsonantal nasals). Plan to finish whichever phonics rules are left in this chapter at the beginning of 2nd Grade.

# 4.2 PHONICS RULES FOR THE PATTERN PHASE

*3rd start here as a review*

**Phonics rules** are the rules that expand the number of words students can decode and encode. They cover the letter combinations that stretch the 26 letters of the Latin alphabet to cover the 40+ sounds in English (see chapter 3.1 #1). The three chapters in section 4 cover 33 phonics rules for you to teach. They are divided into three phases: Phonemic Awareness Phase, Pattern Phase, and Syllable Phase. Mastering these 33 rules will help students develop the pattern layer of the English layer cake (see chapter 1.3 #1). This chapter covers the phonics rules for the Pattern Phase.

Prerequisites for Teaching the Pattern Phase: Full phonemic awareness (i.e., students can encode one sound for each phoneme, including preconsonantal nasals (e.g., *MP, ND, NK, NT*)) (see chapter 4.1 rule 3).

Note: It is fine to teach Phonics Rules 4–8 while students are working towards full phonemic awareness; however, do not start Rules 10–21 until they have mastered phonemic awareness.

It is strongly advised that you go back and review chapter 3.4 Encoding and Decoding, as well as Section 4 Protocol before working with this chapter.

This chapter covers the following phonics rules:

- Rule 9: Encoding and Decoding by Onset/Rimes
- Rule 10: Two Vowels Go Walking: Vowel Teams *AI, OA, EA,* and *AY*
- Rule 11: Diphthongs *OI/OY, OU/OW,* and Their Friends *AU/AW*
- Rule 12: Long Vowels + *R*
- Rule 13: Inflectional Endings #2: *–S, –ES, –ED,* and *–ING*
- Rule 14: The Guardians: Doublers, *–CK, –TCH,* and *–DGE*
- Rule 15: Other Uses for Silent *E*
- Rule 16: Trickster *X*
- Rule 17: *Y* as a Vowel
- Rule 18: Silent Consonants
- Rule 19: Other Vowel Teams
- Rule 20: Compound Words #2
- Rule 21: Homophones

Note: Rules 1–8 are covered in chapter 4.1. Begin 2nd Grade with rule 9 and then go back and teach any of the prior rules you did not teach in 1st Grade.

# Rule 9: Encoding and Decoding by Onset/Rimes

**Phase**: End of the Phonemic Awareness Phase and beginning of the Pattern Phase

**Prerequisites:** CVC words, blends, and full phonemic awareness

**Expected time for students to achieve the 80/80 Rule:** one to two weeks depending on how many phonics rules you introduced in 1st Grade. (Students will continue to practice this process throughout the Pattern Phase with each subsequent phonics rule.)

**Background Information:** Phonics rule 9 encompasses a review of all of the phonics rules taught in the Phonemic Awareness Phase as well as the introduction to a new decoding and encoding process for phonics rules in the Pattern Phase. This lesson has two parts, and they both make use of the process for encoding and decoding by onset and rime as shown in table 4.2.1. The review applies the process for encoding and decoding by onset and rime to word families and is used to review old phonics rules. The introduction to new phonics rules applies the process for encoding and decoding by onset and rime to the introduction of new phonics rules.

**Table 4.2.1: Process for Encoding and Decoding by Onset and Rime**

| Process for Decoding by Onset/Rime | Example |
|---|---|
| 1. Underline the rime. | 1. cli<u>p</u> |
| 2. Say the rime. | 2. "/ip/" |
| 3. Say the onset + rime. | 3. "/kl/ /ip/" |
| 4. Blend the onset and rime together. | 4. "clip" |
| **Process for Encoding by Onset/Rime** | **Example** |
| 1. Say the word. <br> 2. Say the onset and spell it. <br> 3. Say the rime and spell it. <br> 4. Does it look right? | 1. "clip" <br> 2. "/kl/" cl <br> 3. "/ip/" ip <br> 4. clip—"Yes, it looks right." |

## Part One: Word Families (Review of all Phonics Rules Learned to Date)

<u>Background Information</u>: Encoding and decoding by onset/rime is also a way to review old phonics rules while teaching your students something new: word families. A word family is encoding and decoding by onsets and rimes in chains of words that have the same rime (e.g., hand, sand, band, land, grand) (see chapter 1.5 #1 and chapter 3.4 #8). Word families are a subset of encoding and decoding by onset and rime. They are the training wheels of decoding and encoding with onset/rime.

<u>Prerequisites</u>: Students have mastered phonics rule 3 and have full phonemic awareness (i.e., when encoding, they represent each sound in a word with a logical letter choice, which demonstrates they have mastered segmenting sounds).

Note: It is imperative that word families not be used as a crutch to compensate for underdeveloped phonemic awareness. It works, but it comes with a steep price: students will be unable to master multisyllable encoding in later phases.

<u>When to Teach</u>: Plan to schedule word families at the beginning of 2nd Grade Start with rule 9 even if you have not yet taught all of the phonics rules in chapter 4.1. (Phonics rules 5–8 can be taught in either the Phonemic Awareness Phase or the Pattern Phase.)

Introductory Image: First and Last Names

"Just like the members of a family all share the last name of Jones, there are words that have families, too. For example (write on the board): clip, drip, slip, trip, snip all belong to the same family: the *IP* family. Just like people have two parts to their names (write on the board): Judy Jones, Bill Jones and Wanda Jones, we can divide all of the words of the *IP* family into two parts. The onset or first part of the word makes the word unique, the rime or second part of the word tells which family the word belongs to.

"Let's look at the word *clip*. The first part, the letters *CL*, is like a person's first name. It is called the onset. The second part, the letters *IP*, is like a person's last name. It is called the rime. We can put a dash between the onset and rime: cl –ip. We can use the onset and rime to read and spell words faster. Let's try the rest of the words on the list."

Have the students decode each word in the word family using onsets and rime. Have the students help identify the onsets and rime in the list of words. Demonstrate how much faster it is to read words when you can find their onset and rime (e.g., /str/ /ip/ rather than /s/ /t/ /r/ /i/ p/). Then do some more word families together (see table 3.4.5 Rime Chart).

Activities: Practice encoding and decoding with word families using phonics rules the students have already mastered. Include all of the phonics rules you taught in the Phonemic Awareness Phase.

Bookwork: Have the students drawn one or more word family houses in their phonics rules book. See figure 4.2.2.

How to Teach: Review the phonics rules you taught in the Phonemic Awareness Phase using word families. Once students are proficient at decoding and encoding the old phonics rules by onset and rime, teach the rest of the phonics rules in chapter 4.1 (if you have not done so) or go on to rule 10. Use the process shown below.

**Introduction: Decoding and Encoding with Onsets/Rimes for New Phonics Rules**

Background Information: This rule is not a real phonics rule. Instead, it is a process: decoding and encoding by onset/rime (see chapter 3.4 #8).

Prerequisite: Students are familiar with decoding and encoding with word families (i.e., encoding and decoding by onset/rime in chains).

When to Teach: Beginning of Pattern Phase.

How to Teach: Use the teaching rhythm shown in table 4.2.2 to teach all phonics rules in the Pattern Phase.

This teaching rhythm spans multiple days and multiple processes. When you first introduce a new phonics rule for a single-syllable word, use encoding and decoding by phoneme (see chapter 4.1 rule 1). However, once students know the rule, practice encoding and decoding by onset/rimes. Use word families to help students make the transition. Use these two encoding and decoding processes to teach all of the phonics rules for the Pattern Phase. By the end of the phase, students will know their phonics rules and will be able to decode and encode using onset and rimes.

**Table 4.2.2: Teaching Rhythm for Phonics Rules in the Pattern Phase**

| Days One and Two | Days Three (and possibly Four) | Subsequent Days |
|---|---|---|
| <u>Introduce</u> a new phonics rule and practice decoding it by phonemes. | <u>Practice</u> decoding this phonics rule by word families (i.e., chains). | <u>Practice</u> decoding this phonics rule by onset and rime (no chains) as long as it takes for students to get to 80/80. |
| For example,<br><br>1. Underline the vowel letter or letters: l<u>ou</u>t.<br>2. Say the vowel sound: "/ou/."<br>3. Say each sound from beginning to end: "/l/ /ou/ /t/."<br>4. Blend the sounds together: "lout."<br><br>Decode a list of words (not in chains): *pound, spout, loud, etc.* | For example,<br><br>1. Underline the rime: l<u>out</u>.<br>2. Say the rime: "/out/."<br>3. Say the onset + rime: "/l/ /out/."<br>4. Blend the onset and rime together: "lout."<br>5. Read the rest of the words in the word family.<br><br>Decode a list of words in the *out* family: *pout, clout, spout, etc.* | For example,<br><br>1. Underline the rime: l<u>out</u>.<br>2. Say the rime: " /out/."<br>3. Say the onset + rime: "/l/ /out/."<br>4. Blend the onset and rime together: "lout."<br><br>Decode a list of words (not in chains):<br>*ground, rout, pounds, trout, sound, flout, etc.*<br>You can also include nonsense words such as *prout, dound, etc.* |

**The Rule:** NA.

**Bookwork:** NA. Do not put this rule into the phonics rules book because it is a process, not a rule. Instead, follow the recommendations for whichever phonics rule you are teaching for whichever phonics rule you are teaching.

**How to Help Struggling Students:** Make sure students' symbol imagery and phonemic awareness are solid. If not, practice both and continue encoding and decoding by phoneme until they are.

## Rule 10: Two Vowels Go Walking: Vowel Teams *AI, OA, EA,* and *AY*

**Phase:** Beginning of the Pattern Phase

**Prerequisites:** Silent *E* Rule, symbol imagery of 4–5 letters

**Expected time for students to achieve the 80/80 Rule:** 2 weeks with daily practice after introduction

**Background Information:** There are four vowel teams to teach: *AI, OA, EA,* and *AY*. Each pair work together to represent one sound: *AI* and *AY* represent long *A; OA* represents long *O,* and *EA* represents long *E. AY* is used at the end of root words whereas *AI* is used in the middle of root words (e.g., ray/rain).

There are other ways to make these long vowel sounds, most notably with Silent *E*. Use symbol imagery to determine correct spelling. Write the words out both ways and see which one looks right. Is it *bote* or *boat*?

**The Rule:** When two vowels go walking, the first one does the talking.

**Figure 4.2.1: Phonics Rule Book Entry for *Two Vowels Go Walking***

**Introductory Image:** Draw and label a picture of a sail boat floating in a bay with a seal on a nearby rock (see fig. 4.2.1). On the sail write s<u>ai</u>l; on the boat write b<u>oa</u>t; on the water write b<u>ay</u>; and below the seal write s<u>ea</u>l. This drawing will highlight the vowel teams of *AI, OA, AY,* and *EA.* Above or below the picture write: *"When two vowels go walking, the first one does the talking."*

**Activities:** Word sorts where students organize a pre-selected list of words into categories by feature. For example, they are given a list of words with long *O* such as *tone, boat, goal, rope, hole, moan, etc.* They then sort the words into two categories: Words with *O_E* and Words with *OA.*

- *O_E:* tone, rope, mope, pope, hole, home, note, nose, woke, stone, pole, smoke

- *O_A:* boat, goal, moan, loan, load, groan, oak, oath, float, cloak, coach, toast

See chapter 3.3 #2 for more information on word sorts.

**Bookwork:**

- Phonics rule book: Have the students put the phonics rule into their phonics rules book. Have them leave space so they can write in words that follow this rule (see fig. 4.2.1).

- Other written activities for day two: Make a worksheet that features pictures of words that use Two Vowels Go Walking such as *toast, goat, sea, pail, etc.* Include a few words that have short vowels such as *man, rug, etc.*

Have the students circle the pictures where they can hear the long vowel sound and write the spelling next to the picture. Note: Do not try to trick the students by including words that feature long vowel spellings such as Silent *E.* Only include pictures that feature short vowel words and words with Two Vowels Go Walking. You can get pictures from phonics programs or get pictures from *Words Their Way* Appendix C.

**How to Help Struggling Students:** Confirm that students have solid symbol imagery and then have them read lots of phonics readers that feature this rule (e.g., *Frog and Toad*). Do eagle eye noticing tasks for Two Vowels Go Walking (see chapter 3.4 #10).

Note: Remember that encoding mastery is not expected at this time. In 3rd Grade, have students revisit this rule when they begin weekly spelling tests.

## Rule 11: Diphthongs *OI/OY,* *OU/OW,* and Their Friends *AU/AW*

**Phase:** Beginning of the Pattern Phase

**Prerequisites:** Two Vowels Go Walking

**Expected time for students to achieve the 80/80 Rule:** 2–3 weeks with daily practice after introduction

**Background information:** The diphthongs are special vowel teams. They are vowel sounds that make your mouth slide from one position to another. Let's explore what that means. Doctors say, "Open your mouth and say, *AW*." When you make the sound /aw/, your mouth opens wide and stays open the entire sound without changing position. Now think about the sound /ow/ like in the word *out*. Slowly say the sound /ow/. Do you feel how your mouth drops open initially, just like in /aw/, but then your lips pucker forward as if you are about to kiss someone? The sound /ow/ is a **diphthong**, a vowel that moves around in your mouth. It takes two movements of the mouth to make a diphthong as opposed to one for other vowels.

Technically, all of the long vowels are diphthongs. However, there are two special diphthong pairs: *OI/OY* and *OU/OW*. Even though the next pair is not a diphthong, teach it at the same time: *AU/AW*. You can teach these three pairs together or separately.

**The Rule:** There are two ways to spell three different vowel sounds: *OI/OY*, *OU/OW*, and *AU/AW*. As a general rule, *OI*, *OU*, and *AU* are found in the middle of words; *OY*, *OW*, and *AW* are found at the end. For example, *boil, sound, Paul,* and *boy, pow, lawn*. *OW* can also be used to spell the long sound for *O*. For example, *snow*.

**Introductory Images:**

*OI/OY* say "OY" as in *boy*. Example image: draw a picture of a pig and write: *The b<u>oy</u> pig <u>oi</u>nked.*

*OU/OW* says "OW." Example image: draw a picture of an arm in a sling and write: *The patient called <u>out</u>, "<u>Ow</u>! <u>Ou</u>ch!"*

*AU/AW* says "AW." Example image: draw a baby wrapped in a shawl and write: *Baby P<u>au</u>l is wrapped in a sh<u>aw</u>l.*

**Activities:**

1. **Open Sort Spelling Challenge:** Give the students a list of words that contain the letters *OI* and *OY*. Challenge them to sort the words into categories and then spot the spelling pattern. For example, *boil, boy, point, spoil, coy, ahoy, soil, joy, toil, Roy, soy, toy*.

Pattern: *OI* is the spelling used in the middle of words and *OY* is found at the end. Note: This pattern applies to single-syllable words. In longer words, *OY* can appear in the middle: *royal, loyal*, etc.

2. **Word Sort Contrasting the Two Sounds of OW:** After you have introduced the diphthong sound for the letters *OW* (i.e., /ou/ as in *plow*), introduce the long *O* sound of *OW* (e.g., *snow*) through a word sort. Write a list of words where some words have the long *O* sound and others the diphthong. Have the students create a sort sheet with a column for the /ow/ sound and one for the long *O* sound. Have them enter each word into the proper column.

**Bookwork:**

- Phonics rule book: Have the students draw a quick sketch for each rule into their phonics rules book. Have them leave space to add words that follow this rule.

- Other written activities for day two: Make a worksheet that includes pictures of words that use this rule such as *boy, boil*, etc. Have the students circle the pictures that have the targeted sound(s) and write the correct spelling next to each picture.

**How to Help Struggling Students:** Confirm that students have solid symbol imagery and then have them read lots of phonics readers that feature this rule. Do eagle eye noticing tasks for these vowel teams (see 3.4 #10).

## Rule 12: Long Vowels + *R*

**Phase:** Middle of the Pattern Phase

**Prerequisites:** Silent *E*, *R*-controlled vowels, Two Vowels Go Walking, word families, the sight word *our*.

**Expected time for students to achieve the 80/80 Rule:** 2–3 weeks with daily practice after introduction

**Background Information:** There are five long-vowel rimes with *R*: -air (e.g., fair), -ear (e.g., fear), -are (e.g., rare), -ire (e.g., fire), -ure (e.g., pure); two alternate spellings for the letters *OR*: -ore (e.g., core) and –oor (e.g., door); and one diphthong: –our (e.g., sour). The long vowel letters get their full sound AND the letter *R* still acts like a vowel. As a result, it looks like these words have one syllable, but it can sound like they have two (e.g., tire). To avoid this complication, teach the encoding and decoding of these *R* vowels through word families rather than the encoding and decoding process found in table 4.2.2.

**The Rule:** Both the long vowel and the *R* vowel get their full pronunciation as vowels. For example, *fire* = *fie* + *er*.

**Introductory Image:** When the letter *R* follows Two Vowels Go Walking vowel teams, the *R* joins in the talking. It politely waits one beat and says: /r/. For example, ear: /ee/ (clap) /er/ (clap): ear.

**Activities:** Have the class collect words in chains (i.e., word families) for each vowel team. Have the students draw word family houses as shown in figure 4.2.2. Display them in the classroom and ask students to add to them when they find more words for each word family.

**Figure 4.2.2: Word Family House**

**Bookwork:**

- Phonics rule book: Have the students put simplified sketches of word houses in their phonics rules book. Have them leave space to add words that follow this rule.

- Other written activities for day two: Make a worksheet that includes pictures of words that use this rule such as *tear, pair,* etc. Have the students circle the pictures that have the targeted sound(s) and write the correct spellings next to the word.

**How to Help Struggling Students:** When decoding, have the students give the full sound for the long vowel and for the *R* that comes after it. Clap between sounds if needed.

# Rule 13: Inflectional Endings #2: –s, –es, –ed, and –ing

**Phase:** Middle of the Pattern Phase

**Prerequisites:** Encoding the Silent *E* rule; identification of nouns and verbs in grammar; the concept of making a word plural by adding the letter *S*, concept of past tense using –ed; concept of syllables.

**Expected time for students to achieve the 80/80 Rule:** 2–3 weeks with daily practice after introduction. Encoding mastery is not expected at this time. The concept will be retaught in the Syllable Phase (see chapter 4.3 rule 28).

**Background Information:** This is the second of three lessons on inflectional endings (see chapter 4.1 rule 4 and chapter 4.3 rule 28).

Inflectional endings are suffixes put on the end of a word to modify it. The most common inflectional suffixes are:

- –s/–es
- –ed
- –ing

Each of these four suffixes apply to verbs and/or nouns. Note: The dash in front of the letters indicates that these combinations are suffixes and not words that can stand alone.

English-speaking students will pick up the nuances of decoding these endings from the memory and choral reading done in the Emergent Phase and Phonemic Awareness Phase and their inherent knowledge of what sounds right combined with rule 4 in chapter 4.1. However, they will need explicit instruction on how to encode with these endings. The following information is included primarily for spelling.

**Curriculum Connections:** Teach plural nouns in grammar along with this phonics rule (see chapter 3.11 7f). In 2nd Grade, teach the concept of plural nouns in a grammar lesson. Then in a phonics rules lesson, teach the students when to add –es. When planning your lessons, schedule these lessons back to back. You can space out the introduction of –s/–es to coincide with nouns and the introduction of –ed/–ing to coincide with verbs.

**The Rule for –s/–es:** Most plural nouns end in –s. The suffix –es is used when the root word ends with the letter(s): *S, Z, X, CH,* or *SH.* It always gives the root word an extra syllable and makes the sound *is* or *es* (e.g., branches, foxes, buzzes, washes, busses).

Note: The suffix –es is also used with the letter *Y*, but that rule is covered in chapter 4.3 rule 29. Irregular plural nouns such as *children* and *mice* are taught in 4th Grade.

**Introductory Image for –es:** Ask the students to try to say some words ending in the letters *S, Z, X, CH,* or *SH* with just the sound of /s/. (Model how to do so first because it is very hard. For example, say the word *"fox,"* pause briefly, and add the sound /s/.) They will quickly hear that it just does not sound right. Then tell the following story.

*All of the letter children listened to the Mayor and applied his lessons well. For example, they always put the letter S on the ends of words to show that they were plural, just as he told them to. But one day, the Mayor noticed something was wrong. He walked past the word fish and noticed that the letter children had spelled it FISHS. The Mayor tried to sound out the word (say fish /s/), and the letter children fell down, laughing. It sounded ridiculous. Some of the letter children said that they had taken to spelling the word FISHIS because that is how the word sounds. The Mayor said that the letter children were right to put in a vowel letter, but that he could not approve using the letter I because it looks too much like FISH IS. Instead, he decried that they should use the letter E and spell the word FISH with an ES on the end to show there was more than one fish.*

*One letter child complained. He said it was too confusing. When should they use the letter S and when should they use the letters ES? The Mayor said there was a way to tell when to use –S on the end of a word and when to use –ES. He challenged the letter children to find it.*

*Let's see if you can help the letter children find the rule. When do you put an S on a plural word and when do you put on the letters ES?*

**Activity:** Segue right in to an activity to find when to add –s and when to add –es. Give the students a list of plural words that contain both –s and –es. Have them sort the words with you on the board. Make two categories: end in –s and end in –es. Then see if the students can spot the deciding factor. Answer: The words that get an –es are those that have an extra syllable. If the students cannot figure out what changed, have them clap out the syllables in each category.

Note: Although students might notice that the words that get an –es share certain ending letters (e.g., S or Z), focus instruction and practice on whether or not the words get an extra syllable.

**The Rule for –ed:** When adding –ed to the end of a word, consider the root word. The letter E can jump over a single sound and make a vowel say its name. Therefore, if a root word has a short vowel with only one consonant after it, double the final consonant to protect the root word (e.g., beg/begged). If the root word already ends with an E, drop it before adding the –ed (e.g., skate/skated).

Note: If a student finds an irregular past tense verb (e.g., swept), tell her it is irregular and will be taught in 4th Grade.

**Introductory Image:** This story is a continuation of Super *E* or Magic *E* (see chapter 4.1 rule 6).

**Introductory Image from Englishland:** This story uses the umbrella story *Englishland* as it has a grammatical component.

*When it came to spelling verbs, the children of Letter Village ran into a problem. They knew to put an –ed on the end of verbs to show that they had already happened, but it turns out the letter E, if given the chance, would always turn into a superhero and jump over an ending consonant and turn the short vowel into a long vowel. It did this even when it was part of the ending –ed.*

*The letter children never knew what the –ed ending would do to a word. For example, sometimes it behaved itself and helped them change the word* call *into* called *and then other times the E in –ed would all of a sudden turn into a superhero and change the word the children wanted to spell into a completely different word with an altogether different meaning. For example,* pinned *became* pined *(write on the board).*

*A number of the letter children became so frustrated over this trick that –ed sometimes played on them that they went to the Mayor to complain asking him to just get rid of the E in the –ed ending. The Mayor shook his head. "I can't do that," he said. "The letter E does have an important job. There are times when it has to remind the vowel to say its name. However, there is something you children can do to protect those words that have a short vowel." The letter children were mystified. How could they have more power than Super E? One child asked the Mayor, "How?" The Mayor replied, "Remember, although Super E can make a vowel say its name, it only has the strength to bound over one consonant/letter to reach the vowel. So if there is more than one letter separating it from the vowel, E cannot reach the vowel and it keeps its short sound. If you want to protect the short vowel from Super E, just double the final consonant before you add –ed. Then he can't reach it."*

*The letter children decided to see if the Mayor's advice would work. They once again spelled the word* tap *but this time they put a second P on the end of the word before they added on the –ed (write on the board). Sure enough when the E saw how far away the A was, he was quite content to stay put and allow the A in* tapped *to say its short vowel sound. From that day forward, any time a verb had a short vowel sound and only one consonant after it, the letter children doubled the final consonant to protect the short vowel sound before adding –ed. All of the letters were able to play together without any problems.*

**The Rule for –ing:** The suffix –ing follows the same rules as the suffix –ed. When adding –ing to the end of a word, you have to consider the root word. If the root word has a short vowel and one consonant after it, double the final consonant to protect the root word. For example, *beg/begging*. If the root word already ends with an E, drop it before adding the –ing. For example, *skate/skating*.

**Introductory Image:** Tell a story about how the ending –ing copies what its friend –ed does.

**Introductory Image from Englishland: Introducing Doubling with –ing:**

*The ending –ing was best friends with the ending –ed. As good friends often do, they liked to do the same things. So when the ending –ing stood at the end of a word, it started making the vowel say its name, just like –ed.*

*For example, when the letter children formed the word* hop, *the ending –ing stood at the end, reached over the letter P, and made the letter O say its name. As a result, the word now said* hoping *(write the word on the board). The letter children who had spelled the word* <u>hop</u> *were quite upset at this change.*

*But, after their experience with the –ed ending, the letter children were ready for –ing's shenanigans, and they knew what to do! They doubled the last consonant (P) so that the ending –ing could not reach the vowel. This solution worked out great. The word now said* <u>hopping</u> *(write the word on the board).*

*However, the next day, the letter children spelled the word* tape. *(Write the word on the board.) The ending –ing came over to stand at the end of the word. The letter E saw it coming and brightened up. "Now that you are here, you can take over my job!" said E. "We do not both need to make the vowel say its name." The ending –ing agreed that it would do E's job, and everyone was happy. The word said* taping *because the ending –ing made the letter A say its name, and the letter E was free to go help spell other words.*

**Activity:** Have the students act out the suffixes –ed/-ing reaching over to make a short vowel say its name. Make up a list of words, some that need to be doubled and some that do not: pet, trade, trip, sail, etc. Make up letter cards for all of the letters in the list of words plus the letters that will need to be doubled (e.g., the *T* in *pet*, the *P* in *trip*, etc.). Make these letters in a different color. Also make up a card for the suffix –ing or –ed. Hand out letters to a select group of students. Give the suffix card to a responsible student. Hand out the letters that might be doubled to another group of students. Have the remaining students be the judges to decide if a word needs its final consonant doubled. Call out the word to be spelled and have the students who have its letters come up to spell it. Let the child with the suffix try to make the vowel say its name. If she can, have the judges decide if the final consonant needs to be doubled.

**Bookwork:**

- Phonics rule book: Have the students put these rules into their phonics rules book. Have them leave space to write in words that follow these rules.

- Other written activities for day two: kid writing

- –ed: Ask the class to make a list of five things they did last weekend. Then have them go back and see if Super *E*/Magic *E* can make any short vowels say their names. If so, double the final consonant. Have the students use complete sentences to tell what five things they did.

- –ing: Have the class watch you while you are doing something such as <u>tapping</u> your heel. Then ask them to write down what you are doing in a complete sentence (e.g., Ms. Militzer is tapping her heel). Make up a list ahead of time and be sure to include words where the short vowel is doubled and those where it is not (e.g., reading a book, snapping your fingers, writing on the blackboard, etc.) Have students come up and write a sentence on the board. Go over the answers and discuss when the final consonant should be doubled and when it should not.

**How to Help Struggling Students:** NA. Mastery is not expected at this time. This rule will be taught again in 3rd Grade (see chapter 4.3 rule 28). Point out the mistakes they make in their writing and have the students correct them.

## Rule 14: The Guardians: Doublers, –*CK*, –*TCH*, and –*DGE*

**Phase:** Beginning of the Pattern Phase

**Prerequisites:** Silent *E*, Two Vowels Go Walking, inflectional endings

**Expected time for students to achieve the 80/80 Rule:** 2–3 weeks with daily practice after introduction. The goal is mastery of both encoding and decoding.

**Background Information:** In some root words, there is a silent letter whose only job is to guard the short vowel. These silent letters are called the guardians. There are four types: doublers, *CK, TCH, and DGE.*

Root words that have short vowels and end with one consonant letter are in danger of having their vowel become long when vowel suffixes are added. Most root words simply double the final consonant to guard the short vowel, but only when a suffix is added (e.g., beg + ed = begged and tan + ing = tanning) (see chapter 4.2 rule 13 and chapter 4.2 rule 28). However, some root words have an extra letter built in.

**The Rule:** Some root words are spelled with an extra letter to guard the short vowel letter. There are four categories:

1. Double *F, L, S, Z:* The letters *F, L, S,* and *Z* are doubled at the end of words when preceded by a short vowel (e.g., fluff, will, kiss, and buzz) but not for words with long vowel sounds (e.g., leaf or deal).

2. *CK:* The letters *CK* appears on words that have a short vowel followed by the sound /k/ (e.g., lick, cluck, and track) but not words with vowel teams or an extra consonant before the letter *K* (e.g., peek, park, leak, and whisk).

3. *TCH:* The letters *TCH* appears on words that have a short vowel followed by the sound /ch/ (e.g., match, pitch, and retch) but not words with vowel teams or an extra consonant before the letters *CH* (e.g., pooch, inch, and reach).

4. *DGE:* The letters *DGE* appears on words that have a short vowel followed by the sound /j/ (e.g., judge, ridge, and ledge), but not words with long vowels or an extra consonant before the letters *GE* (e.g., page, range, and lunge).

**Introductory Images:** Describe how the guardian letter teams are special combinations of letters that protect short vowels. They stand at the end of words, after a short vowel. They include one silent letter whose only job is to protect the short vowel in the event an ending is added to the word. This silent letter is called the guardian.

1. The letters *F, L, S,* and *Z* recruit their identical twins to help them protect the short vowel: *FF, LL, SS,* and *ZZ*

2. The letter *K* recruits its fraternal twin *C: CK*

3. The consonant team *CH* recruits the letter *T,* the first letter of *team,* and together they form *TCH* (pronounced /ch/).

4. The letters *GE* make the /j/ sound at the end of a word. They recruit the letter *D* to help them protect the short vowel: *DGE* (pronounced /j).

**Activities:**

- Have the students act out the role of guardians protecting the short vowels. Note: Establish firm guidelines before doing this activity. The guardian letters only protect; they never go on the offensive.

- Put up the beginning of a number of identical twin ending words on the board (e.g., ba_ _, fu_ _, cli_ _). Review the four identical twin endings (ll, ss, zz, ff) then ask students to come up and fill in the blanks with possible twin endings. They will discover that some of these word beginnings have more than one possible twin ending (e.g., hill and hiss, fill and fizz, mall and mass, etc.).

**Bookwork:**

- Have the students put these rules into the phonics rules book. Have them leave spaces to write words they find in their independent reading that follow these rules.

## Rule 15: Other Uses for Silent *E*

**Phase:** Middle of the Pattern Phase

**Prerequisites:** Silent *E,* soft and hard sound of *C,* plural nouns

**Expected time for students to achieve the 80/80 Rule:** 2–3 weeks with daily practice after introduction. Emphasize encoding.

**Background:** There are four uses for Silent *E* at the end of words:

- to make a vowel long (e.g., bake) (see chapter 4.1 rule 6)
- to make a *C* or *G* soft (e.g., dance, lodge)
- placed after *V* at the end of words (e.g., give)
- placed after *S* in nouns that are not plural (e.g., mouse)

## The Rules

1. A word cannot end in the letter *J*. Use the letters *GE* instead.

2. A word cannot end with the letter *V*. Put the letter *E* after it. For example, *love, give, gave, leave, etc.* Note that *E* does not always make the vowel long.

3. A word that is not plural cannot end with one letter *S*. When a noun ends in the sound /s/ but is not plural, there are several ways to spell it:
   - Put the letter *E* after the letter *S* as in the word *mouse*.
   - Use the letters *CE* as in the word *dance*.
   - Double the letter *S* as in the word *floss*.

## Introductory Images

1. Make up a story about how you can never end a word with the letter *J* because *J* hates to be last.

2. Describe how you can never end a word with the letter *V* because *V* is a very tippy letter. It stands on a narrow little point. Because the letter *E* is used to being silent on the end of words, it is placed at the end of words that end in the /v/ sound to hold the letter *V* upright. In this case Silent *E* is there to hold up *V* not make the vowel say its name (Bishop 1986, 267).

3. Tell a story about the letter *S*. When nouns end in the /s/ sound, the letter *E* will sometimes stand after them so no one gets confused and thinks the noun is plural (e.g., mouse). However, the letter *S* is so popular that sometimes another letter has to stand in its place such as the letter *C* (e.g., dance). Other times, the letter *S* gives the letter *E* a break and invites its identical twin and they both stand at the end of the word (e.g., floss).

**Activities:** Have the students act out these rules.

## Bookwork:

- Phonics rule book: Have the students put these rules into their phonics rules book. Have them leave space to write in words that follow these rules.

- Other written activities for day two: Make a worksheet that includes pictures of words that use this rule such as *house, horse*, etc. Have the students circle the pictures that have the targeted sound(s) and write the correct spellings next to the word.

**How to Help Struggling Students:** Provide symbol imagery exercises to students who struggle to learn to encode with these Silent *E* words.

# Rule 16: Trickster *X*

**Phase:** Middle of the Pattern Phase

**Prerequisites:** Nonsense words; informal breaking of words into syllables (formal rules to be introduced in the Syllable Phase) (see chapter 3.15 #8)

**Expected time for students to achieve the 80/80 Rule:** One week with daily practice after introduction.

**Background Information:** The letter *X* is a complicated letter. When you teach the alphabet, you introduce the /ks/ sound as in fox but *X* has three possible sounds: /ks/, /gz/, and /z/.

When the letter *X* shows up in the middle of a word, the pronunciation varies. It could be /ks/, /gz/, or both depending on your region. Try a few words to figure out which sound(s) you use in your region. For the word *exit*, do you say eggs-it or eks-it? For the word *example*, do you say *eggs-am-ple* or *eks-am-ple*? Amend the list of sounds to match your region.

There are very few words that begin with the letter *X*. If you are not using nonsense words as part of your practice, begin to do so now. Introduce the idea of people who speak Gobbledygook, a made-up language that sounds like English most of the time but includes lots of silly nonsense words. Have them practice decoding Gobbledygook's silly words. For more information on nonsense words, see chapter 3.4 #2.

**The Rule:** The letter *X* has various pronunciations depending on where it is found in a word.

**Introductory Image:** Tell a story about how *X* is a trickster like the fox and uses different voices depending on where it is located in the word:

- In the beginning of the word, it makes the sound /z/ (e.g., xylophone).
- In the middle of the word, it makes the sound /ks/ (e.g., exit or /gz/ like exam).
- At the end of the word, it makes the sound /ks/ (e.g., fox).

**Activities:** Put up a poem or silly sentence that has many words with the letter *X*. Read the poem. Play eagle eye with words to spy where the *X* is hiding. Then figure out which sound the letter *X* has (see chapter 3.4 #10).

**Bookwork:**

- Phonics rule book: Have the students put these rules into their phonics rules book. Have them leave space to write in words that follow these rules.
- On day two have your students do a word sort with common words that feature the letter *X*. Have the students organize a pre-selected list of words that have the letter *X* into categories based on the sound *X* has. See chapter 3.3 #2 for more information on word sorts.

**Additional Practice:**

1. Review informal syllable breaks before you practice *X* in the middle of words. When practicing, accept any logical break students make for the purposes of practicing *X* (see chapter 3.15 #8).
2. Decode and encode using nonsense words.

## Rule 17: Y as a Vowel

**Phase:** Middle of the Pattern Phase

**Prerequisites:** Informal breaking of words into syllables (see chapter 3.15 #8) and symbol imagery

**Expected time for students to achieve the 80/80 Rule:** 2–3 weeks with daily practice after introduction

**Background Information:** *Y* is the hardest letter to master. It has four possible sounds: /y/, /ĭ/, /ī/, and /ē/ .In addition, it is a consonant at the beginning of words (e.g., yes, yellow, yet) and a vowel in the middle or end of words (e.g., cycle, lady). Furthermore, when it is a vowel, it can stand alone (e.g., fly) or be part of a vowel team (e.g., bay, toy, they). In addition, it can change to the letter I when a suffix is added (see chapter 4.3 rule 29).

**The Rule:** The sound for the letter *Y* depends on where it is found in the word:

- If at the beginning of a word, *Y* says it consonant sound (e.g., /y/ as in yes).

- If located in the middle of a single-syllable word, *Y* has the short vowel sound for the letter *I* (e.g., /ĭ/ as in gym). If located in the middle of a multisyllabic word, *Y* has the long vowel sound for the letter *I* (e.g., /ī/ as in cycle).

- If located at the end of a single-syllable word, *Y* has the long vowel sound for the letter *I* (e.g., /ī/ as in fly). If located at the end of a multisyllabic word, *Y* becomes the long vowel sound for the letter *E* (e.g., /ē/ as in baby).

- In compound words, note the position of the vowel in its root word and apply the rules accordingly (e.g., bodyguard = body + guard; in the word *body,* the letter *Y* is at the end of a multisyllabic word and has the sound /ē/).

**Introductory Images:**

1. Describe *Y* as a chameleon who often changes his sound. Use the list above and put in a different-colored chameleon for each location in the word.

2. Use an explanation from *Englishland*.

*The letters I and E were very popular. They helped to spell lots of words. One group of letter children were getting to the end of some words that needed I and E's sounds, but those two letters were busy spelling other words and were not available. Meanwhile, the letter Y was playing all by himself. He did not show up in a lot of words and had nothing to do. His sound /y/ was not very useful. When he saw that the letter children could not spell their words, he volunteered to take on the sounds of long I and long E. The letter children cheered and welcomed him at the ends of their words. Their problem was solved!*

*The Mayor came over to look at their work. Although he appreciated Y's willingness to help his playmates spell their words, he was afraid that there would be confusion over when Y was saying /ī/ and when he was saying /ē/. To prevent this, he told the letter Y that he could be the sound long I—but only at the end of a word that had one syllable. And he could be the sound long E—but only at the end of a word that had two or more syllables. The letter Y promised. And that is why Y can have the sound long I and long E at the ends of words.* (Note: If you use this image, you can build off of it in chapter 4.3 rule 29.)

**Activities:** Put up a poem or passage with lots of words with the letter *Y.* Read the poem. Play eagle eye with words to spy where the *Y* is hiding (see chapter 3.4 #10). Then use the Mayor's rule to figure out which sound the letter *Y* has. The next day use nonsense word (e.g., yug, slyg, dwy, cytops, etc.) as well as compound words such as *everyone, ladybug,* etc.

**Bookwork:**

- Phonics rule book: Have the students put these rules into their phonics rules book. Have them leave space to write in words that follow this rule.

- Other written activities for day two: Do a word sort with common words that feature the letter *Y.* Have the students organize a list of words that have the letter *Y* into categories based on the sound *Y* has. See chapter 3.3 #2 for more information on word sorts.

**How to Help Struggling Students:** Teach the students to be systematic in decoding with the letter *Y.*

1. Underline the letter *Y.* If it is part of a vowel team such as *AY,* underline the other vowel too. Say the sound of the digraph and read the word.

2. If the *Y* is not part of a vowel team, determine if it is part of a compound word. If so, work with just the word that includes the letter *Y.*

3. Figure out where in the word the *Y* is: beginning, middle, or end. Say its sound.

4. Read the word.

## Rule 18: Silent Consonants

**Phase:** End of the Pattern Phase

**Prerequisites:** None, but teach the more important rules first

**Expected time for students to achieve the 80/80 Rule:** 2–3 weeks with daily practice after introduction. Emphasize decoding.

**Background Information:** English has quite a few silent consonants, many of which are relics of sounds that used to exist in the language. For example, in English's Germanic days, the silent *K* was pronounced in words such as *knight*. These patterns of spellings are archaic, but some of them correspond to the meaning of the word. In addition, some silent letters are pronounced when suffixes are added.

- *WR* only shows up at the beginning of root words. It tends to be about twisting (e.g., wring, wrestle, and write (making twisting lines) (Bishop 1986, 276).

- *GN* can show up at the beginning or end of a root word (e.g., *gnaw* or *sign*). The *G* is always silent when a root word stands alone, but when a Latin suffix is added to the end, sometimes the /g/ is pronounced (e.g., sign becomes signal (sig-nal)).

- *MB* and *MN* are silent at the end of a root word (e.g ., *lamb* and *autumn*, but both are pronounced when you add certain suffixes (e.g., *crumb* and *crumble; condemn* and *condemnation*.

- *GH* has three different sounds: silent after a long vowel sound (e.g., high), /f/ as in *laugh*, and hard *G* as in *ghost*. Teach the first sound. The last two are rare and occur in just a handful of common words. They could be taught in spelling lists in 3rd Grade.

- *OUGH* has six different pronunciations even though it occurs in fewer than 40 words in common usage (Bishop 1986, 203). Do not teach any sound for this particular letter combination. *OUGH* is the one and only example where students should not be taught to decode but rather use the context to read the word. In addition, teach some common *OUGH* words as sight words (see Appendix 4).

- *PH* is not from Old English but from Greek. It has the sound /f/ as in *phone*.

- *KN* only shows up at the beginning of root words. Its words tend to be about knees and knuckles and things related to them (e.g., *knitting* and *knead* (Bishop 1986, 169).

**The Rule:** Teach the sound for each letter combination above.

**Introductory Image:** Describe a dog who usually runs around the yard barking loudly but who has a few spots where she lies quietly in the sun (see chapter 2.1 #4). Like the dog, a few letters usually say their sound, but in some spots in words, these letters are silent. However, you can come up with separate images for letter combinations such as the following:

- *KN: K* and *N* are good friends, but when they get together they act a bit strange. *K* always leads them wherever they go but never makes a sound and *N* does all of the talking.

- *GH:* Use a mnemonic device such as the letters *G* and *H* are so **Good Hearted** that when they come after a vowel, they let their vowel friend say its name and are silent themselves. Optional:

These **good hearted** letters have another side. For Halloween, they dress up as ghosts and ghouls, and the *G* does all the talking as they go out trick-or-treating. In addition, *G* and *H* sometimes play a funny trick: they pretend to be *F* and say its sound /f/ as in rough, tough, laugh, enough.

**Activities:** Play eagle eye (see chapter 3.4 #10). Put up a nursery rhyme or poem that has many of these letter combinations such as the first stanza to "This Old Man." Ask the students to use their eagle eye to find the silent letters (KN is *knick knack* and the MB in *thumb.*) Highlight them and then read the poem, deliberately mispronouncing the words to say each sound.

**Bookwork:**

- Phonics rule book: Have the students put these rules into their phonics rules book. Have them leave space to write in words they find in their independent reading that follow this rule.

**How to Help Struggling Students:** If students have trouble encoding these words, deliberately mispronounce them by saying them the way they look: k-n-i-g-h-t for *knight,* lam-b for *lamb,* etc.

## Rule 19: Other Vowel Teams

**Phase:** End of the Pattern Phase

**Prerequisites:** All of the other phonics rules to date, most sight words

**Expected time for students to achieve the 80/80 Rule:** 2–4 weeks with daily practice after introduction. Emphasize decoding.

**Background Information:** There are many infrequent vowel combinations. Do not teach them all because you will reach a point of diminishing returns. You will have to determine which ones to bring, their order, and how you wish to present them. There are two ways to approach teaching infrequent vowel combinations:

1. Grapheme: Teach each separate letter combination through images, as you did with earlier phonics rules. Select the combinations you plan to teach from Table 4.2.3.

2. Phoneme: Review the spelling of English vowel sounds and introduce infrequent patterns as part of a review of all phonics rules learned to date. Use the vowel sounds found in table 4.2.4.

**Table 4.2.3 Frequency of Uncommon Vowel Teams in Commonly Used Words**

Short E: *EA* (as in bread—156 words)
Long A: *EY* (as in hey—18 words)
    *EI* and/or *EIGH* (as in their or eight)—44 words)
    *EA* (as in great— number of words not listed)
Long E: *IE* (as in chief—71 words)
    *EY* (as in money—43 words)
Long I: *IGH* (as in high—88 words—consider teaching as a word family)
Long U: *EW* (as in few—64 words)
    *EU* (as in feud—27 words)
    *UI* (as in fruit—15 words)
R-Vowels: *EAR* with short vowel (as in heard—31 words)
    *YR* (as in syrup—14 words (including porphyry)

*Source: Material adapted from Hanna Research Project as cited throughout "The ABC's and All Their Tricks: The Complete Reference Book of Phonics and Spelling" by Margaret M. Bishop.*

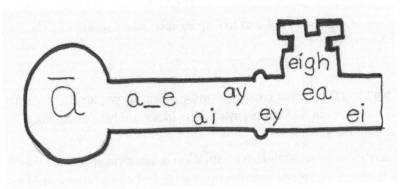

**Figure 4.2.4: Key Display of a Vowel Sound and Its Spellings**

**Table 4.2.4: Various Ways to Spell the 19 English Vowel Sounds (Listed from Most to Least Frequent)**

*Long Vowels:*
/ā/: a, a_e, ai, ay, ei/eigh, ey, ea
/ē/: e , ea, ee, ie, e_e, ey, i, ei, y
/ī/: i_e, i, y, ie, y_e, igh
/ō/: o, o_e, ow, oa, oe
/ū/ pronounced /yoo/: u, u_e, ew, ue
/long oo/: oo, u, o, ou, u_e, ew, ue

*Short Vowels:*
/ă/: a
/ĕ/: e, ea, e_e
/ĭ/: i , y
/ŏ/: o
/ŭ/: u, o, ou
/short oo/: oo, u, ou, o, ould

*R-Vowels*
/ur/ (i.e., /r/): er, ir, ur
/ar/: ar
/or/: or

*Other Vowels:*
/aw/: o, a, au, aw, ough, augh
/oi/: oi, oy
/ou/: ou, ow
/ə/ (i.e., schwa): a, e, i, o

*\*Note: There is one vowel sound that has not been taught: the sound /ə/ or the **schwa**. It makes the sound /ŭ/ as in data. It occurs in unaccented syllables. In some classifications systems, it appears as the 19th vowel sound; however, we do not include it for two reasons: It is taught in Section 4.3 Rule 31 and it is sounds just like the short vowel /ŭ/.*

*Source: Material adapted from Hanna Research Project as cited in Teaching Reading Sourcebook for Kindergarten through Eighth Grade (Honig 2000, 3.19)and The ABC's and All Their Tricks: The Complete Reference Book of Phonics and Spelling" by Margaret M. Bishop.*

**The Rule:** NA—there are multiple ways to spell most English vowel sounds.

**Introductory Image:** There are two possibilities:

1. Invent introductory images for each of the vowel teams you intend to teach (e.g., *OY* and *OW*).
2. Use the image of keys (see fig. 4.2.4) to display each vowel sound and the number of ways that sound can be spelled.

**Activities:** There are two approaches:

1. If you are teaching these letter combinations, play eagle eye (see chapter 3.4 #10). Put up a nursery rhyme or poem that has many of these letter combinations. Ask the students to use their eagle eye to find the silent letters.
2. If you are reviewing vowel sounds, have the class brainstorm ways each vowel sound in English can be spelled. Review each rule as it comes up and teach the new letter combinations as they come up.

**Bookwork:**

- Phonics rule book: There are two approaches:
  1. Have the students record each vowel team in their phonics rules book. Have them leave space to write in words that follow this rule.
  2. Have the students create a page for each vowel sound. There could be one sound per page (i.e., 15–18 pages total) and the students could draw keys for each vowel sound as shown in figure 4.2.4. The student could also make a separate page for short vowels, long vowels, *R*-controlled vowels, and other vowels (i.e., four pages total).
- Other written activities for day two: Continue drawing keys if you are reviewing vowel sounds.

**How to Help Struggling Students:** Make sure symbol imagery is well developed. In addition, review a lot of sight words that have rare vowel teams (e.g., they, enough).

## Rule 20: Compound Words #2

**Phase:** End of the Pattern Phase

**Prerequisites:** Mature symbol imagery (seven+ letters), all previous phonics rules

**Expected time for students to achieve the 80/80 Rule:** Two weeks with daily practice after introduction

**Curriculum Connections:** Review all phonics rules for the Pattern Phase as they show up in compound words.

**The Rule:** Two unrelated words can be combined into one to create an entirely new word. For example, light + house = lighthouse (see chapter 4.1 rule 7).

- Decoding: Look for each word in the compound word and put a break line between them (e.g., homerun home / run).
- Encoding: Have the students tackle each word as a separate word and then put the two words together to make the compound.

**Introductory Image:** (see chapter 4.1 rule 7).

**Activities:**

- Give the students some sentences that contain a number of compound words. Have them underline each compound word and together discuss each word's definition and why they think those two words were combined to form that word. (Most of the time this is obvious but not always (e.g., butterfly).

- On the board write a number of compound words that utilize the phonics rules that you have taught. Analyze each word that makes up the compound word. Have them identify which phonics rule(s) apply for each word. For example, *homerun* is made up of the words *home* and *run*. The word *home* has the Silent *E* rule.

**Bookwork:** See chapter 4.1 rule 7

**How to Help Struggling Students:** Make sure symbol imagery is solid up to seven letters and students are proficient with phonics rules.

## Rule 21: Homophones

**Phase:** End of the Pattern Phase

**Prerequisites:** All previous phonics rules

**Expected time for students to achieve the 80/80 Rule:** 4–6 weeks with daily practice after introduction. Emphasize encoding.

**Background Information:** Homophones are words that are pronounced the same but have different meanings and spellings (e.g., *sale* and *sail)*. They were included in Johnson's dictionary (see chapter 1.3 #3). The initial introduction of homophones occurs at the end of the Pattern Phase (end of 2nd Grade) or the beginning of the Syllable Phase as a review of 2nd Grade phonics rules (beginning of 3rd Grade).

**Curriculum Connections:** If your students have completed all of the words on *The Roadmap to Literacy's* Sight Word List, you can begin giving spelling tests using homophones at the end of 2nd Grade. (Pick 5–6 pairs a week and use them as spelling words.) You can also wait until the beginning of 3rd Grade to begin spelling tests and include homophones as a way of reviewing the phonics rules covered in 2nd Grade (see chapter 3.9 #7).

**Table 4.2.5: Beginning List of Homophones for 2nd/3rd Grade**

| | | | | |
|---|---|---|---|---|
| add/ad | fair/fare | meet/meat | principle/principal | sew/so/sow |
| air/heir | find/fined | might/mite | rain, reign, rein | some/sum |
| ant/aunt | flower/flour | morn/mourn | read/reed | steal/steel |
| ate/eight | for/four/fore | need/knead | real/reel | tail/tale |
| ball/bawl | great/grate | new/knew | red/read | through/threw |
| bare/bear | heard/herd | night/knight | right/write | to/two/too |
| be/bee | here/hear | no/know | road/rode/rowed | toe/tow |
| beat/beet | hi/high | oh/owe | sale/sail | told/tolled |
| blue/blew | hole/whole | one/won | see/sea | way/weigh |
| brake/break | horse/hoarse | or/oar/ore | seem/seam | week/weak |
| by/bye/buy | I/eye | our/hour | sell/cell | weather/whether |
| creek/creak | in/inn | pair/pear/pare | sent/cent/scent | where/wear/ware |
| dear/deer | loan/lone | peace/piece | shoe/shoo | wood/would |
| die/dye | made/maid | plane/plain | side/sighed | |

*Source: Fry 2006, 60–61: List 19.*

Homophones come in different levels. Recommendations for consideration can be found in table 4.2.5. Customize this list for the needs of your class. Note: It is not necessary to teach the entire list at this time. Students will continue to study homophones in later grades.

**The Rule:** Some words sound the same but are spelled different.

**Introductory Images:** Describe Identical twins who dress differently to show they are very different from each other. Some words do the same thing. They sound alike, but they have different spellings to show they are different words.

**Activities:** Read a number of sentences with homophones. Ask your students to listen to each pair of sentences for the words that sound the same. For example, *I* <u>blew</u> *out the candle. Her eyes were* <u>blue</u>.

Write the sentences on the board and have the students identify the homophones. Then have them identify the differences in spelling. Review phonics rules as they come up.

**Bookwork:** Have the students create a quick sketch and a sentence illustrating each pair of homophones. The work can go into a main lesson book or the phonics rules book. Have the students identify the homophones and any phonics rule in the homophones (e.g., the words *pail* and *pale* use two phonics rules: Two Vowels Go Walking and Silent E).

**Other Practice Activities:**

- Help the students find mnemonic tricks or memory tricks (e.g., <u>piece</u> *of pie* or *the princi*<u>pal</u> *is your pal).*

- Deliberately mispronounce a word to hear its silent letters. For example, "It was a new question, but I <u>k-new</u> the answer." or "I will <u>w-rite</u> the letter with my <u>r-i-g-h-t</u> hand." Also, work with your students to make up some of their own ways to remember which spelling goes with which meaning.

- As a review activity at the end of the unit on homophones, give the students a poem where

402

you have deliberately misspelled the homophones. Ask them to underline the misspelled homophones and then fix the spelling. Below is an example based on the introductory lines of "The Woodpecker" by Elizabeth Madox Roberts (1881–1941): "The woodpecker pecked out a little round <u>whole</u> / And <u>maid</u> him a house <u>inn</u> a telephone <u>poll</u>" (Roberts 1922).

**How to Help Struggling Students:** Emphasize memory tricks for spelling. For example, the word *hear* has the word *ear* hidden inside it to show people that they <u>hear</u> with their <u>ears</u>. The word *here* is related to *there* as in *here and there*.

## Conclusion

Ideally, your students should have these phonics rules mastered for use when <u>decoding</u> by the end of 2nd Grade. If not, plan to teach any remaining rules at the beginning of 3rd Grade. The next chapter will present the phonics rules for the Syllable Phase.

# 4.3 PHONICS RULES FOR THE SYLLABLE PHASE

**Phonics rules** are the rules that expand the number of words students can decode and encode. They cover the letter combinations that stretch the 26 letters of the Latin alphabet to cover the 40+ sounds in English (see chapter 3.1 #1). The three chapters in section 4 cover 33 phonics rules for you to teach. They are divided into three phases: Phonemic Awareness Phase, Pattern Phase, and Syllable Phase. Mastering these 33 rules will help students develop the pattern layer of the English layer cake (see chapter 1.3 #1). This chapter covers the phonics rules for the Syllable Phase.

<u>Prerequisites for Teaching the Syllable Phase:</u> Students are able to decode and encode by onset and rime and use symbol imagery for seven letters (i.e., enough for the longest syllables). Note: Some students will not be able to meet the prerequisite for symbol imagery. Teach them these phonics rules anyway, but they will likely need extra practice, particularly with encoding.

It is strongly advised that you to go back and review chapter 3.4 Encoding and Decoding and the Section 4 Protocol found before chapter 4.1 prior to working with this chapter.

This chapter covers the following phonics rules:

- Rule 22: Encoding and Decoding by Syllable
- Rule 23: Open and Closed Syllables
- Rule 24: Big Four Prefixes (un–, dis–, in–, re–)
- Rule 25: Consonant –LE Syllables
- Rule 26: Big Four Suffixes: (–ment, –tive, –tion, –ture)
- Rule 27: Suffixes Beginning with Consonants (–ful, –less, –ness, –ly)
- Rule 28: Suffixes Beginning with Vowels, The 1–1–1 Rule, and Inflectional Endings #3
- Rule 29: When to Change the Letter *Y* to *I*
- Rule 30: Tricky Vowel Junctions
- Rule 31: The Schwa
- Rule 32: The Ending Grid
- Rule 33: Six Syllable Types: Review

## Rule 22: Encoding and Decoding by Syllable

**Phase:** Beginning of the Syllable Phase

**Prerequisites:** Proficiency in encoding and decoding by onset and rime for one-syllable words, proficiency with compound words, and syllable counting (see chapter 3.3 #9)

**Expected time for students to achieve the 80/80 Rule:** NA—will be practiced throughout the Syllable Phase. Initial introduction takes one day.

**Background Information:** This is not a real phonics rule. Instead, it is the third encoding and decoding process: encoding and decoding by syllables.

Teach and practice all phonics rules that cover multisyllable words using encoding and decoding by syllables. It is the most efficient way to decode and encode long words. See chapter 3.4 #9 for more information.

**The Rule:** See table 4.3.2 *Process for* <u>Decoding</u> *Multisyllabic Words* and Table 4.3.3. *Process for* <u>Encoding</u> *Multisyllabic Words.*

### Introductory Image for Decoding

"Who can eat this cucumber all in one bite?" (Hold up giant cucumber.) *"When we have something large to eat, we have to cut it up and eat it in smaller bites. When we have really long words, we have to read them and spell them in smaller bites. Just like with a cucumber, we have to cut long words into syllables before we read or spell them."*

*"Sometimes when you are reading, have you ever come across a really big word that you did not know?"* (Let a student share a story.) *"There is a way you can figure out how to read long words by yourself. I'm going to show you with a long word that I made up:* CONTERANTIVE. (Print your made-up word on the board but <u>do not</u> read it for the students.) *I'm going to break this really long word down into syllables or chunks of sound to make it easier to read."*

Note: It is important to use a nonsense word so that no students will recognize it.

Have the process rules written up on the board and model each step for *conterantive* as shown in table 4.3.1.

### Table 4.3.1: Example Process for Introducing Multisyllabic Decoding

| Write These Steps on the Board | Example |
|---|---|
| 1. Underline vowel <u>sounds.</u><br>2. Break off prefixes and suffixes.<br>3. Try to start every syllable with a consonant.<br>4. Read each syllable separately and then blend together. | 1. c<u>o</u>nt<u>era</u>nt<u>i</u>ve<br>2. c<u>o</u>n/t<u>era</u>n/t<u>i</u>ve<br>3. con / ter / an / tive<br>4. "con…ter…an…tive… conterantive" |

### Sample Script

1. "First, I underline vowel sounds so I can tell how many syllables I have. Each vowel <u>sound</u> forms a syllable. (Underline vowel sounds.) I must underline the *ER* because they are on a vowel team together. I cannot underline Silent *E* because it is silent and cannot form its own syllable. There are (point to each underlined vowel sound and count it aloud) four syllables because each syllable has a vowel sound."

2. "Sometimes words have common beginnings and endings called prefixes and suffixes. I will tell you more about those later. I have to break those syllables off first. (Break off con-and –tive.) I found two of the four syllables."

3. "Now there are only two syllables left to find. Syllables like to start with consonants when they can. I'm going to start at the end and look for clusters of letters that have more than one vowel sound underlined. They need to be broken down into syllables. The letter *I* has a syllable: -tive. The cluster *TERAN* has two vowel sounds. We can break it down into two syllables. The letter

*A* needs to figure out if it can take the letter *R* to be in its syllable as syllables like to start with consonants. It goes to the letter ahead to see if it is a consonant or a vowel. If it is a consonant, then it would join *A's* syllable but if it is a vowel or part of a vowel team, it has to stay in its own syllable. Look at the letter before the *A: R*. The *R* is on a vowel team: *ER*. It cannot join *A's* syllable. I will put in a syllable break between the *R* and the *A*. Now, I have (count the syllables) four syllables. That means I am done splitting my word into syllables."

4. "Now I read each syllable (point to each syllable as you read it) con...ter...an...tive. Blend them together and it says conterantive!"

Model a few long words, have student volunteers come up and do a few two-syllable or three-syllable words, and have the whole class practice a few two syllable words in their practice books. Call on volunteers to share their answers and see if the class agrees. Use words such as:

- gladden (gl<u>a</u>d/d<u>e</u>n)

- decode (d<u>e</u>/c<u>o</u>d<u>e</u>—Note that Silent *E* is part of a vowel team. It does not form its own syllable.)

- perfect (p<u>er</u>/f<u>e</u>ct—Note that the letters *ER* form a vowel team and are treated as a unit.)

- tagging (t<u>a</u>g/g<u>i</u>ng—Note that the double *G* closes the first syllable (see chapter 4.3 rule 23)

## Table 4.3.2: Process for Decoding Multisyllabic Words

| Process for Decoding Multisyllabic Words | Example |
|---|---|
| 1. Underline vowel <u>sounds.</u><br>2. Break off prefixes and suffixes.<br>3. Try to start every syllable with a consonant. Make each vowel grab the letter before it if it is a consonant.<br>4. Read each syllable separately and then blend together. (When a syllable ends in a vowel (open syllable), try reading the vowel as long and short to see which one is right.) | 1. R e <u>u</u> n i f <u>y</u><br>2. R<u>e</u> / <u>u</u> n i f <u>y</u><br>3. R<u>e</u> / <u>u</u> / n <u>i</u> / f <u>y</u><br><br>4. Re...YOU...nEYE....fy, re.... YOU... ni...fy: reunify" |

Note: This table is identical to Table 3.4.8.

Note: Words that have the inflectional suffix *–ing* are fair game as they always form syllables, but words with the suffix *–ed* are tricky because only the words that have the sound /ed/ or /id/ form syllables. For example, tricked (one syllable because the *ED* has the sound /t/) vs. trotted (two syllables because the *ED* has the sound /ed/ or /id/). Do not use words with the suffix *–ed*.

**Introductory Image for Encoding:** First, create a long, made-up word that your class will not be able to spell or choose a real one.

Tell the class, *"When you are spelling really long words, we know that it helps to spell them by syllable. We are going to begin to learn the rules for spelling by syllables. First, let me show you the rules."*

Have the steps written up on the board and model each step as shown in table 4.3.3.

**Table 4.3.3: Process for Encoding Multisyllabic Words**

| Process for Encoding Multisyllabic Words | Example |
|---|---|
| 1. Say the word out loud.<br>2. Say each syllable slowly and write a line as you say it.<br>3. Write down any prefixes or suffixes first.<br>4. Say the remaining syllables and write them down at the same time.<br>5. Put the word together and see if it looks right. | 1. "Comprehend"<br>2. "Com. . .pre. . . hend"<br>3. <u>Com</u> ___ ___<br>4. <u>Com</u> <u>pre</u> <u>hend</u><br>5. Comprehend—"Looks right!"<br>\* Open syllables can have long vowels (see chapter 4.3 rule 23). |

Note: This table is identical to table 3.4.9.

**Activities:** After modeling a few long words, have student volunteers come up and do several two-syllable or three-syllable words, and then have the class practice encoding and decoding several words in their practice books. Call on volunteers to share their answers, including where they broke the word. Have the other students give thumbs up or thumbs down.

**Bookwork:**

- Phonics rule book: NA. Do not put this rule into the phonics rules book because it is a process, not a rule.

- There are no written activities for day two.

**How to Help Struggling Students:** Repetition. Write the process down and practice, practice, practice. If a student still cannot learn the process, sit down with the student to find weak area(s) (see chapter 6.6).

## Rule 23: Open and Closed

**Syllables Phase:** Beginning of the Syllable Phase

**Prerequisites:** Single-syllable words

**Expected time for students to achieve the 80/80 Rule:** 2–3 weeks

**Background Information:** Open and closed syllables are two of six syllable types (see chapter 4.3 rule 33). They are taught in conjunction with rule 22 as students work with them when encoding and decoding multisyllabic words. They are taught as a pair.

The first syllable type is the open syllable. **Open syllables** end with one vowel (e.g., <u>no</u>, <u>sta</u>/tion, con/<u>di</u>/tion). The vowel can be long or short, depending on the origin of the word. For example, the vowel is long in native English words but short in words derived from Latin or French. In general, the vowel in open syllables tends to be long in words with two syllables and tends to be short in words with three or more syllables. This tendency holds true because native English words tend to have one or two syllables.

The second syllable type is the closed syllable. **Closed syllables** have one vowel letter but end with a consonant (e.g., <u>not</u>, <u>ac</u>/tion). The vowel in a closed syllable is always short. The final consonant *closes* the syllable. Ex. *hap/py (*the letter *P* closes the first syllable).

**The Rule:** Open syllables can have long or short vowel sounds, but closed syllables always have short sounds. In general, in two-syllable words, the open syllable is long, but in words with three or more syllables, it is short.

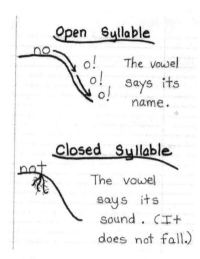

**Figure 4.3.1: Open and Closed Syllables**

**Introductory Image:** Tell a story about a single vowel letter who is hiking through a mountainous terrain alone. When the vowel letter is at the end of the syllable, it falls off the end of the syllable into a ravine and calls out its <u>name</u>, hoping someone will hear. But if there is a consonant after the vowel (i.e., closed syllable), it stops the vowel letter from falling and the vowel says its <u>sound</u>. Vowels on teams (i.e., digraphs) protect each other from falling into a ravine (see fig. 4.3.1).

**Activities:** NA. Move right into encoding and decoding practice and syllable cards.

**Bookwork:**

- Phonics rule book: Have the students put the rules into their phonics rules book. Have them leave space to write in words that follow each rule.

- Other written activities for day two: Have the students make a list of words they find in a book or passage. Have them add these words to their phonics rules book.

**How to Help Struggling Students:**

1. If students have trouble sounding out syllables, do lots of warm-up activities practicing nonsense syllables in isolation (cla, lac, sti).

2. If students have trouble with open syllables, do activities contrasting open and closed syllables. Start with common words such as we/wed; be/bed; hi/hit; go/got; etc. (Be very careful with irregular sight words such as *do*. It is not an open syllable. Otherwise, it would be pronounced *dough*.) Then move to pairs where one word is a syllable and the other is not such as *li/lip; la/lab; tra/trap*, etc. Then transition into pairs of syllables that are not real words: *du/duf; claf/cla; stog/sto*.

3. If students have difficulty counting syllables, practice counting jaw drops (see chapter 3.3 #9).

## Rule 24: The Big Four Prefixes: un–, dis–, in–, re–

**Phase:** Beginning of the Syllable Phase

**Prerequisites:** Decoding process for multisyllabic words, open/closed syllables

**Expected time for students to achieve the 80/80 Rule:** One week with daily practice after introduction

**Curriculum Connections:** Antonyms (see chapter 3.11 #8i)

**Background Information**

Prefixes are common syllables that come at the beginning of words. Prefixes are written with a dash after them to show that something needs to be added there. For example, the word *review* has the prefix *re-*, which means *to do again.* Thus *review* means *to view again.*

The Big Four Prefixes are good beginning prefixes because they are attached directly to root words, words that can stand alone when their affixes have been removed. For example, *view* is a word in its own right before the prefix *re-* is attached to it.

The following four prefixes in table 4.3.4 account for 58% of the prefixes used in English (Bear 2008, 178).

**Table 4.3.4: The Big Four Prefixes**

| Prefix | Meaning | Key Word |
|---|---|---|
| un– | not | unhappy |
| dis– | not | disagree |
| in– | not | injustice |
| re– | again or back | rewind |

*Source: Material adapted from Bear 2008, 178.*

The first three prefixes are added to a root word to create a new word that has the opposite meaning. The suffix *re-* before a word usually means *to do it again* or *go backwards* (e.g., revisit, retype, retrace).

Note: These prefixes do not *always* carry the meaning above. For example, *re-* does not always mean *again.* Alas, the word *retreat* does not mean to give more than one treat!

**The Rule:** Beginning prefixes are added directly onto root words to change the meaning of a word. For example, kind: unkind. To decode, merely break them off.

**Introductory Image from Englishland:** You can use the following story from *Englishland* (see chapter 3.11 Introduction).

*The word* not *was one of the busiest words in Letter Village. He always had to run over and insert himself into sentences (write on the board):*

- *I am* not *happy.*
- *She does* not *agree.*
- *This was* not *justice.*

*At first it was fun to be so useful, but soon he got tired. It was exhausting work showing up in so many sentences!*

*Then, one day the word* not *had a great idea. He grabbed a giant sticker and wrote the prefix "un" on it. Then he stuck it on the front of a word. "This prefix means* not*!" he shouted. "It will take my place so I can be in other sentences."*

*The words in the sentence did not think this was fair so they called the Mayor of Letter Village over to ask him. The*

*Mayor read the two sentences: "I am not happy. I am unhappy." He smiled. "These two sentences mean exactly the same thing!" he said. "The prefix* un *can take the place of the word* not. *The word* not *is free to go!"*

*The word* <u>not</u> *thought he would have tons of time now that he had invented the prefix "un" but so many other sentences needed him that he soon invented two other prefixes "dis" and "in" to help out (write on the board):*

- *She <u>disagrees</u> with the choice.*
- *That soccer move was <u>invalid</u>.*

**Activities:** eagle eye with prefixes (see chapter 3.4 #10).

**Bookwork:**

- Phonics rule book: Have the students put this rule into their phonics rules book. Have them leave space to write in words that follow this rule.
- Other written activities for day two: Have the students make a list of words they find in a book or passage and identify the root word and prefix. Have them add these words to their phonics rules book.

**How to Help Struggling Students:** NA. English-speaking students rarely have trouble with these prefixes as they are so common.

## Rule 25: Consonant –*LE* Syllables

**Phase:** Beginning of the Syllable Phase

**Prerequisites:** Open and closed syllables

**Expected time for students to achieve the 80/80 Rule:** two weeks with daily practice

**Background Information:** There are 10 suffixes that follow the consonant –*LE* pattern: –ble, –cle, –dle, –fle,

–gle, –kle, –ple, –sle, –tle, and –zle. These suffixes violate the open syllable rule. The letter *E* is not pronounced. For example, the words *raffle* and *helpful* have identical sounding suffixes: –fle and –ful. The –fle suffix spelled phonetically would be –*ful*.

**The Rule:** –*LE* attaches itself to the consonant before it to create a suffix. The syllable before it then follows the open/closed syllable rule. For example, ri/fle and rif/fle.

**Introductory Image:** Describe: 1) *LE* as a cowboy, lassoing the consonant before it to create a syllable; 2) *LE* as two friends, inviting a consonant to join them to form a syllable.

**Activities:** NA. Move right into practice encoding and decoding.

**Bookwork:**

- Phonics rule book: Have the students put this rule into their phonics rules book. Have them leave space to write in words that follow this rule.
- Other written activities for day two: Have the students make a list of words they find in a book or passage that contain these suffixes. Have them add these words to their phonics rules book.

**How to Help Struggling Students:** Do symbol imagery exercises with these suffixes if students have trouble learning them.

# Rule 26: The Big Four Suffixes: –ment, –tive, –tion, –ture

**Phase:** Beginning of Syllable Phase

**Prerequisites:** Open/closed syllables

**Expected time for students to achieve the 80/80 Rule:** 2–3 weeks with daily practice after introduction

**Background Information:** The Big Four Suffixes serve as a transition from working primarily with affixes that are attached to root words to affixes that have no root word. They also contain spelling irregularities. Students must approach them as *sight syllables* (i.e., syllables recognized on sight), and learn to read and spell them as such. Although the meaning of the following suffixes is discussed below for your edification, it is not advised to teach their meanings in 3rd Grade. This is because most of the words created by these suffixes are abstract *idea* nouns and best left to 4th Grade when all of your students have completed the nine-year change. See table 4.3.5.

**Table 4.3.5: The Big Four Suffixes, With and Without Root Words**

| –ment | move + -ment = movement | also ce/ment |
| –tive | secret + -tive = secretive | also fes/tive |
| –tion | act + -tion = action | also nation = na/tion |
| –ture | depart + ture = departure | also nature = na/ture |

*–ment:* This suffix is pronounced *"ment"* or *"mint"* depending on region, as in the word *moment*. It is the easiest suffix of the bunch. It has the meaning *"action or process of"* and turns a word into a noun. For example, you can take the verbs *move* and *govern* and create the nouns *movement* and *government*. (Notice how the root word is preserved to show that words that are related in meaning are related in spelling. This concept will become primary in the Latin/Greek Phase.) However, it also can be in words that have no root word such as *moment*.

*–tive:* The suffix *–tive* is only slightly irregular. It is pronounced *"tiv,"* as in *native*. There is a Silent *E* at the end because the letter *V* can never end a word. It also can turn a word into an adjective. For example, you can take the verb *act* and create the adjective *active*. You can take the noun *secret* and create the adjective *secretive*. However, it can also appear in words that have no root word such as *motive*.

*–tion:* The suffix *–tion* is also highly irregular. It is pronounced *"shun,"* as in the word *nation*. When it is attached to a root word, it has the meaning *"act or process"* as in the word *accommodation*. However, it can also appear in words that have no root word such as *motion*.

*–ture:* The suffix *–ture* is highly irregular. It is pronounced *"cher,"* as in the word *nature*. It has a long and complex history in English spelling that is best left for linguistics classes in college. No meaning is given to students.

**The Rule:** NA—just introduce the four suffixes and their pronunciation.

**Introductory Images:** NA—introduce these syllables in words that come from stories or material you are teaching. For example, *agriculture*.

**Activities:** NA— Move right into encoding and decoding practice.

**Bookwork:**

- Phonics rule book: Have the students put these suffixes into their phonics rules book. Have them leave space to write in words that follow this rule.
- Other written activities for day two: Have the students make a list of words they find in a book or passage that contain these suffixes. Have them list these words under the appropriate heading in their phonics rules book.

**How to Help Struggling Students:** If students have difficulty learning the spelling of these suffixes, treat them like sight words and practice them the same way.

## Rule 27: Suffixes Beginning with Consonants (–ful, –less, –ness, –ly)

**Phase:** Beginning of the Syllable Phase

**Prerequisites:** Basic parts of speech: noun, verb, adjective, adverb (see 3.11 #8)

**Expected time for students to achieve the 80/80 Rule:** One week with daily practice after introduction

**Background Information**

Suffixes are common syllables at the <u>end</u> of words. They can carry meaning and/or change a word's part of speech. For example, the word *quick* is an adjective, but when you add the suffix *–ly,* the word becomes an adverb: *quickly.*

Beginning consonant suffixes are attached directly to root words and do not affect the spelling as shown in table 4.3.6.

**Table 4.3.6: Beginning Consonant Suffixes**

| Suffix | Meaning | Key Word |
|--------|---------|----------|
| –ful | full of | joyful |
| –less | without or lacking | soulless |
| –ness | state of or condition of | kindness |
| –ly | characteristic of | quickly |

*Source: Adapted from Fry 2006, 102.*

**The Rule:** You can attach a consonant suffix directly to the end of a root word to add meaning or change its part of speech.

**Introductory Image from *Englishland*:** Build off of the grammar umbrella story of Prince Adverb and his letters –ly (see chapter 3.11 #8c). Tell the students that other parts of speech decided to borrow words from each other. For example, the word *kind* (adjective) was borrowed by Queen Noun. She put –ness on the end, and it became *kindness* (noun).

Teach the meaning of the four suffixes.

**-ful:** The suffix *–ful* means *"full of."* Add it to a root word to create an adjective that means "full of_." For example, *hopeful* means *full of hope* and *respectful* means *full of respect.*

**–less:** The suffix –*less* means "*without*" or "*lacking.*" You add it to a root word to create an adjective that means "*without* _____ *or lacking*_____". For example, *hopeless* means *without hope.* It is spelled with two *S's* to highlight the fact that it is not plural.

**–ness:** The suffix –*ness* means "*state of*" or "*condition of.*" Add it to a root word to create an abstract noun such as *kindness.* The nouns that have the –ness suffix tend not to be people, places, or things but rather ideas (e.g., fondness, fullness, laziness, mildness, rudeness, softness, weakness, etc.).*

**–ly:** The suffix –*ly* is a way to create an adverb. Add it to a root word to tell how something is done or how often something is done. For example, you can take the adjective *happy* and change it into the adverb *happily* as in *I have a happy cat; she purrs happily.* The word *happy* describes the word *cat,* which is a noun, while the word *happily* describes the word *purrs,* which is a verb.

**\*Curriculum Connection:** The suffix –*ness* also creates the fourth type of noun (idea). However, the words it creates tend to be more familiar than and not as sophisticated as those made by the Big Four Suffixes. If you would like to teach its meaning in 3rd Grade, you could do so. You could also wait until the beginning of 4th Grade.

**Activities:** NA— Move right into encoding and decoding practice.

**Bookwork:**

- Phonics rule book: Have the students put these suffixes into their phonics rules book. Have them include their definitions and parts of speech. Have them leave space to write in words that follow this rule.
- Other written activities for day two: Have the students make a list of words they find in a book or passage that contain these suffixes. Have them add these words to their phonics rules book.

**Additional Ways to Practice:** Do exercises to contrast the suffixes –*ful* and –*fle* to show that the former carries meaning, but the latter does not. For example, *graceful* means *full of grace* while *raffle* does not mean *ful of raf.*

- Write a number of words and word parts on the board that could accommodate either a –*ful* suffix or a –*fle* suffix (e.g., help, care, cheer, color, doubt, faith, muf, rif, duf, shuf, waf, snif, etc.). Have students make them into words by adding the right suffix. Have them justify their choice.
- Sort words that have the suffixes –*ful* and –*fle* such as raffle, delightful, baffle, hopeful, etc. Explore the differences between the suffixes –*fle* and –*ful.* (For more on word sorts, see chapter 3.3 #2.)

**How to Help Struggling Students:** Make sure that students are solid on grammar and that they have mature symbol imagery.

# Rule 28: Suffixes Beginning with Vowels, The 1–1–1 Rule, and Inflectional Endings #3

**Phase:** Beginning of the Syllable Phase

**Prerequisites:** Basic parts of speech: noun, verb, adjective, and adverb

**Expected time for students to achieve the 80/80 Rule:** 2–3 weeks with daily practice after introduction. Students have already mastered decoding with these endings; now it is time for them to master <u>encoding</u> with them.

**Background Information:** This is the third and final time to teach inflectional endings (see chapter 4.1 rule 4 and 4.2 rule 13). Present it with additional information on how to deal with suffixes that begin with vowels.

Suffixes that begin with vowels can change the spelling of the root word. There are two things to consider: 1) root words that end in Silent *E*; 2) when to double the final consonant of a root word.

Always drop the Silent *E* in a root word. It is no longer needed:

- Phone: phoned—the letter *E* in the suffix –ed makes the vowel long

- Trace: tracing—the letter *I* makes the letter *C* say /s/ and the letter *A* is long because it is in an open syllable: tra/cing

- Horse: horsing—the word no longer ends in the letter *S* so it cannot be mistaken as plural.

Determine when to double the final consonant in a root word by using the 1–1–1 rule as shown in table 4.3.7.

**Table 4.3.7: The 1–1–1 Rule**

When adding a vowel suffix, double the final consonant of the root word when all three criteria are met:
- 1 short vowel
- 1 consonant after the vowel
- 1 syllable

Examples:
sun + y = sunny (yes)
ripe + er = riper (no—vowel is long)
test + ing = testing (no—two consonants after the vowel)

Advanced Rule (optional): If the word has more than one syllable and the accent is on the last syllable, then double the final consonant.
Ex. begIN + er = beginner; PROgram + ing = programing.

*Source: Adapted from McDonald 2002, 17.*

This rule works because syllables always try to begin with consonants. It is necessary to double the consonant to keep the initial syllable closed. Table 4.3.8 contains some common vowel suffixes.

**Table 4.3.8: Common Vowel Suffixes**

| Suffix | Meaning | Key Word |
|---|---|---|
| –y | characterized by | sunny |
| –er/–est | comparative markers | quicker/quickest |
| –er/–or | one who | teacher/actor |
| –ish | like a | babyish, boyish |
| –ed | past tense marker | tripped |
| –ing | progressive form marker | scanning |

*Source: Adapted from Fry 2006, 102.*

**–y:** The suffix –*y* is a way to create an adjective. You add it to a root word to show that the something is "characterized by or inclined to." For example, the noun *sap* becomes the adjective *sappy* when you add a suffix –y at the end. *Sappy* means something is characterized by *sap*, a sticky, cloying substance. For example, sunny, rainy, mighty, etc. However, there are some words that do not have a root word. *Happy* is not characterized by *hap*.

**-er/-est:** The suffixes *-er/-est* make comparisons. They do not change the part of speech, merely the degree. The suffix -er means "more" and –est means "most.". For example, *taller* means *more tall. Tallest* means *most tall.*

**-er/-or:** The suffixes *-er/-or* can make words into nouns. Both of these suffixes mean "*one who.*" For example, a *teacher* is *one who teaches* and a *sailor* is *one who sails.* Beware of words that do not have root words. For example, a *tailor* is not one who *tails!*

**-ish:** The suffix *-ish* changes words into adjectives. It means "*like a___.*" For example, someone who is *babyish* is someone who acts like a baby.

**-ed:** The suffix *-ed* changes a verb into the past tense or into a past participle. It is only necessary to review past tense in this phase. For example, *played* is the past tense of *play.*

**-ing:** The suffix *-ing* changes a verb into the progressive form or into a present participle. It is only necessary to review the progressive form of the verb in this phase. For example, *playing* is the progressive form of *play.*

**The Rules:**

1. Drop the Silent *E* on the root word before adding the vowel suffix.

2. The 1–1–1–Rule: If a word has: 1 short vowel, 1 consonant after it, and is 1 syllable, double the final consonant before adding a vowel suffix.

**Introductory Images:**

1. Describe *E* as a soldier or worker, relieved of its duties at the end of a shift when someone else takes over.

2. Tell a story about how the extra, final consonant is a guardian letter assigned to protect the vowel when a consonant suffix joins the end of the word.

**Activities:**

1. Word sorts: Evaluate words to see if they follow the 1–1–1 Rule. Sort them into four categories: the three ways they can violate the rule and the ones that get doubled. (For more on word sorts see chapter 3.3 #2.)

2. Before class, write a list of words on the board: *stop, drink, stomp, run, beat, skip, drop, snap, laugh, clip, knit, grade, plan, hem, drip*

   • Review the 1–1–1 Rule.

   • Ask different students to come up and add different vowel suffixes to words. Ask them to explain why they did or did not double the final consonant.

**Bookwork:**

• Phonics rule book: Have the students put these rules into their phonics rules book. Have them include their definitions and parts of speech for the suffixes. Have them leave space to write in words that follow these rules.

• On day two have the students make a list of words they find in a book or passage that contain these suffixes. Have them add these words to their phonics rules book.

**How to Help Struggling Students:** If you choose to teach the advanced rule for the 1–1–1 rule, make sure students are automatic at identifying accented syllable in root words (see chapter 3.3 #9).

## Rule 29: When to Change the Letter *Y* to *I*

**Phase:** Middle of the Syllable Phase

**Prerequisites:** Consonant and vowel suffixes, particularly rule 28

**Expected time for students to achieve the 80/80 Rule:** Two weeks with daily practice after introduction

**Background:** The letter *Y* is a vowel when it is at the end of the word. When you add a suffix to the end of a word, sometimes the letter *Y* changes to the letter *I* and sometimes it does not. To determine when to change *Y* to *I*, look to see if the letter *Y* is part of a vowel digraph. If so, it does not change; if not, it does. See table 4.3.9.

**Table 4.3.9: When to Change *Y* to an *I***

| Root Word ends in Vowel + *Y* | Root Word ends in Consonant + *Y* |
|---|---|
| Do not change the spelling of the root word. For example, played, enjoying, coyness, boys. | Change *Y* to *I* UNLESS you get two letter *I*'s For example, pried, spriest, happiness, but not crying. |
| | Adding the Suffix –s: Change *Y* to *IE* and then add the *S*. For example, cries, spies. |

*Source: McDonald 2002, 15.*

**The Rules:** When adding suffixes to words that end in Y, follow two rules:

1. When a word ends in a vowel + *Y*, add any suffix. For example, paying, playful, plays.

2. When a word ends in a consonant + *Y*, change the *Y* to an *I* <u>unless</u> doing so results in two letter *I*'s (e.g., reply/ replied, pity/pitiful; but babyish not babiish). However, add IE when adding the suffix –S (e.g., spy/spies).

**Introductory Image:** Describe how the letter *Y* got tired of standing in for his friends *I* and *E* at the ends of words (see chapter 4.2 rule 17) so he made them stand in for him for a change.

**Activities:** Have the students dramatize the letter *Y* calling in a favor with his friends *I* and *E*. Play up *Y*'s fatigue when he decides that he just cannot be in a word when all of these extra letters show up at the end.

**Bookwork:**

- Phonics rule book: Have the students put these rules into their phonics rules book. Have them leave space to write in words that follow these rules.

- Other written activities for day two: Have the students make a list of words they find in a book or passage that follow these rules. Have them add these words to their phonics rules book.

**How to Help Struggling Students:** A few students respond better to a formula or flow chart. Try drawing a simple flow chart for them or using a formula if they have trouble learning these rules.

## Rule 30: Tricky Vowel Junctions

**Phase:** Middle of the Syllable Phase

**Prerequisites:** Recognizing vowel digraphs

**Expected time for students to achieve the 80/80 Rule:** One week with daily practice after introduction

**Background:** Sometimes two vowel letters stand next to each other and each one is in a separate syllable. Rather than the two vowels working together as a vowel team, these vowels are working independently.

In some words, it is obvious. For example, in the word *situation*, the letters *U* and *A* are clearly in separate syllables because they do not form a vowel team: si/tu/a/tion. However, in other words, it is ambiguous. For example, in the word *create*, it looks as if the letters *EA* are working together as a vowel team to form the long *E* sound, but they are not. The word is split into the following syllables: cre/ate. The letter *E* is actually part of an open syllable.

It is easy to encode words with tricky vowel junctions because you can hear which vowel belongs in which syllable: *cre-ate*. However, decoding is more complicated. Sometimes it is obvious because the two vowels do not form a vowel team such as in the word *liar*. The letters *IA* do not form a vowel team (although *AI* do). When the vowels do form a digraph, teach the students to flex the pronunciation of the word by breaking the syllables in different ways. Sometimes two vowels are working together, and sometimes they are independent. Try breaking the word both ways and see which sounds right: cr<u>ea</u>te (pronounced *Crete*) or cre/<u>a</u>te (pronounced *create*).

**The Rule:** If two vowels are next to each other, they may or may not be in separate syllables. If they are not vowel digraphs, put them in different syllables. If they are, flex the word by saying it both ways.

**Introductory Image:** Tell the story about desk partners who sometimes work together as a team and sometimes work separately.

**Activities:**

- Put a list of words up on the board and have the students practice flexing the pronunciation of the word by breaking the syllables in different ways. Here is a beginning list of words that have two vowels next to each other: react, lion, cooperate, riot, coexist, realize, liar, reopen, reality

You can also use lots of nonsense words to teach the students to flex the pronunciation.

- Create nonsense words that have vowel junctions that contain vowel teams and random vowels next to each other. Ask the students to use their eagle eyes to find the possible digraphs. Then practice reading them both ways (see chapter 3.4 #10).

**Bookwork:**

- Phonics rule book: Have the students put this rule into their phonics rules book. Have them leave space to write in words that follow this rule.
- Other written activities for day two: Have the students make a list of words they find in a book or passage that follow this rule. Have them add these words to their phonics rules book.

**How to Help Struggling Students:** Insist that they follow the process for breaking words into syllables (see chapter 4.3 rule 22). By breaking off common prefixes and suffixes, it is easier to determine which vowels are working on teams and which vowels are independent agents. For example, in the word *reaction*, breaking off common prefixes and suffixes results in *re/ac/tion*.

## Rule 31: The Schwa ⊠

**Phase:** Middle of the Syllable Phase

**Prerequisites:** Decoding words with three syllables, flexing open syllables, finding the accented syllables (see chapter 3.3 #9).

**Expected time for students to achieve the 80/80 Rule:** 1–2 weeks with daily practice after introduction

**Background Information:** Once students move into words with three or more syllables, they need to learn about the schwa. The schwa is the laziest sound your mouth can make. It is written as an upside down e in a dictionary: ə. It shows up before or after an accented syllable. While the schwa can be spelled with the letters *A, E, I, O,* or *U* it has the sound of short *U*: /ŭ/.

Note: Wait for 4th Grade, when you teach dictionary skills, to teach your students how to write the schwa using the symbol ə.

**The Rule:** The sound /ŭ/ can show up in the syllable before or after the accented syllable. It is called the schwa. It can be spelled with the letters *A, E, I, O,* or *U.*

**Introductory Image:** When people are tired, they can sometimes speak quietly and can even mumble. (Ask if they know anyone who is hard to understand when they first wake up.) Then point out that this happens in Letter Village, especially with the vowel letters. Sometimes when they show up to help spell a word, they are so tired they make the same sleepy sound of /ŭ/, the same sound as short *U* rather than their own sound. For example, the word banana has three *A's* in it, but only one of them is awake and alert and says its sound clearly. The other two just say /u/. See if you can hear the one that speaks clearly:

*Ba/na/na (Write on the board.)*

*/bu /na /nu/ (Write on the board.)*

The middle letter *A* is part of the accented syllable and it says its sound /ă/ while the letter *A* on the right and the one on the left have the sound schwa: /ŭ/. When long words are read or spelled, you have to be aware of the syllables that have the schwa sound and figure out which letter looks right. Even though a schwa vowel may sound like the short *U* (/ŭ/), it almost never is spelled with a *U.*

### Activities:

- Decoding: Practice flexing the accent. Try putting it on different syllables, particularly a middle syllable before a suffix. See which way sounds right.

- Encoding: Practice spelling the schwa sound with different vowel letters. Use symbol imagery to determine which spelling looks right. For example, the word *potato* could be: patato, petato, pitato, potato, putato.

### Bookwork:

- Phonics rule book: Have the students put this rule into their phonics rules book. Have them leave space to write in words that follow this rule.

- Other written activities for day two: Have the students make a list of words they find in a book or passage that follow this rule. Have them add these words to their phonics rules book.

**How to Help Struggling Students:** When encoding words with three or more syllables, the sound /ŭ/ is usually a schwa and thus rarely spelled with the letter *U*. Try other vowels. See if any look right. Symbol imagery is the best way to work with the schwa in the Syllable Phase.

Note: In the Latin/Greek Phase, students will learn to work with **cognates** (related words) to determine which vowel letter goes with a schwa.

## Rule 32: The Ending Grid

**Phase:** Middle of the Syllable Phase

**Prerequisites:** Schwa, the Big Four Suffixes

**Expected time for students to achieve the 80/80 Rule:** 1 week per row = 6 weeks with daily practice after introduction. Emphasize decoding. Students will review encoding with these endings in 4th–6th Grades.

### Background Information

The Ending Grid in table 4.3.10 is a variation of the Ending Grid from the Lindamood-Bell program LiPS®. It is found in the manual *Lindamood Phoneme Sequencing® Program for Reading, Spelling, and Speech* (Lindamood 1998, 364). It is included here as a reference for the teacher. Example words are italicized. Have your students fill out their copies with the suffixes as they learn each row. (See www.waldorfinspirations.com for Ending Grid templates you can download.)

The Ending Grid is a useful tool because it makes it easy for students to learn 35 suffixes. Instead of memorizing each suffix, students can learn seven key suffixes and few tricks. The Ending Grid will become the students' most useful tool for decoding longer words in 3rd Grade and for encoding them in 4th–6th Grades.

Since each suffix contains a schwa, predict that the accented syllable will come on the syllable before it. For example, ba<u>na</u>na, <u>glo</u>rious, etc. This rule will hold true for most words, and it will hold true for all words that have the letter *I* in the suffix (Bishop 1986, 323).

### Table 4.3.10: The Ending Grid

| Vowel says /ŭ/ | -a *banana* | -on *lemon* | -an *human* | -ous *famous* | -al *final* | -ent *silent* | -ence *sentence* |
|---|---|---|---|---|---|---|---|
| -ti says /sh/ | -tia *militia* | -tion *nation* | -tian *Martian* | -tious *cautious* | -tial *partial* | -tient *patient* | -tience *patience* |
| -ci says /sh/ | -cia *Marcia* | -cion *suspicion* | -cian *physician* | -cious *spacious* | -cial *special* | -cient *sufficient* | -cience *conscience* |
| -gi says /j/ | -gia *Georgia* | -gion *region* | -gian *Belgian* | -gious *religious* | X | X | X |
| -si says /zh/ or /sh/ | -sia *Asia* *Russia* | -sion *vision* *mansion* | -sian *Asian* *Russian* | X | X | X | X |
| -i says /ee/ | -ia *media* | -ion *champion* | -ian *Canadian* | -ious *glorious* | -ial *radial* | -ient *ingredient* | -ience *experience* |

*Source: Adapted from Lindamood 1998, 364: Ending Grid.*

**–schwa row (top row):**

Teach the top row as seven suffixes. They are easy to learn because they all have the schwa sound for a vowel. Consequently, the suffixes *–an* and *–on* have the same pronunciation; however, they are easy to tell apart: *–an* is for people and *–on* is for things. Since they all begin with a vowel, they will always try to grab the consonant before if possible to be part of their syllable (e.g., data da/ ta).

**-ti- Row**

This row is easy. –ti- has the sound /sh/ and students are already familiar with the suffix *–tion*. Teach this row second, right after teaching the top row.

**-ci- Row**

This row produces suffixes that sound identical to the –ti- row. It is necessary to use symbol imagery and cognates to predict the correct spelling. Which looks right: facial or fatial? Do you know a cognate, a related word? (face) Use that to predict whether the word has a *C* or a *T*. Examples: *face/facial; part/partial*

**-gi- Row**

This row only has four suffixes. The –gi- makes the sound /j/ (see chapter 4.1 rule 8).

**–si Row**

This row only has three suffixes, but each one has 2 pronunciations: /zh/ and /sh/. /zh/ is the sound *S* has in *pleasure*. If you want, you can teach students that the only time –si- has the sound /sh/ is when it comes after the letters N, L, or S (Lindamood 1998, 364). Examples of /sh/ include *mansion, Russian,* and *expulsion.*

**-i- Row**

This is the hardest row for two reasons. First, these suffixes each have two syllables instead of one: *-ia* is /ee/ /ŭ/. Second, all of these endings begin with a vowel. Thus, they will try to grab the consonant before to be part of their syllable. Example: *-ia* in *media* takes the letter *D* to begin its syllable: me/di/a. As a result, these suffixes are spread out over two syllables. This makes it more challenging to recognize them. Teach this row last.

Note: Have the students keep their copy of the Ending Grid in their phonics rules book.

**Introductory Image:** Ask students if they would rather memorize 35 different suffixes or if they would rather memorize seven and then learn some shortcuts. Then pass out a copy of a blank Ending Grid to each student (see www.waldorfinspirations.com for Ending Grid templates you can download). Review how to read a grid. (This activity should be familiar as the students have been using a multiplication grid in math.) Teach the students the initial seven suffixes on the top row: *-a, -on, -an, -ous, -al, -ent, -ence.* Promise them that once they learn these endings, you will show them how to combine the suffixes with different letters to make new suffixes.

**Activities:**

1. Word Sort for *–an* and *–on* words. Challenge the students to figure out why some words are spelled with the ending *–an* and others with the ending *–on*. Give the class a list of words to sort such as woman, man, onion, nation, Canadian, station, Mexican, construction, Russian, Martian, baton, region, etc. (NB: do not use the word *champion*—it is an exception.) Once the words are sorted, ask the students to figure out the difference. (Answer: the suffix *–an* is for people while *–on* is for things.) If the class needs a hint, use Queen Noun. Have them help her determine what kinds of nouns are in each category.

2. When introducing new suffixes, have the students fill them out on their Ending Grids.

**Bookwork:**

- Phonics rule book: See Activities.
- Other written activities for day two: Have the students make a list of words they find in a book or passage that follow this rule. Have them add these words to their phonics rules book.

**How to Help Struggling Students:** Make sure students understand the concept of a grid. Do symbol imagery exercises with the 35 suffixes.

## Rule 33: Six Syllable Types: Review

**Phase:** End of 3rd Grade (i.e., intermediate Syllable Phase)

Note: The Syllable Phase continues into 4th through 6th Grade as students will need time to master <u>encoding</u> by syllable.

**Prerequisites:** All previous phonics rules

**Expected time for students to achieve the 80/80 Rule:** NA—review

**Background Information:** The students have learned the six syllable types. Review them at the end of 3rd Grade as a review of phonics rules.

1. **Open syllables** end with one vowel (e.g., <u>no</u>, <u>sta</u>/tion, con/<u>di</u>/tion). The vowel tends to be long. (Note: It is long in native English words but short in words derived from Latin/French and some other foreign languages (see chapter 4.3 rule 23).)

2. **Closed syllables** have one vowel letter but end with a consonant (e.g., <u>not</u>, <u>ac</u>/tion). The vowel in a closed syllable is always short. Students have seen this type of syllable in CVC words and blends (see chapter 4.3 rule 23 and chapter 4.1 rules 1 and 3).

3. **Syllables that end with Silent *E*** can be one of several types: 1) Silent *E* (i.e., Super *E* or Magic *E*) or 2) Other Uses for Silent *E* (see chapter 4.1 rule 6 and chapter 4.2 rule 15).

4. ***R*-controlled vowel syllables** end with an *R*-controlled vowel. For example, <u>car</u>, <u>per</u>/son, re/<u>pair</u>, <u>ear</u>/ly (see chapter 4.1 rule 5 and chapter 4.2 rule 12).*

5. **Syllables with Vowel Teams** are syllables (or single-syllable words) that feature a vowel team. For example, <u>sea</u>, <u>stay</u>, <u>tail</u>, <u>beau</u>/ty, <u>rea</u>/son (see chapter 4.2 rules 10, 12, and 19).

6. **Syllables that end with consonant-*LE*** are unaccented final syllables that are made up of a consonant followed by the letters *LE*. For example, ma/<u>ple</u>, puz/<u>zle</u>, and ta/<u>ble</u> (see chapter 4.3 rule 25).

*****Note:** A rule for working with *R*-controlled vowels in multisyllabic words is not given. These syllables are complicated and regional pronunciations vary. For example, the word *bury* can be pronounced *berry* or *burry* (rhymes with *hurry*). If your students need guidance in decoding multisyllabic words with *R*-controlled vowels, teach them to flex the vowel for the *R*-controlled syllable. Have them pronounce the syllable different ways to see which sounds right: for example, var/y (broad *A*); vair/y (long *A*); va/ry (short *A*).

**The Rule:** NA—this is a review.

**Introductory Image:** NA—this is a review.

**Activities:** Encoding and decoding with all syllable types. Have students identify syllable types.

**Bookwork:** If it would help your students, have them write these syllable types in their phonics rules book. However, it is not necessary as this is a review.

**How to Help Struggling Students:** By the end of 3rd Grade, students are expected to be able to <u>decode</u> with these syllable types. If any of your 3rd Grade students struggle with decoding these syllable types, recommend summer tutoring. In 4th Grade, the curriculum shifts from reading skills to subjects. Students will need to be able to decode to handle the curriculum, and decoding will no longer be taught in class.

Note: It is expected that students will need more instruction and practice to master <u>encoding</u> with these six syllable types. Further instruction and practice with these syllable types and phonics rules will be part of the spelling curriculum in Grades 4–6. Only recommend summer tutoring if a student's encoding skills lag significantly behind.

## Conclusion

Phonics rules are the key to learning to decode and encode. Conclude the study of phonics rules by the end of 3rd Grade. You will continue to teach prefixes and suffixes in 4th through 6th Grade, but the emphasis will be on spelling and vocabulary, not decoding.

If you have not finished teaching decoding with these phonics rules, figure out how to modify your schedule in 4th Grade to finish teaching them. It is imperative that the students master them. Otherwise, their reading will suffer in one or more of the following ways: decoding unknown words, reading fluency, and/or vocabulary development. It will also negatively impact their spelling.

# 4.4 CURRICULUM CHART TWO: PHONICS RULES BY PHASE

Phonics rules are part of encoding and decoding, one of the 15 aspects of Language Arts covered in *The Roadmap to Literacy*.

**Curriculum Chart Two: Phonics Rules by Phase**

| Phonemic Awareness | Pattern | Syllable |
|---|---|---|
| 1. Decoding by Phoneme (CVC Words)* <br> 2. Beginning Digraphs <br> 3. Blends <br> 4. Inflectional Endings: –s and –ed | | |
| 5. R-Controlled Vowels *(can be taught in either phase)* <br> 6. Silent E *(can be taught in either phase)* <br> 7. Compound Words #1 *(can be taught in either phase)* <br> 8. Soft C and G *(can be taught in either phase)* | | |
| | 9. Encoding and Decoding by Onset/Rimes* <br> 10. Two Vowels Go Walking <br> 11. Diphthongs and AU/AW <br> 12. Long vowels + R <br> 13. Inflectional Endings #2 <br> 14. The Guardians <br> 15. Other Uses for Silent E <br> 16. Trickster X <br> 17. Y as a Vowel <br> 18. Silent Consonants <br> 19. Other Vowel Digraphs <br> 20. Compound Words #2 <br> 21. Homophones | |
| | | 22. Encoding and Decoding by Syllable* <br> 23. Open and Closed Syllables <br> 24. The Big Four Prefixes <br> 25. Consonant –LE Syllables <br> 26. The Big Four Suffixes <br> 27. Suffixes Beginning with Consonants <br> 28. Suffixes Beginning with Vowels <br> 29. When to Change Y to I <br> 30. Tricky Vowel Junctions <br> 31. The Schwa <br> 32. The Ending Grid <br> 33. Six Syllable Types: Review |
| *These rules are not phonics rules *per se*, but they are the three processes used for encoding and decoding (see chapter 3.4). Use them to teach and practice all phonics rules in their columns. | | |

**Objectives:** By the end of 3rd Grade:

- Students will master decoding words using all 33 phonics rules.
- Students will master encoding words using phonics rules for 1–25 and be in process with rules 26–33.

Students will continue to work on encoding with phonics rules in 4th–6th Grade as part of their spelling program. They will master encoding with the remainder of the phonics rules in this time before moving on to the Latin/Greek Phase where they will learn to decode and encode through advanced units of meaning or morphology.

Note: Although encoding and decoding with phonics rules are a formidable part of the language arts curriculum, keep in mind that phonics rules are only one aspect of literacy. It is just as important that you introduce and practice the other 14 aspects covered in section 3 (see chapter 3.16 Curriculum Chart One and chapter 5.5 #2 Curriculum Chart Three).

# SECTION 5

Curriculum and Lesson Planning

# 5.1 PLANNING A CURRICULUM

In sections 3 and 4, information was presented on what to teach. In this chapter, the focus will be on how to plan a curriculum for the upcoming year. The process includes making a block rotation, researching curriculum materials, creating block plans, and writing daily lesson plans.

This chapter covers the following topics:

1. The Importance of Summer Preparatory Work
2. Scheduling Time for Daily Academic Practice Classes
3. How to Create Your Block Rotation
4. How to Select Curriculum Materials (Summer Preparation Form)
5. How to Make Block Plans
6. How to Make Daily Lesson Plans
7. Other Miscellaneous Prep Work to Do over the Summer
8. How to Deal with a Truncated Schedule

Note: The information in this chapter should be taken as suggestions. Use what is helpful for you and your class.

## 1.   The Importance of Summer Preparatory Work

At the final faculty meeting of the school year, Janet Langley looked around the room at her colleagues. All of the teachers looked burned out or exhausted, except for one, Isabelle Tabacot. That this colleague would be calm and collected was somewhat of a puzzle. She had two young children, was a respected 3rd Grade teacher, and served on various school committees. How could she be so composed after the busiest time of the school year?

Puzzled about how she could maintain her energy and focus even into the final weeks of school, Janet asked how she was able to manage. The answer changed Janet's life.

Isabelle's answer was simple. She said, "I treat this job as a 12-month-a-year position. During the summer I do much of my preparation for the coming year so that I do not have to burn the candle at both ends during the school year."

She went on to explain that as soon as she completed her end-of-year reports in June, she set herself a schedule. Every morning (Monday-Friday) she was at her desk by 9 AM researching and planning her curriculum for the coming year. Around 12:30, she set her work aside and went off with her children to engage in fun summer activities. During the month of July, she took off two solid weeks for a family vacation. During this time the books she read had nothing to do with the upcoming curriculum. Once she returned, she was back at her half-day schedule, adding a few full days in August to get her classroom ready.

She shared that by the time school began, she had:

- her yearly block rotation done
- main lesson block plans sketched out for the entire year
- daily main lesson plans for the first two blocks of the year

She also had:

- a file of possible curriculum stories for the other blocks
- files filled with poems, songs, etc.
- a class play selected
- class projects outlined
- field trips arranged
- guest speakers contacted

As a result, she had little preparation to do over the school year. All she had to do was finalize her daily lesson plans for each block and learn the stories she would tell. In addition, it was easier to write end-of-year reports because she had time to start them in April.

The next year, Janet tried this approach. She planned her curriculum over the summer. When she started teaching in the fall, it was an epiphany. No longer did she have to spend entire weekends wrapping up one block and planning the next. She had time during the year to spend with her family, relax, and have a life outside of work. At the end of the year she did not feel burned out at all. At the final faculty meeting, there were two calm, collected teachers.

Note: To adopt this approach requires one mental shift: the summer is for creating your curriculum for the upcoming year. The following subsections will show you how.

## 2. Scheduling Time for Daily Academic Practice Classes

The first step in planning a curriculum is to guarantee time in the schedule for daily practice.

Over the summer, someone at the school will set the schedule for subject classes such as movement, foreign language, etc. Request that the scheduler set aside one practice class a day for academic practice. Schedule your practice block during these classes. The language arts practice blocks happen during math main lesson blocks and vice versa.

Request one academic practice class each day, preferably during 1st or 2nd period after main lesson when the students are still fresh. (This request will depend upon the scheduling needs of the special subject teachers and the needs of the other grades. It is likely some of your practice classes will have to occur in the afternoon, and that is fine.)

What should not be acceptable is having only one or two academic practice classes a week. This schedule is inadequate, both from the perspective of covering the entire curriculum and from the perspective of brain development. See chapter 1.2 #4 for more information on brain development and chapter 2.3 #7 for more information on truncated schedules.

### 3. How to Create Your Block Rotation

The second step in planning the curriculum is making a block rotation. The block rotation lays out your blocks for the upcoming year in light of the school's academic calendar.

<u>Estimated Time to Complete:</u> one day during the summer

<u>You will need the following items:</u>

1. An academic calendar (i.e., one that goes from July to June). This calendar can be purchased at most office supply stores.

2. Your school's academic calendar for the upcoming school year. It will list dates for in-service days, special school events, and holidays.

<u>Follow these steps:</u>

1. Enter major school dates on your academic calendar: first/last day of school, vacations, festivals, assemblies, holidays, in-service days, etc. Add in the dates for your class play (if applicable) and/ or any planned class trips.

2. Arrange the year into nine blocks, each one three or four weeks. (The ideal is a four-week block however, it is not always possible.) Always begin a new block when returning from a holiday of one week or longer.

3. Alternate blocks between language skills and math in your block rotation. See chapters 5.2 #2, 5.3 #2, and 5.4 #2 for examples for your grade.

Once you have your main lesson blocks scheduled, it is easy to schedule your practice blocks. They will occur during the math main lesson blocks.

You will use this block rotation when you make your block plans. First, though, you will need to assemble your curriculum materials.

### 4. How to Select Curriculum Materials (Summer Preparation Form)

The third step in planning your curriculum is assembling a wide selection of curriculum materials. You will need to find literature curriculum stories, speech activities, write or locate Home Surroundings stories, and decide whether to use another author's umbrella story/ies for language arts or create your own.

<u>Estimated Time to Complete:</u> 4–6 weeks over the summer

<u>You will need the following items:</u>

1. Summer preparation form for your grade (Download this form from www.waldorfinspirations. com.)

2. A selection of books from the *Teacher Literature Resource List* (see Appendix 5) and the resources provided by your school

3. Manilla folders to store copied curriculum materials

Follow these steps:

1. Read through the summer preparation form for your grade.

2. Get books. Decide which books you need from the *Teacher Literature Resource List*. Compare the list against those resource books provided by your school. Order any books needed to fill the gaps (or get them from the library).

3. Read material with an eye to choosing information/stories that would be useful for your curriculum. When you find something, record it on your form, make a copy, and file it.

4. Fill out your entire form. Be sure to get more materials than you can use so that you will have choices when you fill out your block plans.

Note: When filing curriculum materials, organize them into appropriate categories such as poems, tongue twisters, stories, and songs. You can further subdivide these categories by season (e.g., fall/winter/spring); by subject, etc.

You will use these curriculum materials when you make your block plans. To see an example of a summer preparation form, go to chapter 5.2 #3.

## 5.  How to Make Block Plans

The next step in planning a curriculum is to make block plans. There are two types of block plans: main lesson block plans and practice block plans. This subsection will look at how to make both types.

*The Roadmap to Literacy* includes block plan templates for both main lesson and practice blocks Grades 1–3 (see Appendix 1–3). You can use them exactly as written, modify them, or create your own layout, depending on which serves you best.

Note: If you make your own, consult the scheduling subsection in all section 3 chapters for recommendations on how to schedule each aspect of your language arts curriculum. Also refer to the appropriate section 4 chapter to help identify the time parameters for your phonics skills curriculum.

Estimated Time to Complete: one week during the summer You will need the following items:

- your block rotation (see chapter 5.1 #3)

- your completed summer preparation form (This form can be downloaded from www. waldorfinspirations. com.)

- your files of curriculum materials (songs, stories, poems, tongue twisters, etc.)

- block plan templates (see Appendix 1,2, or 3 depending on your grade)

- blank block plans forms (download at www.waldorfinspirations.com or make your own)

Follow these steps:

1. Make copies of blank block plans forms

   a.  1st Grade or 2nd Grade: four main lesson blocks, four practice blocks, one Home Surroundings: Nature Studies Block

   b.  3rd Grade: four main lesson blocks, four practice blocks, one Home Surrounding: Practical Occupations

Note: Make sure you make a copy of the blank block plans for each <u>week</u> of each block. Each block lasts 3–4 weeks (consult your block rotation). You will need one blank block plan for each week of the school year except for Home Surroundings. Around half of your forms should be for main lesson blocks, the others for practice blocks. You should have around 30 copies in total. (There is no form for Home Surroundings because each class will have a different format, depending on what you choose to present in that block. Create your own form to support your ideas for that block.)

2. Fill in each block using your completed summer preparation form and your curriculum materials. Use the block plan templates as a guide. With main lesson blocks, start with the Introduction &/ or Review segment and then fill in the other segments.

You will use your nine completed block plans when you write your daily lesson plans.

To see an example of one week of a monthly block plan, go to chapter 5.2 #5.

## 6.    How to Make Daily Lesson Plans

The fifth step in planning a curriculum is to make a daily lesson plan for each day of a block.

Blank daily lesson plan forms for both main lesson blocks and practice blocks are available at www. waldorfinspirations.com.

<u>Estimated Time to Complete:</u> 2–4 days during the summer

Note: You only need to fill out daily lesson plans for the first block or two (i.e., the first main lesson block and the first language arts practice block) over the summer. Make the other plans one week to one month out as the year progresses. (That way you can adjust the lessons to meet the class.)

<u>You will need the following items:</u>

- blank copies of daily lesson plans (Download from website above or make your own.)
- your completed summer preparation form (see chapter 5.1 #4)
- your files of curriculum materials
- your completed block plan (see chapter 5.1 #5)

<u>Follow these steps:</u>

1. Make enough copies of the daily lesson plan form to have one for each day of your block (~15–20 days).
2. Fill out each day. Get the information from your completed block plan. Flesh it out with notes to yourself on how to deliver the material or what to emphasize.
3. Find the pertinent materials you wish to use from your curriculum materials files.
4. Put all of your materials into a file folder with the daily lesson plan on top. Label it by date.

Note: After you finish teaching the lesson, move those curriculum materials that you will still be working with the next day into the next day's file.

You will use these daily lesson plans as an outline when you teach the class. You will also give them to a substitute teacher on days when you will not be there.

To see an example, go to chapter 5.2 #7.

## 7. Miscellaneous Prep Work to Do over the Summer

There are a few additional things you may want to consider:

- field trips
- class play (Note: It is not necessary to do a play every year. See chapter 2.2 #1 for more information.)
- set up your classroom library (see chapter 3.15 #3)
- guest speakers (if applicable)
- research community service projects (if applicable)
- set up your classroom

## 8. How to Deal with a Truncated Schedule

Some schools have schedules that preclude daily practice (see chapter 2.3 #7). What do you do if you are a 1st or 2nd Grade teacher with a truncated schedule?

Answer: Schedule language arts practice into other classes as best you can. Be aware that this practice is not going to help you address the problem in full, but at least you can try to make the best of the situation until it can be changed. Here are some ideas for ways to work additional reading and writing practice into an abbreviated schedule:

- Have the students read song lyrics in music class. Memory Read familiar songs in 1st Grade and read other songs' lyrics before you introduce the songs in Grades 2 and 3. Model decoding multisyllabic words using lyrics by syllable in 2nd Grade.
- Practice letters and sounds in movement classes. For example, practice literacy skills while playing hopscotch. Students have to say the <u>sound</u> of the letter or word that the beanbag lands on or give a word that ends in that sound or say the sight word that is in the square, etc.
- Use the last 10 minutes of gardening class to practice literacy. Do symbol imagery exercises in the dirt or do some writing in a *Gardening Journal* back in class about what students did in the garden.
- In 1st Grade, work with the Eurythmy teacher to coordinate the curriculum. Ask that she bring poems in Eurythmy that focus on the sounds introduced in main lesson. (Request that the Eurythmy teacher use the English sound/symbol correspondence rather than the German (see chapter 3.1 #2).)
- Have on hand a number of short, individual phonics skill practice activities that students can do when they finish work early in a class.
- Practice phonemic awareness and symbol imagery exercises while waiting for a special subject teacher who is delayed or whenever you have a few spare moments (see chapter 3.3 #2 and chapter 3.5 #3).
- Be creative with the schedule. In 1st Grade, see if there are two classes that you can alternate every other week so that you can free up a class to use for weekly academic practice.

- Most importantly, make sure you are setting aside enough time in the Skills Practice segment of each language arts block to address sight words, spelling, phonics rules, symbol imagery, and phonemic awareness. You may want to adjust your schedule to make sight word chants your Integrated Movement Activity for Transitions to create more time.

Ask yourself where else you can fit in literacy practice. By using economy in teaching, it is possible to work language arts skills into the school day. This situation is far from ideal. Keep lobbying for a full schedule, especially if the 2nd Grade schedule is also truncated.

## Conclusion

The summer is the time to prepare your curriculum. The next three chapters present examples of block rotations, block plans, and daily lesson plans for each grade.

# 5.2 FIRST GRADE CURRICULUM PLANS

In the last chapter, information was presented on how to plan a curriculum. In this chapter, the focus will be on the 1st Grade, with examples of curriculum plans and key teaching moments. This information will help you prepare your specific lesson plans. Because of its importance in setting the tone for the literacy curriculum to come, this chapter will provide you with recommendations for teaching the first week of 1st Grade.

This chapter covers the following topics:

1. Overview of 1st Grade
2. Example Block Rotation
3. Example Summer Preparation Form
4. Advice for Teaching the First Week of School
5. Example Block Plan: Main Lesson Block
6. Example Block Plan: Practice Block
7. Example Daily Lesson Plan 1
8. Example Daily Lesson Plan 2
9. Home Surroundings Block
10. Key Moments in 1st Grade

Note: The information in this chapter should be taken as suggestions. Use what is helpful for you and your class.

## 1. Overview of 1st Grade

Waldorf students begin academic instruction in 1st Grade.

For most of your students, this will be their first introduction to reading, spelling, and writing. (Students coming in from other schools may already know how to read. Also, a few may have taught themselves.) Plan to teach both the Emergent Phase and the Phonemic Awareness Phase in 1st Grade. By the end of the year, your students should be at the end of the Phonemic Awareness Phase (i.e., they should have full phonemic awareness for segmenting sounds and be able to encode and decode with short vowels and consonant blends).

The Emergent Phase is the beginning of the journey to literacy. At the beginning of the phase, students know nothing of letters. They learn to print their names and/or sing "The ABC Song." As they are taught each letter of the alphabet, they learn to name individual sounds, or phonemes. At the end of the phase, they make a breakthrough: they realize that words are made up of separate sounds, they can hear the first sound (or the most prominent sound) in each word, and they can use a letter to represent that sound. Furthermore, they can use their knowledge of letters to help them point to the right word when they memory read. These advances in phonological awareness allow the students to move to the Phonemic Awareness Phase.

It is worth considering an overview of the phase. Table 5.2.1 presents the primary objective and teaching priorities for the Emergent Phase.

### Table 5.2.1: Overview of Objectives for the Emergent Phase

**Primary Teaching Objective for Emergent Phase:** Teach students that letters represent sounds.

**Teaching Priorities for Emergent Phase:**

- alphabet
- phonological and phonemic awareness with an emphasis on materialization techniques for theory of word and first phoneme (chapter 3.3 #2)
- Memory Reading (chapter 3.15 #6)
- handwriting: uppercase and lowercase printing (chapter 3.2 #7)

The Phonemic Awareness Phase represents the next steps in the journey to full phonemic awareness. At the beginning of the phase, students can only discern the first (or most prominent) sound in a word, but by the end, they can separate out all of the sounds in a word (i.e., segment phonemes). At the beginning of this phase, students only know some of the letters of the alphabet, but by the middle of the phase, they have mastered them all. At the beginning, students can only encode one sound in a word, but by the end of the Phonemic Awareness Phase, they can encode one letter for every sound. At the beginning, they can Memory Read, but by the end, they can read simple decodable-text on their own, thanks to their burgeoning knowledge of sight words and decoding (phonics). The Phonemic Awareness Phase marks the biggest transformation in student skills, and it all happens in 1st Grade, brought about by your teaching.

It is worth considering an overview of the phase. Table 5.2.2 presents the primary objective and teaching priorities for the Phonemic Awareness Phase.

### Table 5.2.2: Overview of Objectives for the Phonemic Awareness Phase

**Primary Teaching Objective for Phonemic Awareness Phase:** Help students develop full phonemic awareness (i.e., when encoding, they represent each sound in a word with a logical letter choice, which demonstrates they have mastered segmenting sounds).

**Priorities for Phonemic Awareness Phase:**

- remainder of alphabet (beginning of phase only)
- phonemic awareness: mastering all aspects except manipulating phonemes (see chapter 3.3 #2)
- encoding: making a logical letter match for each sound
- kid writing
- decoding (starting in the middle of the phase)
- reading: memory reading (beginning/middle of phase) and reading decodable-text (middle/end of phase)
- handwriting: uppercase and lowercase printing

In theory, 1st Grade is the beginning of academic work for Waldorf students and all students are in the Emergent Phase. However, many Waldorf students start 1st Grade in the Phonemic Awareness Phase or beyond. It is imperative to assess your rising 1st Grade students to see which phase they are in. Consult chapter 6.2.

Even though it will take you three main lesson blocks to teach the entire alphabet, you can begin kid writing as soon as the majority of your students are in the Phonemic Awareness Phase, regardless of whether they have learned all 26 letters and their phonemes. Furthermore, you can begin reading groups earlier than late spring if there are a number of your students in the Pattern and Syllable Phases. Tailor your lessons to match your students' needs.

## 2. Example Block Rotation

The block rotation lays out your blocks in light of the school's academic calendar for the upcoming year. Use Table 5.2.3 as a guide to make your own (see chapter 5.1 #3).

**Table 5.2.3: Example Block Rotation**

| Block Number and Length | Main Lesson Blocks | Practice Blocks |
|---|---|---|
| First Block (4 weeks) | Language Block One | Math Block One |
| Second Block (4 weeks) | Math Block One | Language Block One |
| Third Block (3 weeks) | Language Block Two | Math Block Two |
| Fourth Block (4 weeks) | Math Block Two | Language Block Two |
| Fifth Block (4 weeks) | Language Block Three | Math Block Three |
| Sixth Block (3 weeks) | Math Block Three | Language Block Three |
| Seventh Block (4 weeks) | Language Block Four | Math Block Four |
| Eighth Block (4 weeks) | Math Block Four | Language Block Four |
| Ninth Block (4 weeks) | Home Surroundings Block | Math and Language Skills |

## 3. Example Summer Preparation Form

The summer preparation form can be used over the summer to plan and organize your curriculum and curriculum materials. It consists of various tables and instructions.

Download this form from www.waldorfinspirations.com. Select the form for 1st Grade and see chapter 5.1 #4 for instructions on how to fill it out.

Notes about the example summer preparation form:

- Unless otherwise indicated, stories noted on this form come from the book *The Complete Grimm's Fairy Tales* edited by James Stein (Random House 1972 edition). Story titles are in quotation marks and the page number is indicated.

- The complete summer preparation form has six areas, but only three areas are included below: 1, 2, and 6.

The rest of this subsection consists of a partially filled out summer preparation form.

**Summer Preparation Form**

**First Grade**

You will need a collection of the following materials to prepare your main lesson blocks and practice blocks for 1st Grade:

1. fairy tales to introduce letters (see chapter 3.1 #7)

2. fairy tales for soul food (see chapter 2.1 #5)

3. nature stories for Home Surroundings Block: (see chapter 5.5 #5 and #6)

4. umbrella stories to introduce grammar (see chapter 3.11 #3)

5. images to introduce phonics rules (see chapter 4.1)

6. poems, tongue twisters, songs, etc. (see chapter 3.10 #4)

Begin your research with books off the Teacher Literature Resource List (see Appendix 5) or similar titles. As you read through the materials, write down possible stories to introduce each concept listed below. You will then select materials off of these lists when you prepare the monthly block plans (main lesson and practice block).

## 1.  Fairy Tales to Introduce Letters Including Related Speech and Songs

Note: Words in bold are images that could be used in the first consonant block where the shape of the letter comes directly from an image out of the story (e.g., the letter *B* emerges from the drawing of the bear) (see chapter 3.1 #7). Individual words that are not in bold are words that could be used as anchor words in the second Consonant Block when the letters do not need to come out of an explicit image.

**Table 5.2.4 Summer Preparation Form (Partially Filled Out): Fairy Tales**

| Concept | Stories and Images | Related Material for Speech/ Song (TT=tongue twister) |
|---|---|---|
| **Letter *A*** | "Iron Hans" (apple) pg. 612<br>"The Hut in the Forest" (animals) pg. 698 | |
| **Letter *B*** | "Snow White and Rose Red" (**Bear**, bag, bird, bush, beard) pg. 664<br>"Queen Bee" (**Bee**) pg. 317 | TT: A big black beetle bit a big black bear on his big black nose.<br>"I am the *B*" (poem)<br>"The Queen Bee" (poem) |
| **Letter *C*** (/k/ hard *C* only) | "The Poor Miller's Boy and the Cat" (cat) pg. 482<br>"Golden Bird" (cage, castle) pg. 272 | |
| **The letter *D*** | "Water of Life" (**Door**) pg.449<br>" Sweetheart Roland" (duck) pg. 268<br>"Cinderella" (doves, birds) pg. 121<br>"The Donkey" (donkey) pg. 632 | TT: Deep in the earth, when days are darkest dwells the summer's dawn. |
| **Letter *E*** | Make up a story about two eagles who have a nest on the edge of a cliff overlooking the Everglades. | The eagles rested in their nest on the edge of a cliff overlooking the Everglades. |
| **Letter *F*** | "Fisherman and His Wife" (**fish**) pg. 103<br>"The Sea Hare" (**fish**) pg. 769<br>"The Three Feathers" (**feathers**) pg. 319 | TT: I found a fish in a fountain pool with fins as fine as a filigree fan. |
| **Letter *G*** (/g/ hard *G* only) | "The Golden Goose" (**Goose**) pg. 322 | "I am the *G*" poem<br>TT: Goodly Gabriel guards the gate.<br>TT: Ghoulish goblins gather the gold. |

## 2. *Soul Food Stories for 7–Year-Olds*

Select stories to use throughout the year (number will vary). Choose fairy tales that you like. These stories will be told for their own sake, not as a vehicle for introducing academic concepts. Consider tales from around the world that match the ethnicity of the students in your class.

Make a copy of each story you record and file it away.

**Table 5.2.5 Summer Preparation Form (Partially Filled Out): Stories for Soul Food**

| Story Title | Why I Like It |
|---|---|
| "The Three Spinners" (pg. 83) | fun |
| "The Straw, the Coal, and the Bean" (pg. 102) | pushiness |
| "The Three Snake Leaves" (pg. 94) | keeping your word, goodness |
| "The Three Little Men in the Wood" (pg. 78) | greed |
| "King Thrushbeard" (pg. 245) | pride |
| "The Poor Miller's Boy and the Cat" (pg. 482) | kindness |
| "The Selfish Giant" by Oscar Wilde | selfishness and kindness |
| "The Bird's Christmas" by F.E. Mann | sharing |

## 3. *Speech*

Collect poems/verses, songs, and tongue twisters for use during the Opening and Speech/Song segments of main lesson.

**Table 5.2.6 Summer Preparation Form (Partially Filled Out): Poems, Tongue Twisters, and Songs**

| Title (type: song, poem, TT-tongue twister) | Source | When to Schedule |
|---|---|---|
| "Bean Bag Song" by Nancy Stewart (movement song) | www.nancymusic.com/SOM/2010/beanbag-song.htm | whenever |
| "Autumn Winds" (song) | http://waldorfmama.typepad.com/waldorf_mama/2009/09/index.html | Fall |
| "Mr. Matthew Mathers" (tongue twister) | Mr. Matthew Mathers, my math master, munches mashed, marmalade muffins. | Main Lesson Block one for letter: *M* |
| "One Finger, One Thumb" (movement song) | https://genius.com/The-wiggles-one-finger-one-thumb-lyrics | whenever |

| "Head, Shoulders, Knees, and Toes" (movement song) | https://www.poetryfoundation.org/poems-and-poets/poems/detail/46944 | whenever |
|---|---|---|
| "In Front, Behind" (poem) | Passed around in various teacher trainings (its author is anonymous.):<br>In front, behind<br>My left, my right<br>Above, below<br>I curl up tight.<br>I stretch my limbs<br>Like a shining star,<br>And to earth bring light<br>From heavens afar. | Opening segment |

This concludes the sample summer preparation form. Use it to help you fill out your own.

Note: Make sure you make a copy of each poem, tongue twister, and song and put it into your files for use during the school year.

## 4. Advice for Teaching the First Week of School

The first week of school is important because it sets the tone for all eight grades.

The first week of school, especially the first day, is a time to lay down the structure and rules that will guide your students for the next eight years. In fact, Steiner dedicated an entire lecture to the first day of 1st Grade in *Practical Advice to Teachers* (lecture 4). The first week is also a time to introduce some of the skills from section 3.

Start the first main lesson block the first <u>full</u> week of school and using the first week of school for other purposes.

### Advice for the First Day of School

Every Waldorf school has its own traditions for the first day. In addition to these events, schedule the following points:

- Opening: Include attendance and Morning Verse. Tell the students that every Waldorf school 1st Grade around the world says this verse every morning. Recite the verse with gestures. The students will learn it over the next few weeks and say it with you; there is no need to teach it formally.
- Skills Practice: Include teaching them "The *ABC* Song" if students do not know it.
- New Learning: (Steiner 2000, 47–61):
  - o Introduce why students come to school (i.e., to learn reading, writing, and arithmetic). The objective is that the students to develop a feeling of wish, hope, and resolve that will later translate into enthusiasm for doing their lessons.
  - o Cultivate a feeling of respect for adults who already know these things.
  - o Teach a lesson on the use of their hands:
    - ▪ Help the students become aware of their right and left hands.
    - ▪ Help them realize what they are for: working.

438

- Day one or day two: Teach a lesson on the straight and curved lines.
    - o Draw the straight line and the curved line on the board.
    - o Have each student come up to the board and draw them as carefully as they can; gently correct as needed.
- Bookwork:
    - o how students are to use and treat their drawing and writing supplies
    - o how to hold a pencil (see chapter 3.2 #2)
    - o having students help each other trace the outline of their hands on paper (Each student then writes his or her name on the paper.)
- Story: Tell a fairy tale. If you want to reinforce the idea of the straight and curved line, the British folktale "Lunsmore of Knockgrafton" found in *The Key of the Kingdom* by Gmeyner and Russell is a possible story. Otherwise, tell a fairy tale you love as soul food.

## Advice for the Rest of the First Week of School

Schedule the following points during the rest of the week based on the number of days available.

Suggestions from Steiner (*Practical Advice to Teachers* (lecture 4)):

- Steiner says, "These examples [i.e. straight and curved lines and form drawing], not the letters of the alphabet, are the proper starting points for the early lessons" (Steiner 2000, 54).
- Review of straight and curved lines: draw the lines on the board and ask the students to name them.
- Form Drawing: See Teacher Literature Resource List (see Appendix 5) for books that address this topic.
- Steiner also has many other suggestions for first week activities but they do not pertain directly to language arts. Waldorf teachers, see *Practical Advice to Teachers* (lecture 4), for more information.

The Roadmap to Literacy Language Arts Suggestions:

- initial introduction of phonological and phonemic awareness (see chapter 3.3 #5)
- initial introduction of symbol imagery (see chapter 3.5 #6)
- initial introduction of concept imagery (see chapter 3.7 #4)
- initial introduction of comprehension (see chapter 3.8 #5)
- initial introduction of speech (see chapter 3.10 #6)
- initial introduction of "The *ABC* Song" (Practice singing it every day. Use Drill Down to prepare students for the introduction of memory reading and the alphabet next week.) (see chapter 2.4 #2 and 3.1 #6)
- initial introduction of handwriting (see chapter 3.2 #6)

In *Practical Advice to Teachers* (lecture 4), Steiner goes on to say that "only when you have taught the children... to use their hands and ears is the time ripe for progressing to the first elements of reading" (Steiner 2000, 54). *The Roadmap to Literacy's* suggestions include advice that will help the students develop their ears (i.e., phonological and phonemic awareness) and a few other skills they will need as well.

If you follow this advice for the first week of school, your students should be ready to start their study of the alphabet during the first full week of school.

Note: For overall (non-language skills) ideas about things to include during the first day and week of school, go to www.waldorfinspirations.com and read the *planning* section of *First Grade*.

## 5. Example Block Plan: Main Lesson Block

The following example block plan in table 5.2.7 is for main lesson block 1 (week one). It was made using Appendix 1A and chapter 5.2 #3 summer preparation form. It is one week of a four-week block plan and is for the first <u>full week</u> of school. It includes the introduction of the alphabet, the introduction of the first letter (*M*), and the introduction of the second letter (*F*). Use this example block plan in conjunction with chapter 5.1 #5 to make your own main lesson block plans.

Note that the archetype of a main lesson is modified to accommodate the demands of teaching the alphabet. The Speech/Song segment is added because the story is part of the Introduction &/or Review segment. See chapter 2.3 #4 for the archetype of a normal main lesson and chapter 3.1 #7 for more information on teaching the alphabet during the first block.

**Table 5.2.7: Example Monthly Block Plan (week of September 10th)**

| Time | Monday | Tuesday | Wednesday | Thursday | Friday |
|---|---|---|---|---|---|
| **Opening 12–15 min.** | "Good Morning Song" Attendance Poem: "In Front, Behind" Morning Verse | | | | |
| **Skills Practice 30 min.** | **Note: by the end of the block, work up to including all of these activities during this segment.**<br><br>**In week one choose two or more of the following:**<br><br>Initial introduction of memory reading: "The *ABC* Song"<br><br>Theory of word: stamping words in three sentences<br><br>Symbol imagery: visualizing straight and curved lines<br><br>Phonological awareness/ syllables: clapping syllables in students' names<br><br>Phonemic awareness/ rhyme: determining which words rhyme in a set of three words<br><br>Phonemic awareness/ blending phonemes: blending three sounds into words (4–6 words)<br><br>Phonemic awareness/ onset and rime: hand spelling (4–6 words) | Memory reading "The *ABC* Song" day two.<br><br>Theory of word: stamping words in three sentences<br><br>Symbol Imagery: visualizing straight and curved lines Phonological awareness/ syllables: clapping syllables in students' names<br><br>Phonemic awareness/ rhyme: determining which words rhyme in a set of three words<br><br>Phonemic awareness/ blending phonemes: blending three sounds into words (4–6 words)<br><br>Phonemic awareness/ onset and rime: hand spelling (4–6 words emphasize onsets, no blends) | **Introduction &/or Review for Letter M (Day Three)**<br><br>Review letter *Mm* include tongue twister.<br><br>Activity B: create *Mm*'s in groups using bodies (10 min.).<br><br>Introduce handwriting (15 min.).<br><br>First demonstrate how to write letters *Mm* on guide line on board then have students form letter on board (one or two to demonstrate).<br><br>Do worksheet for letters *Mm*. | Ibid Tuesday and try the following: Memory reading "The *ABC* Song" day three—find lines in song (e.g., QRS).<br><br>Rhyme: challenge students to find more words that rhyme. | Ibid Thursday and try the following:<br><br>Memory read "The *ABC* Song" locate *M* and *F*, read those lines.<br><br>Symbol imagery: initial introduction of letter drill (*M* and *F*) (see chapter 3.5 #7). |
| **Transition 3–5 min.** | Initial introduction of bean bags: how to handle them | Bean bag exercise to "Bean Bag Song" by Nancy Stewart with Drill Down | | | |

| Time | Monday | Tuesday | Wednesday | Thursday | Friday |
|---|---|---|---|---|---|
| **Introduction &/or Review or Story** 20–30 min. | Fairy Tale: "How the First Letter Was Written" (Kipling) for letter *M* Note: Change hill to a mountain. | Review story using sequential retelling format. Introduction of *M*: introduce letter *Mm* and sound /m/. Write a sentence using the word *mountain* on the Board (see chapter 2.1 #8 for process to introduce sound of /m/). Activity A: ask students to identify classmates whose names begin with the sound /m/. Find /m/ objects in room. (Note: Plant objects before class.) | Fairy Tale: "Fisherman and His Wife" for *F* | Review story using sequential retelling. Introduce letter *Ff* and sound of *F/f/* using the sentence: *The fish was kind*, Activity A: Students identify classmates whose names begin with the /f/ sound. Find /f/ objects in room. (Plant extra objects.) | Review letter *F/f/*. Activity B: Close eyes and raise hand if word begins with /f/. Introduce handwriting for *Ff* (Same format as Wednesday). |
| **Transition** 3–5 min. | IMA: Sing "Head, Shoulders, Knees, and Toes." Directions Game: set up for bookwork | | IMA: " One Finger, One Thumb" movement song Directions Game: set up for bookwork. | | Set up expectation for nature walk (how to behave). |
| **Bookwork** 15–20 min. | Draw a letter picture of a mountain scene from story in main lesson book (see fig. 2.1.1). Include a tall and short mountain. | Paint the letters *Mm*. | Draw a letter picture of fish in the water from story in main lesson book. | Form *Ff* with clay. | Nature walk |
| **Speech/Song** 10–15 min. | Teach the Song "Autumn Winds" verse one. Teach tongue twister (TT): "Mr. Matthew Mathers." | Teach "Autumn Winds" verse two. TT: "Mr. Matthew Mathers." | TT: I found a fish in a fountain with fins as fine as a filigree fan (Vocab: filigree). | "Autumn Winds" sing whole song. | Fairy tale: "The Poor Miller's Boy and the Cat" (for soul food) |

Note: See summer preparation form (chapter 5.2 #3) for sources of material.

## 6. Example Block Plan: Practice Block

The following block plan in table 5.2.8 is for the first language arts practice block (week one). It was made using Appendix 1B and chapter 5.2 #3 summer preparation form. This block would occur right after the first main lesson block. It includes a review of consonants taught in the first language arts main lesson block and a continuation of literacy skills, including the introduction of sight words. Use this example block plan in conjunction with chapter 5.1 #5 to make your practice block plans.

**Table 5.2.8: Block Plan (for week of October 8th)**

| Time | Monday | Tuesday | Wednesday | Thursday | Friday |
|---|---|---|---|---|---|
| Skills Practice 30 – 35 minutes | Symbol Imagery / Visualizing Individual Letters: All letters from Main Lesson Block 1 (5 – 7 min.) | | | | Fun and Games: Sound Bingo Alphabet Clothesline Symbol Imagery Game (See Section 3.1 #10) |
| | Initial Introduction of Sight Words<br>Introduce Words: and, you<br>Chants:<br>And: Arm Tapping<br>You:<br>"I like who?<br>I like YOU!<br>Y- O- U- you!"<br>Do both multiple times<br>(5 – 7 min.) | Review sight words: Flash cards and chants (multiple times with each chant) | | | |
| | Memory Reading Day One: Choral Reading as a whole class with *Autumn Wind* lyrics (Those who are already reading can read silently to themselves.) (See Section 3.15 # 6) (10 min.) | Memory Reading Day Two: Choral Reading in Groups (rows) with *Autumn WInds* (Those who are already reading can read silently to themselves.) | Memory Reading Day Three: Have students locate one line/word in *Autumn Winds*. Include sight word *you*. Section 3.15 # 6) (Those who are already reading can read silently to themselves.) | | |
| | Phonemic Awareness: Rhyming: Big Pig<br><br>Stretchable Fabric Blending phonemes (3 sounds—try 4 if class is ready): 5 - 7 words Hand Spelling and Encoding First sound in word; | Ibid but use Shout Out Rhymes for Rhyming | Ibid Monday | Ibid Tuesday | |
| Bookwork 15 minutes | Handwriting: Ss and Dd | Letter Dictation and Sound Dictation Encoding first sound in words: (fun, man, suds, tab, etc.). (Follow up with Hand Spelling to check.) | Handwriting: Ff and Mm | Letter Dictation and Sound Dictation Encoding first sound in words: (fat mud, ton, sap, etc.). (Follow up with Hand Spelling to check.) | Assessments: Letter and/or Sound Dictation/s (See Section 3.1 #11) Informal Spelling Quiz of Sight Words (see Section 3.6 #10) |

## 7. Example Daily Lesson Plan 1

The following example daily lesson plan in table 5.2.9 is for the first language arts main lesson block (week one), first day. It was made using the example monthly bock plan in table 5.2.7. It includes the introduction of the alphabet and the first letter (see chapter 3.1 #6 and #7). Use this example in conjunction with chapter 5.1 #6 to make your own daily lesson plans.

Note: This lesson occurs the <u>second</u> week of school. For the first week see chapter 5.2 #4.

**Table 5.2.9: Example Daily Lesson Plan**

| | |
|---|---|
| **Daily Lesson Plan for 1st Grade Main Lesson Block One** <br> Day: Monday <br> Date: September 10 <br> Purpose of lesson: introduce memory reading and the alphabet; tell story in preparation to teach the first letter. | |
| **Do Before class:** <br> Write the lyrics to "The *ABC* Song" on the board (make sure each line of the song is its own line in the lyrics). Set out basket of bean bags. | |
| **Opening Time: 8:15–8:30** | "Good Morning Song" <br> Attendance: sing <br> Poem: "In front, Behind" (students to do poem with me) <br> Morning Verse (with gestures) |
| **Skills Practice Time: 8:30–9:00** | **Initial introduction of Memory Reading**: "The *ABC* Song." Sing the song. Open up the board, where the song is written out. Ask students to watch: Sing the song again and point to each letter/word with the pointer as I sing it. Then <u>read</u> the song lyrics and point. Ask the students to "read" along with me. <br><br> **Theory of word**: Stamp words in these sentences: <br> • *Taffy and her Dad climbed through the mountain pass.* <br> • *Thomas tickled his baby sister.* <br> • *The first graders ate chocolate chip cookies.* <br><br> **Symbol Imagery**: Visualize straight and curved lines. <br><br> **Syllables**: Clap syllables in students' first names. Use first two rows. (last two rows tomorrow) <br><br> **Phonemic awareness/rhyme**: which words rhyme in each set? <br> • cat, dog, flat <br> • happy, sunny, money <br> • grow, toe, stone <br> • crazy, spicy, daisy <br> • knew, blue, book <br><br> **Phonemic awareness/blending phonemes**: Blend these sounds into a word: <br> • /z/ /oo/ <br> • /ŏ/ /d/ <br> • /b/ /ĭ/ /g/ <br> • /s/ /ă/ /k/ <br> • /f/ /ĕ/ /d/ <br> • /m/ /ŏ/ /m/ <br><br> **Hand spelling**: <br> • had <br> • lake <br> • zone <br> • mud <br> • gasp |

| Transition 9:00–9:05 | **Initial Introduction of Bean Bags**: Introduce how to hand out, hold, and gather up bean bags then do a bean bag exercise to the "Bean Bag Song." |
|---|---|
| **Introduction &/or Review Or Story Time: 9:05–9:35** | Tell the story "How the First Letter Was Written" (Kipling). Note: Change *hill* to *mountains* when telling story (one tall, one small) |
| **Transition 9:35–9:40** | **IMA**: "Head, Shoulders, Knees, and Toes" song<br>**Directions Game**:<br> • Get out your main lesson book and your crayons.<br> • Open your book to the first page.*<br> • Put your purple crayon on top of the blank page.<br>*Note the students who struggle to identify the first page. Help them learn how to do this. |
| **Bookwork 9:40–10:00** | Review how to treat art supplies: how to hold the crayon.<br>Lead a drawing lesson: draw a picture of a mountain scene from story in main lesson book. (See fig. 2.1.1.) |
| **Speech / Song Time: 10:00 – 10:15** | Teach the song "Autumn Winds."<br><br>Teach tongue twister:<br>"Mister Matthew Mathers, my math master, munches mashed marmalade muffins." |

## 8.   Example Daily Lesson Plan Two

This lesson plan in table 5.2.10 is for the second day of the first main lesson block. It was made using Table 5.2.7. It is included to demonstrate how to build off of Monday's lesson.

**Table 5.2.10: Example Daily Lesson Plan**

| Daily Lesson Plan for 1st Grade Main Lesson Block One<br>Day: Tuesday<br>Date: September 11<br>Purpose of Lesson: Review memory reading and story; introduce the first letter: *M*. | |
|---|---|
| **Do Before Class:**<br> • Plant objects that begin with the letter *M* in the room (mouse, monkey, mail, mittens, mop, etc.).<br> • Tape my picture of mountains from yesterday on the board with space underneath for me to write. | |
| **Opening Time: 8:15–8:30** | "Good Morning Song"<br>Attendance: sing<br>Poem: "In Front, Behind" (with gestures)<br>Morning Verse (with gestures) |

| **Skills Practice Time: 8:30–9:00** | **Memory reading day two:** Choral read "The *ABC* Song" by rows. |
|---|---|
| | **Theory of word:** Stamp words in these sentences: |
| | • *The clowns got out of a very small car.*<br>• *The women boarded the train.*<br>• *Every student said Morning Verse.* |
| | **Symbol imagery:** Visualize pattern of three straight and two curved lines. |
| | **Syllables:** Clap syllables in students' first names. Use last two rows. |
| | **Phonemic awareness/rhyme:** Determine which words rhyme in each set:<br>• riddle, middle, late<br>• hope, fear, rope<br>• late, real, feel<br>• gruel, goose, cruel<br>• kale, Kate, pail |
| | **Phonemic awareness/blending phonemes:** Blend these sounds into a word:<br>• /f/ /ŭ/ /n/<br>• /ă/ /t/<br>• /r/ /ŭ/ /g/<br>• /s/ /ŏ/ /k/<br>• /r/ /ĕ/ /d/<br>• /l/ /ŏ/ /k/ |
| | **Hand spelling:**<br>• head<br>• pun<br>• rail<br>• men<br>• task |
| **Transition<br>9:00–9:05** | **Bean Bags:** Review how to hand out, hold, and gather up bean bags.<br>Pass bean bags around body, handing off to the side with "Bean Bag Song." |
| **Introduction &/or Review Or Story<br>Time: 9:05–9:35** | Review "How the First Letter Was Written" (Kipling) with sequential retelling. Note who struggles or does not participate: ____<br>Write under my mountain picture: *The mountains rose above the plain.*<br>Read the sentence. Point to each word. Underline the word *mountain* and say, "This is how adults write the word *mountain*. When we say *mountain* what is the very first sound we make? (Help the students isolate the /m/ sound: mountain: /m/ emmmmm). That's right, the first sound of mountain is /m/."<br><br>Then underline the letter *m* and say, "When adults want to write the /m/ sound, they use the letter *M*. As we know from our alphabet display, each letter has an adult letter and a child letter. (Point to the *Mm* in the display.) Both of these letters make the /m/ sound and this is how adults write the big or adult letter *M*. (Write the letter *M* on the board. Notice how I begin the letter at the top and draw the line down…finish writing the letter showing the students how to form it properly). And this is how adults write the small, child letter *m*." (Demonstrate on board.)<br><br>Activity A: Review the /m/ sound and have students identify classmates whose names begin with that sound. (No one can say their own first name.) Then ask if anyone has a middle name or last name that begins with the /m/ sound. (Students can offer their own names here.)<br><br>Students find /m/ objects in the room. |

| Transition 9:35–9:40 | IMA: "Head, Shoulders, Knees, and Toes" movement song<br>**Directions Game:**<br>• Clap twice.<br>• Get out your main lesson book and your yellow and purple block crayons.<br>• Open your book to the first blank page after your mountain picture (drawn yesterday).<br>Check to make sure all of the students are on the right page.<br><br>Remind students about their posture: feet firmly on the floor, backs relaxed but straight. |
|---|---|
| Bookwork 9:40–10:00 | First, guide students in drawing a large yellow *moon* (circle) on the center of their page. (Ask students what sound the word *moon* begins with.)<br><br>Then guide them in drawing a large purple *M* and small *m* in the center of their moon with stick crayons. (Note: Stick crayons are used here because this is meant to be an artistic experience of the letter, not a handwriting lesson.) Because this is artistic, do not stress the proper way to form the *Mm*. Proper form will come in tomorrow's handwriting lesson.<br>**Directions Game:**<br>• Put away main lesson book and crayons.<br>• Clap your hands once.<br>• Sit at your desk with your hands folded. |
| **Speech/Song Time:** 10:00–10:15 | Sing the song "Autumn Winds" and say tongue twister: "Mr. Matthew Mathers" (Drill Down). |

## 9. Home Surroundings Block

The Home Surroundings Block will vary based on locale and the needs of your students. It should look different in every Waldorf school and for every class in that school. Decide how best to help your students connect to their local environment. For more information on how to create or find the stories you can use for this block, see chapter 5.5 #5 and #6 and your completed summer preparation form.

Here is a list of possible activities to include in your block plans:

- nature stories (see chapter 5.5 #5)

- nature crafts

- nature walks (Kid Write about what they saw after returning to the classroom.)

- art based on nature

- field trip to a nature center

We encourage you to continue working with aspects of language arts such as kid writing, sight words, phonics rules, reading etc. throughout this block.

## 10. Key Moments in 1st Grade

When you are done preparing your block plans for 1st Grade, proofread them to make sure you have adequately covered all of the key moments. Here is a list:

- initial introduction of consonant (see chapter 3.1 #7)
- initial introduction of handwriting (see chapter 3.2 #6)
- introduction of phonemes (working with sounds not letters-see chapter 3.3 #2)
  - o onset & rime
  - o phoneme matching
  - o blending phonemes
  - o sequencing phonemes
  - o segmenting phonemes
- introduction of materialization techniques for phonemic awareness (see chapter 3.3 #2)
  - o shouting out rhyming words with stomping or clapping
  - o hand spelling
  - o stretching out the sounds in words with stretchable fabric
  - o word sorting
  - o finger spelling
  - o sound and letter boxes
- initial introduction of encoding initial sound in a word (see chapter 3.4 #5)
- initial introduction of symbol imagery (see chapter 3.5 #6)
- initial introduction of sight words (see chapter 3.6 #5)
- initial introduction of concept imagery (see chapter 3.7 #4)
- initial introduction of listening comprehension and HOTS questions (see chapter 3.8 #5)
- initial introduction of speech work for a letter (see chapter 3.10 #7)
- initial introduction of memory reading (see chapter 3.15 #5)

Also make sure you have adequate amounts of practice scheduled.

## Conclusion

*The Roadmap to Literacy* curriculum is designed so that your students will be able to finish both the Emergent Phase and the Phonemic Awareness Phase by the end of 1st Grade. Many students come to 1st Grade already out of the Emergent Phase; with proper instruction, the rest move on to the Phonemic Awareness Phase within the first block(s).

The Emergent Phase ends when students realize that letters represent sounds and have partial knowledge of the alphabet (i.e., enough to begin to use letters to make sound matches in their memory reading). In the Phonemic Awareness Phase, they have to master the rest of the alphabet and develop full phonemic awareness (i.e., when encoding, they represent each sound in a word with a logical letter choice, which demonstrates they have mastered segmenting sounds). Fortunately, the Phonemic Awareness Phase picks up seamlessly from the Emergent Phase. The broad strokes of your classroom instruction will not need to change at the beginning of the Phonemic Awareness Phase. After all, you will still be teaching the alphabet, handwriting, sight words, and memory reading. However, your expectations will change. In addition, many aspects of language arts will deepen and some new ones will be added, including kid writing. By the end of 1st Grade, students should be ready to move on to the Pattern Phase.

# 5.3  SECOND GRADE CURRICULUM PLANS

This chapter presents information for planning the 2nd Grade curriculum. It follows the same format as chapter 5.2, but many of the samples are on the website www.waldorfinspirations.com.

This chapter covers the following topics:

1. Overview of 2nd Grade
2. Example Block Rotation
3. Example Summer Preparation Form
4. Example Block Plan: Practice Block
5. Example Block Plan: Main Lesson Block
6. Example Daily Lesson Plan
7. Home Surroundings Block
8. Key Moments in 2nd Grade

Note: The information in this chapter should be taken as suggestions. Use what is helpful for you and your class.

## 1.  Overview of 2nd Grade

Waldorf students begin language arts instruction a year behind their public school peers. Consequently, they have to make up ground to catch up with them by the end of 3rd Grade. Waldorf students are expected to complete all of the Pattern Phase in 2nd Grade.

In public schools, the Pattern Phase usually begins in 1st Grade and extends into the beginning of 2nd Grade because students master the Emergent Phase and part of the Phonemic Awareness Phase in kindergarten. Waldorf students have to progress faster. With proper instruction and planning on your part, your students will be able to master the Pattern Phase in 2nd Grade because they are older and have the foundations provided by the Emergent and Phonemic Awareness Phases. By the end of 1st Grade, your students should have developed full phonemic awareness (i.e., when encoding, they represent each sound in a word with a logical letter choice, which demonstrates they have mastered segmenting sounds) and be well on their way to mastering symbol imagery. With daily practice, they can easily learn the phonics rules for the Pattern Phase in 2nd Grade.

Phonics rules in the Pattern Phase cover patterns for individual phonemes. Recall that English has three layers: alphabet, pattern, and meaning (see chapter 1.3 #1). These layers represent the three layers of code students need to master to be proficient in English. Students cover the alphabetic (Old English) layer in the Emergent and Phonemic Awareness Phases; they cover the pattern (French/Middle English) layer in the Pattern and Syllable Phases. The Pattern Phase focuses on patterns for single phonemes (e.g., *OA* for long *O* as in *boat*, *EIGH* for long *A* as in *freight*, etc.), while the Syllable Phase focuses on patterns for syllables (i.e., *–tion, -ture*, etc.).

The Pattern Phase contains multiple transitions. Like the Phonemic Awareness Phase, the Pattern Phase focuses on words that are only one syllable long. However, it prepares students for working with syllables.

The first transition is from working with individual phonemes to working with onsets and rimes. In the Phonemic Awareness Phase, students sound out words one phoneme at a time; however, there is a faster way to decode and encode: onset and rimes. Encoding and decoding through onsets and rimes serves as a transition to working with syllables in the Syllable Phase.

The second transition is working with patterns of letters. These patterns include vowel teams such as *OI* and *AY*. as well as longer patterns such as *EIGH*. In the Pattern Phase, students will use their phonemic awareness and symbol imagery skills as the foundation for learning the phonics rules that demonstrate all of the additional ways sounds can be represented in English.

Note: It is imperative that you do not begin the Pattern Phase instruction before your students have developed full phonemic awareness (i.e., when encoding, they represent each sound in a word with a logical letter choice, which demonstrates they have mastered segmenting sounds). Even though students who have weak phonemic awareness often find it easier to learn word families, their weakness in phonemic awareness will come back to haunt them because students need full phonemic awareness to work with syllables in the Syllable Phase. Students who lack it are hobbled in all subsequent phonics, decoding, and encoding work.

Mastery of the Pattern Phase is split. Students master <u>decoding</u> during 2nd Grade, but mastery of <u>encoding</u> spills over into 3rd Grade. This lag happens in all educational systems. It develops when students study patterns because there is more than one way to spell many words. Consequently, it is harder to encode words correctly than it is to decode them.

It is worth considering an overview of the phase. Table 5.3.1 presents the primary objective and teaching priorities for the Pattern Phase.

**Table 5.3.1: Overview of Objectives for the Pattern Phase**

| |
|---|
| **Primary Teaching Objective for Pattern Phase:** Help students develop full symbol imagery for one-syllable words (visualizing up to seven letters). |
| **Teaching Priorities for Pattern Phase:**<br>• symbol imagery<br>• encoding and decoding with phonics rules<br>• reading: decodable-text<br>• writing: kid writing (first half of year) composition (second half)<br>• sight words: finish off the list<br>• grammar (noun/verb and mechanics) |

By the end of 2nd Grade, your students should be able to complete the Pattern Phase. At this point they will have mastered the use of symbol imagery and have the ability to decode with the Pattern Phase phonics rules. They will move into 3rd Grade ready to learn to decode and encode by syllables and to learn the phonics rules that govern that process.

Note: The assumption is that your 2nd Grader students are ready for this phase, but they may not be. Teach to your students' phase, not grade.

## 2. Example Block Rotation

The block rotation lays out your blocks in light of the school's academic calendar for the upcoming year. Use the example in table 5.3.2 as a guide to make your own (see chapter 5.1 #3).

**Table 5.3.2: Example Block Rotation**

| Block Number and Length | Main Lesson Blocks | Practice Blocks |
|---|---|---|
| First Block (4 weeks) | Math Main Lesson Block 1 | Language Practice Block 1 |
| Second Block (4 weeks) | Language Main Lesson Block 1 | Math Practice Block 1 |
| Third Block (3 weeks) | Math Main Lesson Block 2 | Language Practice Block 2 |
| Fourth Block (4 weeks) | Language Main Lesson Block 2 | Math Practice Block 2 |
| Fifth Block (4 weeks) | Math Main Lesson Block 3 | Language Practice Block 3 |
| Sixth Block (3 weeks) | Language Main Lesson Block 3 | Math Practice Block 3 |
| Seventh Block (4 weeks) | Math Main Lesson Block 4 | Language Practice Block 4 |
| Eighth Block (4 weeks) | Language Main Lesson Block 4 | Math Practice Block 4 |
| Ninth Block (4 weeks) | Home Surroundings Block | Language Skills and Math Skills |

## 3. Example Summer Preparation Form

The summer preparation form is the form you can use to plan your curriculum and organize your curriculum materials.

- For templates of 2nd Grade summer preparation form and an example of a partially filled out form, go to www.waldorfinspirations.com. Download the summer preparation form for 2nd Grade. See chapter 5.1 #4 for instructions on how to fill it out.

- To get an idea of how a completed form would look, see chapter 5.2 #3.

## 4. Example Block Plan: Practice Block

If you are following *The Roadmap to Literacy's* block rotation, your first block would be a practice block.

- For a block plan template for 2nd Grade practice block, see Appendix 2B. See chapter 5.1 #5 for instructions on how to fill it out. To get an idea of how a completed form would look, see chapter 5.2 #6.

- For an example of a partially completed form (one week), go to www.waldorfinspirations.com and choose the practice block plan for 2nd Grade.

- If you decide to create your own form, use the scheduling subsection in the section 3 chapters.

## 5. Example Block Plan: Main Lesson Block

If you are following *The Roadmap to Literacy's* block rotation, the first language arts main lesson block will be the second block of the year.

- For a block plan template for 2nd Grade main lesson blocks, see Appendix 2A and 2C. See chapter 5.1 #5 for instructions on how to fill it out. To get an idea of how a completed form would look, see chapter 5.2 #5.

- For an example of a partially completed form (one week), go to www.waldorfinspirations.com. Choose the main lesson block plan for 2nd Grade.

- If you decide to create your own form, use the scheduling subsection in the section 3 chapters.

## 6. Example Daily Lesson Plan

Use your completed block plan forms (both main lesson and practice) as the basis for creating your daily lesson plans.

- For daily lesson plan form, see www.waldorfinspirations.com. See chapter 5.1 #6 for instructions on how to fill it out. To get an idea of how a completed form would look, see chapter 5.2 #7 and #8.

- For an example of a daily lesson plan for the first day of the block, go to www.waldorfinspirations.com.

## 7. Home Surroundings Block

The Home Surroundings Block will vary based on locale and the needs of your students. It should look different in every Waldorf school and for every class in that school. Decide how best to help your students connect to their local environment. For more information on how to create or find the stories you can use for this block, see chapter 5.5 #5 and #7 and your completed summer preparation form.

Here is a list of possible activities to include in your block plans:

- nature stories (see chapter 5.5 #5)

- nature crafts

- nature walks—the class observes nature and writes about what they saw afterward

- art based on nature

- field trip to a nature center

Continue working with aspects of language arts such as composition, phonics rules, reading, spelling, etc. throughout this block.

## 8. Key Moments in 2nd Grade

When you are done preparing your block plans for 2nd Grade, proofread them to make sure you have adequately covered all of the key moments. Here is a list:

- phonics rules for the Pattern Phase (see chapter 4.2)

- introduction of encoding and decoding with onset and rimes (see chapter 3.4 #8 and 4.2 rule 9))

- kid writing (see chapter 3.13 and conclude the second half of the year)

- introduction of composition (see chapter 3.14 #5)

- introduction of cursive writing (see chapter 3.2 #8)

- introduction of grammar (parts of speech) (see chapter 3.11 #7)

- sight words (see chapter 3.6 and complete the second half of the year)

Also make sure you have adequate practice scheduled.

## Conclusion

If you plan your lessons according to *The Roadmap to Literacy*, students will make tremendous progress in language arts in 2nd Grade. In the beginning of the Pattern Phase, they subvocalize when they read, but by the end, most are reading simple chapter books quietly to themselves. In the beginning of the Pattern Phase, their writing is littered with misspellings, but by the end, they can spell most single-syllable words correctly (including sight words and simple homophones). Consult chapter 6.4 for information on how to assess student skills.

# 5.4  THIRD GRADE CURRICULUM PLANS

This chapter presents information for planning the 3rd Grade curriculum. It follows the same format as chapter 5.3. Many examples have been put on the website www.waldorinspirations.com.

This chapter covers the following topics:

1. Overview of 3rd Grade
2. Example Block Rotation
3. Example Summer Preparation Form
4. Example Block Plan: Practice Block
5. Example Block Plan: Main Lesson Block
6. Example Daily Lesson Plan
7. Home Surroundings Block
8. Key Moments in 3rd Grade

Note: The information in this chapter should be taken as suggestions. Use what is helpful for you and your class.

## 1.  Overview of 3rd Grade

This is the year Waldorf students catch up with their public school peers. By the end of 3rd Grade, both Waldorf and public school students should be at the same point: they can decode just about any word and can read grade-appropriate books on their own. They will, however, need to continue their spelling instruction through 8th Grade. By the end of 3rd Grade, Waldorf students should have made the transition from learning to read to reading to learn.

To get to this point, they must master multisyllabic decoding in one year. Fortunately, they can do so because you have laid a good foundation. The students have phonemic awareness and the ability to visualize at least seven letters through symbol imagery. Furthermore, they can decode and encode single-syllable words through onsets and rimes. They are ready to learn to decode and encode multisyllabic words by syllable.

Note: The students only need to master <u>decoding</u> the Syllable Phase phonics rules. They will continue to study and practice <u>encoding</u> with the Syllable Phase phonics rules in 4th Grade, 5th Grade, and 6th Grade when they study spelling. They begin to study spelling this year and have weekly spelling tests that include a review of phonics rules for the Pattern Phase as well as notable exceptions.

It is worth considering an overview of the phase. Table 5.4.1 presents the primary objective and teaching priorities for the Syllable Phase.

**Table 5.4.1: Overview of Objectives for the Syllable Phase**

| |
|---|
| **Primary Teaching Objective for Syllable Phase: Help students develop multisyllabic encoding and decoding.** |
| **Teaching Priorities for Syllable Phase:**<br><br>• encoding and decoding with phonics rules for the Syllable Phase<br><br>• spelling: tests and dictation<br><br>• grammar (more parts of speech and mechanics)<br><br>• reading: decodable-text<br><br>• composition writing (including book reports) |

From 3rd Grade on, students should compose all of their own main lesson book entries, unless they are copying a poem or other literary work from the board or are collaborating with a partner on a writing assignment. Students in 3rd Grade will complete the Syllable Phase phonics rules (see chapter 4.3). While they do not need to master encoding for the Syllable Phase by the end of 3rd Grade, they should be able to correctly encode simple two-syllable words when they write.

Note: The assumption is that your 3rd Grade students are ready for this phase, but they may not be. Teach to your students' phase, not grade.

## 2.   Example Block Rotation

The block rotation lays out your blocks in light of the school's academic calendar for the upcoming year. Use the example in table 5.4.2 as a guide to make your own (see chapter 5.1 #3).

**Table 5.4.2: Example Block Rotation**

| Block Number and Length | Main Lesson Blocks | Practice Blocks |
|---|---|---|
| First Block (4 weeks) | Math Block 1 | Language Block 1 (review) |
| Second Block (4 weeks) | Language Block 1: Grammar | Math Block 1 |
| Third Block (3 weeks) | Math Block 2 | Language Block 2: Grammar |
| Fourth Block (4 weeks) | Language Block 2: Composition | Math Block 2 |
| Fifth Block (4 weeks) | Math Block 3 | Language Block 3: Composition |
| Sixth Block (3 weeks) | Language Block 3: Grammar | Math Block 3 |
| Seventh Block (4 weeks) | Math Block 4 | Language Block 4: Grammar |
| Eighth Block (4 weeks) | Language Block 4: Composition | Math Block 4 |
| Ninth Block (4 weeks) | Home Surroundings: Practical Occupations | Language and Math Skills |

## 3.   Example Summer Preparation Form

The summer preparation form is the form you fill out to plan your curriculum and organize your curriculum materials.

- For templates of 3rd Grade summer preparation form and an example of a partially filled out form, go to www.waldorfinspirations.com. Download the summer preparation form for 3rd Grade. See chapter 5.1 #4 for instructions on how to fill it out.
- To get an idea of how a completed form would look, see chapter 5.2 #3.

## 4. Example Block Plan: Practice Block

If you are following *The Roadmap to Literacy* block rotation, your first literacy block would be a practice block.

- For block plan templates for 3rd Grade Practice block plans, see Appendix 3A and 3C. See chapter 5.1 #5 for instructions on how to fill them out. To get an idea of how a completed form would look, see chapter 5.2 #6.
- For an example of a partially completed form (one week), go to www.waldorfinspirations.com. Choose the practice block plan for 3rd Grade.
- If you decide to create your own form, use the scheduling subsection in the section 3 chapters.

## 5. Example Block Plan: Main Lesson Block

If you are following *The Roadmap to Literacy'* block rotation, your second literacy block would be a main lesson block.

- For block plan templates for 3rd Grade main lesson blocks, see Appendix 3B and 3D. See chapter 5.1 #5 for instructions on how to fill them out. To get an idea of how a completed form would look, see chapter 5.2 #5.
- For an example of a partially completed form (one week), go to www.waldorfinspirations.com. Choose the main lesson block plan for 3rd Grade.
- If you decide to create your own form, use the scheduling subsection in the section 3 chapters.

## 6. Example Daily Lesson Plan

Use your block plan form (both main lesson and practice) as the basis for creating your daily lesson plans.

- For daily lesson plan form, see www.waldorfinspirations.com and chapter 5.1 #6 for instructions on how to fill it out. To get an idea of how a completed form would look, see chapter 5.2 #7 and #8.
- For an example of a daily lesson plan , go to www.waldorfinspirations.com.

## 7. Home Surroundings Block

The ninth block, Home Surroundings (i.e., practical occupations), will vary based on locale and the needs of your students. It should look different in every Waldorf school and for every class in the school. It will be up to you to decide how best to help your students connect to their local environment. When to schedule this block will depend on your location and what you choose to cover. For example, if you live in Vermont and want to teach your students about the maple syrup season, you might choose to schedule this block just prior to spring break. If you live in the foothills east of Sacramento, California, you might choose to schedule it in October when the apple and pumpkin harvest is at its peak (see chapter 2.3 #2 and chapter 5.5 #5 and 8).

Here is a list of possible activities to include in your block plans:

- information about practical occupations (see chapter 5.5 #8)
- practical crafts or projects related to subject(s) of this block
- field trip(s) to view or participate in local occupations that are related to the land (e.g., harvesting local produce, observing local house building, going out on a fishing boat, weaving local baskets, etc.).

We encourage you to continue working with aspects of language arts throughout this block.

## 8.   Key Moments in 3rd Grade

When you are done preparing your four language arts main lesson block plans and your four practice block plans for 3rd Grade, proofread them to make sure you have adequately covered all of the key moments. Here is a list:

- Syllable Phase phonics rules (see chapter 4.3)
- encoding and decoding using the Syllable Phase phonics rules
- introduction to reading nonfiction (optional) (see chapter 3.15 #9)
- introduction of spelling (i.e., weekly spelling words and test) (see chapter 3.9 #5)
- all aspects of 3rd Grade composition (see chapter 3.14 #7)
- book reports (see chapter 3.14 #8)
- grammar curriculum for 3rd Grade (chapter 3.11 #8)

Also make sure you have adequate amounts of practice scheduled.

## Conclusion

If you plan your lessons according to *The Roadmap to Literacy*, your students should be caught up with their public school peers by the end of 3rd Grade in reading, writing, and spelling. Formal reading instruction concludes at the end of 3rd Grade as students move from learning to read to reading to learn. Students will need to be able to read independently and fluently to meet the demands of the 4th Grade curriculum regardless of where they go to school. If a student lags in reading, writing, and spelling skills at the end of 3rd Grade, it is imperative that she is assessed to determine if she needs remediation over the summer (see chapter 6.6).

Note: Even though students need to master Syllable Phase decoding by the end of 3rd Grade, they will have three additional years of spelling instruction in Grades 4–6 to master encoding by syllable.

# 5.5  WORKING WITH STORIES

Stories are important in the Waldorf classroom. Mastering storytelling will be key to preparing and delivering your curriculum.

This chapter covers the following topics:

1. Overview of Stories in the Waldorf Curriculum
2. Curriculum Chart Three: Stories
3. Literature Curriculum Stories
4. Academic Concept Stories
5. Home Surroundings Stories: Introduction
6. Home Surroundings Stories: 1st Grade
7. Home Surroundings Stories: 2nd Grade
8. Home Surroundings Material: 3rd Grade
9. Sacred Nothings
10. Story Bibliography: A List of Recommended Sources

## 1.  Overview of Stories in the Waldorf Curriculum

Stories are an extremely versatile part of the Waldorf curriculum. When preparing your story curriculum, there are three important points to consider: 1) finding or creating the stories you wish to tell; 2) scheduling stories; and 3) the difference between telling and reading stories.

**Stories to Tell:** As a Waldorf teacher, you work with four different types of stories, but you only prepare the first three over the summer:

1. Literature Curriculum Stories
2. Academic Concept Stories
3. Home Surroundings Stories
4. Pedagogical Stories

For a summary of the four types of stories, see chapter 2.1 #5. The first three will be addressed in subsequent subsections in this chapter.

**Scheduling:** The type and purpose of a story affects scheduling. Any story that is told as a vehicle for new academic concepts or information is always told in main lesson, either in the Introduction &/or Review segment or the Story segment; however, if the story is soul food, you can tell the story outside of main lesson.

In "On the Question of the Three-fold Structure of the Main Lesson," Wiechert writes: "There is nothing in Steiner's lectures that dictates the story always come in Main Lesson. In fact, the end of the day is a lovely time to share a story with the students" (Wiechert 2010, 10).

**Telling vs. Reading:** Rudolf Steiner charged teachers to tell stories to their students rather than read them. In *Practical Advice to Teachers*, when Steiner is talking about preparing fairy tales for 1st Grade, he says, "We read aloud as little as possible, but instead prepare ourselves so well that we can bring to them [students] in a narrative way whatever we want to tell them" (Steiner 2000, 168). Furthermore, when you read, the book is between you and the students: the word choice, the sentence structure, and the images all belong to someone else. When you tell a story, you make the story your own in a way you never can do when you read, and thus you make a direct connection with the students.

There is a time and place for reading books aloud to the class: when you share quality literature such as *The Secret Garden*. You can read to the students during snack or in another class such as handwork.

Use this curriculum chart for stories to help organize the story curriculum across Grades 1–3.

## 2. Curriculum Chart Three: Stories

This final curriculum chart covers the types of stories you work with in each grade. See table 5.5.1.

**Table 5.5.1: Curriculum Chart Three: Stories**

|  | 1st Grade | 2nd Grade | 3rd Grade |
|---|---|---|---|
| **Literature Curriculum Stories** | Fairy tales and folk tales from around the world | Fables and legends<br>Saint stories<br>Animal stories | Old Testament stories (i.e., Creation through Moses plus other favorites) |
| **Academic Concept Stories** | Stories/images for phonics rules<br>Umbrella stories for grammar and other new skills | Stories/images for phonics rules<br>Umbrella stories for grammar and other new skills | Stories/images for phonics rules<br>Umbrella stories for grammar and other new skills |
| **Home Surroundings Stories** | Nature stories | Nature stories | NA—Present factual information about Practical Occupations |

The next few subsections will show you how to prepare these three story types over the summer.

## 3. Literature Curriculum Stories

Literature curriculum stories are the first type of stories for you to prepare.

Story Selection

As you read stories and fill out your summer preparation form, keep your purpose in mind: soul food, academic concept story, etc. Find multiple stories that fit the bill. Then choose the stories that you love. If the story resonates with you, you will enjoy learning it and sharing it with your students. In turn, they will love listening to it. (Download story preparation form from www.waldorfinspirations.com.)

<u>During the Summer</u>

- Read a plethora of stories for the upcoming year.
- Select stories that you like and enter them into your summer preparation form. (You will select the actual stories you will use when making block plans from these possibilities.)

<u>When Planning Your Block Plan</u>

- Select the stories you will use during that block.
- The Story segment of main lesson runs 15–20 minutes on average. Most literature curriculum stories are between 10–25 minutes long, although the fables in 2nd Grade are much shorter. If your story is long, schedule it over multiple days or edit it down.

<u>Learning the Story</u>

There are many ways to learn stories. Below is one example:

*The Week before You Tell the Story:*

- While you read your story, make a quick outline of the story. Put in key words and phrases as well as thumbnail sketches (1 minute or less) of key moments in the story. Bullet point outlines work well.
- The next day, tell your story from your outline and time it. Record the time on top of your outline. You will use it to adjust the timing of your main lesson.
- Once you have run through your story, revise your outline. Add more key words or additional thumb-nail sketches as needed or delete material if the story is slightly over time.
- Read your outline for the story. Close your eyes and visualize the story, focusing on the color, the smells, what the main characters look like, how they move, etc. Do this for each scene of the story.
- If you cannot remember, go back and read the story again. Update your outline.

*The Day Before You Tell the Story:*

- Read your outline for the story. Close your eyes and visualize the story, focusing on the color, the smells, what the main characters look like, how they move, etc. Do this for each scene of the story.
- If you cannot remember, go back and read the story again.
- Practice the story if you have time.
- Review the images, scenes, and key words right before bed and then get a good night's sleep.

When you tell the story, recall each image and tell the part of the story that goes with it. For an added layer of support, you can attach your outline to your lesson plan in case you need a few hints.

<u>Telling the Story to Your Class</u>

In the few seconds before you begin, visualize the opening of your story and capture its mood. Both the image and emotion will come through naturally in your voice.

In Grades 1–3 tell the story in a normal voice with few gestures. Do not strive for vocal theatrics or exaggerated dialogue. The students' concept imagery should serve as the basis for comprehension, not your performance. Let the words and images carry the message. Do slow down during sad scenes so the pace of the story carries the emotion and students can experience it.

When telling your story, you should expect for the students to be quiet and attentive (even 1st graders). If you hold the line on this, it will pay off for years to come: your students will know that when you are giving a presentation or telling a story, they are expected to pay attention. Because so much of the Waldorf academic content is delivered orally, it is essential that the classroom environment supports learning through listening. An effective method for gently but firmly holding this line is to stop telling the story whenever a student begins to talk to a neighbor or engage in distracting behavior. Just look at the student (seriously but not glaringly) until she realizes that the storytelling has stopped and she is the reason.

Note: In 1st Grade you may want to create a special ritual around your story. Consider these ideas: close the curtains and light a candle (if permitted by the fire marshal—check with your school); sing a storytelling song or play the lyre before beginning the story; have the children sit around you either on the floor or on chairs. These rituals can help you make a transition, but they are not essential.

## 4. Academic Concept Stories

Academic concept stories are the second type of stories for you to prepare. They require a different approach.

<u>Select or create a story.</u>

Academic concepts stories are a vehicle for bringing new concepts to the class. The story contains an image that you will pull out and use to introduce a new concept, skill, etc. The story can be an individual story or a serial story (umbrella story). You will find examples of these stories in this book, as well as in other resources, but you can also create your own.

If you are considering one of *The Roadmap to Literacy's* academic concept stories, see the chapter 3.11 #6–8 and section 4 phonics rules.

To make up your own academic concept story, use any related incident or image that occurs to you. Use your life experiences, interests, knowledge of the world, etc. to find material for academic concept stories and images. Keep in mind the primary elements:

- character(s)
- plot (conflict/resolution)

Only add in one or two secondary elements if they serve your image:

- setting
- description

Your story should not be elaborate. The point is the image you will pull from it, not the creation of a literary masterpiece.

<u>Timing the Story</u>

These stories tend to be quick. They are usually told in five minutes or less. If they are longer than 10 minutes, schedule the literature curriculum story you were going to tell at the end of main lesson for later on in the day. This practice will keep your main lessons balanced.

<u>Telling the Story</u>

Do not use a ritual to introduce academic concept stories. Just tell the story, pull the image from the story, and immediately introduce the new skill, concept, or material. The only exception is when the story is both an academic concept story and a literature curriculum story. For example, 1st Grade fairy tales are used to meet the developmental needs of students as well as introduce letters of the alphabet. In these cases you can set the stage for the story with your story ritual if you are so inclined.

# 5. Home Surroundings Stories: Introduction

Home surroundings stories are the third type of stories for you to prepare. These stories only apply to 1st and 2nd Grade; in 3rd Grade, switch to presenting facts and real-world experiences. You can find home surroundings stories in books. If you enjoy creating your own stories, try to write a few of your own. The following subsections introduce them and give specific information on how to prepare these stories in each grade.

The following advice comes from Dr. Patrick Wakeford-Evans, a teacher who took two classes through 8th Grade. He writes:

*Geography is a very important aspect in the original curriculum of the Waldorf School. It links, binds, and integrates all of the other subjects into a unity. Unique also to the Waldorf curriculum is the sequence of subjects in geography. Geography begins as local geography and expands out from there. It is taught alongside cultural studies from 1st Grade through 8th Grade.*

*Geography in grades one, two, three, and four begins close to the child. It acquaints the child with home surroundings, proceeds to local geography, and by the end of grade four, expands to include the geography of the whole region, whether it be a state or a unified micro-region.*

*Prior to the nine-year change, children need to be taught through the teacher's imagination. These imaginations inspire the children to have their own feeling-imbued experience of knowledge. This inspiration is achieved through the telling of stories. Stories convey pictures of all things students should know about.*

*The geography curriculum of grades one and two calls for lessons in home surroundings. What is meant by home surroundings? In public schools, children are taught about their neighborhoods as civics lessons. They take field trips to a local fire station, for example, and explore the neighborhood. While this type of lesson is certainly important, Steiner's indication was to acquaint the children with the land, the plants, and the animals in the region where they live. Home Surroundings means becoming acquainted with the eco-systems that surround the children. In biology one might say they need an awareness of the various habitats and their inhabitants. These stories are the first lessons in ecology and nature awareness.*

*In both urban and suburban environments, the wonderful beings of nature dwell and visit the children. There are noisy mockingbirds, squirrels, spiders, and all manner of insects. In addition, there are all kinds of flying creatures like red tail hawks. Depending on where you live, there may even be deer, wild turkeys, and butterflies. In the Sacramento region, you can also hear mysterious tree frogs and coyotes yipping in the distance, spy possums, and even smell skunks.*

*In Waldorf education, one of the important maxims is "characterize, do not define." Waldorf teachers are encouraged to present nature to the students by crafting stories that are true to the facts yet glowing in imaginative portrayal. There are many nature stories to be found in children's literature; however, teachers can also make their own. The stories you create yourself portray nature in imaginative ways. They can be as simple as vivid descriptions of nature or a story that uses literary devices to illustrate facts about the world around them.*

*In his writings, Rudolf Steiner often points out that there is nothing better than stories the teachers invent for the children. The children seem to recognize the love and creativity in a story that a teacher has made 'just for them.'*

<u>Two Approaches to Nature Stories</u>

All nature stories feature the geography of your locale and/or the creatures that live there. However, there are two ways to approach nature stories.

The first approach is to describe one or more local elements. Here is a list of possible topics:

- local flora: trees, bushes, flowers, weeds, vegetables, etc.
- local fauna: insects, reptiles, birds, animals, etc.
- geographical features: rivers, mountains, hills, plains, valleys, etc.
- nature's rhythms: sunrise/sunset, moonrise/moonset, tides, seasons, etc.

Create a story, fable, or description of any of these elements. Just make sure that the description is based on local conditions. For example, if you live in the desert, do not describe mountains with winter snow but the brief spring rains and the profusion of wildflowers afterward.

The second approach includes the description of local element(s) but also introduces a seed-image for a concept that you will teach in a later grade. In Grades 4–8, Waldorf students study many concepts in geography and in science classes. You can plant seeds for these concepts in your nature stories in 1st and 2nd Grade by including a description of something you plan to teach later. When the students get to that subject in a later grade, the territory will be tantalizingly familiar to them because they encountered it in story and images in 1st or 2nd Grade.

You can find inspiration for these seed-images to include in your nature stories from some of the following blocks:

- Animal (4th Grade)
  - life of a specific animal
  - comparing/contrasting two different animals through a conversation between them
- Botany (5th Grade)
  - relationship between insects and plants
  - metamorphosis of caterpillar into butterfly
  - regional plants
  - changes in a deciduous tree through the season (the leaf cycle)
- Chemistry (8th Grade): photosynthesis (i.e., the formation of sugar and carbohydrates) (see the example story for 1st Grade in chapter 5.5 #6)
- Meteorology and Weather (8th Grade)
  - heat build-up and release with winds
  - water cycle (as it relates to the warming and cooling of day and night)
  - clouds
  - sun and wind*
  - sun and moon
  - wind and rain
  - wind and fog
  - the seasons

*For an example of a fable that illustrates how to hold conversations between elements of nature, read Aesop's fable "The North Wind and the Sun," a story where the two argue over who is the more powerful.

Your story creations can be written in the language of a fairy tale, a fable, or a description of everyday events, nature, and people. What is important is that the story brings the students' awareness to the nature that surrounds them in their environment.

Get inspiration to create these stories by doing the following:

- Read books. Get an idea of the facts behind the phenomena. Discover what scientists and others have researched. For example, read descriptions of the real lives of animals in your region.
- Observe nature. Get outside and explore the things you wish to teach with your five senses, your emotions, and your whole being. Take long nature walks. Get acquainted with local flora and fauna by taking trips to nature centers. In addition, take time to look closely at the natural world that is around you. Even mundane observations such as the tenacious nature of dandelions can be fodder for nature stories.

For a delightful story about a ubiquitous weed, see "What the Dandelion Told" by Clara Maetzelfrom in *The Emerald Storybook: Stories and Legends of Spring, Nature and Easter* by Ada M. Skinner. It illustrates how to take simple observations and put them into a story that is suitable for 1st Grade. You could tell this story as is or use it to inspire one of your own. Use the *Teacher Literature Resource List* for a beginning list of books to consult (see Appendix 5).

Once you have completed your research and identified which aspect(s) you wish to bring, you can begin creating your story. Specific guidelines for Grades 2 and 3 are provided in the following subsections. 2nd and 3rd Grade stories have a very different quality than those told in 1st Grade.

# 6. Home Surrounding Stories: 1st Grade

Nature stories for 1st Grade are less realistic than those for 2nd Grade. While they describe nature, they often contain magic and fairies. They have the flavor of a fairy tale and are not completely in this world. This subsection includes a sample nature story for 1st Grade, deconstructs how to create one, and discusses how to prepare to tell the story.

Example Nature Story for 1st Grade: Leaf Day

The story "Leaf Day" is a blend of a story written by Patrick Wakeford-Evans and one written by Jennifer Militzer-Kopperl. It is about the first leaves in spring and contains a seed-image of photosynthesis (an example of the second type of nature story).

*Calvin was a small sugar gnome, so small you could barely see him. He was dressed in brown pants, shirt, and cap, and he had skin and eyes the color of ripe acorns. He lived inside an oak tree.*

*One spring day Calvin was resting in the root-stock of his tree listening to the roots sip up the recent rain water. The winter had been long and cold, but today the soil was pleasantly warm. Up above him, Calvin could hear the streams gurgling and bubbling inside his tree. Today was Leaf Day!*

*Calvin knew he had a lot of work to do. He shook his head and stood up. He took a long drink of sweet sap from the River Phloem and wiped his mouth. Then he fashioned a raft from the sticky sugar logs nearby and climbed aboard. He pushed out into the river using a spindly rootstock as a pole.*

*Calvin poled his way along the river. The sweet sap water ran under him. Up ahead, the river made an abrupt turn where the headwaters of the River Phloem began to flow upwards. Calvin steered his raft to the center of the river and looked up. Above him, he saw a dark tube-like corridor with faint rays of light far in the distance. The river carried him up through the trunk of the mighty oak tree.*

*As the raft soared higher and higher, Calvin felt excited. Today was the day. The sticky green leaves were going to be born this morning. Sugar production was about to start. And Calvin's job as a sugar-gnome was about to begin.*

*Calvin poled along the Phloem River higher and higher. Up ahead a tributary split to the right off from the Phloem. When Calvin reached this split, he steered his raft to the right and entered a smaller river traveling through a limb of his oak tree. He was almost at his destination.*

*Carefully, Calvin steered his raft toward a slender tube and docked it by a small round door. Calvin could see the light outlining the doorframe and feel the warmth coming through the door's cracks. Calvin swung open the door and entered a small, cramped room. Calvin's head almost touched the ceiling. He could reach out and touch the walls. Both the walls and ceiling were wet, and the water on the floor came up to Calvin's knees. Even stranger, the water seemed to be giggling. Calvin looked down and realized that there were undines flowing around his ankles. They had large round heads with two fins on each side. They were hard to see because they were almost transparent. The undines giggled again and swam faster around and around until they disappeared from view.*

*Calvin took a step across the room and opened a window. He pushed his head out the window into a bright world. He was looking out from the tip of a small brownish-red leaf bud on a slender branch. He was on top of the world!*

*The sun was just rising and it felt warm on Calvin's face and ears. Drops of dew clung to the leaf bud. The air was fresh. It smelled damp and warm. Calvin looked up. He could see wide limbs and small branches reaching up to the sky. Everywhere he looked, he could see leaf buds. There must have been thousands of them. They were a grey color, but they had red tips. They rose out of the branches like turrets on a castle. Many of the leaf buds had other sugar gnomes looking out of them too. Calvin smiled and waved to his friends. Then he looked down. Through the bare branches, he could see the tree roots pushing into the soil. It was a long way down. Calvin shivered a bit for he did not like to be so far from the ground.*

*The warm air poured around the leaf bud and around Calvin. The breeze sighed in the branches, and they swayed slightly. The leaf bud abruptly moved side to side, taking Calvin with it. The world jerked back and forth, and Calvin felt dizzy. Then the breeze started laughing as it jostled the leaf bud.*

*"Cut that out!" said Calvin as he and the leaf bud swayed left and right.*

*The breeze settled down and sylphs, who had been playing with the branch, appeared out of the air and sat on the branch next to the leaf bud. They were as large as hummingbirds with wings that fluttered so fast Calvin could scarcely see them. The transparent sylphs continued to make a cool breeze.*

*"Better step back, little sugar gnome," said one of the sylphs, buzzing past the leaf bud. "This leaf is about to open." She was yellow, the color of morning sunlight, and as she flew past, Calvin felt her warmth engulf him.*

*Calvin pulled his head back inside the leaf just in time. Suddenly, the walls and floor lurched from under him! Calvin staggered forward and backward, trying to regain his balance. He reached out for the walls, but they kept moving away from him. The leaf lurched again. Poor Calvin fell backwards into the water and made a huge splash! Before he could stand back up, the entire room transformed before his eyes.*

*The floor and ceiling had flattened out. The room got bigger and bigger as the leaf unfurled. The light got brighter and brighter, and the room got warmer and warmer.*

*Once the leaf stopped moving, Calvin could see that the leaf room was now huge! The ceiling was high above Calvin's head and the walls far away. Calvin picked himself up and shook himself vigorously. Tiny drops flew left and right. He squeezed water out of his clothes and cap, and then Calvin waded over to the window and looked out.*

*The world had been transformed. Everywhere he looked there were sticky green leaves poking out of the leaf buds. Calvin tried to look down, but a giant leaf was blocking his view. He could no longer see the roots of his tree. He tried to look up, but all he saw were little leaf children peeking out of the leaf buds. They whispered together and laughed as the breeze blew through them. "It tickles, it tickles," the leaves said.*

*Suddenly, tiny glowing sylphs came streaming into the leaf room through the window, trailing warmth and light in their wake. They buzzed past Calvin's head and dove into the water that swirled around his legs. Calvin just barely had time to get out of their way. As each sylph dove into the water, it made a tiny splash. The sylphs and undines swirled around in an underwater dance. They danced spirals and circles in the water inside the leaf. As they swirled, Calvin could hear the faint sound of the undines singing:*

> *Sun and rain*
> *Light and air*
> *Make the sugar*
> *Sweet and fair*
>
> *Rain and sun*
> *Air and light*
> *Make the sugar*
> *Taste just right!*

*When the song was done, the sylphs and undines stopped dancing. The sylphs flew back out of the water, and Calvin smelled clean, fresh air in their wake. It smelled green and warm and wet, and he breathed deeply.*

*Now it was time for Calvin to do his job. He waded back to get his raft and his pole. He steered his raft into the leaf room. Since the leaf had opened up, there was plenty of room to maneuver a raft around inside the leaf. Calvin churned the water with his pole, swirling it around and around.*

*Soon the water in the leaf started bubbling. Something went pop! pop! pop! on the surface. Tiny crystals of sugar were bobbing up out of the water. Calvin reached down and held one up.*

*"Look, everyone!" said Calvin. "It's the first sugar of the year. We did it!"*

*The undines lifted their heads out of the water to see. The golden sylphs peeked in through the window. Calvin held up that first sugar crystal. In the warm light of the leaf room, it had an amber glow. Everyone cheered.*

*Then Calvin the sugar-gnome spent the rest of the day carefully steering his raft around the leaf room, scooping up sugar crystals and putting them on his raft. The sun was setting when Calvin's raft was finally full. The load of sugar was almost as tall as he was. Calvin carefully gathered one final sugar crystal from the water and bit into it. It was sweet, even sweeter than the sappy water of the River Phloem. It left sugar crumbs on Calvin's fingers. He licked them off one by one and then licked his lips for good measure. Calvin patted his round tummy and sighed. Nothing tasted as good as the first sugar of spring.*

*Calvin then steered his raft out of the leaf room and back to the River Phloem. The river would take him up around the tree so he could deliver his load of sugar crystals where they were needed for the tree's growth. Calvin had a long night of work ahead of him, but he smiled. He loved to help the undines and sylphs make sugar. He loved to eat the sugar they made. But most of all, he loved to share sugar with his oak tree.*

*The End*

## How to Create a Nature Story for 1st Grade

When creating a nature story for 1st Grade, keep the following points in mind:

1. The story should be about one or more elements of the local environment. For example, "Leaf Day" is about the first leaves of spring.

2. The plot should be very simple and include these elements:

   - Exposition: Introduce character and background (e.g., Calvin is a sugar-gnome who lives in a tree).

   - Inciting Action: Introduce a problem or scenario to begin the plot (e.g., it is Leaf Day).

   - Rising Action: Develop the problem or scenario (e.g., Calvin travels to the leaf and encounters nature spirits).

   - Climax: The high point of the story (e.g., the first sugar crystal is made in the leaf).

   - Falling Action: The after-effects of the climax (e.g., Calvin gathers sugar).

   - Resolution: The conclusion of the story (e.g., Calvin is happy to deliver sugar to the tree).

3. These types of stories tend to have language that is simple yet descriptive. Make sure you include a few new vocabulary words that can be deduced from context (e.g., transparent and maneuver).

4. A nature story contains one or two new concepts suitable for 1st Grade. For example, leaves bud out in spring. Sap flows through trees.

5. Optional: The story can contain a seed-image for a concept that will be taught in a later grade. For example, in 5th Grade introduce the *phloem,* the part of the vascular system of a plant where the sap flows, and in 8th Grade discuss the *Calvin Cycle,* part of photosynthesis where carbon dioxide is converted to sugar.

6. Any 1st Grade story should appeal to a minimum of two of the temperaments. For example, Calvin appeals to phlegmatic students in that he relishes eating sugar; the choleric students will enjoy the fact that his task is demanding and he has to work all night to get it done; the descriptions and actions of the elementals will appeal to sanguine students; and the fact that poor Calvin is afraid of heights and falls into the water can resonate with the melancholic students.

## Adding Nature Spirits to Stories

Nature stories for 1st graders often contain fairies or nature spirits. For example, the undines, sylphs, and gnome in "Leaf Day" illustrate the process of photosynthesis. It is useful to consider what nature spirits are, what they do, and a classification so you can include them in your stories.

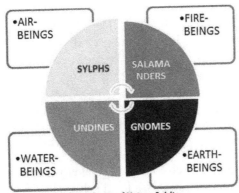

**Figure 5.5.1: Schema of Nature Spirits**

Nature Spirits provide a picture of the workings of nature. They tend to bind or dissolve matter. There are four main categories as shown in figure 5.5.1.

When you create your stories, consider using one or more of the following nature spirits:

- **air beings**: spirits of the air (e.g., zephyrs, mistrals, breezes)
- **sylphs**: small air spirits who care for plants at a local level and foster the flowers
- **fire beings**: spirits of fire such as forest fire or candle flames. (They can weave warmth, including warm days and warmth in fruits.)
- **salamanders**: small fire beings
- **undines**: spirits of the water itself (They are like chemists and carry life. They can be in plants and thus can be quite small.)
- **nymphs**: fresh water spirits who are bound to a particular body of fresh water
- **nixies**: salt water spirits who are bound to a particular body of salt water
- **stone beings**: spirits responsible for large stony areas like continents or mountains
- **gnomes**: small stone beings who are associated with the earth (They tend to make matter solid.)

These nine characters can help you illustrate what is happening in the natural world in a 1st Grade nature story. When it is time to describe elements of nature, find the appropriate nature spirits and add them into your story.

Note: You can also include other nature beings such as dryads (i.e., tree beings).

Timing the Story

Nature stories for 1st Grade tend to be around 8 to 15 minutes but you can adjust up or down as needed.

If you have a long story, consider making an umbrella nature story and telling it over multiple days. For example, "Leaf Day" could be the beginning of an umbrella story that runs for a week. You could take Calvin and his oak tree through all of the seasons of the year, describing what happens to the tree in spring, summer, fall, and winter. "Leaf Day" covers spring; on a subsequent day, you could follow up with summer.

## 7.  Home Surroundings Stories: 2nd Grade

Nature stories for 2nd Grade are more down-to-earth than those for 1st Grade. They are not quite in the real world yet, but they are closer. While they no longer contain fairies, they often contain animals, including ones that talk. This subsection contains a sample nature story for 2nd Grade and deconstructs how to create one. Keep in mind that you do not need to create all of these stories yourself. You can find many stories that pertain to your local environment in books. However, many teachers find that creating a few nature stories for their students can be very rewarding.

Example Nature Story for 2nd Grade: Sal's Journey

This following story "Sal's Journey" was written by Patrick Wakeford-Evans. It is an example of the first type of nature story: a description of the life of the salmon, a local fish in the Sacramento, California area.

*Sal's story began one spring day in the marshy sedges along the edge of the American River. There he and hundreds of his brother and sister salmon emerged from little fish eggs and swirled and darted this way and that in the cool, shallow water.*

*The Majestic Blue Heron stood away from the edge of the river and eagerly watched the new fingerlings dart about, glittering silver in the water. Her tear-shaped body was perched on two long limbs. She had a graceful neck like a swan with a dainty head and a long, pointy orange beak that was dagger sharp.*

*The heron was patient. She waited until the little salmon grew big enough to make an afternoon snack. Then, quick as can be, her neck unfolded and her beak struck the water. The heron struck again and again. Her friends joined her. Of the hundreds of little salmon born in that area of the marsh, only ten survived.*

*Sal and his nine brothers were the lucky ones. As they grew, they became strong and swift with scales that flashed silver in the sun. As soon as they were big enough, they swam away from their marshy home and the hungry herons. They lived in the deeper water of the American River and grew bigger and bigger.*

*Shortly after his first birthday, Sal and his nine siblings felt a yearning. They no longer wanted to live in the swift water of the American River. Instead, they longed for something different. So one day they left their birthplace and began swimming down the river. Like his siblings, Sal eagerly swam around the bends and through the rapids of the American River. Then all of a sudden, they found themselves entering the much wider and slower Sacramento River. As he turned into the river, an inner voice urged Sal and his siblings on, and they swam and swam until finally they came to a bay (the San Francisco Bay). Behind Sal, the water was sweet and fresh; ahead of him the water was salty and brackish. Sal enjoyed the contrast. He stayed in the bay for quite a time, and after a while Sal found it as easy to live in the salty water of the ocean as it had been to live in the fresh water of the river.*

*After some time in the bay, Sal's yearning to move on returned. It led him deeper into the ocean where the water was very salty. The longer he dwelled in the salty sea, the darker his scales became. Sal swam onward until he came to the Salmon Road.*

*The Salmon Road forms a large circle in the Pacific Ocean. The Salmon Road begins and ends in fresh water by a river. Whales and dolphins have their own paths, but only the salmons' path leads back to fresh water.*

*Sal went on many journeys through the currents of the ocean following the Salmon Road. Day turned into night and night turned into day; autumn slid into winter, winter into spring, spring into summer, and summer into autumn. Every few years, Sal and his brothers would come back to the bay where the salty and fresh water met, but then they returned to the ocean and the Salmon Road for it was not yet the right time to leave it.*

*After seven years, Sal returned to the bay. This time when he felt the fresh water, he was filled with a new yearning: he wanted to return to the river where he was born. One by one, Sal and his brothers returned to the bay. They began to grow muscular, and their fish mouths began to curve upward, forming something of a point. They ate as much as they could to grow strong for their journey. They grew stouter and stouter.*

*In the fall, the salmon brothers set off. They swam vigorously out of the bay up into the Sacramento River, jostling and pushing as they swam back towards their birthplace. Their journey was hard. It is an easy thing to swim with the lazy current of the Sacramento River, but quite a different story to swim against its relentless rush of water when traveling back up the river.*

*When they got to the American River, Sal and his brothers turned towards home and their journey became still more difficult. The rapids pummeled their bodies, and they strained with all of their might to swim against the river's currents. They lashed against the currents, straining, sensing that home was just around the bend.*

*First Sal and then his brothers broke through the rapids. They slowed down. There was something about this spot. This bend in the river told him it was time to stop.*

*Sal swam over to the shallow water nearer the river's edge, searching for the perfect spot. He found it among the marshy sedges. He turned back to defend it against his brothers. This was HIS spot and no one else could have it! He used his salmon tusk and his large, muscular body to ward off other salmon. He lashed against his brother and others, hurtling them out of the water and into the air. He was a big, pinkish-red fish, and he defended his territory with single purpose. Many were his mighty battles. Great were the gashes along his sides.*

*Sal was guarding his spot when the female salmon began to arrive. They swam toward the males and their different territories. Then Sal sensed that one of the females was to be his mate. She chose a spot in his territory on the bank of the American River. It was a sandy, gravelly spot hidden in reeds and sedges, far away from the swift currents. Using her fins, she swept away some of the river silt, forming a shallow bowl. There she lovingly gave her eggs, gave her all to fill her little scoured birthing bowl with new life. Sal came forward and blessed it with his own seed.*

*Sal and Sal Mina poured all of their life into that little bowl along the edge of the American River. It had been a long journey, but now it was complete. They stopped swimming and lay still on the water.*

*It was dusk. In the darkening shadows, the masked raccoon ambled along the edge of the river. She spied the bodies of the two fish floating along the edge of the river. She took them out of the water and back to her home in the woods so that her children could be fed. The salmon eggs remained undisturbed in the shallow water, near the reeds and sedges, not far from the trees that are the nesting grounds of the Majestic Blue Heron.*

How to Create a Nature Story for 2nd Grade

When creating a nature story for 2nd Grade, keep the following five points in mind:

1. It is about one or more elements of the local environment. For example, "Sal's Journey" is about the life cycle of a salmon in the local American and Sacramento Rivers.

2. The plot of this story is more complex than the 1st Grade story, but it is still built around a short story plot diagram:

    - Exposition: Introduce character and background (e.g., Sal the Salmon in the American River).

    - Inciting Action: Introduce a problem or scenario to begin the plot (e.g., Sal leaves his birthplace and swims out to the ocean).

- Rising Action: Develop the problem or scenario (e.g., Sal returns home and fights for territory).

- Climax: The high point of the story (e.g., Sal Mina lays eggs and Sal fertilizes them).

- Falling Action: The after-effects of the climax (e.g., Sal and Sal Mina die).

- Resolution: The conclusion of the story (e.g., the raccoon takes their bodies for food and the fish eggs remain undisturbed in the river).

3. The scientific images are more developed than in 1st Grade, but they still remain descriptive. The story always includes a few new vocabulary words that can be deduced from context. For example, *emerge, amble, sedges,* and *brackish.*

4. The story contains one or two new concepts suitable for 2nd Grade. For example, the life cycle of the salmon, a local fish.

5. It appeals to a minimum of two different temperaments. For example, the choleric students will enjoy the description of the salmon's difficult journey back up the river and of his fight to claim territory, and the melancholic students will certainly be touched when the salmon die.

## 8. Home Surroundings Material: 3rd Grade

When students get to 3rd Grade, discontinue nature stories. As they enter the nine-year change, they need information about their environment (i.e., nonfiction).

In 3rd Grade, the Home Surroundings Block changes to Practical Occupations. Rather than stories, bring information about the natural world as it relates to <u>local</u> practical occupations. The curriculum will vary depending on location. For example, it could include fishing in coastal areas, lumber in forested areas, agriculture in farming areas, beekeeping where there are orchards, or the wool industry where sheep are raised. These explorations can then be woven into your local geography curriculum in 4th Grade.

When preparing for this block, research how the land, environment, and resources inform local occupations, trades, and crafts. Then prepare short nonfiction descriptions for your 3rd graders. As much as possible, bring the physical things into the classroom for the students to experience with their senses or take the students on field trips to see them. It might even be possible to find a way for your students to participate in an aspect of a local occupation (e.g., collecting maple syrup in Vermont). However, use your discretion to determine what is or is not appropriate for 3rd graders in general and your students in particular.

## 9. Sacred Nothings

There are two Sacred Nothings related to telling stories: when to schedule stories and how many times to tell a story.

### When to Tell a Story

It has become traditional to always tell the day's main story (literature curriculum story) in main lesson; however, there is nothing wrong with telling a story during snack or at the end of the day. Take advantage of this flexibility when you have a lot to cover in main lesson.

Note: It is good to consider the totality of the day when planning stories. Main lesson is only one class in the day, and stories can occur in other classes such as form drawing, painting, modelling, etc. It is possible to tell too many stories. Christof Wiechert discusses this situation in his article entitled "On the Question of the Three-fold Structure of the Main Lesson" (9–10). Janet Langley has often cautioned teachers that telling too many stories during the week can cause students to have story indigestion, a situation where students have difficulty sleeping because they are struggling to process all of the images from the stories they have heard in the day.

### Telling the Same Story Multiple Times

In kindergarten, Waldorf teachers retell the same story multiple times; however, starting at the beginning of 1st Grade, students should hear a story only once. They understand it the first time and are ready to do something with the information on the second day. They need to review the information, either with questions or creative review activities (see chapter 3.8 #2).

Steiner hints at this development, but he does not develop the idea further. He mentions that once students go through the change of teeth, their mental imagery takes on a different form. Their memory also takes on a different form (Trostli 2004, 18). The story curriculum of 1st Grade changes to meet the newly developing capacities of the students.

Jennifer Militzer-Kopperl sat through a main lesson with 1st graders who were listening to their teacher retell yesterday's story. It was a lovely fairy tale, but most of the students were wilted over their desks, and everyone looked bored. She flashed back to another 1st Grade class she had observed and reflected on the contrast. After telling a fairy tale on day one, that teacher had reviewed the content of the story on day two with simple factual review questions. At the first question, the students sat up and a sea of hands went up. When the teacher insisted that the students answer in complete sentences, almost every hand went up. The students were excited to do the exercise and proud that they could answer in complete sentences.

While kindergartners need to hear a story more than once, 1st Grade students do not.

## 10. Story Bibliography: A List of Recommended Sources

You will need a lot of stories over the years to make a good curriculum.

Compile a collection of books. Your school will likely have books you can use, and your mentor teacher can recommend others. Your local reference desk librarian can also recommend titles. In addition, you can get suggestions from the Teacher Literature Resource List (see Appendix 5). Use it as a jumping-off point for researching your story curriculum, but go beyond it. There are hundreds of possible titles.

## Conclusion

Stories are very important. They will provide the heart of your curriculum in Grades 1–3. Use the summer to read and select a number of great stories for possible use. Make sure you practice your story so you can tell it rather than read it. Use the first three years to practice the art of storytelling, and you will become a master story teller. This skill will be useful in Grades 4–8 when the length of the stories increases.

# SECTION 6

## Assessment and Remediation

# 6.1 INTRODUCTION TO ASSESSMENT

*A 3rd Grade teacher was asked by her new mentor for her student tracking forms so that she could get an idea of the progress her third graders were making in language arts and math. The teacher informed her mentor that she did not need to give planned assessments or officially record student progress because she had been with these students for almost three years and knew where each student was in each academic area.*

*The mentor decided to explore the accuracy of this approach to find out if it was truly as effective as the teacher thought. After writing down a summary of the knowledge the teacher shared about each student, her mentor spent several hours reviewing the 3rd graders' main lesson books, practice books, etc. In the process she discovered a number of discrepancies.*

*First, the 3rd Grade teacher's overall sense of the class as a whole was accurate, but she was unaware of a number of areas where individual students were struggling. For example, there were several students who used uppercase B and D regardless of where they were positioned in a word. When this was pointed out to the teacher, she was a bit surprised. She had not noticed this. Her mentor went on to explain that this error was most probably happening because these students had not learned how to differentiate between a lowercase b and d so they just used the much clearer uppercase letters. (The teacher soon verified that this was true.)*

*After spending some time with one of the class's reading groups, the mentor also discovered two students who still had not developed full phonemic awareness or decoding skills for the Pattern and Syllable Phases. These two students easily read grade-level texts because of their strong visual memories (symbol imagery), but they had no decoding skills when it came to sounding out a word they had never seen. These deficits came as a surprise to the teacher. Initially, she had indicated that they were two of her best readers. She had no idea that they had not developed two core reading skills and were thus in danger of needing reading remediation in the upcoming grades.*

*By skipping assessments, the teacher had unwittingly undermined the education of five of her students. She did not know what she did not know; consequently, her instruction had been compromised. Fortunately, these situations, as well as a few others that her mentor pointed out, were caught in time, and the teacher was able to take steps to remediate the situations. More importantly, she began to do assessments and record their results.*

Assessment is the third leg of the three-legged stool that supports any language arts curriculum: effective instruction, practice, and assessment. Section 5 gives an overview of preparing a Waldorf curriculum for language arts. Section 6 covers all aspects of assessment:

- information on assessment
- how to assess to find your students' phases
- how to assess in each grade
- remedial issues

This chapter covers the following topics:

1. Why Assessment Matters
2. Reframing Attitudes on Assessment
3. Background Information about the Types of Assessments
4. How to Use Informal Assessments
5. How to Use Teacher-Made Assessments
6. How to Use Assessments Created by Educational Testing Groups
7. Standardized Tests
8. Record Keeping for Assessments
9. Benchmarks (Standards): What to Assess
10. How to Use Assessment Results to Improve Your Teaching
11. Giving Feedback to the Students after Assessment
12. When to Intervene
13. Communicating Assessment Results with Parents

## 1. Why Assessment Matters

There are many reasons to assess and keep records.

### Freedom vs. Responsibility

The most important reason to assess is to make sure all of your students are learning. As a Waldorf teacher, you have great freedom to design your own curriculum. The flip side is that you have great responsibility. You are entrusted with the education of a group of students potentially across eight grades. You must make sure that every student in grades one through three masters the foundational academic concepts necessary to transition successfully into the upper grades. Assessment, when used wisely, can help you stay on course and make sure that all of the time you spend on lesson planning produces the outcome that you are striving for: by the end of 3rd Grade, all students are no longer learning to read but are able to read to learn so that they can be successful in any 4th Grade classroom, including yours. Recall that in a Waldorf 4th Grade, the curriculum switches from alternating blocks between math and language arts to a curriculum that includes subject blocks such as local history, geography, and zoology. You will not be teaching reading skills any more (see chapter 2.3 #1).

### Benefits in the Classroom

Assessment benefits you and your students.

Assessment is the GPS to *The Roadmap to Literacy*. Without it, you cannot determine where the students are along the route. English has so many rules and nuances within those rules that it is almost impossible to be aware of what each student in a class knows without some type of assessment.

Assessment helps you figure out where to begin. If you are following *The Roadmap to Literacy*, you will need to determine which phase each student is in to determine which skills and experiences to bring next.

Assessment helps you evaluate the efficacy of your curriculum and improve it as needed. Students are expected to make a certain amount of academic progress each year. Assessment helps you monitor that progress. It helps you ascertain whether the lessons and practice periods have accomplished the task at hand or whether more work is needed. It pinpoints which skills students are struggling with. With the information gleaned from assessment, you are able to adjust your curriculum to provide the exact instruction and/or practice the class and/or individual student needs.

Assessment helps prevent students from slipping through the cracks. Many times a student will have trouble developing one or two skills. If the student finds a way to compensate or hide this fact, you may not be aware of the problem until it is dire. For example, many students who have strong visual memories rely on them rather than developing the phonemic awareness and decoding skills they need to master the code. In the early years, they appear to be good readers; however, around 4th Grade, this compensatory strategy no longer works, and they begin to struggle. Unfortunately, the class is no longer learning reading skills, and these students need to go to tutoring to work on the phonics skills they should have developed in 1st–3rd Grade.

Finally, assessment is what allows you to determine which type(s) of remedial support to offer struggling students. If you offer remedial solutions without first assessing, you are shooting in the dark. If you assess first, you can determine exactly what type of remedial support is needed and you have a benchmark to gauge the effectiveness of that support. (It is common for students to need more than one type of remediation to resolve a problem.)

## Benefits for Your Colleagues and Your Students' Parents

Assessment not only benefits you and your students, it also benefits your colleagues, your students' parents, and eventually your school.

All of your students' teachers will benefit when you use assessments well. If your students struggle to read, write, and/or spell after the 3rd Grade, it impacts their work and behavior in other classes. Students who struggle with grammar struggle with foreign languages in the upper grades. Students who struggle to read or write struggle in all classes that include some element of reading or writing.

Assessments can help parents be more supportive of your program. Parents often feel as if they are taking a risk by putting their children in an alternative school, especially one with no formal grading system until the middle grades (if even then). Assessments that include both your observations and some objective measures give parents feedback that is both personal and objective. When parents get both types of feedback, their anxiety lessens and they are more confident about the choice in education they have made for their child. Parents will then share their support of the school with friends and relatives who might be more likely to enroll their own children. As healthy enrollment increases, the entire school benefits.

Conversely, the lack of assessment can undermine the school's reputation. If their children are struggling and their issues are not identified and addressed in a timely manner, parents often choose to send their children elsewhere and then communicate their displeasure with Waldorf to whomever will listen.

## 2.   Reframing Attitudes on Assessment

If assessment has so many benefits, why is it not used in every 1st-3rd Grade Waldorf classroom?

One reason may be that formal assessment is seldom covered in Waldorf teacher trainings. This lack of information and instruction on how to use assessment can be due to a myriad of reasons (e.g., not enough time, a lack of understanding of its usefulness, etc.). If this training is absent in the curriculum, it leaves graduating teachers without the skills or resources to create an effective assessment program.

Another reason involves a common misperception around assessment: that it is used to assess or judge <u>students</u>. In *The Roadmap to Literacy's* approach to assessment you are not assessing <u>students</u> but their language arts <u>skills</u> so that you can improve their weak areas through instruction and practice. You are not assessing to label (or grade) a student but to figure out which language arts skills the student has mastered and which skills still need work so that you can better teach the student. In the process, you grow as a teacher, and your teaching improves with every assessment you give the class.

If using assessments is uncomfortable for you, read the book *Mindset: The New Psychology of Success* by Carol Dweck. It will help you understand the value of assessments.

## 3. Background Information about the Types of Assessments

Broadly speaking, there are two main types of assessments: informal and formal. In addition, formal assessments can be used for four different purposes. This chapter will look at the types and purposes of assessments and offer some advice on how to work with them.

### Informal Assessments

Observations that are made by the teacher as part of classroom instruction and practice are called **informal assessments**. Informal assessments are the main type of assessment that you will use because they happen daily.

Informal assessments are valuable for several reasons. Their primary value is in providing you with immediate feedback regarding the efficacy of your lesson. If a large group of students is not 'getting it,' you can revise the lesson and find another way to present the information. If only one or two students are struggling with a concept, then you can plan for individualized support. Another value of informal assessments is that you can use them to give students immediate feedback on their work.

An example of an informal assessment is observing the class's energy level during a lesson and observing which students answer questions and the quality of their answers.

### Formal Assessments

Assessments that stand outside of instruction and practice in the classroom are called **formal assessments.** Formal assessments do not happen as frequently as informal assessments, but they are just as important.

Formal assessments are valuable for several reasons. All formal assessments are administered in the same way to every student and are evaluated the same. Consequently, formal assessments are great equalizers: every student in the class does the same work and receives an equal share of your attention. In addition, you can determine exactly which skills you want to examine ahead of time, and you can take time to reflect upon what you are seeing. Most important, formal assessments are efficient: they provide information on each student's skill development that would take days or weeks to gather through informal assessments.

There are three kinds of formal assessments:

1. **Teacher-made assessments** (e.g., a spelling dictation)
2. **Assessments created by an educational testing group** (e.g., *Words Their Way* encoding assessments)

3 **Standardized tests** (i.e., tests mandated by the state) (They only apply to charter schools and some homeschooling parents.)

As a Waldorf teacher, you will have to determine which types of assessments you will use and when. There are some recommendations in chapters 6.3, 6.4, and 6.5 for you to consider.

### Four Uses for Assessments

Assessments can be used in four ways:

1) Screening

2) Progress monitoring

3) Outcome

4) Diagnostic

**Screening Assessments** are assessments that provide information about the base level of skills (or knowledge) that students possess. Use this information to determine where to begin instruction and/or to determine which students need further assessing. Also use a screening assessment if you are considering accepting a new student into the class to determine her skill levels in language arts. Finally, use a screening assessment if you are taking over a class for another teacher and need to get an idea of the whole class's language arts skills.

For example, screen rising 1st graders' knowledge of the alphabet to determine which phase the majority of your class is in at the beginning of the school year.

**Progress Monitoring Assessments** are assessments that monitor whether specific student skills (or knowledge) are progressing appropriately. They show you whether your lessons are adding value. Students should make steady progress. If the class or certain students are bogging down or stuck, it is important to track that fact so that you can try different strategies to help them learn and move on to the next phase. Further progress monitoring can allow you to see whether or not your new strategies were successful. Some students require outside intervention. Your progress monitoring assessment notes will allow you to make the case to parents, care groups, and/or other professionals.

For example, give the same alphabet assessment you used as a screening assessment to the students in the middle of 1st Grade to see exactly how much progress they have made in learning their letters. You can also give a short quiz at the end of each week or two to see which skills students have learned so you can revise your lesson plans for the upcoming week.

**Outcome Assessments** are assessments that are used at the end of a block or a school year to see what students have learned. As a teacher, you use both to prepare your future lessons.

For example, give an assessment of the class's ability to encode words with the phonics rules you have taught over the block. Then use that information to determine which rules still need more practice in the Skills Practice segment of your upcoming practice classes.

**Diagnostic Assessments** are assessments used to diagnose areas of strength and weakness when a student is suspected of having a learning challenge. They are given by outside professionals such as educational psychologists, not classroom teachers.

For example, a public school will test a student to see if she is eligible for an IEP (i.e., an individualized education program) (see chapter 6.6 #11).

Other than diagnostic assessments, all other types of assessments can be done in the classroom.

## 4.    How to Use Informal Assessments

Informal assessments assess participation and provide progress monitoring.

### Background Information

Informal assessments include daily observation of individual students as well as the class as a whole. You are looking at both the students'/class's work as well as their participation. In this manner, they differ significantly from formal assessments, which only consider the students' work.

### How to Use Informal Assessments to Assess Participation

A dull lesson is a dud. Engaged students learn better. Therefore, monitor both the class's participation as well as the participation of individual students.

When you observe the class, consider how engaged the students are. Observe the class's energy level. Are the students' hands raised? Is their attention on you? When they are working, is there a slight hum in the room from engaged, on-task students? When students are participating in classroom movement activities, are they engaged in the movement or merely going through the motions? All of these things are fair game for informal class assessments.

In addition to observing the class as a whole, pay attention to individual students. For example,

- Make notes when you review a student's work such as a kid writing assignment or rough draft of a composition. For example, has the student started using the strategies taught in class such as sight words and specific encoding rules?

- Note how a student does when she comes to the board and corrects the punctuation in a sentence you have written incorrectly.

### How to Use Informal Assessments to Monitor Progress

When you observe an individual student's participation in class, you can monitor this student's language arts skills. Is Samuel now speaking in complete sentences when he answers questions? Is Jane participating in story review? Is Frank using lowercase *b* and *d* correctly? Record these observations in your lesson plans or on a handy check list and plan to transfer them to the students' files (see chapter 6.1 #8).

Student assignments are the most effective way to monitor progress, particularly kid writing assignments. You can assess individual students and the class in the following areas: handwriting, phonemic awareness, sight word spelling, phonics rules, mechanics, etc. For example, you can determine if your class has mastered short vowel sounds or needs more practice. You can determine if Rose, the only student in the Emergent Phase, has started making letter-sound matches for the first sound in a word. Once students' skills grow beyond kid writing into compositions, you can continue to monitor progress in the area of encoding by observing how students apply phonics rules in their own writing. Student writing is a particularly useful way to do informal assessments on comprehension and a student's ability to write clear, coherent sentences.

When it comes to assessing a student's language skills progress, it is better to look at rough drafts and practice books rather than main lesson books. Avoid spending too much time on anything you wrote and they copied as you can only use these assignments to assess handwriting. When you look at the rough draft, study both what the student got right and what the student got wrong to determine current skill development and which skills need further practice. You can then determine how best to further the growth of academic skills.

**Frequency:** Daily

*The Roadmap to Literacy's* **Recommendations**

Informal assessments should make up the bulk of your assessments. They provide the details and specific examples of how students are doing. However, they require formal assessments to balance them out.

Note: It goes without saying that you should never let students help each other on any assignment that you are using as an informal assessment. While there are clear benefits to peer tutoring and having students work together on an assignment, informal assessment is not one of them. In an assessment situation, even an informal one, students must do their own work without any help from anyone else, classmates or teacher.

## 5.  How to Use Teacher-Made Assessments

Teacher-made assessments are most useful for monitoring progress and measuring outcomes. They are important because they supplement your informal assessments.

### Background Information

Teacher-made assessments are typically brief quizzes that reflect your curriculum. They focus on the most important things that you want your students to learn.

### How to Create Teacher-Made Assessments

Since you create the teacher-made assessments yourself, you have a lot of leeway in determining format.

Most written activities/worksheets can be turned into a formal assessment if there is a way to insure that each student does her own work. You can easily make two different assessment forms by mixing up the order of the questions or problems and alternate handing them out.

You can call teacher-made assessments *special assignments* if you want to avoid the term *quiz* in Grades 1–3. Lay out your expectations ahead of time. For example, tell the students:

- Keep your eyes on your own paper.  ✔

- Do your own work. Do not get help from your classmates. ("I want you to tell me what you know, not what your neighbor knows.")

- Put a question mark if you do not know an answer (or leave that one blank).

You can use any activity that will give you feedback on each student's skills including:

- Dictations (see chapter 3.9 #8).

- Reading fluency assessments: Have each student read the same short unfamiliar passage aloud to you in private and note how long it took and their errors. Note: It is easier to use assessments created by educational testing groups for this purpose (see chapter 6.1 #6), but you can make your own.

- Comprehension quizzes: Ask the students a question and have them write the answer in a complete sentence. See factual recall questions and HOTS questions in chapter 3.8 #2. (Grade level: 2nd and 3rd Grade only.)

- Grammar assessments: Give the students a worksheet with a number of sentences on it. Have them underline particular parts of speech and/or add in punctuation as needed. (Grade level: 2nd and 3rd Grade only.)

- Homophone quizzes: Give students a worksheet with a number of sentences that have a blank line where a homophone is needed. Ask them to fill in the blank with a word from a list at the bottom of the sheet. Both words should be available (e.g., blue/blew). (Grade level: 2nd and 3rd Grade only.)

**How to Use Teacher-Made Assessments to Monitor Progress and Determine Outcomes**

Teacher-made assessments are versatile. You can use them to monitor progress and determine what students learned after the lesson is done.

As you teach a new skill, it is good to monitor students' progress in this area. That way, you can determine if more practice is needed and how much. You can then adjust your lessons accordingly.

After you finish teaching a new skill, it is good to give an outcome assessment to determine how successful your lessons were. You can use this information for conferences, report writing, and future lesson planning.

**Frequency:** Weekly, bi-monthly, and/or at the end of the block. Do not use them more frequently than once a week as they interrupt time that could be spent on instruction and practice.

### *The Roadmap to Literacy's* **Recommendations**

The bulk of your <u>formal</u> assessments should be teacher-made assessments. These assessments will match your curriculum perfectly and will help balance out your informal assessments by filling in the missing pieces. While teacher-made assessments are quite useful, if you limit your formal assessment to teacher-made assessments, it is likely that you will still miss some things. That is why it is a good idea to supplement your teacher-made assessments with assessments created by educational testing groups.

## 6. How to Use Assessments Created by Educational Testing Groups

Assessments created by educational testing groups can be used for screening, progress monitoring, and outcome. However, they have the narrowest focus of all the assessments because they focus on just a few key literacy skills. As such, they provide a useful short-cut for assessing a few key aspects of literacy. By using some of these assessments, you do not need to make all of the assessments yourself. Research has shown that the use of these assessments reduces the percentage of students who need reading remediation in 4th and 5th Grade.

**Background Information**

Assessments made by educational testing groups have a very specific purpose: their goal is to change the trajectory for struggling students so that all students learn to read (and then continue to make good progress each year thereafter).

Research has shown that beginning readers who struggle with a few key aspects of literacy (phonemic awareness, letter recognition, etc.) are likely to continue to struggle throughout their academic career. Some researchers have taken this data and created assessments for teachers to use to determine how their students are doing with these key skills so that the teachers can provide additional instruction and practice to help these students. The goal is to close the gap before it widens because students need these key skills in order to progress. When teachers do so, the researchers have found that almost every one of their students learns to read very well. 95% of the students of teachers who use these assessments to help tailor their lessons become successful readers. The percentage of students who struggle to read is reduced to the 2–5% range (Hall 2006, 14). This number represents one student per class or fewer.

This is how the process works: You acquire a set of assessments for the key language arts skills. (They only take a few minutes to administer per student because they target very specific skills.) You administer these assessments three times a year (or as specified by the assessment program):

- at the very beginning of the school year as a screening tool
- at the middle of the school year as a progress monitoring tool
- at the end of the school year as an outcomes assessment

Screening: Screen a few key aspects of your students' skills at the beginning of 1st, 2nd, and 3rd Grade. You use this information to discover which skills your students already have and which need work. You can then determine if you need to provide extra instruction to small groups of students to help them catch up. You also use this information for future progress monitoring.

- 1st Grade screening assessments at the beginning of the year can assess which language arts skills your students have already developed, including your students' phases. There are classes where the majority of students are already in the late stages of the Phonemic Awareness Phase on day one. These assessments will allow you to tailor your lessons so that they match your class's skills.
- 2nd and 3rd Grade screening assessments are also given right at the beginning of the year. The results will help you know which skills need full class review and which skills individual students need to work on. You can then use this information to design the classes in your first language arts practice block to maximum efficiency.

Note: Some teachers may question the wisdom of giving an assessment as soon as their students return from summer break. They point out that students seem to have forgotten much of what they were previously taught over the space of the summer. That is precisely why it is necessary to re-assess: to discover which skills students have forgotten. This information will help you adjust your lesson plans to review and/or reteach weak areas.

Progress Monitoring: You can give the same assessment (or a slight variation of it) in the middle of the school year to monitor progress. You have been monitoring progress with your teacher-made assessments, but this progress monitoring assessment is to be compared against the screening you gave at the beginning of the year. The assessment will tell you if the student has made the expected gains to be on track to learn to read by the end of 3rd Grade. If so, you can continue what you are doing with confidence that it is working. If not, you can try something different. These assessments make sure you did not overlook anything in your informal and teacher-made assessments.

Outcomes Assessment: At the end of the year, you give the same assessment one final time as an outcomes assessment. You will use this information to help you ascertain if the student has made the expected gains through the school year. You can also use the information in your end-of-year report, which lets the parents know how the student is doing. In this report you can make specific recommendations for summer remediation, if needed. When planning for the year to come, you can also use the overall assessment outcomes to help identify a starting point for your fall curriculum.

By using assessments created by educational testing groups to screen, monitor progress, and assess outcome, you can help students whose skills are lagging behind. By creating time in your lessons to work with small groups of students who need extra practice in one or more key aspects of language arts, you give them the chance to catch up in these few key skills at the very beginning of the year. The goal is for them to be able to make adequate progress through the rest of the phases because they never fall seriously far behind in the first place.

Assessments created by educational testing groups are a simple way to spot check key aspects of language arts skill development for every student. You or your mentor can use them as an additional indicator of how each student is progressing and how the class, overall, is moving through the curriculum. Some of these assessments allow you to tailor them to your specific curriculum. These assessments can help you identify any area of the curriculum that requires more practice.

We highly recommend using assessments created by educational testing groups as part of your assessment program.

Sometimes the results of these assessments are communicated in percentiles. The information below will explain what these percentiles are and how they are used. (If you use the reading fluency test, this information will be helpful.)

## How to Interpret the Results Using Percentiles

There are many ways to interpret the results of assessments created by educational testing groups. One is percentiles. You can also use them to understand *The Roadmap to Literacy's* recommendations regarding reading fluency (see chapter 6.1 #9). Finally, if you want, you can find out how your students' or child's performance on the assessment compares to other students' performances.

Note: Keep in mind that you are comparing skills, not children. Students can improve their academic performance with additional instruction and/or practice. Furthermore, the same student is capable of getting a range of scores on the same assessment depending on sleep, hydration, the quality of her breakfast, etc.

**Percentiles** are a measure used to compare students' performances on assessments. Here is how the assessment makers calculate the percentiles. When they create the assessment, they get a very wide range of student scores. They list all of the scores in order and divide them into four equal groups. Scores in the second quarter and third quarter are considered average. The top and bottom quarters are further divided to show how far above or below average a student's score is. To interpret a student's score, use Table 6.1.1.

**Table 6.1.1: Interpreting Percentiles**

| Percentile | Interpretation |
| --- | --- |
| Less than 10th percentile | Low |
| 10th–24th percentile | Low average |
| 25th–75th percentile | Average |
| 76th–90th percentile | Above average |
| Above the 90th percentile | High |

Note: Do not confuse percentages and percentiles. Percentage is calculated by seeing how many answers a student got right. Percentile is calculated by ranking the students' scores and determining where in the lineup each student's performance falls. A student at the 85th percentile achieved higher than 85% of her peers. However, on many standardized tests such as those mandated by the school district at the end of the school year, you would have no way of knowing how many problems she got right or wrong. It is possible that all of the students did rather poorly. Conversely, they all may have done rather well. All you know is that compared to the other students' performances, this student's performance was above average.

## Which Programs to Use

There are many different programs to use. Some of them are programs that are purchased by the school, including two popular programs that are used in some Waldorf schools. Other assessments are located in books that you can purchase yourself for use in your classroom.

The first program is **DIBELs (Dynamic Indicators of Basic Early Literacy Skills)**: DIBELS is a school-wide program that looks at seven key early reading skills students should develop in the first two years of school in order to make sure they will be successful. The skills are listed below with links to show where they appear in the book:

- recognizing initial sounds in words (see chapter 3.3 #2 hand spelling)
- naming letters (see chapter 3.1 and chapter 3.5 #7 letter drill)
- segmenting phonemes (see chapter 3.3 #2)
- decoding nonsense words (see chapter 3.4 #2, #7–9)
- reading fluency (see chapter 3.15 #14)
- retelling stories (comprehension) (see chapter 3.8 #2)
- vocabulary usage (see chapter 3.12 #1, #6–8)

This program provides a complete package of seven assessments that can be used in1st-3rd Grades. Using DIBELS prevents you from having to make your own assessments in these areas.

The second school-wide program is **AIMSweb**. AIMSweb provides assessments for key academic skills in both language arts and math, and it contains assessments for all eight grades. While it also assesses key early reading skills, it has a much broader scope than DIBELS. Furthermore, its information is designed to be shared with parents and school administrators.

Most Waldorf teachers do not have access to these programs. Fortunately, you do not need them. There are books that contain some comparable assessments that you can use.

To assess key aspects of early literacy, use the book *Assessing Reading: Multiple Measures for Kindergarten through Twelfth Grade, 2nd edition* by the Consortium on Reading Excellence (CORE). (Note: This book will often be referred to as *CORE.*) It contains a series of assessments you can give your students, including phonemic awareness, reading fluency, decoding skills (phonics rules), etc. You can pick and choose which assessments would be most useful in your classroom to supplement your teacher-made assessments.

To assess encoding, take a look at Bear's book *Words Their Way.* It contains several assessments you can use for Grades 1–8. Use their *Primary Spelling Inventory* for Grades 1–3. These assessments are very good and can be used to augment your teacher-made assessments.

It is possible to get both of these books new or used online. Both have all of the necessary instructions for administering and scoring their assessments. By investing in these books, you have assessments you can use in key literacy skills that span multiple grades. The assessment program put forth in *The Roadmap to Literacy* uses a blend of both of these books. You can adopt this program in whole or in part for each grade.

## How to Use Assessments Created by Educational Testing Groups to Screen, Monitor Progress, and Determine Outcomes

Follow the recommendations in whichever assessment(s) you choose to use in your classroom. You will find some recommendations to consider in chapters 6.3, 6.4, and 6.5.

**Frequency:** Follow the advice provided with the test. Many tests recommend three times a year: beginning of the year, the mid-point, and end of the year.

## Assessment Recommendations

Using assessments created by educational testing groups is optional. However, it is worth exploring to see which aspects of these assessments would best suit your needs in the classroom. By working with assessments made by educational testing groups, you get a lot of information in a short amount of time. It is much faster to use assessments created by educational testing groups than making up your own teacher-made assessments for every aspect of language arts. In addition, these assessments provide objective proof for your own observations.

Just remember, teachers were not created to serve assessments, but assessments were created to serve teachers. Use only the aspects of the assessments that make your job easier and better.

Recommendations as to which assessments to use are offered in upcoming chapters (see chapters 6.3, 6.4, and 6.5).

## 7. Standardized Tests

Standardized tests are a type of formal assessment that Waldorf teachers seldom use prior to the upper grades. However, information about them is included for charter teachers and homeschool parents. In addition, this information is useful for Waldorf teachers in private schools because some of it applies to assessments used by educational testing groups.

## Background Information

Standardized tests are a subset of formal assessments. Some clarification is needed for when they are useful and when they are harmful.

A standardized test is a test that is administered and scored in a consistent, or standard, way. In a sense, many formal tests are standardized, including those created by educational testing groups; however, when people use the term *standardized test* in the Waldorf community, they are usually referring to the tests mandated by the government that apply to all public schools. These tests are usually done on *scantron* forms or on a computer screen.

Standardized tests can be useful to public school districts and state educational departments. One of their primary uses is to track large trends that are bigger than just one school. For example, if an educational reform such as Common Core has been adopted by a state, a standardized test can monitor how effective it is. From there, changes can be made to the curriculum or how it is used that can benefit students and teachers. They can also provide a picture of the skills of all the students in a geographic area such as a school district, state, or country.

However, standardized tests can be problematic for many reasons:

1. They reflect only one measurement of student achievement and are limited to skills that can be measured with pencil and paper or a keypad on a multiple-choice format.

2. Some students have test anxiety or do not score well for other reasons.

3. These tests are often used to reward or punish schools or teachers. This use is problematic because some aspects of student achievement are outside of a teacher or school's control (see chapter 6.6 #1).

4. If a standardized test is poorly designed, too easy, or too hard, it is not very useful.

5. It can be counter-productive or even detrimental to give them to young students who are not developmentally ready to take such tests.

For these reasons, standardized tests have developed a bad reputation. However, if mandated by the school, they have the potential to be an asset to teachers, schools, students, and communities if used responsibly and in conjunction with other criteria such as student class performance. It is incumbent upon parents and educators to demand that standardized tests be used in a manner that is fair and useful to students, teachers, and schools.

**Which Test:** Depending on your school, the test(s) used will be determined by the state or your school.

**Frequency:** Ibid

The Roadmap to Literacy's Recommendations:

- If you are a homeschool parent, consider opting out of standardized tests given by the state prior to 4th Grade. Young students are not developmentally ready to take such tests.
- If you are a Waldorf charter school teacher, you will have to comply with state regulations for standardized tests. Use the results as one measure to improve your instruction.
- If you are a private 1st-3rd Grade Waldorf school teacher, standardized tests will not apply to you.

## 8.    Record Keeping for Assessments

As a Waldorf teacher, you do not give official grades in Grades 1–3; however, you do keep track of your informal and formal assessments of student progress for use in lesson planning, Parent Conferences, and end-of-year reports. An effective method of record keeping is a combination of informal assessment notes, student files, assessment record book, and individual student portfolios. To this list add records of assessments from educational testing groups, if you have elected to use them.

Note: Make sure you date everything as the assessment loses its value without a date.

**Background Information**

There are several reasons why it is important to keep records of your assessments.

A written record allows you to track progress across the year for both individual students as well as the whole class. It saves you time to have all of the assessment information written down and organized. Without a written record, this comparison is made much more difficult.

In addition, a written record of assessments prevents a subset of students from slipping through the cracks. While an assessment will catch any egregious difficulties, a written record of multiple assessments will pinpoint minor difficulties such as a student who is slow to progress in a particular area, indicating that she needs more practice than she is currently getting.

Finally, a written record of assessment is a godsend to your mentor teacher. It provides a summary of information about the class as a whole and each individual student that can be read in minutes. To present this material orally would take hours and not be as complete. With the written record of assessment in hand, you and your mentor can use your time on more important tasks such as improving your lessons.

Keeping a written record of your assessments is almost as important as doing the assessments themselves. There are several ways to do so.

**Informal Assessment Notes**

The daily lesson plan is an easy way to organize your informal assessments (i.e., your observations of individual students). Just create space in your daily lesson plan for observations and be sure to jot down pertinent notes while you teach or at the end of the day. At the end of each week, transfer the pertinent notes you have for each student into the student's file. In the file, include a separate page called *Student Log: Informal Assessment Notes* as shown in table 6.1.2.

**Table 6.1.2: Example Student Log: Informal Assessment Notes**

Student Log: Informal Assessment Notes for Josey Jones 2017/2018
9/17: no letter/sound matches in encoding
10/1: made her first letter/sound match
10/10: does not volunteer answers in review—(Comprehension?)
11/1: is starting to spell sight words correctly in kid writing
11/17: encoded the first sound of words for >80% of the words she wrote in her kid writing.

**Student Files**

Create a student file for all academic work and your informal assessment notes. Store these files in a filing cabinet or a portable file box. (Purchasing a portable file box with dividers makes transporting student files to and from school easy and secure.) In your file cabinet/box, place a language skill file folder for each student. (It is good to create a second folder for math.) In these files put:

1. Any worksheets that were used for formal assessments

2. Kid writings in 1st/ 2nd Grades and copies of rough drafts of compositions in 3rd

3. Sight word tests in 1st/ 2nd and dictations and spelling tests in 3rd

4. Any other student work that would help you track progress

5. Student Log: Informal Assessment Notes

**Assessment Record Book**

Assessment Record Books are books you can buy to organize your teacher-made assessments. They contain grids for recording assignments/assessments and how students did so that you can see at one glance how the whole class did on a particular assessment or activity (vertical column) or how one student has done (horizontal row) on consecutive assessments such as spelling tests. See table 6.1.3.

**Table 6.1.3: Example Assessment Record**

| 3rd Grade Spelling Tests September 2018 | | | | | | | | | | |
|---|---|---|---|---|---|---|---|---|---|---|
| | 9/10 | 9/17 | 9/24 | 9/30 | | | | | | |
| Alisha | 18/20 | 16/20 | 15/20 | 17/20 | | | | | | |
| Andy | 15/20 | 9/20 | 13/20 | 15/20 | | | | | | |
| Ben | 20/20 | 19/20 | 20/20 | 18/20 | | | | | | |
| Cora | 16/20 | 10/20 | 18/20 | 14/20 | | | | | | |
| Dante | 15/20 | 16/20 | 16/20 | 17/20 | | | | | | |

Note: Dedicate a page (both left and right side when book is open) to a particular subject such as spelling or phonics rules so that you can see the results for the entire year.

**Student Portfolio**

Student portfolios are used for storing oversized objects such as student art and main lesson books, which can be used as informal assessments. Somewhere in the classroom, create a place where you can store your student portfolios. Each portfolio can be made by folding a piece of poster board in half and putting the student name on the board so it is easily visible. Inside this portfolio you can put:

1. Student form drawings

2. Samples of student paintings (You can keep them all until year's end, but it is also nice to periodically send some of them home over the year.)

3. Past main lesson books

Note: Some teachers have started taking pictures of student work with their cell phones and making an electronic record of student work. This method allows them to send more student work (e.g., paintings, compositions, etc.) home with the students.

**Records of Assessments Created by Educational Testing Groups**

If you are using assessments created by educational testing groups, they tend to come with their own means of organizing assessment results. They usually include paper and electronic options. The paper organizational charts tend to be easier and faster to use. If electing to use the paper charts, you could do the following:

- Store the pages in each student's personal file.

- Create a chart of the entire class's performance so you can use the information to group the students.

- Write that information into a page of your assessment record book or print off a blank table and tape that page in.

Between these five tools, you will have a complete record of your formal and informal assessments for each student. Together these records will make it easier to use your assessments to modify your curriculum, to prepare for Parent Conferences, and to write end-of-year reports. However, to do these things effectively you will need appropriate standards or benchmarks.

## 9. Benchmarks (Standards): What to Assess

**Background Information**

Assessments are meaningless without **benchmarks**. Benchmarks, also referred to as **standards**, are the key academic skills (and subject matter or content matter) that students are expected to master in each grade. So what is a benchmark and how does it relate to the curriculum?

The **curriculum** is made up of the skills, concepts, and/or content a teacher is expected to teach in each grade. In Waldorf schools, the curriculum is determined by the faculty, and it can go by different names (e.g., power goals, guidelines, scope and sequence, etc.). The curriculum should meet the following criteria: 1) It identifies every broad subject or skill covered in a grade; 2) It states key content and/or skills to teach. For example, Curriculum Chart One in chapter 3.16 states the 15 language arts skills covered in *The Roadmap to Literacy's* curriculum and breaks these skills down by grade. The curriculum covers what teachers are expected to teach by grade. It is important that they know the parameters of the curriculum they are expected to cover.

In contrast, a benchmark covers what students are expected to learn. A benchmark must meet the following criteria: 1) It states an objective goal; 2) It is quantifiable; 3) It is limited to the outcome, not the process by which to achieve it. The benchmarks are the logical outcome of teaching the curriculum. For example, if teachers teach the curriculum, it should follow that most students achieve the benchmark (see table 6.1.4).

Waldorf teachers take the curriculum and the benchmarks set by their schools and create their own block plans and daily lesson plans. Within the limits set by the curriculum and benchmarks, Waldorf teachers have full freedom to create their own blocks and lessons. For example, they have the freedom to choose the stories, speech exercises (poems, songs, tongue twisters), art projects (paintings, drawings, modeling), drama, field trips, movement exercises, form drawings, etc. that they feel will best suit their individual class. How best to deliver the curriculum to meet the benchmarks is the purview of each individual teacher.

## Benefits of Benchmarks

Schools that develop both a curriculum and benchmarks for each grade are providing a valuable framework. The curriculum gives teachers and parents a clear picture of the school's goals for each skill/subject taught in each grade. Teachers know what is expected of them. Parents know what the curriculum will entail each year and what the academic goals are for that curriculum. They can count on the fact that every child in their family will be taught the same academic curriculum even though each teacher will deliver it through her own unique approach to teaching. Both a clearly articulated curriculum and benchmarks reduce the miscommunications that occur between school and teacher or teacher/school and parents.

Because benchmarks are so useful, it is recommended that a school also develop a curriculum for artistic and physical activity classes and, if the faculty is willing, benchmarks. See www.waldorfinspirations.com for examples of curricula and benchmarks.

## Introduction to *The Roadmap to Literacy's* Benchmarks

Table 6.1.4 contains *The Roadmap to Literacy's* benchmarks for language arts in the first three grades. They are based on the phases students go through in learning to read, write, and spell. They also line up with the language arts curriculum laid out in *The Roadmap to Literacy's* curriculum which is covered in three separate charts (see chapter 3.16, chapter 4.4, and chapter 5.5 #2).

We offer these benchmarks here for your consideration and use. There are a few points to note:

- The benchmarks in table 6.1.4 represent <u>minimal</u> student achievement by the end of the school year for students to be on track to handle a 4th Grade curriculum. If students clear the benchmark, assume that all is well in that area. If students do not, follow-up action is needed to determine why not and what to do about it so the student can clear the benchmark. See subsections in section 3 entitled *How to Help Struggling Students* to get started and then chapter 6.6 if a remedial solution if needed.

- All students are expected to master the benchmarks by the end of the academic year unless otherwise noted.

- The benchmarks are streamlined to reduce redundancy to allow you more time to teach. Every skill taught does not have a benchmark. For example, only two aspects of phonemic awareness are covered rather than all six. Furthermore, if another benchmark covers the same skill either directly or indirectly, it will not be repeated. For example, Spelling only covers the 3rd Grade spelling tests because sight words and encoding cover all aspects of the spelling curriculum in 1st and 2nd Grade. In addition, if students can encode CVC words, it can be assumed that they can also write the sound that goes with each letter without having to have a separate benchmark (and assessment) for that skill.

- The benchmarks are a subset of the curriculum. Be sure to include them in an end-of-year report, but do not base your entire report on them.

- If you start working with *The Roadmap to Literacy* program in 2nd or 3rd Grade, you may need to adjust these benchmarks as well as the curriculum. Teach to your students' phase, not their grade.

*The Roadmap to Literacy*'s benchmarks are found in table 6.1.4.

**Table 6.1.4: *The Roadmap to Literacy*'s Language Arts Benchmarks**

| Language Skill | 1st Grade | 2nd Grade | 3rd Grade |
|---|---|---|---|
| **Sound/Symbol (Alphabet)** | Students can:<br>• Name all letters (uppercase and lowercase).<br>• Give each letter's sound(s) but only short vowel sounds are expected for vowel letters. | NA | NA |
| **Handwriting** | Students can print all uppercase and lowercase letters correctly. | Students can form all uppercase and lowercase cursive letters correctly. | Students can write and read cursive script. |
| **Phonological and Phonemic Awareness: Segmentation** | Students have mastered the following segmentation skills:<br>• sentences into words<br>• words into syllables<br>• single-syllable words into phonemes | NA<br>(Segmentation should have been mastered in 1st Grade. Assess to confirm.) | NA |
| **Phonemic Awareness: Deletion (Note: Deletion is a type of Manipulation)** | Students have mastered the following deletion skills:<br>• initial sound<br>• end sound | Students have mastered the following deletion skills:<br>• initial sound<br>• end sound<br>• blends—initial sound | Students have mastered the following deletion skills:<br>• initial sound<br>• end sound<br>• blends—initial sound<br>• blends—embedded sound |

| Language Skill | 1st Grade | 2nd Grade | 3rd Grade |
|---|---|---|---|
| **Decoding** | Students demonstrate mastery decoding with the following phonics rules:<br>• CVC words<br>• Digraphs: *SH, CH, TH, WH, NG, OO*<br>• Simple blends | Students demonstrate mastery decoding with all phonics rules for single-syllable words. | Students demonstrate mastery decoding with all phonics rules. |
| **Encoding** | Students demonstrate mastery encoding with the following phonics rules:<br>• CVC words<br>• Digraphs: *SH, CH, TH, WH, NG, OO*<br>• Simple blends | Students demonstrate mastery encoding a minimum of the following phonics rules:<br>• Silent *E*<br>• Two Vowels Go Walking<br>• The Guardians<br>• Diphthongs | Students demonstrate mastery encoding:<br>• single-syllable words<br>• two-syllable words with common affixes |
| **Symbol Imagery** | Students can visualize three letters. | Students can visualize seven letters. | Students can visualize two syllables. |
| **Sight Words: Reading** | Students can read 70+ sight words. | Students can read all sight words from *The Roadmap to Literacy* list (i.e., set 1 and set 2). | NA |
| **Sight Words: Spelling** | Students can spell 20+ sight words. | Students can spell 150+ sight words. | NA |
| **Comprehension** | Students can answer factual review questions for stories told in class. | Students can answer factual review questions and HOTS questions for stories told in class and for stories they have read. | Students can answer factual review questions and HOTS questions for stories told in class, factual presentations, and material they have read. |
| **Spelling** | NA—see sight words and encoding. | NA—see sight words and encoding. | Students can spell 3rd Grade level words in context. |
| **Dictation** | NA—see encoding. | Students can take dictation of simple sentences (i.e., subject/ predicate). Example: *The hare ran faster.* | Students can take dictation of sentences up to 7–10 words. Example: *In the forest the students found mushrooms and berries.* |

493

| Language Skill | 1st Grade | 2nd Grade | 3rd Grade |
|---|---|---|---|
| **Grammar: Parts of Speech** | NA | Students can identify the following parts of speech in sentences:<br>• nouns<br>• verbs | Students can identify the following parts of speech in sentences:<br>• nouns<br>• verbs<br>• adjectives<br>• adverbs<br>In addition, they can identify:<br>• possessive nouns<br>• verb tense<br>• being verbs<br>• helping verbs |
| **Grammar: Mechanics** | When writing, students capitalize the first word in a sentence, names, and use periods at the end of sentences. | When writing, students use end punctuation correctly (period, exclamation point, and question mark). | When writing, students use the following correctly:<br>• commas in a list and with quotation marks<br>• quotation marks<br>• apostrophes in possessive nouns and contractions<br>• capitalization of proper nouns |
| **Composition** | NA (See kid writing.) | Students can write brief summaries of stories they have heard or about something they have done (i.e. 3–4 sentences). | Students can write:<br>• a paragraph<br>• 1-3 paragraph summaries for their main lesson books<br>• a thank you note |
| **Reading Fluency** | NA—Students can read simple decodable-text that contains sight words and all phonics rules taught in 1st Grade, but hold off on formal fluency testing. | Students can read 2nd Grade passages from any formal reading fluency program.<br>Reading fluency should be a <u>minimum</u> of 61 correct words per minute with >95% accuracy.<br><br>This fluency score is at or above the 25th percentile for public school students at the end of 2nd Grade.* | Students can read 3rd Grade passages from any formal reading fluency program. Reading fluency should be a <u>minimum</u> of 95 correct words per minute with >95% accuracy.<br><br>This fluency score is at or above the 40th percentile for public school students at the end of 3rd Grade.* |

*These scores come from the Hasbrouck and Tindal *Oral Reading Fluency Norms Grades 1–8 2005* reprinted in *Assessing Reading Multiple Measures* (Diamond 2008, 80). (See chapter 6.4 #3 and 6.5 #3 for more information.)

## 10. How to Use Assessment Results to Improve Your Teaching

Use all of your assessment results to improve your classroom instruction for language arts skills.

**Determining Whether the Class has Achieved Mastery: Using the 80/80 Rule**

Use the 80/80 rule to determine whether the class has achieved mastery and is ready to learn something new.

Recall that the 80/80 rule states that 80% of the students should show mastery of the skill 80% of the time. When using a formal assessment, you can determine quickly whether 80% of the class shows mastery.

We have found the easiest way is to first record the results on a master sheet in the following way:

1. Get a clean copy of the individual assessment activity (e.g., worksheet, spelling test, etc.). This copy will serve as your master sheet.

2. As you look at each student's assessment, make a tick mark beside each item the student missed on the master sheet. For example, if five students misspelled the word *because*, that word on the master sheet should have five tick marks beside it.

3. Once you have recorded all of the students' errors on your master sheet, determine next steps for each of the ticked items.

**How to Use Assessment Results to Improve Lesson Plans for the Whole Class**

If 25% or more of the class is struggling with a language arts skill, consider whether the class needs further instruction and/or more practice. Schedule this work during the Introduction &/or Review and/or Skills Practice segment of your main lesson or language skills practice classes. Set a time to re-assess this skill.

**How to Use Assessment Results to Differentiate Instructions for Small Groups or Individuals**

If a small group of students or just one or two are struggling with a skill, provide further instruction and/or practice outside of formal class lessons.

<u>Small Group Work</u>

1. Use the assessments to determine which student(s) need to work on which skill(s). Use this information to put the students into groups.

2. During a time when the rest of the students are involved in a quiet activity (e.g., putting a final draft into a main lesson book or reading quietly at their desks, etc.), gather the students who need work on a particular item together. Provide them additional instruction or practice.

3. Give students additional work (activities, games, worksheets) to do at home or to do during a practice class to allow them further practice.

4. Set a time for when you will re-assess this skill.

<u>Individual Work</u>

Follow the same steps for small group work but with an individual student.

## 11. Giving Feedback to the Students after Assessment

In Grades 1–3, students do not receive grades; instead, they receive specific feedback from their teacher on their work. It is important to know when to give feedback to students, when not to, and how best to do it so that it is truly effective.

## When Not to Give Feedback

For a formal assessment to provide you with the most accurate information, you should not give any feedback whatsoever while giving the student the assessment. This includes nonverbal cues such as smiling or nodding if she gets one right or shaking your head if she gets one wrong, even if it is done subconsciously. By avoiding personal feedback, you prevent a situation where you unconsciously are giving one student an advantage over another student. The only questions you should answer are ones that clarify the directions.

After an assessment created by an educational testing group is over, do not give any feedback on which answers were right or wrong and why. Doing so invalidates the assessment for reuse in the future. If the students are told the correct answer, they could adjust their answer the next time they take the assessment since these assessments are often reused throughout the year to measure improvement.

## When to Give Feedback

Do give feedback on your teacher-made assessments after the assessment is over. Go over the errors and help the students learn from them.

Do give feedback on informal assessments and daily student assignments. One of the most powerful tools you can use to help students improve is positive feedback. However, there is an effective and an ineffective way to give it.

## How to Give Feedback

It is important to give feedback in a constructive way. Done right, feedback encourages more effort and striving in academic work.

Students learn absolutely nothing from platitudes, even well-meaning ones such as, "Beautiful, well done." or "Good job!" In order for positive feedback to be useful students need to know exactly what was done well and why. For example, if you see that a student who has been struggling to form a lowercase letter *e* correctly is finally getting it, you can point it out by saying, "Look, Leslie, do you see how much better this *e* is than the one you wrote yesterday? See how straight you've drawn the resting line? (See chapter 3.2 #7 for more information.) That's what I'm talking about; well done." Not only will this type of feedback validate the student's efforts to improve and encourage her to focus on improving her handwriting, it will inform those students around her about how you want something done.

Conversely, if you want to let a student know that more is needed, point out the area for improvement and ask her to add more. For example, if the assignment was to write a brief dialogue using basic quotations and a student has forgotten to insert a comma, ask her to put on her *detective hat* and see if she can find what part of the quotation punctuation is missing. Acknowledge her success when she has added it or show her if she does not know it. (Also, make a note that she needs further work here.)

The article "How Can Teachers Develop Students' Motivation–and Success?" by the on-line magazine *Education World* contains an interview with Carol Dweck, author of *Mindsets* and *Self-Theories: Their Role in Motivation, Personality, and Development*. Dweck states that her research has shown a qualitative difference between the two kinds of praises often heard in the classroom. The first type of praise is focused on building up the student's ego, the second on encouraging her striving. Dweck reports that when a student is praised for how smart she is or how good her work is, she develops a self-consciousness that she needs to maintain the appearance of always being smart. Conversely, "praising a student's <u>effort</u> seemed to give students a more hardy sense of themselves as learners, a more healthy desire for challenge, and the skills to cope effectively with setbacks" (Hopkins 2015).

Another way to give positive feedback is to share examples of good work with the class and focus on specific examples. For example, in 3rd Grade give the students a composition assignment that includes the use of adjectives. Select four or five student compositions that are exemplary and read them to the class. (You decide whether or not to identify the author.) Point out what was well done emphasizing the use of adjectives. This way every student in the class will know what you are looking for. Over the course of a main lesson block, strive to share something from everyone.

Likewise, when it comes to the end of a lesson, often teachers will make a blanket statement such as "Well done, class." This praise is counterproductive because there are some students whose work was not well done—and they know it. It is better to say, "I want to thank those of you who were working really hard. I look forward to seeing your work." The more truthful and specific praise is, the more powerful it will be as an agent of improvement.

## 12. When to Intervene

You have assessed your students and found that some are struggling with one or more language arts skills. Now what? Do you intervene or provide more time for them to catch up?

Struggling students need intervention in the form of extra work in their area(s) of weakness. Susan L. Hall writes about this need in the book *I've DIBEL'd, Now What?* She states:

> What has been learned repeatedly in multiple studies is that children who get a slow start in learning to read aren't simply experiencing a developmental lag, but lack critical early reading skills that they will not learn without targeted intervention instruction. If students do not learn these critical early reading skills, they may never catch up. . . . The longer we wait to provide intervention, the more time the intervention takes to be successful. This finding, replicated numerous times, helps teachers confirm that it is critical not to allow a student to get behind in reading. (Hall 2006, 11–12)

This research stands to reason. Learning to read is not a natural part of child development; it is the culmination of education and of concomitant changes in the students' brains (see chapter 1.2). In addition, there are many different skills that students must develop in order to be able to read: letter recognition, phonemic awareness, sight words, decoding, comprehension, fluency, etc. Therefore, use the results of your assessments to figure out which skills your students need more work on. Then organize your class in such a way that you can provide practice for the weak skills.

Developing literacy skills is a marathon, not a sprint. Without help, students who are lagging at the first five or ten signposts are more likely to continue to lag or fall further behind by mile 15, 20, and 25 than to catch up. Researchers have found that "it takes four times as long to remediate a student with poor reading skills in 4th Grade as in late kindergarten or early 1st Grade ([These years correspond to Waldorf 1st and 2nd Grades—sentence added by author)" (Hall 2006, 11). In other words, the longer you wait to intervene, the more ground the student has to make up and the harder it is for everyone involved.

Start by modifying your lessons to provide more instruction and practice in the weak areas and if that fails, consider remedial issues (see chapter 6.6).

## 13. Communicating Assessment Results with Parents

Most schools have either one or two formal parent teacher conferences during the school year. This is a good opportunity to share samples of the student's work, go over her performance in Special Subject classes (that you do not teach), discuss her social relationships with her peers, and review the results of the formal academic assessments she has taken to date. Because these official conferences often have a time limit and are intended to cover the full scope of the student's school experience, it is best to share the assessment results where the student is either at the *achieved* or *developing* level.

If you suspect a problem that requires remediation or special attention, schedule an extra meeting to specifically address this concern. Be mindful that these meetings can be emotionally-laden times for parents. When meeting with parents to share sensitive information, it is helpful to keep the following in mind:

## Preparation for the Meeting

1. If you suspect a concern, do as formal of an assessment as you can to determine exactly what the issue is and the extent of the problem. The more factual information you have combined with your inner sense and knowledge of the student, the more effective you will be in getting your message across. Now would be a good time to use assessments created by educational testing groups.

2. Determine what you would like for the parents to do to help their child. If you are going to make a referral, have names and contact information available for the parents, along with a bit of information about the people/organization that you are referring them too.

3. If you are an inexperienced teacher or are concerned that the conference may get difficult, ask that your mentor be present.

4. Be ready to share the steps that you are willing to take to support the student in the classroom. Also, check to see if there is anything that the school can offer such as Curative Eurythmy and/or remedial support.

5. Have a timeline available to help guide the requested efforts. Be sure to include: 1) the approximate date that outside assessment should occur or the beginning of outside therapies should commence; 2) a schedule of parent/ teacher check-ins and how they will be done (phone, meeting, email, etc.); 3) any other helpful dates that would support the success of the effort.

6. Make three copies of a summary of the above. One would be given to the parents, one held by you, and one given to the office to be placed in the appropriate student file. Check with your school to see if they require or encourage a signature from the teacher and parents on this document.

## At the Meeting

1. Set out some iced tea and cookies and/or fruit in case the parents have not eaten.

2. Thank the parents for being there and for their support of their child, you, and the school.

3. Introduce your mentor if she is present and share her role. If you are new to the school and/or teaching, it may be helpful for her to share her experience with similar situations or to talk about the role of the school such as what it can or cannot offer in the realm of support. If she is there as support for what might become a difficult discussion, acknowledge her role as note taker and someone who will help keep the conversation on track.

4. First, share some of the positive, wonderful things you experience in their child; where she shines academically, artistically, physically, and socially and acknowledge specific support you have received from the parents.

5. Share the reason why you have called the meeting (i.e., your concern and when or why you began to notice the issue).

6. Support your concerns. Share the results of the assessments you have done to support your initial thoughts on the issue. You may also want to contrast their child's work with that of the majority of the class. (If you use specific examples of work, let the students be anonymous.)

7. Lay out your plan of support for the student. Begin with what you can do at school and/or what the school might be able to provide for free (remedial help, Curative Eurythmy, etc.). Follow up with the outside, professional support you are requesting and your request of the parents for their support (be specific).

8. Ask the parents if they have any questions.

9. Go over your suggested timeline for your plan and adjust as necessary.

10. Give parents the written summary of your assessment, recommendations, and timeline (adjusted, if necessary) and thank them for their support.

### After the Meeting

1. Always follow this meeting up with a short email thanking the parents for coming. Share with them something that you have recently done for their child as part of your commitment to the plan. End with acknowledging the date/time for your next official check in.

2. File the communication in the student's file (paper or electronic).

3. Email the parents to acknowledge when they have done something you have requested. A quick note or word of acknowledgement will go a long way in building trust in and enthusiasm for your plan.

In all future communications with the parents, maintain these traits: truthfulness, consciousness, thorough preparation, courtesy, transparency, positive feedback, and encouragement. These traits will be especially useful if the initial plan and/or follow-up strategies prove inadequate and it becomes necessary to recommend an IEP (see chapter 6.6 #11).

## Conclusion

As a teacher, you are responsible for the education of every student in your class. Creative, effective lessons, adequate practice, and assessments will provide the pathway to a stellar education for your students. If what you are doing is ineffective, you must make changes, and assessment will help you identify which changes need to be made, whether they are at a whole class or individual student level.

We would encourage you to build off of Steiner's advice in *Discussions with Teachers*. He states, "If there is something which the pupil cannot do the teacher ought to give himself a bad mark as well as the pupil, for he has not yet succeeded in teaching him how to do it" (Steiner 1983, 163). Additionally, a teacher should give herself a bad mark if she has not assessed a student who is not progressing, figured out what is wrong, tried to address it in class, met with the parents to discuss the problem if her attempts fail, and made recommendations to address the problem outside of class (including an IEP) if it cannot be remediated within the classroom.

Assessment is accountability. Assessment is the third leg of the three-legged stool that supports language arts instruction, along with effective instruction and practice that supports the language arts curriculum. It guarantees that students are making the expected growth towards full literacy. It is imperative that Waldorf teachers take up this mantle. With great freedom comes great responsibility.

# 6.2 WHAT PHASE ARE YOUR STUDENTS IN?

All of your students will travel the same path when developing their literacy skills, but each student will be at a different point along that path. As a teacher, you need to provide all of your students the experiences necessary to complete each of the five phases of literacy. To do that, it will be important to know which phase each of your students is in so that you can support each one's progress. You can ascertain a student's phase by assessing (screening) formally or informally.

This chapter covers the following topics:

1. Signposts for the Phases: A Breakdown of Skill Development by Phase
2. Informal Assessment to Determine Phase
3. Formal Assessments to Determine Phase
4. Split Phases

## 1. Signposts for the Phases: A Breakdown of Skill Development by Phase

*The Roadmap to Literacy* contains many signposts that show which phase a student is in. Furthermore, each phase can be broken down into beginning, intermediate, and advanced stages in three key areas:

- encoding
- decoding
- reading

Archetypal signposts of development are presented in tables 6.2.1–6.2.5. Use this information to determine which phase a student is in (see also table 3.3.1 for signposts specific to the development of phonemic awareness).

Note: A student can be in two different phases. For example, a student could be in the Syllable Phase for reading but the Pattern Phase for encoding. This situation is referred to as **split phases**.

**Table 6.2.1: Signposts for the Emergent Phase**

| | |
|---|---|
| **Beginning** | • Encoding: Student pretends to write by scribbling.<br>• Decoding: NA (Student cannot sound out letters.)<br>• Reading: Student can pretend read only. |
| **Intermediate** | • Encoding: Student pretends to write by using random letters often with no spaces between words.<br>• Decoding: NA (Student cannot sound out letters.)<br>• Reading: Student can memory read but is unaware when she is pointing to the wrong word and often confuses word and syllable. |
| **Advanced** | • Encoding: Student represents first phoneme (or most prominent phoneme) with an appropriate letter. Student starts to put spaces between words.<br>• Decoding: NA (Student cannot sound out letters.)<br>• Reading: In memory reading, student starts to realize when she is off, but needs to start over to fix the mistake. |

**Table 6.2.2: Signposts for Phonemic Awareness Phase**

| | |
|---|---|
| **Beginning** | • Encoding: Student tends to get the first and last consonant sounds in a word.<br>• Decoding: NA<br>• Reading: In memory reading, student does not need to start over when she is off but can find the right word and keep reading. |
| **Intermediate** | • Encoding: Student encodes medial short vowels, initially using point of articulation. Student spells simple blends.<br>• Decoding: Student learns to sound out CVC words.<br>• Reading: Student's memory reading sounds fluent and has expression. Once student learns to sound out CVC words, student begins reading decodable-text (i.e., easy leveled readers) with the assistance of a teacher. Reading is slow and labored. |
| **Advanced** | • Encoding: Student encodes short vowel sounds correctly most of the time. Student uses a letter to encode every sound in a word (not always correctly). Student uses advanced blends correctly, first *DR* and *TR* then preconsonantal nasals (*MP, NG,* etc.).<br>If you have not taught Silent *E*, student may start experimenting by adding an *E* to the ends of words.<br>• Decoding: Student can decode all single-syllable words with short vowels (plus additional phonics rules you have taught(e.g., Silent *E*).<br>• Reading: Student can read easy decodable-text but not fluently or silently. |

**Table 6.2.3: Signposts for the Pattern Phase**

| Beginning | • Encoding: Student uses Silent E correctly.<br>• Decoding: Student can decode phonics rules that have been taught.<br>• Reading: Student reads harder levels of decodable-text. Student starts to read independently. Student may start to read under her breath or begin to read silently. |
|---|---|
| Intermediate | • Encoding: Student uses phonics rules to spell vowel patterns—but not always correctly.<br>• Decoding: Student can decode whichever phonics rules have been taught.<br>• Reading: Student considers herself a reader. Student can read silently and fluency takes off. |
| Advanced | • Encoding: Student spells almost all vowel patterns correctly.<br>• Decoding: Student can decode all vowel patterns.<br>• Reading: Student reads easy chapter books. |

**Table 6.2.4: Signposts for the Syllable Phase**

*Note: The Syllable Phase spans grades 3–6.*

| Beginning | • Encoding: Student spells most single-syllable words correctly. Student spells simple affixes correctly. Student still makes errors with inflectional suffixes.<br>• Decoding: Student can decode words with simple affixes.<br>• Reading: Student reads chapter books at late 2nd and beginning 3rd Grade level. |
|---|---|
| Intermediate | • Encoding: Student spells words with inflectional endings correctly. Student spells basic prefixes and suffixes correctly (-tion, -ture, -ment, -tive, etc.).<br>• Decoding: Student can decode most suffixes but gets confused with advanced suffixes.<br>• Reading: Student reads chapter books at a mid-3rd to beginning 4th Grade level. |
| Advanced | • Encoding: Student spells most suffixes correctly. Student confuses suffixes that sound the same (e.g., -tion/–sion).<br>• Decoding: Student can decode any word.<br>• Reading: Student reads chapter books at a middle 4th -6th Grade level. |

**Table 6.2.5: Signposts for the Latin/Greek Phase**

*Note: The Latin/Greek Phase spans Grades 7 and 8.*

| Beginning | • Encoding: Student spells most words correctly but often makes errors with schwa in words that are derivatives (e.g., misspelling the schwa in confident, forgetting that it is related to the word confide).<br>• Decoding: Student can decode any word.<br>• Reading: Student reads chapter books at 5th/-6th Grade level fluently. |
|---|---|
| Intermediate | • Encoding: Student spells derivatives correctly. Student starts to use Greek and Latin elements.<br>• Decoding: Student can decode any word.<br>• Reading: Student reads chapter books at a middle school grade level. |
| Advanced | • Encoding: Student spells almost everything right but may have difficulty with foreign borrowings.<br>• Decoding: Student can decode any word.<br>• Reading: Student reads chapter books at a middle school grade level or above and uses morphology for new vocabulary. |

## 2.   Informal Assessment to Determine Phase

The easiest way to determine a student's phase is to use informal assessment.

**Encoding:** To assess encoding informally, use a first draft of kid writing or a composition assignment that a student wrote on her own without any help. Match the errors to the phases noted above.

**Decoding:** To assess decoding informally is not recommended. A student may already recognize a word on sight or use contextual clues to figure out a word while reading (see chapter 6.2 #3).

**Reading:** If you choose to assess reading informally, do one of two things. If you suspect the student is in the Emergent Phase or early Phonemic Awareness Phase, ask her to "read" one of her memory reading passages and compare her reading to tables 6.2.1 and 6.2.2. If you suspect the student is in the intermediate Phonemic Awareness Phase or higher, ask the student to read passages of decodable-text she has never seen before and compare to tables 6.2.2, 6.2.3, 6.2.4, and 6.2.5.

Since phases are primarily used to determine what to teach in class, using informal assessment is sufficient most of the time (except for decoding, see above). However, if you are not comfortable assessing informally or just want reassurance that your observations are correct, there are ways to do a formal assessment to determine which phase a student is in.

## 3.   Formal Assessments to Determine Phase

Rather than spend the time creating your own assessment, you can easily use formal assessments created by educational testing groups to assess each student's phase.

**Encoding:** To determine a student's phase in encoding, use the *Primary Spelling Inventory* in *Words Their Way*. This test can be given to the entire class at once. There is a guide in the book that will show you how to score the test and determine stage. The phases outlined in *The Roadmap to Literacy* and their stages align fairly well in encoding but go by different names. See table 6.2.6.

**Table 6.2.6: Assessing Phase for Encoding with *Words Their Way***

| Words Their Way Encoding Stage | The Roadmap to Literacy Phase |
|---|---|
| Emergent | Emergent |
| Letter Name—Alphabetic | Phonemic Awareness |
| Within Word Pattern | Pattern |
| Syllables and Affixes | Syllables |
| Derivational Relations | Latin/Greek |

**Decoding:** To determine a student's phase in decoding, use the book *Assessing Reading Multiple Measures* by the Consortium of Reading Excellence (CORE) and use the *CORE Phonics Surveys* subtest. This test must be given to students individually.

The *CORE Phonics* Surveys subtest has 12 sections which run from subtest A to subtest L. It covers the phonics rules for the Phonemic Awareness Phase, the Pattern Phase, and part of the Syllable Phase. It includes instructions for scoring. The scores can fall into one of three categories:

    1) *Intensive,* which means a student needs both instruction and practice.

    2) *Strategic,* which means a student only needs practice.

    3) *Benchmark,* which means a student has mastered the skill.

See table 6.2.7 for a list of assessments and their corresponding phase.

**Table 6.2.7: Assessing Phase for Decoding with *CORE* Phonics Surveys**

| *CORE* Phonics Survey Assessment | The Roadmap to Literacy Corresponding Phase | |
|---|---|---|
| **Alphabet Skills and Letter Sounds** | **For Subtests A–D:** | |
| A. Letter Names- uppercase<br>B. Letter Names-lowercase<br>C. Consonant Sounds<br>D. Vowel Sounds | If the student scores:<br>  • Intensive<br>  • Strategic<br>  • Benchmark | Then the student is likely in:<br>  • Emergent Phase<br>  • Phonemic Awareness (Beginning)<br>  • PhonemicAawareness (Intermediate) |
| **Reading and Decoding** | **If the student scores *Benchmark*, then the student is likely in the following phase or higher:** | |
| E. Short vowels in CVC words | Phonemic Awareness (Intermediate) | |
| F. Consonant blends with short vowels | Phonemic Awareness (Advanced) | |
| G. Short vowels, digraphs, and the *TCH* trigraph | Phonemic Awareness (Advanced) or Pattern (Beginning) | |
| H. R-controlled vowels | Phonemic Awareness (Advanced) or Pattern (Beginning) | |
| I. Long vowel spellings | Pattern (Beginning) | |

| J. Variant vowels | Pattern (Intermediate) |
|---|---|
| K. Low frequency vowel and consonant spellings | Pattern (Advanced) |
| L. Multisyllabic words | Syllables (Beginning) |

**Reading Fluency:** To determine a student's phase in reading, use the book *Assessing Reading Multiple Measures* by the Consortium of Reading Excellence (CORE) and use the *MASI-R Oral Reading Fluency Measures* subtest. This test must be given to students individually.

The *MASI-R Oral Reading Fluency Measures* subtest has three passages for grade levels 1–6. These grade levels refer to public school grade levels, which means that they will not align with Waldorf schools until the end of 3rd Grade when Waldorf students are at similar reading levels as their public school peers (see chapter 1.1 #4). Therefore, it is necessary to adjust the passage levels:

- 1st Grade Waldorf students: NA. (If you choose to assess at this time, give the 1st Grade passage, starting at the end of 1st Grade.)
- 2nd Grade Waldorf students: Use either the 1st or 2nd Grade passage. Adjust up or down if the passage is too hard or too easy.
- 3rd Grade Waldorf students: Use either the 2nd or 3rd Grade passage. Adjust up or down if the passage is too hard or too easy.

When giving this test, follow the instructions for administration. Follow the scoring instructions to find the *Rate Correct* (i.e., the number of correct words the student read in one minute). Then use Table 6.2.8 to estimate the student's phase.

**Table 6.2.8: Assessing Phase for Reading with MASI-R Oral Reading Fluency**

| MASI-R Passage's Grade Level: | *The Roadmap to Literacy* Corresponding Phase |
|---|---|
| 1st Grade Passage<br>If student scores:<br>• <12 correct words<br>• 12–23 correct words<br>• 23–53 correct words<br>• >53 correct words | Then student is likely in:<br>• Emergent Phase or Phonemic Awareness (Beginning)<br>• Phonemic Awareness (Intermediate)<br>• Phonemic Awareness (Advanced)<br>• Advanced Phonemic Awareness Phase or possibly higher. Try 2nd Grade passage. |
| 2nd Grade Passage<br>If student scores:<br>• <25 correct words<br>• 25–51 correct words<br>• 51–72 correct words<br>• 72–89 correct words<br>• >89 correct words | Then student is likely in:<br>• Phonemic Awareness Phase—try 1st Grade passage<br>• Phonemic Awareness Phase (Advanced) or Pattern Phase (Beginning)<br>• Pattern Phase (Beginning)<br>• Pattern Phase (Intermediate)<br>• Pattern Phase (Advanced) or possibly higher. Try 3rd Grade passage. |

| 3rd Grade<br>If student scores:<br>• <44 correct words<br>• 44–71 correct words<br>• 71–107 correct words<br>• 107+ correct words | Then student is likely in:<br>• Phonemic Awareness Phase or Pattern Phase—try 2nd Grade passage<br>• Pattern Phase (Advanced) or Syllable Phase (Beginning)<br>• Syllable Phase (Beginning or Intermediate)<br>• Syllable Phase (Intermediate)<br>Note: The Syllable Phase continues into 4th and 5th Grades. |
|---|---|

## 4. Split Phases

It is very common for students to be in one phase for one skill but a different phase for a different skill. This is called **split phases**. In one instance it is to be expected; in others it is a problem.

### When Split Phase is Expected

It is common for there to be a mismatch between decoding skills and encoding skills. In the Phonemic Awareness Phase students typically encode better than they decode. By the beginning of the Pattern Phase, students typically decode better than they encode. It is very common to see a student in the Phonemic Awareness Phase successfully encode a word but then struggle to decode the same word when she encounters it in a passage at a later point. By the Pattern Phase, however, students decode better than they encode, and thus students read better than they spell.

This scenario is to be expected. The mismatch between encoding and decoding skills is why there are weekly spelling lists: they provide students the opportunity to practice encoding rules that have already been mastered in decoding while simultaneously memorizing the spelling of words that do not follow the rules.

### When Split Phase is a Problem

In Grades 1–3, it is not uncommon to get a student who is able to read much better than she can encode and/or decode. There are two scenarios where split phases are problematic: contextual readers and accelerated readers who cannot encode. It is necessary to know which one you have as it will affect your instruction.

The more common split phase scenario can be found with students who are **contextual readers**. They use the pictures and contextual language cues to predict what the text will say. They typically use partial print conventions when reading. In other words, they predict the words and content that should come next and then try to match their guesses to the letters they observe in a word and/or known sight words (see chapter 1.6 #4).

It is easy to recognize these readers because their skills are inconsistent:

- In one line, they read a sight word automatically but then cannot read it in the next.
- They cannot decode words in isolation.
- They read one passage fluently but then falter on another at the same level.

In lieu of reading practice, these students need extra encoding and decoding practice, and they need lots of work with nonsense words. If they do not overcome their over-reliance on context, their reading skills will plateau at a 3rd or 4th grade reading level. Contextual clues are insufficient to make up for weak decoding beyond this point.

The second scenario is **accelerated readers who cannot encode**. These students are those 1st and 2nd graders who can read any book put in front of them, including *The Hobbit* and *Harry Potter*, but can only encode at or below grade level.

It is easy to recognize these students because their skills are consistent:

- They can recognize all sight words automatically.
- They decode words out of context automatically.
- Their encoding is at or below grade level. It frequently shows signs that they have not mastered phonemic awareness and/or phonics rules.

It is tempting to let these students go off and read on their own during class, but that is an ineffective use of class time. These students should do extra kid writing practice while the rest of the class practices memory reading or is in reading group. In addition, they need to participate in phonemic awareness, phonics rules introduction, and the concomitant encoding and decoding exercises with the rest of the class. It is imperative that you address their weakness in encoding. Otherwise, there will be problems down the road. In a few years, the rest of the class will catch up in reading and far surpass them in spelling. Despite being able to read, these students still need instruction in basic literacy skills.

## Conclusion

It is important to use both formal and informal assessments to assess phase. Use this information to determine what the students already know and what you need to teach them. The next three chapters will discuss how to assess benchmarks for each grade to make sure each student in your class is on track to finish the phases and develop full literacy skills.

# 6.3  FIRST GRADE ASSESSMENTS

The last chapter presents information on how to assess which phase your students are in, providing a useful screening tool to determine where to start instruction. This chapter covers how to assess benchmarks (standards) to monitor progress and assess outcomes in 1st Grade.

Using *The Roadmap to Literacy* as a metaphor, phases represent the entire route the students must travel to get to full literacy. Benchmarks represent the signposts along the edge of the road. Assessments represent the GPS device that tracks where students are along the road as well as their forward momentum. By comparing the results of the assessments with the benchmarks, you can determine how much progress students have made (progress monitoring) and whether they have met the desired benchmarks by the end of the year (outcomes assessment). By using assessment in this manner, you can determine whether your students' literacy skills are on track.

This chapter contains an overview of benchmarks to assess in language arts in 1st Grade. (Keep in mind that all students are expected to meet the benchmarks in all areas by the end of the year.) This chapter also contains a number of different assessments because assessments should be approached from different angles. There is a time and place for all types of assessments: formal, informal, and assessments created by educational testing groups. The number of options may seem overwhelming, just choose which assessments would work best in your classroom.

Note: Reread 6.1 #3–6 before using this chapter.

This chapter covers the following topics:

1. First Grade Benchmarks
2. How To Use Informal and Teacher-Made Assessments
3. How to Use Assessments Created by Educational Testing Groups
4. End-of-Year Reports

## 1.   First Grade Benchmarks

Benchmarks are the signposts along the road to full literacy. By the end of the school year, all 1st Grade students should be able to meet the following benchmarks. Table 6.3.1 contains the benchmarks for 1st Grade. For a full list of benchmarks, see table 6.1.4.

Note: These benchmarks represent the minimal skill level 1st graders should attain by the end of the year. First graders typically begin the year in the Emergent Phase. However, it is not uncommon for some to be in the Phonemic Awareness or even the Pattern Phase. Therefore, some of your rising 1st Grade students may have already surpassed these benchmarks before starting the 1st Grade. It is imperative that you assess either the summer before or the first week of class to determine which phase your students are in and to plan instruction to meet the students where they are at in order to take them to the next phase. Set higher expectations as needed for those students in the Phonemic Awareness or Pattern Phase.

**Table 6.3.1: Benchmarks for 1st Grade**

| Language Skill | 1st Grade |
|---|---|
| **Sound/Symbol (Alphabet)** | Students can:<br>• Name all letters (uppercase and lowercase).<br>• Give each letter's sound(s) but only short vowel sounds are expected for vowel letters. |
| **Handwriting** | Students can print all uppercase and lowercase letters correctly. |
| **Phonological and Phonemic Awareness: Segmentation** | Students have mastered the following segmentation skills:<br>• sentences into words<br>• words into syllables<br>• single-syllable words into phonemes |
| **Phonemic Awareness: Deletion (Note: Deletion is a type of Manipulation)** | Students have mastered the following deletion skills:<br>• initial sound<br>• end sound |
| **Decoding** | Students demonstrate mastery decoding with the following phonics rules:<br>• CVC words<br>• Digraphs: *SH, CH, TH, WH, NG, OO*<br>• Simple blends |
| **Encoding** | Students demonstrate mastery encoding with the following phonics rules:<br>• CVC words<br>• Digraphs: *SH, CH, TH, WH, NG, OO*<br>• Simple blends |
| **Symbol Imagery** | Students can visualize three letters. |
| **Sight Words: Reading** | Students can read 70+ sight words. |
| **Sight Words: Spelling** | Students can spell 20+ sight words. |
| **Comprehension** | Students can answer factual review questions for stories told in class. |
| **Spelling** | NA—see sight words and encoding. |

| Dictation | NA—see encoding. |
|---|---|
| **Grammar: Parts of Speech** | NA |
| **Grammar: Mechanics** | When writing, students capitalize the first word in a sentence, names, and use periods at the end of sentences. |
| Composition | NA (See kid writing.) |
| **Reading Fluency** | NA—Students can read simple decodable-text that contains sight words and all phonics rules taught in 1st Grade, but hold off on formal fluency testing. |

Note: Many of these benchmarks pertain to kid writing. Therefore, there is no separate benchmark for kid writing because it uses an amalgam of skills.

## 2.   How to Use Informal and Teacher-Made Assessments

You can assess the 15 aspects of language arts both formally and informally in class.

It is possible to assess these skills informally any day you work on them in class. It is possible to assess them formally by making your own formal assessments to use weekly, bi-weekly, or at the end of the block as needed to monitor the growth of students' skills. Table 6.3.2 contains some ideas on how you could assess these skills informally and formally. This list is not exhaustive. You can also supplement your own assessments by using assessments created by educational testing groups (see chapter 6.3 #3).

**Table 6.3.2: Ideas for Assessing Language Arts Informally and Formally in Class**

| Language Skill | Informal Assessment | Formal Teacher-Made Assessments to Be Given during Class |
|---|---|---|
| **1. Alphabet** | Not recommended | Ask the students to write the alphabet (uppercase, lowercase, and/or both). Be sure to cover alphabet display in class. |
| **2. Handwriting** | Observe students' work (handwriting practice, dictation, kid writing, etc.).<br><br>Observe the students' pencil grip and letter formation by wandering around the classroom as they write. (Be sure to correct anything that is done incorrectly.) | Ask the students to copy something from the board using their neatest handwriting. (It could be something to put in their main lesson book or it could be a stand-alone test.)<br><br>Note the following things: mixing uppercase and lowercase letters, letters that are incorrect sizes, letters that go off the line, and letters with descenders that do not descend below the base line (e.g., *y, g, q, p*, etc.). |
| **3. Phonemic Awareness** | Observe kid writing and phonemic awareness exercises. | Use segmentation: Have the students put down a line for each sound they hear in a word (and write the letter that matches the sound if they know it). |

| 4. Decoding/ Encoding | Observe kid writing and spelling dictations. Observe reading groups. | Decoding: NA (Use assessment developed by an Educational Testing Group. See table 6.3.3.)<br><br>Encoding: Make up a list of less-common words with the phonics rule(s) you have been practicing. Ex. CVC: *vet, ham, sip, dud, bog, etc.* Include some nonsense words. Use these words to assess encoding. |
|---|---|---|
| 5. Symbol Imagery | Observe symbol imagery exercises such as syllable cards and mystery word.<br><br>Observe how the students copy from the board (one letter at a time, one word, or groups of words). | Create your own assessment by making cards that have 1–5 random lowercase letters on them such as *lqz*.<br>Show them for 1 second per letter. Take them away.<br>Have the students write down the letters they saw on a piece of paper.<br>(It is good to have 3 cards with 2 letters, 3 with 3 letters, etc.) |
| 6. Sight Words | Observe students' oral reading and kid writing. | Give a spelling test of all of the sight words practiced to date (or just that week). |
| 7. Concept Imagery | Observe student's free renderings of the stories you have told. Make special note of students who struggle to choose a picture or other artistic rendering that does not match the story. | See Comprehension. |
| 8. Comprehension | Observe answers to oral comprehension questions (factual recall questions and simple HOTS questions). | Once your students' are kid writing in the Phonemic Awareness Phase (intermediate or advanced), you can make formal assessments by writing your own comprehension questions and giving the class a very simple written quiz.<br><br>(Example: *What color was the ball the princess dropped down the well?*) (yellow) |
| 9. Spelling | Observe students' kid writing. | Do 1–3 simple dictation sentences using sight words and phonics rules. Ex. *Jan sat by me.* |
| 10. Speech | Observe articulation and grammar. If a student struggles to pronounce a sound (e.g., /r/, /s/, /l/, /w/, /th/, *etc.*), refer the student to speech therapy.<br>Make note of common grammatical problems. Ex. "*Me and him (sic) went out.*" | NA |

| 11. Grammar | Observe use of mechanics (capitalization and punctuation) in kid writing drafts. | NA |
| 12. Vocabulary | Observe students' use of oral language. | NA |
| 13. Kid Writing | NA (There is no informal assessment for kid writing. Instead, you use kid writing to assess for phonemic awareness and sight word spelling.) | NA |
| 14. Composition | NA | NA |
| 15. Reading | Observe students' fluency, phrasing, and errors. | NA |

Keep in mind that you will have to teach the students proper etiquette when giving them an assessment. Students may help each other during regular work time, but insist that students do their own work for formal assessments. Encourage students to leave something blank if they do not know the answer or to take their best guess.

## 3. How to Use Assessments Created by Educational Testing Groups

In addition to the classroom assessments, it is good to use assessments created by an educational testing group three times a year: fall, winter, and spring (see table 6.3.3).

While the content will be the same each time you give an assessment created by an educational testing group, you will use the results in different ways. The fall assessment will allow you to get a baseline read of student skills. Use it to determine what to teach and as the starting point to compare against subsequent assessments. The winter assessment will occur sometime in January/February. Use it as a progress monitoring assessment to supplement your in-class assessments to make sure all students are on track to make the benchmarks by the end of 1st Grade. The spring assessment occurs at the end of the school year. Use it as an outcome assessment to see if students have made benchmark. By supplementing your in-class assessments with these standardized assessments, no students will slip through the cracks.

Please note: Formal teacher-made assessments and assessments made by educational testing groups have different protocols. While it is good to go over the answers in a teacher-made assessment with the class so the students can learn from their mistakes, it is detrimental to go over the answers in an assessment created by an educational testing group. Doing so undermines its usefulness in the future. As you will be using some of these same assessments multiple times a year (and in some cases in subsequent years), do not correct a student or provide any hint as to whether an answer was right or wrong during a formal assessment. This stricture includes nonverbal cues such as a smile or a nod, no matter how subtle.

If your school has access to DIBELS or AIMSweb, use these assessments. If not, use assessments from the books *CORE* and *Words Their Way* (see chapter 6.1 #6). The recommended tests can be found in table 6.3.3.

**Table 6.3.3:**

**Recommended Schedule for Assessments Created by Educational Testing Groups in 1st Grade:** *CORE Reading Assessments* **and** *Words Their Way*

| Language Skill | Fall | Winter | Spring |
|---|---|---|---|
| **Alphabet** | *CORE Phonics Survey: Alphabet Skills and Letter Sounds*<br><br>Part A: Letter Names Uppercase<br>Part B: Letter Names Lowercase | *CORE Phonics Survey: Alphabet Skills and Letter Sounds*<br><br>Part A: Letter Names Uppercase<br>Part B: Letter Names Lowercase<br>Part C: Consonant Sounds<br>Part D: Vowel Sounds | *CORE Phonics Survey: Alphabet Skills and Letter Sounds*<br><br>Part A: Letter Names Uppercase<br>Part B: Letter Names Lowercase<br>Part C: Consonant Sounds<br>Part D: Vowel Sounds |
| **Phonological and Phonemic Awareness** | NA | *CORE Phonological Segmentation Test*—all<br><br>*CORE Phoneme Deletion Test*:<br>Initial Sound<br>Final Sound | *CORE Phonological Segmentation Test*—all<br><br>*CORE Phoneme Deletion Test*:<br>Initial Sound<br>Final Sound |
| **Encoding** | NA | *Words Their Way Primary Spelling Inventory*:<br>Initial Sound<br>Final Sound<br>Short Vowel<br>Digraphs—if applicable<br>Blend—if applicable | Ibid—plus any other feature taught (e.g., long vowel patterns, other vowels, inflected endings) |
| **Decoding** | NA | *CORE Phonics Survey: Reading and Decoding*<br>Part E: Short Vowels in CVC words plus any other elements taught. | *CORE Phonics Survey: Reading and Decoding*\*<br>Part E: Short Vowels in CVC words<br>Part F: Consonant Blends<br>Part G: Digraphs<br>plus any other elements taught. |
| **Sight Words: Reading** | NA | NA (We do not recommend using the *CORE Graded High-Frequency Word Surveys*.) | NA (We do not recommend using the *CORE Graded High-Frequency Word Surveys*. See table 6.3.2.) |
| **Reading Fluency** | NA | NA | Optional: *MASI-R Oral Reading Fluency Measures* (in *CORE* book)1st Grade passages |

Administer the *Words Their Way Primary Spelling Inventory* to the entire class at the same time. It will take less than 15 minutes total. Administer the other assessments to students one-on-one privately. Total time depends on the number of students in the class and how advanced the students' skills are. See table 6.3.4 for estimates. Many of the assessments will not need to be done with every student every time. Once a student has reached mastery in a skill, do not continue to assess it. Consider getting a substitute for a day or using free periods so that you can give the assessments to students one at a time in a private room. Do not let the other students hear you give the assessment in advance as it would compromise the validity of their test scores.

**Table 6.3.4: Estimated Time to Administer**

| Language Skill | Type of Administration | Estimated Time to Administer |
|---|---|---|
| Alphabet | one on one | 5 min./student |
| Encoding | whole class | 10–15 min. |
| Decoding | one on one | 5 min./student |
| Phonological and Phonemic Awareness | one on one | 5 min./student |
| Reading Fluency | one on one | 5 min./student |

The grade levels in the *CORE* testing book refer to public school grade levels. Waldorf students start reading instruction a year later. Therefore, it is necessary to use slightly different scales to interpret the test results than the ones in the book. Use Table 6.3.5.

Here is some advice on how to read Table 6.3.5:

1. The test you will use is identified in the right-hand column (e.g., *CORE Phonics Survey: Alphabet Skills and Letter Sounds*).

2. The subtests are listed after the test's name (e.g., Part A: Letter Names Uppercase).

3. The benchmark score is indicated for each subtest (e.g., +26 (all), which means the student is expected to get all 26 letters right to achieve the benchmark).

Students achieve benchmark if they score at the score indicated in the column.

**Table 6.3.5: Interpreting the Results: Waldorf 1st Grade Benchmarks for *CORE Reading Assessments* and *Words Their Way***

| Language Skill | Benchmarks for Spring, 1st Grade |
|---|---|
| Alphabet | *CORE Phonics Survey: Alphabet Skills and Letter Sounds*<br>Part A: Letter Names Uppercase: +26 (all)<br>Part B: Letter Names Lowercase: +26 (all)<br>Part C: Consonant Sounds: +21 (all)<br>Part D: Vowel Sounds:<br>+ 5 long vowels (all)<br>+ 5 short vowels (all) |

| Phonological Awareness | *CORE Phonological Segmentation Test*<br>Part A: Sentences into Words: +5 (out of 5)<br>Part B: Words into Syllables: + 8 (out of 8)<br>Part C: Words into Phonemes: +9–10 (out of 10) |
|---|---|
| Phonemic Awareness | *CORE Phoneme Deletion Test*<br>Part A: Initial Sounds: +5 (out of 5)<br>Part B: Final Sounds: +5 (out of 5)<br>Part C: First Sound Blends: +3–5 (out of 5)<br>Part D: NA |
| Encoding | *Words Their Way Primary Spelling Inventory*<br>Initial Sound: +7 (all)<br>Final Sound: +7 (all)<br>Short Vowel: +6 or 7 (out of 7)<br>Digraphs: +6 or 7 (out of 7)<br>Blends: +5–7 (out of 7) |
| Decoding | *CORE Phonics Survey: Reading and Decoding*<br>Part E: short vowels in CVC words: +14 or 15 (out of 15)<br>Part F: consonant blends: +10–15 (out of 15)<br>Part G: digraphs +10–15 (out of 15) If you taught *R*-controlled vowels:<br>Part H: *R*-controlled vowels: +10–15 (out of 15) |
| Sight Words | NA<br>(We do not recommend using the *CORE Graded High Frequency Word Surveys*.) |
| Reading Fluency | NA |

By the end of the year, all students are expected to achieve the benchmark for each language skill. If a student does not achieve a benchmark, conduct a further assessment to ascertain why.

## 4. End-of-Year Reports

Use your school's benchmarks (or *The Roadmap to Literacy's* benchmarks) to create a rubric and description of language arts skills to include in your end-of-year report. Here are the steps to follow:

1. Create a description of the language arts skills.

2. Create a rubric.

3. Interpret the rubric.

4. Include areas to work on over the summer.

5. Include other aspects of the curriculum.

### Description of Language Arts Skills

First describe the language arts skills covered in the curriculum such as these:

- alphabet: ability to identify uppercase and lowercase print letters

- handwriting: ability to print uppercase and lowercase letters

- phonemic awareness: segmentation: ability to break words down into individual phonemes

- phonemic awareness: deletion: ability to manipulate sounds in words by deleting sounds
- encoding: ability to segment a word into its sounds and spell it correctly
- decoding: ability to sound out a word to read it correctly
- symbol imagery: ability to visualize letters
- sight words: reading: ability to recognize commonly-used words
- sight words: spelling: ability to spell commonly-used words
- dictation: ability to write short sentences given by the teacher
- mechanics: ability to capitalize names and the first word in a sentence and use periods
- reading: ability to read short, unfamiliar passages

### Rubric

Second, create a rubric. If you adopt *The Roadmap to Literacy's* benchmarks, the rubric could look something like Table 6.3.6.

**Table 6.3.6: End-of-Year Report: Language Arts Rubric**

|  | Achieved | Developing | Area of Concern |
|---|---|---|---|
| **Alphabet** |  |  |  |
| **Handwriting** |  |  |  |
| **Phonemic Awareness: Segmentation** |  |  |  |
| **Phonemic Awareness: Deletion** |  |  |  |
| **Encoding** |  |  |  |
| **Decoding** |  |  |  |
| **Symbol Imagery** |  |  |  |
| **Sight Words: Reading** |  |  |  |
| **Sight Words: Spelling** |  |  |  |
| **Dictation** |  |  |  |
| **Mechanics** |  |  |  |
| **Reading** |  |  |  |

Use your formal assessments (especially those created by educational testing groups) as the basis for filling out this rubric.

### Interpreting the Rubric

Third, give a key to interpret the rubric. For example,

- *Achieved* means that the student has met the benchmark.
- *Developing* means that the student is progressing but needs more practice in order to meet the benchmark.
- *Area of Concern* means that the student needs additional formal instruction and practice to meet the benchmark.

## Areas to Work on Over the Summer

Fourth, describe any *Developing* and/or *Areas of Concern* and make suggestions for how parents could help their child over the summer.

An example would be this excerpt from a 1st Grade end-of-year report: *Samuel's ability to sound out words has steadily improved over the year. However, he often loses his place when he is memory reading a familiar text due to skipping line. I have also noticed that when he is attempting to sound out words in our introductory readers, he tends to hold the book up close to his face. These issues suggest that Samuel might have some vision difficulties. I recommend that you have him assessed over the summer by a vision therapist to ascertain if Samuel needs vision therapy and/or reading glasses. A number of our students have used (insert name) to address difficulties in this area.*

## Other Aspects of the Curriculum

Finally, the end-of-year report should not be limited to academic skills. This rubric for language arts (and another similar one for math that you would create) would only be a part of the report. The rest would then look like a typical Waldorf report with descriptions of class activities and personalized information about how each student is doing socially, physically, artistically, etc. in a written narrative format.

See www.waldorfinspirations.com for examples of rubrics for the other aspects of the curriculum.

In summary, there are many benefits to organizing your end-of-year Reports in this manner. First, the student's academic skills are reported clearly and objectively. It is easier for everyone to interpret the report because there is no ambiguity. Second, it is easier to write your end-of-year reports. Instead of worrying how to present information tactfully yet clearly, you merely check a box. You write an expository paragraph if there is something additional to say. For most students, the rubric plus a short paragraph afterward giving additional information will be sufficient.

## Conclusion

Assessment is like GPS: it enables you to pinpoint where each student is on the road to literacy and to track her progress. A balance of assessments (informal and formal, including assessments created by educational testing groups) is the most effective way to assess. This balance will help you execute your responsibility to teach every student in your class the skills needed for language arts. If a student is not meeting the benchmarks for 1st Grade, consider whether remedial support is needed (see chapter 6.6).

# 6.4 SECOND GRADE ASSESSMENTS

This chapter covers how to assess benchmarks (standards) to monitor progress and assess outcomes in 2nd Grade.

Using *The Roadmap to Literacy* as a metaphor, phases represent the entire route the students must travel to get to full literacy. Benchmarks represent the signposts along the edge of the road. Assessments represent the GPS device that tracks where students are along the road as well as their forward momentum. By comparing the results of the assessments with the benchmarks, you can determine how much progress students have made (progress monitoring) and whether they have met the desired benchmarks by the end of the year (outcomes assessment). By using assessment in this manner, you can determine whether your students' literacy skills are on track.

This chapter contains an overview of benchmarks to assess in language arts in 2nd Grade. (Keep in mind that all students are expected to meet the benchmarks in all areas by the end of the year.) This chapter also contains a number of different assessments because assessments should be approached from different angles. There is a time and place for all types of assessments: formal, informal, and assessments created by educational testing groups. The number of options may seem overwhelming, just choose which assessments would work best in your classroom.

Note: Reread 6.1 #3–6 before using this chapter.

This chapter covers the following topics:

1. Second Grade Benchmarks
2. How To Use Informal and Teacher-Made Assessments
3. How to Use Assessments Created by Educational Testing Groups
4. End-of-Year Reports

## 1. Second Grade Benchmarks

Benchmarks are the signposts along the road to full literacy. By the end of the school year, all second grade students should be able to meet the benchmarks. Table 6.4.1 contains the benchmarks for 2nd Grade. For a full list of benchmark, see table 6.1.4.

The following benchmarks represent the minimal skill level students should attain by the end of the year. Although most students begin the year in the Advanced Phonemic Awareness Phase or the Beginning Pattern Phase, some of them may be in the Syllable Phase. Set higher expectations as needed for these students, but continue to use the 2nd Grade benchmarks for your formal reports.

**Table 6.4.1: Benchmarks for 2nd Grade**

| Language Skill | 2nd Grade |
|---|---|
| Sound/Symbol (Alphabet) | NA |
| Handwriting | Students can form all uppercase and lowercase cursive letters correctly. |
| Phonological and Phonemic Awareness: Segmentation | NA (Segmentation should have been mastered in 1st Grade. Assess to confirm.) |
| Phonemic Awareness: Deletion (Note: Deletion is a type of Manipulation) | Students have mastered the following deletion skills: <br> • initial sound <br> • end sound <br> • blends—initial sound |
| Decoding | Students demonstrate mastery decoding with all phonics rules for single-syllable words. |
| Encoding | Students demonstrate mastery encoding a <u>minimum</u> of the following phonics rules: <br> • Silent E <br> • Two Vowels Go Walking <br> • The Guardians <br> • Diphthongs |
| Symbol Imagery | Students can visualize seven letters. |
| Sight Words: Reading | Students can read all sight words from *The Roadmap to Literacy* list (i.e., set 1 and set 2). |
| Sight Words: Spelling | Students can spell 150+ sight words. |
| Comprehension | Students can answer factual review questions and HOTS questions for stories told in class and for stories they have read. |
| Spelling | NA—see sight words and encoding. |
| Dictation | Students can take dictation of simple sentences (i.e., subject/ predicate). <br> Example: *The hare ran faster.* |
| Grammar: Parts of Speech | Students can identify the following parts of speech in sentences: <br> • nouns <br> • verbs |
| Grammar: Mechanics | When writing, students use end punctuation correctly (period, exclamation point, and question mark). |

| Composition | Students can write brief summaries of stories they have heard or about something they have done (i.e. 3–4 sentences). |
|---|---|
| Reading Fluency | Students can read 2nd Grade passages from any formal reading fluency program.<br><br>Reading fluency should be a <u>minimum</u> of 61 correct words per minute with >95% accuracy.<br><br>This fluency score is at or above the 25th percentile for public school students at the end of 2nd Grade. |

Note: Many of these benchmarks pertain to kid writing. Therefore, there is no separate benchmark for kid writing.

## 2. How to Use Informal and Teacher-Made Assessments

You can assess the 15 aspects of language arts both formally and informally in class.

It is possible to assess these skills informally any day you work on them in class. It is possible to assess them formally by making your own formal assessments to use weekly, bi-weekly, or at the end of the block as needed to monitor the growth of students' skills. Table 6.4.2 contains some ideas on how you could assess these skills informally and formally. This list is not exhaustive. You can also supplement your own assessments by using assessments created by educational testing groups (see chapter 6.4 #3).

**Table 6.4.2: Ideas for Assessing Language Arts Informally and Formally in Class**

| Language Skill | Informal Assessment | Formal Teacher-made Assessments to Be Given during Class |
|---|---|---|
| 1. Alphabet | NA (This should have been mastered in 1st Grade.) | NA (This should have been mastered in 1st Grade.) |
| 2. Handwriting | Observe students' work (handwriting practice, dictation, kid writing, composition, etc.).<br><br>Observe the students' pencil grip and letter formation by wandering around the classroom as they write. (Be sure to correct anything that is done incorrectly.) | Ask the students to copy something from the board using their neatest handwriting. (It could be something to put in their main lesson book or it could be a stand-alone assessment.)<br><br>Mark off for the following things: mixing uppercase and lowercase letters, letters that are incorrect sizes, letters that go off the line, and letters with descenders that do not descend below the base line (e.g., *y, g, q, p*, etc.). |
| 3. Phonemic Awareness | Segmentation: NA (This should have been mastered in 1st Grade.)<br>Deletion: Observe symbol imagery exercises such as syllable cards and mystery word when you ask student to erase a letter and tell you what the new word says. | Segmentation: NA (This should have been mastered in 1st Grade.)<br>Deletion: NA |

| Language Skill | Informal Assessment | Formal Teacher-made Assessments to Be Given during Class |
|---|---|---|
| **4. Decoding/ Encoding** | Observe kid writing and spelling dictations. Observe reading groups. | Decoding: NA (Use assessment developed by an educational testing group. See table 6.4.3.)<br><br>Encoding: Make up a list of words with the phonics rules you have been practicing. Ex. *trail, float, peas, tray* for<br><br>Two Vowels Go Walking.<br><br>Dictate these words to assess encoding. Be sure to include some nonsense words. |
| **5. Symbol Imagery** | Observe symbol imagery exercises such as syllable cards and mystery word.<br>Observe how the students copy from the board (one letter at a time, one word, or groups of words). | Create your own assessment by making cards that have 5–7 random lowercase letters on them such as *lqznt*.<br><br>Show them for one second per letter. Take them away. Have the students write down the letters they saw on a piece of paper.(It is good to have three cards with 5 letters, three with 6 letters, etc.) |
| **6. Sight Words** | Observe students' oral reading. Observe students' kid writing and/ or composition. | Give a spelling test of all the sight words practiced to date (or just that week). |
| **7. Concept Imagery** | See Comprehension. | See Comprehension. |
| **8. Comprehension** | Observe student's answers to oral comprehension questions (HOTS questions and factual recall questions).<br>Observe written summaries. | Write your own comprehension questions and give the class a very simple written quiz. (Example: *How did the sun win the argument with the north wind?* (He warmed the man and made the man take off his jacket.) |
| **9. Spelling** | Observe students' kid writing or compositions. | Give 3–5 simple dictation sentences using sight words and phonics rules. Ex. *Jane was to train for the race.* |
| **10. Speech** | Observe articulation and grammar. If a student struggles to pronounce a sound (e.g., /r/, /s/, /l/, /w/, /th/, etc.), refer the student to speech therapy.<br><br>Make note of common grammatical problems. Ex. "Me and him (sic) went out." | NA |

| Language Skill | Informal Assessment | Formal Teacher-made Assessments to Be Given during Class |
|---|---|---|
| 11. Grammar | Observe use of mechanics (capitalization and punctuation) in kid writing and composition drafts. | Make up your own assessments where students need to identify the nouns and verbs. Ex. *The boat sailed out of the harbor slowly.* |
| 12. Vocabulary | Observe students' use of oral language. | NA |
| 13. Kid Writing | NA (Use kid writing to assess for phonemic awareness and sight words.) | |
| 14. Composition | Observe students' compositions to make sure they are appropriate in length, sentence structure, and grammar. Make sure their content matches the assignment. | NA |
| 15. Reading | Observe students' fluency, phrasing, and errors. | See Comprehension. |

Remind your students to use proper etiquette when they take an assessment. While students may help each other during regular work time, they must do their own work during an assessment. Encourage students to leave something blank, use a question mark, or take their best guess if they do not know the answer.

## 3.  How to Use Assessments Created by Educational Testing Groups

In addition to your own classroom assessments, it is good to use assessments created by Educational Testing Groups three times a year: fall, winter, and spring. If your school has access to DIBELs or AIMSweb, use these assessments. If not, you can use assessments from the books *CORE* and *Words Their Way*. See chapter 6.3 #3 for the protocol for these assessments and see table 6.4.3 for the assessments themselves.

**Table 6.4.3: Recommended Schedule for Assessments Created by Educational Testing Groups in 2nd Grade:** *CORE Reading Assessments* and *Words Their Way*

| Language Skill | Fall | Winter | Spring |
|---|---|---|---|
| **Alphabet** | Only if a student did not master the alphabet in 1st Grade | Ibid | Ibid |
| **Phonological and Phonemic Awareness** | *CORE Phoneme Segmentation Test CORE Phoneme Deletion Test*—all discontinue testing once students have mastered tests. | *CORE* Phoneme Segmentation *Test CORE Phoneme Deletion Test*—all discontinue testing once students have mastered tests. | *CORE Phoneme Segmentation Test CORE Phoneme Deletion Test*—all discontinue testing once students have mastered tests. |
| **Encoding** | *Words Their Way Primary Spelling Inventory*: the entire list (26 words) | *Words Their Way Primary Spelling Inventory*: the entire list (26 words) | *Words Their Way Primary Spelling Inventory*: the entire list (26 words) |
| **Decoding** | *CORE Phonics Survey*: Reading and Decoding: Part E–Part K (all single-syllable words) | *CORE Phonics Survey*: Reading and Decoding: Part E–Part K* Part L: optional *Note: It is not necessary to re-administer parts that students mastered in the fall of 2nd Grade. | *CORE Phonics Survey*: Reading and Decoding: Part E–Part K* Part L *Only administer areas that students have not mastered in fall or winter. |
| **Sight Words: Reading** | NA (We do not recommend using the *CORE Graded High-Frequency Word Surveys.*\*) (see table 6.4.2.) | NA (We do not recommend using the *CORE Graded High-Frequency Word Surveys.*\*) | NA (We do not recommend using the *CORE Graded High-Frequency Word Surveys.*\*) |
| **Reading Fluency** | *MASI-R Oral Reading Fluency Measures* (in *CORE* book) 1st Grade passages or 2nd Grade Passages | *MASI-R Oral Reading Fluency Measures* (in *CORE* book) 2nd Grade passages | *MASI-R Oral Reading Fluency Measures* (in *CORE* book) 2nd Grade passages |

\**CORE Graded High-Frequency Word Surveys* show minimal sight word proficiency and continues to assess sight words through 4th Grade. As such, it is not an ideal fit for *The Roadmap to Literacy* program as it concludes sight word instruction in 2nd Grade.

Administer the *Words Their Way Primary Spelling Inventory* to the entire class at once. It will take around 15 minutes total. Administer the other assessments to students one-on-one privately. Total time depends on the number of students in the class and how advanced the students' skills are. See table 6.4.4 for estimates. Many of the assessment will not need to be done with every student every time. Once a student has reached mastery in a skill, do not continue to assess it. Consider getting a substitute for a day or using free periods so that you can give the assessments to students one at a time in a private room. Do not let the other students hear you give the assessment in advance as it would compromise the validity of their assessment scores.

**Table 6.4.4: Estimated Time to Administer**

| Language Skill | Type of Administration | Estimated Time to Administer |
|---|---|---|
| Encoding | whole class | 10 min. |
| Decoding | one on one | 5 min./student |
| Phonological and Phonemic Awareness | one on one | 5 min./student for Phoneme Segmentation Test 5 min./student for Phoneme Deletion Test |
| Reading Fluency | one on one | 5 min./student |

The grade levels in the *CORE* testing book refer to public school grade levels. Waldorf students start reading instruction a year later. Therefore, it is necessary to use slightly different scales to interpret the assessment results than the ones in the book. Use Table 6.4.5.

Here is some advice on how to read Table 6.4.5:

1. The test you will use is identified in the right-hand column (e.g., *Words Their Way Primary Spelling Inventory*).

2. The subtests are listed under the test's name (e.g., Initial Sound, Final Sound, etc.).

3. The benchmark score is indicated for each subtest (e.g ., +7 (all), which means that a student must get all the questions right to achieve benchmark).

Students achieve benchmark if they score at the score indicated in the column.

**Table 6.4.5: Interpreting the Results: Waldorf 2nd Grade Benchmarks for *CORE* Reading Assessment and *Words Their Way*.**

| Language Skill | Benchmarks for Spring, 2nd Grade |
|---|---|
| Encoding | *Words Their Way Primary Spelling Inventory*<br><br>1. Initial Sound: +7 (all)<br>2. Final Sound: +7 (all)<br>3. Short Vowel: +7 (out of 7)<br>4. Digraphs: +7 (out of 7)<br>5. Blends: +7 (out of 7)<br>6. Long Vowels: +6–7 (out of 7)<br>7. Other Vowels: +5–7 (out of 7)<br>8. Inflected Endings: +5–7 (out of 7) |
| Decoding | *CORE Phonics Survey*: Reading and Decoding<br>Part E: Short Vowels in CVC words: +14 or 15 (out of 15)<br>Part F: Consonant Blends: +14–15 (out of 15)<br>Part G: Digraphs +14–15 (out of 15)<br>Part H: *R*-Controlled Vowels: +14–15 (out of 15)<br>Part I: Long Vowel Spellings: +14–15 (out of 15)<br>Part J: Variant Vowels: +14–15 (out of 15)<br>Part K: Low Frequency Vowels and Consonants: +10–15 (out of 15)<br>Part L: NA |
| Sight Words | NA—We do not recommend using the *CORE Graded High-Frequency Word Surveys*. |

| Phonemic Awareness: Segmentation | *CORE Phoneme Segmentation Test* 14 or 15 ( out of 15) Note: Students are expected to be able to segment words by the end of 1st Grade. This assessment is used to confirm that this skill has been mastered. |
|---|---|
| **Phonemic Awareness: Deletion (Note: Deletion is a type of Manipulation)** | *CORE Phoneme Deletion Test* Part A: Only if benchmark not met in 1st Grade Part B: Only if benchmark not met in 1st Grade Part C: First Sound Blends: +5 (out of 5) Part D: +3–5 (out of 5) |
| **Reading Fluency** | *MASI-R Oral Reading Fluency Measures* (in *CORE* book) 2nd Grade passage: 61 or more correct words/minute Accuracy: 95% or higher<br><br>This fluency score is at or above the 25th percentile for public school students at the end of 2nd Grade. It is the lowest average score (Hasbrouck and Tindal *Oral Reading Fluency Norms Grades 1–8 2005* reprinted in *Assessing Reading Multiple Measures* 80). |

## A Note on Reading Fluency

*The Roadmap to Literacy* reading fluency benchmark is 61 or more correct words/minute. A score of 61 words/minute represents the 25th percentile, the lowest average score for public school 2nd Grade. Some readers familiar with fluency scores may wonder why this number was selected. This score was chosen because Waldorf students begin reading instruction a year later than their public school peers; however, they should be catching up to them by this point in their education.

By the end of the year, all students are expected to score *Achieved* for each benchmark. If a student does not, conduct a further assessment to ascertain why.

By the end of the year, all students are expected to achieve the benchmarks indicated in the above table. If a student does not achieve a benchmark, conduct further assessments to ascertain why.

## 4.   End-of-Year Reports

Use your school's benchmarks (or *The Roadmap to Literacy's* benchmarks) to create a rubric and description of language arts skills to include in your end-of-year report. Here are the steps to follow:

1. Create a description of the language arts skills.

2. Create a rubric.

3. Interpret the rubric.

4. Include areas to work on over the summer.

5. Include other aspects of the curriculum.

### Description of Language Arts Skills

First describe the language arts Skills covered in the curriculum such as these:

- alphabet: ability to identify uppercase and lowercase print letters

- handwriting: ability to print uppercase and lowercase letters

- phonemic awareness: segmentation: ability to break words down into individual phonemes

- phonemic awareness: deletion: ability to manipulate sounds in words by deleting sounds
- encoding: ability to segment a word into its sounds and spell it correctly
- decoding: ability to sound out a word to read it correctly
- symbol imagery: ability to visualize letters
- sight words: ability to recognize commonly-used words
- sight words: ability to spell commonly-used words
- dictation: ability to write short sentences given by the teacher
- mechanics: ability to capitalize names and the first word in a sentence and use periods
- reading: ability to read short, unfamiliar passages

**Rubric**

Second, create a rubric. If you adopt *The Roadmap to Literacy's* benchmarks, the rubric could look something like Table 6.3.6.

**Table 6.4.6: End-of-Year Report: Language Arts Skills**

|  | Achieved | Developing | Area of Concern |
|---|---|---|---|
| **Handwriting** | | | |
| **Phonemic Awareness: Segmentation** | | | |
| **Phonemic Awareness: Deletion** | | | |
| **Encoding** | | | |
| **Decoding** | | | |
| **Symbol Imagery** | | | |
| **Sight Words: Reading** | | | |
| **Sight Words: Spelling** | | | |
| **Dictation** | | | |
| **Grammar** | | | |
| **Mechanics** | | | |
| **Reading Fluency** | | | |

Use your formal assessments (especially those created by educational testing groups) as the basis for filling out this rubric.

**Interpreting the Rubric**

Third, give a key to interpret the rubric. For example,

- *Achieved* means that the student has met the objective.
- *Developing* means that the student is progressing but needs more practice in order to meet the benchmark.
- *Area of Concern* means that the student needs additional formal instruction and practice to meet the benchmark.

**Areas to Work on over the Summer**

Fourth, describe any *Developing* and/or *Areas of Concern* and make suggestions for how parents could help their child over the summer.

For an example see chapter 6.3 #4.

**Other Aspects of the Curriculum**

Finally, the end-of-year report should not be limited to academic skills. This rubric for language arts (and another similar one for math that you would create) would only be a part of the report. The rest would then look like a typical Waldorf report with descriptions of class activities and personalized information about how each student is doing socially, physically, artistically, etc. in a written narrative format.

See www.waldorfinspirations.com for examples of rubrics for the other aspects of the curriculum.

In summary, there are many benefits to organizing your end-of-year reports in this manner. First, the student's academic skills are reported clearly and objectively. It is easier for everyone to interpret the report because there is no ambiguity. Second, it is easier to write your end-of-year reports. Instead of worrying how to present information tactfully yet clearly, you merely check a box. You can write an expository paragraph if there is something additional to say. For most students, the rubric plus a short paragraph afterward giving additional information will be sufficient.

## Conclusion

Assessment is the GPS tool used to make sure your students are on track. Assessments enable you to determine where each student is on the road to literacy and to deduce what each student needs in order to continue the journey. A balance of assessments (informal and formal, including assessments created by educational testing groups) is the most effective way to assess. This balance will help you execute your responsibility to teach every student in your class the skills needed for language arts so that they can reach the advanced level of the Syllable Phase by the end of 3rd Grade. If a student is not meeting the benchmarks for 2nd Grade, consider whether remedial support is needed (see chapter 6.6).

# 6.5  THIRD GRADE ASSESSMENTS

This chapter covers how to assess benchmarks (standards) to monitor progress and assess outcomes in 3rd Grade.

Using *The Roadmap to Literacy* as a metaphor, phases represent the entire route the students must travel to get to full literacy. Benchmarks represent the signposts along the edge of the road. Assessments represent the GPS device that tracks where students are along the road as well as their forward momentum. By comparing the results of the assessments with the benchmarks, you can determine how much progress students have made (progress monitoring) and whether they have met the desired benchmarks by the end of the year (outcomes assessment). By using assessment in this manner, you can determine whether your students' literacy skills are on track.

This chapter contains an overview of benchmarks to assess in language arts in 3rd Grade. (Keep in mind that all students are expected to meet the benchmarks in all areas by the end of the year.) This chapter also contains a number of different assessments because assessments should be approached from different angles. There is a time and place for all types of assessments: formal, informal, and assessments created by educational testing groups. The number of options may seem overwhelming, just choose which assessments would work best in your classroom.

Note: Reread 6.1 #3–6 before using this chapter.

This chapter covers the following topics:

1. Third Grade Benchmarks
2. How to Use Informal and Teacher-Made Assessments
3. How to Use Assessments Created by Educational Testing Groups
4. End-of-Year Reports

## 1.   Third Grade Benchmarks

Benchmarks are the signposts along the road to full literacy. By the end of the school year, all 3rd Grade students should be able to meet the benchmarks. Table 6.5.1 contains the benchmarks for 3rd Grade. For a full list of benchmarks, see table 6.1.4.

**Table 6.5.1: Benchmarks for 3rd Grade**

| Language Skill | 3rd Grade |
|---|---|
| **Sound/Symbol (Alphabet)** | NA |
| **Handwriting** | Students can write and read cursive script. |
| **Phonological and Phonemic Awareness: Segmentation** | NA |
| **Phonemic Awareness: Deletion (Note: Deletion is a type of Manipulation)** | Students have mastered the following deletion skills:<br>• initial sound<br>• end sound<br>• blends—initial sound<br>• blends—embedded sound |
| **Decoding** | Students demonstrate mastery decoding with all phonics rules. |
| **Encoding** | Students demonstrate mastery encoding:<br>• single-syllable words<br>• two-syllable words with common affixes |
| **Symbol Imagery** | Students can visualize two syllables. |
| **Sight Words: Reading** | NA |
| **Sight Words: Spelling** | NA |
| **Comprehension** | Students can answer factual review questions and HOTS questions for stories told in class, factual presentations, and material they have read. |
| **Spelling** | Students can spell 3rd Grade level words in context. |
| **Dictation** | Students can take dictation of sentences up to 7–10 words. Example: *In the forest the students found mushrooms and berries.* |
| **Grammar: Parts of Speech** | Students can identify the following parts of speech in sentences:<br>• nouns<br>• verbs<br>• adjectives<br>• adverbs<br>In addition, they can identify:<br><br>• possessive nouns<br>• verb tense<br>• being verbs<br>• helping verbs |

| Grammar: Mechanics | When writing, students use the following correctly:<br>• commas in a list and with quotation marks<br>• quotation marks<br>• apostrophes in possessive nouns and contractions<br>• capitalization of proper nouns |
|---|---|
| Composition | Students can write:<br>• a paragraph<br>• 1-3 paragraph summaries for their main lesson books<br>• a thank you note |
| Reading Fluency | Students can read 3rd Grade passages from any formal reading fluency program. Reading fluency should be a <u>minimum</u> of 95 correct words per minute with >95% accuracy.<br>This fluency score is at or above the 40th percentile for public school students at the end of 3rd Grade. |

These benchmarks represent the minimal skill level 3rd graders should attain by the end of the year.

## 2.   How to Use Informal and Teacher-Made Assessments

You can assess the 15 aspects of language arts both formally and informally in class.

It is possible to assess these skills informally any day you work on them in class. It is possible to assess them formally by making your own formal assessments to use weekly, bi-weekly, or at the end of the block as needed to monitor the growth of students' skills. Table 6.5.2 contains some ideas on how you could assess these skills informally and formally. This list is not exhaustive. Furthermore, you can also supplement your own assessments by using assessments created by educational testing groups (see chapter 6.5 #3).

**Table 6.5.2: Ideas for Assessing Language Arts Informally and Formally in Class**

| Language Skill | Informal Assessment | Formal Teacher-made Assessments to Be Given during Class |
|---|---|---|
| 1. Alphabet | NA (This should have been mastered in 1st Grade.) | NA (This should have been mastered in 1st Grade.) |
| 2. Handwriting | Observe students' work (handwriting practice, dictations, compositions, etc.). Observe the students' pencil grip and letter formation by wandering around the classroom as they write. (Be sure to correct anything that is done incorrectly.) | Ask the students to copy something from the board using their neatest handwriting. (It could be something to put in their main lesson book or it could be a stand-alone assessment.) Mark off for the following errors for cursive: letter size, letter height, letter shape, not writing on the line, etc. |
| 3. Phonemic Awareness | Segmentation: NA (This should have been mastered in 1st Grade.)<br>Deletion: observe symbol imagery exercises such as syllable cards and mystery word when you ask student to erase a letter and tell you what the new word says. | Segmentation: NA (This should have been mastered in 1st Grade.)<br>Deletion: NA |

| Language Skill | Informal Assessment | Formal Teacher-made Assessments to Be Given during Class |
|---|---|---|
| 4. Decoding/ Encoding | Decoding: Observe reading groups. Encoding: Observe compositions and spelling dictations. | Decoding: NA (Use assessment developed by an educational testing group. See table 6.5.3.) Encoding: Make up a list of words with the phonics rules you have been practicing. Ex. *movement, lotion, rupture, native, etc.* for the Big Four Suffixes. Dictate these words to assess encoding. |
| 5. Symbol Imagery | Observe symbol imagery exercises such as syllable cards and mystery word. Observe how the students copy from the board (one letter at a time, one word, or groups of words). | Create your own assessment by making cards that have multisyllabic nonsense words such as *bluzzle.* Show them for 1 second per letter. Take them away. Have the students write down the letters they saw on a piece of paper. |
| 6. Sight Words | Reading: NA (This should have been mastered in 2nd Grade.) Spelling: Make note of any spelling mistakes in student writing. | Reading: NA (This should have been mastered in 2nd Grade.) Spelling: Include any sight words that were not mastered in 2nd Grade in your weekly spelling words lists and assess from there. |
| 7. Concept Imagery | See Comprehension. | See Comprehension. |
| 8. Comprehension | Observe student's answers to oral comprehension questions (HOTS questions and factual recall questions). | Write your own comprehension questions and give the class written quizzes. (Example: *Why did God decide to flood the Earth?*) |
| 9. Spelling | Observe students' compositions and dictations. | Do 5+ simple dictation sentences using phonics rules and weekly spelling words. Ex. *The children were unhappy because they misplaced their binders.* |
| 10. Speech | NA | NA |
| 11. Grammar | Observe use of mechanics (capitalization and punctuation) in composition drafts. | Make up your own assessments where students need to identify the nouns, verbs, adjectives, and adverbs. Ex. *The old blue boat sailed briskly and merrily out to sea on a sunny day.* |
| 12. Vocabulary | Observe students' use of oral language. | NA |
| 13. Kid Writing | NA (This should have been finished in 2nd Grade.) | NA (This should have been finished in 2nd Grade.) |
| 14. Composition | Observe students' compositions to make sure they are appropriate in length, sentence structure, and grammar. | NA |
| 15. Reading | Observe students' fluency, phrasing, and errors. | See Comprehension |

Keep in mind that you will have to remind the students about proper etiquette when giving them an assessment. Students may help each other during regular work time, but insist that students do their own work for formal assessments. Encourage students to leave something blank, write down a question mark, or take their best guess.

## 3. How to Use Assessments Created by Educational Testing Groups

In addition to the classroom assessments, it is good to use assessments created by educational testing groups three times a year: fall, winter, and spring. For the protocol see chapter 6.3 #3. If your school has access to DIBELs or AIMSweb, use these assessments. If not, you can use assessments from the books *CORE* and *Words Their Way*. A recommended list is found in table 6.5.3.

**Table 6.5.3: Recommended Schedule for Assessments Created by Educational Testing Groups (3rd Grade)**

| Language Skill | Fall | Winter | Spring |
|---|---|---|---|
| **Encoding** | *Words Their Way Elementary Spelling Inventory*: the entire list (25 words) | *Words Their Way Elementary Spelling Inventory*: the entire list (25 words) | *Words Their Way Elementary Spelling Inventory*: the entire list (25 words) |
| **Decoding** | *CORE Phonics Survey*: Reading and Decoding: Part L Any subtests E–K student did not master in 2nd Grade | *CORE Phonics Survey*: Reading and Decoding: Part L* Any subtests E–K student did not master in 2nd Grade *Discontinue administration once student has mastered it. | *CORE Phonics Survey*: Reading and Decoding: Part L* Any subtests E–K student did not master in 2nd Grade *Discontinue administration once student has mastered it. |
| **Sight Words** | NA for most students | NA for most students | NA for most students |
| **Phonological and Phonemic Awareness** | *CORE Phoneme Segmentation Test*— only if not previously mastered *CORE Phoneme Deletion Test*—only sections not already mastered | *CORE Phoneme Segmentation Test*— only if not previously mastered *CORE Phoneme Deletion Test*— only sections not already mastered | *CORE Phoneme Segmentation Test*— only if not previously mastered *CORE Phoneme Deletion Test*— only sections not already mastered |
| **Reading Fluency** | *MASI-R Oral Reading Fluency Measures* (in *CORE* book) 3rd grade passages or 2nd Grade passage if 3rd is too hard | *MASI-R Oral Reading Fluency Measures* (in *CORE* book) 3rd Grade passages | *MASI-R Oral Reading Fluency Measures* (in *CORE* book) 3rd Grade passages |

Administer the *Words Their Way Primary Spelling Inventory* to the entire class at once. It will take about 15 minutes total. Administer the other assessments to students one-on-one privately. Total time depends on the number of students in the class and how advanced the students' skills are. See table 6.5.4 for estimates. Many of the assessment will not need to be done with every student every time. Once a student has reached mastery in a skill, do not continue to assess it. Consider getting a substitute for a day or using free periods to administer the assessments to students one at a time in private. Do not let the other students hear what you are doing or it will compromise the validity of the assessment they take.

**Table 6.5.4: Estimated Time to Administer**

| Language Skill | Type of Administration | Estimated Time to Administer |
|---|---|---|
| Encoding | whole class | 15 min./class |
| Decoding | one on one | 5 min./student |
| Phonological and Phonemic Awareness | one on one | 5 min./student for *CORE Phoneme Deletion Test* |
| Reading Fluency | one on one | 5 min./student |

The grade levels in the *CORE* testing book refer to public school grade levels. Waldorf students start reading instruction a year later. Therefore, it is necessary to use slightly different scales to interpret the assessment results than the ones in the book. Use Table 6.5.5.

Here is some advice on how to read Table 6.5.5:

1. The test you will use is identified in the right-hand column (e.g., *Words Their Way Elementary Spelling Inventory*).

2. The subtests are listed under the test's name (e.g., Initial and Final Sound, etc.).

3. The benchmark score is indicated for each subtest (e.g., +7 (all), which means the student has to get all seven right to achieve the benchmark).

Students achieve benchmark if they score at the score indicated in the column.

**Table 6.5.5: Interpreting the Results: Waldorf 3rd Grade Benchmarks for *CORE Reading Assessments* and *Words Their Way***

| Language Skill | Benchmarks for Spring, 3rd Grade |
|---|---|
| Encoding | Words Their Way *Elementary Spelling Inventory*<br>Initial and Final Sound: +7 (all)<br>Short Vowel: +5 (out of 5)<br>Digraphs: +6 (out of 6)<br>Blends: +7 (out of 7)<br>Long Vowels: +5 (out of 5)<br>Other Vowels: +7 (out of 7)<br>Inflected Endings: +4–5 (out of 5)<br>Syllable Junctures: 4–5 (out of 5)<br>Unaccented Final Syllables: 3–5 (out of 5)<br>Harder Suffixes: 2–5 (out of 5)<br>Bases or Roots: 0–5 (out of 5) |
| Decoding | *CORE Phonics Survey: Reading and Decoding*<br>Part E–J: Any subtests not mastered in 2nd grade<br>Part K: Low Frequency Vowels and Consonants: +14–15 (out of 15)<br>Part L: Multisyllabic Words: +21–24 (out of 24) |
| Sight Words | NA (This should have been mastered in 2nd Grade.) |
| Phonemic Awareness: Segmentation | *CORE Phoneme Segmentation Test*—Only administer if not mastered in 2nd Grade 14 or 15/15<br>Note: Students expected to be able to segment words by the end of 1st Grade. |

| Language Skill | Benchmarks for Spring, 3rd Grade |
|---|---|
| **Phonemic Awareness** | *CORE Phoneme Deletion Test* Part D: +5–5 (out of 5) And Part C if not mastered in 2nd Grade |
| **Reading Fluency** | *MASI-R Oral Reading Fluency Measures* (in *CORE* book) 3rd Grade passage: 95 or more correct words/minute |
| | Accuracy: 95% or higher |

### A Note on Reading Fluency

*The Roadmap to Literacy* reading fluency benchmark is 95 or more correct words/minute. It represents the 40th percentile or above. Some readers familiar with fluency scores may wonder why this number was selected given that the average range for reading fluency at the end of 3rd Grade is 78–137 correct words per minute (i.e., the 25–75th percentiles). The reason is that the 37th/40th percentile represents a threshold. Students above it can handle grade-level work while those below it struggle.

Make sure your students clear this threshold in reading fluency. This is important because in 4th Grade they will no longer be learning to read but rather they will be reading to learn.

By the end of the year, all students are expected to score *Achieved* for each benchmark. If a student does not, conduct a further assessment to ascertain why.

## 4.  End-of-Year Reports

Use your school's benchmarks (or *The Roadmap to Literacy's* benchmarks) to create a rubric and description of language arts skills to include in your end-of-year report. Here are the steps to follow:

1. Create a description of the language arts skills.
2. Create a rubric.
3. Interpret the rubric.
4. Include areas to work on over the summer.
5. Include other aspects of the curriculum.

### Description of Language Arts Skills

First describe the language arts skills covered in the curriculum such as these:

- handwriting: ability to write well in cursive and print
- phonemic awareness: deletion: ability to manipulate sounds in words by deleting sounds
- encoding: ability to segment a word into its sounds and spell it correctly
- decoding: ability to sound out a word to read it correctly
- symbol imagery: ability to visualize syllables and letters
- spelling: mastery of weekly spelling words
- dictation: ability to write sentences given by the teacher
- grammar: ability to identify nouns, verbs, adjectives, and adverbs in sentences

- mechanics: ability to use proper punctuation and capitalization
- composition: ability to compose a standard paragraph, brief book report, and thank you notes
- reading fluency: ability to read unfamiliar passages

**Rubric**

Second, create a rubric. If you adopt *The Roadmap to Literacy's* benchmarks, the rubric could look something like Table 6.5.6.

**Table 6.5.6: End-of-Year Report**

| Language Skill | Achievement | Developing | Area of Concern |
|---|---|---|---|
| **Handwriting** | | | |
| **Phonemic Awareness: Deletion** | | | |
| **Encoding** | | | |
| **Decoding** | | | |
| **Symbol Imagery** | | | |
| **Spelling** | | | |
| **Dictation** | | | |
| **Grammar** | | | |
| **Mechanics** | | | |
| **Composition** | | | |
| **Reading Fluency** | | | |

Use your formal assessments (especially those created by educational testing groups) as the basis for filling out this rubric.

**Interpreting the Rubric**

Third, give a key to interpret the rubric. For example,

- *Achieved* means that the student has met the objective.
- *Developing* means that the student is progressing but needs more practice in order to meet the benchmark.
- *Area of Concern* means that the student needs additional formal instruction and practice to meet the benchmark.

**Areas to Work on over the Summer**

Fourth, describe any *Developing* and/or *Areas of Concern* and make suggestions for how parents could help their child over the summer.

For an example see chapter 6.3 #4.

**Other Aspects of the Curriculum**

Finally, the end-of-year report should not be limited to academic skills. This rubric for language arts (and another similar one for math that you would create) would only be a part of the report. The rest would then look like a typical Waldorf report with descriptions of class activities and personalized information about how each student is doing socially, physically, artistically, etc. in a written narrative format.

See www.waldorfinspirations.com for examples of rubrics for the other aspects of the curriculum.

In summary, there are many benefits to organizing your end-of-year reports in this manner. First, the student's academic skills are reported clearly and objectively. It is easier for everyone to interpret the report because there is no ambiguity. Second, it is easier to write your end-of-year reports. Instead of worrying how to present information tactfully yet clearly, you merely check a box. You can write an expository paragraph if there is something additional to say. For most students, the rubric plus a short paragraph afterward giving additional information will be sufficient.

## Conclusion

Assessment is the GPS tool used to make sure your students are on track. Assessments enable you to determine where each student is on the road to literacy and to deduce what each student needs in order to continue the journey. A balance of assessments (informal and formal, including assessments created by educational testing groups) is the most effective way to assess. This balance will help you execute your responsibility to teach every student in your class the skills needed for language arts so that they can be ready to handle a curriculum that will include subjects. If a student is not meeting the benchmarks, consider whether remedial support is needed (see chapter 6.6).

By the end of 3rd Grade, the students should be at the advanced level of the Syllable Phase. They no longer need to learn to read but can now read to learn. They have mastered basic spelling and writing conventions and can compose main lesson book content on their own. They have a way to go before they have developed full literacy, but they are prepared for whatever 4th Grade class they should attend.

If you have any students who are not at this level, it is imperative that they get immediate remedial support. The curriculum in any 4th Grade assumes that students can read independently, and reading skills are no longer taught. Remedial support will be explored in the next chapter.

# 6.6  WORKING WITH REMEDIAL ISSUES

*By all accounts James should have had no difficulty learning to read. He spent hours looking over his favorite books, had an amazing vocabulary, and loved stories. James entered 1st Grade eager to learn to read, however, by December he had undergone a sea change. This bright, enthusiastic student had become an angry boy who was disruptive in class and who hated school, especially anything involving letters or numbers. What was going on?*

*James' teacher scheduled a conference with his parents. During the conference, his mother recalled that she had vision difficulties when she was young. The teacher and parents agreed that James' mother should take him to a vision therapist (i.e., an optometrist who specializes in vision therapies). The vision therapist assessed James and discovered that he had severe eye tracking issues: He could not focus his eyes on the page. Furthermore, he could not move his eyes along a line of print or a math problem without losing his place. It was no wonder James was angry and disruptive. He was frustrated beyond all measure.*

*The treatment prescribed was four months of daily vision exercises. At the end of this therapy, James began private reading tutoring in order to catch up to his peers. Learning to read was much easier this time around now that his eyes worked together. James mastered the alphabet and soon was reading simple decodable-texts. It took another year of dedicated effort for James to catch up with his classmates, but by the end of 3rd Grade, James was able to read any book he picked up. He loved to read.*

*Thanks to timely action on the part of James's teacher and parents, James resolved his underlying tracking weakness and got remedial reading instruction. These two interventions made it possible for James to enter 4th Grade ready to read to learn.*

This chapter will explore remedial issues. Use this chapter when the subsections in section 3 called *How to Help Struggling Students* are not adequate.

This chapter covers the following topics:

1.  Overview of Learning Problems
2.  Things to Rule Out before Beginning the Remedial Process
3.  Remediating Environmental Factors
4.  Remediating Reflexes
5.  Remediating Physical and Psychological Capacities
6.  Remediating Sensory-Cognitive Functions
7.  Remediating Literacy Instruction
8.  Waldorf Remedial Therapies: Extra Lesson, Therapeutic Eurythmy, Pedagogical Stories (healing stories), and Child Study
9.  What about Dyslexia?

# 1.   Overview of Learning Problems

When students are having difficulty learning despite your best efforts and are failing to meet the benchmarks, it is necessary to figure out if intervention is necessary and if so how best to intervene.

### Is Intervention Necessary? What about the *Dreamy Student*?

We often encounter Waldorf teachers who believe that a number of students who struggle to learn to read are *dreamy* (i.e., late bloomers) and just need extra time to catch up with their peers. While this situation can occur, it is the exception not the rule. More likely, the students have a problem with one or more reading skills and/or underlying capacities. They often try to mask these problems by becoming "transparent," acting out (like James), or taking their cues from other students. If you suspect a late reader, it is necessary first to confirm that the student is making adequate progress in basic reading skills and that there are no underlying issues (vision problems, dyslexia, etc.). This confirmation requires that you do a thorough assessment in the areas of phonemic awareness, decoding, sight words, etc. Address weaknesses that you find. Students do not outgrow weak reading skills and underlying issues; instead they just get further and further behind. If everything checks out fine then give the student until the end of 3rd Grade to develop her skills. If she still struggles, ask the parents to begin reading tutoring with a professional over the summer so that the student can do the reading work of 4th Grade with the class (see chapter 6.1 #12).

### What to Do While Initiating a Remedial Process

While you are initiating a remedial process, the student will still need to function in the classroom. Use accommodations and modifications.

**Accommodations** are slight changes to how the curriculum is taught or practiced to accommodate a challenge. They do not affect learning. For example, you might accommodate a student who needs reading glasses by providing her a book in a larger font. She is still reading the same material as the class.

**Modifications** are changes to the curriculum. They affect what is taught or when the student is expected to learn it. They undermine the purpose of the lesson. For example, you might modify the symbol imagery curriculum for a student who is unable to visualize letters by having her write the letters on a piece of paper. The lesson allows her to participate, but it no longer teaches her to work with symbol imagery. She is no longer expected to learn the same material as everyone else.

These two acceptable changes will give you the flexibility to continue to work with a student in the classroom while addressing her underling challenges.

### How Best to Intervene

While there are many things that can undermine learning, they tend to fall within three broad categories:

1. Ineffective teaching

2. Problems with student capacities

3. Environmental factors

Each one needs to be ruled out before you can conclude that a student is dreamy.

Here is the process to follow. It is important that you go in order. Document all of your findings.

1. Before you begin the remedial process, rule out two things:

    a. Problems with your literacy instruction. Make sure you have provided adequate teaching and practice and have tried to address the problem in class by using the advice given in the subsections *How to Help Struggling Students* at the end of each chapter in section 3.

    b. Problems with the student's visual and/or auditory systems or processing.

2. Then, consider the student's environment. Is something undermining the student's ability to learn?

3. Next, consider the student and her capacities and skills. As a rule of thumb, address any weaknesses in the student's capacities before you provide therapies to provide further literacy instruction.

    a. reflexes (see chapter 6.6 #4)

    b. physical and psychological capacities (see chapter 6.6 #5)

    c. sensory-cognitive functions (see chapter 6.6 #6)

    d. literacy instruction (see chapter 6.6 #7)

The only exception to this process is if you see the student has trouble rhyming and learning phonemic awareness. In this case, consider consulting a reading specialist who is trained in programs for Developmental Dyslexia (see chapter 6.6 #9).

As a teacher, you are responsible for delivering the literacy curriculum as defined by your school's curriculum and benchmarks so that each student is able to successfully make grade (and phase) level progress. However, the only set of variables that is 100% within your jurisdiction is what happens in your classroom. It is not in your purview to address serious student challenges such as issues with reflexes, physical impediments, and/or psychological capacities. However, since they affect your work, it is incumbent on you to understand them and help arrange for remediation if possible.

Fortunately, as a Waldorf teacher, you have opportunities to address weaknesses in student environment and capacities that are not always available to other teachers. In subsequent subsections, you will find an overview of how to remediate common deficits. They include the following points: background information; what you can do as a teacher; what you can do as a faculty; and outside resources.

This program will give you a starting point for planning a remedial intervention.

## 2. Things to Rule Out before Beginning the Remedial Process

There are three areas to rule out before beginning the remedial process:

1. Problems with Instruction

2. Problems with the Student's Eyes

3. Problems with the Student's Ears

## Problems with Instruction

Review your curriculum. Make sure that you are providing instruction at the student's phase and adequate practice for the student to master the curriculum. If either is inadequate, take steps to address the problem(s).

## Problems with the Student's Eyes

There are three common areas to check associated with the student's eyes:

1) Does the student need glasses?

2) Does the student need vision therapy? 3) Does the student have Irlen Syndrome? Rule out all three before beginning a remedial process.

### Need for Glasses and/or Vision Therapy

It is common for students to have difficulty learning to read because of vision problems. These problems can include need for corrective lenses and/or vision therapy.

*What You Can Do as a Teacher*: Screen the student and recommend therapies.

- Informal screening for glasses: Ask the student to read a passage off the board. (Substitute a string of letters if necessary.) Then ask the student to read a passage from a book in a standard-sized font and then one with a larger font. Note any difference in performance and any signs that the student is struggling to see the words such as squinting or holding the book up too close to her face.

- Informal screening for eye tracking: Sit in front of a student. Hold your index finger in front of her nose about 6–12 inches. Ask her to watch your finger with just her eyes. (She cannot move her head.) Slowly move your finger up/down, left/right, and diagonally. Then move your finger in a circle. Observe the child's eyes. A student should be able to follow the motion automatically without her eyes jumping around or struggling to follow your finger. End by bringing your finger to within an inch of the student's nose and observe what the eyes do. They should move together into a cross-eyed position.

If the student fails the informal screening for glasses, ask the parents to have the child screened for glasses. If the student fails the informal screening for eye tracking, ask the parents to have the child's eyes screened for vision therapy.

### Irlen Syndrome

Irlen Syndrome is a situation where a person's eyes are working fine but the brain cannot make sense of the information the eyes are sending it. As a result, a person sees distortions while looking at text. The distortions can take many forms. Letters may jiggle or move around on the page, extra spaces may open up between words or within words, or letters may develop halos of light around them. There are many other forms the distortions can take.

Irlen Syndrome makes learning to read difficult. In general, 12–14% of the population tests positive for Irlen, but the percentage jumps to 45% among students who have difficulty reading (Irlen 2010, 75 and 77). Irlen students sometimes do things to help reduce the distortions such as wear hats with brims inside to block the light, read in the dark, change the angle of the book while they read it, or even shade their eyes. They can also be the students who test fine for reading skills and reading fluency but who still struggle to finish their work. If you suspect that a student in your class has Irlen Syndrome, one possibility is to meet with the parents and request that they consult an Irlen Diagnostician. This person can diagnose Irlen Syndrome and prescribe special glasses known as *Irlen Lenses*. Irlen Lenses look like colored sunglasses. They can come in any color from brown, pink, yellow, green, purple, etc. The student wears the lenses whenever she does academic work.

See Irlen.com to find a list of professionals.

*What You Can Do as a Teacher:*

- Let the student put colored overlays (**Irlen overlays**) over the page to change the background color of the text. The right color can help the majority of students who have Irlen Syndrome. Order a set of 10 colored overlays at http://irlen.mybigcommerce.com/colored-overlays/. Use them for assessment purposes to see which color works best. Once you know the right color(s), consider buying extra overlays that students can use in the classroom or take home or ask parents to do so.

- If many students in the class have trouble (higher than 14%), check the lights in the class. Consider putting in incandescent bulbs if you are able to. If you cannot and you have florescent lights, consider buying a special cover that goes over them.

- If the first two points do not address the problem, go to chapter 6.6 #3 Cleaning up Electromagnetic Pollution.

*What You Can Do as a Faculty:* Replace the school's fluorescent light bulbs and compact fluorescent light bulbs with incandescent bulbs as fluorescent bulbs exacerbate the symptoms of Irlen Syndrome.

### Problems with the Student's Ears

Sometimes students have difficulty hearing, particularly in a classroom setting. These difficulties can stem from a mild to moderate hearing loss to a buildup of ear wax.

*What You Can Do as a Teacher:*

- Do an informal screening for hearing difficulties and refer the student as appropriate. Sit behind a student so that your backs are facing each other. Ask the student to repeat nonsense words that you say: ift, theg, oop, blay, scoofer, oncleptomy, etc. If the student struggles, repeat the experiment with the same list of words but this time facing each other where the student can see your lips. If the student does significantly better when he can see your lips, it is time to consult a professional for a hearing assessment. If the child struggles to repeat the words both ways, it may be a hearing issue or it may be dyslexia.

- Ask the parents to take the child for a hearing screening. Ask that a doctor check ear wax buildup as well.

- In the classroom, seat the child in the front row and insist that the class be perfectly quiet while you speak, especially when giving instructions. Also make sure you face the student when giving instructions or practicing exercises so she can hear better.

Note: There is some indication that chorister work can help students who have mild difficulty hearing the subtle phonemes such as /th/ in thimble and /f/ in feather (Blythe 2005, 67). If that possibility exists in your community, share with the parents.

## 3. Remediating Environmental Factors

Once you have ruled out common problems with the senses, it is time to consider a remedial program. Of the three categories that can undermine learning, the one most often overlooked is the student's environment. As it can be the sole cause of learning problems or a contributing factor, it is good to consider it first.

It is no secret that environmental factors can compromise a student's ability to learn. Students who have not eaten breakfast (or who have eaten a sugary breakfast) perform less well in school. Students whose families are experiencing stress (divorce, job loss, illness in the family, loss of a home, etc.) have a more difficult time learning than others. The reason is straightforward: if basic needs are not met, a student cannot focus on more advanced needs such as education.

## Maslow's Expanded Hierarchy of Needs

Maslow's Expanded Hierarchy of Needs provides a useful tool for identifying environmental factors that can undermine education.

Maslow is a psychologist who categorized and ranked human needs. The needs he identified are included in the left-hand column of Table 6.6.1 whereas *The Roadmap to Literacy's* descriptions of the consequences to students if the need is not met are listed in the right-hand column. The table begins with the most primary needs. Notice that unmet needs on the lower levels (1–4) are impediments to learning while unmet needs at the higher levels (5–7) can be catalysts for learning.

**Table 6.6.1: Maslow's Expanded Hierarchy of Needs and Their Effects on Education**

| Maslow's Hierarchy of Needs (Expanded) | Consequences to Students if the Need is Unmet |
|---|---|
| 1) **Biological and Physiological Needs:** air, food, water, shelter, warmth, sleep, etc. | School will not register at all because the students' bodies will demand that their basic needs be met. *Ex. Sleep-deprived students fall asleep in class.* |
| 2) **Safety Needs:** security, order, law, stability | The students' brains are hijacked. The students will focus on whatever they perceive as the danger at hand. *Ex. Students who are afraid of bullies cannot pay attention to the lesson.* |
| 3) **Love and Belongingness Needs:** friendship, trust and acceptance, affiliating, being part of a group (family and friends) | While these students will likely be able to function intellectually in the classroom, they will be unhappy and a drag on themselves and the other students in the class. *Ex. These students often whine and complain about being excluded from a game at recess.* |
| 4) **Esteem Needs:** self-esteem, achievement, mastery, independence, status, etc. | These students can function in the classroom, but they often have a chip on their shoulders that undermines their performance. *Ex. These students may cheat on their work and/or lie about their test results to make themselves look better.* |
| 5) **Cognitive Needs:** knowledge and understanding, curiosity, exploration, etc. | This is the optimum level for Students in Grades 1–3. *Ex. These students want to participate in well-planned lessons and activities.* |
| 6) **Aesthetic Needs:** appreciation and search for beauty, balance, form, etc. | Students at this level begin to transcend their education. This level pertains more to students in the upper grades because it requires mastery of basic academic and artistic skills. *Ex. Students in 6th or 7th Grade may undergo a sea change in their approach to learning. They may strive for beauty in their work, not because they want to please a teacher or parents but because the work itself pleases them.* |

| 7) **Self-Actualization Needs:** realizing personal potential, self-fulfillment, seeking personal growth and peak experiences | This level is not pertinent in the grades. It may become pertinent in high school and beyond provided that students' lower-level needs are met, they have mastered basic academic and artistic skills, and they have ample opportunity to explore their interests and passions. *Ex. In high school, Bill Gates stayed up late at night and got up early in the morning just to be able to program at a local computer center.* |
|---|---|
| 8) **Transcendence Needs:** helping others to achieve self-actualization | This level is not pertinent to students. Only a few human beings ever reach this level. *Ex. Some healers or spiritual leaders may be at this level.* |

*Source: Maslow's Hierarchy of Needs (Expanded)*
*https://simplypsychology.org/maslow.html*

Students move up or down the *Hierarchy of Needs* depending on the circumstances in their lives. Level 5, Cognitive Needs, is the level where students in Grades 1–3 can fully benefit from instruction. A student's home environment and classroom environment affect levels 1 through 4. Work together with the student's parents to remediate problems on these levels.

There are two environmental solutions to highlight:

- Simplicity Parenting
- cleaning up electromagnetic pollution

**Simplicity Parenting**

The first thing that you can do to help parents provide a home environment that is beneficial to their child is to encourage them to take up Simplicity Parenting.

Simplicity Parenting is a program by Kim John Payne, M. Ed. He has found that many students today who receive diagnoses such as Attention Deficit Disorder (ADD) are just sensitive kids who are so stressed by their environments that their quirks become illnesses. When the stress is removed (or reduced), they no longer qualify for the diagnosis. They become regular children with slight quirks.

Payne has developed a program called Simplicity Parenting that gives advice on how parents can reduce the stress in a child's life. He has targeted four areas to simplify in a child's world: 1) environment; 2) rhythm; 3) schedule; and 4) filtering out the adult world. In his book *Simplicity Parenting: Using the Extraordinary Power of Less to Raise Calmer, Happier, and More Secure Kids,* Payne walks parents through ways they can simplify if they are so inclined. He has found that up to two-thirds of children who undergo Simplicity Parenting no longer qualify for a diagnosis after completing the program (Payne 2009, 28). In other words, they no longer need medication or therapy because the environment was making them sick, and now it is not.

*What You Can Do as a Teacher:* Do a parent evening on Simplicity Parenting.

*What You Can Do as a Faculty:*

- Some Waldorf schools have set up a Simplicity Parenting support group.
- Send a faculty member to a training. See www.simplicityparenting.com.

*Outside Resources:* Contact a Simplicity Parenting Family Life Coach. See www.simplicityparenting.com.

## Cleaning up Electromagnetic Pollution

Electromagnetic pollution is another environmental factor that can interfere with learning. It is generated by modern technology including cell phones, cell towers, Wi-Fi, Smart Meters, faulty wiring, overhead power lines, etc. It can come in many forms, including dirty electricity (high voltage transients that can result when power lines are carrying too high a load, for example) and electrosmog. Even though this pollution cannot be seen, it is ubiquitous in the modern environment, and can be problematic for those sensitive to it.

In the book *Zapped: Why Your Cell Phone Shouldn't be Your Alarm Clock and 1,268 Ways to Outsmart the Hazards of Electronic Pollution*, Ann Gittleman, PhD, cites research from the French INTERPHONE Case-Control Study that found that two minutes on a cell phone can cause changes in the brain that take at least an hour to normalize (120).

In addition, in the book *EMF Freedom: Solutions for the 21st Century Pollution 3rd Edition*, Elizabeth Plourde, PhD, cites research that shows that radiation from cell phones can affect the electrical charge on the cell membrane of red blood cells, causing them to clump together and affecting their ability to carry oxygen (71–73).

Dr. Michela Glockler, M.D. and head of the Medical Section at the Goetheanum (The World Center for Waldorf education and other facets of Rudolf Steiner's work), advises against Wi-Fi in schools. She speculates that Wi-Fi is the asbestos of the 21st century. In other words, it is something universally accepted as safe that is later found to be a serious threat to health only after many people become sick (Koetzsch 2014, 27).

Although it has yet to be acknowledged as a diagnosable illness by the American Medical Association, a condition called electrohypersensitivity (EHS) is recognized by countries such as Canada, France, Norway, etc. These countries have begun treating people for EHS, or extreme sensitivity to electromagnetic pollution in any form. Because the symptoms of EHS can be severe (headaches, insomnia, digestion problems, fatigue, ear ringing, attention problems, and dizziness), it is no wonder that a student with this condition will have difficulty learning, particularly if the school and/or home contains a lot of electromagnetic pollution.

*What You Can Do as a Teacher:*

- Consult the book *Zapped: Why Your Cell Phone Shouldn't Be Your Alarm Clock and 1,268 Ways to Outsmart the Hazards of Electronic Pollution* to learn more about this subject. In particular, consult chapter nine: "Zap-Proof Your Kids." Consider sharing pertinent information at a parent evening.

- Encourage parents not to give their young children cell phones or to allow them to use theirs. A cell phone is not a toy. A child should only use a cell phone in an emergency.

- The same advice applies to tablets and other emitting devices.

- Encourage parents who have children struggling to learn to try minimizing the electromagnetic pollution in their home for one month to see if this reduction has an impact on the student's performance. This should include:

  o Using Ethernet connections for the internet instead of WI-FI or at a bare minimum turning the Wi-Fi off when the family is sleeping.

  o Keep the cell phone (and tablets and other emitting devices) far away from the student. If that is not possible, turn the cell phones to airplane mode as often as possible when around the student. A cell phone that is turned off is still radiating electromagnetic pollution because the phone is programmed to contact cell towers and antennas at all times, even when turned off. *Airplane mode* means it will not try to contact the local cell towers, which makes airplane mode safer. However, if the phone has GPS, it will still emit some radiation because airplane mode does not cover GPS.

- o Getting rid of Smart Meters at home. They generate a field of electro smog. Call the utility companies and opt out of the Smart Meter program.

- o For more information see Katie Singer's "Calming Behavior in Children with Autism and ADHD: The Electromagnetic Radiation (EMR)-Lowering Protocol" (http://www.electronicsilentspring.com/calming-behavior/).

- Reduce the electromagnetic pollution in your classroom. Turn your cell phone to airplane mode when you enter the room. Request that anyone who comes into the classroom do the same.

- Change the lightbulbs. Use old-fashioned incandescent light bulbs whenever possible.

*What You Can Do as a Faculty:*

- Encourage your school to become a cell-phone-free zone as many Waldorf schools are doing. (See Renewal volume 23 #1 Spring/Summer 2014: *Saying Good-Bye to Wi-Fi.*)

- Get rid of Wi-Fi at your school as Dr. Glockler recommends. Use Ethernet cables.

- Get rid of Smart Meters on campus. Call the utility companies and opt out of the Smart Meter program.

- Get rid of old microwave ovens. As they age, their seals become less effective and they emit radiation.

*Outside Resources:* The gold standard for cleaning up the campus is to hire a Certified Building Biology Environmental Consultant (BBEC) who is also a Certified Electromagnetic Radiation Specialist (EMRS). This person can inspect the entire campus and provide information about sources of pollution and ways to address them. Be sure to request that dirty electricity (or high frequency voltage transients) be part of the report. To find a certified professional, consult The International Institute for Bau-Biology & Ecology at http://hbelc.org/find-an-expert/environmental-consultants.

In summary, it is important to work with environmental factors. The best education in the world will not work if the students are compromised by their environment. Work with the faculty and parents to clean up the students' environment. If the environment is compromising the student, your instruction in the classroom will be compromised, regardless of how effective your lessons and delivery are.

## 4. Remediating Reflexes

The second thing to address in your remedial program is reflexes.

Reflexes, or *Early Movement Patterns* as they are sometimes referred to in Waldorf schools, are a sequence of stereotypical movements that young children progress through in their first years of life. They provide the physical foundations for capacities (both physical and psychological). There are two types of reflexes that are important for education: primitive reflexes and postural reflexes. Students need to have worked through both types of reflexes to be ready to learn. If they have problems with reflexes, it could be detrimental to their academic progress.

Primitive and postural reflexes have opposing gestures.

Primitive reflexes are movement reflexes that a baby is born with. These movements help the baby to develop its muscles and its senses. They originate from the most primitive part of the brain: the brain stem. These reflexes help keep a newborn alive and help the baby to develop its first movements outside the womb.

If a primitive reflex remains beyond the age of one, it becomes a problem. Consider the grasp reflex. Put your finger in a baby's palm, and she will grab ahold of it, sometimes with enough strength that you can lift her off the table. However, if a school-aged child retains this reflex, she will not be able adjust her grip on a pencil. Her death grip will make writing difficult until the reflex is resolved.

Primitive reflexes provide early training in a variety of capacities. A baby's first eye tracking is related to a reflex that causes the baby to move its hands across its field of vision. A baby develops the muscles necessary to hold its head up, crawl, and creep thanks to primitive reflexes. Primitive reflexes help the baby develop its senses to a certain point, but if they are not inhibited, they affect the development of a child's capacities.

During a baby's first months, primitive reflexes serve a vital function. But as the child approaches one year, these reflexes should be inhibited and a new set of reflexes should turn on (i.e., the postural reflexes). However, if the child never worked through them during her first year of life, they can still be present.

The gesture of the postural reflexes is to turn on and to stay on for a person's entire life. Postural reflexes support conscious movement. They help coordinate the muscle tension necessary to sit, stand, skip, play sports, etc. It is not necessary to think about the muscle tension needed to do conscious movement thanks to these reflexes.

Postural reflexes should be completely developed by the age of three and a half years. If they are not fully developed, a child will struggle to develop capacities (both physical and psychological).

Researchers at the Institute for Neuro-Physiological Psychology (INPP) such as Sally Goddard Blythe discuss a correlation between retained primitive reflexes and underdeveloped postural reflexes and specific learning difficulties such as dyslexia. They have named the condition Neuro-Developmental Delay (NDD). In Blythe's book *Attention, Balance and Coordination*, NDD is defined as "(1) the continued presence of a cluster of aberrant *primitive* reflexes above the age of one year, and (2) absent or underdeveloped *postural reflexes* above six months of age, and the age of three and a half years" (Blythe 2009, 4). This reveals an immaturity in the functioning of the central nervous system and affects posture, balance, and motor skills. Many learning difficulties including dyslexia have responded positively to treatment of NDD. Reflex problems are the root cause of some students' difficulties in learning to read and write. Recall that 20–30% of students have difficulty recognizing the alphabetic principle (see chapter 1.2 #6). It seems reasonable to assume that some of the students in the bottom group would have an easier time learning if this immaturity were addressed.

Typical signs of reflex problems in the classroom include students who have difficulty sitting at their desks and holding a pencil correctly. You will see these students contorting into various stereotypical positions such as kneeling on their chairs or lying on their desks to write to accommodate retained reflexes. You will also see these students holding their pencils in stereotypical awkward positions to accommodate a retained reflex in the hand. The students are not choosing to engage in these odd behaviors but are accommodating reflex issues. They would like to be able to sit upright and hold a pencil properly, but their bodies will not let them.

Environmental factors can cause reflex issues. Primitive reflexes re-emerge when a person is threatened, and the threat can be physical or psychological. In addition, there is research which indicates that electromagnetic pollution can trigger the re-emergence of reflexes in some individuals (Parsons 2008). In these cases the individuals may not be aware of the pollution, but the cells and tissues of their bodies are being affected by it, and electromagnetic pollution can be registered as a threat.

It is possible to work with reflexes in the classroom. A good program is the INPP School Intervention Program.

**Reflex Programs for Schools**

Sally Goddard Blythe and the INPP have two excellent resources that help teachers address reflexes. The book *Assessing Neuromotor Readiness for Learning: The INPP Developmental Screening Test and School Intervention Programme* by Sally Goddard Blythe contains both an assessment as well as a program. The exercises are to be done over the course of the school year for 15 minutes each day. A series of exercises designed to remediate reflex problems in class can be also be found in *The Well Balanced Child: Movement and Early Learning* by Sally Goddard Blythe 2005 edition (Blythe 2005, 205–233). The exercises are called *Early Morning by the Pond*, a story that contains an image and a description of each exercise. They could easily be worked in to the school day.

Note: There are also hand exercises you can do to remediate reflexes in the hand. See www.waldorfinspirations.com for a demonstration.

*What You Can Do as a Teacher:*

- Take up exercises to work reflexes as appropriate.
- Clean up electromagnetic pollution in the classroom.

*What You Can Do as a Faculty:*

- Encourage the early childhood and kindergarten teachers at the school to take up this work as reflex issues should be completely resolved before a student enters 1st Grade. There are many ways they can do this.
    - o They can teach parents to give newborns and toddler appropriate movement opportunities so the children can work through the reflexes appropriately on their own.
    - o Innovative early childhood instructors are offering workshops and classes that include information on working with reflexes in class so early childhood teachers can work with those children who did not work through their reflexes.
    - o In addition, AWSNA has a wonderful publication called *Developing the Observing Eye: Teacher Observation and Assessment in Early Childhood Education* by Cynthia Murphy-Lang. It has more information on the subject and has beautiful and developmentally appropriate assessments early childhood teachers can do that include reflexes.
    - o Finally, Sally Goddard Blythe's "Early Morning by the Pond" exercises may prove useful (Blythe 2005, 205–233).
- Clean up the electromagnetic pollution in the school.

*Outside Resources:* When reflex issues are quite pronounced and/or are not responding to intervention, it is important to refer students to professionals who can work with them. Sometimes Extra Lesson practitioners have outside training in reflex remediation. Some Occupational Therapists do as well. Research to see who in your community offers this work.

Note: The series of exercises known as *zoo exercises* are not recommended for reflex remediation as they are not presented in a developmental sequence. They are, however, excellent activities for transitional IMA's (see #5 below).

## 5.   Remediating Physical and Psychological Capacities

The third thing to address in your remedial program is physical and psychological capacities. They include movement, psychological functioning, and the senses.

As the child is mastering her reflexes, she simultaneously begins to develop physical and psychological capacities. After the reflex work is finished at age three and a half, the child continues to develop these capacities in the following areas:

1. She is able to perform more difficult, coordinated movements like skipping or swinging a golf club.

2. She begins to strengthen her ability to pay attention and developing her imagination.

3. She matures in her understanding and utilization of the information gained from her senses.

4. She is able to cross the midline freely and develop dominance.

The full flowering of these physical and psychological capacities depends on the maturation of the brain's two hemispheres and the corpus callosum, the connection between the two hemispheres. The brain makes these connections through healthy play. Opportunity for movement is critical for working through primitive reflexes and it remains critical for the development of physical and psychological capacities. As the child plays, she develops the capacities necessary for future academic work. When the child moves freely and interacts with the environment, the child's senses and imagination continue to develop in a healthy way. This exploration helps the sensory-cognitive functions to begin to develop. Play rather than early academics is the appropriate work for developing the brain. This is another reason why Waldorf early childhood education has such an emphasis on play.

In addition, the full flowering of physical and psychological capacities depends on a healthy environment and reflex development (see chapter 6.6 #3 and #4).

### Movement: Developing Physical Capacities

There are many excellent movement-based therapies that you can incorporate into your lessons. In addition to providing therapy, they can also serve as Integrated Movement Activity (IMA) after students have been sitting for too long. Here are four possibilities.

**Brain Gym** consists of a series of simple movements you can use to enhance whole-brain learning. These exercises were designed to be paired with academic skills. They make learning easier. See *Brain Gym: Teacher's Edition Revised* by Paul and Gail Dennison for more information.

**Take Time** includes movement exercises for difficulties in speaking, reading, writing, and spelling. These exercises are sometimes referred to as *Move in Time*. The program include a series of eight specific exercises using a bean bag. Plan to teach the exercises outside of main lesson and then use them as transition activities in main lesson. See the book *Take Time: Movement Exercises for Parents, Teachers, and Therapists of Children with Difficulties in Speaking, Reading, Writing, and Spelling* by Mary Nash-Wortham and Jean Hunt for more information.

**Bal-A-Vix-X** is a series of rhythmic balance, auditory, and vision exercises for brain and body integration invented by Bill Hubert. In essence they are similar to Take Time exercises but they include much more challenging moves that include both sand bag exercises and ball exercises that can be done with a racquetball. They include solo exercises and partner exercises. Plan on teaching the bulk of these exercises outside of main lesson and using just the sand bag exercises as an IMA. See http://www.bal-a-vis-x.com/ for more information.

**Zoo exercises** are a series of movement exercises included in some Waldorf teacher training programs. They feature ways to move like various animal, such as walking like a crab. They are good to use as IMAs during transitions if you are familiar with them.

### Remediating Psychological Issues

It is not advisable to work with psychological problems. If you suspect a psychological problem, request the parents to schedule an appointment with a therapist. Ask your school for a list of recommendations for professionals in the community.

If the problem is one of normal childhood issues such as jealousy or peer relationships, consider using pedagogical or healing stories (see chapter 6.6 #8).

### Remediating Senses/Sensory Integration Difficulties

Some students suffer from difficulties processing information from their senses.

In the book *Sensory Integration and the Child: Understanding Hidden Sensory Challenges*, Ayres states:

> Sensory integration is the organization of sensations for use. Our senses give us information about the physical conditions of our body and the environment around us….Countless bits of sensory information enter our brain at every moment, not only from our eyes and ears but from every place in our body….The brain must organize all of these sensations if a person is to move and learn and behave in a productive manner….When sensations flow in a well-organized or integrated manner, the brain can use those sensations to form perceptions, behaviors, and learning (Ayres 2005, 5).

In some children, sensory integration is compromised. The condition is referred to as *sensory integrative dysfunction* or *sensory integrative disorder*. Ayres describes this condition as a "traffic jam" in the brain. Good sensory processing enables all of the information from the sense to flow easily and smoothly to the correct destination or destinations in the brain. When there is a disorder, some parts of the brain do not get the information they need to do their jobs. Learning and behavioral challenges are the result (Ayres 47–49).

It is not advisable to work with sensory problems or sensory integration problems directly in the classroom. If you suspect a problem, consult a professional. Ask you school for a list of recommendations for professionals in the community.

It is fine to work with problems with the senses indirectly, as part of movement activities in the classroom such as through Bal-A-Vis-X exercises. Do not expect this work to take the place of therapy. It can augment it, however.

Note: Keep in mind that sensory problems can include the need for glasses and hearing aids (see chapter 6.6 #2). Waldorf also recognizes other senses such as balance and proprioception. Therapeutic Eurythmy and Extra Lesson are possible referrals (see chapter 6.6 #8).

*What You Can Do as a Teacher:*

- Incorporate movement exercises into your classroom. Teach movement exercises outside of main lesson and then incorporate them into main lesson as IMAs during transitions.
- If you see signs of difficulty with the senses or with psychological issues, recommend to the student's parents that they contact a professional for a full assessment.

*What You Can Do as a Faculty:*

- Provide parent evenings that educate parents on the importance of play in the preschool years.
- Send members of the faculty for additional training in movement therapies. Both Brain Gym and Bal-A-Vis-X offer trainings.

*Outside Resources:* Many professionals are trained in movement therapies. See who is available in your community. In addition you can consult Therapeutic Eurythmists and Extra Lesson practitioners (see chapter 6.6 #8).

## 6. Remediating Sensory-Cognitive Functions

Sensory cognitive functions are the fourth thing to consider in your remedial program. They emerge as an aspect of physical and psychological capacities in preschool and kindergarten, but they require formal instruction to develop fully.

There are three sensory-cognitive functions: 1) phonemic awareness; 2) symbol imagery; and 3) concept imagery. These functions are the foundations for reading skills. Phonemic awareness supports decoding/encoding skills. Symbol imagery supports sight words. Concept imagery supports using the context (see chapter 1.6 #2–4).

However, if other areas of physical and psychological capacities are insufficiently developed, remediation work addressing sensory-cognitive functions can be compromised. For example, students who have difficulty paying attention have difficulty developing their sensory-cognitive functions.

Lindamood-Bell Learning Processes® offers three programs designed to remediate weaknesses in sensory-cognitive functions. They are:

- *Lindamood Phoneme Sequencing (LiPS)* ® *for Phonemic Awareness*
- *Seeing Stars® for Symbol Imagery*
- *Visualizing and Verbalizing® Program for Cognitive Development, Comprehension, and Thinking for Concept Imagery*

**Lindamood Phoneme Sequencing (LiPS)** ®

*Lindamood Phoneme Sequencing* (LiPS) is considered the gold standard for addressing problems with phonemic awareness. Students who struggle with phonemic awareness learn to use the shape of their mouths while saying a phoneme as a way to jump start phonemic awareness. To be successful with this program, a student should have average to above average language comprehension and attention as the program involves a lot of Socratic dialogue and discovery. The program segues into literacy instruction, including phonics rules and sight words.

**Seeing Stars®: Symbol Imagery for Phonological and Orthographic Processing in Reading and Spelling**

*Seeing Stars®: Symbol Imagery for Phonological and Orthographic Processing in Reading and Spelling* is another Lindamood-Bell program. It teaches symbol imagery or mental picturing in 2D. As symbol imagery and phonemic awareness frequently develop hand in hand, this program uses symbol imagery as a way to develop phonemic awareness. If a student has rudimentary symbol imagery skills, this program can improve them immensely; however, for the small subset of students who cannot visualize letters at all, experience suggests that this program will not be able to teach them to do so. It works best for students who have weak symbol imagery and some phonemic awareness. It can remediate both problems at the same time. It also can improve spelling dramatically.

**Visualizing and Verbalizing® Program for Cognitive Development, Comprehension, and Thinking for Concept Imagery**

*Visualizing and Verbalizing®* is the third Lindamood-Bell program. It teaches students concept imagery, or mental picturing in 3D, and helps them use this function to understand spoken and written language. This program is critical for Waldorf students who cannot follow directions or understand stories. Since Waldorf teachers rely heavily on oral presentation instead of text books, students must develop average to above-average skills in concept imagery. If you have enough students to justify forming a group, you can purchase workbooks online and use them with these students.

Note: It also goes by the name *Visualizing and Verbalizing® for Language Comprehension and Thinking*.

*What You Can Do as a Teacher:*

Working with sensory-cognitive functions should already be part of your literacy program. (See the pertinent chapters in section 3.)

- Consider using part of your reading group time to provide extra instruction and practice to students who struggle. Schedule extra group work for these students.

*What You Can Do as a Faculty:*

- Encourage the early childhood teachers to study the types of phonemic awareness so they can work with it consciously in their programs. Children who are four years old begin to play with rhyming words. Kindergarten students can do phonemic awareness games that do not include letters. Meeting the students with appropriate activities to help foster phonemic awareness would help rising 1st Grade students be ready for academic work (see chapter 3.3 #2).
- Send one or more members of the faculty for training in Lindamood-Bell programs. *Seeing Stars®* is recommended for symbol imagery and *Visualizing and Verbalizing®* for concept imagery. (LiPS® works better in a one-on-one setting rather than in the classroom and is harder to learn.)

*Outside Resources:* If a student has difficulty developing a particular sensory-cognitive function despite the extra work you do in class, you can refer the student to a Lindamood-Bell® Learning Center or find a tutor trained in the program to do one-on-one work with the student. Reading specialists and speech and language therapists often have training in Lindamood-Bell programs. Make sure you have addressed all environmental issues, reflex issues, and physical and psychological capacities prior to starting this work.

## 7. Remediating Literacy Instruction

The fifth and final thing to consider in your remedial program is literacy instruction.

Once you have remediated everything else, it is usually necessary to return to literacy instruction. Learning literacy skills is not part of human development. If a student had challenges that prevented her from learning the first time, she often needs to go back and relearn the information once the challenge is gone.

*What You Can Do as a Teacher:* If there are sufficient students at this level, incorporate this work into a reading group. If the student is too far behind and/or needs one-on-one support, ask that the parents hire a reading tutor.

*What You Can Do as a Faculty:*

- Start a reading program for students who need extra support. (A care group or a committee can get this program going.) See chapter 6.6 #8 for more information.
- *Outside Resources:* Look for tutors trained in reputable literacy programs such as Orton Gillingham (Barton) or the Lindamood-Bell programs. (Check out area reading clinics or private tutors using these programs in your community. Note: Often tutors are affiliated with a particular Waldorf school.)

## 8. Waldorf Remedial Therapies: Extra Lesson, Therapeutic Eurythmy, Pedagogical Stories (Healing Stories), and Child Study

Before arranging for support outside of the classroom for a specific student, it is recommended that a teacher first consult her school's **care group.**

The Waldorf version of remedial support is called a care group. It is a group of teachers who coordinate remedial work and/or services for students in the school who need it. If your school has a care group, consult them to see what kinds of therapies are available through the school. There are four therapies that are Waldorf-specific that they may recommend: Extra Lesson, Therapeutic Eurythmy, child study, and pedagogical stories.

If your school doesn't have a care group, speak with your mentor and any remedial practitioners your school engages for advice on when and if to employ these therapies (especially the first three).

### Extra Lesson

Extra Lesson is a therapeutic approach to addressing learning difficulties. It was developed in the 1940s by Waldorf educator Audrey McAllen. It includes various exercises such as movement exercises, speech exercises, form drawing, bean bag exercises, painting exercises, etc. to address imbalances that can undermine learning. (See http://www.healingeducation.org/about-ahe.html for more information.)

### Therapeutic Eurythmy

Therapeutic Eurythmy is a therapy to address developmental and learning challenges along with other conditions. It is based on modified artistic eurythmy movements (see 2.1 #12). Therapeutic Eurythmy is prescribed by an Anthroposophical Doctor. It must be done by a trained Therapeutic Eurythmist.

### Child Study

Another way to help a student is through child study. Child study occurs during a segment of the faculty meeting which is dedicated to focusing on one particular student who is struggling. The teacher presents a brief physical description and biography of the student, shares examples of the student's class work (academic and artistic), presents a picture of the student in the classroom and with peers, and describes any areas of concern. The faculty then uses an agreed upon process to offer ideas for support of the student, teacher, and the student's parents. (For more information on child study see Christof Wiechert's book: *Solving the Riddle of the Child: the Art of the Child Study*)

### Pedagogical Stories (healing stories)

Employing this particular remedy does not require outside consultation. These stories can be created in advance or on the spot by the teacher to address whole class, group, or individual student issues (see 2.1 #5).

*What You Can Do as a Teacher:*

- Incorporate healing/pedagogical stories into your school day on an as-need basis
- Use Perrow's book *Healing Stories for Challenging Behaviour*
- Meet with the student's parents to learn more about the student and brainstorm ideas for supporting the student. (If possible, visit the child's home so that you can have a better idea of the home environment.)

*What You Can Do as a Faculty:*

- Undertake a Child Study of the student or begin this practice if it is not already established.
- Take steps to get a Therapeutic Eurythmy program and/or an Extra Lesson program established at your school.
- Conduct research on these therapies. Anthroposophy offers a picture of the human being that could be used to add on to the remedial model articulated in *The Roadmap to Literacy*. With this information, teachers would be in a better position to be able to recommend therapies and assess their efficacy.

*Outside Resources:* Therapeutic Eurythmists and Extra Lesson practitioners are available at many Waldorf schools.

## 9. What about Dyslexia?

Dyslexia is a tricky concept. It has had many different definitions, and the definition used affects the options for remediation. In this subsection you will find information about three of the most common definitions and their uses and liabilities.

### Reversals

In popular culture, dyslexia means the individual reverses a letter (or numeral) when encoding or decoding.

Reversals are a symptom of dyslexia. Common reversals include: the letters *b* and *d*, *p* and *q*, as well as the letters *f* and *t*. (Note how the letter reversals can occur around left/right and/or above/below.) Up until the age of eight, the occasional reversal or two is not considered a problem. The eyes are still maturing. After age eight, reversals are a cause for concern as are large numbers of reversals prior to age eight.

Experts have attributed these reversals to many different sources and have come up with remedial programs to address the sources identified. Some students have benefited from some of these programs; other students have not.

Conclusion: There is probably more than one underlying cause for reversals. Some of these programs may prove beneficial for some students. Vision therapy and Irlen overlays/lenses do help some students who see reversals. Other approaches may yield similar benefits. More research is needed to determine best practices for letter reversals and to determine the underlying cause(s).

### Failure to Learn to Read despite Adequate Intelligence

In 1968, the World Federation of Neurology defined dyslexia as "a disorder in children who, despite conventional classroom experience, fail to attain the language skills of reading, writing and spelling commensurate with their intellectual abilities" (Blythe 2009, 366).

While this definition is descriptive, it is not prescriptive. It does not offer any help in determining how to remediate the disorder of dyslexia. The cause of the failure to attain language skills could be just about anything.

## Phonological/Phonemic Awareness Malfunction

Today Developmental Dyslexia is defined as a Phonological weakness that impairs reading at the level of decoding the single word, initially accurately and later fluently (Shaywitz 2003, 140).

Under this definition, dyslexia is a weakness in phonemic awareness (or phonological awareness) that snowballs. In other words, weak phonemic awareness leads to weak decoding, which in turn leads to weak fluency. Remediation can be found in special reading programs designed to target phonemic awareness and phonics rules such as Orton Gillingham programs and Lindamood-Bell programs.

## Our Take

Given that there are three different definitions, what exactly is dyslexia and how do you work with it?

The true dyslexic is someone with Developmental Dyslexia (i.e., someone whose brain is not wired in such a way to support the development of phonological processing). However, this information is of limited usefulness when determining remediation.

The cause of Developmental Dyslexia is unknown. Hereditary factors and/or environmental factors can play a role. Neuro-Developmental Delay (NDD) is a possible candidate (see chapter 6.6 #4).

The symptoms of Developmental Dyslexia appear in pre-school students. One red flag is in rhyming. Children who are four years old frequently begin to rhyme words, as do most kindergartners. Not the developmental dyslexic. Before learning letters, a student with developmental dyslexia struggles with rhyming words. Consequently, this student experiences major difficulties at the beginning of formal reading instruction because phonological and phonemic awareness do not come easily.

These phonemic awareness difficulties then impact a student's ability to learn to break down words into sounds and rebuild them again using the *letter to sound decoding route*, and, in a domino effect, the student does not access the *lexical route* (i.e., the region of the brain that learns to recognize all words instantaneously (see chapter 1.2 #2)). Thus, the student never reaches fluency but continues to sub-vocalize sounds far too long, look at words as if they were pictures, and/or try to guess at words from the illustrations, context, or the first letter. This initial weakness predisposes the dyslexic student to getting stuck in the Emergent Phase or the Phonemic Awareness Phase.

Students with severe Developmental Dyslexia need special instruction and practice to develop phonological and phonemic awareness at the very beginning of their education. It is good to screen them out and provide this instruction before their small weakness snowballs into a bigger problem.

The key to helping a student with Developmental Dyslexia is two-pronged: first, intensive work is needed to build phonemic awareness followed by intensive, structured, daily phonics teaching. Research suggests that a student with Developmental Dyslexia should begin this instruction as soon as possible. There are two reasons. The brain has its own timeline for development. Prior to age six, it is easy for the brain to form neural links for language. Furthermore, from the ages of five to ten there is a pruning process that erases neural cells in the brain that are not used often or not connected (Hempenstall 2006, 18). When students learn to read, they create the *letter to sound decoding route* and the *lexical route* in their brains (see chapter 1.2 #2). If those two pathways are not well myelinated, they may be further compromised during the pruning process. The more practice a student has, the less likely these important pathways will be pruned.

If the Developmental Dyslexia prevents the student from developing the ability to rhyme at age four, the student is already behind the other students before entering 1st Grade. The student should be given the tools to catch up as soon as possible.

**Warning**

Even though Developmental Dyslexia is certainly something that should be considered when a student is showing signs that would lead to that diagnosis, use caution that you not label all reading problems as Developmental Dyslexia or even dyslexia. There are many sources of reading problems, all of which require different forms of remediation. Dyslexia is only one thing that can undermine the acquisition of language skills.

In some instances, a weakness in phonological processing is the root cause of dyslexia and in other instances it is the result of some other problem. Any factor—environmental, instructional, or weakness in student capacities, including but not limited to Developmental Dyslexia—can prevent a student from completing the development of Phonological processing. While the student will need more instruction in phonological processing, she might also need additional therapy and/or environmental modifications to address whatever caused her not to learn in the first place.

Consider Irlen Syndrome. 12–14% of all students have Irlen Syndrome, but that number rises to 45% in students who have difficulty reading.. Having Irlen Syndrome predisposes a student to getting stuck in an early phase (i.e., Emergent or Phonemic Awareness Phase). Because these students have trouble looking at the white page, they will be less likely to get the practice needed to develop phonological processing. They have the defining symptom of Developmental Dyslexia (i.e., weak phonological processing). However, this weakness is a result of their underlying problem, not its cause. Yes, they will need remediation in phonological processing, but as long as the Irlen Syndrome is not addressed, they will still fail to attain the language skills of reading, writing, and spelling commensurate with their intellectual abilities and will still be dyslexic for all practical purposes.

Not all problems with phonological processing stem from Developmental Dyslexia. It is important to determine the cause(s) of the problem before determining the remediation.

*What You Can Do as a Teacher:*

- Observe your students carefully and offer remediation to help any weaknesses observed. Use the advice in this chapter as a starting point and add to it.

- If you see that a 1st Grade student struggles with rhyming and does not improve with practice, the student may have Developmental Dyslexia. Recommend that this student begin therapy to help develop phonological processing.

*What You Can Do as a Faculty*: Discuss early assessment and intervention as a faculty if there are indications that a kindergarten student may have Developmental Dyslexia. (Difficulty with rhyming words and a history of dyslexia in the family are both red flags.) When the student is quite young, the brain is more plastic. Each year this intervention is delayed makes it harder for the dyslexic student to learn to read.

*Outside Resources*: If a student has Developmental Dyslexia, the student will likely need more instruction and practice than can be provided in class. There are two recommended approaches:

- Lindamood-Bell/LiPS®: If the student has severe difficulty with phonemic awareness, recommend that the student do the Lindamood-Bell program *Lindamood Phoneme Sequencing® Program for Reading, Spelling, and Speech* (Lindamood Phoneme Sequencing or LiPS®). It is the gold standard for phonemic awareness problems. It teaches students to use the shape of their mouth to connect to the phonemes. It does require that students have good language comprehension.

- Orton Gillingham: If the student needs more instruction in decoding skills, Orton Gillingham programs are an excellent way to provide it. There are a number of different programs. One that is currently popular is The Barton Reading and Spelling System. It teaches decoding systematically from the middle of the Phonemic Awareness Phase to the end of the Latin/Greek Phase. This program is excellent for remediating decoding issues for the true dyslexic student as it is quite systematic and the dyslexic student needs additional instruction and practice. It does require that students have basic phonemic awareness skills to handle CVC words. If they do not, they need to begin with LiPS.

## 10. Case Studies

Here are some case studies that you might find of interest:

### Lindamood Phoneme Sequencing® Program for Reading, Spelling, and Speech (LiPS®)

At a Lindamood-Bell® Learning Center, a public-school kindergarten student from a dyslexic family began instruction before she learned to read. Every member of her family had struggled to learn to read, and this little girl had all of the symptoms of dyslexia, including difficulty with rhyming. Her family was determined that their youngest member would not have to struggle as they had so she began her treatment for dyslexia before she even started to learn reading.

With special training four hours a day over a period of weeks, the girl was able to develop full phonemic awareness. Her brain was still highly plastic and she was able to overcome the underlying familial weakness in phonemic awareness through intensive, specialized training. When she completed the program, she was at an advanced 1st Grade level in reading and spelling skills. Thanks to early intervention, she never knew she was dyslexic.

### Therapeutic Eurythmy

A middle school student had dysgraphia, a condition that made it difficult for him to use a pen or pencil to write. It was so severe that his mother had taken him out of school and had been homeschooling him for years. He dictated all of his schoolwork to her. The arrangement worked well initially, but it was becoming more onerous with each school year. The boy's workload increased, and his mother had other children who needed her attention.

The student began Therapeutic Eurythmy to address the dysgraphia. One day, his mother was taking dictation for an essay when she was interrupted by a routine household emergency. She came back a few minutes later to find her son busily writing the rest of the essay himself. He looked up and said, "I couldn't wait for you any longer." Dysgraphia resolved, he was able to return to the classroom.

### Visualizing and Verbalizing®

Elizabeth, the new student in Janet Langley's 4th grade class, was able to read well beyond a 4th Grade level; however, Janet noticed that she never raised her hand during reading discussions. This was puzzling since she was quite active in reviews of the stories she told the class during main lesson. After verifying with the student's parents that she was reading every day as requested, Janet began to explore further.

When asked if she enjoyed reading, Elizabeth replied that she did not because she really did not get what the books were about. She said she enjoyed hearing stories and writing stories, but not reading them.

It was around this time that Janet learned about the *Visualizing and Verbalizing®* program offered by Lindamood-Bell. At Janet's request Elizabeth's mother checked into it further and arranged for her daughter to be assessed by a learning specialist. The assessment revealed that even though Elizabeth could decode at a 7th Grade level, she could only comprehend 2nd Grade level text. No wonder Elizabeth did not enjoy reading—none of it made any sense to her because she was unable to create mental pictures of the stories she was reading.

After working with this specialist and the *Visualizing and Verbalizing®* program over the summer, Elizabeth returned to 5th Grade a very different reader. She could now decode at an 8th Grade level and comprehend at a 7th Grade level. As her capacity for concept imagery improved, so did her enjoyment of reading.

Over the years, Elizabeth continued to read. In fact, she went on to get her Master's Degree in Education and is now teaching.

### Extra Lesson

Eleven-year-old Sam, a 4th Grader, had struggled to read for years. Despite all of his teacher's best efforts to tutor him, his decoding skills were still in the Phonemic Awareness Phase. At that time a Waldorf trained remedial or Extra Lesson specialist moved into the area. She began to do a weekly exercise with him called *the Right Angled Triangle*. Within three months Sam was reading at a 5th Grade level. In fact his life had changed so much that he came in one morning with circles under his eyes complaining to his teacher, "Mrs. Langley, the one thing you didn't warn me about learning to read is that you can't stop!" As it turns out he had become so engrossed in the book he had been reading that his mother found him still up at 10 pm with the light on, nose buried in his book.

### Pedagogical (healing) Stories

Jennifer Militzer-Kopperl was working with a student who had behavioral challenges. Her co-workers had the same challenges working with him. The boy needed help, but how could anyone teach him? Jennifer was desperate. She did not have any Waldorf training at the time, but she hit upon an idea to help both of them work together: creating books about him.

Jennifer wrote a series of simple phonics books about the boy to use in place of the regular phonics books they read together during their sessions. These stories changed the tenor of the lessons. The boy used to resist doing reading exercises to the point that he had to be taught in a separate room because he disturbed the other students. However, when the lesson began with a story about him, he settled down. Even better, he took the books home to read to his parents and grandparents. The experience of sharing stories together that were made just for him was profoundly healing for both of them.

### Environmental Case Study: Cleaning up Dirty Electricity, One Form of Electromagnetic Pollution

The following case study comes from the book *Dirty Electricity: Electrification and the Diseases of Civilization 2nd Edition* by Samuel Milham, MD, MPH. Milham is a physician-epidemiologist who specializes in public health with a particular emphasis in the health risks associated with electromagnetic fields.

A school in California was the source of a cancer cluster among faculty. Milham was investigating the school to determine the cause. The school had numerous challenges, including florescent lighting, a cell tower adjacent to campus, and dirty electricity, a form of electromagnetic pollution that occurs when wires are carrying too high of a load. It was noted that the 4th Grade teacher complained that her students were hyperactive and unteachable.

Milham measured the 4th Grade classroom for dirty electricity. A safe reading is less than 50 Graham/Stetzer units. The 4th Grade classroom measured 5,000 Graham/Stetzer units.

Milham provided a simple environmental solution to address the dirty electricity (Stetzerizer filters). The dirty electricity levels dropped back to acceptable levels. Interestingly enough, there was a concomitant change in the students' behavior. The 4th Grade class calmed down and could focus.

The teacher was curious. Were the filters responsible for this change? She unplugged them. Within 30–45 minutes, the students returned to their old ways: hyperactive and distracted. She re-plugged the filters back in. Sure enough, within 30–45 minutes, the students calmed down and focused again. Every time she removed the filters, the same thing happened. Removing the dirty electricity from the environment had a profound effect on the students' ability to learn (Milham 2012, 80).

## 11. What to Do if All Else Fails

Sometimes a student has a problem that defies your ability to help. There are three additional alternatives that could offer insights and/or next steps: IEP, private psycho-educational assessment, or another educational program.

### Individualized Education Program (IEP)

An IEP is an individualized education program. It is used in public schools for students who cannot manage the regular curriculum.

School districts have to determine which students are eligible for an IEP. One method they use is to look for a significant discrepancy between academic achievement and academic potential. This discrepancy usually indicates a learning problem. The school district uses various diagnostic assessments, including IQ testing, to determine eligibility for an IEP, and students who are eligible receive additional services such as remedial education or occupational therapy.

While most Waldorf students are eligible for a free IEP assessment from their local public school, this step should not be undertaken lightly. Diagnostic assessments are long and arduous for the student and represent a considerable investment in time and money for the public school. Only refer a student for IEP/ Diagnostic Assessments if all of the following conditions have been met:

- You suspect a student has a learning challenge.
- You have documented multiple unsuccessful attempts to address it in class.
- You have spoken to the parents and they are open to pursuing the options recommended by the public school's professionals.

You will need to provide information about the student to the school district (usually in questionnaire form) prior to the diagnostic assessment to help pinpoint the possible cause(s) of the student's learning challenges.

### Private Psycho-Educational Assessment

You can request that parents do a private psycho-educational assessment through an educational psychologist. This route is usually quite expensive, but it can be worth it if you suspect a learning problem and the parents do not want to go through an IEP.

### Different School

If all else fails, consider looking for a different school for a student. (Note: This solution may only apply to private Waldorf schools.)

Waldorf education is often referred to as a healing education, and if done well, most students will thrive in its environment. However, in some cases your class and school cannot provide a student with the support system she needs to address her learning challenges. In these cases, you must communicate the problem clearly to the parents and suggest that they investigate the possibility that their child may benefit from a different educational program. Most public schools have learning specialists on staff and their programs should be investigated. If there are alternative private schools in the area that you think might be a solution, give parents that information as well. It will not serve the student, her parents, your class, or you to carry a student whose needs you and your school are unable to meet.

## Conclusion

Learning to read, write, and spell is hard work. It is made harder if there are underlying challenges. When they are present, get your students the help they need in a timely manner. Taking a wait-and-see approach can harm those students who have developmental dyslexia or a deficit in capacities that prevents them from accessing the curriculum.

When it comes to remediation, act as soon as you suspect there is a problem. Try different strategies in the classroom and document your results. If they fail, determine a plan for remediation using the information in this chapter. If it fails, take the problem to someone who can offer further advice.

Giving struggling students extra time to learn to read should be the exception rather than the rule, and it should only apply if you have checked your instruction, the environment, and determined there is no need for a remedial program. Literacy skills build upon each other. To wait without doing due diligence is to allow a student to get even further behind and to gamble it will all come out right at the end.

The advice in this chapter provides a structure for planning a successful remedial intervention. Do not be afraid to use it. Many students have remedial needs that go unaddressed. Those needs hold the students back, and they compound annually as the workload and demands of the classroom increase. They do not go away when the students leave school but continue to hold them back. Every student you help has the potential to go forth in the world, ascend Maslow's *Hierarchy of Needs*, and participate fully in life. Providing support to those students in need is one of the deepest joys of teaching.

# 6.7  FINAL THOUGHTS

We authors have taken language arts instruction in Waldorf Grades 1–3 as far as we can.

We have presented you with a basic understanding of how literacy skills develop and how to teach them in light of English's challenges. We have presented the five phases of language arts development and have given you information so that you can create an artistic and effective curriculum to move your students through these phases.

This book covers a monumental amount of information and took years to write. However, we guarantee that there is room for improvement. Moreover, the issues students face change over time. It will be necessary to keep growing, keep changing, keep questioning, and most importantly, keep exploring. Do not let anything in this book become a new Sacred Nothing. We are not the authority in your classroom; you are. We trust that you, the teacher, will imbue the ideas in *The Roadmap to Literacy* with your own creativity. By bringing your unique talents and gifts to this curriculum and molding it to meet your particular class, you will enliven what are now just words on a page. That process is the *art of teaching*.

It is up to you to apply this information and improve upon it. As you work, share your observations and thoughts with others. If we teachers work together, we can improve language arts instruction in our schools.

At this moment, we conclude the book, and you step forward. Good luck!

Janet Langley and Jennifer Militzer-Kopperl

# APPENDICES AND BIBLIOGRAPHY

# APPENDIX 1A:  BLOCK PLAN TEMPLATE FOR 1st GRADE MAIN LESSON BLOCK 1

|  | **Monday** | **Tuesday** | **Wednesday** | **Thursday** | **Friday** |
|---|---|---|---|---|---|
| **Opening 12–15 min.** | Song<br>Attendance<br>Riddle, Nature Observation, and/or Poem<br>Morning Verse | | | | |
| **Skills Practice 25–35 min.** | • memory reading<br>• theory of word<br>• symbol imagery: lines and letters<br>• clapping syllables<br>• phonemic awareness: rhyme, blending phonemes, and hand spelling<br>• encoding: first sound letter (5 min.).<br><br>Do an Activity B (5–10 min)<br>Introduce handwriting for new letter (15 min.). | | NO SKILLS PRACTICE: Review yesterday's new "letter (5 min.).<br><br>Do Activity B (5 - 10 min.)<br><br>Introduce handwriting for yesterday's letter (15 min.) | Ibid Monday/Tuesday | |
| **Transition 3–5 min.** | Integrated Movement Activity (IMA) | | | | |
| **Introduction &/or Review Or Story 20–30 min.** | Introduction: tell a fairy tale for introduction of a letter tomorrow (15–25 min.). | Review yesterday's story (5–15 min.).<br><br>Introduce new letter from fairy tale (5 min.).<br><br>Do an Activity A (10–20 min.). | Introduction: tell a fairy tale for introduction of a letter tomorrow (15–25 min.). | Same as Tuesday | Review yesterday's letter (5 min.).<br><br>Do an Activity B (5–10 min).<br><br>Introduce handwriting for yesterday's letter (15 min.). |
| **Transition 3–5 min.** | IMA<br>Set up for bookwork. | | | | |
| **Bookwork 15–25 min.** | Draw a picture from the story in main lesson book. | Paint, draw, or sculpt the new letter. | Draw a picture from the story in main lesson book. | Paint or sculpt the new letter. | Go on a nature walk or tell a fairy tale as soul food. |
| **Speech/Song 10–15 min.** | Introduce poem, song, and/or tongue twister (TT). | Practice song, poem, and/or TT. | Ibid Tuesday (or introduce new TT). | Ibid Tuesday | Continue to work on current poem and/or song. |

# APPENDIX 1B: BLOCK PLAN TEMPLATE FOR 1st GRADE PRACTICE BLOCK 1

|  | Monday | Tuesday | Wednesday | Thursday | Friday |
|---|---|---|---|---|---|
| **Skills Practice 30–35 min.** | Symbol imagery/visualizing individual letters: all letters introduced to date (5–7 min) | | | | Fun and games: choose activities for alphabet, symbol imagery, phonemic awareness, concept imagery, and/or sight words. |
|  | Introduce new sight words using chants (5–7 min.). | Practice sight words. | | | |
|  | Memory reading day one: do choral reading as a whole class (silent reading for those who can read) (10 min.). | Memory reading day two: do choral reading using Drill Down. | Memory reading day three: have students locate one line/ word in text (include sight words). | | |
|  | Phonemic Awareness:<br>• rhyming<br>• segmenting: hand spelling<br>• blending<br>• materialization techniques (10 min.) | | | | |
| **Bookwork 15 min.** | Alternate one or more of the following each day in practice book:<br>• letter practice or sound practice<br>• handwriting practice<br>• form drawing exercise<br>• encoding | | | | Assessments: letter practice and/ or sound practice<br><br>informal spelling quiz of sight words |

# APPENDIX 1C: BLOCK PLAN TEMPLATE FOR 1st GRADE MAIN LESSON BLOCKS 2–3

| | Monday | Tuesday | Wednesday | Thursday | Friday |
|---|---|---|---|---|---|
| **Opening** 12–15 min. | Song<br>Attendance<br>Riddle, Nature Observation, and/or Poem<br>Morning Verse | | | | |
| **Skills Practice** 30–40 min. | Symbol imagery: letter drill (5–7 min.)<br>phonemic awareness (15+ min.)<br>encoding (5–7 min.)<br>sight words (3–7 min.) | | Review new letter from Tuesday (5 min.). Activity B (5–10 min.) Introduce handwriting for new letter (15 min.). | Ibid Monday/ Tuesday | Assessments:<br><br>letter practice and/ or sound practice informal spelling quiz of sight words |
| **Transition** 3–5 min. | Integrated Movement Activity (IMA) | | | | |
| **Reading/ Writing** 10–25 min. | Memory reading (10 min.); kid writing (15 min.) | | | | |
| **Introduction &/or Review** 15–25 min. **Note: Includes Story** | Story: tell a fairy tale (to use for letter introduction tomorrow). | Review story (5–15 min.). Introduce letter(s) (5 min.). Activity A (10–15 min.). | Story: tell a fairy tale (to use for letter introduction tomorrow). | Ibid Tuesday | Review new letter from Thursday (5 min.). Activity B (5–10 min.) Introduce handwriting for new letter (15 min.). |
| **Transition** 3–5 min. | Integrated Movement Activity (IMA) | | | | |
| **Bookwork** 15–20 min | Draw a picture from the story in main lesson book. | Paint, draw, or sculpt new letter(s). | Draw a picture from the story in main lesson book. | Paint, draw, or sculpt new letter(s). | Have students practice handwriting in practice book. |
| **Speech / Song** 10–15 min. | Introduce poem, song, and/or tongue twister (TT). | Practice song, poem, and/ or TT. | Ibid Tuesday (You could introduce a new TT.) | Ibid Tuesday | Tell a fairy tale as soul food. |

# APPENDIX 1D: BLOCK PLAN TEMPLATE FOR 1st GRADE PRACTICE BLOCKS 2–3

| | Monday | Tuesday | Wednesday | Thursday | Friday |
|---|---|---|---|---|---|
| **Skills Practice (30–35 min.)** | Letter practice (symbol imagery with letters) (5–7 min.) | | | | Fun and Games:<br><br>Choose activities for alphabet, symbol imagery, phonemic awareness, concept imagery, and/or sight words. |
| | Introduce/practice sight words (5–7 min.). | | | | |
| | Memory reading (Those who are already reading can read silently to themselves.) (10 min.) | | | | |
| | Phonemic awareness (always include):<br>• segmenting<br>• blending (10 min.) | | | | |
| **Bookwork (15 min.)** | Schedule based on phase of majority of class:<br>• Emergent Phase: more work on phonemic awareness<br>• Phonemic Awareness Phase: kid writing (15 min.) | | | | Assessments:<br><br>letter practice and/ or sound practice)<br><br>informal spelling quiz of sight words<br><br>Block 3: encoding quiz |

# APPENDIX 1E: BLOCK PLAN TEMPLATE FOR 1st GRADE MAIN LESSON BLOCK 4

| | Monday | Tuesday | Wednesday | Thursday | Friday |
|---|---|---|---|---|---|
| **Opening** 12–15 min. | Song<br>Attendance<br>Riddle, Nature Observation, and/or Poem<br>Morning Verse | | | | |
| **Skills Practice** 25–30 min. | phonemic awareness (5–10 min.)<br>syllable cards (5 min); mystery word (5 min.)<br>decoding (5 min); encoding (5 min.)<br>sight words: introduce/practice weekly words | | | | Assessments:<br><br>letter practice and/or sound practice (if needed)<br><br>informal spelling quiz of sight words or encoding quiz |
| **Reading/ Writing** 20 min. | 1 reading group<br>kid writing for the other students | | | | |
| **Transition 5–7 min.** | Do an IMA using sight word activities. | | | | |
| **Introduction &/or Review 15–20 min.** Note: Includes Story | Tell a fairy tale or introduce a new phonics rule using an image or umbrella story. | Review Monday's fairy tale or the new phonics rule. | Tell a fairy tale. | Same as Tuesday | Tell a fairy tale as soul food. |
| **Transition** 3–5 min. | IMA (Directions Game to set up for bookwork and/or zoo exercises) | | | | |
| **Bookwork** 20–25 min. | Artwork from story: main lesson book drawing or a painting | Write caption for picture drawn yesterday. If time, write in practice book or phonics rules book. | Ibid Monday | Ibid Tuesday | Have students do additional artwork or writing. |
| **Speech/Song** 10 min. | Introduce poem, song, and/or tongue twister (TT). | Practice song, poem, and/or TT. | Memory Read one of the current poems/ songs. | Same as Wednesday | |

# APPENDIX 1F: BLOCK PLAN TEMPLATE FOR 1st GRADE PRACTICE BLOCK 4

| | Monday | Tuesday | Wednesday | Thursday | Friday |
|---|---|---|---|---|---|
| **Skills Practice 25–30 min.** | Use syllable cards and mystery word for whichever phonics rule(s) you are working on (10–14 min.). | | | | |
| | Introduce/practice week's sight words (5–7 min.). | | | | |
| | Phonemic awareness: practice whichever aspects the class needs more time on (10 min.). | | | | |
| **Introduction &/ or Review 5–10 min.** | Introduce new phonics rule when ready for it (expand time accordingly). Otherwise review: phonics rule taught the day before (or) encoding and decoding with current phonics rule(s) | | | | |
| **Bookwork 15 min.** | Kid writing or reading group | | | | Assessments: informal spelling quiz of sight words encoding quiz |

# APPENDIX 2A: BLOCK PLAN TEMPLATE FOR 2nd GRADE MAIN LESSON BLOCKS 1 AND 2

| | Monday | Tuesday | Wednesday | Thursday | Friday |
|---|---|---|---|---|---|
| **Opening** 12–15 min. | Song<br>Attendance<br>Riddle, Nature Observation, and/or Poem<br>Morning Verse | | | | |
| **Skills Practice** 30–35 min. | Syllable cards (5–7 min.)<br>Mystery word (5–7 min.)<br>Sight words: introduce/practice (5–7 min.)<br>Decoding (5–7 min.)<br>Encoding (5–7 min.) | | | | Assessments:<br><br>give encoding quiz for phonics rules and/or sight words spelling quiz. |
| **Transition** 3–5 min. | poem or song with movements | | | | |
| **Introduction &/or Review** 10–15 min. | Pick one:<br>1. cursive letters<br>2. phonics rule<br>3. mini-lesson from kid writing | Either review phonics rule (practice activity) or review yesterday's story. | Ibid Monday | Ibid Tuesday | Meet with one reading group (silent reading for the rest). |
| **Transition** 3–5 min. | IMA (Directions Game to set up for Bookwork and/or zoo exercises) | | | | |
| **Bookwork** 30–35 min. | 2 reading groups (15 min. each) kid writing and/or phonics worksheet for those who do not have reading group | Do either a drawing, or painting in (main lesson book) from the story. | Cursive practice: do a form drawing <u>or</u> copy entry into main lesson book. | Ibid Monday | Lead students in artwork or a written assignment for main lesson book. |
| **Transition** 3–5 min. | Song or Speech | | | | |
| **Story** 15 –20 min. | Tell a saint story or fable (basis for artwork tomorrow). | Tell a saint story or fable (soul food). | Tell a saint story or fable (soul food). | Ibid Monday | Tell a story for soul food. |

# APPENDIX 2B:  BLOCK PLAN TEMPLATE FOR 2nd GRADE PRACTICE BLOCKS 1–4

|  | Monday | Tuesday | Wednesday | Thursday | Friday |
|---|---|---|---|---|---|
| **Skills Practice 15–20 min.** | syllable cards<br>emphasis on current phonics rule(s) (5–7 min) | | | | **Assessments:**<br><br>give an encoding quiz for phonics rules (see chapter 3.4 #11) or a sight words spelling quiz (see chapter 3.6 #10). |
|  | mystery word<br>emphasis on current phonics rule(s) (5–7 min) | | | | |
|  | introduce/practice weekly sight words (5–7 min) | | | | |
| **Transition 3–5 min.** | Integrated Movement Activity (IMA) | | | | |
| **Introduction &/ or Review 10–15 min.** | Pick one:<br>1.  Introduce a new phonics rule (when the class is ready for one).<br>2.  Do a mini-lesson from kid writing.<br>3.  Review new phonics rule (if introduced in last class) or ongoing practice of encoding and decoding with current phonics rule(s). | | | | |
| **Bookwork 15 min.** | one reading group<br>kid writing or silent reading for the other students | | | | |

# APPENDIX 2C: BLOCK PLAN TEMPLATE FOR 2nd GRADE MAIN LESSON BLOCKS 3 AND 4

| | Monday | Tuesday | Wednesday | Thursday | Friday |
|---|---|---|---|---|---|
| **Opening**<br>**12–15 min.** | Song<br>Attendance<br>Riddle, Nature Observation, and/or Poem<br>Morning Verse | | | | |
| **Skills Practice**<br>**30–35 min.** | • Syllable cards (5–7 min.)<br><br>• Mystery word (5–7 min.)<br><br>• Sight words (5–7 min.)<br><br>• Decoding (5–7 min.)<br><br>• Encoding (5–7 min.) | | | | |
| **Transition**<br>**3–5 min.** | Song or poem with movement | | | | |
| **Introduction &/or Review**<br>**10–15 min.** | Pick one:<br>• new phonics rule<br>• grammar<br>• mini-lesson (kid writing)<br>• composition | Do a practice activity for yesterday's lesson or composition. | Ibid Monday | Ibid Tuesday | Do composition day 3 or lead ongoing practice. |
| **Transition**<br>**3–5 min.** | IMA (Directions Game to set up for bookwork and/or zoo exercises) | | | | |
| **Bookwork**<br>**30–35 min.** | Two reading groups (15 min. each);<br>For remaining students pick from:<br><br>1. Kid writing<br>2. Phonics worksheet<br>3. Grammar worksheet<br>4. Copying a composition into main lesson book | Review story to set up for artwork.<br><br>Lead a painting or drawing from yesterday's story in main lesson book. | Review story to prepare for composition writing (10 min.).<br><br>Teach a composition lesson based on story 20–25 min.). | Ibid Tuesday | Ibid Monday— |
| **Transition**<br>**3–5 min.** | Song or speech work | | | | |
| **Story**<br>**15–20 min.** | Tell a saint story or fable (basis for artwork tomorrow). | Tell a saint story or fable (for tomorrow's composition). | Ibid Monday | Tell a saint story or fable (soul food). | Lead one reading group (silent reading for the others). |

# APPENDIX 3A: BLOCK PLAN TEMPLATE FOR 3rd GRADE PRACTICE BLOCK

**Emphasis: Review 2nd Grade (block one) and follow Composition Block (block three)**

| | Monday | Tuesday | Wednesday | Thursday | Friday |
|---|---|---|---|---|---|
| **Skills Practice 25–30 min.** | Syllable cards <br> • block one: review of 2nd Grade phonics <br> • block three: emphasis on current phonics rule(s) (5–7 min.) | | | | Spelling test and corrections |
| | Mystery word (5–7 min.) | | | | |
| | Weekly spelling words: introduce and practice (15 min.) <br> Note: Block one: initial introduction of spelling program | | | | |
| **Transition 3–5 min.** | Integrated Movement Activity | | | | |
| **Introduction &/or Review OR Bookwork (15 min.)** | Introduction: (pick one) New phonics rule when the class is ready for one <br><br> Ongoing practice of encoding and decoding with current phonics rule(s) <br><br> Review 2nd Grade grammar (Block one only) | Review (pick one): New phonics rule <br><br> Ongoing practice with old phonics rule(s) <br><br> Review 2nd Grade grammar (Block one only) | Composition day one: Students do independent writing. | Composition day two: Students revise and complete day one composition. | Mini-lesson based on composition |

# APPENDIX 3B: BLOCK PLAN TEMPLATE FOR 3rd GRADE MAIN LESSON BLOCKS

**(Emphasis: Grammar)**

| | Monday | Tuesday | Wednesday | Thursday | Friday |
|---|---|---|---|---|---|
| **Opening**<br>**12–15 min.** | Song<br>Attendance<br>Riddle, Nature Observation, and/or Poem<br>Morning Verse | | | | |
| **Skills Practice**<br>**30–35 min.** | Syllable cards (5–7 min.)<br>Mystery word (5–7 min.)<br>Weekly spelling words introduction and practice (15 min.)<br>Grammar practice (old concepts) | | | | Spelling test<br>+ correct<br>(20–25 min.)<br><br>Grammar assignment that doubles as assessment |
| **Introduction &/or Review**<br>**15–20 min.** | Introduce new grammar concept and practice Activity A. | Review new grammar concept and do practice Activity B. | Review Old Testament story (or) introduce new phonics rule. | Review Old Testament story (or) intro/review new phonics rule. | Ibid Thursday |
| **Transition**<br>**5 min.** | Integrated Movement Activity and bookwork set up | | | | |
| **Bookwork**<br>**30–35 min.** | Grammar drawing (or) Composition day three:<br><br>Put last week's composition into a final draft in main lesson book. | Review yesterday's story.<br><br>Lead drawing or painting for yesterday's story for main lesson book. | Review yesterday's story.<br><br>Composition day one:<br>Start a new composition. | Ibid Tuesday | Composition day two: Teach a mini-lesson based on errors.<br><br>Have students revise Wednesday's rough draft. |
| **Transition**<br>**3–5 min.** | Integrated Movement Activity | | | | |
| **Story**<br>**15–20 min.** | Tell an Old Testament story. | | | | |

# APPENDIX 3C: BLOCK PLAN TEMPLATE FOR 3rd GRADE PRACTICE BLOCKS

**(Emphasis: Grammar—to follow Grammar Main Lesson Blocks)**

| | Monday | Tuesday | Wednesday | Thursday | Friday |
|---|---|---|---|---|---|
| **Skills Practice 25–30 min.** | syllable cards (5–7 min.) | | | | spelling test |
| | mystery word (5–7 min.) | | | | |
| | Introduce and practice weekly spelling words (15 min.). | | | | |
| **Transition 3–5 min.** | Integrated Movement Activity | | | | |
| **Introduction &/ or Review** <br> <u>or</u> <br> **Bookwork 15 min.** | Introduce new phonics rule when the class is ready for one. <br><br> Review new phonics rule (if introduced in last class) <br> <u>Or</u> <br> Ongoing practice of encoding and decoding with current phonics Rule(s). | Review new phonics rule <br> <u>Or</u> <br> Ongoing practice of decoding/ encoding with current phonics rule. | Grammar worksheet: review material brought in last Grammar main lesson book. | Grammar worksheet: review of material brought in last Grammar main lesson book. | Grammar worksheet: <br><br> review of material brought in last Grammar main lesson book. <br> <u>Or</u> <br> lead students in ongoing practice of encoding and decoding with current phonics rule(s). |

# APPENDIX 3D: BLOCK PLAN TEMPLATE FOR 3rd GRADE MAIN LESSON BLOCKS

**Emphasis: Composition**

|  | Monday | Tuesday | Wednesday | Thursday | Friday |
|---|---|---|---|---|---|
| **Opening** 12–15 min. | Song <br> Attendance <br> Riddle, Nature Observation, and/or Poem <br> Morning Verse | | | | |
| **Skills Practice** 25–30 Minutes | syllable cards (5–7 min.) <br> mystery word (5–7 min.) <br> weekly spelling words (15 min.) | | | | spelling test |
| **Introduction &/or Review** 15–20 min. | Pick one: <br> Introduce new phonics rule when the class is ready for one. <br> Review new phonics rule (if introduced in last class). <br> Practice encoding and decoding with current phonics rule(s). | | | | |
| **Transition 5 min.** | Integrated Movement Activity + bookwork set up | | | | |
| **Bookwork** 25–30 min. | Composition day three: put last week's composition into a final draft in main lesson book. | Review yesterday's story. <br><br> Lead a drawing or painting for main lesson book. | Review yesterday's story. <br><br> Composition day one: Start a new composition. | Same as Tuesday | Composition day two: teach a mini-lesson based on errors. <br><br> Have students revise Wednesday's rough Draft. |
| **Transition** 3–5 min. | Integrated Movement Activity | | | | |
| **Story** 15–20 min. | Old Testament story | | | | |

Note: Story can be told later in the day if you need more time in main lesson for other things.

# APPENDIX 4: THE ROADMAP TO LITERACY SIGHT WORD LIST

*The Roadmap to Literacy Sight Word List* contains 270 words, divided between two sets. For information on how to use it, please see chapter 3.6 #2 and 3.6 #6–8.

Note:

- **Bold Words** are phonetically irregular
- Words with an asterisk (*) have two pronunciations. Teach both.
- We have omitted the sight words *a* and *I*. Students will learn these words when they learn the letters of the alphabet.

## Set 1: The Most Common Sight Words

The following 20 words are the most frequently written words in the English language. Teach this set first. Teach in any order.

| and | for | **is** | she | **to** |
|-----|-----|--------|------|--------|
| **are** | he | it | that | **was** |
| **as** | **his** | on | **the** | with |
| at | in | **of** | **they** | **you** |

## Set 2: Phonetically Regular and Irregular Sight Words

The following 250 words are the next most commonly used words in the English language. Teach this set second. Teach in any order.

| about | **do** | if | page | **there** |
|-------|--------|------|---------|-----------|
| after | **does** | into | part | these |
| **again** | **don't** | its | **people** | **they** |
| **all** | **done** | just | pick | thing |
| **also** | down | keep | picture | think |
| **always** | draw | kind | play | this |
| am | drink | **know** | please | those |
| an | each | large | **pretty** | though |
| **another** | eat | **laugh** | **pull** | thought |
| **answer** | **eight** | **learn** | **put** | three |
| **any** | **enough** | let | ran | **through** |

575

| | | | | |
|---|---|---|---|---|
| **around** | even | letter | **read\*** | **today** |
| ask | **every** | **light** | red | too |
| ate | **fall** | like | ride | tough |
| **away** | far | **listen** | **right** | try |
| back | fast | little | **rough** | **two** |
| be | **father** | **live\*** | round | under |
| **because** | **find** | long | run | up |
| **been** | first | look | **said** | upon |
| before | five | made | same | us |
| best | follow | make | saw | **use** |
| better | found | **many** | say | **very** |
| big | **four** | may | **school** | **walk** |
| black | **friend** | me | see | **want** |
| blue | **from** | more | **seven** | **warm** |
| **both** | **full** | **mother** | shall | **wash** |
| **bought** | funny | **move** | **should** | **water** |
| boy | gave | much | show | way |
| bring | **get** | must | sing | we |
| **brother** | girl | my | sister | well |
| **brought** | **give** | name | sit | went |
| brown | go | never | six | **were** |
| but | goes | new | sleep | **what** |
| **buy** | going | no | **small** | when |
| by | good | not | so | **where** |
| **call** | got | now | **some** | which |
| came | **great** | number | soon | white |
| can | green | off | sound | **who** |
| **carry** | grow | **often** | spell | **whose** |
| change | had | **old** | start | why |
| **child** | **has** | **once** | stop | will |
| **children** | **have** | **one** | such | wish |
| clean | help | **only** | take | **word** |
| **cold** | her | **open** | tell | **work** |
| **color** | him | or | ten | **would** |
| **come** | **hold** | **other** | **than** | **write** |
| **could** | hot | our | thank | year |
| day | house | out | **their** | yellow |
| did | how | over | them | yes |
| **different** | hurt | own | then | **your** |

# APPENDIX 5: TEACHER LITERATURE RESOURCE LIST

**1st Grade**

- *Grimm's Fairy Tales*
- *Keys of the Kingdom; A Book of Stories and Poems for Children* by Elizabeth Gmeyner
- *The Emerald Story Book; Stories and Legends of Spring, Nature and Easter* by Ada M. Skinner
- *Just So Stories* by Rudyard Kipling
- *The Tales of Tiptoes Lightly* by Reg Down
- *Wise Women: Folk and Fairy Tales from Around the World* by Suzanne Barchers
- *Fairy Tales of Hans Christian Andersen*, Haviland translation (Anchor Books)

**2nd Grade**

- *Old Mother West Wind* by Thorton Burgess
- *Christ Legends* by Selma Lagerlof
- *Animal Stories* by Jacob Streit published by Walter Keller Press Dornach
- *Teaching with the Fables; a Holistic Approach* by Sieglinde de Francesca
- *The Giant at the Ford and Other Legends of the Saints* by Ursula Synge
- *What Animals Say to Each Other; 30 Nature Fables in Rhyme* by Jacob Streit (AWSNA)
- *Columban* by Jacob Streit (AWSNA)
- *Roses in the Snow: A Tale of Saint Elizabeth of Hungary* by Dessi Jackson
- *The Book of Saints and Friendly Beasts* by Abbie Farwell Brown (www.mainlesson.com) The Baldwin Project
- *Paddy Beaver* by Thornton Burgess (also check out his other animal stories including *Sammy Jay*)

**3rd Grade**

- *And it Came to Pass* by Juliet Comton-Burnett (Old Testament Reader adapted from the authorized version)
- *And There Was Light* by Jakob Streit (http://waldorflibrary.org/books/3/ view_bl/121/reading/133/ and-there-was-light-ebook?tab=getmybooksTab&is_show_data=1)
- *Journey to the Promised Land, We Will Build a Temple* by Jakob Streit
- *Stories from the Bible* by Walter de la Mare
- *The Story Bible* by Pearl S. Buck

- *Noah's Ark* by Jerry Pinkney
- *Miriam's Cup: A Passover Story* by Fran Manushkin
- *Seasons of Our Joy: A Modern Guide to Jewish Holidays* by Arthur Waskow
- *Johnny Appleseed* by Reeve Lindbergh

**Poetry 1st through 3rd Grades**

- *A Journey Through Time in Verse and Rhyme* by Heather Thomas
- *Peacock Pie* by Walter de la Mare (and his other books of children's poetry)
- *A Pizza the Size of the Sun* by Jack Prelutsky (and his other books of children's poetry)
- *The Book of a Thousand Poems; A Family Treasury* published by Peter Bedrick Books
- *Favorite Poems Old and New* selected by Helen Ferris
- *Sing a Song of Popcorn* selected by de Regniers, Moore
- *Where the Sidewalk Ends* by Shel Silverstein

**Other Books** (includes Form Drawing)

- *All about Spelling* by Marie Rippel
- *The Blue Book of Grammar and Punctuation; Eleventh Edition* by Jane Straus (exercises for this book at http://www.grammarbook.com)
- *Cambridge Dictionary of American Idioms* by Paul Heacock
- ✓ *Caught 'Ya! Grammar with a Giggle* by Jane Bell Kiester
- *Fee Fi Fo Fun* (and other readers) by Arthur Pittis
- *Grammar-land* by M.L. Nesbitt (2nd and 4th Grade)
- *How to Teach Spelling* by Laura Rudginsky
- *Kid Writing: A Systematic Approach to Phonics, Journals, and Writing Workshop* by Eileen Feldgus
- *Phonemic Awareness: Playing with Sound to Strengthen Beginning Reading Skills* by Jo Fitzpatrick
- *The Singing-Reading Connection Part One* by Shirley Handy
- *Bal-A-Vis-X: Rhythmic Balance/Auditory/Vision eXercises for Brain and brain-Body Integration* by Bill Hubert
- *Take Time: Movement Exercises for Parents, Teachers, and Therapistis of Children with Difficulties in Speaking, Reading, Writing, and Spelling* by Mary Nash-Wortham and Jean Hunt
- *Form Drawing* by Hans R. Niederhauser and Margaret Frohlich
- *Healing Stories for Challenging Behaviour* by Susan Perrow
- *Form Drawing Grades One through Four* by Ernst Schuberth and Laura Embrey-Stine.
- *Specific Skills Series* by Richard A. Boning
- *Spelling Plus: 1000 Words toward Spelling Success* by Susan C. Anthony
- *Quick Word Handbook for Beginning Writers* by Rebecca Sitton

# BIBLIOGRAPHY

Avison, Kevin. Martyn Rawson. 2014. *The Tasks and Content of the Waldorf Curriculum*. Translated by Johanna Collis. Edinburgh: Floris Books.

Ayres, A. Jean. 2005. *Sensory Integration and the Child: Understanding Hidden Sensory Challenges*. Los Angeles: Western Psychological Services.

Bear, Donald R. et al. 2008. *Words Their Way: Word Study for Phonics, Vocabulary, and Spelling Instruction 4th edition*. Columbus: Pearson Prentice Hall.

Bell, Masha. 2004. *Understanding English Spelling*. Cambridge: Pegasus Educational.

Bell, Masha. 2005. "Why English Spelling Should Be Updated." Simplified Spelling Society. Last modified April 17, 2005. http://lrc.salemstate.edu/aske/courses/readings/Why_English_Spelling_Should_Be_Updated.htm

Bell, Masha. 2017. "A Brief History of English Spelling." TESS (The English Spelling Society). http://spellingsociety.org/history#/page/5.

Bell, Nanci. 2001. *Seeing Stars: Symbol Imagery for Phonemic Awareness, Sight Words and Spelling*. San Luis Obispo, CA: Gander Educational Publishing.

Bell, Nanci. 2007. *Visualizing and Verbalizing for Language Comprehension and Thinking, Second Edition*. San Luis Obispo, CA: Gander Publishing.

Bishop, Margaret. 1986. *TheABC's and All Their Tricks: The Complete Reference Book of Phonics and Spelling*. Fenton, MI: Mott Media.

Blythe, Sally Goddard. 2005. *The Well Balanced Child: Movement and Early Learning*. Gloucestershire: Hawthorn Press. [NB: The first edition of this book does not contain "Early Morning by the Pond" exercises.]

Blythe, Sally Goddard. 2009. *Attention, Balance, and Coordination: The A.B.C. of Learning Success*. West Sussex, UK: Wiley-Blackwell.

Blythe, Sally Goddard. 2012. *Assessing Neuromotor Readiness for Learning: The INPP Developmental Screening Test and School Intervention Programme*. West Sussex, UK: Wiley-Blackwell.

Boning, Richard A. 1976. *Getting the Main Idea Booklet E Second Edition*. New York: Barnell Loft.

Bryson, Bill. 1990. *The Mother Tongue: English & How It Got That Way*. New York: Avon Books.

Chaucer, Geoffrey. 2000. *The Canterbury Tales and Other Poems*. Purves, David Laing, ed. Gutenberg Press Etext: http://www.gutenberg.org/cache/epub/2383/pg2383.txt

Dehaene, Stanislas. 2009. *Reading in the Brain: The New Science of How We Read*. New York: Penguin.

Dennison, Paul and Gail. 1989. *Brain Gym Teacher's Edition Revised*. Ventura, CA: Edu-Kinesthetics, Inc.

Diamond, Linda. 2005. "Assessment-Driven Instruction: A Systems Approach" in *IDA Perspectives, vol 31, No. 4, Fall 2005*: 31–37. Appeared in *Assessing Reading Multiple Measures for Kindergarten through Twelfth Grade*.

Diamond, Linda, editor. 2008. *Assessing Reading Multiple Measures for Kindergarten through Twelfth Grade, 2nd Edition. CORE* (Consortium on Reading Excellence, Inc.) Novato: Area Press.

Dweck, Carol. 2016. "How to Best Interpret Growth Mindset Research." *Education World.* January 11, 2016. Dweck, Carol. 2016. *Mindset: The New Psychology of Success*. New York: Random House.

English, Suzanne-Marie. 2012. *The Etiquette of Kindness: It's Not Just About the Right Fork*. Rescue, CA: Pleasant Ranch Publishing.

Feldgus, Eileen. 1999. *Kid Writing: A Systematic Approach to Phonics, Journals, and Writing Workshop, 2nd Edition*. Chicago: Wright Group McGraw-Hill.

Fitzpatrick, Jo. 1997. *Phonemic Awareness: Playing with Sounds to Strengthen Beginning Reading Skills*. Creative Teaching Press. Cypress, CA: Creative Teaching Press.

Florey, Kitty Burns. 2009. *Script & Scribble: The Rise and Fall of Handwriting*. New York: Melville House Publishing.

Fry, Edward. Kress, Jacqueline. 2006. *The Reading Teacher's Book of Lists 5th Edition*. San Francisco, CA: Jossey-Bass.

Gentry, J. Richard. 2007. *Breakthrough in Beginning Reading and Writing*. New York: Scholastic.

Gentry, J. Richard. 2004. *The Science of Spelling*. Portsmouth: Heinemann.

Gentry, J. Richard. 2006. *Breaking the Code: The New Science of Beginning Reading and Writing*. Portsmouth: Heineman.

Gittleman, Ann Louise. *Zapped: Why Your Cell Phone Shouldn't Be Your Alarm Clock and 1,268 Ways to Outsmart the Hazards of Electronic Pollution*. 2010 New York: HarperOne.

Gmeyner, Elisabeth and Russell, Joyce. 1951. *The Key of the Kingdom*. Great Barrington, MA: Bell Pond Books.

Gottgens, Else. 2011. *Waldorf Education in Practice: Exploring How Children Learn in the Lower Grades*. Denver: Outskirts Press, Inc.

Gummere, Francis B., trans., *Beowulf*. 2007. Great Britain: Saland Publishing.

Hall, Susan. 2006. *I've DIBEL'd, Now What? Designing Interventions with DIBELS Data*. Boston: Sopris West Educational Services.

Hempenstall, K. 2006. "What Brain Research Can Tell Us about Reading Instruction." Society for Quality Education September 2006: 17-20. Previously published in *Learning Difficulties Australia Bulletin*, 38(1), 15–16.

Hendrickson, Robert. 2000. *The Facts on File Encyclopedia of Word and Phrase Origins*. New York: Checkmark Books.

Hindes, David. 2006. "Rudolf Steiner on Teaching Left-Handed Children." *Research Bulletin, Autumn 2006, Volume 12 #1.*

Honig, Bill, Diamond Linda, and Gutlohn, Linda. 2000. *Teaching Reading Sourcebook for Kindergarten through Eighth Grade*. Novato, California: Arena Pres.

Hopkins, Gary. 2015. "How Can Teachers Develop Students' Motivation–and Success?" *Education World*. http://www.educationworld.com/a_issues/chat/chat010.shtml.

Hoven, Cynthia. 2012. *Eurythmy Movements and Meditations: A Journey to the Heart of Language*. HeartSong Press.

Howell, Ken. "Performance Criteria for Fluency and Fluency Scores: A Discussion." In *Assessing Reading Multiple Measures for Kindergarten through Twelfth Grade, 2nd Edition*, edited by Linda Diamond, A18–A21, Novato: Arena Press, 2008.

Irlen, Helen. 2010. *The Irlen Revolution: A Guide to Changing Your Perception and Your Life*. Garden City Park: Square One Publishers.

Johnson, Samuel. 1785. *A dictionary of the English language; in which the words are deduced from their originals and illustrated in their different significations by examples from the best writers. To which are prefixed, a history of the language, and on English grammar. In two volumes. 6th edition*. London: J.F. and C. Rivington. http://publicdomainreview.org/collections./samuel-johnsons-dictionary-of-the-english-language-1785/

King, Diana Hanbury. 2000. *English Isn't Crazy!: The Elements of Our Language and How to Teach Them*. Austin, Pro-Ed.

Koetzsch, Ronald, PhD. 2014. "Saying Good-bye to Wi-Fi: A Waldorf School Takes a Precautionary Step." *Renewal* Volume 23 #01 Spring/Summer 2014.

Konnikova, Maria. 2014. "What's Lost as Handwriting Fades." *New York Times* June 2, 2014 Science Times section pages D1 and D4.

Lindamood, Patricia. Lindamood, Phyllis. 1998. *The Lindamood Phoneme Sequencing Program for Reading, Spelling, and Speech: LiPS Teacher's Manual for the Classroom and Clinic 3rd Edition*. Austin: Pro-Ed.

Lubin, Helen. 2007. "Living Language in Waldorf Education." *The Research Bulletin* Spring 2007–Volume 12 #2: 27–31.

Maetzelfrom, Clara. 1929. "What the Dandelion Told." From *The Emerald Storybook: Stories and Legends of Spring, Nature, and Easter* by Ada M. Skinner. New York: Duffield & Company.

Manguel, Alberto. 1996. *A History of Reading*. New York: Viking.

McCrum, Robert. Robert MacNeil and William Cran. 2002. *The Story of English. Third Revised Edition*. New York: Penguin Books.

McDonald, Glen. 2002. *Using Spelling Rules*. St. Louis: McDonald Publishing Company, Inc. Medina, John. 2008. *Brain Rules*. Seattle, WA: Pear Press.

Milham, Samuel. 2012. *Dirty Electricity: Electrification and the Diseases of Civilization 2nd Edition*. Bloomington: Universe Inc.

Murphy-Lang, Cynthia. 2010. *Developing the Observing Eye: Teacher Observation and Assessment in Early Childhood Education*. Ghent, NY: The Association of Waldorf Schools of North America (AWSNA).

Nash-Wortham, Mary and Hunt, Jean. 2003. *Take Time: Movement Exercises for Parents, Teacher, and Therapists of Children with Difficulties in Speaking, Reading, Writing and Spelling.* Stourbridge, England: The Robinswood Press.

Netz, Reviel and Noel, William. 2007. *The Archimedes Codex.* Philadelphia: Da Capo Press/Perseus Books Group.

Niederhauser, Hans R. Frohlich, Margaret. 1984. *Form Drawing.* Spring Valley: Mercury Press.

O'Neil, Gisela. "The Teaching of Handwriting," unpublished paper, 1993 teaching binders, Rudolf Steiner College Library, Fair Oaks, California.

Oxford Dictionary. Online. https://en.oxforddictionaries.com/definition

Parsons, Susan. 2008. "Living with Electrohypersensitivity: A Survival Guide." weepinitiative.org (WEEP: The Canadian Initiative to Stop Wireless, Electric, and Electromagentic Pollution) http://weepinitiative.org/livingwithEHS.html.

Payne, Kim John. 2009. *Simplicity Parenting: Using the Extraordinary Power of Less to Raise Calmer, Happier, and More Secure Kids.* New York: Ballantine Books.

Perrow, Susan. 2008. *Healing Stories for Challenging Behaviour.* Gloucestershire: Hawthorn House.

Pinnell, Gay Su. Irene Fountas. 2007. *The Continuum of Literacy Learning Grades K–2: A Guide to Teaching.* Portsmouth: Heinemann.

Pinnell, Gay Su. Irene Fountas. 2011. *The Continuum of Literacy Learning Grades 3–8: A Guide to Teaching.* Portsmouth: Heinemann.

Plourde, Elizabeth. Marcus Plourde. 2016. *EMF Freedom: Solutions for the 21st Century Pollution 3rd Edition.* Irvine, CA: New Voice Publications.

Roberts, Elizaeth Madox. 1922. "The Woodpecker." *Under the Tree.* New York: B.W. Huebsch, Inc. http://docsouth.unc.edu/southlit/roberts/roberts.html.

Rossetti, Christina. "The Rainbow." https://www.familyfriendpoems.com/poem/the-rainbow-by-christina-rossetti.

Sachem Literacy Coaches. n.d. "Text Level Indicators." Adapted from *The Continuum of Literacy Learning Grades K–2* and *The Continuum of Literacy Learning Grades 3–8* by Pinnell and Fountas. Accessed September 4, 2017. http://www.raising-readers.org/media/cms/Text_Level_Indicators_3F41BEBDDDDAC_73A45638F C38E.pdf.

Shaywitz, Sally. 2003. *Overcoming Dyslexia: A New and Complete Science-Based Program for Reading Problems at Any Level.* New York: Vintage Books.

Singer, Katie. 2014. "Calming Behavior in Children with Autism and ADHD: The Electromagentic Radiation (EMR)-Lowering Protocol (That Has No Cost or Side Effects)." Electronic Silent Spring. http://www.electronicsilentspring.com/calming-behavior/.

Steiner, Rudolf. 1919. "Morning Verse for Lower Grades" (updated July 22, 2016) http://www.waldorfcurriculum.com/Curric/verselower.html

Steiner, Rudolf. 1923. "A Lecture on Eurythmy" (lecture, August 26, 1923) http://wn.rsarchive.org/Lectures/GA279/English/RSP1967/19230826p01.html

Steiner, Rudolf. 1983. *Discussions with Teachers*. Translated by Helen Fox. London: Rudolf Steiner Press.

Steiner, Rudolf. 1984. *Eurythmy as Visible Speech*. London: Rudolf Steiner Press.

Steiner, Rudolf. 1988. *Kingdom of Childhood*. Translated by Helen Fox. Hudson, NY: Anthroposophic Press.

Steiner, Rudolf. 1994. *How to Know Higher Worlds: A Modern Path of Initiation*. Hudson, New York: Anthroposophic Press.

Steiner, Rudolf. 1996. *The Child's Changing Consciousness as the Basis of Pedagogical Practice*. Translated by Roland Everett. Anthroposophic Press.

Steiner, Rudolf. 1998. *Study of Man*. London: Rudolf Steiner Press. Reprinted by Rudolf Steiner College, Fair Oaks, California.

Steiner, Rudolf. 2000. *Practical Advice to Teachers*. Great Barrington, MA: Anthroposophic Press.

Steiner, Rudolf. 2001. *The Renewal of Education*. Great Barrington, MA: Anthroposophic Press.

Steiner, Rudolf. 2003. *Soul Economy*. Translated by Roland Everett. Anthroposophic Press.

Stern, James, editor. 1972. *The Complete Grimm's Fairy Tales*. Based on the translation of Margaret Hunt. New York: Random House.

Stevens, Janet. 1999. *Cook-a-Doodle-Doo!* Boston: Houghton Mifflin, Harcourt.

Stockmeyer, Karl. 1991. *Rudolf Steiner's Curriculum for Waldorf Schools*. Translated by Roland Everett-Zade. East Sussex: Steiner Schools Fellowship Publications.

Thomas, Heather. 2009. *A Journey through Time in Verse and Rhyme*. Edinburgh, Scotland: Floris Books.

Trostli, Roberto. 2004. *Teaching Language Arts in the Waldorf School: A Compendium of Excerpts from the Foundation of Waldorf Education Series*. Fair Oaks, CA: The Association of Waldorf Schools of North America.

Wiechert, Christof. 2010. "On the Question of the Three-fold Structure of the Main Lesson." Translated by John Weedon. *Journal Pedagogical Section at the Goetheanum #38*. Easter 2010: 4–12.

Wiechert, Christof. 2010. "The Educational Practice of the Waldorf Schools." Translated by John Weedon. *Journal: Pedagogical Section at the Goetheanum #39*. Michaelmas 2010: 4–15.

Ziegler, Johannes C. and Goswami, Usha. 2006. "Becoming literate in different language: similar problems, different solutions." *Developmental Science 9:5 (2006): 429–453*.

# GLOSSARY OF TERMS

**Academic Concept Story:** Teacher created stories to introduce a new academic concept. They contain one or more key images that will then be used to teach the new concept. (5.5 #4)

**accommodation:** A slight change to how a lesson is taught or practiced to accommodate a student's learning challenge. It does not change the lesson in any meaningful way. (6.6 #1)

**Activity A/B:** Class (and small group) activities that are part of the initial Introduction &/or Review segments of main lesson. Activity A is any activity that follows the initial introduction and is geared more to the class as a group. Activity B is geared towards smaller groups of the class. (2.3 #4)

**adult writing:** When an adult shows a student who has just completed a *kid writing* assignment how an adult would write the word, title, sentence, etc. (3.13 #5)

**affixes:** Syllables that often carry meaning (e.g., suffixes and prefixes). (3.4 #9)

**AIMSweb:** An assessment used by schools to track student achievement. (6.1 #6)

**alliteration:** The repetition of the first sound in a word (e.g., tongue twisters). (3.3 #2)

**alphabet display:** Pictures of the letters of the alphabet hung in the front of the classroom. It usually contains anchor pictures. (3.1 #3)

**alphabetic layer:** The first layer of the *English Layer Cake*. It illustrates the *alphabetic stage*. (1.3 #1): The first stage of the English language and learning to spell as identified by Bear et al. in *Words Their Way*. (1.3 #4)

**alphabetic principle**: The relationship between letters and phonemes (i.e., letters represent sounds and vice versa). (1.2 #6 and 1.5 #1)

**anchor picture:** A picture of a concrete noun that begins with a specific letter to help students remember the letter's sound. (3.1 #3)

**anchor word:** A word that begins with a specific letter used to help students remember the letter's sound. (3.1 #8)

**assessment created by educational testing groups:** Assessments that focus on a few key literacy skills such as DIBELS and AIMSweb. (6.1 #6)

**Astral Body:** One aspect of the four-fold human being. It refers to the emotional part of the human being and the aspect governed by desires, likes, and dislikes. (2.1 #11)

**Bal-A-Vis-X:** A series of sandbag and ball exercises. (6.6 #5)

**benchmarks** (Standards): A list of skills/content that students are to learn in each grade. (2.3 #1, 6.1 #9)

**birthday verses** (report verses): Individual verses composed by the teacher which students often recite as part of main lesson (usually on the day of the week they were born). (This is considered a Sacred Nothing.) (3.10 #3)

**blend:** Two or three consonants in a cluster (e.g., the letters *DR* in *dragon* and the letters *TCH* in *latch*.). (3.1 #7 and 4.1 rule 3)

**block plan:** The layout of an entire main lesson block or practice block. (5.1 #5 and 2.3 #1)

**block plan templates:** Part of *The Roadmap to Literacy* program that helps teachers lay out block plans. (see Appendices 1–3)

**block rotation:** See main lesson block rotation or practice block rotation. (2.3 #1)

**Body Geography:** A Waldorf variation of Simon Says. (3.7 #5)

**bookwork:** The fourth segment of main lesson. It is the time for the students to take what they have learned and put it down into concrete form through writing and/or drawing. (2.3 #4)

**borders:** The Waldorf practice of including a frame around pages in main lesson books. (This is considered a Sacred Nothing if done without conscious purpose.) (2.2 #1 and 3.2 #3)

**Brain Gym:** Therapeutic movement that makes a useful transition exercise/Integrated Movement Activity. (6.6 #5)

**breathing** (in a lesson): Achieving a balance between activities that require quiet, intense focus and those that allow the students to move, be noisy, or relax. (2.4 #4 and 2.1 #7)

**capacities:** Foundational abilities students should develop before they learn specific academic skills. (1.6 #2)

**chains:** Lists of words where one element changes. The change can be: a letter; the onset (as in *word families*); the rime; or syllable). (3.4 #7)

**choice/contrast:** An educational practice of offering students two possible answers (one right and one wrong) when they are stuck. (3.4 #6)

**choleric:** One of the temperaments identified by Steiner. It refers to people who are go-getters, love action, and are natural leaders. (2.1 #10)

**choral reading:** When students read aloud together, typically memory reading from a passage written on the board in the Emergent and beginning Phonemic Awareness Phase. (3.15 #2)

**circle:** An extended period of time at the beginning of main lesson that includes a plethora of movement, speech, and music activities. (This is a Sacred Nothing when used in the grades.) (2.3 #5)

**closed syllables:** Syllables that have one vowel letter and end with a consonant (e.g., <u>bat</u>/tle <u>ac</u>/tion). (4.3 rule 23)

**cognate:** A word that is related in meaning and spelling (e.g., *grace* and *gracious*). (4.3 rule 31)

**concept imagery:** The ability to visualize in three dimensions, based on oral or written language. (1.6 #2 and 3.7)

**consumable spelling dictionary:** A booklet of commonly-used words for beginning writers. (3.6 #3)

**contextual readers:** Students who use the pictures and contextual language cues to predict what the text will say rather than using decoding and sight words skills. (6.2 #4)

**CORE (Consortium on Reading Excellence, Inc):** A reference to the book *Assessing Reading Multiple Measures for Kindergarten through Twelfth Grade, 2nd edition* put out by *CORE*. It contains assessments teachers can use. (6.1 #6)

**curriculum:** The skills, concepts, and/or content a teacher has to teach in each grade, as determined by her school's faculty. (2.3 #1, 6.1 #9)

**curriculum connection**: A related aspect in a lesson. (Section 4 Protocol)

**CVC words (Consonant-Vowel-Consonant words):** Words spelled with a consonant, short vowel, consonant such as *hit, fan, log, met,* and *hug.* (4.1 rule 1)

**decodable-text:** Leveled readers that use simplified text suited for beginners. They feature common sight words, decodable words with illustrations that match. (3.15 #3)

**decodable-text reading:** Reading that consists of utilizing three reading strategies (sight words, decoding, and contextual clues) while reading unfamiliar, but simple text. (3.15 #2)

**decoding:** The ability to sound out unfamiliar written words. (3.4, 1.2 #1, 1.6 #4)

**DIBELs:** An assessment used by schools to track student achievement. (6.1 #6)

**differentiated instruction:** The practice of giving students different work, depending on their needs/levels. (1.2 #6 and 2.4 #3)

**digraphs:** Two letters that make one sound. They can be consonants or vowels (e.g., *CH* in *chip, OY* in *boy*). They are referred to as *consonant teams* or *vowel teams* in *The Roadmap to Literacy.* (3.1 #2 and 4.1 Rule #2)

**diphthongs:** Two vowel <u>sounds</u> that are connected and make a "gliding" sound such as *OY* in *boy or OW* in *cow,* and long vowels such as the letter I in *hi.*(3.1 #2 and 4.2 rule 11)

**Directions Game:** A way to practice concept imagery. (3.7 #5)

**Drill Down:** Selecting a smaller group of students to do an IMA, speak a verse, etc. in order to gently shift the focus from everyone doing the activity to a few. (2.4 #2)

**Eagle Eye:** A noticing game. (3.4 #10)

**echo reading**: A call-and-response type of reading where the teacher reads a line from a passage on the board while pointing to each word and the student(s) "read" it back. (3.15 #2)

**ego:** One aspect of the four-fold human being. It refers to the distinct individuality of each person. (2.1 #11)

**Elision:** Removing a phoneme, syllable, or word from a spoken word to create a different word. (3.3 #2 and 3.3 #7)

**Emergent Phase:** The first of *The Roadmap to Literacy's* five phases of learning to read and write. (1.5 #1)

**encoding:** To spell words based on matching a letter to each phoneme in a word. (3.4 #1)

**Ending Grid:** A tool to help students memorize various advanced suffixes. (4.3 rule 32)

**English layer cake:** *The Roadmap to Literacy's* analogy to illustrate English's three stages: alphabet, pattern, and meaning (1.3 #1)

**Englishland:** An umbrella story created by the authors for teaching grammar concepts. (3.2 #7 and 3.11 #6–8)

**Etheric Body** (Life Body): One aspect of the four-fold human being. It refers to the part of the human that provides warmth, growth, and healing capacity, etc. (2.1 #11)

**Eurythmy:** An art form invented by Steiner in which music or speech is expressed in bodily movement. (2.1 #12)

**excarnating activities:** Activities that do not require intense focus (listening or work) on the part of the student (e.g., singing, painting, drawing, etc.). (2.3 #4)

**expressive language:** Language that is generated by the student (either spoken or written). (3.8 #1)

**finger spelling:** A materialization technique that is good for segmenting words into phonemes. (3.3 #2)

**fluency:** How quickly and accurately a student can read at grade level. (3.15 #14)

**form drawing:** A type of drawing invented by Steiner that educates the temperaments. It also can help prepare students to learn to print and write cursive. (2.1 #12 and 3.2 #3)

**formal assessments:** Assessments that stand outside of instruction and practice in the classroom. (6.1 #3)

**four-fold human being:** Four aspects of the human being identified by Steiner: physical, etheric, astral, and ego. (2.1 #11)

**free rendering:** An artistic way to review a story created by Else Gottgens. (3.8 #2).

**grapheme:** A written symbol that represents a phoneme (speech sound) (i.e., a written letter). For example, the letters *A, T, P,* and *L.* (1.4 #3 and 3.1 #2)

**guided reading:** Reading done by a student with the support of an adult. (3.15 #2)

**guided writing:** The third of four steps in composition writing where the students write their own compositions by themselves with teacher assistance, as needed. (3.14 #2)

**hand spelling:** A materialization technique to break a word down into onset and rime. (3.3 #2)

**Higher Order Thinking Skills Questions (HOTS questions):** Questions used during story review to develop skills that go beyond mere recall. (3.8 #2)

**Home Surroundings:** A block that focuses on connecting the students to their environmental surroundings. Home Surroundings is called *Nature Studies* in 1st and 2nd Grade and *Practical Occupations* in 3rd Grade. (2.3 #2 and 5.5 #5–8)

**home visit:** When a Waldorf teacher visits a student's home prior to the start of 1st Grade or when accepting a new student into an existing class. (2.1 #13)

**homophone:** Words that sound the same but are spelled differently. (4.2 Rule 21, 6.1 #5)

**incarnating activities:** Quiet activities that require students to focus (e.g., doing bookwork or listening to their teacher present a lesson). (2.3 #4)

**independent reading:** Student reads without support, starting with basic decodable-text. (3.15 #2.)

**inflectional endings (Suffixes):** Suffixes that modify a word such as –ed, –ing, –s. (4.2 rule 13)

**informal assessment:** Daily observation of individual students or the class as a whole. (6.1 #3)

**instructional level:** The zone where the student needs the support of the teacher to be able to apply a new skill and where the most learning occurs. (3.4 #7)

**Integrated Movement Activity (IMA):** Brief movement exercises scheduled during Transitions segment of main lesson. (2.3 #4)

**Introduction &/or Review:** The third segment of *The Roadmap to Literacy* Main Lesson. It is the time for the initial introduction of new concepts, content, or skills. It takes place over two or three days. (2.3 #4)

**Irlen overlays:** Colored overlays used to treat the symptoms of Irlen Syndrome. (6.6 #2)

**Irlen Syndrome:** A condition where a person sees distortions while looking at text. (6.6 #2)

**kid writing:** An educational process where beginning students themselves compose their own simple missives and write down their best guesses at spelling. (3.13)

**Latin/Greek Phase:** *The Roadmap to Literacy's* fifth and final phase taught in 7th and 8th Grades. It focuses on the Latin and Greek roots that found their way into English. (1.5 #1)

**letter drill:** A practice that teaches students to visualize a letter by using symbol imagery. (3.5 #7 and 8)

**letter to sound decoding route:** The route used for reading when a student has to decode (sound out) a word because she does not recognize it automatically. (1.2 #2)

**leveled reader:** A beginning book with controlled vocabulary used for practicing beginning reading skills. (3.15 #2)

**lexical route:** The route used for reading when a person recognizes a word automatically. (1.2 #2)

**Life Body (Etheric Body):** One aspect of the four-fold human being. It refers to the part of the human being that provides the warmth, growth, healing capacity, etc. (2.1 #11)

**Lindamood-Bell Learning Processes®:** A company that has pioneered programs to develop the sensory-cognitive functions that underlie reading and comprehension. (1.6 #2)

**literature curriculum:** Steiner's recommendations for the types of stories to tell students based on grade (e.g., fairy tales for 1st Grade). (2.1 #6)

**long vowels:** One of two possible sounds for each of the vowel letters. (3.1 #2 and *table: 3.1.3*)

**look-say:** A method of reading instruction where students gain familiarity with words by seeing them in print over and over. Dick and Jane readers are examples of look-say readers. (1.6 #3)

**main Lesson (Class):** A two-hour class that explores the main lesson block topic of study; it is scheduled first thing in the day and includes multisensory learning experiences. (2.3 #1)

**main lesson block:** A three-week or four-week unit of study where students focus on one topic. In Grades 1–3, these blocks alternate between a focus on math and language arts. (2.3 #1)

**main lesson block rotation:** The layout of the nine main lesson blocks of the year. (2.3 #1 and *table 5.3.2*)

**main lesson books (MLB):** The books that students create during a main lesson block. (2.1 #1)

**manipulating:** A type of phonemic awareness where students change the sounds in words by adding, subtracting, substituting, or transposing phonemes to form new words. (3.3 #2 and *table 3.5.3*)

**materialization techniques:** Ways to use tangible objects to make abstract elements of speech such as phonemes more concrete for beginning students. (3.3 #2)

**meaning Layer:** The layer of *The English Layer Cake* that corresponds to the *Meaning Stage*. (1.3 #1)

**melancholic:** One of the four temperaments identified by Steiner. It refers to the sensitive people who perceive and remember everything—including every slight and injury. (2.1 #10)

**memory readers:** Collections of poems that your class has memory read together. (3.15 #3.)

**Memory Reading**: Reading that consists of word-to-word matching of spoken word to written word with a text that student has memorized. (1.5 #1 and 3.15 #2.)

**mental picturing**: an umbrella term that refers to any type of mental visualization including concept imagery and symbol imagery. (3.7 #4; 6.6 #6)

**midline barrier**: A hypothetical line that divides the body between left and right sides (i.e., vertical midline) and a hypothetical line that divides the body between top and bottom (i.e., horizontal midline). These barriers limit the range of movement in young children, and they should dissolve before students start school. (2.1 #3)

**midline (dotted)**: A dotted line used in handwriting paper in the early grades to help the students form letters correctly. (*Figure 3.2.7*)

**mini-lesson**: A short lesson designed to reteach something most of the class is struggling with. (3.13 #5)

**modeled writing**: When the teacher demonstrates to her class the process for composing a new type of writing. (3.14 #2)

**Morning Verse**: A verse by Steiner used to open the school day in Waldorf Schools. (2.3 #4)

**morphemes**: Units of meaning. (1.5 #1)

**Move in Time**: See *Take Time*

**mystery word/mystery word game**: A symbol imagery exercise that is used to teach students to visualize letters and decode/encode that is based on an exercise from Lindamood-Bell. (3.5 #3.)

**nine-year change**: The transition students make when they leave behind the magical world of the young child and begin to experience the world in its physical reality. (2.1 #6)

**object words**: Miscellaneous words that begin with a letter that are used as part of the introduction or initial practice activities. (3.1 #8)

**onset**: Any consonant or consonants that come before the rime. For example, in the word *ball*, the onset is *b*. In the word *grail*, the onset is *gr*. (1.5 #1)

**open syllables**: Syllables that end with one vowel (e.g., <u>no</u>, <u>sta</u>/tion, con/<u>di</u>/tion). The vowel can be long or short. (4.3 rule 23)

**Opening**: The first segment of main lesson that contains opening activities. (2.3 #4)

**orthographic stage**: The third and final stage of reading identified by Ute Frith. In this stage students can read automatically and fluently. (1.2 #1)

**pattern layer**: The second layer of the *English Layer Cake* that coincides with the *Pattern Stage*. (1.3 #1)

**Pattern Phase**: *The Roadmap to Literacy's* third phase of learning to read and write. (1.5 #1)

**Pedagogical Section**: A division of the Anthroposophical Society that supports Waldorf education around the world. (1.1)

**pedagogical stories**: Stories teachers tell to address challenging behavior in the classroom. (2.1 #5)

**percentiles**: A unit of measurement used to evaluate students' academic skills on standardized tests. (6.1 #6)

**phlegmatic:** One of the four temperaments identified by Steiner. It refers to the easy-going people who love food, do not get ruffled easily, and feel no need to rush. (2.1 #10)

**phonemes:** Individual speech sounds (e.g., /a/ as in *apple*; /b/ as in *ball*, etc). Phonemes are written inside two forward slashes(e.g. /t/ or /sh/). This shorthand reflects the sound of the letter(s) inside the forward slashes. (1.2 #1 and *table 3.1.2*)

**phonemic awareness:** Awareness of phonemes and ability to manipulate phonemes. (1.4 #2, 1.6 #2 and Chapter 3.3)

**Phonemic Awareness Phase:** *The Roadmap to Literacy's* second phase of learning to read and write. (1.5 #1)

**phonics:** A method of reading instruction that emphasizes teaching children to sound out words. See whole language and look-say. (1.6 #3)

**phonics rules:** Encoding and decoding rules that explain how to use letters and letter combinations to stretch the 26 letters of the Latin alphabet to cover the 40+ sounds in English. (3.1 #1 and section 4)

**phonics rules book:** A small, lined composition book which students use to record their phonics rules. (2.3 #4 and Section 4 Protocol)

**phonological awareness:** An awareness that speech can be broken down into smaller units: 1) word; 2) syllable; 3) phoneme. (1.4 #2)

**phonological stage:** The second of three stages of reading identified by Ute Frith. Students recognize that letters represent sounds and can sound out words, but they are beginning readers and lack fluency. (1.2 #1)

**Physical Body:** One aspect of the four-fold human being. It refers to the part of the human that is perceptible to the eye and provides a vehicle for interaction with the physical world through action, the senses, breathing, and the digestion of food, etc. (2.1 #11)

**pictorial stage:** The first of three stages of reading identified by Ute Frith. Students recognize words as pictures but are not aware that letters represent sounds. (1.2 #1)

**point of articulation:** An unconscious process of using the pronunciation of a vowel letter's name to determine how to encode a short vowel sound. (*table 3.1.4*)

**Practical Life Skills Blocks:** Two or three main lesson blocks in 3rd Grade that focus on practical activities (housebuilding, farming, textiles, shelters) rather than on language arts and math skills. (This is a Sacred Nothing.) (2.3 #3)

**practice block rotation:** The layout of practice blocks over the school year. (2.3 #1, *table: 5.3.2*)

**practice books:** Notebooks students use for writing rough drafts and practice ongoing skills such as encoding and spelling words. They are for more informal assignments. (2.3 #4)

**practice classes:** The classes that occur after main lesson. In *The Roadmap to Literacy*, it refers to the daily language skills practice class held during a math block. (2.3 #1 and 2.3 #6)

**preconsonantal nasals:** End blends made up of the letters *N, M,* or *NG* before another consonant. For example, *ju*<u>*mp*</u> or *ra*<u>*ng*</u>. (4.1 rule 3)

**pretend reading:** Reading that consists of a retelling or paraphrasing of the content of a well-known story without word-to-word matching. (2.1 #2 and 3.15 #2)

**R-controlled vowels:** Vowel teams where the vowel letter or letters are followed by the letter *R*, such as *AR, ER, IR, UR, OR, EAR, AIR,* etc. (4.1 rule 5 and 4.2 rule 12)

**Reading/Writing segment:** An additional lesson segment added to the archetypal main lesson to accommodate the 1st Grade curriculum. (2.3 #4, 3.15 #4, Ap 1A, 1C, 1E)

**receptive language:** Language that is understood by the student (either spoken or written). (3.8 #1)

**reflexes (early movement patterns):** A sequence of stereotypical movements that young children progress through in their first years of life. (6.6 #4)

**report verses:** See *Birthday verses* (3.10 #3)

**responsible innovations:** A term used by Elan Liebner, current head of the Pedagogical Council in the U.S., that refers to positive innovations in Waldorf education. (2.2 #1)

**Review:** The method of going over previous material (academic lessons or stories) to support learning and/or preparation for an assignment. (2.3 #4)

**Rhyming Rime Machine:** *The Roadmap to Literacy's* tool for generating rhyming words. (3.15 #3)

**rime:** The pattern of letters from the vowel to the end of a single-syllable word. For example, in the word *ball*, the rime is *-all*. In the word *grail*, the rime is *-ail*. (1.5 #1)

**Sacred Nothings:** A term penned by Christof Wiechert, past director of the Pedagogical Section of the Anthroposophical Society, that refers to sacrosanct traditions sometimes found in Waldorf classrooms that are of questionable value. (2.2 #1)

**sanguine:** One of the four temperaments identified by Steiner. Sanguines are social, artistic, curious, and enthusiastic. They often lack follow through and can be easily distracted. (2.1 #10)

**school readiness:** A state where students have mature capacities and are ready for formal instruction. (2.1 #3)

**Schwa:** The vowel sound that occurs in unaccented syllables (i.e., /u/). (4.3 rule 31)

**sensory-cognitive functions:** A Lindamood-Bell term for symbol imagery, concept imagery, and phonemic awareness. They represent the junction between skill and ability. (1.6 #2)

**sequential retelling (story retelling):** A type of review where the students retell a story in order (e.g., what happened first, second, etc.). (3.8 #2)

**shared writing:** The second of four steps in composition writing where the teacher and students (or a team of students) compose a writing assignment together. (3.14 #2)

**short vowels:** One of two possible sounds for each of the vowel letters. (3.1 #2 and *table: 3.1.3*)

**sight words:** The short, often highly irregular English words that come from Old English and make up the majority of the words in print. (1.6 #4, 3.5 #1, chapter 3.6, and Appendix 4)

**signposts:** Student achievements that indicate where a student is at along the road to literacy. They can refer to broader achievements that go across grades such as **benchmarks** or specific skills that reflect changes in the students' brains that indicate which phase a student is in. (*table 3.3.1; table 3.13.1; table 6.2.1–6.2.5*)

**silent reading:** The advanced stage of independent reading where students can read quietly to themselves without subvocalization. (3.15 #2)

**simple decodable test:** See *Decodable-text.*

**Six Basic Exercises:** Exercises given by Rudolf Steiner to train thinking, feeling, and willing. (2.1 #14)

**skill:** Academic skills acquired through formal education. (1.6 #2)

**Skills Practice:** The second segment of *The Roadmap to Literacy* main lesson. It is used to practice language arts skills and to warm up for the lesson to come. (2.3 #4)

**soul food stories:** Stories that provide life wisdom and nurture the child's evolving spirit. (2.1 #5)

**Sound/symbol (correspondence):** Recognizing the connection between the grapheme (the written letter) and its phoneme (the letter's sound) (e.g., the phoneme/sound /b/ represents the letter *B* and vice versa). (3.1 #2)

**special subject teachers:** Teachers (other than the main/class teacher) who teach the students. (2.3 #1)

**Speech/Song Segment:** An additional lesson segment added to the archetypal main lesson to accommodate the 1st Grade curriculum. (2.3 #4, 3.15 #4, Ap 1A, 1C, 1E)

**split phases:** When a student's reading, decoding, and encoding skills are not all in the same phase. (6.2 #1)

**standardized test:** A test that is administered and scored in a standard way (usually refers to tests mandated by the government). (6.1 #3 and 7)

**standards:** See *Benchmarks.*

**story:** A segment of main lesson where the story is told. (2.3 #4)

**story frames:** Templates created by Gentry that help students expand the volume of their writing. (3.13 #6)

**Subvocalization:** The stage that precedes silent reading when students read aloud, whisper to themselves, or mouth the words when they read. (3.15 #2)

**summer preparation form:** A *Roadmap to Literacy* form that helps you organize your curriculum materials as you are planning your curriculum over the summer. (5.1 #4)

**syllable cards:** A symbol imagery exercise from the Lindamood-Bell program *Seeing Stars®: Symbol Imagery for Phonological and Orthographic Processing in Reading and Spelling.* It consists of a word or syllable that can be decoded that is used to teach students to visualize letters and decode/encode. (3.5 #3)

**Syllable Phase:** *The Roadmap to Literacy's* fourth phase in learning to read and write. (1.5 #1)

**symbol imagery:** The ability to visualize letters and numerals. (1.6 #2 and 3.5)

**symbol imagery exercises:** Two materialization techniques from the Lindamood-Bell program *Seeing Stars®: Symbol Imagery for Phonological and Orthographic Processing in Reading and Spelling.* (3.3 #2 and 3.5 #3)

**Take Time (Move in Time):** A series of therapeutic bean bag exercises that also make good Integrated Movement Activities. (6.6 #5)

**talking on paper:** An exercise where the students compose their own simple sentence(s) using their best guesses at spelling (i.e., the Waldorf version of kid writing) (3.13 introduction)

**Teacher Literature Resource List:** A list of books recommended by *The Roadmap to Literacy* as a starting point for researching curriculum materials. (Appendix 5)

**teacher-made assessment:** a type of formal assessment made by the teacher. (6.1 #3)

**teaching rhythms:** A template in *The Roadmap to Literacy* program that is used to introduce new material over one or more days. (2.3 #4)

**temperaments:** Four personality types identified by Steiner: choleric, melancholic, phlegmatic, and sanguine. (2.1 #10)

**theory of word:** Being able to break the sound stream down into its separate words. (1.4 #2)

**Transition:** The break between segments of a main lesson (and sometimes a practice class) that are often used for Integrated Movement Activities. (2.3 #4)

**truncated schedules:** Giving 1st Grade and 2nd Grade a shortened school day. (2.3 #7)

**umbrella stories:** Academic concept stories that are serial in nature (i.e., they are told over two or more days). (2.1 #5)

**upside down world:** An Integrated Movement Activity (IMA) to use during transitions where the students drape themselves over their desks, hanging their arms and heads over the front so they can see their feet. (2.3 #4)

**vowel teams:** Two or more vowel letters that represent one sound such as *AI* in *sail, OY* in *boy,* and *OUGH* in *though.* (see *Digraph.*) (1.3 #4)

**whole language:** A method of reading instruction that stresses putting quality literature into children's hands so that they can use their language skills in real situations rather than use the artificial texts favored by phonics and look-say. See phonics and look-say. (1.6 #3)

**whole to parts:** A Waldorf maxim. (2.1 #8)

**word bank:** A list of words that is written on the board so that they can be used in a composition. (3.14 #5)

**word families:** 1) Chains of words that share a common rime (1.5 #1 and *table 1.5.1*); 2) The first step in decoding by onset and rimes. (3.4 #8, 4.2 rule 9, and *table 4.2.2*)

**word identification hub:** *The Roadmap to Literacy* term for the area of the brain that recognizes words automatically (i.e., the *left* occipito-temporal region). (1.2 #3)

**word sorting:** An exercise that involves categorizing words or pictures into categories. (3.3 #2)

**Words Their Way:** A book by Bear et al that provides a useful spelling (encoding) assessment, information on word sorting, and an appendix (i.e., Appendix C) that contains pictures that can be used to create worksheets and games for phonics rules. (6.1 #6)

**zoo exercises:** A series of movement exercises that feature ways to move like various animals, such as walking like a crab. (6.6 #5)

**1–1–1 Rule:** A phonics rule that governs when to double the final consonant when adding a suffix that begins with a vowel. (4.3 Rule 28)

**80/80 Rule (80/80):** A rule from *The Roadmap to Literacy* that covers when to teach a new phonics rule: teach a new phonics rule when 80% of the class can successfully <u>decode</u> using the current rule 80% of the time. (3.4 #2 and Section 4 Protocol)

# Index

Terms are located by chapter rather than page number. Tables, Figures, Appendices, and Glossary noted *Tb., Fig., Ap, and Gl.* Please read material in context.

assessment: section 6; 3.1 #11; 3.2 #11; 3.3 #11; 3.4 #11; 3.5 #12; 3.6 #10; 3.7 #8; 3.8 #9; 3.9 #10; 3.10 #11; 3.11 #10; 3.12 #10; 3.13 #9; 3.14 #10; 3.15 #14

assessment record book: 6.1 #8; Tb. 6.1.3

assessments created by educational testing groups: 6.1 #3 and 6; 6.3 #3; 6.4 #3; 6.5 #3; Tbs. 6.3.3–6.3.5; Tbs. 6.4.3–6.4.5; Tbs. 6.5.3–6.5.5; Gl

astral body: 2.1 #11; Gl

attendance rituals: 3.10 #3

AWSNA: 2.2 #1; 3.10 #8

Bal-A-Vis-X: 2.3 #4; 3.2 #2; 3.9 #11; 6.6 #5; Gl

bean bag exercises: Tb. 5.2.7; Tb. 5.2.9; Tb. 5.2.10 (see also *Take Time* and *Bal-A-Vis-X*)

benchmarks: Tb. 6.1.4; 2.1 #1; section 4 Protocol; 6.1 #9; 6.3 #1; 6.4 #1; 6.5 #1; Tb. 3.1.9; Tb. 3.2.1; Tb. 3.3.4; Tb. 3.4.10; Tb. 3.5.3; Tb. 3.6.1; Tb. 3.8.2; Tb. 3.9.3; Tb. 3.11.3; Tb. 3.13.2; Tb. 3.14.4; Tb. 3.15.4; Tb. 6.3.1; Tb. 6.4.1; Tb. 6.5.1; Gl

birthday verse: foreword; 3.10 #3; Gl

blending phonemes: 3.3 #2; Tb. 3.4.4; Tb. 4.1.1; Tb. 5.2.7–Tb. 5.2.10; Ap 1A, 1B, and 1D

blends: 3.1 #7; 4.1 rule 3; Tbs. 4.1.2–4.1.4; Tb. 6.2.2; Tb. 6.3.1; Tb. 6.3.3; Tb. 6.3.5; Tb. 6.4.1; Gl

block crayons: 2.2 #1; 3.2 introduction

block plan templates: Ap 1A-1F; Ap 2A-2C; Ap 3A–3D; Gl

block plans: 2.3 #1; 5.1 #5; 5.2 #5 and 6; 5.3 #4 and 5; 5.4 #4–5; Tb. 5.2.7; Tb. 5.2.8; Gl

block rotation: 2.3 #1 and 2; 5.1 #3; 5.2 #2; 5.3 #2; 5.4 #2; Tb. 5.2.3; Tb. 5.3.2; Tb. 5.4.2; Gl

Body Geography: 3.7 #5; Gl

book report: 3.14 #4 and 8

bookwork: 2.3 #4 and 6; Tbs. 5.2.7–5.2.10; Gl

borders: 2.2 #1; 3.2 #3; Gl

brain: 1.2; 1.5 #2; 3.1 #1; 3.2 #1; 3.4 #1; 6.6 #4, 5, and 9 (see also *letter to sound decoding route, lexical route,* and *word identification hub*)

Brain Gym: 2.3 #4; 3.2 #2 and 3; 6.6 #5; Gl

breathing: 2.1 #7; 2.3 #4; Gl

capacities: 1.6 #2; 2.1 #3; 6.6 #1, 5, and conclusion; Gl

capitalization: 3.11 #6a and 8h; 3.14 #10; 6.5 #4; Tb. 6.1.4; Tb. 6.3.1; Tb. 6.5.1; Tb. 6.5.2

care group: 6.6 #7 and 8

cell phone: 3.7 #1; 6.1 #8; 6.6 #3

chains: 3.4 #7, 8, and 9; 4.2 rule 9; Tb. 4.2.2

chanting: 3.6 #6–9; 3.9 #2, 6, and 11; Fig. 3.6.1

choice/contrast: 3.4 #5 and 6; 3.13 #2 and 5; Tb. 3.3.3

choleric: 2.1 #10; 3.15 #3; 5.5 #6 and 7; Gl

choral reading: 3.15 #2 and #7; Tb. 3.15.1; Tb. 5.2.8; Gl

circle: 2.2 #1; 2.3 #5; Gl

fluency (reading fluency): 1.1 #3; 3.6 #1; 3.8 #10; 3.15 #1 and 14; 6.1 #6; 6.4 #3; 6.5 #3; Tb. 6.1.4; Tb. 6.2.8; Tbs. 6.3.1–6.3.6; Tbs. 6.4.1—6.4.6; Tbs. 6.5.1–6.5.6; Gl

form drawing: 2.1 #12; 2.2 #1; 3.2 #3 and 8; Fig. 2.1.2; Gl

formal assessment: 6.1 #3 and 5; 6.2 #3; 6.3 #2 and 3; 6.4 #2 and 3; 6.5 #2 and 3; Tb. 6.3.2; Tb. 6.3.3; Tb. 6.4.2; Tb. 6.4.3; Tb. 6.5.2; Tb. 6.5.3; Gl

four-fold human being: 2.1 #11; Gl

free rendering: 2.2 #1; 3.8 #2, 5, and 6; Gl

Gentry; J. Richard: 1.2 #6; 1.5 #2; 1.6 #2; 3.3 #2; 3.5 #1; 3.6 #1; 3.13 #5 and 6

German: 1.1 #1; 1.3 #1–4; 3.1 #2 and 3; 3.10 #9; 3.11 #1 and 2; 5.1. #8

Gottgens; Else: 2.2 #1; 3.8 #2; 3.13 #1

grammar: 3.11; 3.16; 6.3 #1 and 2; 6.5 #4; Tb. 3.11.1; Tb. 3.11.3; Tb. 6.1.4; Tb. 6.3.1; Tb. 6.3.2; Tb. 6.4.1; Tb. 6.4.2; Tb. 6.5.1; Tb. 6.5.2; Tb. 6.5.6

grapheme: 1.4 #3; 3.1 #2; 3.2 #3; Gl

guided reading: 3.15 #2, 7, and 8; Tb. 3.15.1; Gl

guided writing: 3.14 #2 and 5; Gl

hand spelling: 3.1 #10; 3.3 #2; Tb. 3.3.2; Tbs. 5.2.7–5.2.10; Gl

handwriting: 3.2; 3.16; 6.5 #4; Tb. 3.2.1; Tb. 5.2.7; Tb. 5.2.8; Tb. 6.1.4; Tb. 6.3.1; Tb. 6.3.2; Tb. 6.3.6; Tb. 6.4.1; Tb. 6.4.2; Tb. 6.5.1; Tb. 6.5.2; Fig. 3.2.1–3.2.12

Higher Order Thinking Skills Questions (HOTS): 3.8 #2, 5, 6, and 7; 3.14 #3 and 7; Tb. 6.3.2; Tb. 6.4.2; Tb. 6.5.2; Gl

Home Surroundings: 2.3 #2; 5.2 #9; 5.3 #7; 5.4 #7; Gl

Home Surroundings stories: 2.1 #5; 5.5 #1, 5, 6, and 7; Tb. 5.5.1

home visit: 2.1 #13; 3.1 #4; Gl

homophones: 1.3 #3; 1.5 #1; 4.2 rule 21; Tb. 4.2.5

I Spy: 3.3 #10; 3.4 #10

idioms: 3.12 #8

incarnating activities: 2.3 #4; Gl

independent reading: 3.15 #2, 7, 8, 9, and 11; Tb. 3.15.1; Gl

independent writing: 3.14 #2 and 5

Individualized Education Program (IEP): 6.6 #11

inference: 3.8 #2

inflectional ending/inflectional suffix: 4.1 rule 4; 4.2 rule 13; 4.3 rule 28; Gl

informal assessment: 6.1 #3, 4, and 8; 6.2 #2; 6.3 #2; 6.4 #2; 6.5 #2: Tb. 6.3.2; Tb. 6.4.2; Tb. 6.5.2; Gl

instructional level: 3.4 #7, 8, and 9; 3.9 #7; 3.13 #2 and 5; 3.15 #10

Integrated Movement Activities (IMAs): 2.3 #4 and 5; 3.6 #9; 3.7 #5; 3.10 #6; 6.6 #4 and 5; Tbs. 5.2.7 and 5.2.9; Ap 1A, 1C, and 1E; Ap 2A-2C; Ap 3A–3D; Gl

Introduction &/or Review (segment): 2.3 #4 and 6; Tb. 5.2.7; Tb. 5.2.9; Tb. 5.2.10; Gl

Irlen Syndrome/Irlen (colored) overlays: 3.2 #12; 3.6 #11; 3.9 #11; 6.6 #2 and 9; Gl

spelling: 3.9; 3.16; 3.12 #2; 6.5 #4; Tbs. 6.3.1–6.3.3; Tb. 6.3.5; Tb. 6.1.4; Tb. 3.9.1–3.9.3; Tbs. 6.4.1–6.4.2; Tbs. 6.5 1–6.5.3; Tb. 6.5.6

spelling assessment dictation: 3.9 #8

spelling dictionary: See *consumable spelling dictionary*

split phase: 6.2 #4; Gl

standardized tests: 6.1 #3 and 7

standards: See *Benchmarks*

Steiner, Rudolf: foreword; 1.1 introduction, #3, and 4; 1.3 introduction, #2, 3, and 4; 1.4 introduction and #3; 1.6 introduction, #1, and 5; 2.1 #4 and 6–14; 2.2 introduction, #1, and 2; 2.3 #2, 3, and 4; 3.1 #2, 3, 7, and 9; 3.2 #1 and 3; 3.10 #1, 3, 4, and 9; 3.11 #1, 2, 3, and 7; 3.13 #1; 3.14 #1; 5.2 #4; 5.5 #1, 5, and 9; 6.1 conclusion

story: 5.5; 2.1 #5; 2.2 #1; 2.3 #4; Gl

story frames: 3.13 #6; Gl

story indigestion: 5.5 #9

story review (segment): 3.8 #2 and 5–7; 3.13 #5; Tb. 3.8.1; Tb. 3.8.2

straight and curved lines: 5.2 #4 and 5

structure words: 3.7 #4; Tb. 3.7.1

student file: 6.1 #8

subject (of a block): 1.1 #2; 2.3 #1

subject (of a sentence): 3.11 #8a

substitution (of phonemes): 3.3 #2

subvocalization: 3.15 #2; 6.6 #9; Gl

suffix: 3.4 #9; 4.3 rules 26–28; Tb. 4.3.5–4.3.10

summary (written): 3.14 #7

summer preparation form: 5.1 #4; 5.2 #3; 5.3 #3; 5.4 #3; Tbs. 5.2.4–5.2.6; Gl

syllable: 4.3; 1.4 #2; 3.3 #1, 5, 6, and 9; 3.16; Tb. 5.2.7; Tb. 5.2.9; Tb. 5.2.10; Fig. 4.3.1

syllable cards: 3.5 #3; Tb. 3.5.1; Ap 1E and 1F; Ap 2A–2C; Ap 3A–3D; Gl

Syllable Phase: 4.4; 1.5 #1; 3.3 #9; 3.4 #9; 3.5 #10; 3.15 #9; 3.16; 5.4 #1; Tb. 1.5.2; Tb. 1.6.3; Tb. 3.15.1; Tb. 5.4.1; Tb. 6.2.4; Tb. 6.2.6; Gl

symbol imagery: chapter 3.5; 3.16; 1.5 #1; 1.6 #2–4; 3.4 #10 and 11; 3.6 #7; 3.9 #2; 6.5 #4; Tb. 1.6.1; Tb. 1.6.2; Tbs. 3.5.1–3.5.3; Tbs. 5.2.7–5.2.10; Tb. 6.1.4; Tb. 6.3.1; Tb. 6.3.2; Tb. 6.3.6; Tb. 6.4.1; Tb. 6.4.2; Tb. 6.5.1; Tb. 6.5.2; Tb. 6.5.6; Fig. 3.5.1; Gl

symbol imagery exercises (i.e., syllable cards and mystery word): 3.3 #2; 3.5 #3; Tb. 3.3.2; Tb. 3.5.1; Tb. 3.5.2; Ap 1E–1F; Ap 2A–2C; Ap 3A–3D; Gl

symbol imagery game: 3.1 #10; Tb. 5.2.8

synonym: 3.11 #8i; 3.12 #7

Take Time: 3.2 #2; 3.9 #11; 4.1 rule 2; 6.6 #5; Gl. (see also *Bean Bag Exercises*)

talking on paper: 3.13 Introduction and #1; Gl

Teacher Literature Resource List: 5.1 #4; Ap 5; Gl

# ABOUT THE AUTHORS

**Janet Langley** is an experienced Waldorf teacher and mentor. She walked into her first Waldorf classroom in 1986 and was instantly enamored with what she saw unfolding before her eyes: the warm environment, the enthusiastic students, a permeation of the arts, and the palpable love that existed between student and teacher. This experience led her to enroll her daughter in a Waldorf School and ultimately to become a teacher, herself. She graduated her first Waldorf class in 2001 and her second class in 2008. She has since been a school mentor, evaluator, teacher training instructor, creator of several workshops including: Working with *Consensus as a Spiritual Deed* and *The Roadmap to Literacy: Teaching Foundational Literacy Skills* and co-creator of the website: www.waldorfinspirations.com. Although her work as a mentor and adult educator has been very rewarding, Janet's greatest joys are derived from the wonderful connections she still has with her former students and being able to make this book available to teachers.

Janet likes to travel with Jerry-her husband of 45 years, ski, read, swim, go for walks in the woods, and spend as much time as possible with her daughter and two grandsons.

**Jennifer Militzer-Kopperl** has been a private Remedial Specialist since 2005. She graduated from Grand Valley State University with a degree in Russian Studies (1994) and went on to complete two years of graduate work at The University of Kansas in Slavic Languages and Literatures. She took a job at Lindamood-Bell Learning Processes® teaching remedial reading, math, and language comprehension. Soon after she realized that she had found her vocation: remedial education. She returned to school to get a degree in Waldorf education (Rudolf Steiner College, Fair Oaks, 2005) and has been working with Waldorf students ever since.

The inspiration to write this book came when she realized that most of her Waldorf students fit a certain profile and that she could explain the roots of the problem and how to fix it by using her background in foreign languages and linguistics. She thought her observations could help current Waldorf teachers and future generations of students so she began offering various workshops on remedial reading to area Waldorf schools, including *How English Reading and Spelling Conventions Work* and *Teaching "Reading" Grades 1 – 3*. She wrote this book with Janet Langley in order to engage a larger audience.

Jennifer Militzer-Kopperl lives with her husband, Ben, and their two cats.

CPSIA information can be obtained
at www.ICGtesting.com
Printed in the USA
FSHW020744140920
73666FS

9 781545 660232